British Qualifications 2012

42ND EDITION

A Complete Guide to Professional, Vocational & Academic Qualifications in the United Kingdom

LONDON PHILADELPHIA NEW DELHI

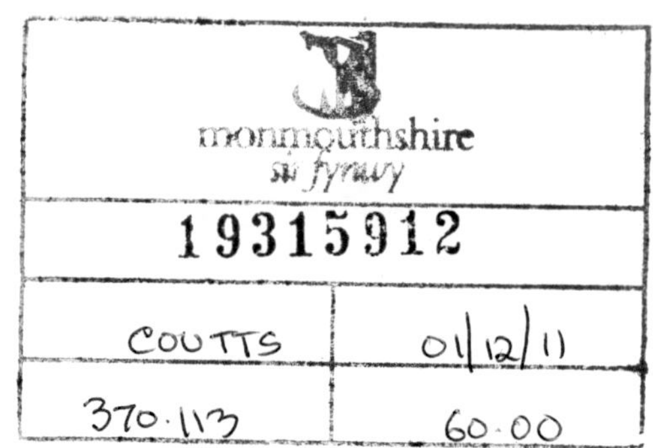

Publisher's note

Every possible effort has been made to ensure that the information contained in this book is accurate at the time of going to press, and the publishers and authors cannot accept responsibility for any errors or omissions, however caused. No responsibility for loss or damage occasioned to any person acting, or refraining from action, as a result of the material in this publication can be accepted by the editor, the publisher or any of the authors.

First published in Great Britain in 1966

Forty-second edition published in Great Britain and the United States in 2012 by Kogan Page Limited

Apart from any fair dealing for the purposes of research or private study, or criticism or review, as permitted under the Copyright, Designs and Patents Act 1988, this publication may only be reproduced, stored or transmitted, in any form or by any means, with the prior permission in writing of the publishers, or in the case of reprographic reproduction in accordance with the terms and licences issued by the CLA. Enquiries concerning reproduction outside these terms should be sent to the publishers at the undermentioned addresses:

120 Pentonville Road
London N1 9JN
United Kingdom
www.koganpage.com

1518 Walnut Street, Suite 1100
Philadelphia PA 19102
USA

4737/23 Ansari Road
Daryaganj
New Delhi 110002
India

© Kogan Page, 2012

British Library Cataloguing-in-Publication Data

A CIP record for this book is available from the British Library.

ISBN 978 0 7494 6411 0
E-ISBN 978 0 7494 6412 7
ISSN 0141-5972

Typeset by AMA DataSet Ltd, Preston
Production managed by Jellyfish
Printed and bound by CPI Group (UK) Ltd, Croydon, CR0 4YY

19315912

£5-00

British Qualifications 2012

A

NOT FOR LOAN

MONMOUTHSHIRE LIBRARIES

19315912

PUBLISHER'S NOTE

This 42nd edition of *British Qualifications* has been considerably revised and updated to reflect the many changes in degree, diploma and certificate courses and to take account of legislative reforms affecting the structure of higher and further education over the past year.

The editor and compilers are most grateful to the academic registrars and the secretaries of the many bodies they have contacted for information and advice. Without their cooperation, the revision and updating of *British Qualifications* would not have been possible.

Masters in Business Administration (MBA) Studied in London at

Kensington College of Business

has been granted approval to offer the following MBA programmes validated and awarded by the University of Wales:

- MBA in (Banking & Financial Institutions Management)
- MBA in (Finance)
- MBA in (Healthcare Management)
- MBA in (Human Resource Management)
- MBA in (Information Technology Management)
- MBA in (Management of Innovation Technology & Change)
- MBA in (International Management)
- MBA in (Marketing)
- MBA in (Retail Management)
- MBA in (Travel Tourism & Hospitality Management)
- MBA
- MSC in (Computing)

COURSE CONTENT AND ASSESSMENT:

The course contains nine modules in which seven compulsory modules, two optional modules and a project. The assessments are exams and course work based. Students have to pass 9 modules plus the Dissertation to be awarded the MBA.

Masters in Business Administration (MBA)
These degrees are validated and awarded by the University of Wales, UK. For further details regarding the University and its validation services, please log on to www.wales.ac.uk/validation or email validation@wales.ac.uk

PRIFYSGOL CYMRU
UNIVERSITY OF WALES

Tuition fee of the MBA Programme is £7450 (£1000 scholarship is available)
Kensington College of Business

Masters Degrees

Masters in Business Administration

Energy Management
General Management
Tourism Management
Hospitality Management
Health Management
Management Consultancy

Masters in Computing

Computer Systems
Computer Networks
Business Information Technology

MSc Money Finance and Investment

QUALITY
Degrees awarded by leading UK universities

AFFORDABILITY
Affordable tuition fee with instalment plan

FLEXIBILITY
Accelerated programmes with up to three start dates per year

Courses commence: October, January & July of each year

CITY OF LONDON COLLEGE

A University Sector Premier College

Bachelors Degrees

International Business
International Finance
Tourism Management
Business Information Technology
Computing

Higher National Diploma awards

Business - Computing & Systems Development - Travel & Tourism Management
Hospitality Management - Health & Social Care Management - Accounting

ONE OF THE LONGEST ESTABLISHED COLLEGES IN LONDON WITH OVER 30 YEARS' RECORD OF SUCCESS

+44 (0)207 247 2166

WWW.CLC-LONDON.AC.UK

CONTENTS

REFERENCES

Association of MBAs (AMBA) (annual) *AMBA – Financial Times Guide to Business Schools,* AMBA, London

Committee of Vice-Chancellors and Principals (CVCP) (annual) *University Entrance: The official guide,* CVCP, London

Department for Education and Skills (DfES) (2003) *The Future of Higher Education,* The Stationery Office, London [online] http://www.dfes.gov.uk/hegateway/strategy/hestrategy/foreword.shtml

DfES (2004) *Five-Year Strategy for Children and Learners,* DfES, London

Qualifications and Curriculum Authority (QCA) (2004) *New Thinking for Reform: A framework for achievement,* QCA, London (July)

HOW TO USE THIS BOOK

You may find these notes helpful when using the book.

Part 1 presents an overview of the further and higher educational systems currently in operation in the United Kingdom, including a discussion of the major reforms that have taken place over the past year and their impact.

Part 2 takes a look at the teaching establishments whose qualifications are listed in Part 4 of the book, offering an explanation of the different types of institution, their place in the overall system and the levels of qualification that they award.

Part 3 presents a detailed description of vocational qualifications awarded by many of the professional associations included in Part 5, including an explanation of validating, examining and awarding bodies.

Part 4 is a directory of qualifications awarded by universities in the United Kingdom (ordered by university name). There is a brief introduction detailing admission to degree courses, degree structure and the various categories of degree available.

Part 5 is a directory of qualifications awarded by professional, trade and specialist associations in the United Kingdom (ordered by profession / discipline), including certificates, diplomas, NVQs and SVQs. A short introduction explains the functions of professional associations and how to gain membership.

Part 6 describes various bodies involved in the accreditation of colleges in the independent sector of further and higher education.

Part 7 is a list of study associations and learned societies.

Also included (at the beginning of the book) is a list of all abbreviations and designatory letters used throughout *British Qualifications*.

INDEX OF ABBREVIATIONS AND DESIGNATORY LETTERS

AAB	Associate of the Association of Book-keepers
AACB	Associate of the Association of Certified Bookkeepers
AACP	Associate of the Association of Computer Professionals
AAFC	Associate of the Association of Financial Controllers and Administrators
AAIA	Associate of the Association of International Accountants
AAMS	Associate of the Association of Medical Secretaries, Practice Managers, Administrators and Receptionists
AASI	Associate of the Ambulance Service Institute
AASW	Advanced Award in Social Work
AAT	Association of Accounting Technicians
ABC	Awarding Body Consortium
ABDO	Associate of the British Dispensing Opticians
ABE	Association of Business Executives
ABEng	Associate Member of the Association of Building Engineers
ABHA	Associate of the British Hypnotherapy Association
ABIAT	Associate Member of the British Institute of Architectural Technologists
ABIPP	Associate of the British Institute of Professional Photography
ABMA	Associate of the Business Management Association
ABPR	Association of British Picture Restorers
ABRSM	Associated Board of the Royal Schools of Music
ABS	Association of Business Schools
ABSSG	Associate of the British Society of Scientific Glassblowers
ACA	Associate of the Institute of Chartered Accountants in England and Wales
ACA	Associate of the Institute of Chartered Accountants in Ireland
ACB	Association of Certified Bookkeepers
ACC	Accredited Clinical Coders
ACCA	Associate of the Association of Chartered Certified Accountants
ACCA	Association of Chartered Certified Accountants
ACE	Association for Conferences and Events
ACEA	Associate of the Institute of Cost and Executive Accountants
ACertCM	Archbishop of Canterbury's Certificate in Church Music
ACGI	Associate of City and Guilds of London Institute
ACIArb	Associate of the Chartered Institute of Arbitrators
ACIB	Associate of the Chartered Institute of Bankers
ACIBS	Associate of the Chartered Institute of Bankers in Scotland
ACIBSE	Associate of the Chartered Institution of Building Services Engineers
ACIH	Associate of the Chartered Institute of Housing
ACII	Associate of the Chartered Insurance Institute
ACILA	Associate of the Chartered Institute of Loss Adjusters
ACIM	Associate of the Chartered Institute of Marketing
ACIOB	Associate of the Chartered Institute of Building
ACIS	Associate of the Institute of Chartered Secretaries and Administrators
ACIT	Advanced Certificate in International Trade
ACLIP	Certified Affiliate of CILIP
ACMA	Associate of the Chartered Institute of Management Accountants
ACP	Association of Child Psychotherapists
ACP	Associate of the College of Preceptors

ACP	Association of Computer Professionals
ACPM	Associate of the Confederation of Professional Management
ACPP	Associate of the College of Pharmacy Practice
ACT	Associate of the College of Teachers
ACYW	Associate of the Community and Youth Work Association
ADCE	Advanced Diploma in Childcare and Education
ADCM	Archbishop of Canterbury's Diploma in Church Music
AdDipEd	Advanced Diploma in Education
ADI	Approved Driving Instructor
AECI	Association Member of the Institute of Employment Consultants
AEWVH	Association for the Education and Welfare of the Visually Handicapped
AFA	Associate of the Faculty of Actuaries
AFA	Associate of the Institute of Financial Accountants
AFBPsS	Associate Fellow of the British Psychological Society
AFCI	Associate of the Faculty of Commerce and Industry Ltd
AffBMA	Affiliate of the Business Management Association
AffIManf	Affiliate of the Institute of Manufacturing
AffIMI	Affiliate of the Institute of the Motor Industry
AffIMS	Affiliate of the Institute of Management Specialists
AffInstM	Affiliate of the Meat Training Council
AffIP	Affiliate of the Institute of Plumbing
AffProfBTM	Affiliate of Professional Business and Technical Management
AFIMA	Associate Fellow of the Institute of Mathematics and its Applications
AFISOL	Aerodrome Flight Information Service Officer's Licence
AFPC	Advanced Financial Planning Certificate
AFRCSEd	Associate Fellow of Royal College of Surgeons of Edinburgh
AGCL	Associate of the Guild of Cleaners and Launderers
AGI	Associate of the Greek Institute
AGSM	Associate of the Guildhall School of Music and Drama
AHCIMA	Associate of the Hotel and Catering International Management Association
AHFS	Associate of the Council of Health Fitness and Sports Therapists
AHRIM	Associate of the Institute of Health Record Information and Management
AIA	Associate of the Institute of Actuaries
AIA	Association of International Accountants
AIAgrE	Associate of the Institution of Agricultural Engineers
AIAT	Associate of the Institute of Asphalt Technology
AIBCM	Associate of the Institute of British Carriage and Automobile Manufacturers
AIBMS	Associate of the Institute of Biomedical Science
AICB	Associate of the Institute of Certified Book-Keepers
AIChor	Associate of the Benesh Institute of Choreology
AICHT	Associate of the International Council of Holistic Therapists
AICM(Cert)	Associate Member of the Institute of Credit Management
AICS	Associate of the Institution of Chartered Shipbrokers
AICSc	Associate of the Institute of Consumer Sciences Incorporating Home Economics
AIDTA	Associate of the International Dance Teachers' Association
AIE	Associate of the Institute of Electrolysis
AIEM	Associate of the Institute of Executives and Managers
AIExpE	Associate of the Institute of Explosive Engineers
AIFA	Associate of the Institute of Field Archaeologists
AIFBQ	Associate of the International Faculty of Business Qualifications
AIFireE	Associate of the Institution of Fire Engineers
AIFP	Associate of the British International Freight Association

AIGD — Associate of the Institute of Grocery Distribution
AIHort — Associate Member of the Institute of Horticulture
AIIMR — Associate of the Institute of Investment Management and Research
AIIRSM — Associate of the International Institute of Risk and Safety Management
AIL — Associate of the Institute of Linguists
AILAM — Associate of the Institute of Leisure and Amenity Management
AIMBM — Associate of the Institute of Maintenance and Building Management
AIMC — Associate of the Institute of Management Consultancy
AIMgt — Associate of the Institute of Management
AIMIS — Associate of the Institute for the Management of Information Systems
AIMM — Associate of the Institute of Massage and Movement
AInstAM — Associate of the Institute of Administrative Management
AInstBA — Associate of the Institute of Business Administration
AInstBCA — Associate of the Institute of Burial and Cremation Administration
AInstBM — Associate of the Institute of Builders' Merchants
AInstCM — Associate of the Institute of Commercial Management
AInstM — Associate of the Meat Training Council
AInstPkg — Associate of the Institute of Packaging
AInstPM — Associate of the Institute of Professional Managers and Administrators
AInstSMM — Associate of the Institute of Sales and Marketing Management
AInstTA — Associate of the Institute of Transport Administration
AInstTT — Associate Member of the Institute of Travel and Tourism
AIOC — Associate of the Institute of Carpenters
AIOFMS — Associate of the Institute of Financial and Management Studies
AIP — Associate of the Institute of Plumbing
AIQA — Associate of the Institute of Quality Assurance
AIS — Accredited Imaging Scientist
AISOB — Associate of the Incorporated Society of Organ Builders
AISTD — Associate of the Imperial Society of Teachers of Dancing
AISTDDip — Associate Diploma of the Imperial Society of Teachers of Dancing
AITSA — Associate of the Institute of Trading Standards Administration
AIVehE — Associate of the Institute of Vehicle Engineers
AIWSc — Associate Member of the Institute of Wood Science
ALCM — Associate of the London College of Music
ALI — Associate of the Landscape Institute
ALS — Associate of the Linnean Society of London
AMA — Associate of the Museums Association
AMABE — Associate Member of the Association of Business Executives
AMAE — Associate Member of the Academy of Experts
AMASI — Associate Member of the Architecture and Surveying Institute
AMBA — Association of MBAs
AMBA — Non-Teacher Associate Member of the British (Theatrical) Arts
AMBCS — Associate Member of the British Computer Society
AMBII — Associate Member of the British Institute of Innkeeping
AmCAM — Associate of the Communication Advertising and Marketing Education Foundation
AMCT — Associate of the Association of Corporate Treasurers
AMCTHCM — Associate Member of the Confederation of Tourism, Hotel and Catering Management
AMI — Association Montessori Internationale
AMIA — Affiliated Member of the Association of International Accountants
AMIAgrE — Associate Member of the Institution of Agricultural Engineers
AMIAP — Associate Member of the Institution of Analysts and Programmers

AMIAT	Associate Member of the Institute of Asphalt Technology
AMIBC	Associate Member of the Institute of Building Control
AMIBCM	Associate Member of the Institute of British Carriage and Automobile Manufacturers
AMIBE	Associate Member of the Institution of British Engineers
AMIBF	Associate Member of the Institute of British Foundrymen
AMICE	Associate Member of the Institution of Civil Engineers
AMIChemE	Associate Member of the Institution of Chemical Engineers
AMIED	Associate Member of the Institution of Engineering Designers
AMIEE	Associate Member of the Institution of Electrical Engineers
AMIEx	Associate Member of the Institute of Export
AMIHIE	Associate Member of the Institute of Highway Incorporated Engineers
AMIHT	Associate Member of the Institution of Highways and Transportation
AMIIE	Associate Member of the Institution of Incorporated Engineers
AMIIExE	Associate Member of the Institution of Incorporated Executive Engineers
AMIIHTM	Associate Member of the International Institute of Hospitality Tourism & Management
AMIISE	Associate Member of the International Institute of Social Economics
AMIM	Associate Member of the Institute of Materials
AMIManf	Member of the Institute of Manufacturing
AMIMechE	Associate Member of the Institution of Mechanical Engineers
AMIMechIE	Associate Member of the Institution of Mechanical Incorporated Engineers
AMIMI	Associate Member of the Institute of the Motor Industry
AMIMinE	Associate of the Institute of Mining Engineers
AMIMM	Associate Member of the Institution of Mining and Metallurgy
AMIMS	Associate Member of the Institute of Management Specialists
AMInstAEA	Associate Member of the Institute of Automotive Engineer Assessors
AMInstBE	Associate Member of the Institution of British Engineers
AMInstE	Associate Member of the Institute of Energy
AMInstR	Associate Member of the Institute of Refrigeration
AMInstTA	Associate Member of the Institute of Transport Administration
AMIPlantE	Associate Member of the Institution of Plant Engineers
AMIPR	Associate Member of the Institute of Public Relations
AMIPRE	Associate Member of the Incorporated Practitioners in Radio and Electronics
AMIQ	Associate Member of the Institute of Quarrying
AMIQA	Associate Member of the Institute of Quality Assurance
AMIRTE	Associate Member of the Institute of Road Transport Engineers
AMISM	Associate Member of the Institute for Supervision & Management
AMIStrutE	Associate Member of the Institution of Structural Engineers
AMITD	Associate Member of the Institute of Training and Development
AMIVehE	Associate Member of the Institute of Vehicle Engineers
AMNI	Associate Member of the Nautical Institute
AMPA	Associate Member of the Master Photographers Association
AMProfBTM	Associate Member of Professional Business and Technical Management
AMRAeS	Associate Member of the Royal Aeronautical Society
AMRSH	Associate Member of the Royal Society for the Promotion of Health
AMS	Associate of the Institute of Management Services
AMS(Aff)	Affiliate of the Association of Medical Secretaries, Practice Managers, Administrators and Receptionists
AMSE	Associate Member of the Society of Engineers (Inc)
AMSPAR	Association of Medical Secretaries, Practice Managers, Administrators and Receptionists

AMusEd	Associate Diploma in Music Education
AMusLCM	Associate in Music of the London College of Music
AMusTCL	Associate in Music of Trinity College of Music
AMWES	Associate Member of the Women's Engineering Society
ANAEA	Associate of the National Association of Estate Agents
ANCA	Advanced National Certificate in Agriculture
AOP	Association of Photographers
AOR	Association of Reflexologists
APA	Accreditation of Prior Experience
APC	Assessment of Professional Competence
APCS	Associate of the Property Consultants Society
APMI	Associate of the Pensions Management Institute
APMP	Association for Project Management Professional
AQA	Assessment & Qualifications Alliance
ARAD	Associate of the Royal Academy of Dancing
ARAM	Associate of the Royal Academy of Music
ARB	Architects Registration Board
ARCM	Associate of Royal College of Music
ARCO	Associate of the Royal College of Organists
ARCS	Associate of the Royal College of Science
AREC	Associate of the Recruitment and Employment Confederation
ARELS	Association of Recognised English Language Services
ARELS-FELCO	Association of Recognised English Language Teaching Establishments in Britain
ARIBA	Associate of the Royal Institute of British Architects
ARICS	Associate of the Royal Institution of Chartered Surveyors
ARIPHH	Associate of the Royal Institute of Public Health and Hygiene
ARPS	Associate of the Royal Photographic Society
ARSC	Associate of the Royal Society of Chemistry
ARSCM	Associate of the Royal School of Church Music
ARSM	Associate of the Royal School of Mines
AS	Advanced Supplementary level
ASCA	Associate of the Institute of Company Accountants
ASCT	Associate of the Society of Claims Technicians
ASDC	Associate of the Society of Dyers and Colourists
ASE	Associate of the Society of Engineers (Inc)
ASI	Ambulance Service Institute
ASI	Architecture and Surveying Institute
ASIAffil	Affiliate of the Ambulance Service Institute
ASIS	Accredited Senior Imaging Scientist
ASLC	Advanced Secretarial Language Certificate
ASMA	Associate of the Society of Sales Management Administrators Ltd
ASNN	Associate of the Society of Nursery Nursing
AssCI	Associate of the Institute of Commerce
AssociateCIPD	Associate of the Chartered Institute of Personnel and Development
AssociateIEEE	Associate of the Institution of Electrical and Electronics Engineers Incorporated
AssociateIIE	Associate of the Institution of Incorporated Engineers
AssocIMechIE	Associate of the Institution of Mechanical Incorporated Engineers
AssocIPD	Associate of the Institute of Personnel & Development
AssocIPHE	Associate of the Institution of Public Health Engineers
AssocMIWM	Associate Member of the Institute of Wastes Management
AssocTechIIE	Associate Technician of the Institution of Incorporated Engineers
ASTA	Associate of the Swimming Teachers' Association

ASVA	Associate of the Incorporated Society of Valuers and Auctioneers
ATC	Art Teacher's Certificate
ATCL	Associate of Trinity College of Music
ATCLicence	Air Traffic Controller's Licence
ATCLTESOL	Associate Diploma in the Teaching of English to Speakers of Other Languages, Trinity College
ATD	Art Teacher's Diploma
ATI	Associate of the Textile Industry
ATII	Associate of the Chartered Institute of Taxation
ATPL	Airline Transport Pilot's Licence
ATSC	Associate of the Oil and Colour Chemists' Association
ATSC	Associate in the Technology of Surface Coatings
ATT	Association of Taxation Technicians
ATT	Member of the Association of Taxation Technicians
ATTA	Association of Therapy Teachers Associate
ATTF	Association of Therapy Teachers Fellow
ATTM	Association of Therapy Teachers Member
AWeldI	Associate of the Welding Institute
BA	Bachelor of Arts
BA(Econ)	Bachelor of Arts in Economics & Social Studies
BA(Ed)	Bachelor of Arts (Education)
BA(Lan)	Bachelor of Languages
BA(Law)	Bachelor of Arts in Law
BA(Music)	Bachelor of Music
BABTAC	British Association of Beauty Therapy and Cosmetology Ltd
BAC	British Accreditation Council for Independent Further and Higher Education
BAC	British Association for Counselling
BAcc	Bachelor of Accountancy
BACP	British Association for Counselling Psychotherapy
BADA	British Antique Dealers' Association
BADN	British Association of Dental Nurses
BAE	British Association of Electrolysists Ltd
BAGMA	British Agricultural and Garden Machinery Association
BAgr	Bachelor of Agriculture
BAO	Bachelor of Obstetrics
BAP	British Association of Psychotherapists
BArch	Bachelor of Architecture
BASELT	British Association in State English Language Teaching
BBO	British Ballet Organisation
BChD	Bachelor of Dental Surgery
BChir	Bachelor of Surgery
BCL	Bachelor of Civil Law
BCom	Bachelor of Commerce
BCombStuds	Bachelor of Combined Studies
BComm	Bachelor of Communications
BCS	Bachelor of Combined Studies
BCS	British Computer Society
BD	Bachelor of Divinity
BDA	British Dietetic Association
BDes	Bachelor of Design
BDS	Bachelor of Dental Surgery
BEconSc	Bachelor of Economics

BECTU	Broadcasting, Entertainment, Cinematograph and Theatre Union
BEd	Bachelor of Education
BEng	Bachelor of Engineering
BEng and Man	Bachelor of Mechanical Engineering, Manufacture and Management
BER	Board for Engineers' Regulation
BFA	Bachelor of Fine Arts
BFin	Bachelor of Finance
BHA	British Hypnotherapy Association
BHI	British Horological Institute Ltd
BHS	British Horse Society
BHSAI	British Horse Society's Assistant Instructor's Certificate
BHSI	British Horse Society's Instructor's Certificate
BHSII	British Horse Society's Intermediate Instructor's Certificate
BHSIntSM	British Horse Society's Intermediate Stable Manager's Certificate
BHSSM	British Horse Society's Stable Manager's Certificate
BIA	Beauty Industry Authority
BIAT	British Institute of Architectural Technologists
BIBA	Bachelor of International Business Administration
BIE	British Institute of Embalmers
BIFA	British International Freight Association
BIPP	British Institute of Professional Photography
BIS	British Interplanetary Society
BKSTS	British Kinematograph Sound and Television Society
BLD	Bachelor of Landscape Design
BLE	Bachelor of Land Economy
BLEng	Bi-Lingual Engineer
BLib	Bachelor of Librarianship
BLing	Bachelor of Linguistics
BLitt	Bachelor of Letters
BLS	Bachelor of Library Studies
BM	Bachelor of Medicine
BMA	British Medical Association
BM, BCh	Conjoint degree of Bachelor of Medicine, Bachelor of Surgery
BM, BS	Conjoint degree of Bachelor of Medicine, Bachelor of Surgery
BMedBiol	Bachelor of Medical Biology
BMedSci	Bachelor of Medical Sciences
BMedSci(Speech)	Bachelor of Medical Sciences (Speech)
BMet	Bachelor of Metallurgy
BMid	Bachelor of Midwifery
BMidwif	Bachelor of Midwifery
BMSc	Bachelor of Medical Sciences
BMus	Bachelor of Music
BN	Bachelor of Nursing
BNNursing	Bachelor of Nursing, Nursing Studies
BNSc	Bachelor of Nursing
BNurs	Bachelor of Nursing
BOptom	Bachelor of Optometry
BPA	Bachelor of Performing Arts
BPharm	Bachelor of Pharmacy
BPhil	Bachelor of Philosophy
BPhil(Ed)	Bachelor of Philosophy (Education)
BPL	Bachelor of Planning

BSc	Bachelor of Science
BSc(Archit)	Bachelor of Science (Architecture)
BSc(DentSci)	Bachelor of Science in Dental Science
BSc(Econ)	Bachelor of Science in Economics
BSc(MedSci)	Bachelor of Science (Medical Science)
BSc(Social Science)	Bachelor of Science (Social Science)
BSc(Town & Regional Planning)	Bachelor of Science (Town & Regional Planning)
BSc(VetSc)	Bachelor of Science (Veterinary Science)
BScAgr	Bachelor of Science in Agriculture
BScEng	Bachelor of Science in Engineering
BScFor	Bachelor of Science in Forestry
BScTech	Bachelor of Technical Science
BSocSc	Bachelor of Social Science
BSSc	Bachelor of Social Science
BSSG	Member of the British Society of Scientific Glassblowers
BTEC	Business and Technology Education Council
BTech	Bachelor of Technology
BTechEd	Bachelor of Technological Education
BTEC HC	Business and Technology Education Council Higher Certificate
BTEC HD	Business and Technology Education Council Higher Diploma
BTEC HNC	Business and Technology Education Council Higher National Certificate
BTEC HND	Business and Technology Education Council Higher National Diploma
BTechS	Bachelor of Technology Studies
BTh	Bachelor of Theology
BTheol	Bachelor of Theology
BTP	Bachelor of Town Planning
BVC	Bar Vocational Course
BVetMed	Bachelor of Veterinary Medicine
BVMS	Bachelor of Veterinary Medicine
BVM&S	Bachelor of Veterinary Medicine
BVSc	Bachelor of Veterinary Science
C&G	City and Guilds
CA	Member of the Institute of Chartered Accountants of Scotland
CAA	Civil Aviation Authority
CABE	Companion of the Association of Business Executives
CACHE	Council for Awards in Children's Care and Education
CAE	Certificated Automotive Engineer
CAE	Companion of the Academy of Experts
CAM	Communication Advertising and Marketing Education Foundation
CAS	Certification of Accountancy Studies
CASS	Certificate of Applied Social Studies
CAT	Certificate for Accounting Technicians
CAT	College of Advanced Technology
CATS	Postgraduate Qualification by Credit Accumulation and Transfer
CBA	Companion of the British (Theatrical) Arts
CBAE	Companion of the British Academy of Experts
CBIM	Companion of the British Institute of Management
CBiol	Chartered Biologist
CBLC	Certificate in Business Language Competence
CBSSG	Craft Member of the British Society of Scientific Glassblowers
CCETSW	Central Council for Education and Training in Social Work

CChem	Chartered Chemist
CCol	Chartered Colourist
CCST	Certificate of Completion of Specialist Training
CDBA	Certified Doctor of Business Administration
CDipAF	Certified Diploma in Accounting and Finance
CEE	Extended European Command Endorsement
CeFA	Certificate for Financial Advisers
CEM	Certificate in Executive Management
CeMAP	Certificate in Mortgage Advice and Practice
CEng	Chartered Engineer
CertAMed	Certificate in Aviation Medicine
CertArb	Certificate in Arboriculture
CertBibKnowl	Certificate of Bible Knowledge
CertCIH	Chartered Institute of Housing recognised Housing Qualification
CertCM	Certificate of Cash Management
CertDesRCA	Certificate of Designer of the Royal College of Art
CertEd	Certificate in Education
CertEPK	Certificate of Essential Pensions Knowledge
CertHE	Certificate of Higher Education
CertHSAP	Certificate in Health Services Administration Practice
CertHSM	Certificate in Health Services Management
CertMFS	Certificate in the Marketing of Financial Services
CertOccHyg	Certificate in Operational Competence in Comprehensive Occupational Hygiene
CertRP	Certificate in Recruitment Practice
CertTEL	Certificate in the Teaching of European Languages
CertTESOL	Certificate of Teaching of English to Speakers of Other Languages
CertTEYL	Certificate of Teaching of English to Young Learners
CertYCW	Certificate in Youth and Community Work
CETHV	Certificate of Education in Training as Health Visitor
CEYA	Council for Early Years Awards
CFS	Certificate in Financial Services
CFSP	Certificate in Financial Services Practice
CGeol	Chartered Geologist
CGLI	City & Guilds of London Institute
CHARM	Centre for Hazard and Risk Management
ChB	Bachelor of Surgery
CHD	Choral-Training Diploma
ChM	Master of Surgery
CHP	Certificate in Hypnosis and Psychology
CHRIM	Certified Member of the Institute of Health Record Information and Management
CIAgrE	Companion of the Institution of Agricultural Engineers
CIArb	Chartered Institute of Arbitrators
CIB	Chartered Institute of Bankers
CIBM	Corporate Member of the Institute of Builders' Merchants
CIBS	Chartered Institute of Bankers in Scotland
CIBSE	Chartered Institution of Building Services Engineers
CIC	Construction Industry Council
CIEx	Companion of the Institute of Export
CIFE	Conference for Independent Further Education
CIH	Chartered Institute of Housing
CII	Chartered Insurance Institute
CILA	Chartered Institute of Loss Adjusters

CILIP	Chartered Institute of Library and Information Professionals
CIM	Chartered Institute of Marketing
CIMA	Chartered Institute of Management Accountants
CIMediE	Companion of the Institution of Mechanical Engineers
CIMgt	Companion of the Institute of Management
CIOB	Chartered Institute of Building
CIP	Certificate of Institute Practice
CIPD	Chartered Institute of Personnel and Development
CIPFA	Chartered Institute of Public Finance & Accounting
CIPS	Chartered Institute of Purchasing and Supply
CISOB	Counsellor of the Incorporated Society of Organ Builders
CIT	Certificate in Information Technology
CIWEM	Chartered Institution of Water and Environmental Management
CL(ABDO)	Diploma in Contact Lens Practice of the Association of British Dispensing Opticians
CLAC	Commercial Language Assistant Certificate
CLAIT	Computer Literacy & Information Technology
CLC	Council for Licensed Conveyancers
CLE	Limited European Command Endorsement
ClinPsyD	Doctorate in Clinical Psychology
CMA	Certificate in Management Accountancy
CMathFIMA	Fellow of the Institute of Mathematics and its Applications
CMBA	Certified Master of Business Administration
CMBHI	Craft Member of the British Horological Institute
CMC	Certified Management Consultants
CMet	Chartered Meteorologist
CMIWSc	Certified Member of the Institute of Wood Science
CMS	Certificate in Management Studies
CNAA	Council for National Academic Awards
COA	Certificate of Accreditation
COBC	Certificate of Basic Competence
CoEA	Certificate of Educational Achievement
COES	Certificate of Educational Studies
CofE	Church of England
CofS	Church of Scotland
CompBCS	Companion of the British Computer Society
CompIAP	Companion of the Institution of Analysts and Programmers
CompIEE	Companion of the Institution of Electrical Engineers
CompIGasE	Companion of the Institution of Gas Engineers
CompIManf	Companion of the Institute of Manufacturing
CompIMS	Companion of the Institute of Management Specialists
CompIP	Companion of the Institute of Plumbing
CorporateIRRV	Corporate Member of the Institute of Revenues, Rating and Valuation
COSCA	Confederation of Scottish Counselling Agencies
CPA	Chartered Patent Agents
CPC	Certificate of Professional Competence, the Institute of Transport Administration
CPD	Continuing Professional Development
CPE	Common Professional Exam
CPEA	Certificate of Practice in Estate Agency
CPFA	Member of Chartered Institute of Public Finance and Accountancy
CPhys	Chartered Physicist of the Institute of Physics
CPIM	Certificate in Production and Inventory Management

CPL	Commercial Pilot's Licence
CPM	Certified Professional Manager
CPP	Certificate of Pre-school Practice
CPR	Chartered Professional Review
CProfBTM	Companion of Professional Business and Technical Management
CPS	Certificate in Pastoral Studies and Applied Theology
CPSC	Certificate of Proficiency in Survival Craft
CPsychol	Chartered Psychologist, British Psychological Society
CPT	Continuing Professional Training
CPVE	Certificate of Pre-Vocational Training
CRAeS	Companion of the Royal Aeronautical Society
CRAH	Central Register of Advanced Hypnotherapists
CRCW	Church Related Community Workers
CRNCM	Companion of the Royal Northern College of Music
CSCT	Central School for Counselling Training
CSD	Chartered Society of Designers
CSE	Certificate of Secondary Education
CSM	Certificate in Safety Management
CSMGSM	Certificate in Stage Management (Guildhall School of Music and Drama)
CStat	Chartered Statistician
CSYS	Certificate of Sixth Year Studies
CTABRSM	Certificate of Teaching of the Associated Board of the Royal School of Music
CTextATI	Associate of the Textile Institute
CTextFTI	Fellow of the Textile Institute
CTHCM	Confederation of Tourism, Hotel and Catering Management
CVA	Certificated Value Analyst
CVM	Certificated Value Manager
CVT	Certified Vehicle Technologist
DA	Diploma in Anaesthetics
DAdmin	Doctor of Administration
DAES	Diploma in Advanced Educational Studies
DArch	Doctor of Architecture
DAvMed	Diploma in Aviation Medicine
DBA	Doctor of Business Administration
DBE	Diploma in Business Engineering
DBO	Diploma of the British Orthoptic Society
DBS	Diploma in Business Studies
DCC	Diploma of Chelsea College
DCDH	Diploma in Child Dental Health
DCE	Dangerous Cargo Endorsements
DCE	Diploma in Childcare and Education
DCG	Diploma in Careers Guidance
DCH	Diploma in Child Health
DChD	Diploma of Dental Surgery
DChM	Diploma in Chiropodial Medicine, Institute of Chiropodists and Podiatrists
DCHT	Diploma in Community Health in Tropical Countries
DCL	Doctor of Civil Law
DCLF	Diploma in Contact Lens Fitting
DClinPsych	Doctor of Clinical Psychiatry
DCLP	Diploma in Contact Lens Practice
DCR(R)or(T)	Diploma of the College of Radiographers
DD	Doctor of Divinity

DDH(Birm)	Diploma in Dental Health, University of Birmingham
DDOrthRCPSGlas	Diploma in Dental Orthopaedics of the Royal College of Physicians and Surgeons of Glasgow
DDPHRCS(Eng)	Diploma in Dental Public Health, Royal College of Surgeons of England
DDS	Doctor of Dental Surgery
DDSc	Doctor of Dental Science
DEBA	Diploma in European Business Administration
DEdPsy	Doctor of Educational Psychiatry
DEM	Diploma in Executive Management
DEng	Doctor of Engineering
DES	Department of Education and Science (now the Department for Education)
DETR	Department of the Environment, Transport and the Regions
DFin	Doctor of Finance
DFSM	Diploma in Financial Services Management
DGA	Diamond Member of the Gemmological Association and Gem Testing Laboratory of Great Britain
DGDPRCSEng	Diploma in General Dental Practice, Royal College of Surgeons of England
DGM	Diploma in Geriatric Medicine
DGO	Diploma in Obstetrics and Gynaecology
DHC	Doctorate in Healthcare
DHE	Diploma in Horticulture, Royal Botanic Garden, Edinburgh
DHMSA	Diploma in the History of Medicine, Society of Apothecaries of London
DHP	Diploma in Hypnosis and Psychotherapy
DIA	Diploma of Industrial Administration
DIB	Diploma in International Business
DIC	Diploma of Membership of Imperial College of Science and Technology, University of London
DIH	Diploma in Industrial Health
DipABRSM	Diploma of the Associated Board of the Royal Schools of Music
DipAD	Diploma in Art and Design
DipAdvHYP	Diploma in Advanced Hypnotherapy
DipAE	Diploma in Adult Education
DipAgrComm	Diploma in Agricultural Communication
DipArb	Diploma in Arbitration
DipArb	Diploma in Arboriculture
DipArch	Diploma in Architecture
DipASE(CofP)	Graduate Level Specialist Diploma in Advanced Study in Education, College of Preceptors
DipASSc	Diploma in Arts and Social Sciences
DipAT	Diploma in Accounting Technology
DipAvMed	Diploma in Aviation Medicine
DipBA	Diploma in Business Administration
DipBldgCons	Diploma in Building Conservation
DipBMA	Diploma in Business Management
DipCAM	Diploma in the Communication Advertising and Marketing Education Foundation
DipCD	Diploma in Community Development
DipCHM	Diploma in Choir Training, Royal College of Organists
DipClinPath	Diploma in Clinical Pathology
DipCOT	Diploma of the College of Occupational Therapists
DipCP	Diploma of the College of Teachers
DipCT	Diploma in Corporate Treasury Management
DipDerm	Diploma in Dermatology

DipEd	Diploma in Education
DipEF	Diploma in Executive Finance
DipEH	Diploma in Environmental Health
DipEM	Diploma in Environmental Management
DipEMA	Diploma in Executive and Management Accountancy
DipEngLit	Diploma in English Literature
DipFD	Diploma in Funeral Directing, National Association of Funeral Directors
DipFS	Diploma in Financial Services
DipGAI	Diploma of the Guild of Architectural Ironmongers
DipGrTrans	Diploma in Greek Translation
DipGSM	Diploma of the Guildhall School of Music and Drama
DipHE	Diploma of Higher Education
DipHS	Diploma of the Heraldry Society
DipIEB	Diploma of the International Employee Benefits
DipISW	Diploma of the Institute of Social Welfare
DipLE	Diploma in Land Economy
DipLP	Diploma in Legal Practice
DipM	Postgraduate Diploma in Marketing
DipMedAc	Diploma in Medical Acupuncture
DipMetEng	Diploma in Meteorological Engineering
DipMFS	Diploma in the Marketing of Financial Services
DipMth	Diploma in Music Therapy
DipOccH	Diploma in Occupational Health
DipOccHyg	Diploma of Professional Competence in Comprehensive Occupational Hygiene
DipPDTC	Diploma in Professional Dancers Teaching Course
DipPharmMed	Diploma in Pharmaceutical Medicine
DipPhil	Diploma in Philosophy
DipProjMan	Diploma in Project Management
DipPropInv	Diploma in Property Investment
DipRAM	Diploma of the Royal Academy of Music
DipRCM	Diploma of the Royal College of Music
DipRMS	Diploma of the Royal Microscopical Society
DipSc	Diploma in Science
DipSM	Diploma in Safety Management
DipSurv	Diploma in Surveying
DipSW	Diploma in Social Work
DipTCL	Diploma of the Trinity College of Music, London
DipTCR	Diploma in Organ Teaching
DipTESOL	Diploma in Teaching of English to Speakers of Other Languages
DipTHP	Diploma in Therapeutic Hypnosis and Psychotherapy
DipTM	Diploma in Training Management, Institute of Personnel and Development
DipTransIoL	Diploma in Translation, Institute of Linguists
DipUniv	Diploma of the University
DipVen	Diploma in Venereology, Society of Apothecaries of London
DipWCF	Diploma of the Worshipful Company of Farriers
DIS	Diploma in Industrial Studies
DLang	Doctor of Language
DLit(t)	Doctor of Letters or Literature
DLO	Diploma of Laryngology and Otology
DLORCSEng	Diploma in Laryngology and Otology, Royal College of Surgeons of England
DLP	Diploma in Legal Practice
DM	Doctor of Medicine

DMedRehab	Diploma in Medical Rehabilitation
DMedSc	Doctor in Medical Science
DMet	Doctor of Metallurgy
DMJ(Clin) or DMJ(Path)	Diploma in Medical Jurisprudence (Clinical or Pathological), Society of Apothecaries of London
DMRD	Diploma in Medical Radio-Diagnosis
DMRT	Diploma in Radiotherapy
DMS	Diploma in Management Studies
DMU	Diploma in Medical Ultrasound
DMus	Doctor of Music
DMusCantuar	Archbishop of Canterbury's Doctorate in Music
DNSc	Doctor in Nursing Science
DO	Diploma in Ophthalmology
DO	Diploma in Osteopathy
DocEdPsy	Doctorate in Educational Psychology
DOpt	Diploma in Ophthalmic Optics
DOrth	Diploma in Orthoptics
DOrthRCSEdin	Diploma in Orthodontics, Royal College of Surgeons of Edinburgh
DOrthRCSEng	Diplomate in Orthodontics, Royal College of Surgeons of England
DP	Diploma in Psychotherapy
DPA	Diploma in Public Administration
DpBact	Diploma in Bacteriology
DPD(Dund)	Diploma in Public Dentistry, University of Dundee
DPH	Diploma in Public Health
DPharm	Diploma in Pharmacy
DPhil	Diploma in Philosophy
DPHRCSEng	Diploma in Dental Public Health, Royal College of Surgeons of England
DPM	Diploma in Psychological Medicine
DPodM	Diploma in Podiatric Medicine
DProf	Doctor of Professional Studies
DPS	Diploma in Professional Studies
DPSE	Diploma in Pastoral Studies and Applied Theology
DPsychol	Doctor of Psychology
DrAc	Doctor of Acupuncture
Dr(RCA)	Doctor of the Royal College of Art
DRCOG	Diploma of the Royal College of Obstetricians and Gynaecologists
DRDRCSEd	Diploma in Restorative Dentistry, Royal College of Surgeons of Edinburgh
DRE	Diploma in Remedial Electrolysis, Institute of Electrolysis
DRI	Diploma in Radionuclide Imaging
DRSAMD	Diploma in the Royal Scottish Academy of Music and Drama
DSA	Diploma in Secretarial Administration
DSc	Doctor of Science
DSc(Econ)	Doctor of Science (Economics) or in Economics
DSc(Eng)	Doctor of Science (Engineering)
DSc(Social)	Doctor of Science in the Social Sciences
DScEcon	Doctor in the Faculty of Economics and Social Studies
DSCh(Ox)	Diploma in Surgical Chiropody (Oxon), Oxford School of Chiropody and Podiatry
DScTech	Doctor of Technical Science
DSocSc	Doctor of Social Science
DSSc	Doctor of Social Science
DSTA	Diploma Member of the Swimming Teachers' Association
DTCD	Diploma in Tuberculosis and Chest Diseases

DTech	Doctor of Technology
DTI	Department of Trade and Industry
DTMH	Diploma in Tropical Medicine and Hygiene
DTM&H	Diploma in Tropical Medicine and Hygiene
DTp	Department of Transport
DUniv	Doctor of the University
DVetMed	Doctor of Veterinary Medicine
DVM	Doctor of Veterinary Medicine
DVM&S	Doctor of Veterinary Medicine and Surgery
DVS	Doctor of Veterinary Surgery
DVSc	Doctor of Veterinary Science
ECBL	European Certification Board for Logistics
ECDL	European Computer Driving Licence
ECG	Executive Group Committees (of the Board for Engineers Registration)
EDBA	Executive Diploma in Business Accounting
EdD	Doctor of Education
EDH	Efficient Deck Hand
EdPsyD	Doctor of Educational Psychology
EEAC	European Executive Assistant Certificate
EFB	English for Business
EFL	English as a Foreign Language
EHO	Environmental Health Officer
EIS	Educational Institute of Scotland
EITB	Engineering Industry Training Board
EMBA	European Master of Business Administration
EMBS	European Master of Business Sciences
EMFEC	East Midland Further Education Council
EN	Enrolled Nurse
EN(G)	Enrolled Nurse (General)
EN(M)	Enrolled Nurse (Mental)
EN(MH)	Enrolled Nurse (Mental Handicap)
ENB	English National Board
EngC	Engineering Council
EngD	Doctor of Engineering
EngTech	Engineering Technician
ENS	Electronic Navigational System
ESD	Executive Secretary's Diploma
ESOL	English for Speakers of Other Languages
ESSTL	Engineering Services Training Trust Ltd
EurIng	European Engineer
EuroBiol	European Biologist
FABE	Fellow of the Association of Business Executives
FACB	Fellow of the Association of Certified Bookkeepers
FACP	Fellow of the Association of Computer Professionals
FAE	Fellow of the Academy of Experts
FAFC	Fellow of the Association of Financial Controllers and Administrators
FAIA	Fellow of the Association of International Accountants
FAMS	Fellow of the Association of Medical Secretaries, Practice Managers, Administrators and Receptionists
FAPM	Fellow of the Association for Project Management
FASI	Fellow of the Ambulance Service Institute
FASI	Fellow of the Architecture and Surveying Institute

FASP	Fellow of the Association of Sales Personnel
FBA	Fellow of the British Academy
FBA	Fellow of the British (Theatrical) Arts
FBCS	Fellow of the British Computer Society
FBDO	Fellow of the Association of British Dispensing Opticians
FBDO(Hons)	Fellow of the Association of British Dispensing Opticians with Honours Diploma
FBDO(Hons)CL	Fellow of the Association of British Dispensing Opticians with Honours Diploma and Diploma in Contact Lens Practice
FBEI	Fellow of the Institution of Body Engineers
FBEng	Fellow of the Association of Building Engineers
FBHA	Fellow of the British Hypnotherapy Association
FBHI	Fellow of the British Horological Institute
FBHS	Fellow of the British Horse Society
FBID	Fellow of the British Institute of Interior Design
FBIDST	Fellow of the British Institute of Dental and Surgical Technologists
FBIE	Fellow of the British Institute of Embalmers
FBIPP	Fellow of the British Institute of Professional Photography
FBIS	Fellow of the British Interplanetary Society
FBMA	Fellow of the Business Management Association
FBPsS	Fellow of the British Psychological Society
FCA	Fellow of the Institute of Chartered Accountants in England and Wales
FCAM	Fellow of the Communication Advertising and Marketing Education Foundation
FCB	Fellow of the British Association of Communicators in Business Ltd
FCBSI	Fellow of the Chartered Building Societies Institute
FCCA	Fellow of the Association of Chartered Certified Accountants
FCEA	Fellow of the Institute of Cost and Executive Accountants
FCGI	Fellowship, City & Guilds
FChS	Fellow of the Society of Chiropodists and Podiatrists
FCI	Faculty of Commerce and Industry
FCI	Fellow of the Institute of Commerce
FCIArb	Fellow of the Chartered Institute of Arbitrators
FCIB	Fellow of the Chartered Institute of Bankers
FCIBS	Fellow of the Chartered Institute of Bankers in Scotland
FCIBSE	Fellow of the Chartered Institute of Building Services Engineers
FCIH	Fellow of the Chartered Institute of Housing
FCII	Fellow of the Chartered Insurance Institute
FCIJ	Fellow of the Chartered Institute of Journalists
FCILA	Fellow of the Chartered Institute of Loss Adjusters
FCIM	Fellow of the Chartered Institute of Marketing
FCIOB	Fellow of the Chartered Institute of Building
FCIPD	Fellow of the Chartered Institute of Personnel and Development
FCIPS	Fellow of the Chartered Institute of Purchasing and Supply
FCIS	Fellow of the Institute of Chartered Secretaries and Administrators
FCIT	Fellow of the Chartered Institute of Transport
FCLIP	Chartered Fellow of CILIP
FCLS	First Certificate for Legal Secretaries
FCMA	Fellow of the Chartered Institute of Management Accountants
FCMA	Fellow of the Institute of Cost and Management Accountants
FCMC	Fellow Grade Certified Management Consultants
FCOphth	Fellow of the College of Ophthalmology
FCOptom	Fellow of the College of Optometrists
FCoT	Ordinary Fellow of the College of Teachers

FCPM	Fellow of the Confederation of Professional Management
FCPP	Fellow of the College of Pharmacy Practice
FCSP	Fellow of the Chartered Society of Physiotherapy
FCT	Fellow of the Association of Corporate Treasurers
FCoT	Fellow of the College of Teachers
FCTHCM	Fellow of the Confederation of Tourism, Hotel and Catering Management
FCYW	Fellow of the Community and Youth Work Association
FDSRCPSGlas	Fellow in Dental Surgery of the Royal College of Surgeons of Glasgow
FDSRCSEd	Fellow in Dental Surgery of the Royal College of Physicians and Surgeons of Edinburgh
FDSRCSEng	Fellow in Dental Surgery of the Royal College of Surgeons of England
FE	Further Education
FEANI	Fédération Européene d'Associations Nationales d'Ingénieurs
FECI	Fellow of the Institute of Employment Consultants
FEFC	Further Education Funding Council
FEIS	Fellow of the Educational Institute of Scotland
FFA	Fellow of the Faculty of Actuaries
FFA	Fellow of the Institute of Financial Accountants
FFARCSEng	Fellow of the Faculty of Anaesthetists of the Royal College of Surgeons in England
FFARCSIrel	Fellow of the Faculty of Anaesthetists of the Royal College of Surgeons in Ireland
FFAS	Fellow of the Faculty of Architects and Surveyors (Architects)
FFCA	Fellow of the Association of Financial Controllers and Administrators
FFCI	Fellow of the Faculty of Commerce and Industry
FFCS	Fellow of the Faculty of Secretaries
FFHom	Fellow of the Faculty of Homeopathy
FFPHM	Fellow of the Faculty of Public Health Medicine, Royal College of Physicians of London and Edinburgh and Royal College of Physicians and Surgeons of Glasgow
FFPHMIrel	Fellow of the Faculty of Public Health Medicine, Royal College of Physicians of Ireland
FFRRCSIrel	Fellow of the Faculty of Radiologists, Royal College of Surgeons in Ireland
FFS	Fellow of the Faculty of Architects and Surveyors (Surveyors)
FGA	Fellow of the Gemmological Association and Gem Testing Laboratory of Great Britain
FGCL	Fellow of the Guild of Cleaners and Launderers
FGI	Fellow of the Greek Institute
FGSM	Fellow of the Guildhall School of Music and Drama
FHCIMA	Fellow of the Hotel and Catering International Management Association
FHFS	Fellow of the Council of Health, Fitness and Sports Therapists
FHG	Fellow of the Institute of Heraldic and Genealogical Studies
FHRIM	Fellow of the Institute of Health Record Information and Management
FHS	Fellow of the Heraldry Society
FHSM	Fellow of the Institute of Health Services Management
FHT	Federation of Holistic Therapies
FIA	Fellow of the Institute of Actuaries
FIAB	Fellow of the International Association of Book-keepers
FIAEA	Fellow of the Institute of Automotive Engineer Assessors
FIAgrE	Fellow of the Institution of Agricultural Engineers
FIAP	Fellow of the Institution of Analysts and Programmers
FIAT	Fellow of the Institute of Asphalt Technology
FIBA	Fellow of the Institution of Business Agents
FIBC	Fellow of the Institute of Building Control

FIBCM	Fellow of the Institute of British Carriage and Automobile Manufacturers
FIBCO	Fellow of the Institute of Building Control Officers
FIBE	Fellow of the Institution of British Engineers
FIBF	Fellow of the Institute of British Foundrymen
FIBiol	Fellow of the Institute of Biology
FIBM	Fellow of the Institute of Builders' Merchants
FIBMS	Fellow of the Institute of Biomedical Science
FIBMS	Fellow of the Institute of Medical Laboratory Sciences
FICA	Fellow of the Institute of Company Accountants
FICB	Fellow of the Institute of Certified Book-Keepers
FICE	Fellow of the Institution of Civil Engineers
FIChemE	Fellow of the Institution of Chemical Engineers
FIChor	Fellow of the Benesh Institute of Choreology
FICHT	Fellow of the International Council of Holistic Therapies
FICM	Fellow of the Institute of Credit Management
FICorr	Fellow of the Institute of Corrosion
FICS	Fellow of the Institute of Chartered Shipbrokers
FICW	Fellow of the Institute of Clerks of Works of Great Britain Incorporated
FIDTA	Fellow of the International Dance Teachers' Association
FIED	Fellow of the Institution of Engineering Designers
FIEE	Fellow of the Institution of Electrical Engineers
FIEM	Fellow of the Institute of Executives and Managers
FIEx	Fellow of the Institute of Export
FIExpE	Fellow of the Institute of Explosives Engineers
FIFBQ	Fellow of the International Faculty of Business Qualifications
FIFireE	Fellow of the Institution of Fire Engineers
FIFM	Fellow of the Institute of Fisheries Management
FIFST	Fellow of the Institute of Food Science and Technology
FIGasE	Fellow of the Institution of Gas Engineers
FIGD	Fellow of the Institute of Grocery Distribution
FIGeol	Fellow of the Institute of Geologists
FIHEc	Fellow of the Institute of Home Economics Ltd
FIHIE	Fellow of the Institute of Highway Incorporated Engineers
FIHort	Fellow of the Institute of Horticulture
FIHT	Fellow of the Institution of Highways and Transportation
FIIE	Fellow of the Institution of Incorporated Engineers
FIIHTM	Fellow of the International Institute of Hospitality Tourism & Management
FIIM	Fellow of the International Institute of Management
FIIMR	Fellow of the Institute of Investment Management and Research
FIIRSM	Fellow of the International Institute of Risk and Safety Management
FIISE	Fellow of the International Institute of Social Economics
FIISec	Fellow of the International Institute of Security
FIL	Fellow of the Institute of Linguists
FILAM	Fellow of the Institute of Leisure and Amenity Management
FILT	Fellow of the Institute of Logistics and Transport
FIM	Fellow of the Institute of Materials
FIMA	Fellow of the Institute of Mathematics and its Applications
FIManf	Fellow of the Institute of Manufacturing
FIMarE	Fellow of the Institute of Marine Engineers
FIMatM	Fellow of the Institute of Materials Management
FIMBM	Fellow of the Institute of Maintenance and Building Management
FIMechE	Fellow of the Institute of Mechanical Engineers

FIMechIE	Fellow of the Institute of Mechanical Incorporated Engineers
FIMF	Fellow of the Institute of Metal Finishing
FIMgt	Fellow of the Institute of Management
FIMI	Fellow of the Institute of the Motor Industry
FIMIS	Fellow of the Institute for the Management of Information Systems
FIMM	Fellow of the Institute of Massage and Movement
FIMM	Fellow of the Institution of Mining and Metallurgy
FIMM	International Federation of Manual Medicine
FIMS	Fellow of the Institute of Management Specialists
FIMunE	Fellow of the Institution of Municipal Engineers
FInstAEA	Fellow of the Institute of Automotive Engineer Assessors
FInstAM	Fellow of the Institute of Administrative Management
FInstBA	Fellow of the Institute of Business Administration
FInstBCA	Fellow of the Institute of Burial and Cremation Administration
FInstBM	Fellow of the Institute of Builders' Merchants
FInstBRM	Fellow of the Institute of Baths and Recreation Management
FInstCh	Fellow of the Institute of Chiropodists
FInstCM	Fellow of the Institute of Commercial Management
FInstD	Fellow of the Institute of Directors
FInstE	Fellow of the Institute of Energy
FInstLEx	Fellow of the Institute of Legal Executives
FInstMC	Fellow of the Institute of Measurement and Control
FInstNDT	Fellow of the British Institute of Non-Destructive Testing
FInstP	Fellow of the Institute of Physics
FInstPet	Fellow of the Institute of Petroleum
FInstPkg	Fellow of the Institute of Packaging
FInstPM	Fellow of the Institute of Professional Managers and Administrators
FInstPS	Fellow of the Institute of Purchasing and Supply
FInstR	Fellow of the Institute of Refrigeration
FInstSMM	Fellow of the Institute of Sales and Marketing Management
FInstTA	Fellow of the Institute of Transport Administration
FInstTT	Fellow of the Institute of Travel and Tourism
FInstWM	Fellow of the Institute of Wastes Management
FInstWM	Fellowship of the Institute of Wastes Management
FIntMC	Fellow of International Management Centre
FIOC	Fellow of the Institute of Carpenters
FIOM	Fellow of the Institute of Operations Management
FIOP	Fellow of the Institute of Plumbing
FIOP	Fellow of the Institute of Printing
FIOSH	Fellow of the Institution of Occupational Safety and Health
FIPA	Fellow of the Institute of Practitioners in Advertising
FIPD	Fellow of the Institute of Personnel Development
FIPI	Fellow of the Institute of Professional Investigators
FIPlantE	Fellow of the Institution of Plant Engineers
FIPR	Fellow of the Institute of Public Relations
FIQ	Fellow of the Institute of Quarrying
FIQA	Fellow of the Institute of Quality Assurance
FIR	Fellow of the Institute of Population Registration
FIRSE	Fellow of the Institution of Railway Signal Engineers
FIRTE	Fellow of the Institute of Road Transport Engineers
FIS	Fellow of the Institute of Statisticians
FISM	Fellow of the Institute for Supervision & Management

FISOB	Fellow of the Incorporated Society of Organ Builders
FISTC	Fellow of the Institute of Scientific and Technical Communicators
FISTD	Fellow of the Imperial Society of Teachers of Dancing
FIStrucE	Fellow of the Institution of Structural Engineers
FISW	Fellow of the Institute of Social Welfare
FIT	Foundation Insurance Test
FITD	Fellow of the Institute of Training and Development
FITSA	Fellow of the Institute of Trading Standards Administration
FIVehE	Fellow of the Institute of Vehicle Engineers
FIWM	Fellow of the Institute of Wastes Management
FLAW	Foreign Languages at Work
FLCM	Fellow of the London College of Music
FLCSP	Fellow of the London and Counties Society of Physiologists
FLI	Fellow of the Landscape Institute
FLIC	Foreign Languages for Industry and Commerce
FLS	Fellow of the Linnean Society of London
FMA	Fellow of the Museums Association
FMAAT	Fellow Member of the Association of Accounting Technicians
FMPA	Fellow of the Master Photographers Association
FMR	Fellow of the Association of Health Care Information and Medical Records Officers
FMS	Fellow of the Institute of Management Services
FMusEd	Fellowship in Music Education
FN	Fellow of the Nautical Society
FNAEA	Fellow of the National Association of Estate Agents
FNAEAHon	Honoured Fellow of the National Association of Estate Agents
FNCP	Fellow of the National Council of Psychotherapists
FNI	Fellow of the Nautical Institute
FNIMH	Fellow of the National Institute of Medical Herbalists
FPC	Financial Planning Certificate
FPC	Foundation for Psychotherapy and Counselling
FPCS	Fellow of the Property Consultants Society
FPMI	Fellow of the Pensions Management Institute
FPodS	Fellow of the Surgical Faculty of the College of Podiatrists
FProfBTM	Fellow of Professional Business and Technical Management
FRAeS	Fellow of the Royal Aeronautical Society
FRAS	Fellow of the Royal Astronomical Society
FRCA	Fellow of the Royal College of Anaesthetists
FRCGP	Fellow of the Royal College of General Practitioners
FRCM	Fellow of the Royal College of Music
FRCO	Fellow of the Royal College of Organists
FRCO(CHM)	Fellow of the Royal College of Organists (Choir-training Diploma)
FRCOG	Fellow of the Royal College of Obstetricians and Gynaecologists
FRCP	Fellow of the Royal College of Physicians of London
FRCPath	Fellow of the Royal College of Pathologists
FRCPEdin	Fellow of the Royal College of Physicians of Edinburgh
FRCPsych	Fellow of the Royal College of Psychiatrists
FRCR	Fellow of the Royal College of Radiologists
FRCS(Irel)	Fellow of the Royal College of Surgeons in Ireland
FRCSEd	Fellow of the Royal College of Surgeons of Edinburgh
FRCSEd(C/TH)	Fellow of the Royal College of Surgeons of Edinburgh, specialising in Cardiothoracic Surgery

FRCSEd(Orth)	Fellow of the Royal College of Surgeons of Edinburgh, specialising in Orthopaedic Surgery
FRCSEd(SN)	Fellow of the Royal College of Surgeons of Edinburgh, specialising in Surgical Neurology
FRCSEng	Fellow of the Royal College of Surgeons of England
FRCSEng(Oto)	Fellow of the Royal College of Surgeons of England, with Otolaryngology
FRCSGlasg	Fellow of the Royal College of Physicians and Surgeons of Glasgow
FRCVS	Fellow of the Royal College of Veterinary Surgeons
FREC	Fellow of the Recruitment and Employment Confederation
FRHS	Fellow of the Royal Horticultural Society
FRIBA	Fellow of the Royal Institute of British Architects
FRICS	Fellow of the Royal Institution of Chartered Surveyors
FRIN	Fellow of the Royal Institute of Navigation
FRINA	Fellow of the Royal Institution of Naval Architects
FRIPHH	Fellow of the Royal Institution of Public Health and Hygiene
FRNCM	Fellow of the Royal Northern College of Music
FRPharmS	Fellow of the Royal Pharmaceutical Society of Great Britain
FRPS	Fellow of the Royal Photographic Society
FRS	Fellow of the Royal Society
FRSC	Fellow of the Royal Society of Chemistry
FRSCM	Fellow of the Royal School of Church Music
FRSH	Fellow of the Royal Society for the Promotion of Health
FRTPI	Fellow of the Royal Town Planning Institute
FSAPP	Fellow of the Society of Advanced Psychotherapy Practitioners
FSBP	Fellow of the Society of Business Practitioners
FSBT	Fellow of the Society of Teachers in Business Education
FSCT	Fellow of the Society of Claims Technicians
FSDC	Fellow of the Society of Dyers and Colourists
FSE	Fellow of the Society of Engineers (Inc)
FSElec	Fellow of the Society of Electroscience
FSG	Fellow of the Society of Genealogists
FSG(Hon)	Honorary Fellow of the Society of Genealogists
FSGT	Fellow of the Society of Glass Technology
FSIAD	Fellow of the Society of Industrial Artists and Designers
FSMA	Fellow of the Society of Martial Arts
FSMA	Fellow of the Society of Sales Management Administrators Ltd
FSNN	Fellow of the Society of Nursery Nursing
FSS	Fellow of the Royal Statistical Society
FSSCh	Fellow of the British Chiropody and Podiatry Association
FSSF	Fellow of the Society of Shoe Fitters
FSTA	Fellow of the Swimming Teachers' Association
FSVA	Fellow of the Incorporated Society of Valuers and Auctioneers
FTCL	Fellow of the Trinity College of Music
FTI	Fellow of the Textile Institute
FTII	Fellow of the Chartered Institute of Taxation
FTSC	Fellow of the Oil and Colour Chemists' Association
FTSC	Fellow in the Technology of Surface Coatings
FWeldI	Fellow of the Welding Institute
FYDA	Associate Fellowship of the Youth Development Association
GAGTL	Gemmological Association and Gem Testing Laboratory of Great Britain
GAI	Guild of Architectural Ironmongers
GASI	Graduate Member of the Ambulance Service Institute

GBSM	Graduate of the Birmingham School of Music
GCE	General Certificate of Education
GCE A	General Certificate of Education Advanced Level
GCE O	General Certificate of Education Ordinary Level
GCGI	Graduateship, City & Guilds
GCL	Guild of Cleaners and Launderers
GCSE	General Certificate of Secondary Education
GDC	General Dental Council
GIBCM	Graduate of the Institute of British Carriage and Automobile Manufacturers
GIBiol	Graduate of the Institute of Biology
GIEM	Graduate of the Institute of Executives and Managers
GIMA	Graduate of the Institute of Mathematics and its Applications
GIMI	Graduate of the Institute of the Motor Industry
GInstP	Graduate of the Institute of Physics
GIntMC	Graduate of the International Management Centre
GIS	Graduate Imaging Scientist
GLCM	Graduate Diploma of the London College of Music
GMAT	Graduate Management Admissions Test
GMC	General Medical Council
GMDSS	Global Maritime Distress & Safety System
GMInstM	Graduate Member of the Meat Training Council
GMus	Graduate Diploma in Music
GMusRNCM	Graduate in Music of the Royal Northern College of Music
GNSM	Graduate of the Northern School of Music
GNVQ	General National Vocational Qualifications
GradAES	Graduate of the Royal Aeronautical Society
GradBEng	Graduate Member of the Association of Building Engineers
GradBHI	Graduate of the British Horological Institute
GradDip	Graduate Diploma
GradIAP	Graduate of the Institution of Analysts and Programmers
GradIBE	Graduate of the Institution of British Engineers
GradIElecIE	Graduate of the Institution of Electrical and Electronics Incorporated Engineers
GradIIE	Graduate of the Institution of Incorporated Engineers
GradIISec	Graduate of the International Institute of Security
GradIManf	Graduate of the Institute Manufacturing
GradIMF	Graduate of the Institute of Metal Finishing
GradIMS	Graduate of the Institute of Management Specialists
GradInstNDT	Graduate of the British Institute of Non-Destructive Testing
GradInstP	Graduate of the Institute of Physics
GradInstPS	Graduate of the Institute of Purchasing and Supply
GradIOP	Graduate of the Institute of Printing
GradIPD	Graduate of the Institute of Personnel and Development
GradIS	Graduate of the Institute of Statisticians
GradISCA	Graduate of the Institute of Chartered Secretaries and Administrators
GradMechE	Graduate of the Institution of Mechanical Engineers
GradMIWM	Graduate Member of the Institute of Wastes Management
GradRNCM	Graduate of the Royal Northern College of Music
GradRSC	Graduate of the Royal Society of Chemistry
GradSMA	Graduate of the Society of Martial Arts
GradStat	Graduate Statistician
GraduateCIPD	Graduate of the Chartered Institute of Personnel and Development
GraduateIEIE	Graduate of the Institution of Electrical and Electronics Incorporated Engineers

GradWeldI	Graduate of the Welding Institute
GRC	General Readers Certificate
GRC	Grade Related Criteria
GRIC	Graduate Membership of the Royal Institute of Chemistry
GRSC	Graduate of the Royal Society of Chemistry
GRSM	Graduate Diploma of the Royal Manchester School of Music
GRSM(Hons)	Graduate of the Royal Schools of Music
GSMA	Graduate of the Society of Sales Management Administrators Ltd
GSNN	Graduate of the Society of Nursery Nursing
GTC	General Teaching Council
HABIA	Hairdressing and Beauty Industry Authority
HC	Higher Certificate
HCIMA	Hotel and Catering International Management Association
HD	Higher Diploma
HDCR (R) or (T)	Higher Award in Radiodiagnosis or Radiotherapy, College of Radiographers
HEFCE	Higher Education Funding Council for England
HFInstE	Honorary Fellow of the Institute of Energy
HNC	Higher National Certificate
HND	Higher National Diploma
HonASTA	Honorary Associate of the Swimming Teachers' Association
HonDrRCA	Honorary Doctorate of the Royal College of Art
HonFAE	Honorary Fellow of the Academy of Experts
HonFBID	Honorary Fellow of the British Institute of Interior Design
HonFBIPP	Honorary Fellow of the British Institute of Professional Photography
HonFCP	Charter Fellow of the College of Preceptors
HonFEIS	Honorary Fellow of the Educational Institute of Scotland
HonFHCIMA	Honorary Fellow of the Hotel, Catering and Institutional Management Association
HonFHS	Honorary Fellow of the Heraldry Society
HonFIEE	Honorary Fellow of the Institution of Electrical Engineers
HonFIExpE	Honorary Fellow of the Institute of Explosives Engineers
HonFIGasE	Honorary Fellow of the Institution of Gas Engineers
HonFIMarE	Honorary Fellow of the Institute of Marine Engineers
HonFIMechE	Honorary Fellow of the Institution of Mechanical Engineers
HonFIMM	Honorary Fellow of the Institution of Mining and Metallurgy
HonFInstE	Honorary Fellow of the Institute of Energy
HonFInstMC	Honorary Fellow of the Institute of Measurement and Control
HonFInstNDT	Honorary Fellow of the British Institute of Non-Destructive Testing
HonFIQA	Honorary Fellow of the Institute of Quality Assurance
HonFIRSE	Honorary Fellow of the Institution of Railway Signal Engineers
HonFIRTE	Honorary Fellow of the Institute of Road Transport Engineers
HonFPRI	Honorary Fellow of the Plastics and Rubber Institute
HonFRIN	Honorary Fellow of the Royal Institute of Navigation
HonFRINA	Honorary Fellow of the Royal Institution of Naval Architects
HonFRPS	Honorary Fellow of the Royal Photographic Society
HonFSE	Honorary Fellow of the Society of Engineers (Inc)
HonFSGT	Honorary Fellow of the Society of Glass Technology
HonFWeldI	Honorary Fellow of the Welding Institute
HonGSM	Honorary Member of the Guildhall School of Music and Drama
HonMIFM	Honorary Member of the Institute of Fisheries Management
HonMInstNDT	Honorary Member of the British Institute of Non-Destructive Testing
HonMRIN	Honorary Member of the Royal Institute of Navigation
HonMWES	Honorary Member of the Women's Engineering Society

HonRAM	Honorary Member of the Royal Academy of Music
HonRCM	Honorary Member of the Royal College of Music
HonRNCM	Honorary Member of the Royal Northern College of Music
HonRSCM	Honorary Member of the Royal School of Church Music
HSC	Higher School Certificate
HSE	Health & Safety Executive
HTB	Hairdressing Training Board
HTC	Higher Technical Certificate
IAAP	International Association for Analytic Psychology
IAB	International Association of Book-Keepers
IABC	International Association of Business Computing
IAC	Investment Advice Certificate
IAgrE	Institution of Agricultural Engineers
IAP	Institution of Analysts and Programmers
IAQ	Investment Administration Qualification
IAT	Institute of Asphalt Technology
IBA	Institute of Business Administration
IBC	Institute of Building Control
IBE	Institution of British Engineers
IBF	Institute of British Foundrymen
IBMS	Institute of Biomedical Science
ICAEW	Institute of Chartered Accountants in England and Wales
ICAI	Institute of Chartered Accountants in Ireland
ICAS	Institute of Chartered Accountants of Scotland
ICB	Institute of Certified Book-Keepers
ICE	Institution of Civil Engineers
ICEA	Institute of Cost and Executive Accountants
ICG	Institute of Careers Guidance
IChemE	Institution of Chemical Engineers
ICIOB	Incorporated Member of the Chartered Institute of Building
ICM	Institute of Commercial Management
ICM	Institute of Complementary Medicine
ICM	Institute of Credit Management
ICMQ	International Capital Markets Qualification
ICSA	Institute of Chartered Secretaries and Administrators
ICSF	Intermediate Certificate of the Society of Floristry
IDA	Improvement and Development Agency
IDTA	International Dance Teachers' Association Ltd
IED	Institution of Engineering Designers
IEE	Institution of Electrical Engineers
IEM	Institute of Executives and Managers
IEng	Incorporated Engineer
IETTL	Insulation and Environmental Training Trust Ltd
IEx	Institute of Export
IExpE	Institute of Explosives Engineers
IFA	Institute of Field Archaeologists
IFA	Institute of Financial Accountants
IFA	Insurance Foundation Certificate
IFBQ	International Faculty of Business Qualifications
IFM	Institute of Fisheries Management
IFST	Institute of Food Science and Technology (UK)
IHBC	International Health & Beauty Council

IHIE	Institute of Highway Incorporated Engineers
IHort	Institute of Horticulture
IHT	Institute of Highways and Transportation
IIA	Institute of Internal Auditors
IIE	Institution of Incorporated Engineers
IIExE	Institution of Incorporated Executive Engineers
IIHHT	International Institute of Health & Holistic Therapies
IIHTM	International Institute of Hospitality Tourism & Management
IIRSM	International Institute of Risk and Safety Management
ILAM	Institute of Leisure and Amenity Management
ILE	Institution of Lighting Engineers
ILEX	Institute of Legal Executives
ILT	Institute of Logistics and Transport
IMarE	Institute of Marine Engineers
IMBM	Institute of Maintenance and Building Management
IMC	Institute of Management Consultancy
IMechE	Institution of Mechanical Engineers
IMF	Institute of Metal Finishing
IMI	Institute of the Motor Industry
IMIBC	Incorporated Member of the Institute of Building Control
IMInstAEA	Incorporated Member of the Institute of Automotive Engineer Assessors
IMIS	Institute for the Management of Information Systems
IMM	Institution of Mining and Metallurgy
IMS	Institute of Management Specialists
IncMWeldI	Incorporated Member of the Welding Institute
InstAEA	Institute of Automotive Engineer Assessors
InstAM	Institute of Administrative Management
InstBCA	Institute of Burial and Cremation Administration
InstE	Institute of Energy
InstPet	Institute of Petroleum
IOB	Institute of Brewing
IOC	Institute of Carpenters
IoD	Institute of Directors
IOM	Institute of Operations Management
IOP	Institute of Packaging
IOSH	Institution of Occupational Safety and Health
IOTA	Institute of Transport Administration
IPA	Institute of Practitioners in Advertising
IPD	Initial Professional Development
IPD	Institute of Personnel and Development
IPFA	Member of the Chartered Institute of Public Finance and Accountancy
IPlantE	Institution of Plant Engineers
IPR	Incorporated Professional Review
IPR	Institute of Public Relations
IPSM	Institute of Public Service Management
IQ	Institute of Quarrying
IQA	Institute of Quality Assurance
IRMT	International Register of Massage Therapists
IRRV	Corporate Member of the Institute of Revenues, Rating and Valuation
IRRV	Institute of Revenues, Rating and Valuation
IRSE	Institution of Railway Signal Engineers
IRTE	Institute of Road Transport Engineers

ISEB	Information Systems Examinations Board
ISM	Incorporated Society of Musicians
ISM	Institute for Supervision & Management
ISMM	Institute of Sales and Marketing Management
ISRM	Institute of Sport and Recreation Management
ISTD	Imperial Society of Teachers of Dancing
IStructE	Institution of Structural Engineers
ITEC	International Therapy Examination Council
ITIL	IT Infrastructure Library
ITSA	Institute of Trading Standards Administration
IVehE	Institute of the Vehicle Engineers
IVM	Institute of Value Management
IWSc	Institute of Wood Science
JEB	Joint Examination Board
JET	Jewellery, Education and Training
JP	Justice of the Peace
LA	Library Association
LABAC	Licentiate Member of the Association of Business and Administrative Computing
LAE	Licentiate Automotive Engineer
LAEx	Legal Accounts Executive
LAMDA	London Academy of Music and Dramatic Art
LAMRTPI	Legal Associate Member of the Royal Town Planning Institute
LASI	Licentiate of the Ambulance Service Institute
LASI	Licentiate of the Architecture and Surveying Institute
LBEI	Licentiate of the Institution of Body Engineers
LBIDST	Licentiate of the British Institute of Dental and Surgical Technologists
LBIPP	Licentiate of the British Institute of Professional Photography
LCCI	London Chamber of Commerce and Industry
LCCIEB	London Chamber of Commerce and Industry Examinations Board
LCEA	Licentiate of the Association of Cost and Executive Accountants
LCFI	Licentiate of CFI International (Clothing and Footwear Institute)
LCGI	Licentiate, City & Guilds
LCIBSE	Licentiate of the Chartered Institution of Building Services Engineers
LCP	Licentiate of the College of Preceptors
LCSP	London and Counties Society of Physiologists
LCSP(Assoc)	Associate of the London and Counties Society of Physiologists
LCSP(BTh)	Member of the London and Counties Society of Physiologists (Beauty Therapy)
LCSP(Chir)	Member of the London and Counties Society of Physiologists (Chiropody)
LCSP(Phys)	Member of the London and Counties Society of Physiologists (Physical and Manipulative Therapy)
LCT	Licentiate of the College of Teachers
LDS	Licentiate in Dental Surgery
LDSRCPSGlas	Licentiate in Dental Surgery of the Royal College of Physicians and Surgeons of Glasgow
LDSRCSEd	Licentiate in Dental Surgery of the Royal College of Surgeons of Edinburgh
LDSRCSEng	Licentiate in Dental Surgery of the Royal College of Surgeons of England
LFA	Licentiate of the Institute of Financial Accountants
LFCI	Licentiate of the Faculty of Commerce and Industry
LFCS	Licentiate of the Faculty of Secretaries
LFS	Licentiate of the Faculty of Architects and Surveyors (Surveyors)
LGCL	Licentiate of the Guild of Cleaners and Launderers
LGSM	Licentiate of the Guildhall School of Music and Drama

LHCIMA	Licentiate of the Hotel and Catering International Management Association
LHG	Licentiate of the Institute of Heraldic and Genealogical Studies
LI	Landscape Institute
LicentiateCIPD	Licentiate of the Chartered Institute of Personnel and Development
LicIPD	Licentiate of the Institute of Personnel & Development
LicIQA	Licentiate of the Institute of Quality Assurance
LICW	Licentiate of the Institute of Clerks of Works of Great Britain Incorporated
LIDPM	Licentiate of the Institute of Data Processing Management
LIEM	Licentiate of the Institute of Executives and Managers
LIIST	Licentiate of the International Institute of Sports Therapy
LILAM	Licentiate of the Institute of Leisure and Amenity Management
LIM	Licentiate of the Institute of Materials
LIMA	Licentiate of the Institute of Mathematics and its Applications
LIMF	Licentiate of the Institute of Metal Finishing
LIMIS	Licentiate of the Institute for the Management of Information Systems
LInstBCA	Licentiate of the Institute of Burial and Cremation Administration
LInstBM	Licentiate of the Institute of Builders' Merchants
LIOC	Licentiate of the Institute of Carpenters
LIR	Licentiate of the Institute of Population Registration
LISTD	Licentiate of the Imperial Society of Teachers of Dancing
LISTD(Dip)	Licentiate Diploma of the Imperial Society of Teachers of Dancing
LittD	Doctor of Letters
LIWM	Licentiate of the Institute of Wastes Management
LLB	Bachelor of Law
LLCM	Performers Diploma of Licentiateship in Speech, Drama and Public Speaking
LLCM(TD)	Licentiate of the London College of Music and Media (Teachers' Diploma)
LLD	Doctor of Law
LLM	Master of Law
LM	Licentiate in Midwifery
LMIFM	Licentiate Member of the Institute of Fisheries Management
LMInstE	Licentiate Member of the Institute of Energy
LMPA	Licentiate Member of the Master Photographers Association
LMRTPI	Legal Member of the Royal Town Planning Institute
LMSSALond	Licentiate in Medicine, Surgery and Obstetrics & Gynaecology, Society of Apothecaries of London
LMusEd	Licentiate Diploma in Music Education
LMusLCM	Licentiate in Music of the London College of Music
LMusTCL	Licentiate in Music, Trinity College of Music
LNCP	Licentiate of the National Council of Psychotherapists
LPC	Legal Practice Course
LRAD	Licentiate of the Royal Academy of Dancing
LRAM	Licentiate of the Royal Academy of Music
LRCPEdin	Conjoint Diplomas Licentiate of the Royal College of Physicians of Edinburgh
LRCPSGlasg	Conjoint Diplomas Licentiate of the Royal College of Physicians and Surgeons of Glasgow
LRCSEdin	Conjoint Diplomas Licentiate of the Royal College of Surgeons of Edinburgh
LRCSEng	Licentiate of the Royal College of Surgeons in England
LRPS	Licentiate of the Royal Photographic Society
LRSC	Licentiate of the Royal Society of Chemistry
LRSM	Licentiate Diploma of the Royal Schools of Music
LSBP	Licentiate of the Society of Business Practitioners
LSCP(Assoc)	Associate of the London and Counties Society of Physiologists

LTCL	Licentiate of Trinity College of Music
LTh	Licentiate in Theology
LTI	Licentiate of the Textile Industry
LTSC	Licentiate of the Oil and Colour Chemists' Association
LVT	Licentiate Vehicle Technologist
MA	Master of Arts
MA(Architectural)	Master of Arts (Architectural Studies)
MA(Econ)	Master of Arts in Economic and Social Studies
MA(Ed)	Master of Arts in Education
MA(LD)	Master of Arts (Landscape Design)
MA(MUS)	Master of Arts (Music)
MA(RCA)	Master of Arts, Royal College of Art
MA(SocSci)	Master of Arts (Social Science)
MA(Theol)	Master of Arts in Theology
MAAT	Member of the Association of Accounting Technicians
MABAC	Member of the Association of Business and Administrative Computing
MABE	Member of the Association of Business Executives
MAcc	Master of Accountancy
MACP	Member of the Association of Computer Professionals
MAE	Member of the Academy of Experts
MAgr	Master of Agriculture
MAgrSc	Master of Agricultural Science
MAMS	Member of the Association of Medical Secretaries, Practice Managers, Administrators and Receptionists
MAMSA	Managing & Marketing Sales Association Examination Board
MAnimSc	Master of Animal Science
MAO	Master of Obstetrics
MAP	Membership by Assessment of Performance
MAPM	Member of the Association for Project Management
MAppSci	Master of Applied Science
MAQ	Mortgage Advice Qualification
MArAd	Master of Archive Administration
MArb	Master of Arboriculture
MArch	Master of Architecture
MArt/RCA	Master of Arts, Royal College of Art
MasFCI	Master of the Faculty of Commerce and Industry
MASHAM	Management and Administration of Safety and Health at Mines
MASI	Member of the Architecture and Surveying Institute
MBA	Master of Business Administration
MBAE	Member of the British Association of Electrolysists
MB, BCh	Conjoint Degree of Bachelor of Medicine, Bachelor of Surgery
MB, BChir	Conjoint Degree of Bachelor of Medicine, Bachelor of Surgery
MB, BS	Conjoint Degree of Bachelor of Medicine, Bachelor of Surgery
MB, ChB	Conjoint Degree of Bachelor of Medicine, Bachelor of Surgery
MBChA	Member of the British Chiropody and Podiatry Association
MBCO	Member of the British College of Ophthalmic Opticians
MBCS	Member of the British Computer Society
MBEng	Member of the Association of Building Engineers
MBHA	Member of the British Hypnotherapy Association
MBHI	Member of the British Horological Institute
MBIAT	Member of the British Institute of Architectural Technologists
MBID	Member of the British Institute of Interior Design

MBIE	Member of the British Institute of Embalmers
MBII	Member of the British Institute of Innkeeping
MBioc	Master of Biochemistry
MBKS	Member of the British Kinematograph, Sound and Television Society
MBM	Master of Business Management
MBMA	Member of the Business Management Association
MBSc	Master in Business Science
MBSSG	Master of the British Society of Scientific Glassblowers
MCAM	Member of the Communication Advertising and Marketing Education Foundation
MCB	Mastership in Clinical Biochemistry
MCB	Member of the British Association of Communicators in Business
MCBDip	Member of the British Association of Communicators in Business who hold the Association's Certificate and Diploma
MCC	Master of Community Care
MCCDRCS(Eng)	Member of the Royal College of Surgeons of England, Clinical Community Dentistry
MCD	Master of Civic Design
MCDH	Master of Community Dental Health
MCGI	Membership, City & Guilds
MCGPIrel	Member of the Irish College of General Practitioners
MCh	Master of Surgery
MChD	Master of Dental Surgery
MChem	Master of Chemistry
MChemA	Master of Chemical Analysis
MChemPhys	Master of Chemical Physics
MChemPST	Master of Chemistry Polymer Science and Technology
MChir	Master of Surgery
MChOrth	Master of Orthopaedic Surgery
MChS	Member of the Society of Chiropodists and Podiatrists
MCIArb	Member of the Chartered Institute of Arbitrators
MCIBS	Member of the Chartered Institute of Bankers in Scotland
MCIBSE	Member of the Chartered Institution of Building Services Engineers
MCIH	Corporate Member of the Chartered Institute of Housing
MCIJ	Member of the Chartered Institute of Journalists
MCIM	Member of the Chartered Institute of Marketing
MCIOB	Member of the Chartered Institute of Building
MCIPD	Member of the Chartered Institute of Personnel and Development
MCIPS	Member of the Chartered Institute of Purchasing and Supply
MCIT	Member of the Chartered Institute of Transport
MCIWEM	Member of the Chartered Institution of Water and Environmental Management
MCLIP	Chartered Member of CILIP
MCom	Master of Commerce
MCommH	Master of Community Health
MComp	Master of Computer Science
MCOptom	Member of the College of Optometrists
MCoT	Member of the College of Teachers
MCPM	Member of the Confederation of Professional Management
MCPP	Member of the College of Pharmacy Practice
MCQ	Multiple Choice Question paper
MCSD	Member of the Chartered Society of Designers
MCSP	Member of the Chartered Society of Physiotherapy
MCT	Member of the Association of Corporate Treasurers

MCTHCM	Member of the Confederation of Tourism, Hotel and Catering Management
MCYW	Member of the Community and Youth Work Association
MD	Doctor of Medicine
MDA	Master of Defence Administration
MD; ChM	Conjoint Doctorate in Medicine, Doctorate in Surgery
MDCR	Management Diploma of the College of Radiographers
MDent	Master of Dental Science
MDes	Master of Design
MDes(RCA)	Master of Design, Royal College of Art
MDORCPSGlas	Membership of Dental Orthopaedics, Royal College of Physicians and Surgeons of Glasgow
MDra	Master of Drama
MDS	Master of Dental Surgery
MDSc	Master of Dental Science
MEBA	Master of European Business Administration
MECI	Member of the Institute of Employment Consultants
MEd	Master of Education
MEd(EdPsych)	Master of Education (Educational Psychology)
MEdStud	Master of Educational Studies
MEng	Master of Engineering
MEnv	Master of Environmental Studies
MEnvSci	Master of Environmental Science
MESc	Master of Earth Sciences
MFA	Master of Fine Art
MFC	Mastership in Food Control
MFCM	Member of the Faculty of Community Medicine
MFDO	Member of the Faculty of Dispensing Opticians
MFDS	Member of the Faculty of Dental Surgery
MFGDPEng	Membership in General Dental Practice, Royal College of Surgeons of England
MFHom	Member of the Faculty of Homeopathy
MFM	Master of Forensic Medicine
MFPHM	Member of the Faculty of Public Health Medicine, Royal College of Physicians of London and Edinburgh and Royal College of Physicians and Surgeons of Glasgow
MFPHMIrel	Member of the Faculty of Public Health Medicine, Royal College of Physicians of Ireland
MFTCom	Member of the Faculty of Teachers in Commerce
MGDSRCSEd	Membership in General Dental Surgery, Royal College of Surgeons of Edinburgh
MGDSRCSEng	Membership in General Dental Surgery, Royal College of Surgeons of England
MGeog	Master of Geography
MGeol	Master of Geology
MGeophys	Master of Geophysical Sciences
MHCIMA	Member of the Hotel and Catering International Management Association
MHM	Master of Health Management
MHort(RHS)	Master of Horticulture, Royal Horticultural Society
MHSM	Member of the Institute of Health Services Management
MIAB	Member of the International Association of Book-keepers
MIAEA	Member of the Institute of Automotive Engineer Assessors
MIAgrE	Member of the Institution of Agricultural Engineers
MIAP	Member of the Institution of Analysts and Programmers
MIAT	Member of the Institute of Asphalt Technology
MIBC	Member of the Institute of Building Control

MIBCM	Member of the Institute British Carriage and Automobile Manufacturers
MIBCO	Member of the Institution of Building Control Officers
MIBE	Member of the Institution of British Engineers
MIBF	Member of the Institute of British Foundrymen
MIBiol	Member of the Institute of Biology
MIBM	Member of the Institute of Builders' Merchants
MICB	Member of the Institute of Certified Book-Keepers
MICE	Member of the Institute of Civil Engineers
MIChemE	Member of the Institution of Chemical Engineers
MICHT	Member of the International Council for Holistic Therapies
MICM	Member of the Institute of Credit Management
MICM(Grad)	Graduate Member of the Institute of Credit Management
MICorr	Member of the Institute of Corrosion
MICS	Member of the Institute of Chartered Shipbrokers
MICSc	Corporate Member of the Institute of Consumer Sciences Incorporating Home Economics
MICW	Member of the Institute of Clerks of Works of Great Britain Incorporated
MIDTA	Member of the International Dance Teachers' Association
MIED	Member of the Institution of Engineering Designers
MIEE	Member of the Institution of Electrical Engineers
MIEM	Member of the Institute of Executives and Managers
MIEx	Member of the Institute of Export
MIEx(Grad)	Graduate Member of the Institute of Export
MIExpE	Member of the Institute of Explosives Engineers
MIFA	Member of the Institute of Field Archaeologists
MIFireE	Member of the Institution of Fire Engineers
MIFM	Registered Member of the Institute of Fisheries Management
MIFST	Member of the Institute of Food Science and Technology
MIGasE	Member of the Institution of Gas Engineers
MIGD	Member of the Institute of Grocery Distribution
MIHEc	Member of the Institute of Home Economics
MIHIE	Member of the Institute of Highway Incorporated Engineers
MIHM	Member of the Institute of Healthcare Management
MIHort	Member of the Institute of Horticulture
MIHT	Member of the Institution of Highways and Transportation
MIIA	Member of the Institute of Internal Auditors
MIIE	Member of the Institution of Incorporated Engineers
MIIExE	Member of the Institution of Incorporated Executive Engineers
MIIHTM	Member of the International Institute of Hospitality Tourism & Management
MIIM	Member of the Institute of Industrial Managers
MIIM	Member of the International Institute of Management
MIIRSM	Member of the International Institute of Risk and Safety Management
MIISE	Member of the International Institute of Social Economics
MIISec	Member of the International Institute of Security
MIL	Member of the Institute of Linguists
MILAM	Member of the Institute of Leisure and Amenity Management
MILT	Member of the Institute of Logistics and Transport
MIM	Professional Member of the Institute of Materials
MIMA	Member of the Institute of Mathematics and its Applications
MIManf	Member of the Institute of Manufacturing
MIMarE	Member of the Institute of Marine Engineers
MIMatM	Member of the Institute of Materials Management

MIMBM	Member of the Institute of Maintenance and Building Management
MIMC	Member of the Institute of Management Consultancy
MIMechE	Member of the Institution of Mechanical Engineers
MIMechIE	Member of the Institution of Mechanical Incorporated Engineers
MIMF	Member of the Institute of Metal Finishing
MIMI	Member of the Institute of the Motor Industry
MIMinE	Member of the Institution of Mining Engineers
MIMIS	Member of the Institute for the Management of Information Systems
MIMM	Member of the Institute of Massage and Movement
MIMM	Member of the Institution of Mining and Metallurgy
MIMS	Member of the Institute of Management Specialists
MInstAEA	Member of the Institute of Automotive Engineer Assessors
MInstAM	Member of the Institute of Administrative Management
MInstBA	Member of the Institute of Business Administration
MInstBCA	Member of the Institute of Burial and Cremation Administration
MInstBE	Member of the Institution of British Engineers
MInstBM	Member of the Institute of Builders' Merchants
MInstCF	Master Fitter of the National Institute of Carpet and Floorlayers
MInstChP	Member of the Institute of Chiropodists & Podiatrists
MInstCM	Member of the Institute of Commercial Management
MInstD	Member of the Institute of Directors
MInstE	Member of the Institute of Energy
MInstLEx	Member of the Institute of Legal Executives
MInstMC	Member of the Institute of Measurement and Control
MInstNDT	Member of the British Institute of Non-Destructive Testing
MInstP	Member of the Institute of Physics
MInstPet	Member of the Institute of Petroleum
MInstPkg	Member of the Institute of Packaging
MInstPkg(Dip)	Diploma Member of the Institute of Packaging
MInstPM	Member of the Institute of Professional Managers and Administrators
MInstPS	Corporate Member of the Institute of Purchasing and Supply
MInstPSA	Member of the Institute of Public Service Administrators
MInstR	Member of the Institute of Refrigeration
MInstSMM	Member of the Institute of Sales and Marketing Management
MInstTA	Member of the Institute of Transport Administration
MInstTT	Full Member of the Institute of Travel and Tourism
MInstWM	Member of the Institute of Wastes Management
MIOC	Member of the Institute of Carpenters
MIOFMS	Member of the Institute of Financial and Management Studies
MIOM	Member of the Institute of Operations Management
MIOP	Member of the Institute of Printing
MIOSH	Member of the Institution of Occupational Safety and Health
MIP	Member of the Institute of Plumbing
MIPA	Member of the Institute of Practitioners in Advertising
MIPD	Member of the Institute of Personnel and Development
MIPI	Member of the Institute of Professional Investigators
MIPlantE	Member of the Institution of Plant Engineers
MIPR	Member of the Institute of Public Relations
MIPRE	Member of the Incorporated Practitioners in Radio & Electronics
MIQ	Member of the Institute of Quarrying
MIQA	Member of the Institute of Quality Assurance
MIR	Member of the Institute of Population Registration

MIRRV	Member of the Institute of Revenue, Rating and Valuation
MIRSE	Member of the Institution of Railway Signal Engineers
MIRTE	Member of the Institute of Road Transport Engineering
MISM	Member of the Institute for Supervision & Management
MISOB	Member of the Incorporated Society of Organ Builders
MISTC	Member of the Institute of Scientific and Technical Communicators
MIStrucE	Member of the Institution of Structural Engineers
MISW	Member of the Institute of Social Welfare
MITAI	Member of the Institute of Traffic Accident Investigators
MITSA	Member of the Institute of Trading Standards Administration
MIVehE	Member of the Institute of Vehicle Engineers
MIWM	Member of the Institute of Wastes Management
MIWPC	Member of the Institute of Water Pollution Control
MJur	Master of Jurisprudence
MLA	Master of Landscape Architecture
MLang	Master of Languages
MLangEng	Master of Language Engineering
MLD	Master of Landscape Design
MLE	Master of Land Economy
MLI	Member of the Landscape Institute
MLing	Master of Languages
MLitt	Master of Letters
MLPM	Master of Landscape Planning and Management
MLS	Master of Library Science
MM	Master of Midwifery
MMA	Master of Management and Administration
MMAS	Master of Minimal Access Surgery
MMath	Master of Mathematics
MMedE	Master of Medical Education
MMedSci	Master of Medical Science
MMet	Master of Metallurgy
MML	Master of Modern Languages
MMS	Member of the Institute of Management Services
MMSc	Master of Medical Sciences
MMus	Master of Music
MMus(Comp)	Master of Music (Composition)
MMus(Perf)	Master of Music (Performance)
MMus, RCM	Master of Music, Royal College of Music
MMusArt	Master of Musical Arts
MN	Master of Nursing
MNAEA	Member of the National Association of Estate Agents
MNatSc	Master of Natural Science
MNCP	Member of the National Council of Psychotherapists
MNeuro	Master of Neuroscience
MNI	Member of the Nautical Institute
MNIMH	Member of the National Institute of Medical Herbalists
MNRHP	Full Member of the National Register of Hypnotherapists and Psychotherapists
MNRHP(Eqv)	Full Member (Equivalent) of the National Register of Hypnotherapists and Psychotherapists
MNTB	Merchant Navy Training Board
MObstG	Master of Obstetrics and Gynaecology
MOptom	Master of Optometry

MOrthRCSEng	Membership in Orthodontics, Royal College of Surgeons of England
MPA	Master of Public Administration
MPaedDenRCSEng	Membership in Paediatric Dentistry, Royal College of Surgeons of England
MPC	Master of Palliative Care
MPH	Master of Public Health
MPharm	Master of Pharmacy
MPharmSci	Master of Pharmaceutical Science
MPhil	Master of Philosophy
MPhil(Eng)	Master of Philosophy in Engineering
MPhys	Master of Physics
MPhysGeog	Master of Physical Geography
MPlan	Master of Planning
MPPS	Master of Public Policy Studies
MPRI	Member of the Plastics and Rubber Institute
MProf	Master of Professional Studies
MProfBTM	Member of the Professional Business and Technical Management
MPS	Member of the Pharmaceutical Society of Northern Ireland
MPsychMed	Master of Psychological Medicine
MPsychol	Master of Psychology
MQB	Mining Qualifications Board
MRad	Master of Radiology
MRad; MRad(D)	Master of Radiology (Radiodiagnosis) or (Radiotherapy)
MRAeS	Member of the Royal Aeronautical Society
MRCGP	Member of the Royal College of General Practitioners
MRCOG	Member of the Royal College of Obstetricians and Gynaecologists
MRCP	Member of the Royal College of Physicians of London
MRCP(UK)	Member of the Royal College of Physicians of the United Kingdom
MRCPath	Member of the Royal College of Pathologists
MRCPEdin	Member of the Royal College of Physicians of Edinburgh (superceded by MRCP(UK))
MRCPGlasg	Member of the Royal College of Physicians of Glasgow (superceded by MRCP(UK))
MRCPIrel	Member of the Royal College of Physicians of Ireland
MRCPsych	Member of the Royal College of Psychiatrists
MRCSEd	Member of the Royal College of Surgeons of Edinburgh
MRCSEng	Member of the Royal College of Surgeons of England
MRCVS	Member of the Royal College of Veterinary Surgeons
MRDRCS	Membership in Restorative Dentistry, Royal College of Surgeons of England
MREC	Member of the Recruitment and Employment Confederation
MREHIS	Member of the Royal Environmental Health Institute of Scotland
MRes	Master of Research
MRIN	Member of the Royal Institute of Navigation
MRINA	Member of the Royal Institution of Naval Architects
MRIPHH	Member of the Royal Institute of Public Health and Hygiene
MRPharmS	Member of the Pharmaceutical Society of Great Britain
MRSC	Member of the Royal Society of Chemistry
MRSH	Member of the Royal Society for the Promotion of Health
MRSS	Member of the Royal Statistical Society
MRTPI	Member of the Royal Town Planning Institute
MS	Master of Surgery
MSA	Marine Safety Agency
MSAPP	Member of the Society of Advanced Psychotherapy Practitioners

MSBP Member of the Society of Business Practitioners
MSBT Member of the Society of Teachers in Business Education
MSc Master of Science
MSc(Econ) Master of Science in Economics
MSc(Ed) Master of Science in Education
MSc(Eng) Master of Science in Engineering
MSc(Entr) Master of Entrepreneurship
MSc(Mgt) Master of Science in Management
MScD Master of Dental Science
MScEcon Master in Faculty of Economic and Social Studies
MSCi Master of Natural Sciences
MScTech Master of Technical Science
MSE Member of Society of Engineers (Inc)
MSF Member of the SMAE Institute
MSFA Advanced Financial Planning Certificate
MSIAD Member of the Society of Industrial Artists and Designers
MSMA Member of the Society of Martial Arts
MSocSc Master of Social Science
MSSc Master of Social Science
MSSc Master of Surgical Science
MSSCh Member of the British Chiropody and Podiatry Association
MSSF Member of the Society of Shoe Fitters
MSt Master of Studies
MSTA Member of the Swimming Teachers' Association
MSTI Certificate of Insurance Work
MSurgDentRCSEng Membership in Surgical Dentistry, Royal College of Surgeons of England
MSW Master of Social Work
MTCP Master of Town and Country Planning
MTD Master of Transport Design
MTech Master of Technology
MTh Master of Theology
MTheol Master of Theology
MTP Master of Town Planning
MTPI Master of Town Planning
MTropMed Master of Tropical Medicine
MTropPaediatrics Master of Tropical Paediatrics
MUniv Master of University (Honorary)
MURP Master of Urban and Regional Planning
MusB Bachelor of Music
MusD Doctor of Music
MVC Management Verification Consortium
MVM Master of Veterinary Medicine
MVSc Master of Veterinary Science
MWeldI Member of the Welding Institute
MWES Member of the Women's Engineering Society
MYD Member of the Youth Development Association
NACOS National Approval Council for Security Systems
NAEA National Association of Estate Agents
NAG National Association of Goldsmiths
NAMCW National Association for Maternal and Child Welfare
NC National Certificate
NCA National Certificate in Agriculture

NCC	National Computing Centre
NCC	Navigational Control Course
NCDT	National Council for Drama Training
NCTJ	National Council for the Training of Journalists
NCVQ	National Council for Vocational Qualifications
ND	Diploma in Naturopathy
NDD	National Diploma in Design
NDF	National Diploma in Forestry
NDH	National Diploma in Horticulture
NDSF	National Diploma of the Society of Floristry
NDT	National Diploma in the Science and Practice of Turfculture and Sports Ground Management
NEBOSH	National Examination Board in Occupational Safety and Health
NEBS	National Examining Board for Supervision & Management
NFTS	National Film and Television School
NICCEA	Northern Ireland Council for the Curriculum, Examinations and Assessment
NID	National Intermediate Diploma
NIM	Northern Institute of Massage
NNEB	National Nursery Examination Board
NRHP	National Register of Hypnotherapists and Psychotherapists
NRHP(Affil)	Affiliate of the National Register of Hypnotherapists and Psychotherapists
NRHP(Assoc)	Associate of the National Register of Hypnotherapists and Psychotherapists
N-SHAP	National School of Hypnosis and Psychotherapy
NTTG	National Textile Training Group
NUJ	National Union of Journalists
NVQ	National Vocational Qualifications
NWRAC	North Western Regional Advisory Council for Further Education
OCR	Oxford, Cambridge & RSA Examinations
ODLQC	Open & Distance Learning Quality Council, formerly CACC, Council for Accreditation of Correspondence Colleges
ONC	Ordinary National Certificate
OND	Ordinary National Diploma
OSCE	Objective Structured Clinical Exam
PBTM	Professional Business and Technical Management
PCN	Personnel Certification in Non-Destructive Testing Ltd
PDP	Professional Development Programme
PESD	Private and Executive Secretary's Diploma, London Chamber of Commerce and Industry
PgC	Postgraduate Certificate
PGCE	Postgraduate Certificate in Education
PGCert	Postgraduate Certificate
PgD	Postgraduate Diploma
PGDip	Postgraduate Diploma
PGDip(Comp)	Postgraduate Diploma in Composition
PGDip(LCM)	Postgraduate Diploma of the London College of Music
PGDip(Perf)	Postgraduate Diploma in Performance
PGDip(RCM)	Postgraduate Diploma of the Royal College of Music
PGDipMin	Postgraduate Diploma in Ministry
PGDipMus	Postgraduate Diploma in Music
PhD	Doctor of Philosophy
PhD(RCA)	Doctor of Philosophy (Royal College of Art)
PIC	Professional Investment Certificate

PIFA	Practitioner of the Institute of Field Archaeologists
PIIA	Practitioner of the Institute of Internal Auditors
PInstNDT	Practitioner of the British Institute of Non-Destructive Testing
PJDip	Professional Jewellers' Diploma
PJGemDip	Professional Jewellers' Gemstone Diploma
PJManDip	Professional Jewellers' Management Diploma
PJValDip	Professional Jewellers' Valuation Diploma
PPL	Private Pilot's Licence
PPRNCM	Professional Performance Diploma of the Royal Northern College of Music
PQS	Professional Qualification Structure
PQSW	Post-Qualifying Award in Social Work
PRCA	Public Relations Consultants Association
PSC	Private Secretary's Certificate
PSD	Private Secretary's Diploma
PTA	Pianoforte Tuners' Association
PVM	Professional in Value Management
QC	Queen's Counsel
QCA	Qualifications and Curriculum Authority
QCG	Qualification in Careers Guidance
QDR	Qualified Dispute Resolver
QICA	Qualification in Computer Auditing
QIS	Qualified Imaging Scientist
QPA	Qualification in Pensions Administration
QPSPA	Qualification in Public Sector Pensions Administration
RA	Royal Academician
RAD	Royal Academy of Dancing
RADA	Royal Academy of Dramatic Art
RAM	Royal Academy of Music
RANA	Royal Animal Nursing Auxiliary
RAS	Royal Astronomical Society
RBS	Royal Ballet School
RC	Roman Catholic
RCM	Royal College of Midwives
RCN	Royal College of Nursing
RCSLT	Royal College of Speech and Language Therapists
RCVS	Royal College of Veterinary Surgeons
REA	Regional Examining Body
REC	Recruitment and Employment Confederation
Ret'dABID	Retired Associate of the British Institute of Interior Design
Ret'dFBID	Retired Fellow of the British Institute of Interior Design
Ret'dMBID	Retired Member of the British Institute of Interior Design
RGN	Registered General Nurse
RHS	Royal Horticultural Society
RHV	Registered Health Visitor
RIBA	Royal Institute of British Architects
RICS	Royal Institution of Chartered Surveyors
RINA	Royal Institution of Naval Architects
RJDip	Diploma for Retail Jewellers
RJGemDip	National Association of Goldsmiths Gemstone Diploma
RM	Registered Midwife
RMN	Registered Mental Nurse
RMS	Royal Microscopical Society

RNMH	Registered Nurse for the Mentally Handicapped
RP	Registered Plumber
RPS	Royal Photographic Society
RSA	Royal Society of Arts
RSBEI	Registered Student of the Institution of Body Engineers
RSC	Royal Society of Chemistry
RSCN	Registered Sick Children's Nurse
RSP	Registered Safety Practitioner
RTO	Recognised Training Organisation
RTPI	Royal Town Planning Institute
SA	Salvation Army Management
SBP	Society of Business Practitioners
SCAA	School Curriculum and Assessment Authority
ScD	Doctor of Science
SCE	Scottish Certificate of Education
SCLS	Second Certificate for Legal Secretaries
SCMT	Ship Captain's Medical Training
SCOTVEC	Scottish Vocational Education Council
SCPL	Senior Commercial Pilot's Licence
SE	Society of Engineers
SEE	Society of Environmental Engineers
SEFIC	Spoken English for Industry and Commerce
SenAWeldI	Senior Associate of the Welding Institute
SEng	Qualified Sales Engineer
SenMWeldI	Senior Member of the Welding Institute
SF	Society of Floristry Ltd
SFA	Securities and Futures Authority
SFInstE	Senior Fellow of the Institute of Energy
SG	Society of Genealogists
SGT	Society of Glass Technology
SHNC	Scottish Higher National Certificate
SHND	Scottish Higher National Diploma
SIEDip	Securities Industry Examination Diploma
SInstPet	Student of the Institute of Petroleum
SITO	Security Industry Training Organisation Ltd
SLC	Secretarial Language Certificate
SLD	Secretarial Language Diploma
SNC	Scottish National Certificate
SND	Scottish National Diploma
SNNEB	Scottish Nursery Nurses Examination Board
SPA	Screen Printing Association
SPRINT	Sport Play and Recreation Industries National Training Executive
SQA	Scottish Qualifications Authority
SRD	State Registered Dietician
SRN	State Registered Nurse
SSC	Secretarial Studies Certificate, London Chamber of Commerce and Industry
STA	Specialist Teacher Assistant (CACHE)
STA	Swimming Teachers' Association
STAT	Society of Teachers of the Alexander Technique
StudentIEE	Student of the Institution of Electrical Engineers
StudentIIE	Student of the Institution of Incorporated Engineers
StudentIMechE	Student of the Institution of Mechanical Engineers

StudIAP	Student of the Institution of Analysts and Programmers
StudIManf	Student Member of the Institute of Manufacturing
StudIMS	Student of the Institute of Management Specialists
StudProfBTM	Student of the Professional Business and Technical Management
StudSE	Student of the Society of Engineers (Inc)
StudSElec	Student of the Society of Electroscience
StudWeldI	Student of the Welding Institute
SVQ	Scottish Vocational Qualification
TC	Technician Certificate
TCA	Technician in Costing and Accounting
TCA	Technician of the Institute of Cost and Executive Accountants
TCert	Teacher's Certificate
TD	Technician Diploma
TDCR	Teacher's Diploma of the College of Radiographers
TechICorr	Technician of the Institute of Corrosion
TechMIWM	Technician Member of the Institute of Wastes Management
TechRICS	Technical Surveyor of the Royal Institution of Chartered Surveyors
TechRMS	Technological Qualification in Microscopy, Royal Microscopical Society
TechRTPI	Technical Member of the Royal Town Planning Institute
TechSP	Technician Safety Practitioner
TechWeldI	Technician of the Welding Institute
TEMOL	Training in Energy Management through Open Learning
TI	Textile Institute
TIMBM	Technician of the Institute of Maintenance and Building Management
TMBA	Teacher Member of the British (Theatrical) Arts
TnIMBM	Technicians of the Institute of Maintenance and Building Management
TOEFL	Test of English as a Foreign Language
TPP	Test of Professional Practice
TVM	Trainer in Value Management
UCAS	Universities and Colleges Admissions Service
UCL	University College London
UEB	United Examining Board
UKCC	United Kingdom Central Council
UKCP	United Kingdom Council for Psychotherapy
UMIST	University of Manchester Institute of Science and Technology
URC	United Reformed Church
VetMB	Bachelor of Veterinary Medicine
VTCT	Vocational Training Charitable Trust
WCMD	Welsh College of Music and Drama
WES	Women's Engineering Society
WJEC	Welsh Joint Education Committee
WMAC	West Midlands Advisory Council for Further Education
WSA	West of Scotland Agricultural College
YHAFHE	Yorkshire and Humberside Association for Further and Higher Education
ZSL	Zoological Society of London

Part 1

Introduction

Since its first publication in 1970, *British Qualifications* has charted a number of fundamental changes in further and higher education provision in the UK. Major advances in technology and more flexible delivery and attendance patterns have created different types of learning opportunity, encouraging an ever more diverse student population to access education at all levels. The range of subjects delivered has grown beyond all recognition. New areas of research have been established and developed into major subject specialisms. Employers and professional bodies have collaborated to develop subject areas aligned to changing industry requirements. Flexibility and choice are the hallmarks of today's system, and anyone new to higher education might well be bewildered by the sheer variety of degree pathways available. The capacity to combine and mix modules and subjects has in fact grown beyond anything that could have been imagined in 1970.

Traditional boundaries between academic and vocational pathways continue to break down, and today most degrees have a vocational slant. Extended industry and professional placements, sponsored research projects, practitioner input and field-based assignments are common features in many degrees, and provide an important link into practice at the early stages of learning. Overall in 20 years, universities have doubled in size and the responsibilities they have taken on have expanded considerably.

Collaboration between further and higher education (HE) institutions has enabled a substantial amount of HE-level provision to be delivered in further education institutions. Clear progression routes have been established for some time.

Considerable breadth of provision is now available in further education. Not only has the sector grown to accommodate sub-degree provision, it has continued to deliver a wide range of pre-and post-18 vocational qualifications, which include technical, occupational and professional awards.

Today, certain types of external qualification cross the boundaries between further and higher education. Several higher education institutions (HEIs) – particularly those that gained university status in the 1990s and more recently in 2005 – deliver advanced professional qualifications and higher national diplomas or certificates awarded by awarding bodies like Edexcel, OCR and SQA. At the same time there has been a significant shift towards further education's involvement in delivery of these types of qualification, and a greater input from private sector colleges.

EDUCATION REFORM

The Higher Education Act 2004 introduced in 2006/07 brought new student support and tuition fee arrangements. For full-time UK and EU undergraduate students, institutions may charge up to £3,290 (2010/11 figures). However, following the Browne Review of 2010, it is proposed that universities will be able to charge full-time UK and EU undergraduate students up to £9,000 a year as part of a reorganization of higher education funding and student finance. You will find further authoritative, official information about universities and colleges in the UK at the Unistats website, http://unistats.direct.gov.uk/. Information on student finance can be found at www.direct.gov.uk.

As well as implementing reforms, the further and higher education sectors contribute to UK economic performance and the delivery of the government's policies on HE. As part of this shared responsibility a great deal of effort is being made to increase access to and participation in education, particularly among individuals who have not had much involvement in the past. The general availability of modular study programmes and related credit recognition of units, and greater use of ICT and e-learning resources, have done a lot to create more flexible methods of delivery and attendance requirements in further and higher education.

FOUNDATION DEGREES

Foundation degrees (FDs) were established to give people the intermediate technical and professional skills that are in demand from employers, and to provide more flexible and accessible ways of studying. They are a higher level qualification awarded by universities. The qualification can be 'built up' from a range of relevant learning experiences, to allow for extremely flexible and adaptable qualifications that can be 'tailored' by employers to support their workforce and business development needs. They offer opportunities for employment and career advancement. Progression routes include links with associated professional qualifications and/or direct entry to the final year of a relevant Honours-level degree. FDs are offered by universities, colleges and other providers.

The first FDs in 2001 were studied by 4,000 students. In 2010, there were just over 99,700 enrolled on FDs. There are now hundreds of FD courses available, both full-time and part-time. Foundation degree forward (fdf) was established in the 2003 Higher Education White Paper; it is the centre of expertise on Foundation degrees and its website www.fdf.ac.uk/ provides up-to-date information and guidance on all aspects of FDs for students, employers and institutions, including the full range of courses and illustrative case study material.

POLICY AND REGULATION

National priorities for further and higher education are now set by the UK and Scottish parliaments and the Welsh and Northern Ireland assemblies, following devolution in 1999/2000. Policy development, planning and implementation rest with the government departments responsible for each national education brief – the Department for Business, Innovation and Skills (BIS), the Department for Employment and Learning Northern Ireland (DELNI), the Scottish Government, and the Department for Children, Education, Lifelong Learning and Skills (DCELLS) in Wales.

In England, delivery of further education is subject to external audit and public reporting by the Office for Standards in Education, Children's Services and Schools (Ofsted). In Scotland, the Scottish Funding Council (SFC) has overall responsibility for planning, funding and quality assurance of further education through its work with Her Majesty's Inspectorate of Education (HMIE).

DCELLS is responsible for planning, funding and promotion of all post-16 education in Wales. Estyn (the Welsh-language acronym for Her Majesty's Inspectorate for Education and Training in Wales, website: www.estyn.gov.uk) is the appointed authority for audit of the quality of provision and related areas.

The Department for Employment and Learning (DELNI) is responsible for planning and funding of further education provision in Northern Ireland. Inspection and audit are undertaken by the Education and Training Inspectorate on behalf of the Department (www.delni.gov.uk, www.etini.gov.uk).

QUALITY ASSURANCE

A degree of convergence does exist in the area of quality assurance of qualifications at Level 3 and below. England, Wales and Northern Ireland share a common qualifications system, and the regulators in each country (listed below) work together in regulating qualifications for use across the three countries. Scotland has a separate qualifications system, although there is close correlation across all four countries, particularly in the area of vocational qualifications.

The following four bodies are responsible for the accreditation and standards of external qualifications and for curriculum and assessment for ages 3–16:

- England: Ofqual: Office of the Qualifications and Examinations Regulator;
- Northern Ireland: Council for Curriculum, Examinations and Assessment (CCEA*);
- Scotland: Scottish Qualifications Authority (SQA*);
- Wales: Department for Children, Education, Lifelong Learning and Skills (DCELLS).

*CCEA is also an Awarding Body for qualifications in Northern Ireland, which include National Qualifications to A level. SQA is also an Awarding Body that develops and validates SQA-branded qualifications including National Qualifications (Access, Intermediate, Higher and Advanced Higher Levels), Higher National Certificates and Diplomas, Scottish Vocational Qualifications and Scottish Professional Awards.

In higher education the responsibility for standards and quality rests firmly with each institution. All institutions work with the independent Quality Assurance Agency for Higher Education (QAA) for England, Northern Ireland, Scotland and Wales. Institutional audits and subject-level reviews have been undertaken by QAA since 2001. It publishes its findings on its website as publicly accessible information; see www.qaa.ac.uk.

Given the scale and diversity of degree provision in the present-day higher education sector, there has been a need to clarify what can reasonably be expected from undergraduate and postgraduate programmes. QAA has responded to this requirement and developed a code of practice for higher education providers, and subject benchmark statements indicating the expected standards of degrees across a range of subjects.

QUALIFICATION FRAMEWORKS

In further response to the breadth and diversity of qualifications available, a number of national qualification frameworks have been introduced. The framework concept is closely associated with greater transparency and comparability between types of qualification, particularly between those that were traditionally classified as academic or vocational. Common characteristics of all frameworks include universal adoption and understanding of qualification titles, and national tariffs of credits that recognize relevant levels of achievement.

The framework for Higher Education Qualifications in England, Wales and Northern Ireland (FHEQ) applies to degrees, diplomas, certificates and other academic awards by higher education providers (Figure 1.1). The Scottish Credit and Qualification Framework (SCQF) was developed by SQA, the Scottish Executive, QAA (Scottish Office) and Universities for Scotland. It provides an overview of all levels of national and higher qualifications provision in Scotland (Figure 1.2).

The Qualifications and Credit Framework (QCF) is a new framework for recognizing and accrediting qualifications in England, Wales and Northern Ireland. The intention behind the reform was to make the system and qualifications offered far more relevant to the needs of

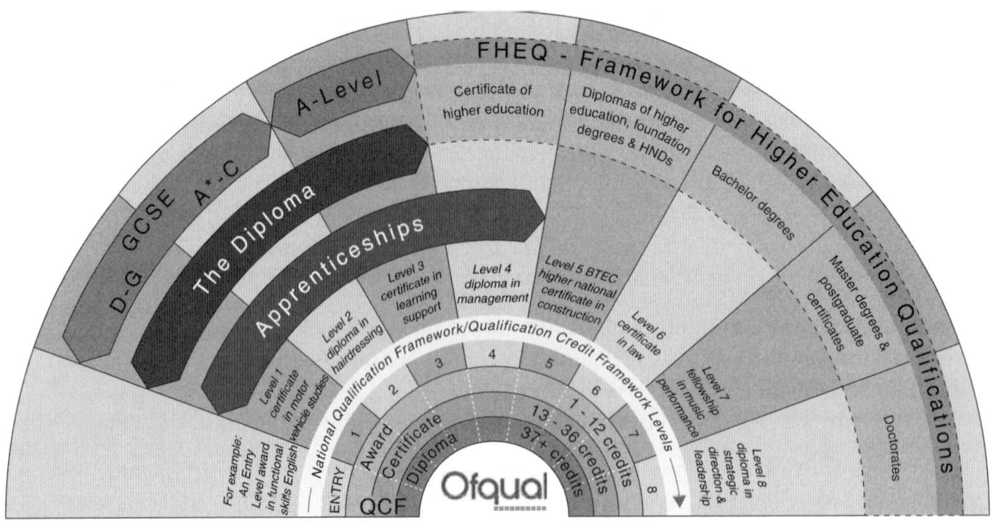

Figure 1.1 Framework for Higher Education Qualifications in England, Wales and Northern Ireland
Source: www.qaa.ac.uk

employers, with more flexibility for learners. Every unit and qualification in the framework has a credit value (where one credit represents 10 hours) and a level between Entry level and level 8. There are three sizes of quali?cation in the QCF:

Awards: 1–12 credits
Certificates: 13–36 credits
Diplomas: 37 credits or more

This means that each qualification title contains the level (from Entry to level 8), the size (Award/Certificate/Diploma) and the details of the content of the qualification. For a full list of accredited qualifications please visit the National Database of Accredited Qualifications at www.accreditedqualifications.org.uk. This is a fully searchable database of qualifications that are accredited by Ofqual, DCELLS and CCEA.

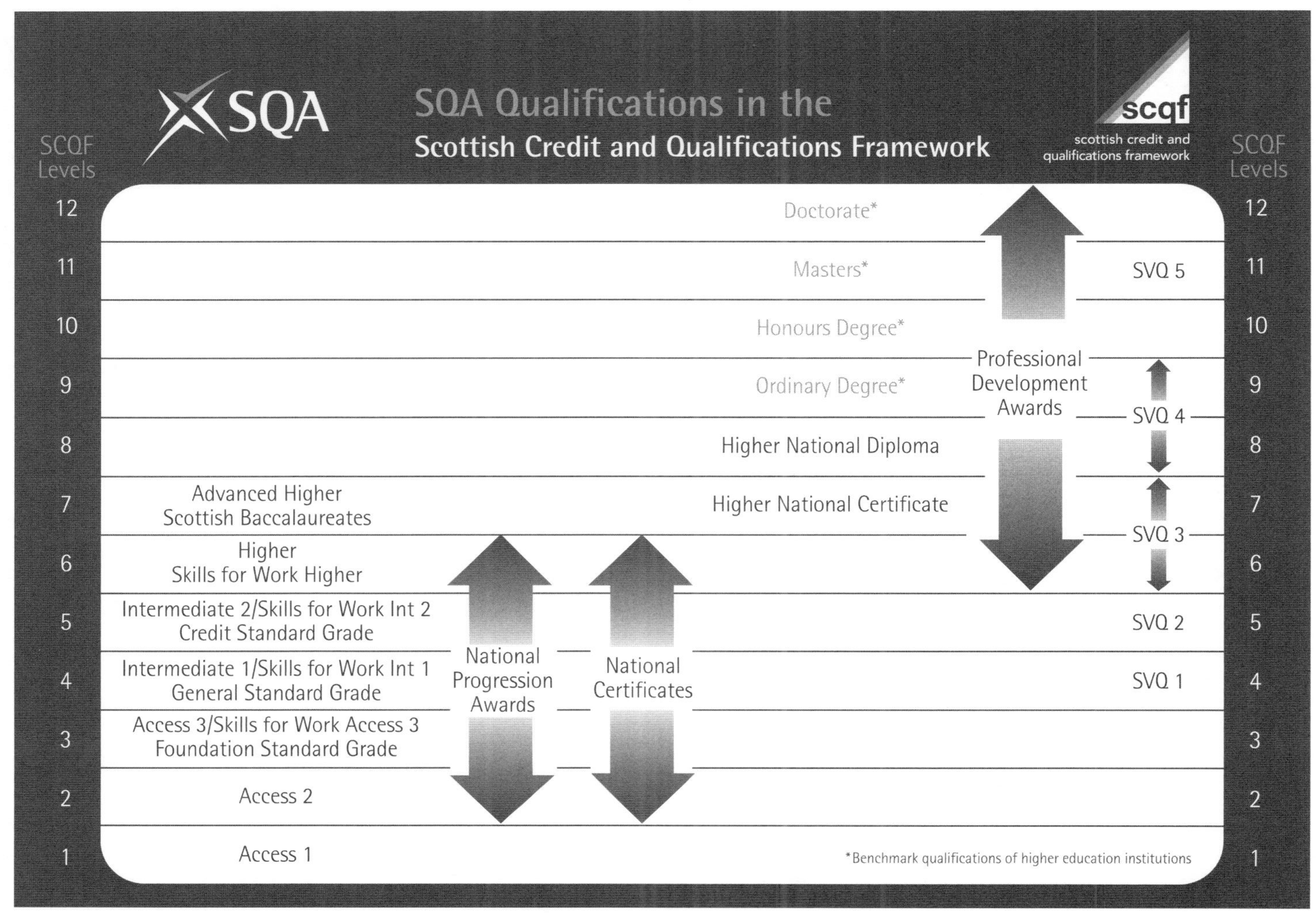

Figure 1.2 Framework for Higher Education Qualifications in Scotland

Part 2

Teaching Establishments

The statutory responsibility for the provision of education in the United Kingdom lies with the Department for Education and the Department for Business, Innovation and Skills (BIS) in England, the Welsh Assembly Government's Department for Children, Education, Lifelong Learning and Skills (DCELLS), the Education Department of the Scottish Government and the Department of Education and Department of Employment and Learning in Northern Ireland. In the United Kingdom the statutory system of public education has three progressive stages: primary education (up to the age of 11 or 12), secondary education (up to age 16), and further education (post-16).

This section briefly describes further and higher provision and the main types of institution.

FURTHER AND HIGHER EDUCATION

'Higher education' is a generic term that broadly defines any course of study leading to a qualification at level 4 and above in the National Qualifications Credit Framework for England, Wales and Northern Ireland, and level 6 and above in the Scottish Credit and Qualifications Framework.

Higher education incorporates study towards a wide range of qualifications including Foundation, undergraduate and postgraduate degrees, certificates and diplomas awarded by individual universities and other higher education institutions (HEIs) with degree-awarding powers.

It can also include study towards general, technical or occupationally-related diplomas and certificates awarded by the large unitary awarding bodies. Unitary awarding bodies are characterized by their breadth of provision, from GNVQ and A levels through to qualifications at level 5 and above in the national frameworks.

The other category that can be characterized as higher education includes post-experience education above level 4 (and level 7 in Scotland). This includes qualifications available from awarding bodies that represent a particular sector, occupation or technical/craft area, and professional institutions that are also approved as awarding bodies.

Higher education can take place in universities and HEIs (which continue to provide the majority of undergraduate and postgraduate courses). It can also take place in colleges of further education. A significant number of colleges deliver parts of, and in some cases entire, Foundation and undergraduate degree courses in agreement with a selected university partner that is responsible for Quality Assurance and final awards.

In general terms, further education is available for students who are over the age of 16 and still in full-time education, and for adults aged 19 and over. Further education provision includes GCSEs, A levels and other types of general and vocational qualifications below level 4 (and level 6 in Scotland) in the National Qualifications Frameworks.

All qualifications are awarded by approved external awarding bodies that include AQA, City & Guilds, Edexcel, LCCI, OCR, OCN and SQA in Scotland. This also includes qualifications below level 4 (level 6 in Scotland) that have a craft or technical focus or are related to an occupation/sector. At the time of writing, readers who want to find out more about approved qualifications below level 4 will find The Register of Regulated Qualifications website informative (http://register.ofqual.gov.uk/). It contains details of all those qualifications that are accredited by the regulators of external qualifications in England (Ofqual), Wales (DCELLS) and Northern Ireland (CCEA).

FURTHER AND HIGHER EDUCATION INSTITUTIONS

England and Wales

There is a wide range of further and higher education establishments, including colleges with various titles. There are also a number of independent specialist establishments, like secretarial and correspondence colleges.

According to latest figures available, there were 115 universities, 165 higher education institutions and 419 further education colleges (of which 95 were sixth form colleges) in the UK in 2010. Of the universities, 89 are in England (including The Open University), 10 are in Wales, 14 are in Scotland and two are in Northern Ireland. Courses include those for first and second degrees, certain graduate-equivalent qualifications, and the examinations of the principal professional associations. These institutions also provide courses leading to important qualifications below degree level, such as Foundation degrees, Higher National Diplomas and Certificates, and Diplomas of Higher Education.

Most colleges of further education specialize in providing courses that lead to qualifications below degree level, such as A levels and BTEC qualifications. Some offer degree courses, including in many cases Foundation degrees.

Students aged 16–18 who have been ordinarily resident in the UK for three years and European Union nationals normally have the right to attend a full-time course without paying tuition fees. Colleges are free to determine fee levels for other students.

Scotland

There are 41 colleges of further education in Scotland which provide a broad mix of courses, many awarded by the Scottish Qualifications Authority (SQA). Most courses of higher education at or near degree level and beyond are provided by the 14 universities, The Open University in Scotland and the 19 other HEIs. These institutions offer a range of vocationally-oriented courses ranging from science, engineering and computing to health care, art and design, music and drama, and teacher training, as well as the more traditional 'academic' courses. All the universities and HEIs are funded by the Scottish Funding Council.

Northern Ireland

Responsibility for the further education sector in Northern Ireland rests with the Department for Employment and Learning (DELNI) which directly funds colleges. There are six further education colleges, and these offer a wide range of vocational and non-vocational courses for both full-time and part-time students.

Queen's University Belfast and the University of Ulster receive funding from the Department for Employment and Learning, Northern Ireland.

Many of the courses in both universities are designed to suit the needs of industry, commerce and the professions. Agricultural, horticultural and food colleges in Northern Ireland are administered through the Department of Agriculture, as in Scotland.

UNIVERSITIES AND HE COLLEGES

Universities are self-governing bodies, largely financed by the government through the Higher Education Funding Councils in the UK. They generally derive their rights and privileges from Royal Charter or Act of Parliament, and any amendment of their charters or statutes is made by the Crown acting through the Privy Council on the application of the universities themselves. The universities alone decide what degrees they award and the conditions on which they are awarded; they alone decide which students to admit and which staff to appoint. However, government policies have started to influence admission criteria, particularly in the area of widening access and participation in higher education. Student fees set by universities are also subject to strict guidelines set by the government.

Institutions receiving funding from Higher Education Funding Council for England (Source: Higher Education Funding Council for England)

The 19 schools and institutes of the University of London which receive funds directly from the HEFCE are marked *.

Anglia Ruskin University; Aston University; University of Bath; Bath Spa University; University of Bedfordshire; Birkbeck College*; University of Birmingham; University College Birmingham; Birmingham City University; Bishop Grosseteste University College Lincoln; University of Bolton; Arts University College at Bournemouth; Bournemouth University; University of Bradford; University of Brighton; University of Bristol; Brunel University; Buckinghamshire New University; University of Cambridge; Institute of Cancer Research*; Canterbury Christ Church University; University of Central Lancashire; Central School of Speech and Drama*; University of Chester; University of Chichester; City University, London; Conservatoire for Dance and Drama; Courtauld Institute of Art*; Coventry University; Cranfield University; University for the Creative Arts; University of Cumbria; De Montfort University; University of Derby; Durham University; University of East Anglia; University of East London; Edge Hill University; Institute of Education*; University of Essex; University of Exeter; University College Falmouth; University of Gloucestershire; Goldsmiths, University of London*; University of Greenwich; Guildhall School of Music and Drama; Harper Adams University College; University of Hertfordshire; Heythrop College, University of London*; University of Huddersfield; University of Hull; Imperial College London; Keele University; University of Kent; King's College London*; Kingston University; Lancaster University; University of Leeds; Leeds College of Music; Leeds Metropolitan University; Leeds Trinity University College; University of Leicester; University of Lincoln; University of Liverpool; Liverpool Hope University; Liverpool Institute for Performing Arts; Liverpool John Moores University; University of London; University of the Arts, London; London Business School*; London School of Economics and Political Science*; London School of Hygiene and Tropical Medicine*; London Metropolitan University; London South Bank University; Loughborough University; University of Manchester; Manchester Metropolitan University; Middlesex University, London; Newcastle University; Newman University College; University of Northampton; Northumbria University; Norwich University College of the Arts; University of Nottingham; Nottingham Trent University; The Open University; School of Oriental and African Studies*; University of Oxford; Oxford Brookes University; School of Pharmacy*; University of Plymouth; University College Plymouth Marjon; University of Portsmouth; Queen Mary, University of London*; Ravensbourne; University of Reading; Roehampton University; Rose Bruford College; Royal Academy of Music*; Royal Agricultural College; Royal College of Art; Royal College of

Music; Royal Holloway, University of London*; Royal Northern College of Music; Royal Veterinary College*; St George's, University of London*; St Mary's University College; University of Salford; University of Sheffield; Sheffield Hallam University; University of Southampton; Southampton Solent University; Staffordshire University; University Campus Suffolk; University of Sunderland; University of Surrey; University of Sussex; Teesside University; Trinity Laban Conservatoire of Music and Dance; UCL*; University of Warwick; University of the West of England, Bristol; University of West London; University of Westminster; University of Winchester; University of Wolverhampton; University of Worcester; Writtle College; University of York; York St John University.

Universities receiving funding from the Department for Employment and Learning in Northern Ireland (source: Higher Education Funding Council for England)

Queen's University Belfast; University of Ulster.

Higher Education Institutions receiving funding from the Scottish Funding Council (Source: Scottish Further and Higher Education Funding Council)

University of Aberdeen; University of Abertay Dundee; University of Dundee; Edinburgh College of Art; Edinburgh Napier University; University of Edinburgh; Glasgow Caledonian University; Glasgow School of Art; University of Glasgow; Heriot-Watt University; The Open University in Scotland; Queen Margaret University, Edinburgh; Robert Gordon University; Royal Scottish Academy of Music and Drama; Scottish Agricultural College; University of St Andrews; University of Stirling; University of Strathclyde; University of the Highlands and Islands; University of the West of Scotland.

Institutions receiving funding from the Higher Education Funding Council for Wales (source: Higher Education Funding Council for Wales)

Aberystwyth University; Bangor University; Cardiff University; University of Glamorgan; Glyndwr University; University of Wales, Trinity Saint David (Lampeter campus); University of Wales, Newport; The Open University in Wales; Swansea Metropolitan University; Swansea University; University of Wales Trinity Saint David (Carmarthen campus); UWIC (University of Wales Institute, Cardiff).

OTHER HE ORGANIZATIONS

There are a number of other organizations involved in shaping the Higher Education sector, for example the British Academy, the General Medical Council and Research Councils UK. You can find a full list of these organizations on the Universities UK website, www.universitiesuk.ac.uk.

Part 3

Qualifications

INTRODUCTION

Definition of Common Terms

A number of terms are commonly used as synonyms for qualifications, for example, 'examinations' and 'courses'. This can hide important differences of meaning and lead to confusion and misunderstanding. In some contexts it may be important to make these differences explicit in order to guard against exaggerating or diminishing the level of achievement, which is an essential core of the concept of qualification. It is especially important to clarify the difference in meaning between 'examination', 'course' and 'qualification'.

Examination

An examination is a formal test or assessment. It can focus on one or more of the following: knowledge, understanding, skill or competence. An examination may be set as a written test, an oral test, an aural and oral test (eg a foreign language test) or a practical test. In the past, most forms of external assessment in FE were based on a model of examination dominated by the psychometric model, designed to discriminate between individuals – normative referencing – and took the form of written tests. There was considerable variation in different kinds of written examination, ranging through essays, question and answer, and 'multiple response'. Today, largely as a result of the introduction of National Vocational Qualifications (NVQs), the purpose and format of many examinations have been reappraised, and criterion-referenced examinations that focus on achievement (and in the case of NVQs, competence) are increasingly common. Many forms of assessment are now an integral part of the learning process, with a formative as well as a summative function rather than a separate, terminal, summative function.

Course

A course implies an ordered sequence of teaching or learning over a period of time. A course is governed by regulations or requirements, frequently imposed by an external awarding body and sometimes by the institution providing the course. An important distinguishing feature between different courses is the length of time allocated to study: it can vary from a few days to several years. Some courses offer a terminal award on the basis of course completion, and these courses are set for a given period of time. Other 'set period' courses may prescribe examinations; these can include continuous assessment, terminal testing or a combination of both. In other courses, the programme of study may be accomplished at a faster or slower rate; such courses normally enjoin continuous assessment or a terminal examination, or both. Many courses require attendance at an institution, while distance learning, correspondence courses, and various forms of flexible-learning courses are usually free of these requirements, although some of these courses may require occasional attendance for residential components or face-to-face tutoring. A successful examination result usually confers a qualification or an award.

Qualification

A qualification is normally a certificated endorsement, from a recognized awarding body, that a level or quality of accomplishment has been achieved by an individual. Qualifications are usually conferred on successful completion of an examination, although not all examinations necessarily offer qualifications. An examination may offer an award that is a part-qualification. For example, an NVQ candidate may acquire a unit of competence that is a part-qualification building towards a full statement of competence – an NVQ. A first-year student on an HND course may be required to pass all first-year examinations in order to be permitted to continue into the second year; in a sense, that student is 'qualified' to continue the course but no qualification is awarded. Some award-bearing examinations may be fully recognized and certificated qualifications in themselves (eg a BTEC HNC) but only part-qualifications for a profession (eg Chartered Engineer).

Apparent anomalies do exist. Some professional bodies and trade associations award qualifications that are recognized within the profession or association but that are not obtained by examination. They are usually awarded on the basis of experience, and payment of a fee, and denote membership or acceptance. When the body also offers an examination route to the same qualification, successful examinees are usually known as 'graduate members'.

There are a number of accreditation authorities that approve qualifications. There are also many specialist and general validating, examining and awarding bodies that are responsible for the design and assessment of qualifications.

ACCREDITING REGULATORY BODIES

England

Sector Skills Councils

The Alliance of Sector Skills Councils launched in April 2008 is an organization that supports the network of licensed UK Sector Skills Councils (SSCs). These are employer-led, independent organizations that cover specific work sectors across the UK (currently accounting for approximately 90 per cent of the UK workforce). With the influence granted by licences from the governments of England, Scotland, Wales and Northern Ireland, and with private and public funding, this independent network engages with the education and training supply-side, such as universities, colleges, funders and qualifications bodies, to increase productivity at all levels in the workforce. Details are listed in Table 3.1.

Table 3.1 Sector Skill Councils

Asset Skills
Sector: Property and planning, housing, cleaning sectors and facilities management
Tel: 0845 678 2 888
E-mail: info@assetskills.org
Website: www.assetskills.org

Cogent
Sector: Chemical and pharmaceutical, oil, nuclear, gas, petroleum and polymer
Tel: 01925 515200
E-mail: info@cogent-ssc.com
Website: www.cogent-ssc.com

ConstructionSkills
Sector: Construction
Tel: 0344 994 4400
E-mail: call.centre@cskills.org
Website: www.cskills.org

Creative & Cultural Skills
Sector: Crafts, music, performing, heritage, design and arts
Tel: 020 7015 1800
E-mail: info@ccskills.org.uk
Website: www.ccskills.org.uk

Energy & Utility Skills
Sector: Energy, waste and utilities
Tel: 08450 779922
E-mail: enquiries@euskills.co.uk
Website: www.euskills.co.uk

e-skills UK
Sector: IT and telecoms
Tel: 020 7963 8920
E-mail: info@e-skills.com
Website: www.e-skills.com

continued

Table 3.1 *Continued*

GoSkills
Sector: Passenger transport
Tel: 01216 355520
E-mail: info@goskills.org
Website: www.goskills.org

Improve Ltd
Sector: Food and drinks manufacturing and processing
Tel: 08456 440448
E-mail: info@improveltd.co.uk
Website: www.improveltd.co.uk

IMI The Institute of the Motor Industry
Sector: Retail motor industries
Tel: 01992 511521
E-mail: imi@motor.org.uk
Website: www.motor.org.uk

Lantra
Sector: Environmental and land-based
Tel: 02476 696996
E-mail: connect@lantra.co.uk
Website: www.lantra.co.uk

People 1st
Sector: Hospitality, leisure, travel and tourism
Tel: 01895 817000
E-mail: info@people1st.co.uk
Website: www.people1st.co.uk

Proskills UK
Sector: Process and manufacturing
Tel: 01235 833844
E-mail: info@proskills.co.uk
Website: www.proskills.co.uk

SEMTA
Sector: Science, engineering and manufacturing technologies
Tel: 0845 643 9001
E-mail: customerservices@semta.org.uk
Website: www.semta.org.uk

Skills for Care & Development
Sector: Social care, children, early years and young people's workforces in the UK
Tel: 01133 907666
E-mail: sscinfo@skillsforcareanddevelopment.org.uk
Website: www.skillsforcareanddevelopment.org.uk

Skills for Health
Sector: UK Health
Tel: 01179221155
E-mail: office@skillsforhealth.org.uk
Website: www.skillsforhealth.org.uk

Skills for Justice
Sector: Policing and law enforcement, youth justice, custodial care, community justice, courts service, prosecution services, forensic science, fire rescue services and legal services
Tel: 01142 611 499
E-mail: info@skillsforjustice.com
Website: www.skillsforjustice.com

Skills for Logistics
Sector: Freight logistics and wholesaling industry
Tel: 01908 313360
E-mail: info@skillsforlogistics.org
Website: www.skillsforlogistics.org

SkillsActive
Sector: Sport and recreation, health and fitness, outdoors, playwork and caravanning industry
Tel: 02076 322000
E-mail: skills@skillsactive.com
Website: www.skillsactive.com

continued

Table 3.1 *Continued*

Skillsset
Sector: TV, film, radio, interactive media, advertising, animation, computer games, facilities, photo imaging, publishing, fashion and textiles
Tel: 02077 139800
E-mail: info@skillsset.org
Website: www.skillset.org

Skillsmart Retail
Sector: Retail
Tel: 02074 625060
E-mail: contactus@skillsmartretail.com
Website: www.skillsmartretail.com

SummitSkills
Sector: Building services engineering
Tel: 01908 303960
E-mail: enquiries@summitskills.org.uk
Website: www.summitskills.org.uk

The Alliance of Sector Skills Councils (ASSC)
Tel: 08450 725600
E-mail: info@sscalliance.org
Website: www.sscalliance.org

The Qualifications and Curriculum Development Agency (QCDA)

53–55 Butts Road, Earlsdon Park, Coventry CV1 3BH, Tel: 0300 303 3010, e-mail: info@qcda.gov.uk

QCDA is a public body, sponsored by the Department for Education, that is currently responsible for the development of the national curriculum, qualifications and delivery of assessment.

Ofqual: Office of the Qualifications and Examinations Regulator

Ofqual's role is to ensure all learners get the results they deserve, standards are maintained, and their qualifications are correctly valued and understood, now and in the future. It regulates exams, qualifications and tests in England and vocational qualifications in Northern Ireland.

In 2009, the government passed the Apprenticeship, Skills, Children and Learning Act, which established Ofqual as the regulator of qualifications, examinations and tests in England. Ofqual commenced work as a fully independent non-ministerial government department on 1 April 2010. Ofqual is now accountable to parliament rather than to government ministers.

Scotland

Scottish Qualifications Authority (SQA)

Customer Contact Centre, Tel 0845 279 1000; Fax 0845 213 5000; e-mail customer@sqa.org.uk

The Scottish Qualifications Authority (SQA) is the national accreditation and awarding body in Scotland. SQA is an executive non-departmental public body (NDPB) sponsored by the Scottish Government's Learning Directorate.

SQA works in partnership with schools, colleges, universities and industry to provide high-quality, flexible and relevant qualifications and assessments — embedding industry standards where appropriate. It strives to ensure that SQA qualifications are inclusive, accessible to all, that they provide clear progression pathways, facilitate lifelong learning and recognize candidate achievement.

People take SQA qualifications at all stages of their lives — at school, at college, at work, and in their leisure time. There are qualifications at all levels of attainment. SQA is responsible for three main types of qualification: units, courses and group awards. Most SQA-awarded qualifications are made up of a combination of units, which can also be used in their own right. Each unit represents approximately 40 hours of teaching with additional study. Units are achieved by passing an assessment.

Courses consist of Standard Grades and six National Courses levels — Access 2 & 3, Intermediate 1 & 2, Higher, Advanced Higher and the Scottish Baccalaureate. They are mainly taken at school but some colleges may also offer provision at some levels.

National Qualification Group Awards are designed to be taken at college — National Certificates (NCs), Higher National Certificates and Diplomas (HNCs and HNDs) and National Progression Awards (NPAs) — and the workplace: Scottish Vocational Qualifications (SVQs), Professional Development Awards (PDAs) and Customised Awards. A private company or training provider must become an 'approved centre' to deliver SQA qualifications, or work in partnership with a college or training provider.

Standard Grades and National Courses

Standard Grades are generally taken over two years in the third and fourth years of secondary school. The courses are made up of different parts, called elements, usually with an exam at the end of fourth year.

National Courses, with the exception of Access level, are made up of three units plus an external assessment usually an examination. These can be taken in the fourth, fifth and sixth years at school.

There is a comprehensive appeals system for those who do not perform as well as expected.

Higher National Qualifications

Higher National Certificates (HNCs) and Higher National Diplomas (HNDs) are developed by SQA in partnership with further education colleges, universities, and industry and commerce. They are credible, flexible qualifications that are designed to deliver the skills and knowledge to meet the needs of today's businesses.

National Progression Awards (NPAs)

NPAs are designed to assess a defined set of skills and knowledge in specialist vocational areas. They are mainly used by colleges for short programmes of study.

National Certificates

National Certificates are primarily aimed at 16–18-year-olds and adults in full-time education, normally at a college. They prepare candidates for employment or further study, by developing a range of knowledge and skills.

Scottish Vocational Qualifications (SVQs)

SVQs are based on job competence, and recognize the skills and knowledge people need in employment. SVQs can be attained in most occupations and are available for all types and levels of job. They are primarily delivered to candidates in full-time employment and in the workplace.

Professional Development Awards (PDAs)

PDAs are qualifications for people who are already in a career and who wish to extend or broaden their skills. In some cases they are designed for people wishing to enter employment. PDAs can be taken at college or the workplace.

Customised Awards

Though these qualifications meet the needs of the majority of organizations, SQA also offers specially designed vocational qualifications at any level to meet an organization's need for skills and expertise.

Scottish Credit and Qualifications Framework

The SQA is a partner in a 'credit' system called the Scottish Credit and Qualifications Framework (SCQF), which helps to understand Scottish qualifications and how they relate to one another by making clear the credit value of each type of qualification available in Scotland. The framework has 12 levels: from Level 1 for very basic education to Level 12 for doctoral degrees.

More information about SQA and its qualifications can be found at its website www.sqa.org.uk

VALIDATING, EXAMINING AND AWARDING BODIES/ORGANIZATIONS

A large number of external bodies provide qualifications recognized by accrediting and regulatory bodies. Not all qualifications are available across the entire further education sector: some colleges specialize in particular vocational areas while others are involved in more general adult education provision.

The Federation of Awarding Bodies (FAB) is a trade federation and membership organization for vocational awarding bodies. At the time of writing there are over 100 Ofqual recognized awarding bodies that are full members of FAB. It also has associate members. Find more information at www.awarding.org.uk.

is important to contact the examining or awarding bodies directly to find which colleges deliver the qualifications desired. However, most colleges deliver courses leading to qualifications awarded by the sample selection of organizations listed in the following section:

ABC Awards

Robins Wood House, Robins Wood Road, Aspley, Nottingham NG8 3NH, Tel: 0115 854 1616; Fax: 0115 854 1617; e-mail: enquiries@abcawards.co.uk; website: www.abcawards.co.uk

ABC Awards is a vocational awarding organization with accredited QCF qualifications in all sectors. Many of ABC's qualifications are included in the Foundation Learning Catalogue and are recognized as being eligible for apprenticeships and additional and specialist learning for diplomas. ABC Awards is dedicated to working with centres to deliver exceptional and flexible qualifications.

AQA

Stag Hill House, Guildford, Surrey GU2 7XJ, Tel: 01483 506 506; Fax: 01483 300 152;
e-mail: mailbox@aqa.org.uk; website: www.aqa.org.uk

AQA is the largest of the English exam boards currently awarding around 45 per cent of full course GCSEs and 44 per cent of A Levels nationally. As an awarding body AQA offers a broad range of qualifications available through academic or vocational pathways including GCEs, GCSEs, Entry Level Certificates, Basic and Key Skills, Vocationally Related Qualifications and others such as the Diploma, the Extended Project Qualification, and the AQA Baccalaureate among others.

ASDAN

Wainbrook House, Hudds Vale Road, St George, Bristol BS5 7HY, Tel: 01179 411126, e-mail: info@asdan.org.uk; website: www.asdan.org.uk

ASDAN is established as a registered charity for 'The advancement of education, by providing opportunities for all learners to develop their personal and social attributes and levels of achievement through ASDAN awards and resources, and the relief of poverty, where poverty inhibits such opportunities for learners.' ASDAN offers the following qualifications:

- Wider Key Skills Levels 1–3
- Basic Skills (Skills for Life/Adult Literacy and Numeracy (ALAN)) Levels 1 and 2
- Diploma in Life Skills Entry Levels 1–3
- Certificate of Personal Effectiveness (CoPE) Levels 1–3
- CoPE Through Levels 1–3
- Award of Personal Effectiveness (AoPE) Levels 1 and 2
- Personal and Social Development (PSD) Entry 1–3 and Levels 1 and 2
- Community Volunteering Qualifications (CVO) Levels 1–3 and Volunteering at an Event Levels 1 and 2
- Employability Entry 2, Entry 3, Levels 1–3 including General, Careers Education and Enterprise Education Pathways
- Personal Progress Qualifications Entry 1

To find out more about ASDAN visit www.asdan.org.uk.

City & Guilds

1 Giltspur Street, London EC1A 9DD, Tel: 0844 543 0000; Fax: 0207 294 2400,
website: www.cityandguilds.com

City & Guilds is a leading vocational educational organization, offering more than 500 work-related qualifications worldwide. Around 2 million people every year start City & Guilds qualifications, which span from basic skills to the highest level of professional achievement.

With over 130 years of experience, City & Guilds offers a wide range of qualifications from agriculture to engineering; hairdressing to health and social care; IT to tourism; and photography to catering. They are developed with the help of industry experts and are workplace-relevant, so these qualifications equip people for doing a real job — benefiting them and their employer.

City & Guilds qualifications develop both knowledge and practical skills. They are available at nine levels and are suitable for anyone, whether they are beginners or advanced in their career or area of study. Assessment is based on any combination of examination, projects or coursework. The organizations that offer City & Guilds qualifications include schools, colleges, training organizations, companies and adult education institutes. Depending on the organization, it is possible to study full-time, part-time or through distance learning.

Edexcel Foundation

190 High Holborn, London WC1V 7BH, Tel. 0845 618 0440; website: www.edexcel.org.uk

Edexcel is the UK's largest awarding body, operating in over 85 countries and offering a range of international qualifications including GCEs, GCSEs, vocational and business learning and adult literacy and numeracy qualifications that are offered in schools and colleges, through training providers or in the workplace. Edexcel's BTEC qualifications provide a range of widely accessible, high-quality education programmes of study directly related to employment. Edexcel approves nationally recognized qualifications and Certificates of Achievement that equip students both for employment and for further study. These include adult learning qualifications and NVQs. They are delivered through a network of approved centres around the world. It collaborates closely with industry, government and others to ensure that Edexcel programmes serve the interests of individuals, employers and the nations they are taken in.

EDI plc

International House, Siskin Parkway, Middlemarch Business Park, Coventry CV3 4PE,
Tel: 08707 202909; Fax: 02476 516505; e-mail: enquiries@ediplc.com; website: www.ediplc.com

Education Development International plc (EDI) is a leading provider of education and training qualifications and assessment services. In the UK, EDI is accredited by the government to award a wide range of vocational qualifications, including apprenticeships and diplomas. EDI's expertise is in quality assuring work-based training programmes working closely with employers and over 1,500 private training providers and further education colleges. Internationally, EDI trades under the London Chamber of Commerce and Industry brand and offers a range of business and English language qualifications which have a history that can be traced back to 1887. LCCI International Qualifications are widely used in South East Asia and over 100 countries around the world.

The EDI website has a search facility: www.ediplc.com/Qualifications_Search.asp

NCFE

Citygate, St James' Boulevard, Newcastle upon Tyne NE1 4JE, Tel: 0191 239 8000; Fax: 0191 239 8001; e-mail: info@ncfe.org.uk; website: www.ncfe.org.uk

NCFE is a national awarding organization and registered educational charity. It currently offers over 420 nationally accredited qualifications from Entry level up to and including Level 4 as well as NVQs, Functional Skills, Diplomas, Apprenticeships and Key Skills. Further qualifications are in development. The NCFE website has a qualifications finder search facility at www.ncfe.org.uk/QualificationFinder.aspx

OCR

1 Hills Road, Cambridge, CB1 2EU, Tel: 01223 553998; Fax: 01223 552627;
e-mail: general.qualifications@ocr.org.uk; website: www.ocr.org.uk

OCR is at the forefront of developing qualifications for the 21st century. It offers a wide range of general and vocational qualifications, from GCSEs, A levels and Diplomas to OCR Nationals, NVQs and specialist qualifications. You can find a full index of OCR qualifications at: www.ocr.org.uk/qualifications/index.html

WJEC

245 Western Avenue, Cardiff CF5 2YX, Tel: 02920 265000, e-mail: info@wjec.co.uk; website: www.wjec.co.uk

WJEC is an examining board offering the following major qualifications: General Certificate of Secondary Education (GCSE); Entry Level (EL) and Advanced (A)/Advanced Supplementary (AS) levels and the Welsh Baccalaureate, a new overriding qualification for Wales available at different levels and incorporating GCSEs, A Levels, GNVQs or NVQs. In addition WJEC provides Key/Essential Skills, Functional Skills (in England), Project and Extended Project and Principal Learning qualifications.

JCQ: Joint Council for Qualifications

Sixth Floor, 29 Great Peter Street, London, SW1P 3LW, Tel: 020 7638 4132; Fax: 0207 374 4343; e-mail: info@jcq.org.uk; website: www.jcq.org.uk

The Joint Council for Qualifications (JCQ) was established in 2004 (superseding the Joint Council for General Qualifications, 1998–2003) and consists of AQA, City & Guilds, CCEA, Edexcel, OCR, SQA and WJEC, the seven largest providers of qualifications in the UK, offering GCSE, GCE, Scottish Highers, Entry Level, Vocational and vocationally-related qualifications. The JCQ enables member awarding bodies to act together on a number of issues including providing, wherever possible, common administrative arrangements for the schools and colleges and other providers that offer their qualifications and dealing with the regulators; in responding to proposals and initiatives on assessment and the curriculum.

The Register of Regulated Qualifications contains details of recognized awarding organisations and regulated qualifications in England (Ofqual), Wales (DCELLS) and Northern Ireland (Ofqual for vocational qualifications and CCEA for all other qualifications). The website also carries a full alphabetical list of awarding bodies offering qualifications accredited by the regulatory authorities in England, Wales and Northern Ireland. For more information see www.register.ofqual.gov.uk.

Part 4

Qualifications Awarded or Validated by Universities

ADMISSION TO DEGREE COURSES

Higher Education Institutions (HEIs)

Most institutions have a general requirement for admission to a degree course; special requirements may be in force for particular courses. Requirements are usually expressed in terms of subjects passed at GCE A level and the Higher Grade of the SCE. The universities have a clearing-house to handle applications for university courses: UCAS, www.ucas.ac.uk. All intending students who live in the UK may obtain information on application procedures from their schools or colleges, or directly from UCAS. The scheme covers all universities and all medical schools. UCAS also has specialist services: the Graduate Teacher Training Registry (GTTR), the UK Postgraduate Application and Statistical Service (UKPASS) and the Conservatoires UK Admissions Service (CUKAS).

HEIs have specific schemes to encourage access and participation in higher education. These can include partnerships with further education colleges that run access to higher education courses.

The Open University

For admission to most first-degree courses, no formal educational qualifications are necessary. However, students who have successfully completed one or more years of full-time study at the higher education level (or its equivalent in part-time study) may be eligible for exemption from some credit requirements of the BA degree. The Open University handles its own admissions.

Business schools

The degrees awarded by the various university business schools are postgraduate and therefore normally require an honours degree as part of their entrance qualification.

AWARDS

The awards made by the universities may be separated into the following categories: first degrees; higher degrees; honorary degrees; first diplomas and certificates; higher diplomas and certificates.

First degrees

Nomenclature

Various names are given to the first degrees at British universities. At most universities the first degree in Arts is the BA (Bachelor of Arts) degree and the first degree in Science is the BSc (Bachelor of Science) degree. But at the universities of Oxford and Cambridge and at several new universities, the BA is the first degree gained by students in both arts and science. In Scotland the first arts degree at three of the four old universities is Master of Arts (MA). There are numerous variations on the bachelor theme, eg BSc (Econ) (Bachelor of Science in Economics), BCom (Bachelor of Commerce), BSocSc (Bachelor of Social Science), BEng (Bachelor of Engineering) and BTech (Bachelor of Technology). The first award in medicine is the joint degrees of MB, ChB (Bachelor of Medicine, Bachelor of Surgery), the designatory letters of which vary from university to university.

Structure of courses

First-degree courses vary considerably in structure, not only between one university and another but also between faculties in a single university. The degree examination is usually in two sections, Part I coming after one or two years of the course and Part II, 'finals', at the end of the course. The first-degree system at some Scottish universities differs substantially from that in English and Welsh universities (see below).

Bachelor degrees

These degrees, sometimes known as 'ordinary' or 'first' degrees, lead to qualifications such as Bachelor of Arts (BA), Bachelor of Science (BSc) or Bachelor of Medicine (MB). Each university decides the form and content of its own degree examinations. These vary from university to university.

The first-degree structure in all British universities is based on the Honours degree. Successful candidates in Honours degree examinations are placed in different classes according to their performance, first class being the highest. The other classes given vary from university to university, but the classification most often used is: Class I; Class II (Division 1); Class II (Division 2); Class III. Most graduates who go on to higher academic qualifications, and those entering, for example, the higher grades in the Civil Service or research, normally have a good class Honours degree.

You can find out more about recognized UK degrees at the BIS website; www.bis.gov.uk.

Number of subjects studied

Excluding medicine and dentistry, the broad subject areas are Arts (or Humanities), Social Science, Pure Science and Applied Science. Most students study one main subject selected from one of these areas. It is possible to distinguish many types of degree course according to the number of subjects studied; these types are a variation on three main categories:

1. honours course in one to three subjects with or without examinable subsidiary subjects;
2. pass or ordinary courses in one to three subjects with or without examinable subsidiary subjects;
3. common studies for pass and honours in one to three subjects, with or without examinable subsidiary subjects.

Length of degree course

First-degree courses may be preceded by a preliminary year, from which students with the appropriate entry qualifications may be exempted. At most universities honours and pass courses in arts, social science, pure and applied science last three or four years, but courses in architecture, dentistry and veterinary medicine usually last five years, and complete qualifying courses in medicine up to six years. Courses in fine arts and pharmacy may last four years; four-year courses exist mainly in double honours schools especially when they involve foreign languages and a period of study abroad, and in the technological universities where some courses include a period of integrated industrial training (sandwich courses).

The Scottish first degree

The distinctive feature of first degrees at some Scottish universities is the Ordinary MA course, which has no counterpart in England and Wales, and the Ordinary BSc course. The function of the Ordinary MA is to provide a broad, general education. Scottish undergraduates are required to show during their first two years of study, over a range of subjects, that they are fit to go on to an honours degree course, which takes a further two years to complete.

Aegrotat degrees

Candidates who have followed a course for a degree but have been prevented from taking the examinations by illness may be awarded a degree certificate indicating that they were likely to have obtained the degree had they taken the examinations.

Higher degrees

These comprise:

- some Bachelor's degrees: BPhil, BLitt, etc;
- Master's degrees: MA, MSc, etc;
- Doctor of Philosophy: PhD or DPhil;
- Higher Doctorates: DLitt, DSc, etc.

At Oxford and Cambridge the degree of MA is conferred on any BA of the university without any further course of study or examination after a specified number of years and on payment of a fee. Candidates for a Master's degree at other universities (and at some for the degrees of BPhil, BLitt and BD, which are of equivalent standing) are normally required to have a first degree, although it need not have been obtained in the same university. Master's degrees are taken after one or two years' full-time study. The PhD requires at least two or more usually three years of full-time study.

In some universities and faculties students may be selected for a PhD course after an initial year's study or research common to both a PhD and a Master's degree. Candidates for a Master's degree are required either to prepare a thesis for presentation to examiners, who may afterwards question them on it orally, or to take written examination papers; they may be required to do both. All PhD students present a thesis; some may be required to take an examination paper as well. MPhil, MSc and similar degrees are usually awarded at the end of a one- or two-year course in a special topic on the results of a written examination or a thesis. Higher doctorates are designated on a faculty basis, eg DLitt (Doctor of Letters) and DSc (Doctor of Science). Candidates are usually required to have at least a Master's degree of the awarding university. Senior doctorates are conferred on more mature and established people, usually on the basis of published contributions to knowledge.

Foundation degrees

Foundation degrees were established to give people the intermediate technical and professional skills that are in demand from employers and to provide more flexible and accessible ways of studying. Increasing opportunities for employment and career advancement are priorities; foundation degree content and assessment are therefore designed in consultation with employers. Additional progression routes include links with associated professional qualifications and/or direct entry to the final year of a relevant Honours level degree. Provision is available across a range of further education colleges and a number of HEIs.

Honorary degrees

Most universities confer honorary degrees on people of distinction in academic and public life, and on others who have rendered service to the university or to the local community. Normally degrees awarded are at least Foundation level.

Diplomas and certificates of higher education

Courses for first diplomas and certificates are relatively simple in structure; they usually reach a level lower than that required for the award of a degree. There is usually a carefully defined course in a specialized or vocational subject, lasting one or two years, followed by all candidates. Most courses are full time.

Postgraduate diplomas and certificates

Diplomas (eg in public health, social administration, medicine and technology) are awarded either on a full-time or less often part-time basis according to the subject and the university. Candidates must usually be graduates or hold equivalent qualifications. Diplomas are awarded after formal courses of instruction and success in written examinations. A Certificate or Diploma in Education is awarded to graduates training to become teachers after one year's full-time study and teaching practice.

Postgraduate courses

A number of courses for graduates or people with equivalent qualifications are offered in further education establishments. They include short specialist courses in Management and Business Studies and secretarial courses for graduates.

Business schools

A Master of Business Administration (MBA) is an internationally recognized postgraduate qualification intended to prepare individuals for middle to senior level general managerial positions. Most programmes contain as their core a number of subjects considered essential for understanding the operations of any enterprise. These are: accounting and finance, operations management, business policy, economics, human resource management, marketing, information systems and strategic planning.

Unlike any other Master's programme, the MBA is not only postgraduate, it is also strongly post-experience. A minimum of three years' (often more) work experience at an appropriate level of responsibility is generally expected of applicants. The requirement for a first degree (or equivalent) is sometimes waived for those holding an impressive track record of over five years at managerial level. Approximately one-third of MBA students have an engineering or information technology background. Many undertake the qualification to facilitate change from technical or specialist positions to more generalist ones.

The MBA was conceived originally in the United States at the beginning of the 20th century. Introduced in the United Kingdom in the late 1960s, it did not grow in popularity until the late 1980s. The popularity of this degree in the United Kingdom can be seen in the rapid expansion in the number of providers.

The Association of MBAs (AMBA) operates a system of accreditation. The accreditation process, which is internationally recognized for all MBA, DBA and Masters in Business and Management (MBM) programmes, measures individual MBA programmes against specific accreditation criteria. Further information, including a list of accredited MBA programmes, can be obtained from the Association of MBAs, 25 Hosier Lane, London EC1A 9LQ, Tel: 0207 246 2686, e-mail: info@mba-world.com, website; www.mbaworld.com.

The Association of Business Schools (ABS)

137 Euston Road, London NW1 2AA, Tel: 020 7388 0007, Fax: 020 7388 0009, e-mail: abs@the-abs.org.uk, website; www.the-abs.org.uk

The ABS is the representative body for management and business education and all the United Kingdom's leading business schools. The ABS works broadly in three main areas: policy development, promotion and representation and training and development.

The ABS is able to provide general information about the wide range of courses and programmes provided by the United Kingdom's business schools.

First awards

- **BA, BEd, BEng, LLB, BSc:** with 1st Class, 2nd Class (Divisions 1 and 2), 3rd Class Honours or Pass; or unclassified with or without Distinction.
- **MEng:** awarded to students who successfully complete a course of study that is longer and more demanding than the BEng first degree course in Engineering.
- **GMus (Graduate Diploma in Music):** awarded to those students who complete three years' approved full-time study (or equivalent) in Music and who demonstrate competence in musical performance.
- **DipHE (Diploma of Higher Education):** equivalent in standard and often similar in content to the first two years of an Honours degree course.
- **Certificates of Higher Education:** equivalent to the first year of an Honours degree course.

Higher awards

- **MA, MBA, MEd, MSc:** for successful completion of an approved postgraduate course of study of 48 weeks' duration (or the part-time equivalent).
- **MPhil, PhD:** for successful completion of approved programmes of supervised research.
- **DSc, DLitt and DTech:** for original and important contributions to knowledge and/or its applications.
- **Postgraduate Diploma:** awarded for the successful completion of an approved postgraduate course of study of 25 weeks' duration (or the part-time equivalent).
- **Postgraduate Certificate:** awarded for the successful completion of postgraduate/post-experience courses of 15 weeks' duration (or the part-time equivalent).
- **Postgraduate Certificate in Education (PGCE):** awarded on completion of a one-year full-time course; candidates must be British graduates or hold another recognized qualification.
- **Diploma in Professional Studies:** available in the fields of education and nursing, health visiting, midwifery and sports coaching. Students normally hold an initial professional qualification. A minimum of two years' experience is normally expected.

UNIVERSITY OF ABERDEEN
www.abdn.ac.uk

College of Arts and Social Sciences; www.abdn.ac.uk/about/social-sciences/php

Aberdeen Business School; www.abdn.ac.uk/business

accounting, economics, enterprise, entrepreneurship, finance, innovation, international relations, macroeconomics, management studies, property & real estate management, MBA programmes; MA(Hons), MBA, MRes, MSc, PgCert, PhD

School of Divinity, History & Philosophy; www.abdn.ac.uk/sdhp

cultural history, divinity, history (medieval, early modern, Irish, Scottish, Scandinavian), history of art, art in Scotland, art & business, philosophy, religious studies, theology, ministry, biblical theology, church history, social anthroplogy, visual culture; BD, BTh, DMin, LicTh, MA(Hons), MLitt, MTh, PgDip, PhD

School of Education; www.abdn.ac.uk/education

early/childhood studies, primary education, professional development, TQFE, secondary education, tertiary education, autism, adult literacy, inclusive practice; BA(Hons), BEd(Hons), MEd, MPhil, MRes, MSc, Mus(Hons), PGCert, PGDE, PGDip, PhD

School of Language & Literature; www.abdn.ac.uk/sll

Celtic, comparative literature, creative writing, English/literature/language, film & visual culture, French, German & Hispanic studies, Irish–Scottish studies, linguistics, medieval studies, modern thought, the novel, sociolinguistics, language & linguistics; MA, MA(Designated), MA(Hons), MLitt, PhD

School of Law; www.abdn.ac.uk/law

law,legal practice, European, international commercial/business/private/oil & gas law, criminal justice, human rights, sustainable development; LlB, LlB(Hons), LlM, MPhil, PhD

School of Social Science; www.abdn.ac.uk/socsc

anthropology, gender studies, politics & international relations, social anthropology, sociology, religion & society, globalization, Europolitics & society, sex, gender & violence, strategic studies; MA(Hons), MA, MLitt, MPhil, MRes, MSc, PGDip, PhD

College of Life Sciences and Medicine; www.abdn.ac.uk/clsm

School of Biological Sciences; www.abdn.ac.uk/biologicalsci

animal ecology, biology, cell & molecular systems, conservation biology, environmental science/sustainability/microbiology, forestry, immunology, drug development, global health, medical physics, nursing/midwifery/health care, psychology, plant & soil science/biology, marine biology, parasitology, molecular nutrition,wildlife management, zoology; BSc(Hons),MPhil, MSc, MSc/PGDip, MRes, PhD

School of Medical Science; www.abdn.ac.uk/sms
biochemistry, biomedical sciences, biotechnology, genetics, health & human nutrition, immunology, microbiology, molecular biology, pharmacology, physiology, primary care, sport & exercise science, sports studies, applied marine & fisheries ecology; BSc(Hons), MPhil, MSc, MSc/PGDip, PhD

School of Medicine & Dentistry; www.abdn.ac.uk/medicine-dentistry
dentistry, health science/studies, medicine; BDS, BSc, MA, MBChB, MMedSci, MPhil, MSc, PhD

School of Psychology; www.abdn.ac.uk/psychology
patient safety, psychology, social cognition, neuroscience; BSc(Hons), MA, MRes, MSc

Rowlet Institute of Nutrition and Health Studies; www.rowletac.uk
impacts on human health; BSc(Hons), MSc, MSc/PgDip, PhD

College of Physical Sciences; www.abdn.ac.uk/about/physical-sciences.php

School of Engineering; www.abdn.ac.uk/engineering
chemical engineering, civil engineering, electrical & electronic engineering, mechanical engineering, project management, safety engineering, energy futures, subsea engineering, oil & gas structures; BEng(Hons), BScEng, EnD, MEng, MSc

School of Geosciences; www.abdn.ac.uk/geosciences

Dept of Archaeology; www.abdn.ac.uk/archaeology
archaeology with anthropology/Celtic civilization/history/geography, archaeology of the north; BSc(Hons), MA(Hons), MPhil, PhD

Dept of Geography & the Environment; www.abdn.ac.uk/geography
geography, geoscience, marine & coastal resource management, urban/rural planning, property, rural surveying, spatial planning, sustainable rural development, environmental management; BSc(Hons), MA(Hons), MSc, PgDip/Cert, PhD

Dept of Geology & Petroleum Geology; www.abdn.ac.uk/geology
oil & gas enterprise management, geology, geoscience, petroleum geology; BSc(Hons), MA(Hons), MRes, MSc, PgDip/Cert, PhD

Centre for Planning & Environmental Management; www.abdn.ac.uk/cpem
geographical & spatial planning, property, urban planning, real estate, rural planning & environmental management, sustainable rural development, land economy; BSc(Hons), MA(Hons), MSc

School of Natural & Computing Sciences; www.abdn.ac.uk/sncs

Chemistry; www.abdn.ac.uk/chemistry
chemistry, biomedical materials, chemical science, environmental chemistry, materials, medicinal chemistry; BSc(Hons), MChem, MSc, PgDip, PhD

Computing Science; www.csd.abdn.ac.uk
artificial intelligence, business information systems, computing science, business computing systems, computing & e-business, software project management, information systems/technology, electronic commerce technology, natural language generation; BSc(Hons), MA(Hons), MSc, MSci, PhD

Mathematics; www.maths.abdn.ac.uk/
engineering mathematics, mathematics/physics/computing science/education, pure mathematics; BSc(Hons), MA(Hons), MSc, PhD

Physics; www.abdn.ac.uk/physics
physical sciences, physics, physics with chemistry/geology/philosophy/engineering/mathematics/education; BSc(Hons), MSc(Hons)

UNIVERSITY OF ABERTAY, DUNDEE
www.abertay.ac.uk

School of Arts, Media & Computer Games www.abertay.ac.uk/studying/schools/amg;

computer arts, computer games/technology/design/production/applications, creative sound production, visual communication & media design, creative sound production; BA(Hons), BSc(Hons), DipHE, MProf, MSc/PGDip

School of Computing & Engineering Systems; www.abertay.ac.uk/ces

computing, networks/security, IT, intelligence, security informatics, internet computing, engineering systems, adaptive sytems, ethical hacking & countermeasures, web design/development; BSc(Hons),MSc,DipHE,PGDip

Dundee Business School; www.abertay.ac.uk/studying/schools/dbe

accountancy, business administration/studies, enterprise, Europe (economy, business law, management), entrepreneurship, finance, HRM, international management, law, marketing, management accounting, oil & gas accounting, retail marketing, tourism, golf management, biotechnology; BA (Hons), GradCert, MBA, MSc, PGDip

The School of Contemporary Sciences; www.abertay.ac.uk/studying/schools/cs

bioinformatics, biomedical sciences, medical biotechnology, civil engineering, energy & environmental management, environment & business industrial environment, food biotechnology/product design, nutrition, consumer science, forensic sciences, health sciences, medical biotechnology, policy & security, renewable energy, urban water, water pollution control; BSc(Hons), DipHE, MSc, MTech, PGDip

The School of Social & Health Sciences; www.abertay.ac.uk/studying/schools/shs

behavioural science, counselling, criminological studies, forensic psychobiology, media, culture and society, mental health/nursing, psychology, public administration, social & health science, sociology, sports/coaching, golf, sport & exercise/management/nutrition/psychology, sports development; BA(Hons), BSc(Hons), GradCert, MSc, PGDip, DipHE

ABERYSTWYTH UNIVERSITY
www.aber.ac.uk

School of Art; www.aber.ac.uk/en/art

art/history, fine art, museum & gallery studies; BA(Hons), MA, MPhil, PhD

Institute of Biological, Environmental & Rural Sciences; www.aber.ac.uk/en/ers

agriculture, animal science/zoology, biochemistry, biology, conservation/countryside management, microbiology, environmental/science/biology, equine science, genetics, marine & freshwater biology, tourism & recreation; BSc(Hons), MPhil, MSc, PhD

Dept of Computer Science; www.aber.ac.uk/en/cs

business IT, computer graphics, internet engineering, mobile wearable computing, open source computing, robotics, software engineering, artificial intelligence; BEng, BSc(Hons), HND, MEng, MSc, PhD

School of Education & Lifelong Learning; www.aber.ac.uk/en/sell

childhood studies, lifelong learning, education; BA(Hons), BSc(Hons), MPhil, PGCE, PGDip, PhD

Dept of English & Creative Writing; www.aber.ac.uk/en/english

creative writing, English literature, literary/classical studies, American studies; BA(Hons), MA, PhD

Dept of European Languages; www.aber.ac.uk/en/eurolangs

French, German, Italian, European culture, Romance languages, Spanish; BA(Hons), MA, PhD

Institute of Geography & Earth Sciences; www.ies.aber.ac.uk/en/ges

environmental earth/science, geography, GIS and remote sensing, glaciology, human/physical geography, local and regional economic development, quaternary environmental change; BSc(Hons), MPhil, MRes, MSc, PhD

Dept of History & Welsh History; www.aber.ac.uk/en/history

economic/social/European/medieval & modern history, contemporary politics, Welsh history, history & media, early British/18th-century history, history of medicine, Celtic history; BA(Hons), MA, PhD

Dept of Information Studies; www.dis.aber.ac.uk/en/dis

business information, historical & archival/information & library studies, records mang, information management/systems; BA(Hons), BSc(Econ), Dip/Cert, MPhil, MSc(Econ), PhD

Dept of International Politics; www.aber.ac.uk/en/interpol

European studies, intelligence & strategic studies, international history/strategic studies/third world/military history, international relations, military history, political studies, intelligence studies, peace conflict & security, international politics & the third world; BSc(Econ), MA, MSc, MSc(Econ), PhD

Dept of Law and Criminology; www.aber.ac.uk/en/law-criminology

business law, criminal law, criminology with applied psychology/law, European law, human rights, law; BA(Hons), BSc(Econ), LlB, LlM, PhD

School of Management and Business; www.aber.ac.uk/en/smb

accounting & finance, business, business economics/finance, economics, entrepreneurship, marketing,international business/finance, management; BSc(Econ), MBA, MSc(Econ), PhD

Institute of Mathematical & Physical Sciences; www.aber.ac.uk/en/maps

applied mathematics, statistics, computer science, pure mathematics, physics, planetary and space physics, space science, theoretical physics, astrophysics, robotics; BSc(Hons), MMath, MPhys, PhD

Dept of Psychology; www.aber.ac.uk/en/psychology

psychology, BSc(Econ), BSc(Hons), PhD

Dept of Sport & Exercise Science; www.aber.ac.uk/sport/exercise

sport & exercise science, equine & human sport exercise, exercise psychology/physiology/biomedicine; BSc(Hons), PhD

Dept of Theatre, Film & Television Studies; www.aber.ac.uk/en/tfts

drama & theatre, film & television, film studies, media & communication, performance, scenography/theatre design, scriptwriting, Welsh medium courses; BA(Hons), MA, MPhil, PhD

Dept of Welsh; www.aber.ac.uk/cymraeg-welsh

Breton, Welsh & Celtic languages, Celtic studies, Irish, Welsh 1st language, medieval Welsh literature; BA(Hons), MA

ANGLIA RUSKIN UNIVERSITY
www.anglia.ac.uk

Faculty of Arts, Law and Social Sciences; www.anglia ac.uk/en/home/faculties/alss

Dept of English, Communication, Film & Media; anglia.ac.uk/ruskin/en/home/faculties/alss/deps/english_media

English language/literature/teaching, TESOL, film/media studies, sports journalism, writing, applied linguistics, intercultural communication, publishing; BA(Hons), MPhil, PhD

Anglia Law School; www.anglia.ac.uk/ruskin/en/home/faculties/alss/deps/law

criminology, international business/ law, legal practice, professional legal studies; BA(Hons), LlB, LlD, LlM

Cambridge School of Art; www.anglia.ac.uk/ruskin/en/home/faculties/alss/deps/csoa

animation, children's book illustration, computer games, fashion/interior design, film, TV & theatre, fine art, illustration, photography, graphic design; BA(Hons), FdA, MA, MFA

Dept of Humanities & Social Sciences; www.anglia.ac.uk/ruskin/en/home/faculties/alss/deps/hss

criminology, forensic science, history, English, philosophy, psychosocial studies, public service, sociology, transnational crime; BA(Hons), FdA, MPhil, PhD

Dept of Music & Performing Arts; www.anglia.ac.uk/ruskin/en/home/faculties/alss/deps/music

contemporary theatre, creative music technology, drama/music/ therapy, performing arts, pop music, film studies; BA(Hons), FdADip, MA, MPhil, PhD

Ashcroft International Business School; www.anglia.ac.uk/ruskin/en/home/faculties/aibs

accountancy, business/economics/corporate management, finance, enterprise & entrepreneurship, HRM, international business/tourism management, leadership, marketing; BA(Hons), BSc(Hons), MA, MBA, MSc, CertHE, HNC, HND

Faculty of Education; www.anglia.ac.uk/ruskin/en/home/faculties/education

early childhood, education studies, ESOL, EYPS, FE/HE, learning through technology, PGCE primary and secondary courses, primary education/with modern foreign languages, teaching and learning assistants, teaching English (literacy), teaching mathematics (numeracy); BA(Hons), Diplomas, FdA/FdSc Professional Practice, MA, PGCE, UnivCert

Faculty of Health and Social Care; www.anglia.ac.uk/ruskin/en/home/faculties/hsc

children & young people's nursing, case management, children and family, community public health nursing, health care, management and leadership in social care, midwifery, operating dept practice, perioperative care, physiotherapy, radiotherapy, oncology, nursing (adult, child, learning disabilities, mental health, young people), social work/policy, youth and community work; BSc(Hons), FdSc, Cert HE, Dip HE, MSc, PGDip/Cert

Faculty of Science and Technology; www.anglia.ac.uk/ruskin/en/home/faculties/fst

Dept of Built Environment; www.anglia.ac.uk/ruskin/en/home/faculties/fst/departs/builtenv

architecture/technology, building surveying, civil engineering, construction management, environmental planning, project management, quantity surveying, real estate management, structural engineering, sustainable construction, town planning; BSc(Hons), FdSc, MSc, PGCert, PGDip

Dept of Computing & Technology; www.anglia.ac.uk/ruskin/en/home/faculties/fst/departments/comptech

animation/audio, video and music technology, business information systems/technology, computer games/ networking/ science, computing, music technology, electronics, engineering management, forensic computing, information security, integrated engineering, mechanical engineering, mobile telecommunication, multimedia, network/network security; BEng(Hons), BSc(Hons), HND

Dept of Vision and Hearing Science; www.anglia.ac.uk/ruskin/en/home/departments/vision-hearing

ophthalmics, optometry, hearing aid technology; BOptom(Hons), BSc(Hons), FdSc, UnivCert

Dept of Psychology; www.anglia.ac.uk/ruskin/enhome/departments/psychology

cognitive neuroscience, abnormal/clinical/child psychology, criminology; BSc(Hons), MSc

Dept of Life Sciences; www.anglia.ac.uk/ruskin/en/home/faculties/fst/deps/lifesciences

animal behaviour/welfare, biomedical sciences, cell & molecular biology, coaching, conservation, ecology, equine studies, forensic science, marine/wildlife biology, microbiology, sports coaching & PE, zoology; BSc(Hons), FdSc, MSc, PGDip

Degrees validated by Anglia Ruskin University offered at:

COLCHESTER INSTITUTE
www.colchester.ac.uk

Art, Design and Media
art, fashion textiles, fine art, graphic design, media/video production; BA(Hons), FdA, HNC, MA

Business & Management
accountancy, business, e-business, hospitality, logistics & transport, public services, sport, tourism; BA(Hons), DipMan, Foundation degree, HNC, HND, PgDip/Cert

Computing & Administration
computing, business administration, systems support, web design; Bsc(Hons), BTEC, Dipl Man, NC

Construction
brickwork, construction/sitesupervision management, plumbing,woodcraft/carpentry/joinery/cabinet making, electrical installations; BSc(Hons), FD, HNC, NVQs 4 & 5

Education
lifelong learning, literacy & ESOL, continuing education, TESOL teacher training; BA(Hons), Cert Ed, EFT, ESOL, FD, PGCE

Engineering
acoustics & noise control, electrical/electronic, mechanical engineering; C&G Certs, Dipl in Acoustics, FD, HNC

Health & Care
counselling, health, social care; BA(Hons), FD, DipHE

Hospitality & Food Studies
food & drink service, food preparation & cooking, hospitality supervision; Dips, Nat Dip, NVQs

Music & Performing Arts
acting, jazz and popular music, music, musical/technical theatre; BA(Hons), FD, MA

ASHRIDGE
www.ashridge.ac.uk

executive coaching, management, organization consulting/change, sustainability & responsibility; Doc Orgn Consulting, ExecMBA, MBA, MSc

ASTON UNIVERSITY
www.aston.ac.uk

Aston Business School; www.aston.ac.uk/aston-business-school
accounting, business & management, business computing & IT, economics, finance, HRM, international business & management/economics/modern language/commercial law, investments, IT project management, law, financial regulation, strategy, administration, marketing, mathematics with economics, management & strategy; BSc(Hons), DBA, Foundation degree, LlB, LlM, MBA, PhD,FD

Centre for Learning, Innovation and Professional Practice; clipp/ www.aston.uk.ac
curriculum & learning development, teaching, media & learning technologies; MA, PG Cert

School of Engineering and Applied Science; www.aston.uk.ac/eas

Chemical Engineering & Applied Chemistry
applied/biological chemistry, chemical engineering, chemistry; BE Eng, MEng, MChem

Computer Science
computing science, computing for business, multimedia computing BSc

Electronic Engineering
communications engineering, computer science, electrical & electronic engineering, internet systems; BSc, BEng

Engineering Systems & Management
construction management/project management; BSc

Technology & Enterprise Management
technology & enterprise management; BSc

Logistics & Transport Management
logistics, transport management; BSc

Mathematics
mathematics, mathematics with computing; BSc

Mechanical Engineering & Design
electromechanical engineering, mechanical engineering, design engineering; BEng, MEng

Product Design
industrial/ engineering/medical/automotive product design, product design & management, sustainable product design; BSc

School of Life and Health Sciences; www.aston.uk.ac/life-health-sciences
applied & human biology, audiology, biomedical science, cognitive neurosciences, health psychology, hearing aid audiology, optometry, pharmacy, psychiatric pharmacy/ therapeutics, psychology; BSc(Hons), GradDip, FD MPharm, MRes, MSc, PGCert/Dip, PhD

School of Languages and Social Sciences; www.aston.uk.ac/ls

Modern Languages & Translation Studies
French, German, Spanish, translation studies, international business & modern languages studies,

International Relations, Politics & European Studies
sociology/politics, international relations and business/politics/public policy & management/sociology

English Studies
English language/range of subjects for combined honours

Sociology & Public Policy & Management
social sciences, sociology, business/computer science/ international relations/politics, public policy & management & business; BA(Hons), BSc(Hons), MA, MPhil, MRes, MSc, PhD

BANGOR UNIVERSITY
www.bangor.ac.uk

College of Arts and Humanities; www.bangor.ac.uk/cah

Creative Studies & Media; www.bangor.ac.uk/creative.industries
creative/film studies, journalism, media studies, theatre, professional writing, creative writing

English; www.bangor.ac.uk/english
creative writing, English literature/language, journalism, publishing, theatre/film studies, Arthurian legend, medieval & early modern literature

History, Welsh History & Archaeology; www.bangor.ac.uk/history
archaeology, contemporary/medieval & early modern/Welsh history, heritage, Celtic archaeology, political & social sciences

School of Linguistics & English Language; www.bangor.ac.uk/linguistics
creative writing, English language/literature, applied/ cognitive/anthropological linguistics, bilingualism

School of Modern Languages; www.bangor.ac.uk/ml
French, German, Italian, Spanish, mid European languages & cultures, translation studies

School of Music; www.bangor.ac.uk/music
music/technology, composition, elecroacoustics, sacred music

Theology & Religious Studies; www.bangor.ac.uk/trs
religious studies, theology, study of religion

School of Welsh; www.bangor.ac.uk/ysgolygymraeg; details of courses provided in Welsh language, Welsh, bilingualism
BA(Hons), BD, BMus, Dip, MA, MMus, MPhil, MTh, PgDip, PhD

College of Business, Social Sciences & Law; www.bangor.ac.uk/cbss

Bangor Business School; www.bangor.ac.uk/business
accounting, banking, business studies, economics, finance, leisure/management, marketing, administration, ICT, social authority law, Islamic justice, information management; BA, BSc(Hons), MA, MSc, MBA

School of Social Sciences; www.bangor.ac.uk/so
criminology & criminal justice, health & social care, social policy/work/studies/research, sociology; BA(Hons), MA, DipPG, PhD, MPhil

School of Law; www.bangor.ac.uk/law
law, criminal justice, law & devolved goverments, company/commercial/family & welfare/media/international law, intellectual property; BA(Hons), DBA, HND, LlB, LlM, MA, MBA, MSc, MPhil, PGDip, PhD

School of Education and Lifelong Learning; www.bangor.ac.uk/sell

childhood studies, design & technology, secondary education, post-11 learning support studies, early childhood & learning support studies, primary education, PGCE primary/secondary, lifelong learning; BA Cert, Dipl, FdA, HNC/HND

Academic Development Unit; www.bangor.ac.uk/adu
Welsh for adults; PGCertHE, BSc(Hons), EdMed, FdA, MA, MEd, MMusD, MPhil, MTh, PGCE, PhD

College of Natural Sciences; www.bangor.ac.uk/cns

CNS School of Biological Sciences; www.bangor.ac.uk/biology
medical/molecular biology, biology, biomedical science, ecology, molecular biology, zoology, animal behaviour/ecology/conservation/marine zoology, genetics, ecology; BSc(Hons), Dipl, MA, MBiol, MPhil, MRes, MSc, MZool, PhD

School of Environment, Natural Resources, & Geography; www.bangor.ac.uk/senrgy
agriculture, conservation, environmental conservation/management, countryside management, environmental planning/science, forest ecosystems, forestry, geography, sustainable development, terrestrial and marine ecology; BA/BSc(Hons), BSc(Hons), MA, MEnvSci, MPhil, MSc, PhD

School of Ocean Sciences; www.bangor.ac.uk/sos
coastal/geological oceanography, marine biology/& geology/environmental studies/science/vertebrate zoology, oceanography, marine science, ocean science, geological oceanography; BSc(Hons), MMBiol, MMSci, MOcean, MPhil, MSc, PhD

Welsh Institute for Natural Resources; www.bangor.ac.uk/wnr

College of Health & Behavioural Sciences; www.bangor.ac.uk/cohabs

School of Healthcare Sciences; www.bangor.ac.uk/healthcaresciences
health studies/science, critical care, midwifery, nursing, occupational therapy, pharmacology, operating dept practice, public health, radiography, social care; BN(Hons), BSc(Hons), BMidw, DipHE, GradCert/Dip, MPhil, PhD

School of Medical Sciences; www.bangor.ac.uk/sms
behavioural neurology, clinical & functional brain imaging, molecular science for medicine; MSc, PGDip/Cert(HE), BMed Sci,BSc PhD

School of Psychology; www.bangor.ac.uk/psychology
child & language development, clinical & health psychology, neuropsychology, psychology, applied behavioural analysis, consumer psychology; BSc(Hons), MSc, PhD, MRes, MA

School of Sport, Health & Exercise Science; www.bangor.ac.uk/sport
sport science, sport, health & exercise, physical education, exercise science, physiology, exercise psychology, outdoor activities; BSc(Hons), MPhil, MSc, PhD

Institute of Medical & Social Research; www.bangor.ac.uk/imscar
dementia & ageing, health economics, public health; PhD

College of Physical and Applied Sciences; www.bangor.ac.uk/copas

School of Chemistry; www.chemistry.bangor.ac.uk/
analytical chemistry, chemistry, biomolecular sciences, environmental/marine chemistry, molecular science for medicine; BSc, MChem, MSc, PGDip, PhD, MPhil

School of Electronics; www.eng.bangor.ac.uk/
computer systems engineering, electronic engineering, electronics (hardware systems/software programming), electronics for business, music technology, broadband communications, optoelectronics, nanotechnology; BEng(Hons), BSc(Hons), MEng (Hons), MSc, PhD

School of Computer Science; www.cs.bangor.ac.uk
computer science/animation, internet systems and e-commerce, creative technologies, information & communications technology, computer systems engineering, electronic engineering; BA(Hons), BEng(Hons), MEng(Hons), MPhil, MRes, MSc, PhD

UNIVERSITY CENTRE BARNSLEY
www.barnsley.hud.ac.uk

Art & Design;
contemporary crafts design/visual arts; BA(Hons)

Construction;
construction, project management; BSc(Hons), FdSc, HNC

Business Management;
business administration/management; BA (Hons), FdA, MBA

Computing;
animation, digital film, film, multimedia, music and enterprise; BA(Hons), FdSc

Early Years & Childhood Studies;
early years, the children's workforce; FdA, BA(Hons)

Education & Training;
early years, education & training, numeracy for teachers, post-compulsory education & training, professional development; BA(Hons), CertEd, FdA, MA/PGDip/PGCert, PGCE

Film;
digital film & visual effects, film, animation, music; BA(Hons)

History;
history, English literature, humanities; BA(Hons)

Journalism & Media;
journalism, media production; FdA

Multimedia;
multimedia/computing; BSc(Hons),FdSc

Music;
music production & sound recording, popular music & promotion; BA(Hons)

Professional Development for Staff in Education;
education & training, literacy & numeracy, professional development; BA, MA, PGDip/Cert

Psychology;
psychological studies; BSc(Hons)

Sciences;
resource & waste management; Dip

Social Sciences;
social sciences; BSc(Hons)

Teaching;
PC Education & training; CertEd, PGCE

UNIVERSITY OF BATH
www.bath.ac.uk

Faculty of Engineering and Design; www.bath.ac.uk/engineering

Architecture & Civil Engineering; www.bath.ac.uk/ace

architectural engineering: environmental design, architecture, civil engineering, conservation buildings/gardens, facade engineering; BEng, BSc, EngD, MArch, MEng, MPhil, MSc, PGCert, PhD

Chemical Engineering; www.bath.ac.uk/chem-eng

biochemical/chemical engineering, environmental management; transport phenomena; BEng, EngD, MEng, MPhil, MSc, PhD

Electronic & Electrical Engineering; www.bath.ac.uk/elec-eng

communication/computer systems engineering, digital communications, electrical & electronic/electrical power engineering, mechanical engineering, mechatronics, space science & technology, wireless systems; BEng, EngD, MEng, MPhil, MSc, PhD

Mechanical Engineering; www.bath.ac.uk/mech-eng

aerospace engineering, automotive engineering, innovation/ & engineering design, fluid power engineering, mechanical/ manufacturing engineering, mechatronics, technology management, adv design & innovation; EngD, MEng, MPhil, MSc, PhD

Faculty of Humanities and Social Science; www.bath.ac.uk/hss

Dept of Economics; www.bath.ac.uk/economics

economics/& finance, international development, politics, international money & banking, economics (development); BSc(Hons), MPhil, MRes, PhD

Dept of Education; www.bath.ac.uk/education

childhood, youth & education studies, coach education, teacher training,, TESOL, sports performance, TESOL; BA(Hons), EdD, FdSc, MA, MPhil, MRes, PGCE, PhD, ProfPGCE

Dept of European Studies & Modern Languages; www.bath.ac.uk/esml

contemporary European politics, international politics/security/relations, interpreting, translating, modern languages & European studies, politics, economics; BA(Hons), BSc(Hons), MA, MPhil, PGDip, PhD

Dept of Psychology; www.bath.ac.uk/psychology

health/psychology, science, risk & health communication, applied cognition, social processes; BSc(Hons), MPhil, MSc, PhD

Department of Social and Policy Sciences; www.bath.ac.uk/soc-pl

business & community, death & society, European social policy/research/ sciences, social work & applied social studies, sociology, wellbeing & human dev; BSc, MPhil, MRes, MSc, PhD

Faculty of Science; www.bath.ac.uk/science

Dept of Biology & Biochemistry; www.bath.ac.uk/bio-sci

biology, biochemistry, biosciences, molecular & cellular biology, developmental biology, evolution & population biology, medical bioscience, molecular plant science, protein structure; BSc(Hons), MPhil, MRes, PhD

Dept of Chemistry; www.bath.ac.uk/chemistry

chemistry/for drug discovery; BSc(Hons), MChem, MSci, PhD

Dept of Computer Science; www.bath.ac.uk/comp-sci

advanced computer systems, computer information systems, computer science; BSc(Hons), EngD, MComp, MSc, PhD

Dept of Mathematics; www.bath.ac.uk/math-sci

mathematical biology/sciences, mathematics, modern applics of mathematics, statistics; BSc(Hons), MMath, MSc, PhD

Dept of Natural Sciences; www.bath.ac.uk/nat-sci

biology, chemistry, pharmacology, physics; BSc(Hons), MSci

Dept of Pharmacy & Pharmacology; www.bath.ac.uk/pharmacy

pharmaceutical practice & therapeutics, pharmacology, pharmacy; MPharm, MPharmacol, PhD

Dept of Physics; www.bath.ac.uk/physics

mathematics and physics, physics/with computing, nanoscience, medical physics, photonics; BSc, MSc, MPhil, MPhys, PhD

School of Management; www.bath.ac.uk/management

accounting & finance, international management, management, marketing, innovation & technology management; BSc(Hons), DBA, EngD, MBA, MPhil, MRes, MSc, PhD

School for Health; www.bath.ac.uk/health

health practice, health care/informatics, information governance, sport & exercise science, sports physiotherapy, sport & exercise/medicine; BSc(Hons), MD, MPhil, MS, PGDip, PhD

BATH SPA UNIVERSITY
www.bathspa.ac.uk

Bath School of Art & Design; www.artbathspa.com

art/design, ceramics, fine art, graphic communication, fashion design, ceramics, digital/3D design, interactive multimedia, media communication, textile design; BA(Hons), FdA, MFA, MPhil, PhD

Development & Participation; www.bathspa.ac.uk/schools/development-and-participation; QTLS

lifelong learning, student study skills

School of Education; www.bathspa.ac.uk/schools/education

early years/education,,global citizenship,, primary education studies/for teaching assistants, PGCE (primary (3–11)/middle years (7–14)/ secondary (11–16); range of subjects), professional studies, TESOL; FD, GradCert, MA/MTeach, PGCE, PGCert/Dip

School of Humanities & Creative Industries; www.bath-spa.ac.uk/schools/humanities-and cultural-industries

creative media practice/writing, film & screen skills, media communications, English literature, publishing; study of religions, philosophy & ethics, history; BA(Hons), MPhil, PhD.MA

Music & the Performing Arts; www.bathspampa.com

commercial music, creative arts, music technology, dance, drama, performing arts, music, theatre production, arts management; BA(Hons), FdA, FdMus, MA, PhD

School of Science, Society & Management; www.ssmbathspa.com

biology, business & management, development/geography, diet & health, environmental science, food & nutrition, GIS, health studies, heath & social care management, human nutrition, psychology, sociology; BA(Hons), BSc (Hons), BA/BSc, MPhil, MSc, PhD, FDA, DipHE

UNIVERSITY OF BEDFORDSHIRE
www.beds.ac.uk

Faculty of Creative Arts, Technologies & Science; www.beds.ac.uk/departments/cats

Bedfordshire Institute of Media and the Creative & Performing Arts; www.beds.ac.uk/departments/bim

Div of Art & Design

advertising design, animation, art and design, fashion design, fine art, graphic design, illustration, interior architecture, photography & video art, art design & internet technologies

Div of Journalism & Communication

creative writing, journalism, media, mass communication arts/practices/performances, PR, sport/ broadcast journalism

Div of Media Arts & Production

media production (moving image, new media, radio, scriptwriting), documentary, music technology, internet technologies, TV production

Div of Performing Arts & English

dance & professional practice, education studies, English studies, performing arts, theatre & profession practice; BA(Hons), FdA, MA, MRes, PhD

Dept of Computer Science & Technology; www.beds.ac.uk/departments/computing

computer science/ networking, information systems, mobile computing, computer games development, software engineering, AI and robotics, computer security & forensics, applied computing & IT, computer animation, business info systems, computer & internet applications, computing & entrepreneurship, telecommunications management; BSc(Hons), FdSc, MSc

Div of Science

biomedical science, biotechnology, biological sciences, forensic science, medical science, nutritional sciences, pharmacology; BSc(Hons), FdSc, MSc, PgCert, PgDip, MPhil, PhD

Faculty of Health and Social Sciences; www.beds.ac.uk/departments/healthsciences

Dept of Acute Health Care; Dept of Community Services; Dept of Midwifery & Child Health

midwifery, nursing (adult, children, mental health, learning disabilities, mental health, operating dept practice, osteopathy, care management, complementary therapy, dental nursing/practice management, clinical science, health studies, leadership, medical education/simulation, patient safety, palliative care, psychological intervention, sexual health, public health nursing; BSc(Hons), FdA, FdSc, MSc, PGDip/ Cert, DipHE, FdA/Sc, MOst

Dept of Applied Social Studies; www.beds.ac.uk/departments/appliedsocialstudies

applied social studies, criminology, early years/child and adolescent studies, counselling health and social care, social work, sociology, young people's services, youth & community studies, public policy; BSc(Hons), FdA, FdSc, MSc, ProfDoc

Div of Psychology; www.beds.ac.uk/departments/psychology

applied/health psychology, counselling and therapies, criminal behaviour, criminology, crime, criminal behaviour; BSc(Hons), CertHE, FdA, MSc, PhD

Div of Sports Therapy; www.beds.ac.uk/departments/spoth

sports therapy; BSc(Hons)

Bedfordshire & Hertfordshire Postgraduate Medical School; www.beds.ac.uk/departments/bhpms

diabetes, dental/medical education, public health, sexual health, medical simulation; MA, MSc, PGDip, PGCert

Institute for Health Research; www.beds.ac.uk/researchir

psychological approach to health & management, public health, research & evaluation; MSc, PhD

Institute of Applied Social Research; www.beds.ac.uk/research/lasr

applied public policy, children's & young people's services, Europerspectives, leadership; ProfDoc, MA

University of Bedfordshire Business School www.beds.ac.uk/departments/ubbs

Depts of Accounting & Finance, Marketing, Strategy & HRM, Business Systems, Law (School of), Language & Communication

accounting, finance, banking investment; advertising, marketing, PR, business/management, logistics & supply chain management, marketing communications, international/HRM, business administration; business decison making/strategy, e-business; engineering/business management, project management; law, international commercial law, Islamic finance and banking; applied linguistics, (ETL), intercultural communication, public service interpreting; BA(Hons), BSc(Hons), DBA, FdA, LIB, LIM, MA, MBA, MSc, PGCErt, LLM

Faculty of Education, Sport & Tourism; www.beds.ac.uk/es;

primary education/QTS, early years, primary languages, specialist maths, post-compulsory education, lifelong learning, PGCE secondary education (range of subjects), chemistry/maths enhancement, applied education, childhood & youth/disability studies, footbal studies, PE, sports management/studies, event management, sport/international tourism management; PGCE, BA(Hons), BEd(Hons), MA, FdA, PGCSMT

THE QUEEN'S UNIVERSITY OF BELFAST
www.qub.ac.uk

School of Biological Sciences; www.qub.ac.uk/schools/schoolofbiological sciences

agricultural biochemistry, biological sciences, environmental biology, food quality, safety & nutrition, genetics, land use & environmental management technology, land environmental sustainability, marine biology, microbiology, molecular biology, rural sustainability, zoology; BSc(Hons), MSc, PGDip, PhD

School of Chemistry and Chemical Engineering; www.ch.qub.ac.uk

chemistry, medicinal chemistry, chemistry with forensic analysis, chemical engineering, chemical enzymology, process engineering; BSc(Hons), MSci, BEng, MEng, MSc, PGDip, PhD

School of Education; www.qub.ac.uk/schools/school of education

applying psychology to education, arts, autistic spectrum disorders, coaching & mentoring, education, e-learning, diversity and inclusion, counselling, initial teacher education, leadership & management in education, management & business studies, primary school experience, principles & practice of education, inclusion & special education, lifelong learning; TESOL; AdvCertEd, DASE, EdD, MA, MEd, MSc, MSSc, PGCE, PGDip/Cert, UnivCert, BA(Hons)

School of Electronics, Electrical Engineering and Computer Science; www.qub.ac.uk/schools/eeec

business IT, computing and IT, computer & electronic security, computer games design & development, computer science, creative multimedia, educational multimedia, electrical & electronic engineering, electronics, telecommunications, software & electronic systems engineering, advanced wireless communication; BEng, BSc, MEng, MSc, MPhil, PhD

School of English; www.qub.ac.uk/schools/SchoolofEnglish

creative writing, English language & linguistics, Irish writing, linguistics, medieval studies, modern literary studies, modern poetry, reconceiving the Renaissance; BA(Hons), MA, PhD

School of Geography, Archaeology and Palaeoecology; www.qub.ac.uk/schools/gap

archaeology, dating & chronology, geography, landscape, heritage & environment, palaeoecology. geography; BA(Hons), BSc(Hons), MSc, PhD

School of History and Anthropology; www.qub.ac.uk/schools/SchoolofHistoryandAnthroplogy

ancient history, anthropological studies, ethnomusicology, Irish history, modern history, social anthropology, cognition & culture; BA(Hons), GradDip, MA, MPhil, PhD

School of Languages, Literatures and Performing Arts; www.qub.ac.uk/schools/SchoolofLanguages Literatures andPerformingArts

drama studies, film studies,performance, French/German/Irish & Celtic/ Spanish & Portugese studies, visual arts, Irish translation studies, translation; BA(Hons), MA, PhD

School of Law; www.law.qub.ac.uk/law/with politics

law/with politics, common & civil law, environmental law, criminal justice, legal science, criminology, governance, international commerce, human rights; LlB, LlM, MSSc, MLSc, PGdip, MPhil, PhD

Queen's University Management School; www.qub.ac.uk/schools/mgt

accounting, finance, actuarial science & risk, business economics/management, economics, management, international business, environmental management, financial regulation sustainabilty & corporate responsibilty; BSc(Hons), MSc, MScs, MBA, PhD

School of Mathematics and Physics; www.qub.ac.uk/schools /Schoolof MathematicsandPhysics

applied/pure mathematics, computer science & physics, operational research, statistics, astrophysics, physics with medical applications, theoretical/plasma physics, vacuum technology; BSc(Hons), GradDip, MSc, MSci, PhD

School of Mechanical and Aerospace Engineering; www.qub.ac.uk/schools/SchoolofMechanicaland AerospaceEngineering

aerospace engineering, mechanical & manufacturing engineering, product design & development, polymers enginering; BEng, MEng, MSc

School of Medicine, Dentistry and Biomedical Sciences; www.qub.ac.uk/schools/mdbs

medicine, biomedical science, clinical education, dentistry, surgery, molecular medicine, mental health, obstetrics, public health, pain science, health & social care; BCh, BAO, BSc(Hons), BDS, DAO, Diploma, MB, MD, MSc

School of Music and Sonic Arts; www.mu.qub.ac.uk

music, composition, creative practice, ethnomusicology, jazz, pop, Irish traditional music, musicology, music technology, performance, sonic arts, sound design/engineering; BMus, BSc(Hons), MA, PhD

School of Nursing and Midwifery; www.qub.ac.uk/schools/SchoolofNursingandMidwifery

nursing – adult/children's/learning disability/mental health, maternal and child health, midwifery, continuing professional development, clinical practice; BSc(Hons), Diploma, MPhil, PhD, DNursingPractice

School of Pharmacy; www.qub.ac.uk/schools/SchoolofPharmacy

clinical pharmacy, community pharmacy, pharmacist prescribing, pharmacy practice; MPharm, MSc, PGCert/Dip

School of Planning, Architecture and Civil Engineering; www.qub.ac.uk/schools/SchoolofPlanningArchitectureand CivilEngineering

architecture, civil engineering, durability of structures, environmental engineering/planning, management, spatial regeneration, urban & rural design, water resources, sustainable design; BSc(Hons), MSc, MArch, MPhil, PhD

School of Politics, International Studies and Philosophy; www.qub.ac.uk/schools/SchoolofPoliticsInternationalStudies andPhilosophy

cognitive science, comparative ethnic conflict, gender & society, European Union policies, international relations/studies, Irish politics, law with politics, legislative studies & practice, philosophy, politics,, economics & philosophy, violence, terrorism and security; BA(Hons), LlB, MA, MRes, MPhil, PhD

School of Psychology; www.psych.qub.ac.uk

atypical child development, educational child and adolescent psychology, political psychology, applied/clinical psychology; BSc(Hons), MSc, DocClinPsych, PhD DocEducational

School of Sociology, Social Policy and Social work; www.qub.ac.uk/schools/SchoolofSociologySocialPolicy SocialWork

applied social studies,criminology, childhood studies, gender studies, social policy, social research methods, sociology; BA(Hons), BSW, MA, MSc, DChild Stud

UNIVERSITY OF BIRMINGHAM
www.bham.ac.uk

College of Arts and Law; www.colleges.bham.ac.uk/artslaw

Institute of Archaeology and Antiquity; www.iaa.bham.ac.uk

antiquity, archaeology (classical/conflict/European/Greek/practical), ancient history, heritage management, Egyptology, anthropology, Byzantine, Ottoman & modern Greek studies, classics, classical literature & civilization, cuniform & ancient near eastern studies, Egyptology, Roman history, E Mediterranean history, Greece and the Greeks, museums management, Ottoman studies; BA(Hons), MA, MPhil, diploma, PhD

Birmingham Law School; www.law.bham.ac.uk

law, commercial law, criminal law & criminal justice, European law, international commercial law; GradDip; LlB, LlM, MPhil/MJur/PhD

English, Drama and American & Canadian Studies; www.weblearn.bham.ac.uk

American & Canadian studies, English & American literature & film history, creative writing, directing & dramaturgy, playwriting studies, drama & theatre arts, English language/literature, Shakespeare studies, film studies, film & TV; BA(Hons), BSc(Hons), MPhil, PhD

School of History and Cultures; www.historycultures.bham.ac.uk

African studies, history(ancient & medieval/economic & social/modern) archaeology & anthropology, Caribbean literature, cultural heritage of Shakespeare's England, early modern history, history of Christianity, modern European history, Reformation & early modern studies, 20th-century British history, war studies, West Midlands history, air power, 1st/2nd world war studies; BA(Hons), MA, MPhil, PGDip, PhD

School of Languages, Cultures, Art History and Music; www.about.bham.ac.uk/colleges/artslaw/lcam

Centre for European Languages & Culture

modern languages, film studies, cultural enquiry, European studies, French, gender studies, German, Hispanic, Italian, modern, translation studies

Centre for Modern Languages

Japanese

Dept of History of Art

history of art

Dept of Music

composition, editing, musicology, performance, performance practice; BA, MA, BMus,MA, MPhil,PhD

The School of Philosophy, Theology and Religion; www.about.bham.ac.uk/colleges/artslaw/ptr

biblical studies, electronic scholarly editing, global ethics, history of Christianity, inter-religious relations, cognitive science, Islam and Christian–Muslim relations, Islamic studies, philosophy of language and linguistics/of mind and psychology/of religion and ethics, evangelical & charismatic studies, human rights & values, practical theology, Quaker studies, religion & culture, Sikh studies, theology & religion, ethics; BA(Hons), BMus, MA, MPhil, PhD

College of Engineering and Physical Sciences; www.about.bham.ac.uk/colleges/eps

School of Chemistry; www.chem.bham.ac.uk

chemical biology, chemistry &/with analytical science/bioorganic chemistry/pharmacology, materials chemistry, molecular processes & theory, molecular synthesis

School of Chemical Engineering; www.eng.bham.ac.uk/chemical

chemical engineering, air pollution management & control, biochemical engineering, energy engineering, formulation engineering, food safety, hygiene & management, air pollution control

School of Civil Engineering; www.eng.bham.ac.uk/civil

civil engineering, energy engineering, geotechnical engineering, railway systems engineering & integration, road management & engineering, transport technology, construction management, water resources technology & management

School of Computer Science; www.cs.bham.ac.uk

artificial intelligence, computer science, software engineering, computer security, electronic & software engineering, intelligent systems engineering, internet software systems, natural computation

School of Electrical, Electronic and Computer Engineering; www.eece.bham.ac.uk

communications engineering/networks, electronic & electrical engineering, software engineering, digital entrepreneurship, electromagnetic sensor networks, RF engineering, computer engineering, embedded systems, interactive digital media, satellite & mobile communication

School of Mathematics; www.mat.bham.ac.uk

pure/applied mathematics, mathematics, operation research, statistics & economics, mathematics in computing & biology, statistics

School of Mechanical Engineering; www.eng.bham.ac.uk/mechanical

mechanical engineering, engineering/operations/project management, manufacturing processes, systems engineering, vehicle technology

School of Metallurgy and Materials; www.eng.bham.ac.uk/metallurgy

materials/for sustainable energy technologies, metallurgy, biomaterials, nuclear engineering, science & engineering of materials, sports science & materials technology

School of Physics and Astronomy; www.ph.bham.ac.uk

medical & radiation physics, physics, physics & astrophysics/ technology of nuclear reactors/nanoscale physics/particle physics & cosmology, theoretical physics, & applied mathematics, radioactive waste management & decommissioning; BEng, BNatSci, BSc(Hons), DEng, MEng, MPhil, MRes, MSc, MSci, PGDip/Cert, PhD

College of Life and Environmental Sciences; www.about.bham.ac.uk/colleges/les

School of Biosciences; www.biosciences.bham.ac.uk

analytical genomics, biochemistry, genetics, molecular biotechnology, microbiology, molecular cell/plant/environmental/human/medical biology,ornithology, toxicology

School of Geography, Earth and Environmental Sciences; www.gees.bham.ac.uk

air pollution management & control, applied meteorology & climatology, enterprise, environment & place, environmental geoscience/health/management/planning, geography, geology, hydrotechnology, public & environmental health science, safety & the environment, resource & applied geology, river environmental planning, palaeobiology & palaeoenvironment, urban & regional planning

School of Psychology; www.psychology.bham.ac.uk

psychology, brain injury, clinical criminology/psychology, cognition & computational neuroscience, cognitive behaviour therapy/neuropsychology & rehabilitation, criminological psychology, forensic psychology, neuroscience

School of Sport and Exercise Sciences; www.sportex.bham.ac.uk

sport & exercise, sports science/& materials technology/mathematics; BSc(Hons), Clin, ForenPsyD, MPhil, MRes, MSc, PhD, PsyD, PGDip, PhD, PGDips

College of Medical and Dental Sciences; www.about.bham.ac.uk/colleges/mds

The Five Schools of the College are: Cancer Sciences, Clinical & Experimental Medicine, Dentistry, Health & Population Sciences, Immunity & Infection; biomedical materials science, cancer, cardiovascular sciences, dental hygiene & therapy, dental surgery, dentistry, health sciences, hormones & genes, immunity & infection, medical science, medicine, surgery, neuroscience, nursing, physiotherapy; BDS, BMedSci, BSc(Hons), BNurs, DDS, MBChB, MD

College of Social Sciences; www.about.bham.ac.uk/colleges/socialsciences

Birmingham Business School; www.business.bham.ac.uk

accounting & finance, banking, business & American studies, business management/with communications, development economics, economic policy/& international business, economics, environmental & natural resource economics, urban & regional planning, HRM, international accounting & finance, international business/economics/marketing/money &

banking, investments, management, marketing/communications, mathematical economics & statistics/finance, money, planning with economics, political science, social policy, spatial planning, strategic marketing & consulting, urban & regional studies, urban governance; BSc Economics, BSc(Hons), Dip, MSc, MBA, DBA, MPhil, PhD PGCert, PGDip, UCert

School of Education; www.education.bham.ac.uk

golf management, autism/spectrum disorders, bilingualism in education, childhood, culture & education, education for health professionals, educational psychology, English language & literature/international studies in education, IT and education, leadership in education, learning and learning contexts, learning difficulties/ disabilities, multisensory impairment (deafblindness), sport, physical education & coaching science, social, emotional and behavioural difficulties, sports coaching, teacher training (early years, primary, secondary subject courses) – (English, geography, history and citizenship, mathematics, modern foreign languages, PE, RE, biology, chemistry, physics), TEFL, visual impairment; AdCert, BA(Hons), BPhil, ChildPsyD, EdD, EdPsychD, MEd, MPhil, PGCE, PGCert/Dip, PhD

School of Government and Society; www.about.bham.ac.uk/colleges/socialsciences/governmentsociety

Poltical Science & International Studies; political science, African studies, anthropology, economics, Russian studies, social policy, sociology, social & political theory, political economy/science/theory, international relations, European politics, society & economics, Central & East European studies, international development, urban development, development/aid management, public administration/service, poverty reduction, local government, social care & wellbeing, criminal justice, politics & religion; BA(Hons), BSc(Hons), GradDip/Cert, MA, MPhil, MSc, PhD

The School of Social Policy (The Health Services Management Centre; Institute of Applied Social Studies); www.hsmc.bham.ac.uk; www.iass.bham.a.uk

partnership in/health and social care, health care & policy improvement, policy into practice, planning, poltiiical science, leadership for health services, leading public service change and organizational development, public service commissioning, social policy, social work; MA, MSc, PGDip

Degrees validated at the University of Birmingham offered at:

SCHOOL OF EDUCATION, SELLY OAK
www.education.bham.ac.uk

applied golf management studies, autism, bilingualism in education, childhood, culture & education, dyslexia studies, education for health professionals, English language and literature in education, educational psychology, hearing impairment, inclusion & special educational needs, international studies in education, IT & education, leaders & leadership in education, learning & learning contexts, learning difficulties/ multisensory impairment, sports coaching, teacher training – primary courses; early years, general primary/secondary subject courses (English, geography, history & citizenship, mathematics, modern foreign languages, PE, professional development, RE, biology, chemistry, physics), TEFL, visual impairment; AppEd, BA, ChildPsyD, EdPsychD, MPhil, PhD, PGCE

UNIVERSITY COLLEGE BIRMINGHAM
www.ucb.ac.uk

business & marketing, childhood & education, hospitality, food & events management, recreational sport & tourism, sports therapy, salon management; BA(Hons), BSc(Hons), FdA Dip HE, FdSc, MA, MSc, PGCE, PGDip/Cert

BIRMINGHAM CITY UNIVERSITY
www.bcu.ac.uk

Birmingham Institute of Art and Design; www.bcu.ac.uk/bid

animation, architecture, art/& education, fashion promotion/styling, digital/games/interior design, art practice, design, fashion design/retail management, fine art, gemmology/horology/jewellery & silversmithing, history of art & design, landscape architecture/studies, theatre, performance & event/product/urban/textile/graphic design, visual communication; BA(Hons), BTEC, CertHE/DipHE, HND, MA, MPhil, PgCert/PgDip, PhD

Birmingham City Business School; www.bcu.ac.uk/business-school

accountancy, advertising, business & management/administration, business law/psychology/information technology/management, clinical risk, internal audit practice, risk management, business studies, economics, finance & consultancy, business, international HRM; BA(Hons), DBA, HND, MBA, MPhil, MSc, PhD

Faculty of Education, Law and Social Sciences; www.bcu.ac.uk/elss

School of Education; www.bcu.ac.uk/els

children & integrated professional care, early childhood/education studies, early years, post-compulsory education & training, secondary/art & design/drama/education, mathematics, music, primary education / with QTS, subject enhancement in mathematics; BA(Hons), FD, FC, CA, MPhil, PGDip/Cert, PGCE, PhD,PGCE

The School of Law; www.bcu.ac.uk/law

corporate & business law, international human rights, legal studies, law, law with American legal studies/criminology/business law/human rights, legal practice; GradDip, MPhil/PhD, HND, LlB(Hons), PGCert/PGDip/LLM

School of Social Sciences; www.cu.ac.uk/social sciences

criminal investigation/policing, criminology/& security studies, housing practice, forensic social sciences, sociology,sustainable communities; BA(Hons), BSc(Hons), CertHE, FdA, MA, MPhil, MSc, PGCert, PGDip, PhD

Faculty of Health; www.bcu.ac.uk/health

advanced health care, child care, health and social care/ wellbeing (exercise science/nutrition science/individuals and communities), health promotion & public health, mental health, midwifery, nursing (adult, child learning disability), operating dept practice, perioperative specialist practice, radiography, rehabilitation work (visual impairment), social work, speech & language therapy, strategic leadership; BSc(Hons), DipHE, FdA, MPhil, MSc, PgCert, PGDip, PQ, PhjD

Faculty of Performance, Media and English; www.bcu.ac.uk/pme

Birmingham Conservatoire; www.conservatoire.bcu.ac.uk

jazz, performance/& pedagogy music/technology, pop music studies; AdvPGDip, BMus(Hons), HND, MA, MMus, MPhil, PGCert, PhD

Birmingham School of Media; www.bcu.ac.uk/mediacourses

journalism, freelance photography/media, music industries, PR, radio production, broadcast/online journalism, event & exhibition management, media & communication, television & interactive content, web & new media; BA(Hons), PGDip, MA, MPhil, PhD,HND

Birmingham School of Acting; www.bsa.bcu.ac.uk

community & applied theatre/dance theatre, physical theatre, professional voice practice acting, stage management; BA(Hons), MA, PgDip

School of English; www.lmds.bcu.acuk/English

English/ & media/drama/creative writing, English literature/language, linguistics, writing, philosophy; BA(Hons), Diploma, MA, MPhil, PhD

Faculty of Technology, Engineering and the Environment; www.bcu.ac.uk/tee-landing

business information & business systems technology, computer games technology, computer networks/& security, computer science/technology, computing & sound & multimedia technology, television technology & production; automotive engineering, computer-aided automotive design, management of manufacturing systems, mechanical engineering, motorsports technology, architectural technology, building surveying/services engineering, construction/management & economics, construction quantity surveying, estate management practice, planning & development, property & construction, real estate; BSc, HNC, FdSc, MSc, PgCert, PgDip

BISHOP GROSSETESTE UNIVERSITY COLLEGE
www.bgc.ac.uk

early childhood/children & youth work, learning support, drama in the community, early childhood studies, education (non-QTS), primary education with QTS, heritage studies, education studies in art & design/drama/English/geography/history/mathematics/music PGCE (primary/secondary), English literature; BA(Hons), FdA, GradDip, MA, PGCE

EAST LANCASHIRE INSTITUTE OF HIGHER EDUCATION AT BLACKBURN COLLEGE
www.blackburn.ac.uk

Vocation qualifications (BTEC, City & Guilds etc)
Courses offered at University Centre, Blackburn College: applied psychology, business accounting/studies, complementary medicine, design (contemporary textiles/graphic communication/illustration and animation/interiors/moving image/new media) digital media design, disability studies, early years childcare, educational studies, ciivil/electrical/electronic engineering, English financial services, fine art (integrated media), hospitality management, housing studies, criminology, HRM, journalism, law/with psychology,legal studies, marketing, mechanical engineering, photographic media, social sciences, sociology, sustainable construction, telecommunications,working with children & young people; BA(Hons, Ord), BEng(Hons, Ord), BSc(Hons, Ord), DMS (validated externally), FD, HNC, HND, LlB (validated by Lancaster), LlM, MBA, MSc

BOURNEMOUTH UNIVERSITY
www.bournemouth.ac.uk

The School of Applied Sciences; www.bournemouth.ac.uk/applied-sciences

prehistoric & Roman archaeology, archaeology & geography, archaeological, anthropological & forensic sciences, biological/ forensic/environmental science, animal and landbased studies, biological/forensic anthropology, anthropology & heritage, conservation, ecology & environmental change; BSc(Hons), BA(Hons), MSc, PhD

The Business School; www.business.bournemouth.ac.uk

accounting, business/& project management, economics, finance, risk management, international business finance/management/commercial law, intellectual property, law and taxation, management; BA(Hons), LlB(Hons), LlM, MA, MBA, MPhil, MSc, PhD

School of Design, Engineering & Computing; www.dec.bournemouth.ac.uk

design business management, engineering design innovation, engineering project management, sustainable product design, design engineering, industrial/product design, games/music & audio technology, computer games, psychology, clinical psychology, ageing neuropsychology, cognitive neuropsychology, business computing/information technology, web systems, internet/multimedia comunication systems, software engineering/product design, forensic computing & security, digital media, multimedia business & entrepreneurship, network systems management, advanced computing, applied data analysis, smart systems, software systems/sustainable network systems, wireless & mobile networks; BSc(Hons), FD, HNC, HND, MA, MPhil, MSc, PhD

School of Health and Social Care; www.bournemouth.ac.uk/hsc
nutrition, early years care, operating dept practice, paramedic science, adult/child health nursing, learning disability, mental health, children & family studies, nurse practitioner, midwifery, exercise science, occupational therapy, physiotherapy, social work, sociology, social policy; AdvDip, BA(Hons), BSc(Hons), DipHE, FdA, FdSc, MPhil, PGDip/Cert, PhD, Dr Prof Practice

The Media School; www.media.bournemouth.ac.uk
advertising, marketing/communications, communication & media, 3D computer animation arts, computer visualization, digital cinematography, English, cinematography, global computer animation practice, music/technology, contemporary theatre performance/dance/ music/theatre, photography, PR, radio production, software design for games, scriptwriting for film and TV, TV and film production, politics & media, screenwriting; BA(Hons), BSc(Hons), FdA, MA, MBA, MPhil, MSc, PhD, DProfD

School of Tourism; www.bournemouth.ac.uk/tourism
events management, leisure marketing, applied animal management, tourism & hospitality, European tourism management, tourism management & marketing/planning; FDA, FDSc, BA(Hons), BSc(Hons), MA, MSc, PhD

UNIVERSITY OF BRADFORD
www.bradford.ac.uk

School of Computing, Informatics and Media; www.scim.brad.ac.uk
Computing: advanced computer science, artificial intelligence for games computing, business computing, computer science/for games, forensic computing, ICT with business/law/marketing, informatics, intelligent systems & robotics, internet computing, mobile computing applications, networks & performance engineering, software development applications/ engineering
Media: digital media, digital & creative enterprise,- digital arts, film production,technology, film studies, informatics, media studies with cinematics/computer animation/digital imaging/TV/, media technology and production,TV production, web design & technologies,
Mathematics; www.maths.brad.ac.uk applied mathematics, computational mathematics
Creative technology: advanced computer animation and special effects, computer animation, graphics for games, informatics, interactive systems & video games design, visual computing effects production; BA(Hons), BSc(Hons), MAMSc, FdSc

School of Engineering, Design and Technology; www.eng.brad.ac.uk
automotive design technology, automotive engineering quality improvement, civil & structural engineering, clinical technology, electrical & electronic engineering, power electronics, information technology management, industrial engineering, manufacturing engineering/management, mechanical/& automotive engineering, medical engineering, personal, mobile & satellite communications, product design, technology management, wireless sensor & embedded systems; BEng, BSc, FD, MEng, MPhil, MSc, PhD

School of Health Studies; www.brad.ac.uk/ acad/health
cancer care, dementia care, diagnostic radiography, health, wellbeing & social care, midwifery, nursing (adult branch/mental health branch/child branch), nursing practice (acutely ill adult/cancer & palliative care/pain management/tissue viability) nursing studies (adult, child, mental health), occupational therapy, physiotherapy, sexual health; tomography, angiography; AdvDip, BSc(Hons), CertHE, DipHE, FD, MSc, MPhil, PGDip/Cert, PhD

School of Life Sciences; www.brad.ac.uk/ acad/lifesci

Div of Archaeological Geographical & Environmental Sciences
archaeological prospection/sciences, analytical science, archaeology, environmental management/ science, forensic & archaeological sciences, forensic archaeology & crime scene investigation, human

osteology & palaeopathology; BA, BSc, CertHE, MA, MSc, MPhil, PhD

Div of Biomedical Sciences

biomedical science, cellular pathology, chemical & forensic science, medical biochemistry, medical microbiology, optometry, pharmacology; BSc(Hons), MSC, PgD

Bradford School of Pharmacy

clinical pharmacy, pharmacy, pharmaceutical services/management, and medicines control, prescribing; DPharm, MSC, MPharm

Dept of Chemical and Forensic Sciences

chemistry/with pharmacy for forensic science, forensic & bimolecular science/medical science, medical chemistry & anti-cancer drug development; BSc(Hons), MPhil, PhD

Div of Optometry

optometry; BSc, MPhil, PhD

The School of Lifelong Education and Development; www.brad.ac.uk/admin/conted/cfa

aviation management, coaching & mentoring, community interpreting/justice/regeneration, HE practice, integrated emergency mangt, regeneration mangt, TESOL/applied linguistics, training & development; FD, Certs, MA, MSc, PGDip/Cert

The School of Management (inc Law); www.brad.ac.uk/acad/management

accounting, business studies, finance, financial planning, business & management studies, HRM, international business & management, law, financial management, European management, marketing; BA(Hons), BSc(Hons), DBA, LlB, GradDip(Law), MBA, MRes, PhD

The School of Social and International Studies; www.brad.ac.uk/acad/ssis

creative writing, development studies, economics, English, history, interdisciplinary human studies, international development/relations, mental health studies, peace studies, philosophy, politics, law, psychology, social policy, social work, sociology, working with children, young people & families; BA(Hons), BSc(Hons), MA, MPhil, PhD, PGDip

Degrees validated by University of Bradford offered at:

BRADFORD COLLEGE
www.bradfordcollege.ac.uk

accounting, animal care, art & design, beauty therapy, business & management, business computing, business studies, catering & hospitality, cutural studies, community & social care, computing & ICT, civil engineering, counselling & pyschology, early years, education, engineering, construction management, English & communication, fashion & textiles, fashion design, foreign languages, graphic media/design, games development, hairdressing, health & nutrition, illustration, interior design, law, mechanical engineering, marketing, mathematics, media & creative writing, music, opthalmic dispensing, PCET, performing arts, pharmacy, photography, print making, public services, quantity surveying, science, social work/care. sport & leisure, sports coaching, teaching/ESOL, TU studies, travel & tourism, visual culture/arts, youth & community studies; BSc(Hons), CertHE, DipHE, Foundation degrees, HNC, HNDBA(Hons), LlB(Hons), MA, MEd, PGDipCert

UNIVERSITY OF BRIGHTON
www.brighton.ac.uk

Faculty of Arts; www.arts.brighton.ac.uk

School of Architecture and Design, School of Arts and Media, School of Humanities

architecture, interior/architecture & urban studies, interior design, arts & cultural res, design & craft, history of design arts, sustainable design, fashion & business/dress history, textiles design, fine art(painting/printmaking/sculpture), critical fine art practice, inclusive arts practice, digital media/& sound arts, graphic design, moving image, sequential design, illustration, performance & visual practices/arts – theatre/dance, music & visual art, film and screen studies, history of decorative art and crafts, history of design and material culture, museum & heritage studies, visual culture, English language teaching studies, media-assisted language teaching, TESOL/TEFL; broadcast /creative media, linguistics, history, English language/literature/studies, culture, media, philosophy of languge, culture, politics, war, conflict & modernity, humanities, applied ethics, cultural & critical theory, media studies; radio /TV production, broadcast media/journalism, creative media, photography; BA(Hons), FdSA, Grad Dip, MA, MDes, MFA, MPhil, PGDip/Cert, PhD

Faculty of Education and Sport; www.brighton.ac.uk/fes

Chelsea School; www.brighton.ac.uk/chelsea

physical education with QTS, sport and exercise science/leisure management, sport coaching, sport journalism studies

School of Education; www.brighton.ac.uk/education

early years care & education/professional status, learning & development, English literature & education, information technology education, key stage 2/3 English /ICT mathematics/education, secondary design & technology/mathematics/science, PGCE primary education, secondary (numerous subjects), knowledge enhancement courses, post-compulsory education, professional education studies, professional studies in learning and development/primary education, RE, working with young people, youth work

School of Service Management; www.brighton.ac.uk/ssm

food & culinary arts, food services wellbeing, hospitality & event management, international event management, tourism/travel management, retail management/enterprise/marketing, tourism & international development/social anthropology, travel & tourism marketing; BA(Hons), FdA, MA, MSc, PhD

Centre for Learning and Teaching; www.brighton.ac.uk/clt

learning & development; learning & teaching in HE; BA(Hons), BSc(Hons), CertEd, EdD, FdA, MA, MPhil, MPhil/PhD, MSc, PGCert, PGCE, PhD

Faculty of Health and Social Science; www.brighton.ac.uyk/fhss

School of Applied Social Science; www.brighton.ac.uk/sass

applied psychology, community psychology, counselling and psychotherapy, criminology, mental health, politics, psychology, psychosocial studies, social policy/science/work, sociology, substance misuse, therapeutic counselling, public admin; BA(Hons), MA, MPhil, MSc, PGDip/Cert, PhD

School of Health Professions; www.brighton.ac.uk/sohs

clinical education, diabetes, clinical biomechanics, health through occupation, occupational therapy, physiotherapy/and education/management, podiatry, community healthcare rehabilitation science, sports injury management; BS(Hons), MSc, PGDip/Cert, PhD, Prof Doc

School of Nursing and Midwifery; www.brighton.ac.uk/snm

acute & critical care, acute clinical practice, adult/child/mental health nursing, children, family & public health, clinical studies, community specialist practice, health & social care, health studies nurse practitioner, midwifery, paramedic practice, professional practice, specialist community public health nursing; BSc(Hons), FdSc, MPhil, MRes, MSc, PGDip/Cert, PhD

Brighton Business School; www.brighton.ac.uk/bbs

accounting, business administration/management, finance, business studies, change management, economics, finance, international business, investment, knowledge & innovation, law with business, marketing (branding, international, social), personnel & development, HRM, professional accounting; ACCA, BA(Hons), LlB, MBA, MSc

Faculty of Science and Engineering; www.brighton.ac.uk/scieng

School of School of Computing, Engineering & Mathematics; www.bighton.ac.uk/cem

business computer/information systems, computer science (games), digital media, digital games production, European computing, internet computing, software engineering, computing, information systems, internet & distributed systems, user experience, electrical & electronic engineering, digital electronics, communication, automotive electronic engineering, information studies, mathematics/& computing, mathematics with business/finance, aeronautical engineering, mechanical/manufacturing/automobile engineering, product innovation & design, product design technology, sports/ sustainable product design; BSc(Hons), FdSc, MA, MComp, MPhil, MSc, PGDip/Cert

School of Environment and Technology; www.brighton.ac.uk/set

Built Environment: architectural technology, building studies, building surveying, construction management, environmental assessment & management, facilities management, project management for construction, sustainability of the built environment, town planning; civil engineering, environmental engineering; environmental/hazards/management and assessment/sciences, environment & media studies, GIS & sustainability of the built environment, GIS/water & environmental management; geography, earth & ocean science, environmental geology, geology; BA/BSc(Hons), BEng(Hons), BSc(Hons), FdSc, FdEng, MEng, MPhil, PGDip/Cert, PhD

School of Pharmacy and Biomolecular Sciences; www.brighton.ac.uk/pharmacy

analytical chemistry with business, biomedical sciences, clinical pharmacy practice, pharmacology, ecology, industrial pharmaceutical studies, biomedical sciences, chemical sciences; BSc(Hons), MSc, MPharmHons, MPhil, MRes, PGDip, PhD

Brighton and Sussex Medical School; www.bsms.ac.uk

cardiology, medical education, diabetes, health or social care, global health, oncology, infectious disease, primary care, psychiatry, medicine, nephrology, public health, surgery; BM, BS, MD, MPhil, MSc, PGDip/Cert, PhD

Institute of Postgraduate Medicine

UNIVERSITY OF BRISTOL
www.bris.ac.uk

Faculty of Arts; www.bris.ac.uk/arts

School of Arts; www.bris.ac.uk/arts

Dept of Archaeology & Anthroplogy; www.bris.ac.uk/archanth;

archaeology, anthropology, archaeological & anthropological sciences, conflict/landscape/maritime archaeology, social anthropology, ancient history, archaeology for screen media, historical archaeology of the modern world

Dept of Drama, Theatre, Film, Television; www.bris.ac.uk/drama

screen & performance, documentary practice, cinema studies, drama, film & TV production, performance research

Dept of Music; www.bris.ac.uk/music

British music, composition, medieval music, music/theory, musicology, performance, Russian music

Dept of Philosophy; www.bris.ac.uk/philosophy

philosophy, philosophy & history of science/law/biology & cognitive science, logic & philosophy of mathematics; BA(Hons), BSc(Hons), MA, Mlitt, MMus, MSci, PGDip, PhD

School of Humanities; www.bris.ac.uk/humanities

Dept of Classics & Ancient History; www.bris.ac.uk/classics

ancient history, ancient history & archaeology, classical studies, classics, history

Dept of English; www.bris.ac.uk/english

English, English and philosophy/classical studies/drama, English literature/& community engagement, modern & contemporary poetry, romanticism, Shakespeare, late medieval & early modern literature

Dept of History; www.bris.ac.uk/history

empires, contemporary history, histories, peoples, cultures, medieval and early modern history, Russian history, ancient history

Dept of Art History; www.bris.ac.uk/arthistory

art histories and interpretations, history of art

Dept of Theology and Religious Studies; www.bris.ac.uk/thrs

biblical studies, theology & religious studies, Buddhist studies, philosophy & ethics, reception of the bible: tradition, theology, & culture, medieval studies

School of Modern Languages; www.bris.ac.uk/sml

French, German, Hispanic, Portuguese & Latin American studies/history, Italian, Russian, Russian studies (includes Czech); Mandarin, translation,

European literatures, modern languages, Russian history, literary & cultural studies, linguistics; BA(Hons), MA, MLitt, MPhil, PGDip, PhD

Faculty of Engineering; www.bris.ac.uk/engineering

Dept of Aerospace Engineering; www.bris.ac.uk/aerospace

aerospace systems design/engineering, aeronautical engineering

Dept of Civil Engineering; www.bris.ac.uk/civilengineering

civil engineering, water & environmental management

Dept of Computer Science; www.cs.bris.ac.uk

computer science/& electronic/mathematics, internet technologies with security, machine learning & data mining, high performance computing, creative technologies

Dept of Electrical and Electronic Engineering; www.bris.ac.uk/eeng

optical communications, communication networks & signal processing, computer science & electronics, electrical & electronic engineering, communications engineering, image & video communications, wireless communication systems & signal processing

Dept of Engineering Mathematics; www.enm.bris.ac.uk

advanced computing, data mining, machine learning, artificial intelligence, logic programming, computing molecular biology/neuroscience, pattern anlaysis, engineering mathematics

Dept of Mechanical Engineering; www.bris.ac.uk/mecheng

mechanical engineering, adv robotics engineering; BSc(Hons), BEng, EngDPGCert MEng, MSc, PhD

Faculty of Medical and Veterinary Science; www.bris.ac.uk/mvs

Dept of Biochemistry; www.bris.ac.uk/biochemistry

biochemistry/with molecular biology & biotechnology, medical biochemistry, quantitative cell imaging

Dept of Cellular and Molecular; Medicine; www.bris.ac.uk/cellmolmed

cancer biology, immunology, medical /microbiology, pathology, transfusion & transplantation science, virology, cellular & molecular medicine

Bristol Veterinary School; www.bris.ac.uk/vetscience

animal behaviour & welfare, meat science & technology, veterinary cellular & molecular science, veterinary nursing & bioveterinary science, veterinary science

Dept of Physiology & Pharmacology; www.bris.ac.uk/phys-pharm

cardiovascular science, cell signalling & cell biology, neuroscience, pharmacology, physiological science; BSc(Hons), BVS, MD, MSc, MSci, PhD

Faculty of Medicine and Dentistry; www.bris.ac.uk/fmd

medicine, surgery, dentistry, dental implantology, health care ethics & the law, molecular neuroscience, orthodontics, palliative medicine, reproduction & development, stem cells and regeneration, social medicine; MB, BDS, BSc(Hons), ChB, ChM, DDS, Diploma, DPDS, MClinDent, MD, MMedEd, MSci, PhD

Faculty of Science; www.bris.ac.uk/science

School of Biological Sciences; www.bris.ac.uk/biology

biology, botany, ecology and management of the natural environment, geology & biology, psychology, zoology, palentology & evolution, ecology

School of Chemistry; www.chm.bris.ac.uk/

chemistry, chemical physics, inorganic & materials chemistry, organic & biological chemistry, physical & theoretical chemistry, chemical synthesis

School of Earth Sciences; www.gly.bris.ac.uk/

archaeological & anthropological sciences, biology, environmental geoscience, geology, palaeobiology & evolution,, science of natural hazards

Dept of Experimental Psychology; www.psychology.psy.bris.ac.uk/

biological psychology, cognition, computational/clinical/applied neuroscience, neuropsychology, psychology, vision sciences

School of Geographical Sciences; www.ggy.bris.ac.uk/

geography, human/physical geography, society & space, science of natural hazards, environmental policy

Dept of Mathematics; www.maths.bris.ac.uk/

applied/pure mathematics, biology & mathematics, economics & mathematics, mathematics, mathematics & computer science/philosophy/physics/statistics, statistics

Dept of Physics; www.phsy.bris.ac.uk/

astrophysics, astronomy, correlated electron systems, mathematics and physics, micro- and nanol materials, nanophysics & soft matter, particle physics, physics/& philosophy, quantum photonics, theoretical physics; BSc(Hons), DSc, LlB, MRes, MSci, MSc, PhD, UGCert

Faculty of Social Science and Law; www.bris.ac.uk/fss

Bristol Institute for Public Affairs; www.bris.ac.uk/bipa

Graduate School of Education; www.bris.ac.uk/education

education, education, technology & society, science & education, TESOL,systems learning & leadership, PGCE in range of subjects

School for Policy Studies; www.bristol.ac.uk/sps

early/childhood studies, international health, social policy & politics, inclusion policy & practice, public policy, social work, children & young people

School of Applied Community and Health Studies; www.bris.ac.uk/sachs

Centre for Deaf Studies; Centre for Hearing & Balance Studies; Centre for Personal & Professional Development

audiology, deaf/deafhood studies, counselling, audiological audiological rehabilitation adv clinical audiology,

Norah Fry Research Centre

educational psychology, inclusive theory and practice: empowering people with learning disabilities

Centre for Personal and Professional Development

counselling, creative writing for therapeutic purposes

School of Economics, Finance & Management; www.bristol.ac.uk/efm

accounting, finance, management, econometrics, public policy, investment, strategic management, economics, economics & mathematics/politics/ philosophy

School of Law; www.bris.ac.uk/law

law, law with chemistry, law and French/ German, socio-legal studies, adv studies legal system

School of Sociology, Politics & international relations; www.bristol.ac.uk/spais

politics, international relations, European governance, gender, international security/development, development studies, development & security, economics, philiosphy, social policy, sociology, contemporay identities, ethnicity & multiculturism, social & cultural theory, social science, politics & mod language, E.Asian development & the global economy; BA(Hons), BSc(Hons), DSocSci, EdD, LlB, LlD, LlM, MEd, MPhil, MSc, MSci, PCGE, PhD,Dip

UNIVERSITY OF THE WEST OF ENGLAND, BRISTOL
www.uwe.ac.uk

Faculty of Business & Law; www.uwe.ac.uk/bl

Bristol Business School; www.uwe.ac.uk/bbs

business enterprise/management, business studies/ with accounting & finance/economics/HRM/marketing/tourism, coaching & mentoring, international business, accounting/money, banking & finance, economics, financial management, marketing/communications, tourism management, business & law/ management, leadership & management in health & social care, international HRM/management/tourism/ events, coaching & mentoring; BA(Hons), BSc(Hons), MA, MBA, MSc, PhD

Bristol Law School; www.law.uwe.ac.uk

commercial law, criminology, criminal law, contract law, public law, environmental law & sustainability, European business law, European & international law, international economic/banking & financial/ trade law, industrial law, law; LlB, LlM, PhD

Faculty of Creative Arts, Humanities & Education; www.uwe.ac.uk/cahe;

Dept of Art & Design; www, uwe.ac.uk/cahe/ad

animation, art & visual culture, art, media & design by project, creative practices, design: craft, fashion design, fashion design/textile design, photography, printmaking; BA(Hons), FdA, MA, MPhil, PhD

Dept of Culture, Media & Drama; www.uwe.ac.uk/cahe/cmd

drama, creative writing, film studies, English, media & cultural studies, journalism, media practice & culture

Dept of Education; www1.uwe.ac.uk/ssh/education

applied social research, careers guidance, early childhood studies, early years education, education in professional practice, initial teacher education, PGCE lower primary – early years (3–7)/secondary/post-16 training, post-compulsory education and training, upper primary (7–11), primary education, learning & skills, special education, schools support staff; ASR, BA(Hons), CertEd, DipHE, MA, MPhil, MSc PGCert/Dip, PhD

Dept of History, Philosophy & Politics; www.uwe.ac.uk/cahe/hpp

history, international history/politics/relations, philosophy, politics, European philosophy, human rights, peace & conflict; BA(Hons)MA, MPhil, PhD, PGDip

Dept of English, Linguistics & Communication; www.uwe.ac.uk/cahe/elc

English/language, drama, English & history/journalism/ philosophy/film studies, media & cultural studies, intercultural communication, translation; BA(Hons), MA, MPhil, PhD

Faculty of Environment and Technology; www.uwe.ac.uk/et

Dept of Computer Science & Creative Technologies; www.uwe.ac.uk/et/cst

audio music tehnology/production, computer science for games/security/systems integration, computing, creative music technology, enterprise/forensic computing, games technology/information technology, IT management for business, information & library management, multimedia computing, software engineering, web design; BSc(Hons), MSc, MPhil, PhD

Dept of Construction & Property; www.uwe.ac.uk/et/cp

building/quantity surveying, business in property, building services engineering, construction/project management, housing defects & maintenance planning, property development & planning/investment, real estate/management, law for construction professional; FDA, BA(Hons), BSc(Hons) MSc, MPhil, PhD

Dept of Engineering, Design & Mathematics; www.uwe.ac.uk/et/edm

aerospace engineering/manaufacture, creative product design, design for smart products, electrical & electronic engineering, engineering/management, manufacturing process improvement, mathematics, mechanical engineering, motor sport engineering, product design technology, adv technology in electronics, adv engineering/robotics, statistics; BEng, MEng, BSc(Hons), MPhil, PhD

Dept of Geography & Environmental management; www.uwe.acf.uk/et/gem

civil engineering, geography, environment management, tourism/management, planning, climate change & environment management, environmental consultancy, river & coastal engineering; BA(Hons), BSc(Hons), GradDip, MPhil, PhD

Dept of Planning & Architecture; www.uwe.ac.uk/et/pa

architecture, architectural technology & design, environment engineering/planning, geography, town & country planning, built & natural environments, spatial/transport planning, urban design, participation & neighbourhood renewal; BA(Hons), BSc(Hons), BArch, MA, MSc, MPlan, MPhil, PhD

Faculty of Health & Life Sciences; www.uwe.ac.uk/hls

Dept of Allied Health Professions; www.uwe.ac.uk/hls/ahp

diagnostic imaging, paramedic science, physiotherapy, health professions, occupational therapy, radiotherapy & oncology, sports therapy & rehabilitation, medical ultrasound, nuclear medicine; FdSc, BSc(Hons), MSc, PGDip/Cert, MPhil, PhD

Dept of Applied Sciences; www.uwe.ac.uk/hls/as

applied/biomedical sciences/(clinical), biological science, conservation biology, environmental health/science, forensic science/biology/chemistry/photography, human biology, integrated wildlife conservation, sport science, biosensing technologies, science communication, medical microbiology, molecular biotechnology, haematology, immunology, cellular pathology, clinical chemistry; FdSc, BSc(Hons), MSc, MRes, ProfDoc, PGCert, MPhil, PhD

Dept of Health & Applied Social Sciences; www.uwe.ac.uk/hls/hass
criminology, criminal justice, sociology, early childhood studies, environmental health, public health, social work/with adults, working with children, young people & their families, substance misuse, psychosocial studies, leadership & management in health & social services, special community public health; FdA, BSc(Hons), BA(Hons), MSc, PGDip/Cert, GradDip, MPhil, PhD

Dept of Nursing & Midwifery; www.uwe.ac.uk/hls/nm
adult/children's/mental health/learning disability nursing, midwifery, health & social care practice, health professions, advanced practice, child & adolescent mental health, clinical research, psychosocial interventions, specialist practice; FdSc, BSc(Hons), MSc, PGDip/Cert, PRofDoc, MPhil, PhD

Dept of Psychology; www.uwe.ac.uk/hls/psychology
psychology, psychology & criminology/education/sociology, health psychology, pscho-social studies, research methods, counselling; BA(Hons), BSc(Hons), MSc, DPS, ProfDoc, MPhil, PhD

Hartpury College (Associate Faculty); www.hartpury.ac.uk
agricultural business management, animal behaviour & veterinary science/welfare, animal science, bioveterinary science, conservation & countryside management; equine/business management/dental science/performance/sports science; coaching science, sport & exercise management, sport/events/management/studies/business management/coaching performance equine veterinary nursing, veterinary nursing science/physiotherapy; BA(Hons), BSc(Hons), FdSc, FdA, MA, MSc, PGDip/Cert

BRUNEL UNIVERSITY
www.brunel.ac.uk

School of Arts; www.brunel.ac.uk/about/acad/sa
contemporary literature & culture/performance making, creative writing, digital games theory and design documentary practice, drama, cult film & TV, English/literature, games design, campaigning &/journalism, modern drama studies, 21st century/music, musical composition/performance, sonic arts; BA(Hons), BMus, MA, MMus, MPhil, PhD

Brunel Law School; www.brunel.ac.uk/about/acad/bls
law, legal practice, consumer affairs, European and international commercial law, intellectual property/economic/international economic and trade/international human rights law, international & comparative criminal justice; CPE, European Masters, GradDip, LlM, LLB, MPhil, PhD

School of Engineering and Design; www.brunel.ac.uk /about/acad /sed
advanced manufacturing systems, engineering management, packing technology, design & branding, integrated product design, multimedia design & 3D technologies, broadcast media des, computer networks/systems, data communication systems, electrical/electronic/computer engineering, sustainable electrical power, wireless communication systems, advanced engineering design/mechanical engineering, aerospace/aviation engineering, automotive & motorsport engineering, biomedical engineering, building services engineering/management, sustainable energy technologies; BA(Hons), BEng, BSc(Hons), EngD, MEng, MPhil, MSc, PhD

Brunel Business School; www.brunel.ac.uk /about/acad/bbs
business & management, accounting, marketing, international business, corporate brand management, global supply chain management, HRM, HR and employment relations, international business management; BSc, MSc, MBA, PhD

School of Health Sciences and Social Care; www.brunel.ac.uk/about/acad/health
biomedical sciences, biochemistry/forensics/genetics/human health/immunology, occupational therapy, physiotherapy, social work, public health nursing, specialist social work, health promotion and public health, neurorehabilitation, occupational therapy, molecular medicine, cancer research, hand therapy, youth & community work; BSc, BA, MSc, MA, PGDip, PGCert

School of Information Systems, Computing and Mathematics; www.brunel.ac.uk/about/acad/siscm

artificial intelligence, computational mathematics with modelling, computer science, computing, digital media & games, financial computing/maths, information systems (business/e-commerce/human–computer interaction/social web), mathematics, modelling and management of risk, network computing, software engineering,, financial mathematics, statistics, systems integration; BSc, MSc, MTech, PhD

School of Social Sciences; www.brunel.ac.uk/about/acad/sss

accounting, economics, finance, social anthropology, anthropology and psychology/sociology, business economics/ finance, history, international money/ politics/relations, investment, media and communications, media studies, politics, psychology, public policy, child welfare; BA, BSc, MRes, MSc, PhD

School of Sport and Education; www.brunel.ac.uk/about/acad/sse

sport sciences (coaching/human performance/sport development/PE & youth sport), contemporary education, PE, child welfare & protection, education, English/secondary, information & communication technology, mathematics, science, sport & exercise psychology; BA,BSc, MSc,MA, PGCert,,EdD, MPhil, PhD

University Specialist Research Institutes offer postgraduate degree opportunities

UNIVERSITY OF BUCKINGHAM
www.buckingham.ac.uk

Buckingham School of Business; www.buckingham.ac.uk/business

accounting, business, business enterprise, communication studies, economics, finance, financial management, information systems, international financial services, management, marketing, media communications; BSc(Econ)(Hons), BSc(Hons), CMS, MBA, MSc/Diploma

School of Humanities; www.buckingham.ac.uk/humanities

Dept of Education; www.beds.ac.uk/departments/schoolofeducation/education

Teacher Training: PGCE, QTS, educational leadership, performance management; MEd

Dept of Economics & International Studies; www.beds.ac.uk/international

biography, business journalism, business, communication studies, business/economics, EFL, English literature, EFL/ESL, English studies/for teaching, French, global affairs, history, information systems, international business & trade, international studies, journalism, law, media studies/communication, military history, politics, psychology, security & intelligence studies, Spanish, TESOL; BA(Hons), BSc(Econ)Hons, DPhil, MA, MPhil, MSc

Dept of Modern Foreign Languages; www.buckingham.ac.uk/mfl

range of languages taught for part of joint degrees

Dept of English; www.buckingham.ac.uk/english

foundation English, English language/literature, communication studies, media, journalism, biography, English studies for teaching

London Studies; www.buckingham.ac.uk/london

biography, decorative arts & historic interiors, military history, war studies

Buckingham Law School; www.buckingham.ac.uk/law

law, common law, international & commercial law, joint degrees; Cert. Dip, LlB,LlM

School of Sciences & Medicine; www.buckingham.ac.uk/sciences

School of Medicine; www.buckingham.ac.uk/medicine

graduate entry, PG medical school, general internal medicine, clinical science; Clinical MD, MBBS, MSc

Dept of Applied Computing; www.buckingham.ac.uk/applied computing

applied computing, computing, innovative computing; BSc, Cert Comp, MSc, PGDip, PhD

Dept of Psychology; www.buckingham.ac.uk/psychology

psychology, adult dyslexia; BSc(Hons), MPhil, MSc, PhD

Clore Laboratory; www.buckingham,ac.uk/clore

diabetes, obesity & metabolic research, molecular genetics, biochemistry, pharmacology, nutrition; DPhil, MPhil, MSc

BUCKINGHAMSHIRE NEW UNIVERSITY
www.bucks.ac.uk

Faculty of Design, Media & Management; www.bucks.ac.uk/about/structure/academic/faculties/design-media-management

School of Applied Management & Law; www.bucks.ac.uk/about/structure/academic-schools/applied-management-law

business, international management, sports management & science & finance, events & festival management, law, commercial pilot training

School of Design, Craft & Visual Arts; www.bucks.ac.uk/about/structure/academicschools/design-craft-visual-arts

conservation & interpretation of cultural artefacts, new media, internet technologies, creative industries, visual imagery

School of Applied Production & New Media; www.bucks.ac.uk/about/structure/academicschools/music-entertainment-image

commercial music, film and entertainment, art/music management, creative industries, new media, production, journalism, scriptwriting, performance

Faculty of Society and Health; www.bucks.ac.uk/about/structure/faculties/society-and-health

School of Social Sciences, Primary Care & Education; www.bucks.ac.uk/about/structure/academicschools/social-care-education

community health care, public health practice, mentorship/practice teacher/practice education, social work, mental health nursing, education, psychology/cognitive behavioural therapy, criminology/police studies

School of Advanced and Continuing Practice; www.bucks.ac.uk/about/structure/academicschools/advanced-continuing-practice

cancer and palliative/critical/respiratory care, nurse practitioner (acute care/emergency care/primary care), advanced practice

School of Pre-qualifying Nursing; www.bucks.ac.uk/about/structure/academicschools/pre-registration-nursing

BA(Hons), BSc(Hons), Certs, DMS, GradDip, FD, HNC, HND, LlB(Hons), LlM, MA, MBA, MCommunMan, MSc, PhD, FD

UNIVERSITY OF CAMBRIDGE
www.cam.ac.uk

School of Arts and Humanities; www.csah.cam.ac.uk

Faculty of Architecture and History of Art; www.aha.cam.ac.uk
architecture, environmental design, design in the built environment, history of art, medieval art & architecture, Renaissance art & architecture, 20th-century art & theory, western & non-western cultural exchange; BA, MPhil, MSt, PhD

Faculty of Asian & Middle Eastern Studies; www.ames.cam.ac.uk
Chinese studies, Hebrew and Semitic studies, Japanese studies, Middle Eastern & Islamic studies, Korean studies, Arabic & Persian studies, East Asia, Southern Asia studies, Assyriology, Egyptology; BA, MPhil, PhD

Faculty of Classics; www.classics.cam.ac.uk classics & Latin literature, history, philology and linguistics, philosophy; BA, MPhil, PGCE

Faculty of Divinity; www.divinity.cam.ac.uk
biblical studies, church history, historical & systematic theology, religious studies & the philosophy of religion, the Christian tradition; BA, MPhil, PhD, PGDip

Faculty of English; www.english.cam.ac.uk
American literature, Anglo-Saxon, Norse & Celtic, English & applied linguistics, medieval/English literature, European languages & literatures, English studies: criticism & culture/18th-century & romantic studies; language for literature; BA, MLitt, MPhil, PhD

Faculty of Modern and Medieval Languages; www.mml.cam.ac.uk
Depts of French, German & Dutch, Italian, Spanish & Portuguese, European literature, linguistics, modern Greek, neo-Latin, Russian studies, screen & media cultures, Slavonic studies; BA, MPhil, PhDE

Faculty of Music; www.mus.cam.ac.uk
ethnomusicology, historical musicology, music/with education studies, analysis, practical musicianship, tonal compositions & analysis & repertoire, musical composition, science & music, choral studies; BA, MPhil, PhD, MMusD

Faculty of Philosophy; www.phil.cam.ac
ethics, experimental psychology, history of philosophy, logic, metaphysics, philosophy of science, political philosophy, aesthetics, mathematical logic, ancient philosophy; BA, MPhil, PhD

School of Humanities and Social Science; www.cshss.cam.ac.uk

Faculty of Archaeology and Anthropology; www.archanthcam.ac
archaeological heritage & museum, archaeology, archaeology of the Americas, biological anthropology, Egyptian archaeology, European prehistory, human evolutionary studies, medieval archaeology, Mesopotamian studies, palaeolithic & mesolithic archaeology, social anthropology, south Asian archaeology; BA, MPhil, PhD

Faculty of Economics; www.econ..cam.ac.uk
asset pricing, behavioural economics, British industrialization, economics of networks, economics of poor countries, industrial organization, microeconomics, politics, quantitative methods, microeconomics, macroeconometrics, economics; BA, Diploma, MPhil, PhD

Faculty of Education; www.educ.cam.ac.uk
arts culture & education, child & adolescent counselling, citizenship & wellbeing in schools, critical approaches to children's literature, education, educational leadership & school improvement, inclusive & special psychology & education, mathematics, PGCE; early years, primary, secondary, second language education; BA, MEd, PGCE, PGDip/Cert, PhD

Faculty of History; www.hist.cam.ac.uk
American history, British political & constitutional history, economic history, European history, extra-European history, medieval history, political thought; BA, MPhil, PhD

Faculty of Law; www.law.cam.ac.uk
criminological research, criminology, international law, law, legal studies, large range of legal topics at Master level; BA, Diploma, LLD, LLM, MLitt, MPhil, PhD

Institute of Criminology; www.crim.cam.ac
applied/criminology, penology & management, applied criminology & police management; MPhil, MSt, PhD

Faculty of Politics, Psychology, Sociology and International Studies; www.ppsis.cam.ac.uk

Politics and International Studies; www.ppsis.cam.ac.uk
history of political thought, international relations, modern world politics, the political theorists, politics, representative democracy; BA, MPhil, MSt, PhD

Dept of Social and Developmental Psychology
psychology, social and developmental psychology

Dept of Sociology
sociology, modern society & global transformations; BA, MPhil, PhD

Centre for Family Research
bioethics & the family, early social development & the family, genetics, health & families, non-traditional families, parent, children & family relationships; MPhil, PhD

History and Philosophy of Science; www.hps.cam.ac.uk
history, classical traditions in the sciences, metaphysics, epistemology & the sciences, modern medicine & biological sciences, history & philosophy of the mind, natural philosophies; Renaisscance to Enlightenment, science in society; BA, MPhil, PhD

Land Economy; www.landecon.cam.ac.uk
environmental policy, land economy, planning, growth & regeneration, real estate finance; BA, MPhil, PhD

Centre of Latin American Studies; www.latin-america.cam.ac.uk
economic issues in contemporary Latin America, history of South American external relations, Latin American literary culture/film and visual arts, race & ethnicity/anthropology/sociology & politics in Latin America; MPhil, PhD

Centre of African Studies; www.africa.cam.ac.uk
African studies; MPhil

Centre of South Asian Studies
modern South Asian studies; MPhil

Development Studies Committee; www.devstudies.cam.ac.uk
development studies; MPhil

School of Biological Sciences; www.cam.ac.uk/sbs

Faculty of Biology; www.cam.ac.uk

Depts of Biology, Experimental Psychology, Genetics, Pharmacology, Physiology, Development & Neuroscience, Plant Science, Veterinary Medicine, Zoology
agriculture, biochemistry, biotechnology & pharmacological industries, experimental psychology, genetics, genomes & gene products, health, integrated functional systems, pathology, pharmacology, physiology, development & neuroscience, plant sciences, zoology; BA, MPhil, PhD

Faculty of Veterinary Medicine

Department of Veterinary Medicine; www.vet.cam.ac.uk/
Clinical Course: veterinary science, preclinical course; MPhil, VetMB

Wellcome Trust Centre for Stem Cell Research; www.cscr.cam.ac.uk

stem cell biology; PhD

Wellcome Trust/Cancer Research UK Gurdon InstituteTechnology; www.gurdon.cam.ac.uk

cellular & molecular biology, developmental, cell & cancer biology; PhD

School of Technology; www.tech.ac.uk

Faculty of Engineering; www.eng.cam.ac.uk

engineering (aerospace & aerothermal) civil, electrical & electronic, engineering for sustainable development, environmental, industrial systems, information & computer, manufacture & management, mechanical, nuclear energy, construction eng; BA(Hons), MEng, MPhil, PhD

Faculty of Business & Management (Judge Business School); www.jbs.cam.ac.uk

courses include: finance & accounting, international business, management science & operations, equity/derivatives, investment, Asian capital markets, entrepreneurship, value creation, leadership, real estate, risk management, venture capital, econometrics; MBA, MFin

Computer Laboratory; www.clcam.ac.uk

adv/computer science, network architecture, internet useriterface, forensic signal analysis, language processing, embedded sytems, programming logic etc; BA, MPhil, PhD

Department of Chemical Engineering & Biotechnology; www.ceb.cam.ac.uk

advanced chemical engineering, bioscience enterprise, biotechnology, chemical engineering; BA/MEng, MPhil, PhD

Cambridge Programme for Sustainability Leadership; www.cpi.cam.ac.uk

sustainable business, sustainability leadership; sustainable cities biodiversity, health care services, built environment; MSt, PGCert

School of Physical Sciences; www.cam.ac.uk/about/physsci

Dept of Applied Mathematics & Theoretical Physics

mathematical science; www.physci.cam, ac.uk/about the school/dampt

Institute of Astronomy; www.physci.cam/about the school/astronomy

theoretical & observational astronomy

Faculty of Earth Sciences; www.physci.cam.ac.uk/earthsciences

earth sciences, environment, environmental science, palaeontology, geophysics, minerals physics/science; BA, MPhil, PhD

Dept of Geography; www.physci.cam.ac.uk/about the school/geography (inc Scott Polar Research Institute);

geography/historical & cultural, spaces of economy & society, environmental processes, environment & development; BA, MPhil, PhD

Dept of Material Science & Metallurgy; www.physci.cam.ac.uk/aboutthe school/materialsscience

metals, alloys, ceramics, polymers, composites, semiconducting/magenetic/superconducting/ferroelectric/biomedical materials

Isaac Newton Institute for Mathematical Sciences www.physsci.cam.ac.uk/aboutthe school/newton

applied mathematics & theoretical physics, computational bilology, mathematics, mathematics with physics, pure mathematics & mathematical statistics, statistical science; BA, MPhil, PhD, MMath, MAdvStud

Dept of Physics; www.physci.cam.ac.uk/abouttheschool/physics

physics, astrophysics, atomic/high energy/quantum & condensed matter/thin film magenetism; BA, MPhil, MSci, PhD

Dept of Pure Mathematics & Mathematical statistics; www.physci.cam.ac.uk/about the school/dpmss

School of Clinical Medicine; www.medschl.cam.ac.uk

Dept of Clinical Biochemistry (Metabolic Research Laboratories); www.clbc.cam.ac.uk

biomedical research, diabetes, molecular cell biology of membrane traffic pathways, obesity & other related endocrine and metabolic disorders; PhD

Dept of Clinical Neurosciences (Cambridge Centre for Brain Repair; Neurology Unit; Neurosurgery; Wolfson Brain Imaging Centre); www.neurosciences.medschl.am.ac.uk

brain repair, neurology, neurosurgery, brain imaging; MB/PhD

Dept of Haematology; www.haem.cam.ac.uk

transfusion medicine diagnostics development; PhD

Dept of Medical Genetics; www.cimr.cam.ac.uk/medgen

genetics of inflammatory disorders, juvenile diabetes, autoimmune liver disease; BChir, MB, MD, PhD

Dept of Medicine

anasthesia, clinical pharmacology

Obstetrics & Gynaecology

Oncology

Paediatrics

Psychiatry

brain mapping, developmental psychiatry

Public Health & Primary Care

general practice & primary care research, clinical gerentology

Radiology

Surgery

orthopaedic research

CAMBRIDGE INTERNATIONAL COLLEGE
www.cambridgecollege.ac.uk

accounting, finance, business, economics, commerce, communication, tourism, hospitality, management, leadership, marketing, sales, advertising, personnel, HR, logistics purchasing; BA, Diplomas

CANTERBURY CHRIST CHURCH UNIVERSITY
www.canterbury.ac.uk

Faculty of Arts and Humanities; www.canterbury.ac.uk/arts-humanities

Art
fine art, applied/visual art, ceramics, sculpture, printmaking

English & Language Studies
English/literature, children's literature, creative writing, Victorian literature

History & American studies
American studies, Canadian studies, archaeology, history

Media
digital media, film, radio & TV, multimedia journalism, graphic design, web design

Music
access to music, commercial music production, creative music technology, performing arts

Theology & Religious Studies
theology, religious studies; BA, BSC, MA, MPhil, PhD, PGDip, FD

Faculty of Business and Management; www.canterbury.ac.uk/business-management

The Business School; www.canterbury.ac.uk/business-management/business-school
accounting & finance, advertising management, business & management, business management/studies, economics, entrepreneurship, HRM, logistics, management studies, managerial finance, marketing, strategic management

Centre for Leadership & Management; www.canterbury.ac.uk/business-management/CLMD
coaching, leadership development, organizational development, personal effectiveness, project management, recruitment and selection, team dev, management studies; BSc(Hons), MA, MBA, MPhil/PhD, MSc, PGDip/Cert

Faculty of Education; www.canterbury.ac.uk/ education
early/childhood studies, early years/professional status/ studies, educational studies, enabling learning, institutional development, leadership & management for learning, lifelong learning, literacy & learning, religion in education, school development, teaching skills for life – numeracy, literacy/ESOL, PGCE; primary teaching, post-compulsory primary education, teaching & learning, modular (primary/secondary), PE, RE, post-primary education, professional development; BA(Hons), EdD, EYPS, FDA, MA, MPhil/PhD

Faculty of Health and Social Care; www.canterbury.ac.uk/health/home

Department of Allied Health Professions; www.canterbury.ac.uk/health/allied-health-professions
advanced occupational therapy practice, clinical reporting, diagnostic radiography, health & social care, medical imaging, occupational therapy, radiography, speech language therapy

Centre for Health and Social Care Research; www.canterbury.ac.uk/health/health-social-care-research

Dementia Services Development Centre South East; www.dementiacentre.canterbury.ac.uk/
mental health, public health

Dept of Health, Well-being & the Family; www.canterbury.ac.uk/health
midwifery, child nursing, health and social care, health studies (health promotion, public health, maternal and child health, practice-based play therapy), mental health nursing, health-wellbeing-

family, interprofessional health & social care, social work children & families

Department of Nursing and Applied Clinical Studies; www.canterbury.ac.uk/health/nursing-applied-clinical-studies

adult nursing, advancing nursing practice, cancer care, clinical practice, gerontology and dementia related studies, health & social care, practice development/education, public & community health, workforce analysis & development, optical dispensing

Department of Social Work, Community & Mental Health; www.canterbury.ac.uk/health/social-work-community-mental-health

children & families, health & social care, mental health & learning disabilities, nursing studies (mental health), social work, specialist social work with adults/in mental health services, young children, their families & carers; Adv Dip, BSc(Hons), DipHE, Foundation Degree, GradCert, MA, MPhil/PhD, MRes, MSc

Faculty of Social and Applied Sciences; www.canterbury.ac.uk/social applied-science

Dept of Applied Psychology; www.canterbury.ac.uk/social-applied-sciences/aspd

applied social & psychological development, clinical psychology, cognitive behavioural therapy and psychological wellbeing practice, psychology, sport & exercise psychology

Dept of Applied Social Science; www.canterbury.ac.uk/social-applied-sciences

global governance/politics, politics & governance/international relations, sociology & social science

Dept of Computing; www.canterbury.ac.uk/social-applied-sciences/computing, internet computing

business computing, computing, cybercrime forensics, forensic computing, internet computing

The Department of Law and Criminal Justice Studies; www.canterbury.ac.uk/social-applied-sciences/crime-and-policing

law & legal studies, applied criminology, crime & policing/policing studies, forensic investigation

Dept of Geographical and Life Sciences; www.canterbury.ac.uk/social-applied-sciences/geographical-and-life-sciences

conservation, environmental biology/science, geography, integrated science, urban and regional studies, GIS

Dept of Sports Science, Tourism and Leisure; www.canterbury.ac.uk/social-applied-sciences/sport-science-tourism-and-leisure

sport & exercise science/exercise psychology, leisure management, tourism and leisure studies, tourism management, physical education & sport; BA/BSc, MBA, MSc, MA, Adv Dip, Grad Cert, PGDip, FD

CARDIFF UNIVERSITY
www.cardiff.ac.uk

Welsh School of Architecture; www.cardiff.ac.uk/archi

architecture, environmental design of buildings, sustainable energy & environment, urban design, sustainable development; BSc, DipProfStudies, MA, MArch, MPhil, MSc, PhD

School of Biosciences; www.cardiff.ac.uk/bios

biochemistry, biology, biomedical science – anatomy/neuroscience/physiology, dental hygiene/therapy, medical pharmacy, genetics, microbiology, molecular biology, zoology; BSc(Hons), MRes, MSc, PhD, BDS, MBBCh

Cardiff Business School; www.cardiff.ac.uk/carbs

accounting, banking, business economics, business management – human resources/international/logistics & operations/marketing, economics, finance, financial economics, HRM, international economics, international transport, lean operations, management studies, marine policy, marketing, port and shipping administration, public /policy/administration, strategic marketing; BSc, BScEcon, MBA, MPA, MSc, PhD

School of Chemistry; www.cardiff.ac.uk/chemy

chemical biology, chemistry, chemistry with physics/industrial experience, inorganic chemistry, organic synthesis, physical organic chemistry, solid state and materials chemistry, molecular modelling, sustainable chemistry, theoretical and computational chemistry; BSc, MChem, MPhil, PhD

School of City & Regional Planning; www.cardiff.ac.uk/c/plan

city & regional planning, geography (human) & planning, geography/planning, international planning, regeneration studies, sustainability, planning and environmental policy, transport, urban design, housing, regeneration studies; BSc, MSc, PhD

School of Computer Science & Information; www.cardiff.cs.cf.ac.uk

computer science, information systems/computer vision and computer graphics/knowledge and information systems/distributed and mobile systems/computing/computer systems engineering, strategic information systems, information security and privacy, computer systems & maths; BSc, MSc, PhD

School of Dentistry; www.cardiff.ac.uk/denti

dental surgery, dental therapy & hygiene, implantology, oral diseases, orthodontics, tissue engineering; BDS, BSc(Hons), MClinDent, MD, MPhil, MSc, PhD

School of Earth and Ocean Sciences; www.cardiff.ac.uk/earth

earth sciences, environmental geoscience/hydrogeology, exploration and resource geology, geobiology, geology, marine geography, geoscience; BSc, MESc, MPhil, MSc, PhD

School of Engineering; www.cardiff.ac.uk/engin

architectural/civil/environmental/clinical engineering, communication engineering and signal processing, computer systems/electrical and electronic engineering, electronic and communications/environmental/geoenvironmental/integrated engineering, mechanical/medical/orthopaedic/structural engineering, sustainable energy and environment, electro-energy engineering hydroenvironmental engineering, magnetics; BEng, EngD, MEng, MPhil, MSc, PhD

School of English, Communication & Philosophy; www.cardiff.ac.uk/encap

applied linguistics, communication, creative writing, critical & cultural theory, analytic mid-European philosophy, English language/literature, ethics & social philosophy, forensic linguistics, language and communication, philosophy, analytic mid-European philosophy; BA, Diploma, MA/Dip, MPhil, PhD

School of European Studies; www.cardiff.ac.uk/euros

French, German, Spanish, Italian, European/European Union studies, international relations, political theory, law, politics translation studies, politics & public policy, Welsh politics & government; BA, BScEcon, LlB, MA, MScEcon, MPhil, PhD

School of Healthcare Studies; www.cardiff.ac.uk/sohcs

healthcare science, intra & perioperative practice, medical illustration, neurorehabilitation, neuro-musculoskeletal physiotherapy, occupation & health, occupational therapy, operating department practice, physiotherapy, radiography & imaging, radiotherapy & oncology, sports physiotherapy, surgical care practice; CertHE, DipHE, MPhil, MSc, PGDip/Cert, PhD

School of History and Archaeology; www.cardiff.ac.uk/hisar

ancient and medieval warfare, ancient history, archaeology, care of collections, conservation, early Celtic studies, early medieval society and culture, European neolithic, history and archaeology of the Greek and Roman world, medieval/history, Byzantine studies, medieval British studies/history, Welsh history; BA, BSc, MA, MPhil, MSc, PhD

Journalism Media and Cultural Studies; www.cardiff.ac.uk/jomec

international journalism/PR/political communications, science, media and communication, journalism, media & cultural studies; BA, MA, MPhil, MSc, PGDip, PhD

School of Law; www.law.cf.ac.uk

canon law, commercial law, European legal studies, human rights, medical practice, law, international commercial law, law & criminology/politics/sociology/French/German/Welsh, social care, governance development, law; LlB, LlM, MPhil, PhD

Centre for Lifelong Learning

languages, business & management, computer studies, law, science & environment, social studies

School of Mathematics; www.cardiff.ac.uk/maths

analysis, computing in the physical sciences, mathematics/& its applications, numerical analysis, operational research & statistics and risk; BSc, MMath, MPhil, MSc, PhD

Manufacturing Engineering Centre; wwwmec.cg.ac.uk

industrial engineering and systems engineering, manufacturing engineering; MPhil, PhD

School of Medicine; www.cardiff.ac.uk/medic

advanced surgical practice, bioinformatics, child health, critical care, dermatology, diabetes, anaesthesia, geriatric medicine, intensive care medicine, learning disabilities, geriatric medicine, public health, genetics, medicine, obstetrics & gynaecology, occupational health, oncology, paediatrics, pain management, palliative medicine, primary care & public health, psychiatry, therapeutics, wound healing; MBBCh, MD, MPH, MPhil, MSc/PGDip/Cert, PhD

School of Music; www.cardiff.ac.uk/music

composition, ethnomusicology, music, musicology, performance studies; BA/BMus, MA, MMus, PhD

School of Nursing & Midwifery Studies; www.cardiff.ac.uk/sonims

adult/child/community public health nursing, advanced practice, health studies, independent prescribing, mental health, non-medical prescribing, nursing children and young people with cancer; BMid, BN, BSc(Hons), DipHE, DNurs, DocProf, MPhil, MSc, PGDip/Cert, PhD

School of Optometry & Vision Sciences; www.cardiff.ac.uk/optom

clinical investigation, vision sciences, optometry, visual neuroscience & molecular biology, structural biophysics; BSc, MPhil, PhD

School of Pharmacy; www.cardiff.ac.uk/phring

clinical pharmacy, clinical research, community pharmacy, non-medical prescribing, pharmaceutical medicine, pharmacy, international pharmacological economics; Dipl, MPharm, MPhil, MSc, PhD

School of Physics and Astronomy; www.astro.cardiff.ac.uk

astrophysics, biophotonics, physics, medical physics, astronomy, theoretical and computational physics; BSc, MPhil, MPhys, PhD

Postgraduate Medical and Dental Education; www.cardiff.ac.uk/pgmde

dental/medical education, general/ hospital practice, IM & T

School of Psychology; www.cardiff.ac.uk/psych

clinical psychology, educational psychology, psychology; BSc, DEdPsych, DClinPsych, GradDip, PhD

School of Religious and Theological Studies; www.cardiff.ac.uk/relig

chaplaincy studies, Christian doctrine/ethics, church history, religious & theological studies, Indian religions, Islam, practical theology; BA, DipD, MA, MPhil, MTh, PhPG

School of Social Sciences; www.cardiff.ac.uk/socsci

criminal justice, criminology, social sciences, education, equality and diversity, social policy/work, social science research methods, sociology; BA, BSc, DHS, DSW, EdD, MA, MSc, PGCE

School of Welsh; www.cardiff.ac.uk/welsh

Welsh, Welsh ethnological studies, Welsh history, early Celtic studies, medieval British studies; BA, MA, PhD

UNIVERSITY OF CENTRAL LANCASHIRE
www.uclan.ac.uk

School of Art, Design & Performance; www.uclan.ac.uk/schools/adp

3D design, acting, animation, arts health, art & design, ceramics, computer games, contemporary theatre & performance, dance, performance, & teaching, fine art/studio practice, contemporary visual arts, drawing, design enterprise, digital design for fashion, Eastern fashion design, drawing, fashion brand management/promotion, games design, graphic design, children/books/illustration, interior design, music production/theatre, product design, surface pattern, textiles; MA, MBA, MPhil, PGCert/Dip, PhD, UniCert

School of Built & Natural Environment; www.uclan.ac.uk/schools/ built_natural_environment;
architecture/technology, building conservation & regeneration, building services & sustainable engineering, building/quantity surveying, construction law, construction/project management, construction economics/facilities management, environment hazards/management, project management, geography, sustainable energy management; BSc(Hons), BA(Hons), FdSc, PGDip/Cert, MSc

School of Computing, Engineering & Physical Sciences; www.uclan.ac.uk/ schools/computing_engineering_physical;
Computing; computer games/networks, computing, database systems, digital signal image processing, forensic computing, information systems, internet/ agile software/design, IT security, mobile interactive technology, multimedia/games development, network computing, renewable/wind energy engineering, software engineering
Engineering: electronic computing, robotics & mechatronics, digital computing, electronic design automation, computer-aided engineering; motorsports/engineering, mechanical maintenance engineering; Nuclear Engineering
Physics & Mathematics: mathematics, physics, astrophysics, astronomy; BSc(Hons), BEng(Hons), MPhys, MSc, FdSc, MPhil, PhD

School of Dentistry, & Institute for Postgraduate Dental Education; www.uclan.ac.uk/health/schools/ dentistry_at_uclan/
aesthetic dental implantology, clinical periodontology, dental surgery, dentistry, endodontology, oral surgery, orthodontic therapy, restorative cosmetic dentistry; BDS, CertHE, MSc, PGDip, Adv Cert

School of Education and Social Sciences; www.uclan.ac.uk/aschools/ education_social_sciences
Criminology: criminal justice, law, criminology, forensic science, criminal investigation, police
Deaf Studies: British sign language/English interpreting & translation/communication, deaf studies
Education: children, schools & family, children & young people, adult literacy, ESOL, lifelong learning, post-comp education
Equality & Diversity; promoting equality & managing diversity/workplace, developing partnership
Ethnicity & Human Rights
History: history, modern world history, museums and heritage
Islamic Studies
Philosophy: philosophy/mental health, values & environment
Politics: politics & international relations
Religion, Culture & Society
Sociology; BA(Hons), BSc(Hons), MA, Mhil, PGCE, PhD, UnivCert, PGCert

School of Forensic and Investigative Sciences; www.uclan.ac.uk/schools/ forensic_investigative/
archaeology/of death, osteroarchaeology, fire engineering/leadership studies/investigation/safety, forensic chemistry/archaeology, police & criminal investigation; BA(Hons), BEng, BSc(Hons), FdSc, MPhil, PhD

School of Health; www.uclan.ac.uk/ schools/school_of_health
prereg nursing (mental health/children/adult), professional practice, clinical knowledge, skills enhancement, psychosocial care, children, public & families, paramedical practice, operating dept practice, counselling, integrated healthcare; psychotherapy; BA(Hons), BSc(Hons), MA, MSc, PGcert/Dip. DipHE, UnivCert

School of Journalism, Media and Communication; www.uclan.ac.uk/ schools/journalism_media_communication
journalism (various), film/production & media studies, web & multimedia, screenwriting, idigital media, media practice/technology, photography, modern & contemporary literature, English language/lliterature & linguistics, creative writing, dance & theatre, play writing, publishing, American studies; BSc(Hons), BA(Hons), MA, MPhil, PGDip, PGCert, PhD

Lancashire Business School; www.uclan.ac.uk/schools/lbs
accounting, advertising, finance, business/administration, management, digital/marketing, business information technology/project management/studies/systems, economics, European business management, financial management, global business, health service management, HRM, international business, logistics & supply chain management, strategic communications, oil & gas management, sports/PR, retail management, sustainable business; BA(Hons), DBA, MA, MBA, MSC, PGDip/Cert

Lancashire Law School; www.uclan.ac.uk/schools/lancashire_law_school
advanced legal practice, employment /European commercial law, forensic & legal medicine, human rights, law, criminology, senior status, legal practice, medical law & bioethics; BA(Hons), BA/BSc, LlB, LLM, MA, MPhil, PGDip

School of Languages and International Studies; www.uclan.ac.uk/schools/languages_and_international;
business English, English for foreigners, modern foreign languages, intercultural communication, interpretation & translation, TESOL; BA(Hons), MPhil, PhD

School of Pharmacy and Biomedical Sciences; www.uclan.ac.uk/schools/pharmacy
pharmacy,biomedical science, cancer biology & therapy, non-medical prescribing, physiology & pharmacology, clinical pharmaceutical pract/technology, industrial pharmaceutics; BSc(Hons), MPharm, MSc, PGDip/Cert, PhD

School of Psychology; www.uclan.ac.uk/schools/psychology
applied psychology, forensic psychology, child development, social psychology, sport & exercise psychology, health psychology, neuropsychology; BSc(Hons), GradDip, MSc

School of Social Work; www.uclan.ac.uk/health/schools/school_of_social_work/
care, community and citizenship, child health & social care, safeguarding children, social policy/work; BA(Hons), MA, PGCert

School of Sport, Tourism and the Outdoors; www.uclan.ac.uk/management/ssto
leisure (management),sport/management/coaching/development/event management/PR studies, sports policy & community development, adventure sports coaching/leadership/management, international/tourism management, hospitality, sports/ event management, outdoor leadership; BA(Hons), FdA, MA/PGDip/PGCert

UNIVERSITY OF CHESTER
www.chester.ac.uk

Faculty of Applied Sciences; www.chester.ac.uk/faculties#A

Dept of Biological Sciences; www.chester.ac.uk/biology
animal behaviour, animal/zoo management, biomedical sciences, biology, diabetes management, forensic biology; BSc, MSc, PhD

Computer Science and Information Systems; www.chester.ac.uk/csis
computer science, computing, digital technology/media, e-business, internet, multimedia technology, programming, information systems, web-based technology; BSc(Hons), MPhil, PhD, FD

Dept of Clinical Science; www.chester.ac.uk/cens;
cardiovascular rehabilitation, exercise & nutrition science, weight management; MSc, PhD, MPhil

Centre for Public Health Research; www.chester.ac.uk/cphr
public health, research methods; MSc

Centre for Science Communication

Centre for Research into Sport & Society; www.chester.ac.uk/scicom;
sociology of sport & exercise; MSc, PhD

Dept of Sport & Exercise Science; www.chester.ac.uk/sport
sport science/development, sport coaching, fitness health, sport & exercise science; BA, BSc, MSc

Faculty of Arts & Media; www.chester.ac.uk/faculties#B

Dept of Art & Design; www.chester.ac.uk/art & design;
art & design, fine art, graphic design, photography; BA(Hons), MA, MSc

Dept of Media; www.chester.ac.uk/media
advertising, commercial music, digital photography, radio/TV prodn, film studies, sports/journalism, media studies; BA(Hons)

Dept of Performing Arts; www.chester.ac.uk/departments/performing-arts
drama, dance & music/theatre studies/pop music, performance; BA(Hons), MA

Faculty of Business, Enterprise & Lifelong Learning; www.chester.ac.uk/faculties#C

Chester Business School; www.chester.ac.uk/chester-business-school
business administration/management/studies, accounting, information systems, international business, finance, HRM, management, marketing, tourism & events management, tourism management, strategy; BA(Hons), BA/BSc, FdA, MBA, MPhil, PhD

Centre for Work Related Studies; Professional Development Unit; Work Based Learning Office; www.chester.ac.uk/pdu
goverment, civil service, management & leadership or business, education; FD, BA, MA

Faculty of Education & Children's Services; www.chester.ac.uk/education

children and young people, families, early childhood studies, continuing professional development, early years practice, education, PGCE secondary/primary/early years, teaching assistance; teacher ed, teaching & learning, coaching; BA(Hons), BEd, EdD, FdA, MA, MEd, PGCE

Faculty of Health and Social Care; www.chester.ac.uk/health

childen, young people & families, community health, mental health pract, nursing, health & social care, midwifery, public health, social work, art therapy, medical prescribing, professional studies; FD, BA(Hons), BSc(Hons), MA, MSc, PGCert, PhD

Faculty of Humanities; www.chester.ac.uk/faculties#F

English; www.chester.ac.uk/english
creative writing, English/ language, 19th-cent literature and culture, modern & contemporary fiction; BA, MA, PhD

History and Archaeology; www.chester.ac.uk/departments/history-and-archeology
archaeology, history, military history; BA(Hons), MA, MPhil, PhD

Dept of Modern Languages; www.chester.ac.uk/languages
European languages & cultures, French, German & Spanish; BA(Hons), MA, PGCert/Dip

Theology & Religious Studies; www.chester.ac.uk/trs
Christian youth work, religious studies, practical/theology; BA(Hons), BTh, Dip HE, FdA, MA, MPhil, MTh, PhD

Faculty of Social Sciences; www.chester.ac.uk/faculties#G

Geography and Development Studies; www.chester.ac.uk/geography
geography, international development studies, natural hazard/environmental management; BA(Hons), MA, MSc, PhD

Dept of Psychology; www.chester.ac.uk/psychology
psychology; BA(Hons), BSc(Hons)

Dept of Social Science & Counselling; www.chester.ac.uk/scc
criminology, sociology, community studies, politics, psychological trauma, crime & justice, counselling; BA, BSc, MA, MSc

Law School; www.chester.ac.uk/law
law, family law (criminal justice, human rights & discrimination)

UNIVERSITY OF CHICHESTER
www.chiuni.ac.uk

dance, English, creative writing, fine art, history, media production/studies, music/marketing, musical theatre, commercial music, performing arts, theology; accounting, finance, business studies, event management, finance, HRM, IT management for business, marketing, management, tourism management; teacher & learning support, teacher education; graduate teacher programme; primary/

secondary,teaching, teaching assistants, language development, TESOL, PE, RE, childhood & youth: childhood studies, early childhood education, mathematics education, teaching & learning support, teaching psychology, counselling: social work & social care; sport counselling/exercise psychology/ development/therapy; adventure education, sports, exercise & health sciences/psychology, substance misuse; BA(Hons), BSc(Hons), FD, GradDip/Cert, MA, PGCE, MSc, MSW

CITY UNIVERSITY LONDON
www.city.ac.uk

School of of Arts; www.city.ac.uk/arts

Cultural Policy and Management; www.city.ac.uk/cpm

culture, policy & management, creative industries, information in the cultural sector, innovation, creativity, leadership; FD, MA, MSc, BA(Hons)

Faculty of Journalism; www.city.ac.uk/ journalism

broadcast/TV/investigative/magazine/newspaper/ science/international/financial/ journalism, creative writing, electronic publishing, publishing studies; BA(Hons), MA, MSc, PhD

Dept of Music; www.city.ac.uk/music

music composition (electroacoustic/instrumental and vocal), music performance, musicology/ethnomusicology, culture studies, creative practice; BMus, DMA, MA, MMA, MPhil, PhD

Centre for Translation Studies; www.city.ac.uk/

audiovisual translation, legal translation, principles and practice of translation; Dip, MA, PGCert

Cass Business School; www.cass.city.ac.uk

Faculty of Actuarial Science and Insurance; www.cass.city.ac.uk/facact

actuarial management, actuarial science, insurance; BSc(Hons), MSc, Dip, PhD, MPhil

Faculty of Finance; www.cass.city.ac.uk/ facfin

accounting, corporate finance, econometrics, investment & risk management, mathematical finance, asset management

Faculty of Management; www.cass.city.ac.uk/facmana

accounting, finance, banking & international insurance, actuarial management/science, banking & international finance, business studies, energy, trade & finance, European business, finance and investment, financial mathematics, investment & financial risk management, management, mathematical trading, quantitative finance, real estate, voluntary sector management, charity accounting/marketing/fundraising, NGO management; BSc(Hons), MBA, MEb, MPhil, MSc, PGDip, PhD

School of Engineering and Mathematical Sciences; www.city.ac.uk/sems

aeronautical engineering, air safety management/ transport engineering/transport operations/management, aircraft maintenance management, analysis and design of structures for hazards, architecture, automotive & motorsport engineering, biomedical engineering, civil engineering/structures, construction management, clinical engineering with healthcare technology management, computer science, computer systems engineering, construction management, electrical/electronic engineering, energy engineering, energy & environmental technology & economics, maritime operations & management, mathematical science with statistics/computer science, mathematics & finance, mechanical & automotive engineering, mechanical engineering, media communication systems, multimedia, power systems and energy management, project management, software engineerings, statistics, surveying, systems & control, telecommunications/& networks; BEng, BSc(Hons), MEng, MMath, MPhil, MSc, PgDip, PhD

Centre for Mathematical Science; www.city.ac.uk/sems/mathematics;

mathematics, finance, mathematical science with statistics/computer science/finance/economics; BSc, MMath, PhD

School of Community and Health Sciences; www.city.ac.uk/communityandhealth

adult nursing, anatomy, applied biological sciences, biochemistry, genetics, microbiology, nutrition, pathophysiology, pharmacology, physiology; BSc, DipHE, PGDip

Interdisciplinary Studies in Professional Practice; www.city.ac.uk/communityandhealth/spp;
interprofessional practice, health management, clinical leadership, disabilty & social inclusion, disabilty studies; MPhil, PhD

Language and Communication; www.city.ac.uk/lcs
human communication, joint professional practice, speech & language therapy; BSc(Hons), MSc

Mental Health and Learning Disabilities; www.city.ac.uk/sonm/nursing/mental-health-nursing
mental health nursing, BSc, DipPG, Dip

Midwifery and Child Health; www.city.ac.uk/sonm/midwifery-child-health
child health/nursing, midwifery; BSc, DipHE, PGDip

Optometry and Visual Science; www.city.ac.uk/optometry
advanced/ophthalmic dispensing, applied vision research, clinical/optometry, visual neuroscience, visual psychophysics & perception; BSc, MSc, FD, PGDip

Public Health, Primary Care and Food Policy; www.city.ac.uk/communityandhealth/phpcfp
education, food policy, practice development, primary care (district nursing, practice nursing), specialist nursing (health visiting, school nursing); MSc, PGDip, Dip

Radiography; www.city.ac.uk/radiography
nuclear medicine technology, radiography, oncology/diagnostic imaging; BSc(Hons), FD, GradDip Cert, MSc, PhD

School of Informatics; www.soi.city.ac.uk

Centre for Health Informatics; www.soi.city.ac.uk/organisation/chi
health informatics; MSc, MPhil, PhD

Centre for Human Computer Interaction Design; www-hcid.soi.city.ac.uk
human-centred systems; MSc, PhD

Centre for Software Reliability; www.csr.city.ac.uk
MSc, MPhil, PhD

Department of Information Science; www.soi.city.ac.uk/business
systems analysis, e-business systems, human-centred systems, information leadership

Department of Computing; www.soi.city.ac.uk
artificial intelligence, business computing systems, computer science, electronic publishing, games technology, health informatics, human computer interaction, leadership in the cultural sector, information systems, library science, music technology, software development, software engineering; BSc(Hons), MA, MScMIl, MInnov

City Law School; www.city.ac.uk/law

law, int banking/commercial/competition law/energy litigation. maritime law, energy law, competition law, criminal litigation, civil litigation dispute resolution, EU commercial law; LlB, LlM, MPhil, PhD, MJur, Grad Dip

School of Social Sciences; www.city.ac.uk/social

Department of Economics; www.city.ac.uk/economics

accountancy, int business economics, economics, economic evaluation in health care, economic regulation and competition, financial economics, health economics; BSc, MSc, PhD

Department of International Politics; www.city.ac.uk/intpol

international politics/& sociology, global political economy; BSC, MA, PhD

Department of Psychology; www.city.ac.uk/psychology

counselling psychology, clinical supervision, health psychology, organizational psychology/organizational behaviour, psychology, psychology and health; BSc, MSC, PhD

Dept of Sociology; www.city.ac.uk/sociology

criminology, criminal justice, global migration, human rights, international communications & development, media studies, international politics, social research methods, sociology, surveillance studies, political communication, transnational media & communication; BEng, BSc(Hons), DPsych, GradDip/Cert, MA, MSc, PhD, ProfDoc

Degrees validated by City University offered at:

GUILDHALL SCHOOL OF MUSIC & DRAMA
www.gsmd.ac.uk

acting, training actors, music, music composition, music therapy, performance, singing, electronic music, technical theatre arts, stage management; BA(Hons), BMus,MA, MMA/DMA, MMP, MMus, MPerf, PGDip

LABAN
www.laban.org

choreography, dance, dance studies/theatre/performance, music, performance,composition, creative practice; PGCE; BA(Hons), MA, MPhil, MSc, PGDipls, PhD

SCHOOL OF PSYCHOTHERAPY & COUNSELLING PSYCHOLOGY AT REGENT'S COLLEGE
www.spc.ac.uk

counselling, psychology, psychotherapy, mediation; DCounsPsy, MA, MPhil/PhD, PGDip

THE NORDOFF-ROBBINS MUSIC THERAPY CENTRE
www.nordoff-robbins.org.uk

music therapy; MMusTherapy, PGDip, MPhil,PhD

COVENTRY UNIVERSITY
www.coventry.ac.uk

Coventry School of Art & Design; www.coventry.ac.uk/artanddesign

Dept of Design & Visual Arts
fashion, art, graphic design; BA(Hons)

Dept of Industrial Design
automotive/& transport design 3D/automotive/bike/boat transport/vehicle des, automotive engineering, engine des, vehicle dynamics/structures, inclusive/industrial product des, consumer product/industrial product/sports/toy, rehabilitation engineering; BA(Hons), BSc(Hons), MA, MDes

Dept of Media & Communication
advertising, culture, health/global journalism, media/production, photography, communication; BA(Hons), MA, PGDip/Cert

Dept of Performing Arts
dance making, e-music, music, music technology/composition, theatre, performance, performing arts innovation & enterprise, professional practice; BA(Hons), BSc(Hons)

School of Lifelong Learning; www.coventry.ac.uk/SOLL
enterprise & global entrepreneurship, leadership career development, management practice, project management, FD, BA(Hons), MA, PGdip/Cert, Msc

Faculty of Business, Environment & Society; www.coventry.ac.uk/bes

Coventry University Business School; www.coventry.ac.uk/bes/cubs
accountancy, advertising, banking & finance, business decision management, biotechnical technology,

economics, engineering/project management, enterprise & entrepreneurship, finance, financial/international business economics, global business, HRM, information technology, international business/law/management/marketing/sport management/tourism management/banking, investment, law, leisure management, logistics, management information systems, management for construction, marketing, risk & disaster/sport business management, sport & exercise therapy, strategic marketing, supply chain management; BSc(Hons), MA, MSc, MBA, LlM, BA(Hons), PGDip/Cert

Coventry University Law School; www.coventry.ac.uk/besl/aw

law and business/international studies, diplomacy law and global change, global development and international law/business law; LlB, LlM, MSc

Department of Geography, Environment & Disaster Management; www.coventry.ac.uk/bes/ged

climate & environmental management, disaster management & emergency planning, reconstruction & development, environmental management, geography, global sustainability, natural hazards, international tourism management, oil & gas management; Prof Dip, PGCert, BA, BSc, MA, MSc, MBA, MPhil, PhD

School of International Studies & Social Science; www.coventry.ac.uk/bes/isss

community & social action, terrorism, international crime & global security, terrorism, international relations, politics, sociology, diplomacy, law & social change, 20th century/history; MA, PhD, MPhil

Faculty of Engineering & Computing; www.coventry.ac.uk/engineeringandcomputing

aerospace systems engineering/technology, architecture, architectural design technology/engineering, automotive engineering/aviation management, avionics technology, building/services engineering/surveying, business information technology, civil engineering, computer hardware & software/science, computers, networking & communications technology, construction/management, creative computing, e-commerce, electrical systems/engineering, electronic engineering, engineering mathematics, ethical hacking & network security, European construction engineering studies/information technology/ business management/logistics, global logistics & management, informatics, internet & enterprise computing, IT, logistics business management, manufacturing systems engineering, mathematical sciences, mathematics & statistics, mechanical engineering/mechatronics, motorsport engineering, multimedia computing, quantity surveying, rehab engineering, software engineering, structural engineering; BEng, BSc(Hons), MEng, MSc, Mphil, Phd, DEng

Faculty of Health & Life Sciences; www.coventry.ac.uk/hls

Dept of Clinical Psychology; www.coventry.ac.uk/HLS/ClinPsych

clinical psychology; DocClinPsych

Dept of Nursing, Midwifery & Health Care

adult/children & young people nursing, cancer care for teenagers & young adults, learning disability/mental health nursing, midwifery, paramedic science, complex life threatening care, emergency care, long term conditions, applied health & social care, assistive technology, operating dept practice; BSc(Hons), DipHE, FdSc, MSc, PGDip/Cert

Dept of Physiotherapy & Dietetics

dietetics, manual therapy, neurological/clinical physiotherapy, sports & exercise nutrition; BSc(Hons), MSc

Dept of Psychology; www.coventry.ac.uk/psychology

applied/occupational/clinical/forensic psychology, crime, health/sport psychology, parapsychology, criminology, reading development, sociology; BSc(Hons), MSc

Dept of Social & Community Studies

applied community & social studies, criminological social sciences, criminology & law/psychology, forensic science, mental health studies, practice education, social & health care management, social work, youth work, criminology and law/sociology/psychology, career guidance

Dept of Occupational Therapy; www.coventry.ac.uk/OT

occupational therapy, neurological occupational OT, assistance techniques; BSc, MSc, Dip

Dept of Biomolecular & Sports Sciences; www.coventry.ac.uk/HLS/BSS;

analytical chemistry/biological/forensic sciences, biomedical science/technology, environmental health, forensic & investigative science, human bioscience, medical and pharmacological science, nutrition &

food science, sport, exercise, nutrition & health, sports therapy, biomolecular & sport /exercise science; HND, BSc(Hons), PGCert/Dip.MSc, PhD

CRANFIELD UNIVERSITY
www.cranfield.ac.uk

School of Applied Sciences; www.cranfield.ac.uk/sas

manufacturing, materials & nanotechnology, motorsport, business & IS, economics and management, engineering,environment & water, offshore, welding; EngD, MPhil, MSc, MTech, PhD

Cranfield Defence and Security; www.cranfield.ac.uk/cds

defence acquisition/leadership/sensors & data fusion/ simulation & modelling and logistics, explosives ordnance, forensics, global security, guided weapons, information operations/management, international defence/marketing/ security, military aerospace/electronic systems/OR/vehicle technology, project management, resilience, scientific computation, security sector management; EngD, MSc, PGDip/Cert, PhD

School of Engineering; www.cranfield.ac.uk/soe

aerospace, air transport, astronautics, applied mechanics, automotive engineering, computation, engineering, renewable/energy, carbon capture & transport, human factors, safety, power and propulsion, process & systems engineering; EngD, MSc, PhD

Cranfield Health; www.cranfield.ac.uk/health

bioinformatics, analytical biotechnology, clinical research/information, nanomedicine, translational medicine, clinical research, environment & health, food chain systems, molecular medicine, toxicology & epidemiology; DM, MSc

Cranfield School of Management; www.cranfield.ac.uk/som

business performance, complex systems, economics, enterprise, entrepreneurship, finance & management, information systems, international HRM, managing organizational performance, logistics & supply chain management, management development, management knowledge and strategic change, marketing & sales management, operations management, organization studies, programme & project management, strategic marketing; DBA, MBA, MSc, PhD

UNIVERSITY OF CUMBRIA
www.cumbria.ac.uk

Faculty of the Arts, Business & Science; www.cumbria.ac.uk/about us/faculties/ ABS

Arts, Media, Performance & Humanities; drama, religious studies, creative writing, English, TESOL, fine art, graphic design, photography, performing arts

Business: applied computing, business management, management/studies sustainability, leadership, sustainability,

Science & Natural Resources: forestry, wildlife conservation, outdoor studies, sustainable environment; BA(Hons), BEng(Hons)

Faculty of Education;cumbria.ac.uk/ about us/faculties/FacultyEducation

early years/QTS, primary ed/inclusive ed/special needs, secondary ed/QTS/mathematics/PE, learning & teaching in HE, TESOL, PGCE, primary ed/QTS, secondary/QTS in range of subjects; BA(Hons), MA,PGDip/Cert, PGCE

Facultyof Health & Wellbeing; www.cumbria.ac.uk/about us/ facultyofHealthWellbeing;

health care practice, person-centred therapy/counselling, nursing, trauma & loss, psychotherapy, care & management, mentally disordered offenders, autistics, addictive behaviour, adv nurse practiononer, district/practice nursing, primary health care, health visiting, school nursing, sexual health, non-medical prescribing, occupational health, teaching in HE, child & family studies, midwifery, children's & young people's mental health, nursing (all branches), physiotherapy, occupational therapy, stroke rehabilitation, social work, coaching & sport development, sport & exercise science/therapy, PE; BA, BSc(Hons), GradDip, MA, MSc, PgC,UC, UAD, DipHE, FdA, MPhil, PhD

DE MONTFORD UNIVERSITY
www.dmu.ac.uk

Faculty of Art and Design; www.dmu.ac.uk/faculties/art_and_design

architecture/design, design/crafts/products, fashion/design/fabrics, fine art, graphic/footwear/furniture/game art/interior design, photography, entrepreneurship, innovation, art & design; BA(Hons), BArch(-Hons), BSc(BAHons), DipHE, MA, MSc, MPhil, PGDip, PhD

Faculty of Business and Law; www.dmu.ac.uk/faculties/business_and_law

business man/studies, accounting,criminal justice, economics, finance, HRM, marketing, goverment, media, retail, business/employment/environment/foodmedical/sports law; BA(Hons), BSc(Hons), DipHE, GDL/CPE, HND, LlBHons, LLM, LPC, MA, MPhil, MBA, MSc, PGDip/Cert, PhD

Faculty of Health and Life Sciences; www.dmu.ac.uk/faculties/his

audiology, biomedical/medical science, clinical technology, health sudies, children/families, nursing, midwifery, pharmacy/biotechnology, criminology, dental tech, enviroment, forensic science, health/psychology, social work, youth work; BA(Hons), BSc(Hons), DipHE, FdA, MA, MPharm(Hons), MSc, PGDip, RSHDip

Faculty of Humanities; www.dmu.ac.uk/faculties/humanities

creative writing, arts & festival management, film studies, PR, TV writing, dance, drama, education, English, history, international relations, journalism, media studies, music; BA(Hons), MA, PGDip

Faculty of Technology (Computer Science and Engineering); www.dmu.ac.uk/faculties/technology

audio recording/technology, business information systs, computers/security/science/games/business, green energy, intelligent systems, microelectronics, creative sound technology, digital video, electronic/mechanical engineering, engineering design, forensic computing, info/comm tech, mechatronics, media production/technology, multimedia computing, music technology, radio prodn, software engineering, climate change; BEng, BSc(Hons), HND, MPhil, MSc, PGDip, PhD

UNIVERSITY OF DERBY
www.derby.ac.uk

Faculty of Art, Design, and Technology; www.derby.ac.uk/adt

Art & Design: applied art & design, fine art, film & TV prodn, photography, textiles, visual communication,graphic design, illustration; Humanities: American studies, creative writing, English, film & TV, history, media; Technology: architecture & built environment, electrical/electronic, mechanical/civil/manufacturing engineering, construction, product desuign, music & media technology; BA(Hons), MDes, PhD, Univ Cert/Dip, BEng, FdSc/Eng

Faculty of Business, Computing and Law; www.derby.ac.uk/bcl

Derbyshire Business School

accountancy & finance, business, coaching, enterprise, HRM, leadership, marketing, purchasing & supply, management

Law & Criminology

law, business, international/social & public/commercial/corporate & financial/transnational law; criminology, crime & justice, legal practice

Computing & Mathematics
computing forensics/games/networks, security, information science/technology, mobile device systems, graphics prodn, games, mathematics/studies; BA(Hons), BSc(Hons), FD, LlBHons, LlM, MA, MPhil/PhD, MSc, PGDip/Cert

Faculty of Education, Health and Sciences; www.derby.ac.uk/ehs

Education & Social Sciences
education studies, teacher education, early childhood/years, primary ed, lifelong learning, children's & young peoples' services, pop culture & media, sociology, social studies

Health & Social Care
nursing studies (adult/mental health/public health), community specialist practitioner, long term conditions, occupational therapy, health care practice, radiography

Science
biological science, geography,geology, environmental science, forensic science, psychology, sport & exercise science; Adv Dip, BA(Hons), BEd, BSc(Hons), EdD, FdA, HNC/HND, jtHons, MA, MSC, PGCert/Dip, PGCE, PhD, Univ Cert/Dip

DONCASTER BUSINESS SCHOOL
www.don.ac.uk/dbs

business administration/management, strategic personnel & management, leadership & management, HRM, marketing; CIM, CIPD, CIPS, HND/BA(Hons), MBA, MSc

UNIVERSITY OF DUNDEE
www.dundee.ac.uk

College of Art, Sciences and Engineering; www.dundee.ac.uk/case

School of Architecture; www.dundee.ac.uk/architecture
architecture, advanced sustainability of the built environment, architectural humanities/technology & the environment/communications

School of Computing; www.computing.dundee.ac.uk
applied computing, artificial intelligence, business intelligence, computing/science, design ethnography, digital internet design, information technology, interactive media design, vision & imaging

Duncan of Jordanstone College of Art and Design; www.dundee.ac.uk/djcad
animation, art & digital film, art philosophy, design – graphics/interior & environmental/interactive media/ jewellery and metal/textiles, digital interaction, exhibitions, fine art, illustration, media arts & imaging, forensic/media/medical art

School of Engineering, Physics and Mathematics; www.dundee.ac.uk/eps
sustainability of built environment, biomedical engineering, civil engineering, concrete engineering & environmental management, electronic engineering, physics, renewable energy, display technology, electronic circuit design & manufacture, earthquake and offshore engineering, mathematics, mechanical engineering & mechatronics, product design, renewable energy & environmental modelling, structural engineering; BEng, BSc, CertHE, DipHE, MArch, MEng, MA, MSc, MSci, PhD,PGDE,PGDip

College of Arts and Social Sciences; www.dundee.ac.uk/artsoc

School of Business www.dundee.ac.uk/ business
accountancy, finance, business management, international finance/business, economics, corporate governance, HRM, marketing, management, strategic financial management Islamic accounting & finance, strategic financial management

Continuing Education; www.dundee.ac.uk/conted;

CPD, communication & languages, community outreach; MA

School of Education, Social Work and Community Education; www.dundee.ac.uk/eswce

community learning & development, education, PGCE primary/secondary (chemistry, physics, maths), CPD, childhood studies, teaching qual (FE/HE), social work, childhood studies, children/adult care & protection

Interdisciplinary Disability Research Institute (IDRIS)

Institute for Research and Innovation in Social Services (IRISS)

School of Humanities; www.dundee.ac.uk/humanities

Centre for Archive and Information Studies; www.dundee.ac.uk/cias

archives & records management/information rights, family & local history digital appl

Communication and Language Studies; www.dundee.ac.uk/language studies;

French, German, Spanish

English; www.dundee.ac.uk/English

English, English and film studies, women, culture & society, creative writing, philosophy & literature

European Studies

History; www.dundee.ac.uk/history

early America, European history, Greater Britain in the twentieth century, history, Scottish/church history, urban and cultural history, church history

Philosophy; www.dundee.ac.uk/philosophy

European philosophy, philosophy/and literaure, continental/recent analytic philosophy, history of philosophy, philosophy of science

Politics; www.dundee.ac.uk/politics

European politics, international relations & politics/geoplitics, international politics & security

Women, Culture & Society

School of Law; www.dundee.ac.uk/law

commercial & international commercial law, company law & corporate/international criminal justice/human rights, private/ international law, public law, Scottish law, comparative law

Graduate School of Natural Resources Law, Policy and Management; www.dundee.ac.uk/postgradschool

Centre for Energy, Petroleum and Mineral Law and Policy

energy/mineral/petroleum/environmental law & policy, natural resources law & policy, international oil & gas management

UNESCO Centre for Water Law, Policy and Science

water law, water governance & conflict resolution, water resources management & law

School of Psychology; www.dundee.ac.uk/psychology

psychology, psychological research methods, visual/cognition, eye movements, language & communication

School of Social and Environmental Sciences; www.dundee.ac.uk/social science

Environmental Science: environmental science/with geography

Geography: applied population & welfare geography, environmental remote sensing, social research methods, sustainable catchment management

Town & Regional Planning: environmental sustainability, geography & planning, community regeneration, spatial planning, European/international urban conservation; MA(Hons), MLitt/MSc, MSc, LlB, LlM, PhD, PGCert, BAcc, BIAcc, BIFin, BSc(Hons)

College of Life Sciences; www.lifesci.dundee.ac.uk

anatomical sciences, biochemistry, biomedical/biological sciences, drug discovery, cancer biology, crops for the future, drug design & discovery, environmental biology/science, forensic anthropology/art, human anatomy, medical art, microbiology, molecular biology, molecular genetics, neuroscience, pharmacology, physiological sciences, sports biomedicine; BSc(Hons), MRes, MSc, PhD

School of Research

Centre for Anatomy and Human Identification; www.lifesci.dundee.ac.uk/CAHId

Biological Services (CLS); www.lifesci.dundee.ac.uk/biolservices

Div of Cell and Developmental Biology; www.lifesci.dundee.ac.uk/cdb

Div of Cell Biology and Signalling; www.lifesci.dundee.ac.uk/cbi

CRUK Nucleic Acid Structure Research Group; www.lifesci.dundee.ac.uk/nasg

gene regulation & expression

Molecular Microbiology; www.lifesci.dundee.ac.uk/mmb

Div of Molecular Medicine; www.lifesci.dundee.ac.uk/mm

Div of Molecular Physiology; www.lifesci.dundee.ac.uk/mp

Div of Plant Sciences; www.lifesci.dundee.ac.uk/pl

Div of Signal Transduction Therapy; www.lifesci.dundee.ac.uk/dstt

TMRC Research Lab

BSc(Hons), MRes, MSc, PhD

College of Medicine, Dentistry and Nursing; www.dundee.ac.uk/cmdn

School of Dentistry; www.dundee.ac.uk/dentalschool

oral health science, prosthodontics, dental surgery, cancer biology

School of Nursing and Midwifery; www.dundee.ac.uk/medden

advanced practice, nursing, palliative care, midwifery, infection prevention & control, health studies, community health nursing, mental health, physiotherapeutics, clinical assessment governance

School of Medicine; www.dundee.ac.uk/medschool

anaesthesia, cardiovascular lung biology cancer, diabetes, health skills, immunology, medical science, medicine, molecular medicine, neuroscience, oncology, orthopaedic & trauma surgery, orthopaedic and rehabilitation technology, palliative care, primary care, psychiatry cognitive behavioural psychotherapy, psychological therapy in primary care, public heath, surgery; BDS, BHealthN, BM, BMSc, BN, BSc, DDSc, DipCert, MA, MBChB, MChOrth, MD, MDSc, MFM, MMAS, MMSc, MNurs, MPH, MPhil, MSc, MSSc

Biomedical Research Institute

Div of Clinical & Population Sciences & Education

Centre for Primary Care & Population Research

Dental Health Services & Research Unit (DHSRU)

Institute for Health Skills & Education

Dundee Epidemiology and Biostatistics Unit

Institute of Cardiovascular Research Centre for Neuroscience

Centre for Oncology & Molecular Medicine

DURHAM UNIVERSITY
www.dur.ac.uk

Faculty of Arts and Humanities; www.dur.ac.uk /arts.humanities

Dept of Classics and Ancient History; www.dur.ac.uk/classics

ancient history & archaeology, ancient history, classics, ancient, medieval & modern history, ancient epic/histiography/philosophy, classical tradition, Greece, Rome & the Near East

Dept of English Studies; www.dur.ac.uk/english.studies

English literature & philosophy/history, medieval & renaissance/romantic and Victorian literary studies, poetry, 20th-century literary studies

Dept of History; www.dur.ac.uk/history

history, medieval history, early modern/modern history, research methods (economic and social history)

Dept of Music; www.dur.ac.uk/music

music (ethnomusicology/composition/electroacoustic studies/performance), musicology

School of Modern Languages and Cultures; www.dur.ac.uk/mlac

Arabic, culture & medieval and renaissance studies, French, German, Hispanic studies, Italian, Russian, Chinese, the photographic image, 17th century studies, translation studies, culture & difference

Dept of Philosophy; www.dur.ac.uk/philosophy

history & philosophy of science & medicine, philosophy/ politics & economics (PPE), psychology, metaphysics, ethics, Buddhism, aesthetics

Dept of Theology and Religion; www.dur.ac.uk/theology.religion

biblical studies, Christian theology (Anglican, Catholic studies), religion and society, theology & philosophy/religion/European studies; BA(Hons), GDip, MA, MLitt, MMus, MTh, PhD

Faculty of Science; www.dur.ac.uk/science.faculty

School of Biological and Biomedical Sciences; www.dur.ac.uk/biological.sciences

biology, biomedical sciences, cell biology, ecology, evolution & behaviour, molecular biology & biochemistry, natural sciences, zoology

Dept of Chemistry; www.dur.ac.uk/chemistry

chemistry, biochemistry, materials/adv computational, catalysis, organometallic, inorganic materials, optical & molecular chemistry, physical/organic/polymer chemistry, structural chemistry

Dept of Engineering and Computer Science; www.dur.ac.uk/ecs/computing.science

advanced software engineering, aeronautics, civil/electronic/mechanical/electrical engineering, communications/computer engineering, computer science, design, general engineering, internet and distributed systems technologies, internet systems and e-business, new and renewable energy, design & operations engineering

Dept of Earth Sciences; www.dur.ac.uk/earth.sciences

earth/environmental, geology, geophysics, geosciences

Dept of Mathematical Sciences; www.dur.ac.uk/mathematical.sciences

mathematics, biomathematics, elementary particle theory, mathematical sciences

Dept of Physics; www.dur.ac.uk/physics

physics, astronomy, theoretical physics, particle theory

Dept of Psychology; www.dur.ac.uk/psychology

cognitive neuroscience/applied/developmental psychopathology, psychology; BA(Hons), BEng, BSc(Hons), MA, MChem, MEng, MMath, MPhil, MPhys, MSc, MSci, PhD

Faculty of Social Science and Health; www.dur.ac.uk /science.health

School of Applied Social Sciences; www.dur.ac.uk/sass

crime, children & young persons, criminology & criminal justice, social policy, social work, society & politics, social research, managing community practice, community and youth work, sociology, sport

Dept of Anthropology; www.dur.ac.uk/anthropology

anthropology, development/evolutionary/biologicall anthropology, health and human sciences, medical anthropology, wellbeing, culture & development, sociocultural anthropology

Dept of Archaeology; www.dur.ac.uk/archaeology

archaeology/& ancient civilizations, conservation of archaeological & museum objects, museums & artefacts, palaeopathology

Durham Business School; www.dur.ac.uk/dbs

accounting & finance, business/finance, corporate & international finance, economics, entrepreneurship, financial management, HRM and organizational behaviour, international banking/money, investment, marketing psychology, public management, strategy and organization, strategic marketing

School of Education; www.dur.ac.uk/education

educational assessment, education studies, initial training PGCE primary/secondary, practice of education, primary education

Dept of Geography; www.dur.ac.uk/geo

risk & environmental hazards, geography, contemporary human geography

School of Government and International Affairs; www.dur.ac.uk/sgia

Arab world studies, defence, development, diplomacy, conflict prevention & security, international relations/studies, Islamic finance, politics; BA(Hons), DBA, EdD, MA, MA(Ed), MBA, MAnth, MSc, MScW, PGCE, PGCert/Dip, PhD

Durham Law School; www.dur.ac.uk
European trade/international trade & commercial law, law, society & law, legal studies

School of Medicine & Health; www.dur.ac.uk/school.health
clinical management, health research methods, history & philosophy of science, interdisciplinary mental health, medical education, public policy and health; BA(Hons), BA(Ed), BSc(Ed), BSc(Hons), Cert Leg Stud, LlB, LlM, MA, MBBS, MPhil, PGCert, PGCert/Dip, PGCE, PhD, MA

Degrees validated by Durham University offered at:

CRAMNER HALL, ST JOHN'S COLLEGE
www.cranmerhall.com

theology and ministry; BA, MA, diploma/ certificate

NEW COLLEGE DURHAM
www.newdur.ac.uk

accounting, administration, business management, graphic design, information technology management, complementary healthcare, counselling, WESOL & modern languages, podiatry, social work, sport & exercise,BA(Hons), BSc(Hons), FD, HND, HNC

ROYAL ACADEMY OF DANCE
www.rad.org.uk

ballet education, ballet teaching studies, Benesh, dance education, movement notation; BA(Hons), Dip/CertHE, MTeach(Dance), licenciate

USHAW COLLEGE
www.ushaw.ac.uk

theology & ministry; BA, Certs, Dipls, MA, PGCert/Dip

UNIVERSITY OF EAST ANGLIA
www.uea.ac.uk

Faculty of Arts and Humanities; www.uea.ac.uk/hum

American Studies; www.uea.ac.uk/ams
American studies/literature, & American history/English history/politics, & creative writing

School of World Art & Museum Studies; www.uea.ac.uk/art
archaeology, anthropology & art history, gallery & musem studies, the Americas, ancient & African art, art history, material & visual culture, contemporary art, cultural heritage & museology

School of Film & Television Studies; www.uea.ac.uk/ftv
film & TV studies, film/English/American studies, media studies

School of History; www.uea.ac.uk/his
modern history, history, history and politics/languages, landscape/medieval/mod European history

School of Literature and Creative Writing; www.uea.ac.uk/lit
creative writing, drama, scriptwriting & performance, English & American literature, critical writing, culture & modernity, life writing, literature & history

School of Language and Communication Studies; www.uea.ac.uk/lcs
cross-cultural communication/business & management, language studies, international development, film & TV, French, media, Spanish, Japanese, applied translation studies, language/conflict & intercultural communication

School of Music; www.uea.ac.uk/mus
music, music & technology, creative entrepreneurship, performance, conducting

School of Political, Social and International Studies; www.uea.ac.uk/psi
culture, literature, broadcast journalism, European studies/politics, international relations/& politics, philosophy/& politics, international/public policy & management, social & political theory, society, culture & media; BA(Hons), MA, MMus, MPhil, PGDip, PhD, MRes

Faculty of Health; www.uea.ac.uk/foh

School of Allied Health Professions; www.uea.ac.uk/ahp
occupational therapy, physiotherapy, speech & language therapy, clinical education, muscoskeletal research & practice, stroke recovery

School of Medicine, Health Policy & Practice; www.uea.ac.uk/med
medicine, surgery, clinical psychology, health economics/ research. CPD

School of Nursing and Midwifery; www.uea.ac.uk/nam
acute, critical and emergency practice, midwifery practice, nursing (adult, children's, mental health, learning disabilities), nurse practitioner (advanced practice), policy, planning & leadership, operating department practice, HE community healthcare

Institute of Biomedical and Clinical Science; www.uea.ac.uk/foh/research/Institutes/biomed
infection & immunity, nutrition & healthy ageing

Health and Social Science Research Institute; www.uea.ac.uk/foh/research/Institutes/hss
health economics, medical statistics, mental health & psychological sciences, public health & health services research, stroke & rehabilitation, shared decision making

Education in Health Institute; www.uea.ac.uk/foh/research/Institutes/educationinhealth
medical education, interprofessional education, educational theory; BA(Hons), BSc(Hons), ClinPsyD, DipHE, Foundation degrees, MBBS, MClinEd, MD, MHeaRes, MPhil, MSc, PGDip, PhD

Faculty of Science; www.uea.ac.uk/sci

School of Biological Science; www.uea.ac.uk/bio
applied ecology, conservation, biochemistry, ecology, biological sciences, biomedicine, cell biology, microbiology, plant science, biotechnology for a sustainable future, genetics & crop improvement, molecular biology/biochemistry/medicine

School of Chemical Science; www.uea.ac.uk/che
chemistry, adv organic chemistry, analytical science, biological and medicinal chemistry, chemical physics, forensic chemistry/science, pharmaceutical chemistry, archeometry & provenancing

School of Computing Science; www.uea.ac.uk/cmp
actuarial sciences, applied computing science, information systems, business statistics, computational biology, computer graphics/systems engineering/science, computing for business, games development, geoinformatics, imaging & multimedia, knowledge discovery & data mining, software engineering

School of Environmental Sciences; www.uea.ac.uk/env
applied ecology, environmental social science, atmospheric sciences, climate change/science, environmental assessment & management/chemistry/earth sciences, environmental geography & international

development/ geophysics, geophysical sciences, meteorology & oceanography

School of Natural Science; www. uea.ac.uk/ sci/natsci; natural science

School of Mathematics; www.uea.ac.uk/ mth
mathematics, mathematics with economics/statistics/ computing, maths education, energy & enviromental management

School of Pharmacy; www.uea.ac.uk/pha
general pharmacy practice, industrial/pharmacy; BSc(Hons), GradDip, MPhil, MSc, MSci, PGDip, PhD

Faculty of Social Sciences; www.uea.ac.uk/ssf

School of Economics; www.uea.ac.uk/eco
economics & accountancy, business economics, business finance & economics, economics with economic psychology, environmental/experimental/industrial economics, international business finance, media economics, politics, international relations

School of Education and Lifelong Learning; www.uea.ac.uk/edu
adult literacy, advanced educational practice, counselling/ focusing-orientated psychotherapy, early years, education studies, lifelong learning & development:mathematics education, PGCE primary / secondary teacher training, teacher education PE & sport, professional studies

School of International Development; www.uea.ac.uk/dev
international development with economics/overseas experience/sociology/anthropology/environment & society, agriculture & rural development, development economics/studies, education & development, conflict, governance/gender analysis/globalization/ media/climate change/environment/water security & international development, international relations & development studies

Norwich Law School; www.uea.ac.uk/law
law, employment law, European legal systems, information, technology & intellectual property law, international commercial & business law/ competition law & policy/trade law, law with American law/ French law & language, legal studies, media law, policy and practice

Norwich Business School; www.uea.ac.uk/ nbs
accounting & finance/management, brand leadership, international business management/accounting & financial/HRM, management consultancy, marketing, strategic information systems, strategic supply chain management, strategic carbon management

School of Social Work and Psychology; www.uea.ac.uk/swp
child & family research/ psychology, psychology, social work; BA(Hons), BSc(Hons), CPE/Dip, DEd, GradDip, LlBHons, LLM, MA, MA/DipSW, MBA, MPhil, MRes, MSc, MScEd, PGCert, PGDip, PhD

Degrees validated by University of East Anglia offered by:

CITY COLLEGE NORWICH
www.ccn.ac.uk

business computing, business management, child care & education, culinary arts, early childhood studies, engineering (civil, electrical, electronic, mechanical), English, financial services/retail: insurance, health & exercise, health studies, hospitality management/tourism, interactive media, journalism, leisure & events management, licensed retail, psychology, public sector management, social work, teaching assistants, travel & tourism, music marketing; BA(Hons), BSc(Hons), FdA, FdSc, HNC, HND

OTLEY COLLEGE
www.otleycollege.ac.uk

agriculture, animal studies, arboriculture, business solutions, conservation, construction, engineering, fishery studies, florestry, food skills, horse studies, horticulture, land & countryside, leisure learning, sport & outdoors

UNIVERSITY OF EAST LONDON
www.uel.ac.uk

School of Architecture and the Visual Arts; www.uel.ac.uk/ava

animation, architecture, contemporary visual media, design, digital/graphic arts, illustration, fashion, moving images, fine art, photography, printmaking, textiles, landscape architecture, sustainability; BA(Hons), BSc/BA, FdA, GradCert, MA, MArch, MPhil, MSc, PGC, PhD, ProfDoc

School of Combined Honours; www.uel.ac.uk/combined

range of subjects for which combined honours courses are conducted

School of Computing, Information Technology and Engineering; www.uel.ac.uk/cite

bus inf systems/technology, civil engineering, computing, construction management, computer games/networks, systems eng/games/networks/technology, computing, digital media, electronics, electrical & electronic eng, information security systems, IT, mathematics, mobile computing/communications multimedia, music tech, product design, software eng, surveying, & mapping sci, surveying; BA/BEng(Hons), BA/BSc, BSc(Hons), MPhil, MSc, PhD, ProfDoc

Royal Docks Business School; www.uel.ac.uk/business

accounting, investment/risk management, money/banking, finance, project management, retail, brand management, business admin/economics/investment/management, marketing, music industry, sports/tourism management; BA(Hons), DBA, HND, LlB, MA, MBA, MPhil, MSc, PGDip, PhD

Cass School of Education; www.uel.ac.uk/education

early childhood, secondary/primary education, childcare, internation education, English language, playwork, teacher training, teaching assistants, youth studies & community work; BA(Hons), EdD, FdA, MA, PGCE, PGDip, ProfDoc, UnivCert

School of Health and Bioscience; www.uel.ac.uk/hal

bioscience, biochemistry, biomedical science, biotechnology, conservation & ecology, health studies/science, medical/microbiology, paediatrics, toxology, public health, pharmacology, physiotherapy, podiatory, sports science; BA(Hons), BSc(Hons), FdSc, MPhil, MSc, PGCert, PhD, ProfDoc

School of Law; www.uel.ac.uk/law

law, criminal justice, criminology, human rights, international law & finance/world economy, Islamic & Middle East law, refugee studies, terrorism; BA(Hons), BSc(Hons), LlB, LlM, MSc, PostGDip

School of Psychology; www.uel.ac.uk/psychology

counselling, mentoring, pysychology, critical/developmental/forensic/educational/child psychology, psychosocial studies; BA(Hons), BSc(Hons), ClinPSyD, FdA, GradDip/Cert, MA, MSc, ProfDoc, UnivCert

School of Humanities and Social Sciences; www.uel.ac.uk/hsocialsciences

advertising, anthroplogy, communication studies, computer games, cultural studies, dance, information technology, film/video studies, Eng literature, history, refugee studies, international development/politics/relations, journalism, media studies, music culture, social policy, social work/enterprise, sociology, theatre studies, voluntary sector studies; BA(Hons), BMus, BSc(Hons), FdA, GradDip/Cert, MA, ProfDoc, UnivCert

THE UNIVERSITY OF EDINBURGH
www.ed.ac.uk

College of Humanities and Social Sciences; www.hss.ed.ac.uk

School of Arts, Culture and the Environment; www.ed.ac.uk/schools-departments/arts-culture-environment
architecture, sustainable design, urban design, project management, design & digital media, digital composition, the city, landscape architecture, fine art, history of art/middle ages, modern art, Scottish art, music, performance, music technology, digital/composition, musicology, sound design, sustainable/ urban design, composition for screen, cultural studies

The Business School; www.business-school.ed.ac.uk
analysis, accounting & finance, business studies, carbon finance/management, economics,international business & emerging markets, management science, marketing

School of Divinity; www.div.ed.ac.uk
divinity, biblical studies, ethics, ministry, philosophy & theology, religious studies, theology, world Christianity

School of Economics; www.ed.ac.uk/schools-departments/economics
asset pricing, corporate finance, economics, international money & finance, economics analysis, econometrics/finance, macroeconomics, microeconomics

School of Health in Social Science; www.ed.ac.uk/schools-departments/health
advancing nursing practice, applied psychology for children & young people, clinical psychology, counselling, nursing studies, psychotherapy, social science in health

School of History, Classics and Archaeology; www.shc.ed.ac.uk
American history, diaspora & migration studies, ancient philosophy, medieval history, intellectual history, Scottish history, modern British & Irish history, social & cultural history, classical art & archaeology,Celtic, Scottish studies, classics, gender history, archaeology (European/forensic/Mediterranean), osteoarchaeology, social anthropology

School of Law; www.law.ed.ac.uk
law (English, family, criminal, European, public health, international private, competition/innovation, international economic), trusts, international tax law, criminal & global crime

School of Literatures, Languages and Cultures; www.ed.ac.uk/schools-departments/literatures-languages-cultures
Asian studies, Celtic & Scottish studies, comparative literature, European languages & cultures, English literature, European theatre, film studies, Islamic & Middle Eastern studies, literature & transatlanticism, medieval studies, translation, word & music studies

Moray House School of Education; www.education.ed.ac.uk
childhood practice, applied sport science, community education, dance science & education, e-learning, leadership, headship, inclusive & special education, language – theory, practice & literacy, language teaching, management of training & development, outdoor education, performance psychology, PE, primary education, sport & recreation management, TESOL, university teaching

School of Philosophy, Psychology and Language Science; www.ppls.ed.ac.uk
ancient philosophy, artificial intelligence, psychology, cognitive science, English language, epistemology, ethics, history & theory of psychology, human cognitive neuropsychology, linguistics, philosophy, aesthetics, knowledge, Wittgenstein, epistemology, logistics, Hellenistic philosophy, metaethics, psychology/ of individual differences, mind & language/ cognition

School of Social & Political Science; www.sps.ed.ac.uk
politics & international relations, science, innovation & technology, social anthropology, social policy, social work, sociology; BA(Arch), BD, BEd(Hons), BMedSci, BMus, BN, BSc(Hons), DD, DLitt, DMus, DClinPyschol, EdD, LlM, MA, MA(Hons), MBA, MLA, MPhil/PhD, MSc, MTeach, MTh/Sc, PGDip-Cert, PGDE

College of Medicine and Veterinary Medicine; www.ed.ac.uk/schools-departments/medicine-vet-medicine

animal biology, biomedical & clinical sciences, clinical skills, dental primary care, diagnosis, medicine, oral health science/surgery, orthodontics, paediatric dentistry, pharmacology, therapeutics, posthodontics, public health, pyschological medicine, surgery, transfusion, transplantation and tissue banking, veterinary medicine & surgery

School of Clinical Sciences and Community Health; www.ed.ac.uk/schools-departments/clinical-sciences

clinical & surgical sciences, community health sciences, medical and radiological sciences, reproductive and developmental sciences, postgraduate dental education

School of Biomedical Sciences; www.ed.ac.uk/schools-departments/biomedical-sciences

biomedical sciences, translational medicine, international animal health, biodiversity, wildlife, global health

School of Molecular and Clinical Medicine; www.mcm.ed.ac.uk

clinical brain services, neuroimaging, molecular medicine, transfusion, transplantation & tissue banking

The Royal (Dick) School of Veterinary Studies; www.ed.ac.uk/schools-departments/vet

veterinary medicine & surgery, population medicine & veterinary public health; BSc(Hons), MBChB, MSC, BVMS, DipCert, MPhil,PhD

College of Science and Engineering; www.scieng.ed.ac.uk

School of Biological Sciences; www.ed.ac.uk/schools-departments/biology

biochemistry, biodiversity & taxonomy of plants, bioinformatics, biological sciences, biotechnology, cell biology, developmental/evolutionary/medical/molecular/reproductive biology, drug discovery & translational biology, ecology, plant science, pharmacology, zoology, quantitative genetics & genome analysis, molecular genetics, physiology, neuroscience

School of Chemistry; www.chem.ed.ac.uk

chemical physics, chemistry/with environmental & sustainable chemistry/materials chemistry, medicinal & biological chemistry

School of Engineering; www.see.ed.ac.uk

Chemical Engineering with environmental engineering/management, materials & processes, energy systems

Civil and Environmental Engineering: civil engineering, civil and environmental engineering/construction management, structural engineering with architecture, structural & fire safety engineering

Electronics and Electrical Engineering: electrical engineering, renewable energy, electronics, computer science, bioelectronics, communications, software engineering, mechanical engineering, energy systems, integrated micro and nano systems, digital communications

Mechanical Engineering: advanced materials applications, electrical & mechanical engineering, fluid and particle dynamics, manufacturing & process optimization, materials & processes, mechanical engineering with management/structural mechanics

Institute for Energy Systems: environmental mitigation, energy delivery, renewable energy, restructuring and regulation

General Engineering

School for Informatics; www.inf.ed.ac.uk

informatics, artificial intelligence, cognitive science, computational linguistics/physics, computer science, software engineering/computer science,analytical & scientific databases, bioinformatics, systems & synthetic biology, informatics & economics, intelligent robotics, knowledge management, representation & reasoning, learning from data, music informatics, natural languages & language engineering, neural computation & neuroinformatics

School of Geosciences; www.geos.ed.ac.uk

Ecological Sciences,Geography,Earth Science: geography, physical geography, geology, geophysics, archaeology, GIS, meteorology, conservation & eco-management, environmental studies, earth sciences, ecolological economics, forestry, ecology & environmental science, integrated resource management, environment & development, carbon capture & storage/management

School of Mathematics; www.maths.ed.ac.uk

pure/applied mathematics, financial mathematics/& optimization, mathematical physics, mathematics &

statistics/management/physics/artificial intelligence/ computer science/philosophy operational research,-geometry & topology

School of Physics and Astronomy; www.ph.ed.ac.uk

astrophysics, chemical physics, computational physics, distributed scientific computing, geophysics, physics and computer sci/mathematics/meteorology/ music, high performance computing; BEng, BSc, MChem, MChemPhys, MEarthSci, MEng, MInf, MPhil, MPhys, MS, MSc, MSci, PGDip, PhD

EDINBURGH NAPIER UNIVERSITY
www.napier.ac.uk

The Business School; www.napier.ac.uk/business-school

Accounting, Economics and Statistics

accounting, corporate strategy/finance, economics, entrepreneurship, finance, financial services, HRM, international finance, investment promotion & economic development, management, law, marketing management, wealth management; BA(Hons), DBA, MPhil, MSc, PhD

Management & Law

business management, business studies, finance, coaching, entrepreneurship, health & social welfare law, HRM, international business management/ studies, managerial leadership, marketing; BA/ BA(Hons), BMA, LlB, LlM, MBA, MSc

Marketing Tourism and Languages

hospitality/marketing/ management, festival & event management, entrepreneurship/language/HRM, heritage and cultural tourism management, consumer studies, intercultural business communication/ with TESOL, international business languages/marketing, languages, marketing management, tourism/and airline management; BA, BA(Hons), MSc

Faculty of Engineering, Computing and Creative Industries; www.napier.ac.uk/fecci

School of Computing

advanced networking, applied informatics, business information systems/technology, computer networks & distributed systems, computing security & forensics, computing, digital media/networking, embedded computer systems, interactive media design/systems/entertainment & games development, mobile/network computing, web-based systems, security & digital forensics, software engineering, web technology; BEng, BSc, MPhil, MSc, PhD

Arts & Creative Industries

adv film practice, acting, advertising, PR, creative advertising/writing, communication, design & digital arts, English, film, graphic design, interaction/interdisciplinary design, interior architecture, journalism, music (pop), photography, product design, publishing, screen project development, screenwriting, sound production, TV; BA/BA(Hons), BDes, BDes(Hons), BMus, BMus(Hons), MDes, MFA, MSc, PGCert/Dip

Engineering & the Built Environment

architectural technology & building performance, automation & control, building surveying, built environment, timber engineering, civil engineering, communication engineering, computer-aided design, construction & project management, electronic/computer/electrical engineering, digital systems, energy & environmental engineering, engineering design, environmental sustainability, materials engineering, mechanical engineering, mechatronics, polymer engineering, product design engineering/ manufacture, project management, property & construction management, property development & valuation, investment, quantity surveying, renewable energy, safety & environmental management, sports technology, structural engineering, timber industry management, transport management/planning and engineering, transportation engineering; BSc/BSs(Hons), BEng, BEng/Hons, MEng, MSc, MSci, PGCert/Dip

Faculty of Health, Life & Social Science; www.napier.ac.uk/fhlss

Life, Sport & Social Sciences

career guidance & development, complementary healthcare (aromatherapy/reflexology), complementary therapies practitioner, criminology, psychology, sociology, social science, social research; aquatic ecosystem management, biological science, biotechnology, animal biology, biomedical science, conservation & management of protected areas, marine & freshwater biology, pharmaceutical design, exercise physiology, sports science/coaching/injury/ psychology, sport performance enhancement, wildlife biology & conservation; BSc(Hons), MSc, BA(Hons), PGCert/Dip

School of Nursing, Midwifery and Social Care

adv/profession practice – intellectual disabilities/ palliative care/cancer care/midwifery/neonatal nursng/child protection/diabetes nursing, counselling, health admin, midwifery, nursing – adult, child, learning disabilities, mental health, intellectual disability, mental health, midwifery, social care, veterinary nursing; BMid, BN, DipHE, MSc, PGDip/ Cert

UNIVERSITY OF ESSEX
www.essex.ac.uk

Faculty of Humanities and Comparative Studies; www.essex.ac.uk/hcs

Art History & Theory

literature, film studies, art history & theory, Latin American/contemporary art, gallery studies, cultural/ critical curating

History

history (modern, social & cultural, American, film studies, joint honours in range of subjects, cultural & social, digital, local, community & family

Department of Literature, Film, and Theatre Studies

comparative literature, creative writing, drama/& literature, English language, English & United States literature, literature & film studies/history of art/ sociology/philosophy/history, literature/myth, literature and the unconscious, wild writing: literature, science & the environment

Dept of Philosophy; www.essex.ac.uk/ philosphy

philosophy/religion & ethics, numerous joint hons degrees, ethics, politics & public policy, philosophy & health care ethics/law, philosophy law & human rights/ politics & environmental issues

Latin American Studies

European Studies

European studies/with politics or modern languages

American studies

American (US) studies with politics/criminology

Humanities

BA(Hons), CertHE, Dip/MA, FdA, MA, MFA, MPhil, PGCert, PhD

Faculty of Social Sciences; www.essex.ac.uk/ss

Dept of Economics; www.essex.ac.uk/ economics

accounting & financial economics, applied economics & data analysis, business economics, econometrics, economics, economics with mathematics, financial/ international/management economics

Dept of Government; www.essex.ac.uk/ government

European integration/politics, global & comparative politics, ideology & discourse analysis, international development/relations/& media, philosophy, politics & economics, political behaviour/economy/ theory, politics, politics and law/ sociology/ human rights, public opinion and polling

Dept of Languages and Linguistics; www.essex.ac.uk/linguistics

applied/ linguistics, English language/& literature/ sociolinguistics, teaching English, language disorders, Portuguese, Spanish, TEFL, phonology, syntax, literature & mod langauges

Dept of Sociology; www.essex.ac.uk/ sociology

sociology – social sciences/humanities/criminology, criminology & social legislation, organized crime, terrorism & society, joint hons incl social psychology, media, business, media, culture & society; BA(Hons), BSc(Hons), Diploma, GradDip, MA, MPhil, MRes, MSc, PGDip, PhD, ProcDoc

Faculty of Law and Management; www.essex.ac.uk/lm

Essex Business School; www.essex.ac.uk/ebs

Centre for Global Accountability; Centre for Entrepreneurship Research; Essex Finance Centre; Essex Management Centre

accounting, economics, finance, financial management, banking, business management, marketing, HRM, international enerprise & entrepreneurship, social & community enterprise, global project & innovation management, management & organizational dynamics

Human Rights Centre; www.essex.ac.uk/humanrightscentre

human rights & Latin American studies/law/philosophy/politics/sociology, int rights law, humanitarian law, healthcare law, philosophy, law & human rights

School of Law; www.essex.ac.uk/law

law/& philosophy/politics/human rights, English & French laws, European business law, EU law, international law, health care law, human rights law, information technology, media and e-commerce, humanitarian law, international trade law, public law, environmental governance; BA(Hons), BSc(Hons), DocProg, LlM, LLB, MPhil, MSc, PhD

Faculty of Science and Engineering; www.essex.ac.uk/se

Dept of Biological Sciences; www.essex.ac.uk/bs

biochemistry, biological sciences, biology, biomedical science, biotechnology, cardiac rehabilitation, ecology, environmental governance, natural world, environmental resource management, genetics, marine biology, molecular medicine, natural environment & society, science & society, sports & exercise science, plant biotechnology, wild writing

School of Computer Science and Electronic Engineering; www.essex.ac.uk/csee

computer games/networks/science/systems engineering, IT & commuications technology, computers and electronics, data communication, electronics engineering, telecommunications engineering, telecommunications & data communications

School of Health and Human Sciences; www.essex.ac.uk/hss

adult/mental health nursing, midwifery, health/social services, clinical psychology, counselling psychology, speech & language/occupational therapy, physiotherapy, healthcare practice, CPD

Department of Mathematical Sciences; www.essex.ac.uk/maths

mathematics & computing/economics/biology/finance, cryptography & network security, discrete mathematics & its applications, biomathematics, financial decision making, econometrics, statistics & data analysis, mathematics for secondary teaching

Dept of Psychology; www.essex.ac.uk/psychology

psychology, cognitive psychology/neuropsychology/neuroscience, development perception & social & health psychology, research methods in psychology; BA(Hons), BEng, BSc(Hons), GradDip, MA, MPhil, MRes, MSc, PGDip, PhD, ProfDoc

Degrees validated by the University of Essex offered at:

WRITTLE COLLEGE
www.writtle.ac.uk

agriculture, animal science & management, business management, conservation, design, equine, floristry, horticulture, sport; BA(Hons), BSc(Hons), CertMS, Certs, DipMS, FDAs, Higher Certs, MA, MBA, MSc

UNIVERSITY OF EXETER
www.exeter.ac.uk

University of Exeter Business School; www.business-school.exeter.ac.uk

accounting, finance, business, economics, management, marketing, leadership, tourism, employability; BA(Hons), MBA, MPhil, MSc, PGDip/Cert, PhD

College of Engineering, Mathematics & Physical Sciences; www.emps.exeter.ac.uk/engineering

Computing: IT management for business, computer science, networking, electronics, applied artificial intelligence
Engineering: civil/environmental/electronic/mechanical/materials engineering, engineering and management, adv/mathematics, computer science, biosystems engineering, urban water systems
Geology: applied/engineering geology, geotechnology, mining geology
Mathematics & Computer Science: mathematics(climate science, mathematical biology), mathematics with computer science/ accountancy/economics/finance/engineering/physics), applied artificial intelligence, bioinformation & systems biology, biosystems engineering, financial management
Medical Imaging: diagnostic radiography
Minerals & Mining Engineering: minerals/mining engineering, mining geology, surveying & land/environment
Physics & Astronomy: physics, astrophysics, medical imaging, biomedical physics, quantum systems, electromagnetic materials, nanomaterials;
Renewable Energy; BSc(Hons), BEng, MEng, MSc, MPhil, PhD

College of Humanities; www.humanities.exeter.ac.uk

Archaeology; archaeology & forensic science, anthropology, ancient history, heritage management, bioarchaeology, experimental/landscape archaeology, material culture studies
Classics & Ancient History; ancient history, classical studies, classics, art history/art & archaeology, ancient drama & society, Hellenistic culture, Roman myth & history, food & culture
Drama: drama, theatre practice – appl theatre, drecting, physical performance, actor training, playwriting, dramaturgy, staging Shakespeare
English: English/studies, film, creative writing, criticism & theory, the 20th century, Victoran studies
Film Studies: film studies/with English, modern languages
History: ancient/modern/maritime/medieval/naval history, Arabic/M East studies, comb degs
Modern Languages: French, German, Italian, Hispanic studies, Russian, literature, linguistics, literary & applied translation

College of Life & Environmental Sciences; www.lifesciences.exeter.ac.uk

Biosciences: biology & animal behaviour, human bioscience, clinical/environmental science, biocatalysis, medical/bioinformatics, systems biology, food security & sustainability, applied ecology, conservation & diversity
Geography: geography, environmental science/management, conservation biology, climate change, critical human geography, sustainable development, energy policy
Psychology; psychology, animal behaviour, social & organizational psychology, psychological/cognitive therapies, sports exercise science
Sport and Health Sciences: sport & health science paediatric exercise, sport & exercise medicine/science/psychology, exercise, human biosciences, sports science; BSc(Hons), MPhil, BA(Hons), DocCiniPsychology, MSc, PhD, PGCert/Dip, MRes, BClinSci

College of Social Science & International Studies; www.social sciences.exeter.ac.uk

Arab & Islamic studies; Arab/Islamic studies, Kurdish/East/Persian/Palestine/Gulf/Iranain studies, ethnopolitics, Middle East history, north African politics

Graduate School of Education;

creative art, special educational needs, TESOL, technology, creativity training, educational psychology, childhood & youth studies, English & education, sport science
PGCE: primary art/music/science/modern foreign languages, early years, secondary sciences/design & technology/English with media/drama/modern foreign languages/geography/information, communication technologies

School of Law:

law, European (German/French) law, European studies, international business/international & comparative public law, international human rights law

Politics & International Relations: politics, international relations/studies
Sociology & Philosophy; sociology, philosophy, archaeology & anthropology, political economy, genetics & society, history & philosophy of biology, philosophy & sociology of science; BA(Hons), MA, PhD, MPhil, MA, PhD, LlB, LlM, MRes, DEdPsych, EdD, MEd

Peninsula College of Medicine and Dentistry; www.pms.exeter.ac.uk
clinical sciences, infection prevention & control, remote healthcare, clinical education, dentistry, clinical education, enviromental & human health, medicine, surgery; BClinM, BDS, BMMS, MPhil, MD/MS, PhD, MSc

Degrees validated by University of Exeter offered at:

UCP MARJON-UNIVERSITY COLLEGE PLYMOUTH ST MARK & ST JOHN
www.ucpmarjon.ac.uk

children, youth & community, drama, education & teacher training, English language, literature & creative writing, leadership, live music, media, sport, outdoor, coaching & PE; BA(Hons), BA/BSc, BEd, FdA church college certs; GTP, MA, MEd, MPhil, PGCE

UNIVERSITY COLLEGE FALMOUTH (INC DARTINGTON COLLEGE OF ARTS)
www.falmouth.ac.uk

3D design, advertising, art & performance/environment, choreography, contemporary crafts, creative events management, creative music technology, curatorial practice, dance, digital animation, English with creative writing/media, fashion design, film, fine art, garden design, graphic design, illustration, interior design, journalism, media studies, music performance/theatre/composition, photography, popular music, PR, professional writing, radio production, screen & media performance,sportswear design,TV production, textile design, theatre (design and production, directing, performance, writing); BA(Hons), FdA, MA, MPhil, PGDip, PhD

UNIVERSITY OF GLAMORGAN
www.glam.ac.uk

Cardiff School of Creative and Cultural Industries; www.ccc.glam.ac.uk
computer/animation, art/production & design, computer music, drama, theatre, fashion & retail/interior design, film studies, video, games art, graphic communication, visual effects, journalism, music/sound technology, pop, computer music, photography, media production/communication/technology, radio, scripwriting, visual art; BA(Hons), FdA, MA, MPhil

Faculty of Health, Sport and Science; www.hesas.glam.ac.uk
Health & Social Care: chiropractic, clinical physiology, counselling, psychotherapy, diagnostic clinical ultrasound, nursing (children, adult, mental health, learning disabilities), midwifery, pharmacology & prescribing, social work & social care
Science: astronomy, chemistry, pharmaceutical science, biology, geology, geography, natural history, forensic & police science
Sport & Coaching; sports health & exercise, youth sport, nutrition, physical activity, psychology, rugby, football; BA(Hons), BSc(Hons), BN, FoundCerts, HEDip, HNC, HND, MA, MPhil, MSC/PGD/, PGC, PhD

Faculty of Advanced Technology; www.fat.glam.ac.uk
built environment, construction technology/project management, quantity surveying, real estate, building services/civil/structural engineering,

environmental management, international development,engineering technology, mechanical/manufacturing engineering, energy systems, lighting/live events technology, aeronautical engineering/systems, aircraft maintenance, avionics, electrical & electronic engineering, mobile technology, computer systems, mechatronics, electronic/mobile/communications/ product design, IT, embedded systems, mobile/ satellite communications, optical & communications networks, business & computing, mobile computing, computer games, software, computer forensics & security, mathematics, computing/financial mathematics; BEng(Hons), BSc, BSc(Hons), CertHE, DipHE, HNC, HND, MEng

Glamorgan Business School; www.bus.glam.ac.uk

forensic/international accounting, business management/enterprise/communications, forensic audit, international fashion/financial systems, Islamic banking & finance, strategic/HRM, marketing, procurement, PR, transport & logistics, tourism event/sport management, logistics/supply chain management, transport; ACCA, BA(Hons), BSc(Hons), DBA, DocLC, FdA, MBA, MPhil, MSc

Faculty of Humanities and Social Sciences; www.hass.glam.ac.uk

Visual Art: art & design, art practice

Criminology: criminal justice, police studies,forensic science/law/psychology/sociology

Education & Careers: early years development, education, childhood & youth, career guidance

Community Regeneration

Early Years, Childhood & Adolescence; early years, education, childhood & youth, social justice, play/ therapy

English & Creative Writing: creative & professional writing, English/literature/joint degrees, professional Welsh, Gothic studies, literature, culture & society

History; history and joint degrees, social & cultural history, research history

Languages: applied language studies, professional Welsh/TESOL/joint degrees, Spanish

Law: law/accountancy/business/criminology/sociology, legal practice, international/commercial law

Psychology: psychology, criminology, education/ sociology, applied/developmental/sport/health psychology, therapeutic psychology

Public Services: public/emergency services, health/& public service management, public leadership

Sociology: sociology with criminology, education.history/law/psychology, youth & social justice

The Centre for Lifelong Learning; www.cell.glam.ac.uk

TESOL; BA(Hons), BA/BSc, BSc(Hons), DocPublServ, FCert, FdA, GradDip Law, LlB(Hons), LlM/PhD/PgD, MA/PDip/Cert, MSc, PGD/PGC

The Centre for Lifelong Learning; www.cell.glam.ac.uk

astronomy, business courses, community courses/ regeneration, communication technology, craft and design, creative industries, environmental studies, information, languages, social sciences; BA(Hons), BSc(Hons), FdA, GCert/Dip/MA/MSc

UNIVERSITY OF GLASGOW
www.gla.ac.uk

College of Arts; www.gla.ac.uk/ colleges/arts

archaeology, arts & media informatics, American studies, 19th-century art, Celtic civilization/studies, classics, comparative literature, Czech, decorative arts, dramaturgy, English/English literature, history, European studies, film & TV studies, French, Gaelic, German, Greek, history, history of art, Italian, Latin, modern & contemporary art, music, philosophy, pop/ sonic arts, Polish, Russian, Scottish literature/history, Slavonic/Chinese studies, Spanish, textile conservation, theatre studies, theology & religious studies; BD(Min), BMus, DLitt, MA, MAHons, MLitt, MPhil, MTh, PhD

College of Medical Veterinary & Life Sciences; www..gla.ac.ukcolleges/mvls

School of Life Sciences; www.gla.ac.uk/ schools/lifesciences

anatomy, biochemistry, bioinformatics, biomedical/ biological sciences, biotechnology, ecological & environmental biology/management, computing/& physiology, genetics, immunology, marine & freshwater biology/ecology & enviromental management, medical/& veterinary microbiology, microbiology, molecular & cellular biology, neuroscience, nutrition, molecular/parasitology, pharmacology, physiology, plant science, sports medicine/science, virology, zoology, human biology, virology

School of Medicine; www.gla.ac.uk/medicine,

dentistry, medicine, health care, immunology, nursing (community, adult, surgical, children, public health), child health, clinical nutrition/pharmacy/physics/psychology, primary dentistry, oral surgery, orthodontics, radiation physics, primary healthcare, pediatric science, medical genetics, public health, physiology, sport science & nutrition, sports /& exercise medicine, surgical oncology, translational medicine

School of Veterinary Medicine; www.gla.ac.uk/schools/vet

veterinary biosciences, veterinary medicine/surgery/public health; BSc, BSc(Vet Sci), BVMS, MVPH, PhD B(MedSci), MBChB, MD, MML, MMLE, MPC, MPH, PhD, BDS, BSc(Dent Sc), DDS, MSc

College of Science & Engineering; www.gla.acuk/colleges/scienceengineering

School of Chemistry; www.gla.ac.uk/schools/chemistry

chemistry, physical/medical chemistry, environmental science

School of Engineering; www.gla.ac.uk/schools/engineering

aerospace/aeronautical engineering, aeronautics, architecture, automotive engineering, avionics, biomedical engineering, civil engineering, electronics & software engineering/music, electronic design, mechanical design/engineering, mechatronics, microcomputer systems engineering, product design engineering, embedded systems engineering, geotechnics, global water sustainabilty, signal processing, space systems ananlysis & design/engineering, structural engineering & mechanics, sustainable energy/world resources, telecommunications electronics

School of Computing Science; www.gla.ac.uk/schools/computing

computing science, neuroinformatics, electronic & software engineering/development, mobile/software engineering. information retrieval/security/technology

School of Geographical & Earth Sciences; www.gla.ac.uk/schools/ges

earth science, geography, applied population & statistical mapping, freshwater/coastal/aquatic sytems science, geoinformatic technology & mapping science, human geography, landscape monitoring, marine systs, science, international development

School of Mathematics & Statistics; www.gla.ac.uk/schools/mathematicsstatistics;

applied/pure mathematics, mathematical sience, statistics, biostatistics, environmental/social statistics, financial modelling/finance

School of Physics & Astronomy; www.gla.ac.uk/schools/physics

astronomy, chemical/theoretical physics, astrophysics, advanced materials, energy & the environment, global security, life sciences

School of Psychology; www.gla.ac.uk/schools/psychology

psychology, brain imaging, psychological science; BEng, BSc, EngD, MEng, MSc, PGDip, PhD, EngD, PGDip

College of Social Sciences; www.gla.ac.uk/schools/social sciences

University of Glasgow Business School; www.gla.ac.uk/schools/business

accountancy, business economics/finance/admin, financial services, banking, Chinese studies, economics, environmental & sustainable development, international finance, financial economics/forecasting/modelling/risk management, international management/marketing, HR, public admin; BA BSc, MA, MAQ(SocSci), MAcc, MBA, MFin, MSc, PhD

School of Education; www.gla.ac.uk/schools/education

adult & continuous education, childhood practice, education (primary, secondary), ELT, literature & literacy, community development, addiction, music, RE, English language teaching, inclusive education, organization leadership, psychological studies, teaching adults, technological education, young people, social inclusion & change; BA(Hons), BTechEd, BTechS, EdD, MA, MA(Hons), MEd, MLitt, MSc, MusicBEd, PhD

School of Interdisciplinary Studies; www.gla.ac.uk/schools/interdisciplinary

environmental stewardship, health & social studies, liberal arts (history/humanities/literature/philosophy), primary education with TQ, applied carbon management, managing health & wellbeing, tourism, heritage & development; BSc, MA, MLitt, PGCert/Dip

School of Law; www.gla.ac.uk/schools/law

law, contemporary law & practice, corporate & financial/medical law, intellectual property & digital environment, international competition/commercial law, law & security, professionl legal practice, social law studies; MRes, LlB, LlM, MRes, PgDip/Cert, PhD

School of Social & Political Science; www.ac.uk/schools/socialpolitical

Central & east European studies, economic & social history, politics, public policy, sociology, city/regional planning, criminology,, criminal justice, equality & human rights, Euro politics/law, global health/economy/security, housing studies, international politics/relations, political ommunication, Russian, Central & East European studies, social science, sociology, spatial planning, transnational crime, urban policy/practice/regeneration; MA, MA(SocSci), MSc, MRes, CPD, MLitt, EdD, PhD

GLASGOW CALEDONIAN UNIVERSITY
www.caledonian.ac.uk

School of the Built & Natural Environment; www.caledonian.ac.uk/bne

building services engineering/ surveying, construction management, energy & environmental engineering, environmental civil engineering/management & planning, fire risk engineering, real estate & property management & valuation, quantity surveying, sustainable energy technology, waste management; BSc/BEng, BSc(Hons), MSc, MPhil, PhD

Caledonian School of Business; www.caledonian.ac.uk/cbs

accountancy, banking, business & management/studies, economics,entertainment & events management, fashion, finance, global supply chain & logistics, HRM, innovation & enterprise marketing, investment, international trade, journalism, media, risk management, marketing, retailing, risk sports, travel, tourism; BA/BA(Hons), MRes, PhD

School of Engineering and Computing; www.caledonian.ac.uk/sec

3D computer animation, instumentation systs, audio technology with multimedia/electronics, computer & communication systems, engineering, computer games (design, software), computer-aided mechanical engineering. computing (information/networks, web systems, digital/forensics security/systems engineering, electrical power, electronics/forensics/engineering, graphic design for digital media, interactive media, mechanical & power plant systems/ mechanical electronic systems engineering, mechatronics, network security/systems support,robotics, telecommunications engineering, wireless communication; BA/BA(Hons), BEng/BEng(Hons), BSc/BSc(Hons), DipHE, MA/PGD, MSc/PGD, PhD

School of Health; www.caledonian.ac.uk/health

health & social care, primary care, dietetics, cardiac rehabilitation, occupational therapy, physiotherapy, podiatrics, radiography, social work, nursing (adult/child/mental health/learning disabilities), community health, operating dept practices, diagnostic imaging; BSc(Hons), BA(Hons), GradCert, MPhil, MSc, PgCert/Dip, PhD, ProfDoc, BMidwifery, BN

School of Life Sciences; www.caledonian.ac.uk/sls

biochemistry, biological & biomedical sciences, cell & molecular biology, dietetics, food bioscience, forensics, human biology/biosciences, microbiology, nutrition, optometry, pharmacology, clinical physiology, psychology, vision sciences; BSc, BSc(Hons), DipHE, DPsych, MSc, OpthDisp, PGCert/Dip, PhD, MRes

School of Law and Social Sciences; www.caledonian.ac.uk/sls

business law, law, European/& international trade/business law, international contracting/law and IT, social sciences, Scottish/history; BA(Hons), LlB, LlM, MSc, PGD/C, PhDBA/BA(Hons)

THE GLASGOW SCHOOL OF ART
www.gsa.ac.uk

architecture; interior/silversmithing & jewellery/fashion & textiles design, environmental art, fine art, photography, painting & printmaking, historical and critical studies, product engineering, visual communication; BA(Hons), BEng, BArch,DipArch, MA, MArch, MDes, MEng, MPhil, MRes, PhD

UNIVERSITY OF GLOUCESTERSHIRE
www.glos.ac.uk

The university is now organized into the following academic departments:

Accountancy & Finance; Art & Design; Business & Management; Communication & Media Production, Computing; Education; Events, Tourism & Hospitality; Health & Social Care; Humanities: Natural & Social Sciences; Sport & Exercise

The large number of courses offered lead to the following qualifications: honours degrees, foundation degrees, Higher National Diplomas and postgraduate Master degrees designated as follows: BA/BA(Hons), BSc/BSc(Hons), DipSW, HND,BEd,LlB MA, MPhil, MRes, MSc, PGCert, PGDip, MBA, CMS, DMS

UNIVERSITY OF GREENWICH
www.gre.ac.uk

School of Architecture and Construction; www.gre.ac.uk/schools/arc

architecture, building surveying/rehabilitation, construction/surveying, design & construction management, digital/graphic design, housing, real estate, fine art, garden design/history, landscape architecture/management, land use, occupational safety, photography, quantity surveying, urban design, visual arts, web design; BA(Hons), BSc(Hons), Certs, Dip, HNC, HND, MA, MSc, MPhil, PGDip, PhD

The Business School; www.gre.ac.uk/schools/business

accounting, international/banking, business administration/administration/entrepreneurship & innovation, advertising, business in Europe, business logistics & transport management, business management/studies, economics, events management, finance, financial information systems, HRM, investment, international business/banking, marketing, logistics, marketing/communications, multimedia, PR, project management, public services, purchasing & supply chain management/e-logistics, leisure & tourism management; BA(Hons), BSc(Hons), Certs, DBA, FD, HNC, HND, MA, MBA, MSc, PGDip, PhD

School of Computing & Mathematical Science; www.gre.ac.uk/schools/cms

business computing/information systems/information technology/intelligence, computer science, computer security & forensics, computer systems & networking, computing (with games development, digital multimedia), data warehousing/animation & production/film production/TV & interactive media, embedded computer systems, film & TV production, financial mathematics, games, IT/systems & digital media, internet computing, mathematics & computing, mathematics for decision science, mathematics, statistics & computing, mobile computing & communications, networks, software engineering, web technologies; BSc(Hons), FDSc, MA, MEng/BEng, MPhil, MSc, PhD

School of Education; www.gre.ac.uk/education

childhood studies, secondary design & technology with QTS, early years, education, lifelong learning, primary education with QTS/French, secondary education/design & technology, learning, teaching & training with digital techn, youth & community work; BA(Hons), BELT, Cert, DipHE, EdD, FD, MA, MPhil, MSc, PGCert/Dip, PhD,P GCE

School of Engineering; www.gre.ac.uk/schools/engineering

civil engineering, communications systems engineering, computer networking, electrical & electronic engineering, engineering management, games & entertainment systems, information & communications technology/management, internet technology, manufacturing systems, marine engineering, mechanical engineering, project management, public health/water environment engineering, software engineering; BEng(Hons), BSc(Hons), HNC, HND, MEng, MSc

Greenwich Maritime Institute; www.gre.ac.uk/schools/gmi

maritime history/management, international maritime policy; MA, MBA, MPhil, PhD

School of Health and Social Care; www.gre.ac.uk/schools/health

child development, childhood studies, counselling, heath & wellbeing/social care, early years, mental health work, midwifery, nursing (adult, child/learning disabilities, mental health), paramedic science, primary care professional practice, psychology, public health, social work & social care, therapeutic counselling; BA(Hons), BSc(Hons), DipHE, FD, GradDips, MA, MPhil, PGCert, PhD

School of Humanities and Social Sciences; www.gre.ac.uk/schools/humanities

creative writing, criminal justice & legal studies, criminal psychology, criminology, drama, English, film studies, history, international studies/law/politics, journalism and PR, Japanese languge teaching, justice & legal studies, language & culture, law, media and creative arts/communication/philosophy, media writing, French, German, Italian, Spanish, philosophy, politics, sociology, TESOL ELT; BSc(Hons), BA(Hons), FD, LlB, MA, MPhil, MSc, PGCert, PGDip, PhD

Medway School of Pharmacy; www.gre.ac.uk/schools/studying/index/html

medicines management, general/pharmacy practice, independant/supplementary prescribing; BSc(Hons), FdMM, FdPP, MPharm, MSc, PGCert/Dip

Natural Resources Institute; www.gre.ac.uk/schools/nri

rural development dynamic, food safety & quality management, natural resources; BSc(Hons), MPhil, MSc, PhD

School of Science; www.gre.ac.uk/schools/science

biomedical sciences, biosciences, biotechnology, chemical & life sciences, forensic science, environmental & earth sciences, geography, GIS, human nutrition, natural resources, pharmaceutical science/studies, professional football coaching sport science, sustainability; BSc(Hons), HNC, HND, MPhil, MSc, PGDip, PhD

GRIMSBY INSTITUTE OF FURTHER AND HIGHER EDUCATION
www.grimsby.ac.uk

animal care, business & law, computing, construction, creative arts, electrical/electronics engineering, hair & beauty, health & child care, humanities & science, manufacturing & logistics, mechanical engineering, media/writing, refrigeration, sports & fitness, teacher education, travel & tourism; BA(Hons), BSc(Hons), FdA, FdEd, FdSc, HEdDip, HNC, HND, MA, MBA, MSc, PGCE

HARPER ADAMS UNIVERSITY COLLEGE
www.harper-adams.ac.uk

agricultural, engineering, animals, business, countryside management/& environment, retail, food studies, rural affairs estate management, management, marketing, leisure & tourism, veterinary/physiotherapy/pharmacy, sustainable agriculture; BSc(Hons), FdSc, MBA, MSc, PGDip/Cert

HERIOT-WATT UNIVERSITY
www.hw.ac.uk

School of the Built Environment; www.hw.ac.uk/sbe

architectural engineering,civil & structural engineering, quantity/building surveying, construction project management/& surveying, foundation engineering, built environment, real estate management/investment and finance/planning; environmental engineering, building conservation, housing and regeneration, sustainable community design, urban and regional planning, planning & property development, water resources and catchment development; BSc(Hons, Ord), BEng, MEng, MRes, MSc, PGDip/Cert, PhD

School of Mathematical and Computer Sciences; www.macs.hw.ac.uk

actuarial mathematics/science, advanced internet applications, applied mathematical sciences, artificial intelligence, computer science, computer systems management, creative software systems, financial mathematics, information systems, information technology (business/software systems), mathematics, mathematical, statistical & actuarial sciences, quantitative risk management, software engineering, statistical modelling, statistics; BSc(Hons), MEng, MMath, MRes, MSc, PGDip/Cert, PhD

School of Engineering and Physical Sciences; www.eps.hw.ac.uk

biochemistry, chemistry/with forensic materials, computational chemistry, forensic science, materials/pharmaceutical chemistry, nanotechnology; biochemical engineering, bioprocessing, chemical engineering with pharmaceutical chemistry/nanotechnology & microsystems/oil & gas technology, sustainability engineering, petroleum/pipeline engineering; physics, mathematical engineering physics, nano-technology and microsystems, photonics, optoelectronic devices, physics with environmental, applied optics, lasers, plasmas, theoretical physics; computer vision and robotics, computing & electronics, electrical & electronic engineering (computer & internet engineering/microwaves & electronics/mobile & digital comms/power & HV engineering/real time control & robotics/sustainability), information technology (embedded systems/mobile communications, applied systems), microsystems, photonics and optoelectronic devices, renewable energy and distributed generation, sustainability engineering, system level integration, vision, image and signal processing, automotive engineering, mechanical engineering, creative 3D digital technologies, design & management, forensic materials, materials for sustainable and renewable energies, renewable/energy engineering, robotics & cybertronics; BEng, BSc(Ord,Hons), EngD, MChem, MEng, MPhil, MPhys, PhD

School of Life Sciences; www.hw.ac.uk/sls

applied psychology (forensic science), psychology, psychology with human health; applied marine biology, biological sciences (cell and molecular biology/food science/human health/microbiology), bioprocesses, biotechnology, biology, microbiology; brewing and distilling; food science/safety and health, technology and food science; marine science, applied marine biology, climate change: managing the marine environment, environmental analysis & assessment, marine biodiversity & biotechnology, marine resource development & protection, spacial planning; BSc(Hons), MSc/Cert/Dip, PGDip, PhD

School of Management and Languages; www.hw.ac.uk/sml

accountancy & business law/finance, business; business management with HRM/marketing, enterprise, economics, international fashion marketing/management, logistics & supply chain management, management with business law/enterprise/HRM/marketing/operations management, maritime logistics & supply chain management, social sciences, strategic project/investment management
Languages and Intercultural Studies: Arabic–English translating & conference interpreting, applied languages & translating (French/German) (French/Spanish) (German/Spanish), Chinese–English translating and conference interpreting/computer-assisted translation tools, international management & languages, interpreting studies & skills, British sign language; BA(Hons, Ord), GradDip, MA(Hons), MSc

Heriot-Watt Institute of Petroleum Engineering; www.pet.hw.ac.uk

geoscience for subsurface exploration appraisal & development, marine resource management, petroleum engineering, renewable energy development, reservoir evaluation & management; MPhil, MSc, PhD

School of Textiles and Design; www.tex.hw.ac.uk

design for textiles, fashion, fashion communication/marketing & retailing/menswear/technology/womenswear, interior des, fashion & textiles design/textiles innovation and new applications/management; BA, BSc(Hons,Ord), MA, MSc

Edinburgh Business School; www.ebsglobal.net

accounting, competitive strategy, consumer behaviour, corporate governance, strategic/credit/financial risk management, derivatives, developing effective managers and leaders, economics, employee relations, finance, development leadership, HRM/dev and planning, int marketing, leadership,mergers & acquisitions, project management, retailing, planning; DBA, MBA, MSc

Degrees validated by Heriot-Watt University offered at:

EDINBURGH COLLEGE OF ART
www.eca.ac.uk

architecture/conservation, animation, art or design, contemporary art (theory/practice/photography), fashion, film directing, glass, graphic design, illustration, int design, jewellery & silversmithing, landscape architecture, performance costume, product design,-textiles, urban design; BAArch, BA(Comb), BSc(Hons, Ord), MAHons, MPhil, MSc, PhD

UNIVERSITY OF HERTFORDSHIRE
www.herts.ac.uk

Business School; www.herts.ac.uk/schools-of-study/courses/business

accounting/with mod languages/European studies, organizational change, business adminstration/economics/studies, corporate governance, public services, economics, events management, finance, financial management/modelling, global business, hospitality, HRM, information systems, investment management, marketing, tourism; BA/BSc, BA(Hons), BSc, DBA, DMan, MA, MBA, MPhil, MSc, PGCert/Dip, PhD

School of Computer Science; www.herts.ac.uk/courses/schools-of-study/computer-science

artificial intelligence, business computing, computer science, distributed systems, e-learning technology,entertainment systems, information technology, mobile computing, mutimedia technology, networks, robotics, secure computing systems, software eng, web-based systsems; BSc(Hons), MEng, MPhil, MSc, PGCert/Dip, PhD

School of Creative Arts; www.herts.ac.uk/courses/schools-of-study/creative-arts

digital/animation, games art, character creation, contemporay applied arts, engineering product design, fashion, film & TV directing/producing/screenwriting, fine art, graphic design, illustration, interactive media software, contemporary textiles, art therapy, modelling, interior/industrial/model/ multimedia/design, music composition/technology/entertainment industry management, photography, screen cultures, sound design, special/visual effects; BA(Hons), MA, PgCert/Dip, MSc, MPhil, PhD

School of Education; www.herts.ac.uk/courses/schools-of-study/education

deaf children education, early years, leading learning, primary/secondary education; BA(Hons), BEd, EdD, FdA, MA, MPhil, PGCert/Dip, PGCE, PhD

School of Engineering & Technology; www.hearts.ac.uk/courses/schools-of-study/engineering-and-technology

aerospace engineering/systems, pilot studies, automotive engineering, motorsport technology, computer & network technology, digital film & TV technology, data communication networks, embedded intelligent systems, film & TV prodn, mechanical engineering, multimedia technology, internet engineering, audiovisual digital broadcasting, digital communications/systems, electronics/electrical/computer engineering, adv digital systems, biometrics & cybersecurity, broadband communication systems, manufacturing management, operations & supply chain management, internet technology; BSc(Hons), BEng, MEng MSc, PgDip/Cert, MPhil, PhD

School of Health and Emergency Professions; www.herts.ac.uk/courses/schools-of-study/health-and-emergency-professions
diagnostic imaging/radiography, dietetics, medical imaging, oncology, paramedic science, physiotherapy, radiation sciences, radiotherapy, sport & exercise rehabilitation, ultrasound; BSc(Hons), DHRes, FD, MPhil, MSc, PGCert/Dip, PhD

School of Humanities; www.herts.ac.uk/courses/schools-of-study/humanities
acting & screen performance, American studies, creative writing, English language & communication/literature, ELT, film, languages, history, journalism, media cultures, mass communication, new media publishing, philosophy; BA(Hons), MA, MPhil, PGCert/Dip, PhD

School of Law; www.herts.ac.uk/courses/schools-of-study/law
commercial law, e-commerce law, international law, telecomm law, legal practice, maritime law; BSc(Hons), Diploma, LlB(Hons), LlM, MPhil, PGDip, PhD, Univ Cert

School of Life Sciences; www.herts.ac.uk/courses/schools-of-study/life-sciences
biochemistry, bioinformatics, biological/biomedical/science, biotechnology, environmental management, exercise science, genetics, geography, molecular biology, pharmaceutical science, pharmacology, physiology, sports studies/therapy,sustainable planning/transport, water & environmental management; BSc/BSc(Hons), MSc, PgCert/Dip

School of Nursing, Midwifery & Social Work; www.herts.ac.uk/courses/schools-of-study/nursing-and-midwifery/
nursing (prequal & postqual, adult, child, mental health, learning disabilities), health visiting, social work/intervention midwifery (pre & postqual) and women's health, nursing (learning disability), social work, specialist community nursing; BSc/BSc(Hons), DipHE, DipHE Nursing, MSc, NVQs, PGDip/PGCert

School of Pharmacy; www.herts.ac.uk/courses/schools-of-study/pharmacy
advancing pharmacy practice, medicinal chemistry, pharmacy; MPharm, MPhil, MSc, PGCert/Dip, PhD

School of Physics, Astronomy and Mathematics; www.herts.ac.uk/courses/schools-of-study/physics-astronomy-and-mathematics
astrophysics, financial market analysis, financial maths, mathematics, physics; BSc(Hons), MPhil, MSc, PhD

School of Post Graduate Medicine; www.herts.ac.uk/courses/schools-of-study/postgraduate-medicine
clinical practice, dermatology skills & treatment, health law & ethics, health & medical education, mental health practice, psychiatric practice, western medical acupuncture, skin integrity skills & practice; MD, MSc, PGCert/Dip

School of Psychology; www.herts.ac.uk/courses/schools-of-study/psychology
business psychology, psychology, cognitive behavioral therapy/neuropsychology, psychotherapy & disability, clinical/health psychology, therapeutic counselling, mental health studies/primary care, occupational/organizational psychology; BSc(Hons), DClinPsy, MSc, PGDip

Degrees validated by the University of Hertfordshire offered at:

HERTFORDSHIRE REGIONAL COLLEGE
www.hrc. .ac.uk

3D dimensional design, art & design, business, early years, engineering, fine art practice, graphic design, IT. performing arts, teacher training; BA(Hons), BSc, C&G, FD, N/HD

NORTH HERTFORDSHIRE COLLEGE
www.nhc.ac.uk

performing arts, business, finance, HRM, early years, health & social care, IT, multimedia, beauty therapy, management studies; BA, BSc, FD, N/HND

OAKLANDS COLLEGE
www.oaklands.ac.uk

animal care, business, childcare, computing, engineering, art/fashion, ELT, health & social care, hospitality,land-based studies, IT, media/music, equine studies, retail, sports studies, teacher training; C&G, FD, Dips, HNC, HND, Nat Dips NVQs

WEST HERTS COLLEGE
www.westherts.ac.uk

accounting, advertising, art & design, beauty, business & management, care & early years, construction, counselling, ESOL, forensic science, holistic therapies, hospitality & catering, information technology, legal executive, management studies, marketing, media & photography, performing arts & music, personal development, public services, retail, sport, teaching & training, travel; BA(Hons), BTEC, C&G, College Cert/Dips, Nat Dips, PGDip

THE UNIVERSITY OF HUDDERSFIELD
www2.hud.ac.uk.sas

School of Applied Sciences; www2.hud.ac.uk/sas

Chemical & Biological Sciences: analytical/chemistry, biochemistry, biology (molecular,cellular), chemical engineering, chemistry, food science/nutrition, forensic & analytical science, medical biochemistry/biology/genetics, pharmaceuticals, pharmacy, public health

Logistics & Hospitality Management: leisure management, air transport & logistics management, transport & supply chain management, global logistics, hospitality management, events management, travel & tourism, transport; BA(Hons), BSc(Hons), HND, MA, MChem, MPharm, MSc, MSci, PhD

School of Art, Design and Architecture; www2.hud.ac.uk/ada

3D, art, communication design, construction, costume,digital media/arts production, exhibition & retail design, fashion, fashion and textiles buying/management/retailing/design with marketing/production, fine art,contemporary arts, graphic design, illustration, interior design, multimedia design/games, photography, product design, project management, spatial design, sustainable architecture, surface/transport design, textile design & crafts; BA(Hons), BSc(Hons), CerHE, DipHE, FdA, FdSc, MA, MArch, MSc

University of Huddersfield Business School; www2.hud.ac.uk/uhbs

accountancy, advertising, brand management, business administration/information management/law & management/project management, business studies, commercial law, management, e-business. entrepreneurship, European business, events management, financial services, finance, global business, hospitality management, HRM, international business, logistics & supply chain management, marketing, journalism, law, legal practice, management studies, marketing communications, international/marketing, media relations, PR, retail, risk, disaster & environmental management, small business, travel & tourism; BA(Hons), FdA, GradDipLaw, HND, LlB(Hons), LlM, MBA, MSc, PGCE, PGDip, PGDip/Cert

School of Computing and Engineering; www2.hud.ac.uk/ce
automotive design/engineering/systems design and analysis/technology, motorsport engineering/design, computing science/studies/in business, computer-aided design/engineering, computer control systems/engineering, communications/electronic/electrical engineering, software development, music technology/audio systems,pop music prodn, energy engineering, engineering & technology management, mechanical engineering, computer games design/ technology, digital films & visual effect, video/ animation, interactive multimedia, web technology; BEng(Hons), HNC, HND, MEng, MSc, PhD, UniFdCert

School of Education and Professional Development; www2.hud.ac.uk/edu
teacher training (primary, secondary, lifelong learning), youth & community work, childhood studies, early years, counselling, guidance, learning support, multimedia & e-learning, religion & education,literacy/ESOL, education & training; BA(Hons), CertEd, FdA, MA, PGradDip/Cert, PSCE

Human and Health Sciences; www2.hud.ac.uk/hhs
criminology, public management, international/politics, sociology, behavioural sciences, counselling, district nursing, exercise, physical activity & health, health, community studies, midwifery, occupational therapy, perioperative skills, physiotherapy, podiatry, psychology, social work, nursing (adult, child, learning disability, mental health), perioperative practice, child/welfare, safeguarding, health studies; DipHE, MA, MSc, PGDip/Cert, PhD,ProfDoc

Music, Humanities and Media; www2.hud.ac.uk/mhm
British sign language, Chinese (Mandarin), French, German, Italian, Japanese, Spanish, Urdu, drama, English/literature, creative writing, digital/broadcast journalism, oral/history, literary studies, interpretation, politics, humanities, music/ technology/performance/production, popular music, sociology, technical theatre; BA(Hons), FdA, MA, MPhil, PdF, PhD

UNIVERSITY OF HULL
www.hull.ac.uk

Faculty of Arts and Social Sciences; www.hull.ac.uk/fass
American studies, archaeology, arts & new media, British politics, creative writing, criminology, digital media, drama, economics, English, film studies, forensic science, French,German, Spanish, Italian, translation studies, TESOL, gender studies, geography, globalization & governance, history (20th century, medieval, maritime, military, European, imperial), history of art, music/technology, jazz and pop music, internet computing, media studies, theatre & performance, philosophy, politics, globalization & governance, psychology, social policy/work, sociology, Spanish law, religion, theology, travel studies, war & security studies, web design

School of Law
law (commercial, international, business, human rights, environmental, French, Spanish, German, European public) legal studies, criminology, restorative justice; BA(Hons), BMus, BSc(Hons), LlB, LLM, MA, MEd, MMus, MPhil, MR/MRes, PGDip/Cert, PhD

The Hull University Business School; www.hull.ac.uk/hubs
accounting, advertising, business/economics/management/analytics, financial management, HRM, international business, logistics, marketing management, money, banking, finance, sport, leisure, tourism, supply chain management; BA(Hons), BSc(Hons), MBA, MPhil, MRes, MSc, PhD

Faculty of Health and Social Care; www.hull.ac.uk/fhsc
community care, dental nursing, nursing (adult, children's, learning disabilities, acute /mental health, community), gatroenterology, leadership, midwifery, non-medical prescribing, operating dept practice, critical/emergency/neonatal care, public health; Adv Diploma, BSc(Hons), FD, MPhil, MRes, PhD,Univ Cert,PGDip

The Hull York Medical School; www.hyms.ac.uk
anatomy, cancer, cardiovascular medicine, child health, clinical sciences, clinical techniques & skills,

cognitive behavioural therapy, dermatology, evidence-based decision making, gastrointestinal medicine, immunology, medicine, mental health, metabolic & renal medicine, pathology, person-centred care, population health & medicine, reproduction, respiration, surgery; BSc, MBBS, MPhil, MA,MRes, MSc/Dip/Cert, PGCert/Dip, PhD

Faculty of Education; www.2.hull.ac.uk/ifl

early childhood studies/years, education & learning/society, primary education (QTS), e-learning, inclusive education, learning & support, lifelong learning, TESOL, English literacy, inclusive education, mathematics, PGCE primary/secondary, primary teaching, special needs; BA, EdD, FD, GradCert, MA, MEd, MPhil, MSc, PGCE, PhD

Postgraduate Medical Institute; www2.hull.ac.uk/pgmi

biomedicine, cell & molecular medicine, cardiology, clinical psychology, diabetes, metabolic bone health, obstetrics & gynaecology, oncology, psychiatry & primary care, respiratory medicine; MD, MPhil, PhD

Faculty of Science; www.hull.ac.uk/science

Biological Sciences: aquatic zoology, biology, biomedical science, coastal marine biology, ecology, human biology, marine & freshwater biology, molecular bioscience, pharmaceutical science, zoology
Chemistry: chemistry, forensic/analytical science, pharmaceutical science, molecular medicine, nanotechnology, toxology
Computer Science: computer & business informatics, computer science/engineering, design & technology, electronic/medical product design, games development, computer software/systems engineering, information technology, computer graphics/games programming, distributed/financial systems development
Engineering: engineering, electronic engineering, mechanical engineering, medical engineering, medical product design, product innovation, wireless systems engineering, logistics technology, embedded systems, automatic control
Geography: human/physical geography, environmental management, GIS & enviromental modelling
Physics: physics, astrophysics, statistical & quantum physics, MRI, spectroscopy, nanotechnology
Sports Science, Health & Exercise: coaching, sports & exercise science, rehabilitation
Environmental & Marine Science: environmental science, coastal/marine biology, ecology
Estuarine & Coastal Studies: marine biology
Psychology: psychology, cognitive & clinical neuroscience, cognition & perception, clinical psychology; BA, BEng, BSc, BSc/MEng, MPhil, MPhys, MPhysGeog, MRes, MSc, PhD

Degrees validated by the University of Hull offered at:

BISHOP BURTON COLLEGE
www.bishopburton.ac.uk

agriculture, animal management, design, early years, environmental conservation, equine, floristry, food, garden design & management, management, planning & development, public services, sport, teacher training; BA(Hons), BSc(Hons), BSc(Ord), BTECExtel, FD, FdSc, HNC, MSc, PGCE

DONCASTER COLLEGE
www.don.ac.uk

business/administration, building services, animation & games, criminal justice, construction, counselling, dance, digital performance/entertainment, early years, education, English, film & TV, fine art, engineering, fashion & textiles, hospitality & catering, graphic design, HRM, media, music/music technology, public services, sport & leisure; BA(Hons), BSc, BSc(Hons), FD, HNC, HND, MA, MSc, NVQs, PCE, PGCert

IMPERIAL COLLEGE, LONDON
www3.imperial.ac.uk

Faculty of Engineering; www3.engineering.imperial.ac.uk

aeronatical engineering, composites, adv computational methods (aeronautics-flow,fluid-structure interaction); bioengineering, biochemical engineering/with biomaterials/biomechanics/medical physics, neurotechnology; chemical technology, chemical engineering, process systems eng, structured product, biotechnology; civil/structural engineering, structured steel design, concrete structures, earthquake structures, environmental eng, geotechnics, transport; computing, computer science (games, vision, artificial intelligence, software engineering, biology, medicine); earth science & engineering, geology, geophysics, environmental/petroleum geoscience/geophysics, materials & energy finance; electronic/electrical engineering, analog & digital integrated circuit design, information systems engineering, communications & signal processing, control systems, material science, aerospace materials, biomaterials, tissue engineering, nuclear engineering, advanced materials, materials; adv/mechanical engineering, nuclear engineering, innovation design engineering; BEng, MA, MEng, MSc, MSci, PhD

Faculty of Medicine; www1.medicine.imperial.ac.uk

medicine, biomedical research, cancer biology, drug discovery, epidemology, haematology, immunology, epidemiology, molecular medicine, molecular medicine, neuroscience, paediatrics, preventative cardiology, pharm & translational allergy, physiology & public health, reproductive biology, surgery/technology/education, translational medicine, virology; BSc, CAS, MB BS, MEd, MPH, MRes, MSc, MSci, PhD

Imperial College Business School; www3.imperial.ac.uk/business-school

accounting/management analysis, management, actuarial finance, business economics/strategy, entrepreneurship, finance, innovation, international health management, management, managerial economics, marketing, metals-energy finance, organizational behaviour, project management, risk management and financial engineering, strategic marketing; BSc, MBA, MSc, PhD

Dept of Humanities; www3.imperial.ac.uk/humanities

foreign languages (French, German, Italian, Mandarin Chinese), history of medicine, languages for science, scientific, technical, medical translation; MPhil, MSc, PhD

Faculty of Natural Sciences; www3.imperial.ac.uk/naturalsciences

chemical biology, chemistry and management/medicinal chemistry/molecular physics,,green chemistry, nanomaterials, plastic electronics

Life Sciences: biochemistry, biology, biology with management/microbiology, bioimaging sciences, biomedical science, biotechnology,drug dicovery, ecology and environmental biology, microbiology, plant biology, zoology

Mathematics: applied/pure mathematics, mathematical finance, mathematical physics, statistics

Physics: physics, optics and photonics, photonics, plastic electronics, quantum fields and fundamental forces, theoretical physics, theory and simulation of materials; BSc, MRes, MSci, PhD

KEELE UNIVERSITY
www.keele.ac.uk

Faculty of Health; www.keele.ac.uk/facs/health

School of Medicine; www.keele.ac.uk/depts/schoolofmedicine

biomedical engineering, cell and tissue engineering, clinical practice/pathology, primary care, parasitology, vector biology, foundation medical practice, geriatric medicine, medical education, medical science, medical ethics & law, medicine, surgery

School of Pharmacy; www.keele.ac.uk/schools/pharm

clinical (hospital) pharmacy, community pharmacist, prescribing adviser, medical/non medical/practice-based prescribing, medicines management

Nursing and Midwifery; www.keele.ac.uk/depts/ns

acute care, adult/childrens nursing, clinical practice, critical care, end of life care, generic route, high dependency care, learning disability nursing, long term conditions, maternal and infant health, midwifery, operating dept practice, pre-registration – mental health nursing, rheumatology nursing

School of Health and Rehabilitation; www.keele.ac.uk/depts/pt

anatomical science, health science, neurological rehabilitation, neuromusculoskeletal healthcare, osteopathy, pain science management, physiotherapy; MBChB, BSc, MSc, MSci, MPharm, PGCert, MMedSci, MPhil, PhD, MD

Faculty of Humanities and Social Sciences; www.keele.ac.uk/facs/humass

Keele Management School; www.keele.ac.uk/schools/ems

accounting, finance, actuarial science, business management/ economics, economics, finance & IT/management, HRM, international business, management, management & IT, marketing; MA, MBA, MSc, PGCert, PGDip, UnivCert

School of Humanities; www.keele.ac.uk/schools/hums

American studies/literature and culture, English, creative writing, film studies, English and American literatures, humanities, Victorian studies, early modern history, history, local and public history, medieval cultural history, film studies, media communication/global media & culture, music, music technology, popular music, performance, composition

Keele Law School; www.keele.ac.uk/depts/law

child care law & practice, gender, sexuality & human rights, globalization & justice, medical ethics & law, law, law with politics/criminology, social science research in law

School of Politics, International Relations and Philosophy; www.keele.ac.uk/spire

diplomatic studies, environmental politics, European politics & culture, global security, globalization & justice, human rights, international relations, philosophy, politics, climate change

School of Public Policy and Professional Practice; www.keele.ac.uk/schools/pppp

Education: creative and critical practice, development, educational leadership/studies, mathematics development, PGCE (subject enhancement, pre-teaching training), teaching & learning, social work, clinical management & leadership, mathematics CPD for teachers, education, health executive, public policy, gerontology, health services management, HE teaching & learning, communiity health, geriatric medicine, professional leadership & management; GradDip Law, EdD, LlB, LLM, MA, MBA, MRes, MSc, PGCE, PGDip/Cert, PhD

Faculty of Natural Sciences; www.keele.ac.uk/facs/sci/

School of Computing and Mathematics; www.scm.keele.ac.uk

actuarial science, computer science, creative computing, finance and IT, information systems, IT management for business, mathematics (pure, applied, statistics), project management, smart systems, web & internet technologies

School of Life Sciences; www. keele.ac.uk/depts/bi

biochemistry, biology, biomedical science, European scientific research training, human biology, molecular parasitology and vector biology, neuroscience

School of Physical and Geographical Sciences; www.keele.ac.uk/schools/dps/

chemistry, medicinal chemistry, analytical, materials & surface chemistry, spectroscopy, bioinorganic chemistry, chemical ecology, green chemistry and clean energy, integrated macromolecular structure, organic chemistry, photochemistry, porous materials, solid state and computational chemistry, zeolite research; applied environmental science, earth science, environment and sustainability, green technology, geography, geology, geoscience, human geography, physical geography: forensic science; astrophysics, physics

School of Psychology; www.keele.ac.uk/depts/ps

psychology, child social development, clinical psychology, counselling psychology/supervision, psychology/of health & wellbeing, supervision; BA, BSc, DClinPsy, DSc, MGeoscience, MRes, MSc, PGCert, PGDip, PhD

UNIVERSITY OF KENT
www.kent.ac.uk

Faculty of Humanities; www.kent.ac.uk/humanities

Kent School of Architecture; www.kent.ac.uk/architecture
architecture, architectural visualization, European architecture, urban design, interiors, arhitecture & cities

School of Arts; www.kent.ac.uk/arts
drama & theatre studies,, European theatre, film studies, fine arts, history & philosophy of art/aesthetics, music technology, performance arts/practice, event & experience studies

School of English; www.kent.ac.uk/english
English/American literature, post-colonial studies, creative writing, critical theory, Dickens & Victorian culture, medieval & early modern studies

School of European Culture & Languages; www.kent.ac.uk/secl
classical & archaeological studies, comparative literature, English language, French, German, Hispanic studies, history of archaeology, Italian, language & linguistic studies, modern European literature, philosophy, religious studies

School of History; www.kent.ac.uk/history
American studies, history of science, modern history, technology & medicine, medieval & modern studies, propaganda & war, war studies, war, media & modernity; BA(Hons), BSc(Hons), MA, MArch, MDram, MPhil, PhD

Faculty of Science; www.kent.ac.uk/stms

Dept of Bioscience; www.kent.ac.uk/bio
biochemistry, biological/medical science, biology, biomedical imaging, reproductive medicine & ethics, cancer biology, science, community & society

School of Computing; www.sc.kent.ac.uk/
computer science – artificial intelligence/consulting/networks, computing & business administration, computer intelligence, business information, computer security, networks & security, multicore systems, business/IT, molecular computing

School of Engineering and Digital Arts; www.eng.kent.ac.uk;
advanced/electronic/computer systems engineering, architectural vision, broadband /mobile communication, computer animation, digital visual effects/arts, electronic & communications engineering, drama & multimedia, information security/biometrics, multimedia technology, web computing, wireless communication & signal processing

School of Mathematics, Statistics & Actuarial Science; www.kent.ac.uk/IMS
actuarial science, pure/applied maths, statistics, finance, investment, risk

Medway School of Pharmacy; www.kent.ac.uk/msp
medicine management, pharmaceutical practice, pharmacy, independant & supplementary prescription

School of Physical Sciences; www.kent.ac.uk/physical-sciences
astrophysics, applied optics, astronomy, forensic chemistry/science, functional materials, imaging, physics, planetary/space science; BA(Hons), BEng, BSc(Hons), DClinPsych, MD, MRes, MPhil, MSc, Msurg, PCert, PDip, PhD,

Faculty of Social Sciences; www.kent.ac.uk/socsci

School of Anthropology and Conservation; www.kent.ac.uk/sac
anthropology (social/biological/medical), biodiversity conservation & management, conservation biology, environmental anthropology, ethnicity, ethnobotany, evolution & human behaviour, conservation & int wildlife trade/tourism, social/visual anthropology, wildlife conservation; BA(Hons), BSc(Hons), MA, MSc, PhD

Kent Business School; www.kent.ac.uk/kbs
accounting, business administration, business/management studies, finance, financial services/management, HRM, international business, logistics, management science, marketing management, sustainability management, tourism management, value chain management; BA(Hons), BBA, BSc(Hons), MBA, MEBA, MPhil, MSc

School of Economics; www.kent.ac.uk/economics

agricultural economics, applied environmental economics, econometrics, economics, finance, financial economics,, economic development, international finance; BSc(Hons), MPhil, PhD, MSc

Kent Law School; www.kent.ac.uk/law

criminal justice, English, French, German, Spanish or Italian law, European legal studies/law, international environmental/commercial law, international criminal justice, medical law & ethics, public international law, senior status; BA(Hons), LlB, LlM, MPhil, PhD

Centre for Journalism; www.kent.ac.uk/journalism

journalism, multimedia journalism, journalism & the news industry; BA(Hons)

School of Politics and International Relations; www.kent.ac.uk/politics

comparative federalism, conflict, peace & security, European governance, international conflict analysis/law/relations/security, politics, political theory, security & terrorism; BA(Hons), MA, MPhil, PhD

Dept of Psychology; www.kent.ac.uk/psychology

applied psychology, cognition, cognitive psychology/neuropsychology, forensic psychology, group processes & intergroup relations, psychology, social psychology; BSc(Hons), MPhil, MSc, PhD

School of Social Policy, Sociology and Social Research; www.kent.ac.uk/sspssr

criminal justice studies, criminology, cultural studies, environmental social science, health & social care, intellectual & development disabilities, international/social policy,sociology, social work/science, migration studies, substance misuse management; BA(Hons), BSc(Hons), Certificate and Diplomas, MA, MPhil, MSc, PhD

Centre for Sports Studies; www.kent.ac.uk/sports-studies

health & fitness, rehabilitation, sport science/therapy, sports & exercise management/science; BA, BSc, BSc(Hons), MA

KINGSTON UNIVERSITY
www.kingston.ac.uk

Faculty of Art, Design and Architecture; www.kingston.ac.uk/faculties/#design

architecture, art & design/history/market, building surveying, design, contemporary design, curating, product space, fashion, film studies/making, fine art (painting, sculpture, intermedia, print), games development, garden design, graphic design, historic building conservation, illustration & animation, interior design, landscape architecture/planning/urbanism, museum & gallery studies, photography, planning & sustainability, product & furniture design, property planning & development, quantity surveying consultancy, real estate management, residential property, sustainable place making & urban design, user experience design, visual & material culture; BA(Hons), FdA, FDA, FdSc, MA, MSc, PGCert/Dip

Faculty of Arts and Social Sciences; www.fass.kingston.ac.uk

applied development/international business/financial economics, business & economic forecasting, international politics & economics; child centred interprofessional practice, children's special educational needs/inclusive education, early years education & childcare/management & leadership/teaching, primary/secondary teaching (QTS), English language teaching, continuous professional development; creative writing, English language, & communication, English literature, film studies, French, journalism, media and cultural studies, Spanish; writing fiction/chilren's literature/travel, language dance, drama, film studies/making, music, music education/performance/technology, performance, classical theatre, pop music, playwriting, electroacoustic composition; BA(Hons), MA, PgCert/Dip, EdD

Faculty of Law & Business; www.business.kingston.ac.uk

Kingston Business School: accounting, banking, finance, business, management, business information technology & management, marketing & communications, creative industries, general management, leadership, HRM, services management

Kingston School of Law: law, criminality, international/corporate & financial/community/employment law, human rights, immigration law, international commercial law, conflict, international relations, legal studies; BA(Hons), BSc(Hons), DBA, FdA, GradDip Law, HND, LlM, MA, MBA, MSC, PhD

Faculty of Computing, Information Systems and Mathematics; www.cism.kingston.ac.uk

computer science, computer-generated images/ vision, electronic commerce, embedded systems, informatics, health-related computing, IT for e-business, IT business support, games & graphics, actuarial mathematics, medical technologies, networking and data communications information security, software engineering, statistics, web development, wireless communications; BSc(Hons), FdSc, HND, MComp, MPhil, MSc, PhD

Faculty of Engineering; www.engineering.kingston.ac.uk

advanced industrial & manufacturing systems, advanced product design engineering, aerospace/ aircraft engineering/maintenance, astronautics & space technology, automotive engineering, aviation studies for commercial pilots, civil engineering, construction law/management, embedded systems, engineering projects & systems management, mechanical engineering, mechatronic systems, motorsport engineering, renewable energy engineering, structural design, sustainable concrete structures; BEng, BSc(Hons), FdSc, HND, MEng, MSc, PhD

Faculty of Health & Social Care Sciences; www.healthcare.kingston.ac.uk

advanced practice (health care), biomedical science/ clinical practice, exercise & nutrition, medical technologies, healthcare practice/information/education, health management/information, long-term condition, maternal & child health, social work midwifery/registered midwife, nursing, nutrition, paramedic science, physiotherapy, radiography, rehabilitation, social care, BSc(Hons), DipHE, FdSc, MREs, MPhil, MSc, MSw, PGCert/Dip, PhD

Faculty of Science; www.kingston.ac.uk/ science

applied/analytical chemistry, applied & environmental geology, biochemistry, biology, biomedical science, biotechnology, cancer biology, chemistry, cell & molecular biology, communication systems, games development, computer graphics technology/generated imagery, computing, earth systems science, environmental management/science/studies/& earth resource management, exercise, nutrition & health, forensic biology, forensic analysis, gemmology & applied mineralogy, applied GI, geography, geology/ applied and environmental, GIS, hazards & disaster management, human biology, human geography, media technology, medical biochemistry, nutrition, paramedic sciences, pharmaceutical analysis/science, sports science, TV & video technology, sustainable development/environment & change; BSc(Hons), FdSc, MPharm, MPhil, MSc, PhD, PGCert/Dip

LANCASTER UNIVERSITY
www.lancs.ac.uk

Faculty of Arts and Social Sciences; www.lancs.ac.uk/fass/faculties

European Languages and Cultures; www.lancs.ac.uk/fass/eurolang

German, Italian, French, Spanish, modern languages, film studies, modern European history, European institutions & policy/languages & cultures

Applied Social Science; www.lancs.ac.uk/ fass/appsocsci

criminology, social work

Educational Research; www.lancs.ac.uk/ fass/edres

education, research, psychology in education

English and Creative Writing; www.lancs.ac.uk/fass/english

English language/literature, theatre studies, creative writing, contemporary literature

History; www.lancs.ac.uk/fass/history

medieval & renaissance/modern European/ social history

Lancaster Institute for the Contemporary Arts; www.lancs.ac.uk/fass/licr

contemporary/creative arts, fine art, marketing & design, music, pop music, music technology, sustainability, innovation & design, theatre studies, film & culture studies, design/management & policy

School of Law; www.lancs.ac.uk/fass/law
law, bioethics, medical law, European legal studies, humanitarian /international, business & corporate, international human rights/law, law & criminology, management & law

Linguistics & English Language; w www.ling.lancs.ac.uk
English language/the media, applied/linguistics, creative writing, teaching English (TESOL), language studies/testing, discourse studies, sociolinguistics

Politics, Philosophy & Religion; www.lancs.ac.uk/fass/ppr
politics, international relations/law, religious studies, philosophy, diplomacy, foreign policy, international law, religion, conflict, development & security, conflict resolution & peace studies

Sociology; www.lancs.ac.uk/fass/sociology
sociology, society technology and nature, gender and women's studies, social research, society, technology & nature; BSc(Hons), LlB, LlM, MA, MPhil, MSc, PGD, PhD

School of Health and Medicine; www.lancs.ac.uk/shm/faculties

Biomedical & Health Sciences; www.lancs.ac.uk/shm/bls
biochemistry/with biomedicine or genetics, medical statistics, cell biology, clinical psychology, learning disabilities, life care, premedical studies, public mental health

Medicine; www.lancs.ac.uk/shm/med
basic biomedical research, medical education, medical statistics & epidemiology, medicine, sociology of medicine, clinical psychology; BSc(Hons), CertHE, DClinPsych, MBChB, MBiomed, MD, MHospice leadership, MPhil, MRes, MSc, PgDip/Cert, PhD

Lancaster University Management School; www.lums.lancs.ac.uk

accounting, advertising, banking, business studies, e-business, European management, finance, financial management/analysis, HR, information technology, international business, knowledge management, logistics & supply chain management, management & law/organizational change, management/ science & operations/analytics/organization, marketing, market analytics, money, operational research, project management, quanitative finance; BA(Hons), BBA, BSc(Hons), LlM, MBA, MPhil, MRes, MSc, PhD

Faculty of Science and Technology; www.lancs.ac.uk/shm/sci-tech/faculties

Computing & Communication; www.lancs.ac.uk/sci-tech/departments/computing_and_communication
computer science, communication systems engineering/ & electronics, cyber security, software engineering, IT for creative industries, distributed systems engineering, DSP & intelligent systems, human–computer interaction, management & IT, mobile & ubiquitous computing, media production & distribution, telecommunications mobile broadband communications/systems, multimedia networking, network & internet systs, social network technologies

Engineering; www.engineering.lancs.ac.uk
engineering, electronic/electrical engineering. mechatronic/mechanical engineering, nuclear engineering, sustainable engineering, computer systems engineering, decommissioning & environmental clean-up, microelectronics, safety engineering

Lancaster Environment Centre; www.lec.lancs.ac.uk
biology, biological science, biophotonics, conservation science, contaminated land, ecology/energy & environment, development, environmental informatics/management/pollution & protection/science/ technology, biochemical toxology, earth science, plant sciences, resource and environmental management, sustainable water management, volcanology & geological hazard

Mathematics and Statistics; www.maths.lancs.ac.uk
applied social statistics, computer science and mathematics, statistics, environmental/financial mathematics/& philosophy/statistics/psycholog/theoretical physics, quantitative methods/finance

Natural Sciences; www.naturalsci.lancs.ac.uk
combined science, combined technology, natural sciences

Physics; www.lancs.ac.uk/depts/physics
astrophysics, cosmology, biomedical physics, physics, space science, theoretical physics/with mathematics, particle physics

Psychology; www.psych.lancs.ac.uk
development psychology/disorders, language, speech & learning, psychology, psychology of advertising, social psychology;

BEng(Hons), BSc(Hons), MChem, MEng(Hons), MPhil, MPhys(Hons), MRes, MSc, MSci(Hons), PGDip, PhD

Degrees validated by Lancaster University offered at:

BLACKPOOL AND THE FYLDE COLLEGE
www.blackpool.ac.uk

construction, art, media and performance, business management, catering & food prodn, society, health & childhood, autosport, computing & automotive engineering, catering, food production, hair, beauty and related therapies, tourism, leisure & hospitality; FD, HNC, HND, BEng, BA(Hons), BSc/(Hons)

EDGEHILL UNIVERSITY
www.edgehill.ac.uk

Faculty of Education; www.edgehill.ac.uk/education

education with QTS (creative art, design & technology/ secondary education, early years, English, secondary education, mathematics, mod foreign langs, primary education, RE, science, PE, science key stage 2/3/secondary education/PE/secondary science, 14–19/11–16 education, childhood & early years, e-learning, inclusive & special needs, educational psychology PGCE (business education/creative media/design & technology/English/geography/history/info & communication technology/mathematics/mod langs/music/PE); BA(Hons), BSc(Hons), CertHE, Foundation degrees, PGCE, MA, MTL

Faculty of Health; www.edgehill.ac.uk/health

Nursing

cognitive behavioural therapies, applied health & social care, integrated practice (early years and children), midwifery, nursing studies (adult, learning disabilities, mental health, children's), operating dept practice, paramedic science, substance misuse interventions, respiratory care, surgery; BSc(Hons), Dip/CertHE, FDA, FdSc, MCh, MPhil, MSc, PhD

Faculty of Arts and Science

Business School; www.edgehill.ac.uk/business

accounting, business, management/administration, Chinese studies, HRM, int business, leisure & tourism, marketing, advertising, communications, management development, computing (control & embedded systems, information systems, software), IT for business, web systems, information security & IT management

Dept of English and History; www.edgehill.ac.uk/history

Chinese studies, creative writing, English language/literature, film studies, history, culture

Law & Criminology; www.edgehill.ac.uk/law

criminology, law, international sports regulation, law, law with management

Media; www.edgehill.ac.uk/media

digital SFX/animation, advertising, film & TV production, journalism, media, film & television or music & sound, PR, television production management

Dept of Natural, Geographical and Applied Sciences; www.edgehill.ac.uk/ngas

biogeography, biology, conservation management, environmental science, geography, geology, human/physical geography

Performing Arts; www.edgehill.ac.uk/performingart

theatre, dance, design for performance, drama/ visual theatre/music & sound, performance & health, making performance

Dept of Social & Psychological Sciences; www.edgehill.ac.uk/dsaps;

psychology, childhood & youth studies, social work & sociology, social research methods

Dept of Sport & Physical Activity; www.edgehill.ac.uk/sport
coach education, physical education & school sport, sport & exercise psychology/science, sports development/studies/therapy, football rehabilitation; BA(Hons), BSc(Hons), FDA, FDSc, LlB(Hons), MA, MSc, PhD, MBA

UNIVERSITY OF LEEDS
www.leeds.ac.uk

Faculty of Arts; www.leeds.ac.uk/arts

School of English; www.leeds.ac.uk/english
American literature & culture, English language/literature, modern & contemporary/Renaissance literature, post-colonial literary & cultural studies, romantic literature & culture, theatre & global studies, theatre making/studies, Victorian literature

School of History; www.leeds.ac.uk/history
history, international history & politics, medieval history, modern history, race & resistance, social & cultural history

School of Humanities; www.leeds.ac.uk/humanities
classical civilization/studies, classics, Greek, Latin, philosophy, development studies, health care ethics, history and philosophy of science, pastoral studies, mind and knowledge, philosophy of religion/physics, religion/theology and public life/pastoral care, religious studies, science communication, theology

Institute for Colonial and Post-colonial Studies; www.leeds.ac.uk/icps
post-colonial literary & cultural studies, race & resistance, world cinema, modern languages & cultures

School of Modern Languages and Cultures; www.leeds.ac.uk/smlc
Arabic & Middle Eastern studies, Chinese, Japanese, South/East Asian studies, French, German, Italian, linguistics & phonetics, modern languages & cultures, professional language & intercultural studies, Russian, Spanish, Portuguese and Latin American studies, translation & interpreting, world cinema; BA(Hons), MA, MPhil, PGDip, PhD

Faculty of Biological Studies; www.fbs.leeds.ac.uk

biochemistry, biology, bioscience (biotechnology/bioinformatics & computational biology/human disease & therapy/infection & immunology/plant science), ecology & environmental biology, biodiversity & conservation, genetics, human physiology, medical biochemistry/microbiology/sciences, microbiology, neuroscience, pharmacology, virology, molecular biology, sport & exercise sciences, zoology; BSc(Hons), MRes, MSc, PhD

Faculty of Business; www.fbs.leeds.ac.uk

Leeds University Business School; www.leeds.ac.uk/lbs
accounting, advertising & design, banking, business economics, computing & management, corporate communications & PR, diversity management, economics, actuarial/finance, financial economics/mathematics/risk, HRM, international business/finance/marketing management, management, organizational psychology, textile innovation, manufacturing leadership, marketing, transport studies; BSc(Hons), ExecMBA, MA, MBA, MPhil, MSc, PhD

Faculty of Education, Social Sciences & Law; www.essl.leeds.ac.uk

School of Education; www.education.leeds.ac.uk
childhood studies, clinical education, deaf education, ICT, lifelong learning, mathematics/science education, PGCE biology/chemistry/English/mathematics/modern foreign languages/physics, children with learning difficulties/developmental disorders, special educational needs, teaching, teaching English (TESOL) for young learners/studies/teacher education

School of Law; www.law.leeds.ac.uk
criminal law & rights law, European law/& society, international & comparative criminal justice, law, policing, European & international business law/corporate law/trade law, intellectual property law, European human rights law, senior status

School of Politics and International Studies; www.leeds.ac.uk/polis

global development, politics (parliamentary, political theory), international relations/development, conflict, development & security, conflict, terrorism & insurgency

School of Sociology and Social Policy; www.sociology.leeds.ac.uk

disability studies. crime, gender studies, global genders, social & political theory, international social transformation, racism & ethnicity studies, social science/policy, sociology; BA(Hons), LLM, MA, MEd, MPhil, MSc, PGCert, PGCE, PhD

Faculty of Engineering; www.engineering.leeds.ac.uk

School of Civil Engineering; www.engineering.leeds.ac.uk/civil

architectural engineering, civil & environmental engineering/structural engineering/with construction management, international construction management/public health engineering, environmental engineering, engineering project management

School of Computing; www.engineering.leeds.ac.uk/comp

artificial intelligence, computer science/& mathematics, computing/ for business management, information technology

School of Electronic and Electrical Engineering; www.engineering.leeds.ac.uk/elec

electrical engineering, electronic/& communications engineering, mechatronics & robotics, music, multimedia & electronics, nanotechnology, nanomaterials & adv devices, renewable energy sytems, broadband wireless & optical comm, embedded systems

Mechanical Engineering; www.engineering.leeds.ac.uk/mech

aeronautical & aerospace engineering, automotive engineering, mechanical engineering, mechatronics & robotics, medical engineering, oilfield corrosion engineering, nuclear engineering, tribology & engineering interfaces

School of Process, Environmental and Materials Engineering; www.engineering.leeds.ac.uk/speme

aviation technology, pilot studies, chemical & energy/ materials/minerals engineering/pharmaceutical engineering, chemical engineering, computational fluid dynamics, energy & environment, computational fluid mechanics, fire & explosion, petroleum engineering; BEng, MEng, MSc, MSc(Eng), MPhil, PhD

Faculty of the Environment; www.leeds.ac.uk/foe

School of Earth & Environment; www.see.leeds.ac.uk

engineering geology, environment & business/management, climate science/change, environmental sustainability/management/science/conservation, exploration geophysics, geochemistry, geological/ geophysical sciences, hydrogeology, physics of the earth & atmosphere, sustainability (transport/business environment & corporate responsibility/environmental consultancy/environment & development/ environmental politics & policy)

School of Geography; www.geog.leeds.ac.uk

geography, activism & society, catchment dynamics, geography/with transport planning, geography–geology, GIS, human geography, hydrology, social & cultural geography

Institute for Transport Studies; www.its.leeds.ac.uk

economics with transport studies, geography with transport planning, management with transport planning, planning, transport economics, engineering/environment, sutainabilty (transport)

Earth & Biosphere Institute; www.earth.leeds.ac.uk/ebi

global change & the biosphere; BA(Hons), BSc(Hons), MA, MGeol, MGeophys, MRes, MSc, DGCert/Dip, PhD

Faculty of Mathematics and Physical Science; www.maps.leeds.ac.uk

School of Chemistry; www.chemistry.leeds.ac.uk

chemistry, chemical process, colour & imaging science, analytical chemistry, medicinal chemistry, polymer & surface coatings science, chemical biology & drug design

School of Food Science and Nutrition; www.food.leeds.ac.uk

food biotechnology/quality & innovation, nutrition, food studies/science

School of Physics and Astronomy; www.physics.leeds.ac.uk
astrophysics, nanotchnology, physics, medical physics, quantum technologies, theoretical physics

School of Mathematics; www.amsta.ac.uk
actuarial/financial mathematics, mathematics/with finance, statistics /with applications to finance, atmosphere ocean dynamics; BSc(Hons), MChem, MMath, MNatSci, MPhil, MPhys, MSc, PhD

Faculty of Health and Medicine; www.leeds.ac.uk/medhealth

Leeds Dental Institute; www.leeds.ac.uk/dental
hygiene & therapy, dental nursing/surgery/technology/therapy, dental public health

Leeds Institute of Medical Education; www.leeds.ac.uk/medicine/lime
medicine, surgery, child health, clinical embryology/psychology, health informatics/management, planning & policy, hospital management, medical physics/imaging, nutrition, obesity & health, primary care education/healthcare, psychiatry, psychoanalytic observational studies, public health, statistical epidemiology, systematic family therapy, healthcare ethics

School of Healthcare; www.lhealthcare.leeds.ac.uk/
adult/child nursing, clinical physiology, counselling, diagnostic imaging, audiology, medicines management, mental health, midwifery, nursing, public health, radiography, social work

School of Medicine; www.leeds.ac.uk/medicine
child health, clinical embryology/psychology, family therapy, health informatics/management, hospital management, medical physics/imaging, medicine, nutrition, obesity & health, patient safety, primary health care, psychiatry, psychoanalytical observation, public health, statistical epidemiology, surgery

Institute of Psychological Sciences; www.psych.leeds.ac.uk
biological/cognitive/sport & exercise psychology, psychological approach to health, memory & its disorders; BHSc, BSc(Hons), CPD, DClinPsych, GradDip, MA, MBChB, MD, MMedSci, MPH, MPsycObs, MSc, PGDip/Cert, PhD

Faculty of Performance, Visual Arts and Communication; www.leeds.ac.uk/pvac

Institute of Communication Studies; www.ics.leeds.ac.uk
broadcast journalism, cinema & photography, communications studies, international/political communications, journalism, new/media industries, TV production

School of Design; www.design.leeds.ac.uk
textile & performance clothing, advertising & design, art & design, design & colour technology/technology management, fashion design, graphic and communication design, textile innovation & branding

School of Fine Art, History of Art and Cutural Studies; www.leeds.ac.uk/fine.art
art gallery and museum studies, art history with museum studies, cultural studies, fine art, history of art

School of Music; www.ics.leeds.ac.uk/music
composition, psychology of music, music, multimedia & electronics, pop & world music, music technology, musicology, performance

School of Performance & Cultural Industries; www.ics.leeds.ac.uk/paci
choreography, culture, creativity & entrepreneurship, dance, managing performance, performance culture, theatre & performance, writing for performance and publication; BA(Hons), GradDip, MFA, BMus, BSc(Hons), MA, MMus, MSc, PhD

Degrees validated by University of Leeds offered at:

ASKHAM BRYAN COLLEGE
www.askham-bryan.ac.uk

agriculture, animal management, business & IT, countryside & environment, engineering, plant & construction, equine, floristry, food, forestry & arboriculture, horticulture, land management, sports & leisure, surface & greenkeeping, teacher education; BA(Hons), BSc(Hons), Nat Dips, FD

COLLEGE OF THE RESURRECTION

www.mirfield.org.uk

theology & pastoral studies; BA(Hons), DipHE, MA, MPhil, PGDip, PhD

LEEDS COLLEGE OF ART

www.leeds-art.ac.uk

art & design, creative advertising, digital film, games & animation, fashion, fine art, furniture making, graphic design, interior design, photography, printed textiles & surface pattern design, visual communication; BA(Hons), FD, HNC, National Diploma

LEEDS COLLEGE OF MUSIC

www.lcm.ac.uk

classical/pop music, composition, jazz, music production, musicology, performance, composition; BA (Hons), FD, MA, PGDip

LEEDS TRINITY & ALL SAINTS

www.leedstrinity.ac.uk

Faculty of Arts and Social Sciences; www.leedstrinity.ac.uk/departments/fass

English, history, psychology, sport, health, leisure & nutrition, theology & religious studies, Victorian studies; BA(Hons), BSc(Hons), MA, MSc, PGCE

Faculty of Education

Catholic education, children, young people & families, PGCE programmes, primary education, secondary education, teaching assistants; BA(Hons), FD, MA, PGCert, PGCE

Faculty of Media, Business & Marketing; www.leedstrinity.ac.uk/departments/FMBN

broadcast/magazine/print journalism, business & management, business studies, management, marketing, media, film & culture, public communications, PR, sports journalism; BA(Hons), MA/PGDip, MB

NORTHERN SCHOOL OF CONTEMPORARY DANCE

www.nscd.ac.uk

contemporary dance, choreography; BPA(Hons), PgDip, MA,FD

YORK ST JOHN UNIVERSITY

www.yorksj.ac.uk

Faculty of Arts

film & TV production, music composition/performance, American studies, creative writing, dance, documentary/film production, English literature, film/literary studies, fine arts, history, media, music, product design, theatre; FD, BA(Hons), PgCert/Dip, MA

Faculty of Education & Theology

PGCE, primary/secondary education, religious studies, theology & ministry, Christian theology/studies teacher education; MFL, BA(Hons), GradDip, PgDip

Faculty of Health & Life Sciences

counselling, occupational therapy, physiotherapy, psychology, CPD & lifelong learning, sport; BA(Hons), MA, PgDip/Cert

York St John Business School

international/business/management, HRM, business IT, web technologies, English language & linguistics, international tourism/ marketing management, tourism management, global marketing, languages, leadership & management, innovation & change, TESOL, web technologies; BA(Hons), FD, MA, PGDip/Cert,MBA

LEEDS METROPOLITAN UNIVERSITY
www.leedsmet.ac.uk

Faculty of Arts & Society; www.leedsmet.ac.uk/as

The Leeds School of Architecture, Landscape & Design; www.lmu.ac.uk/as/ald

urban design, garden art, interior architecture, design (appl textiles/digital/furniture/play/product), landscape architecture

School of Civil Engineering & Construction Management; www.lmu.ac.uk/aet/benv

building studies, engineering studies, civil engineering, construction/commercial/management, strategic/ project management, adv engineering management, facilities management; architectural technology, building/quantity surveying, housing, human geography/& planning, planning law & practice, project management, town & regional planning, heritage planning, construction law & dispute res

School of Computing; www.leedsmet.ac.uk/aet/computing

business information systs, computer forensics, computing, computer security & ethical hacking, systems & networking, green computing, mobile & distr computer networks, web applications, software development/engineering, mobile device applications, adv engineering management, information technology/systems/management

School of Music; www.leedsmet.ac.uk/aet/music

music performance/production/technology, audio post-production, moving image, music for interactive games, sound design

School of Interactive Media; www.leedsmet.ac.uk/aet/interactive-media

broadcast media technologies, photographic journalism, computer animation, games design, digital imaging/video, mobile device development, multimedia/entertainment /creative technology

The Leeds School of Contemporary Art & Graphic Design; www.lmu.ac.uk/as/cagd

graphic/art & design, contemporary fine art practices, fine art

School of Cultural Studies; www.lmu.ac.uk/as/cs

English, English literature, history, media, communication, culture, cultural planning & policy, English contemp literature, screen media cultures

Film, Television, and Performing Arts; www.lmu.ac.uk/as/ftpa

animation, art, contemporary dance/performance, creative enterprise, events performance, dance, film and moving image production, film & TV production, filmmaking, performance/works

School of Social Science; www.lmu.ac.uk/as/sss

criminology, politics, psychology & society, social sciences, sociology, working with young people, youth work & community development; BA(Hons), BSc(Hons), DipHE, FdAA, GradCert, MPhil, MRes, MSc, PGDip

Faculty of Business and Law; www.leedsmet.ac.uk/fbl

Leeds Business School; www.leedsmet.ac.uk/fbl/leeds_business_school

accounting, advertising, business, business studies, economics for business, finance, HRM, international business/communications, journalism, management, marketing, organizational behaviour, PR, purchasing & supply/logistics, strategy & business analysis

Leeds Law School; www.leedsmet.ac.uk/lbs/law

law, law with criminology, legal practice, commercial/employment/family/property/business law, personal injury; BA(Hons), HND, LlB(Hons), LlM, MA, MSc, PGDip/Cert, MBA

Faculty of Health & Social Sciences; www.leedsmet.ac.uk/hss

accupuncture, applied psychology, social work/science, psychotherapy, biomedical sciences (human biology, microbiology, physiology), counselling, health, public health nursing, nursing (adult health/mental health/district nursing), osteopathy, practice/community children' s nursing, occupational therapy, physiotherapy, psychology and criminology, nutrition, safety, health & environmental management, social work, speech & language therapy, sport & exercise therapy, therapeutic counselling, youth work, playwork; BA(Hons), BSc(Hons), CertHE, HNC, MA, MSc, PGDip/Cert, Prof Dip

Carnegie Faculty www.leedsmet.ac.uk/carnegie

English language teaching, material development, business & EFL/marketing/tourism management, language studies, French, German, Spanish, contemporary European studies, international tourism & hospitaility/business management/leadership & management, retail business management, international/resort/student hospitality management, consumer/retail marketing, international business admin, strategic sales, sports/events management, conference & exhibitions management, culture/sports events, international festival management; BA(Hons), BSc(Hons), FdSc, MSc, PGCE, PGCert/Dip/MA, PhD, HND

UNIVERSITY OF LEICESTER
www.le.ac.uk

College of Arts, Humanities and Law; www2.le.ac.uk/colleges/artshumlaw

School of Archaeology & Ancient History; www.le.ac.uk/ar

ancient history, archaeology, classical Mediterranean, historical archaeology, history of the Roman world

School of English; www.le.ac.uk/ee

American studies/history, English studies, history of art, visual culture, modern literature & creative writing, Victorian studies

Dept of History of Art and Film; www.le.ac.uk/ha

the country house in art, history & culture, film studies and the visual arts, history of art, humanities, film & film cultures

School of Historical Studies; www.le.ac.uk/hi

contemporary history, English local history, history, history and politics/international relations/ancient history, European urbanization, archaeology, urban history/change, social change & resistance

School of Law; www.le.ac.uk/law

law (European Union/ international/international/commercial/public/employment), law with French law, European law & integration, human rights, legal research

School of Modern Languages; www.le.ac.uk/ml

European studies, French, German, Italian, modern language studies, Spanish, humanities, translation studies

Museum Studies; www.le.ac.uk /ms

art museum & gallery studies, digital heritage, interpretive studies, learning & visitor studies; BA(Hons), BSc(Hons), LlB, LlM, MSC, MA/GradDip, MPhil, PhD

College of Science and Engineering; www2.le.ac.uk/colleges/science

Dept of Chemistry; www.le.ac.uk/ch

biochemistry, chemistry, cancer chemistry, biological/physical chemistry, forensic science, green/pharmaceutical chemistry

Dept of Computer Science; www.cs.le.ac.uk

advanced computational methods/distributed systems/software engineering, computer science, computers, computing,, web applications & services

Dept of Engineering; www2.le.ac.uk/departments/engineering

advanced control & dynamics, advanced engineering, aerospace engineering, communications & electronic engineering, control & signal processing, electrical engineering, embedded systems & control engineering, general engineering, information & communication engineering, mechanical engineering, software

Dept of Geography; www.le.ac.uk/geography

environmental informatics, geography, geology, GIS, global environmental change, human/physical geography, sustainable management of natural resources, social change & resistance, geospatial intelligence

Dept of Geology; www2.le.ac.uk/departments/geology

applied & environmental geology, crustal processes, geology, borehole/geophysics, palaeobiology

Centre for Interdisciplinary Science; www2.le.ac.uk/departments/interdisciplinary-science

communication science, complex systems, evolution, laboratory science, mathematics for science, nanoscale frontiers, sustainable livelihoods in Africa, virtual worlds

Dept of Mathematics; www2.le.ac.uk/departments/mathematics

actuarial science, computational mathematics, financial mathematics, mathematical modelling, mathematics

Dept of Physics and Astronomy; www2.le.ac.uk/departments/physics

astronomy, physics, radio & space plasma physics, physics with nanotechnology/astrophysics/space science & technology/planetary science; BA(Hons), BSc(Hons), BEng/MEng, MA, MChem, MComp, MGeol, MMath, MPhil, MPhys, MSc, MSci, PGDip, PhD

College of Medicine, Biological Sciences and Psychology; www2.le.ac.uk/colleges/medbiopsych

School of Biological Sciences; www.le.ac.uk/lbs

biochemistry, bioinformatics, biological science, biology, cell physiology & pharmacology, genetics, medical biochemistry/genetics/microbiology, clinical science, microbiology, molecular biology/genetics/toxicology, pharmacology, zoology

School of Medicine, Leicester Medical School; www.le.ac.uk/sm/le

cancer studies & molecular medicine, cardiovascular sciences, health sciences, infection, medical statistics, molecular pathology/toxicology, occupational psychology, operating dept practice, pain management, physiotherapy, primary care research, social science applied to health, child & adolescent mental health

School of Psychology; www2.le.ac.uk/departments/psychology

clinical/forensic psychology, cognitive neuroscience, psychology; DocClinPsych, BSc, MBChB, MBioSci, MD, MSc, PostgradDip/Cert, PhD

College of the Social Sciences www.le.ac.uk/colleges/socsci

Dept of Criminology; www.le.ac.uk/criminology

applied/clinical/criminology, terrorism, security & policing

Dept of Economics; www2.le.ac.uk/ec

banking & finance, business/financial economics, economics, business analysis & finance, money, public sector economics

Dept of Education; www.le.ac.uk/education

educational studies, learning & teaching, dyslexia, education leadership, mentoring & coaching, teaching assistants, international education, teaching mathematics, PGCE primary/scondary education, TESOL & applied linguistics

The Centre for Labour Market Studies; www2.le.ac.uk/departments/clms

HRM, HRM & training, performance management/industrial relations & workplace learning

Institute of Lifelong Learning; www2.le.ac.uk/departments/lifelong-learning
higher education, humanities & arts, counselling/drugs & alcohol, managing political & community orgs, emergency planning, risk crisis, disaster management

School of Management; www.le.ac.uk/ulsm
accounting, finance, management studies/economics/politics, marketing; MBA

Dept of Media & Communication; www.le.ac.uk/mc
communications & globalization, media & society/PR/advertising, media & sociology, mass communications, new media governance & democracy

Dept of Politics and International Relations; www.le.ac.uk/politics
American intervention, contemporary history, diplomatic studies, economics, politics & sociology/history/management, ethics/& international relations, S African foreign policy, negotiation

Dept of Sociology; www.le.ac.uk/sociology
sociology, civil society, social research; BA(Hons), DocSocSci, EdD, FD, MA, MBA, MPhil, MSc, PGCE, PGDip/Cert, PhD

Degrees validated by the University of Leicester offered at:

NEWMAN UNIVERSITY COLLEGE
www.newman.ac.uk

art & design, counselling, creative arts, drama, early years, education studies, English/literature, history, information technology, management & business, media & communication, theology, psychology, science/biology, PE & sports studies, teacher training, working with cildren, young people & families, youth & community work; BA/BSc(Hons), FD,MA, MPhil, PGCE, PhD

UNIVERSITY OF LINCOLN
www.lincoln.ac.uk

Faculty of Agriculture, Food and Animal Science; www.lincoln.ac.uk/afas
agriculture & environment, bioveterinary science, clinical/animal behaviour & welfare, conservation biology, equine science/sports science, food manufacture/technology; BSc, FdSc, MPhil, MSc, PhD

Faculty of Art, Architecture & Design; www.lincoln.ac.uk/aad
animation, architecture/sustainable, art & design, conservation of historic objects/studies/restoration, creative advertising, construction project management, contemporary lens media, design/exhibition & museums, development & regeneration, fashion studies, fine art, graphic design, illustration, interactive design, interior design/architecture, product design, urban design; BA(Hons), BArch, GradDip, MA, March, MPhil, PhD

Faculty of Business & Law; www.lincoln.ac.uk /bl
accountancy, advertising, branding, business administration/management/studies, European business/marketing/law, finance, hospitality, HRM, HRD, international business/management studies/marketing strategy/tourism, law & business/criminology, logistics, marketing, PR, tourism/marketing/management, sports business; BA(Hons), BSc(Hons), LlB(Hons), LlM, MA, MBA, MPhil, MRes, MSc, PhD

Faculty of Health, Life & Social Sciences; www.lincoln.ac.uk/hlsc
acupuncture, biomedical science, clinical/forensic psychology, contemporary culture & communication, criminology/and international relations/politics/forensic investigation, employment-based social work, forensic science, globalizing justice, golf science, health & social care, health science, herbal medicine, human nutrition, international relations politics/

social policy, nursing (adult), psychology with criminology/marketing/social policy/child studies, social policy/care/science, sport/development, coaching & exercise science; BA(Hons), BSc(Hons), CertHE, DClinPsy, MA, MClinRes, MPhil, PGCert, PhD

Faculty of Media, Humanities and Technology; www.lincoln.ac.uk/mht

21st-century writing, audio production, American studies, community radio, computer games production/information systems/science, creative writing, criminology, dance, digital imaging, media & photography/drama, documentary production, film & TV, English, games/computing, history, medieval studies, arts/sports journalism, culture & communications, web technology, politics, PR, theatre & consciousness

Lincoln School of Engineering; www.lincoln.ac.uk/engineering

mechanical engineering; BA(Hons), BS(Hons), FdA, MA, MComp, MPhil, MRes, MSc, PhD

Centre for Educational Research & Development; www.lincoln.ac.uk/cerd

educational development, HE teaching & learning; EdD, PhD, PGCE

School of Theology & Ministry Studies; www.lincoln.ac.uk/home/theology

theology; BA(Hons), Cert/Dip Theology, MA, FD

Degrees validated by the University of Lincoln offered at:

EAST RIDING COLLEGE
www.eastridingcollege.ac.uk

access to higher education, art, design and media, business & administration, construction, early years, health & social care, education & training, information technology, sport & recreation; BSc(Hons), DIDA, FD, HNC/D,PGCE

HULL COLLEGE
www.hull-college.ac.uk

Hull School of Art & Design

animation, appl creative media, architectural design, contemporary fine art practice, design, games/graphic design, illustration, interactive multimedia, lens-based photo media & communications, TV & film design, visual arts, web design; BA(Hons), FD, HNC

Business, Computing and Professional Development

business, prof dev, computing, education, IT & software design, retail; BA(Hons), FD

Construction and Engineering

construction/management, electrical/electronic/mechanical/chemical engineering, engineering techn; BSc/BEng, FD, HNC, HND

Health and Science

biomedicine, chemistry, childcare & working with young people, counselling, criminology, health, social care; BSc(Hons), FD, HNC, HND

Performance Arts

acting, broadcast media, dance, music performance, production & community performance, stage management & technical theatre, musical/ touring & community theatre; BA, FD

Sport and Leisure

ICFT for travel & tourism, tourism planning and the environment, marketing & event management, travel operations; HNC/D

NORTH LINDSEY COLLEGE
www.northlindsey.ac.uk

business & management, children's services, computing, counselling, education, English, history, health & social care, social science, sport & exercise; BA(Hons), Dips, FdA/Sc, HNC, HND

UNIVERSITY OF LIVERPOOL
www.liv.ac.uk

Faculty of Health & Life Sciences; www.liv.ac.uk/health_and_life_sciences

Biomedical Sciences:
physiology/for health practitioners, cellular & molecular physiology, pharmacology, anatomy, human biology

Dentistry:
dental hygiene/therapy/surgery, conscious sedation, orthodontics

Health Sciences:
diagnostic radiography, nursing, allied health professional, midwifery, occupational therapy, orthoptics, physiology, radiotherapy, health sciences

Medicine:
medicine, surgery, medical education, cancer studies, infection & host defences, reproduction & developmental medicine

Psychology
psychology, addictive behaviour, critical & major incidents, investigative forensic psychology, research methods

Life Sciences:
biochemistry, biological sciences, genetics, life sciences/medicine, microbiology, microbiotechnology, molecular biology, tropical disease bilogy, zoolology, advanced biological science (numerous subjects)

Veterinary Science:
veterinary science, bioveterinary science, infection biology, epidemiology, disease ecology, evolution; BSc(Hons), BN, BVSc, BDS, MBChB, FD, PGCert/Dip, MRes, MSc, MPhil, PhD, MD BDS, MChOrth, MCommH, MClinPsychol, MDS, MPH, MRCPsych, MTCH&CP, MTropMed, MTropPaed

Faculty of Humanities & Social Sciences; www.liv.ac.uk/humanities_and_social_sciences/hss

School of the Arts; www.live.ac.uk/arts

Architecture:
architecture, architectural design, sustainable architecture, contemp architectural technology

Communications & Media:
communications, business studies, media, pop music, English, politics, Italian

English Language:
applied linguistics, TESOL, English

English:
English, medieval, renaissance, 18th, 19th century literature, 20th century poetry, science fiction, corpus linguistics, discourse analysis language teaching

Music:
music, pop music, music industry, musicology, composition, performance

Philosophy:
philosophy & maths, politics, art, aesthetics & cultural institutions, philosophy as a way of life, metaphysics, language, mind

School of History, Language & Culture

History:
history – social & economic, modern (record management

Irish Studies:
Irish studies & English language & literature, history/politics, understanding conflict

Politics:
politics, international politics & policy & international business, international relations & security, politics & Irish studies/mass media

Archaeology, Classics & Egyptology:
ancient history, archaeology/of ancient cultures, evolutionary anthropology, Egyptian archaeology, classics & modern languages, Egyptology, paleoanthropology, Manx studies, 18th century worlds

Culture, Language & Area studies:
French, German, Hispanic studies, Italian, modern European languages, Euro film studies, classical studies, business studies, critical theory, gender studies, colonial/post-colonial slavery

School of Law & Social Justice

Liverpool Law School:
law/and business. international (human rights) law, European/international business law, law, medicine & healthcare, technology & intellectual property law

Sociology & Social Policy:
sociology, sociology & social policy/criminology, research methods, cities, culture & regeneration

School of Management

University of Liverpool Management School: accountancy, business economics/studies, international business, consumer/marketing, business finance & management, economics & finance, football industry, entrepreneurship, public administration, HRM, e-business strategy & systems, operations & supply chain management; BA(Hons), MA, MMus, MPhil, MBA, PhD

Faculty of Science & Engineering; www.liv.ac.uk/science.and.engineering

School of Engineering;

aerospace engineering, maritme/civil engineering, materials science & engineering, mechanical engineering, aerospace & mechanical systems, adv engineering materials/manufacture, energy manufacture, laser applications, product design & management simulation in aerospace engineering

Electrical Engineering & Electronics & Computer Science;

avionic systems, pilot studies, computer science, electronic engineering, electrical engineering, electronics, communications engineering, mechatronics & robotic systems, medical electronics & instrumentation, BioMEMS, organic & silicon electronics, intelligence automation & industrial automation, plasma & complex systems, signal processing & communication, computer science/information systems, internet computing, software development, computers & games theory

School of Environmental Sciences; www.liv.ac.uk/environmental-sciences

civic design, ecology, the environment, geography, geology, geophysics, ocean science, marrine biology, town & regional planning, environmental management & planning, urban regeneration, marine planning & management, globalization & development, environmental & climate change, conservation & resource management

School of Physical Sciences

Chemistry:

chemistry, medicinal chemistry, pharmacy, adv chemical science (organic/chemical sysnthesis/ biomedical chemistry/nanosciene with interfacial science/ materials chemistry

Mathematical Sciences:

mathematics, pure/applied mathematics, mathematical sciences, maths with joint subjects, financial mathematics, mathematical/theoretical physics, statistics & probability

Physics:

physics, astronomy, astrophysics, mathematical/theoretical physics, nuclear science, medical applications, new technology, radiometrics, radioactive waste, advanced science; BSc(Hons), MChem, BEng, MEng, DEng, MPhil, MMath, MPhys, MESci, MRes, MSc, PhD, MSc(Eng)

Degrees validated at the University of Liverpool offered by:

LIVERPOOL HOPE UNIVERSITY
www.hope.ac.uk

accounting, business management, childhood & youth studies, creative/practice & performing arts, computing, criminology, dance, design, drama & theatre studies, education (early childhood studies/ special education/mentoring & coaching/teaching & learning), English language/literature, film studies, fine art, geography, health, healthcare, nutrition & fitness, history, human biology, information technology, international studies, law, marketing, mathematics, media, music, nutrition, philosophy & ethics/ religion, politics, psychology, social policy/work, sport psychology/studies, teacher training, theology & religious studies, tourism, art history & curating, Christian chaplaincy/education leadership/theology, Muslim studies, criminal justice, environment management, global cultures/politics, HRM, music in cultural history, networks & security, popular literature; BA(Hons), BMin, BSc(Hons), BDes, FdA, FdSc, MA, MBA, MMin, MPhil, PGCE, PhD

LIVERPOOL JOHN MOORES UNIVERSITY
www.ljmu.ac.uk

Faculty of Business and Law; www.ljmu.ac.uk/BLW

Liverpool Business School; www.ljmu.ac.uk

accounting, business/studies/communications/management, finance, HRM, management, marketing, personnel dev, executive leadership, information & library management, international accounting/finance, banking/business/management/law, operations management

School of Law; www.ljmu.ac.uk/LAW

law, criminal justice, forensic psychology, international business & commercial law, legal practice, criminology, law and commerce, TESOL; BA(Hons), BSc(Hons), DBA, HND, LlB, LlM, MA, MBA, MPhil, M, Res, MSc, PgDip/Cert

Faculty of Education, Community and Leisure; www.ljmu.ac.uk/ECL

CPD, adv educational practice, coaching, dyslexia/leadership & community nutrition, early years, dance studies, secondary & vocational education (information technology, leisure & tourism, mathematics, PE, science, design & technology, modern languages), early childhood studies (0–8 years), education studies & English/applied community studies/special and inclusive education, environmental educational tourism, events management, food & nutrition, outdoor education, PE, primary & secondary education, mathematics, science education, primary early years (primary French (TS)), psychology and sport science, school sport management/development, sport & physical activity/ technology, teacher training courses (primary, secondary), work-related learning; BA(Hons), BSc(Hons), EdD, FD, MA, MPhil, MRes, PGCert, PgDip, PhD

Faculty of Media, Arts & Social Science; www.ljmu.ac.uk/MAS

Liverpool School of Art & Design; www.ljmu.ac.uk/LSA

architecture, graphic design, illustration, history of art, fine art, interior design, pop music, urban design

Liverpool Screen School; www.ljmu.ac.uk/LSS

creative writing, film studies, English, drama, media studies, international/journalism, screen & interactive media, screen/writing

School of Humanities & Social Science; www.ljmu.ac.uk/HSS

criminology, psychology, sociology, English, modern/history, mass communications, media, culture, communication, literature, cultural history, critical & creative arts, social science; cultural leadership; BA, BA(Hons), BDes, DipArch, DipHE, MA, MPhil, MRes, PG, PGCE, PhD

Faculty of Science; www.ljmu.ac.uk/faculties/scs

School of Sport & Exercise Science; www.ljmu.ac.uk/sps

sport science, science & football, exercise sciences, app sports psychology/physiology, biomechanics of gait & posture, clinical exercise physiology

School of Pharmacy & Biomolecular Sciences; www.ljmu.ac.uk/PBS

biomedical sciences, biochemistry, biotechnology, forensic science, applied chemical & pharmaceutical science, clinical/pharmacy, virology

School of Natural Sciences & Psychology; www.ljmu.ac.uk/NSP

animal behaviour, forensic anthropology, human/forensic/applied psychology, health/occupational psychology, geography, zoology, biology, environmental science, wildlife conservation, criminal justice; BSc(Hons), MPhil, MPhys, MRes, MSc, PGCE, PhD

Astrophysics Research Institute; www.ljmu.ac.uk/astro

physics, astronomy, astrophysics

Faculty of Technology & the Environment; www.ljmu.ac.uk/faculties/TAE

School of Computing & Mathematical Sciences; www.ljmu.ac.uk/cmp

computer animation & visualization, adv/computer studies/ forensics, computing information systems, IT & multimedia, computer games techn, web computing, software engineering, wireless & mobile computing, computer & network security, business mathematics

School of Engineering & Terchnology; www.ljmu.ac.uk/ENC

mechanical, electrical, electronic, marine, automotive, engineering, product innovation & development, broadcast & media production, computer technology, microelectronics, electric machines & drives, design mechanics & materials, sport technology

School of the Built Environment; www.ljmu.ac.uk/BLT

architectural technology, building surveying, civil engineering, commercial property development, project management, construction, quantity surveying, real estate management, environmental planning, building service engineering, water, energy & environment; BA(Hons), BSc(Hons), FdSc, HND/C, MPhil, MSc, PgCert, PGCE, PgDip, PhD

Faculty of Health & Applied Social Services; www.ljmu.ac.uk/faculties/HEA

child nursing, care practice, environmental health, health and social care, health sciences, midwifery, nursing (adult/child/mental health/paramedic practice), public health, social work, specialist community practitioner, counselling, psychotherapy, adv paediatric nursing; BA(Hons), BSc, DNurs, DMidw, DPH, DipHE, FD, FdA MPhil, MRes, MSc, PGDip/Cert

UNIVERSITY OF THE ARTS LONDON
www.arts.ac.uk

Camberwell College of Art & Design; www.camberwell.arts.ac.uk

3D design, art & design, book arts, conservation, conservation, designer–maker, design practice, digital arts, drawing, graphic design, fine art, visual art, illustration, painting, printmaking, sculpture; BA(Hons), Dip, FdA, MA, MPhil, PGDip, PhD

Central Saint Martins College of Art & Design; www.csm.arts.ac.uk

acting, architecture: spaces and objects, art & design, character animation, criticism, curation & communication/design, exhibition studies, fashion, creative practice for narrative, European classical acting, fashion, fine art, graphic design, images in creative industries, industrial design, innovation management, international communication & curating, jewellery design, performance design & practice, moving images, performance, photography, product design, directing, writing, textile design; BA(Hons), FdA, FD, GradDip, MA, MPhil, PGCert/Dip, PhD

Chelsea College of Art & Design; www.chelsea.arts.ac.uk

art theory, art & design, curating, fine art, graphic design communication, graphic design, interior & spatial design,, textile design; BA(Hons), FdA, Foundation Dip, GradDip, MA, MPhil, PGCert/Dip, PhD

London College of Communication; www.lcc.arts.ac.uk

3D design, animation, architecture, artefact & spatial design, book arts, curation & criticism, design, digital arts/media, documentary research, events management, film, video & broadcast, games design, graphic design, illustration, industrial/interior design, interactive media, journalism, marketing, advertising, media & cultural studies, photography, print media & production, printmaking, product design, PR, publishing, retail, screenwriting, travel & tourism, typography; BA(Hons), FdA, ABCDip, MA, MDes, MRes, MSc, PgDip

London College of Fashion; www.fashion.arts.ac.uk

beauty therapy, broadcasting, buying & merchandising, cosmetic science, costume, curation & criticism, design, digital arts/media, drawing, fashion, textiles, fashion journalism/ management/marketing/promotion/production, film, TV & video, footwear, graphic design, make-up & image styling, media & cultural studies, pattern cutting, photography, PR/retail management, surface design, technical effects, theatre design & performing arts, visual design & display; BA(Hons), BSc(Hons), diplomas, FD MA, PgDip/Cert

Wimbledon College of Art; www.wimbledon.arts.ac.uk

acting & directing, animation, costume, design, digital arts/media, film video & broadcast, drawing, fine art, interactive media, painting, pattern cutting, printmaking, sculpture, sonic arts, theatre; design & performing arts/technical arts; BA(Hons), FdA, MA

LONDON CONTEMPORARY DANCE SCHOOL
www.theplace.org.uk

advanced dance training, choreography, contemporary dance, dance training and education, improvisation, performance; BA, PGDip

LONDON METROPOLITAN UNIVERSITY
www.londonmet.ac.uk

Faculty of Applied Social Sciences; www.londonmet.ac.uk/depts/dass

community sector management, youth studies/work, organization & community development, regeneration, housing & planning, community/district/occupational health/practice/school/public health/mental health nursing, health studies, public health & social care, social policy, anthropolgy, sociology, social work, migration & social cohesion, criminology/& law; digital media, crime, safety, security, security intelligence, mass communications, media studies, organisation & community dev, bioethics, health visiting, labour & TU studies, sustainable, information & knowledge management, international journalism, woman & child abuse; BA(Hons), BSc(Hons), MA, MPhil, MRes, MSc, PGCert/Dip, PhD

Faculty of Architecture and Spacial Design; www.londonmet.ac.uk/architecture

architectural history, architecture, interior architecture & design, design & urban cultures, energy & sustainability, cities, digital design systems, rapid design & rare resources, renewable energy, spacial planning & urban design; BA(Hons), MA, MSc, PhD, ProfDip

Faculty of Computing; www.londonmet.ac.uk/depts/cctm

Communications Technology

communications systems, computer networking/systems engineering, digital computer networks, electronic & computer/communications engineering, electronics, telecommunications & network eng, embedded systems, information and communications technology support, mobile & satellite communication, network management & security

Computing

business computing, business IT, computer forensics/science, computing, internet computing, IT security, mobile computing, software engineering, data mining, information systems dev/technology, distributed systems, mobile computing

Mathematics

computing, mathematics, decision science, financial mathematics, mathematical sciences, mathematics, statistics

Multimedia

computer animation, multimedia solutions(/games/e-learning/internet), digital solutions, e-learning technology, IT consultancy, interactive media & games; BSc(Hons), FdSc, MEng, MRes, MSc, PhD

Faculty of Humanities, Arts, Language and Education; www.londonmet.ac.uk/depts/hale

School of Humanities, Arts and Language; www.londonmet.ac.uk/depts/hale

American studies, translation studies, Caribbean studies, creative writing, creative/cultural industries, equality & diversity, migration & social cohesion, English /literature, film studies, filmmaking, game studies, history, interpreting/public service, journalism, performing arts, philosophy, professional writing, screenwriting, French/Spanish/and Latin American studies, TESOL, theatre studies

School of Education; www.londonmet.ac.uk/education

early childhood studies, early years teaching, Jewish education, leading and managing school development, learning & teaching in HE, music education with QTS, therapy and education; BA(Hons), BEd, FdA, MA, PGCE, PGDip/Cert

Faculty of Law, Governance and International Relations; www.londonmet.ac.uk/ depts/hale/lgr

law, business/international/European/human rights/ law, international banking & insurance law/, trade, transport & maritime law, comparative IP law, European law, human rights and social justice, Asia Pacific studies, governance & international relations/ law, international development, peace & conflict studies, politics, European studies, public service management, international relations & globalization, public administration; BA(Hons), BSc(Hons), FdG, LlB, LlM, MA, PGCE

Faculty of Life Sciences; www.londonmet.ac.uk/depts/fls

School of Human Science; www.londonmet.ac.uk/depts/hhs

biochemistry, bioethics, biological sciences, biomedical sciences, chemistry, medical microbiology, food science, forensic & bioanalytical science, pharmaceutical sciences, genetics, health promotion, herbal medicinal science, home economics, human biology/ nutrition, public health/sports/dietetics, medical bioscience, medical genetics, nutrition, personal training and fitness consultancy, pharmaceutical science, pharmacology, sports and exercise science, PE, public health, nutrition, fitness evaluation, sports therapy, sustainability in the food industry

School of Psychology; www.londonmet.ac.uk/depts/dops

psychology, addiction/business/consumer/forensic/ health/occupational/sport & performance psychology, cognitive behaviour therapy; BSc(Hons), DipHE, FdSc, GradDip/Cert, MOst, MOstMed, MSc, Prof Doc

London Metropolitan Business School; www.londonmet.ac.uk/lmb

computer/forensic accounting, advertising & marketing communication, arts management, finance, aviation management, banking, business, business economics/enterprise/IT/admin business/operations management/psychology, corporate finance and investment/treasury management, social responsibility, derivatives, international/economics, European business, events (marketing) management, fashion marketing, financial communications/ economics/ markets & derivatives/with information systems, financial regulation/and compliance management, HRM strategy, insurance, international business and banking/finance/marketing/entrepreneurship/business finance/economics and finance, financial risk/ service regulation, arts & heritage management, international hospitality management/hotel & restaurant management, international sustainable tourism/ tourism management, trade, transport, investment/ fund management, law, leadership, marketing, music and media marketing/PR, music industry management, philosophy, politics, economics, purchase & supply chain management, retail management, security management, int sports management, strategic management, sustainable business, tourism; DPS, FdSc, GradConv, HND, MA, MBA, MSc, PGDip,

Sir John Cass Dept of Art Media and Design; www.londonmet.ac.uk/jcmd

communications management, conservation, curating the contemporary, design, digital film & animation, film production, fine art, furniture design, graphic design, inclusive design, jewellery design, manufacture & design for polymer products, media, musical instruments, photography, plasic product design, polymers, polymer science & engineering, design product & management, research for disability, restoration & conservation, textile design; BA(Hons), BSc(Hons), FdA, MA, MPhil, MSc, PhD

THE LONDON SCHOOL OF OSTEOPATHY
www.lso.ac.uk

osteopathy; MOst

LONDON SOUTH BANK UNIVERSITY
www.lsbu.ac.uk

Faculty of Arts and Human Sciences; www.lsbu.ac.uk/#ahs

Arts, Media ; www.lsbu.ac.uk/ahs/departments/artsmedia
digital film & video/media arts/photography, game cultures, music & sonic media; BA(Hons), MA, MPhil, PhD

Culture, Writing & Performance; www.lsbu.ac.uk/ahs/departments/cwp
critical/arts management, creative writing, drama & performance, English, media studies, film studies, cultural studies, multimedia journalism, creative producing, media writing, theatre practice; BA(Hons), MA, PhD, MPhil

Education; www.lsbu.ac.uk/departments/education
early years, education for sustainability, graduate teacher programme/PGCE with QTS (primary/secondary maths), HE, learning and teaching, post-compulsory education, secondary mathematics;(BA(-Hons), Cert, FdA, MA, PgDip/Cert,EdD,PGCHE

Law; www.lsbu.ac.uk/#ahslaw
common law, crime & litigation, international human rights and development, law, legal studies, criminality; GradDip, LlB(Hons), LLM,CPE

Psychology; www.lsbu.ac.uk/#ahspsycho
addiction psychology & counselling, investigative forensic psychology, psychology, criminology, clinical psychology, child development; BSc(Hons), GradDip, MSc, PhD

Social and Policy Studies; www.lsbu.ac.uk/ahs/departments/socialpolicy
criminology (with law/psychology), international politics, refugee studies, social policy, social research methods, sociology; BA(Hons), BSc(Hons), MSc, PhD, PGDip/Cert

Urban, Environmental & Leisure Studies; www.lsbu.ac.uk/ahs/departments/uels
built environment studies, housing studies, international tourism & hospitality/travel management, leisure & events management, international/hospitality & food management, planning policy and practice, town planning, urban planning design, sustainable communities, urban and environmental planning/regeneration and community development; BA(Hons), FdA, HNC, MA, MSc, PGCert/Dip,MPhil,PhD

Faculty of Business; www.bus.lsbu.ac.uk

Accounting & Finance, Business
accounting, banking, business/administration/studies, computing, charity marketing/fundraising/finance, international finance, investment, quantitative finance & business analysis, enterprise/small business, finance, marketing

Computing & Information Management
business intelligence, business IT/information technology/intelligence, enterprise/human centred/multimedia computing, computer systems management, information technology, internet & database systems, managing business technology, mobile computing, web dev

Management, Human Resources & Marketing; Public, Voluntary, Not for Profit
business administration, charity marketing & fundraising, management, international health services & hospital management, international/HR, HRM/D/practice Eurasian business management, international business/management/marketing learning & development practice, public administration, marketing/communications/management, voluntary administration; MA, MBA, PGDip/Cert, MSc, BTEC, HND, DMS, CM, BSc(Hons), BA(Hons)

Faculty of Engineering, Science & Built Environment; www.lsbu.ac.uk/esbe

Dept of Applied Science; www.lsbu.ac.uk/esbe/deparments/appsci
applied biology, applied science, bioscience, chemical & process engineering, biochemistry, culinary art, engineering, environmental biology food & nutrition, food safety & control, food science, forensic science, human biology, integrated sciences, microbiology, petroleum engineering, sport & exercise science; BA(Hons), BEng(Hons), BSc(Hons), FdSc, MSc/PgCert/PgDip

Dept of Engineering & Design; www.lsbu.ac.uk/esbe/departments/engdes
computer-aided design/engineering, computer systems & networks(ing), electrical & electronic

engineering, engineering product design, mechanical engineering/design, mechatronics/engineering, power distribution, product design/ computing, sports product design, telecommunications & computer networks engineering, design & manufacturing management, embedded & distributed systems, manufacturing management, quality engineering management; BEng(Hons), BSc(Hons), FdEng, HNC, HND, MRes MSc, PgDip

Dept of the Built Environment; www.1lsbu.ac.uk/esbe/departments/builtenv

architecture, architectural technology, built environment, quantity surveying, construction/management/project management, planning buildings for health, property development & planning mang, building/surveying, real estate; BA(Hons), FdSc, HNC, PgDip/Cert, MSc

Dept of Urban Engineering; www1.lsbu.ac.uk/esbe/departments/urbeng

architectural engineering, building services engineering, civil engineering, railway civil engineering, environmental & architectural acoustics, sustainable energy systems; BEng(Hons), BSc(Hons), FdEng, HNC, HND, MSc, PgDip/Cert

Faculty of Health & Social Care; www.lsbu.ac.uk/faculties/hsc

Nursing: health care/studies, nursing (adult)Allied Health Services: therapeutic radiography, adv cardiac catheter pract/neuromuscoskeletal mang, occupational therapy, breast imaging, clin ultrasound, non-medical prescribing, adult/neonatal/children's/mental health/learning disability nursing, child health studies; Mental Health & Learning Disabilities; acute & psychiatric intensive care, cognitive behaviour therapy, forensic/mental health; Midwifery & Women's Health; midwifery, non-medical prescribing; Radiography; diagnostic/therapeutic radiography; Operating Dpt Practice; Physioterapy; Occupational Therapy; Social Work; Primary & Social Care; adv nurse practitioner, career guidance/education, leadership & service improvement, practice education , primary care, public health & health promotion, school nursing; FdSc, BSc, BSc(Hons), DipHE(Hons), MSc, PgDip/Cert, PhD, University AdvDip, ProfDoc, MCMAc

UNIVERSITY OF LONDON; BIRKBECK
www.bbk.ac.uk

School of Arts; www.bbk.ac.uk/arts

English & humanities, European cultures & languages, history of art & screen media, media & cultural studies, Iberian & Latin American studies, French, Spanish, German, Japanese, Polish

School of Business, Economics and Informatics; www.bbk.ac.uk/business

computer science & information systems, economics, mathematics & statistics, management, organizational psychology, business studies; BSc, CertHE, MPhil, PhD MSc, MRes

School of Law; www.bbk.ac.uk/law

law, law (public/company/medical/European), criminology, human rights etc; LlB, MPhil, PhD

School of Science; www.bbk.ac.uk

Blogical Sciences: pharmacy, biodiversity & conservation, biomedicine, chemical & molecular biology, biological science; Earth and Planetary Sciences; environmental/geology, earth science, planet science & astronomy; Psychological Sciences: psychology; BSc, MPhil, PhD,FD

School of Social Sciences, History and Philosophy; www/bbk.ac.uk

applied linguistics & communication, geography, environment & development studies, history, classics & archaeology, philosophy, politics, psychosocial studies, social policy & education; BA, BSc, MA, MRes, MPhil, PhD, CertHE

UNIVERSITY OF LONDON; UNIVERSITY COLLEGE LONDON (UCL)
www.ucl.ac.uk

UCL School of Life and Medical Science (including UCL Medical School); www.ucl.ac.uk/slms

adv paediatrics, adv ageing & mental health, adv aesthetic dentistry, audiology/for ENT, audiological science, audiovestibular medicine, biochemistry, biological sciences, biology of vision, biomedical sciences, biotechnology, brain & mind sciences, cancer, cardiorespiratory physiotherapy, cell & gene therapy, child & adolescent mental health, clinical & applied paediatric neuropsychology, clinical biochemistry/dentistry/neuroscience/experimental medicine, clinical ophthalmology, clinical & public health nutrition, cognitive & decision sciences/neuroscience/behaviour therapy, community child health, conservative dentistry, dental public health/sedation & pain management, drug design, endodontology, environmental biology, genetics of human disease, global health & development, haemaglobinopathy, health informatics, health psychology, healthcare, history of medicine, immunology, implant dentistry, infection & immunity, international child health, language sciences, linguistics, medical education, medical mycology, medicine, mental health science, molecular biology/medicine, musculoskeletal science,nanotechnology & regenerative medicine, neuroimaging, neuroscience, oral & maxillofacial surgery/medicine, orthodontics, paediatric dentistry, paediatric neuropschycology, paediatrics, periodontology, pharmacology, phonetics, phonology, physiology, pragmatics, prenatal genetics & fetal medicine, prosthodontics, radiation biology, reproductive science & women's health, restorative dental practice, sexually transmitted infections and HIV, social cognition, social epidemiology, special care dentistry, speech & language sciences, speech, language & cognition, sports & exercise medicine, surgical science, syntax, synthetic biology, theoretical psychoanalytical studies, trauma & orthopaedics, urology, voice pathology, zoology; BSc(Hons), DipCDSc, IbSc, MBBS, MClinDent, MD(Res), MPhil, MRes, MSc, MSci, PGCert/Dip, PhD

The Bartlett, Faculty of the Built Environment

Built Environment; www.barlett.ucl.ac.uk

advanced architectural studies, architectural design/history, architecture, building & urban design in development, built environment, sustainable heritage, construction management, environmental design & engineering/sustainable heritage, construction economics & management, development administration & planning, environment & sustainable development, facility & environment management, international planning, light & lighting, mega infrastucture planning, professional practice, project & enterprise management, real estate & planning, sustainable urbanism, social development practice, spacial planning, strategic management of projects, town & country planning, urban design/development planning/economic development/management/regeneration/studies; BSc(Hons), Diplomas, EngD, MA, MArch, MPhil, MSc, PhD, MArch, PGDip, MRes

Faculty of Engineering Sciences; www.ucl.ac.uk/engineering

Civil, Environmental & Geomatic Engineering; www.rege.ucl.ac.uk

civil engineering, earthquake engineering with disaster management, environmental engineering/mapping, environmental systems engineering, GIS, hydrographic surveying, photogrammetry, remote sensing, surveying, transport studies

Biochemical Engineering; www.ucl.ac.uk/biochemeng

biochemical engineering

Chemical Engineering; www.ucl.ac.uk/chemeng

chemical engineering/with biochemical engineering, chemical process engineering

Computer Science; www.cs.ucl.ac.uk/

computer science, computational analysis, computational statistics & machine learning, computer graphics, vision & imaging, financial systems engineering, human–computer interaction with ergonomics, information security, machine learning, mathematical computation, networked computer systems, software systems engineering

Electronic and Electrical Engineering; www.ee.ucl.ac.uk
communications engineering/computer science/nanotechnology, electrical & electronic engineering, internet engineering, nanotechnology, photonics systems, spacecraft technology & satellite communications, telecommunications/engineering, wireless & optical communications

Management Science and Innovation; www.ucl.ac.uk/msi
information management for business, entrepreneural finance, managing high-tech organizations, decision & risk analysis, business strategy, leadership, ethics, community, organizational behaviour, managing technology enterpreneurship

Mechanical Engineering; www.ucl.ac.uk/mecheng
engineering with business finance, marine engineering, mechanical engineering, naval architecture, power systems engineering, biomaterials & tissue engineering

Medical Physics & Bioengineering; www.ucl.ac.uk/medphys
human physiology, medical imaging, medical physics, radiation physics, physics & engineering in medicine

Security & Crime Science; www.ucl.ac.uk/scs
crime analysis/science/detection/prevention community safety, countering organised crime & terrorism; BEng, BSc, Certs, MEng, MPhil, MRes, MSc, PgDip, PhD

Faculty of Mathematical and Physical Sciences; www.ucl.ac.uk/maps-faculty

Chemistry; www.chem.ucl.ac.uk
chemistry, chemical physics/biology, nanotechnology, medicinal/computational/inorganic/materials/physical chemistry, organic synthesis

Earth Sciences; www.es.ucl.ac.uk
earth science, environmental geoscience, geology, geophysical hazards, geophysics, geosciences, natural hazards for insurers

Mathematics; www.ucl.ac.uk/mathematics
mathematics with mathematical physics/economics/modern languages/management studies/physics/statistical science, mathematical modelling, pure/applied mathematics

Physics and Astronomy; www.phys.ucl.ac.uk
astronomy, astrophysics, physics, theoretical physics, biological physics, medical physics, molecular & positron physics, condensed matter & materials

Science and Technology Studies; www.ucl.ac.uk/sts
history, philosophy & social studies of science, science, communication & policy & technology studies

Space and Climate Physics; www.mssl.ucl.ac.uk
astrophysics, climate extremes, imaging, space plasma physics, plasma science, solar & stellar physics

Statistical Science; www.ucl.ac.uk/stats
economics, finance, mathematics, statistical science, statistics, statistics & management for business; BSc, BSc(Econ), EngD, MRes, MSc, MSci, PhD

Faculty of Arts & Humanities; www.ucl.ac.uk/ah

European social & political studies, Dutch, French, German, Italian, Russian, Spanish, Scandanavian studies, European history, law, philosophy, politics, history & philosophy of science, economics, English language & literature, English linguistics, issues in modern culture, Shakepeare in history, old & middle English literature, film studies, French, modern languages, language & culture, French & francophone studies, adv translation, German, German studies, Greek & Latin, languages & literature, ancient world studies, reception of classical world, Hebrew & Jewish studies, Jewish history, language & culture, Holocaust studies, modern Israeli studies, history (central & E Europe), library & information studies, electronic communication & publishing, archive & information studies, digital humanities publishing, Italian, Italian and design/history of art, contemporary Italian culture & history, philosophy, philosophy of mind & language, politics & modern philosphy, metaphysics & epistemology, history of philosophy, Scandinavian Studies, Icelandic, Viking studies; Spanish and Latin American Studies; Hispanic/ Latin-American studies, translation theory & practice;

Slade School of Art:
painting, fine art, sculpture, media, history & theory of art, critical studies; BA(Hons), BFA, MA, MPhil, MRes, PhD, MFA

Faculty of Law; www.ucl.ac.uk/laws

law, law & adv studies/another legal system (Australia,Singapore), French/German/Hispanic law, competition/comparative/corporate law, criminal justice & social welfare, environmental law & policy, EU/human rights/intellectual property law, international banking & finance/commercial law international law, jurisprudence & legal theory, legal history, litigation & dispute resolution, public law; LlB and Baccalaureus Legum, LlBHons, LlM, MPhil, PhD

Faculty of Historical and Social Sciences; www.ucl.ac.uk/shs

Anthropology; www.ucl.ac.uk/anthropology

anthroplogy, digital/social & cultural anthropology, culture, materials & design, environment and development, human evolution & behaviour, medical anthropology, materials & visual culture, paleoanthropology; BA(Hons), BSc(Hons), MA, MPhil, MRes, MSc, PhD

Archaeology; www.ucl.ac.uk/archaeology

archaeology & anthropology, African archaeology, archaeology of eastern Mediterranean/& Middle East, artefact studies, classical archaeology & classical civilization, comparative art & archaeology, conservation for archaeology & museums, cultural heritage studies, Egyptian archaeology, environmental archaeology, forensic archaeological science, GIS, managing archaeological sites, maritime archaeology, museum studies, palaeoanthropology & palaeolithic archaeology, principles of conservation, public archaeology, skeletal & dental bioarchaeology, technology & analysis of archaeological materials; BA(Hons), BSc(Hons), MA, MPhil, MSc, PhD

Economics; www.ucl.ac.uk/economics

applied/economics, statistical methods, microeconomics, macroeconomics, international trade, industrial economics, economics of growth/corporate finance/information, economic development, urban economics, economic policy; BSc(Hons), MSc, PhD

Geography; www.geog.ucl.ac.uk

aquatic science, ecology, global migration, globalization, GIS, natural resources/water management, population/political/physical/human geography, quaternary science, remote sensing, urban studies; BA(Hons), BSc(Hons), MSc, PhD

History; www.ucl.ac.uk/history

history,ancient history, Egyptology, late antique & Byzantine studies, European history, history of political thought & intellectual history; BA(Hons), MA, MPhil, PhD

History of Art; www.ucl.ac.uk/art-history

history of art/with material studies, contemporary art & globalization, popular imagery in 19th century, race/place/exotic/erotic, the writing of art, early modern horror; BA(Hons), MA, MPhil, PhD

Political Science; www.ucl.ac.uk/ssp

political studies, international relations, European social & human rights, security studies, democracy & democratization, European public policy, global government & ethics, international public policy, legal & political theory; MA, MPhil, MSc, PhD

School of Slavonic and Eastern European Studies; www.ssees.ucl.ac.uk

central SE/E European studies, politics, security & integration, social science, history 2008–2009, identity, culture and power, politics & East European studies, institutions, development and globalization, Russian & East European literature & culture, state & society; BA(Hons), MA, MPhil, MRes, PhD

UNIVERSITY OF LONDON; COURTAULD INSTITUTE OF ART www.courtald.ac.uk

conservation of easel paintings, curating the art museum, history of art, painting conservation (wall painting); BA(Hons), GradDip, MA, PGDip, MPhil, PhD

UNIVERSITY OF LONDON; GOLDSMITHS
www.goldsmiths.ac.uk

Dept of Anthropology; www.gold.ac.uk/anthroplogy

anthropology, media, development & rights, cultural politics, history, sociology, social/visual anthropology, community & youth work, development & rights, health with body in 21st century; BA(Hons), MPhil, PhD, MRes

Dept of Art; www.gold.ac.uk/art

fine art & history of art, art writing, curating; BA(Hons), MFA, MPhil, PhD

Centre for English Language & Academic Writing; www.gold.ac.uk/eap;

humanities, social science, media, communication, creative & culture industries, counselling, therapy etc; GradDip, IntCert

Centre for Cultural Studies; www.gold.ac.uk/cultural-studies

cultural studies/industry, interactive media: critical theory & practice, post-colonial culture & global policy; MA, MPhil, PhD

Dept of Computing; www.gold.ac.uk/computing

cognitive computing, computational arts, computer games & entertainment, computer studio art/technology, computing & interactive design, creative computing, creative & cultural entrepreneurship, digital computing/technology, music computing; BMus, BA/BSc(Hons), MFA, MPhil, MSc, PhD

Dept of Design; www.gold.ac.uk/design

design, design & technology education, computing & interaction design, design & innovation/environment, design – critical practice/education/futures, creative & cultural entrepreneurship; BA(Hons), BA/BSc(Hons), BEng/MEng, MPhil, MRes, PhD

Dept of Drama; www.gold.ac.uk/drama

applied drama: theatre in educational, community & social contexts, arts administration & cultural policy, contemporary African theatre & performance, creative & cultural entrepreneurship, musical theatre, performance & culture, performance making, writing for performance, drama/& theatre arts; BA(Hons), MA, MPhil, PhD

Dept of Educational Studies; www.gold.ac.uk/educational-studies

artist teachers, education, language & identity/culture & society, public service professionals, teacher training (PGCE) – primary/secondary art & design, design & technology, drama, English, geography, mathematics, modern languages, music, biology, chemistry, general science or physics; BA(Hons), DPS, MA, MPhil, PhD

English and Comparative Literature; www.gold.ac.uk/ecl

American literature, applied linguistics, comparative literature, creative/& life writing, drama, English, history, media & modern literature/languages; BA(Hons), MA, MPhil, MRes, PhD

Dept of History; www.gold.ac.uk/history

history, history & anthropology/history of ideas/politics; BA (Hons), MA, MPhil, MRes, PhD

Institute for Creative and Cultural Entrepreneurship; www.gold.ac.uk/ccl

creative & cultural entrepreneurship; MA, MPhil, PhD

Dept of Media and Communications; www.gold.ac.uk/media-communications

anthropology & media, media & communications/sociology/modern literature, brand development, creative & cultural entrepreneurship, digital media/journalism, filmmaking, gender & culture, image & communication, electronic graphics, TV/journalism, radio screen documentary, screen & film studies, script writing, media & communications, political communication; BA(Hons), MA, MPhil, PhD, MRes

Dept of Music; www.gold.ac.uk/music

arts administration & cultural policy, composition, contemporary & pop music, creative practice/& entrepreneurship, ethnomusicology, historical musicology, music, music computing/ performance and related studies, studio composition; BMus(Hons), BMus/BSc(Hons), MA, MMus, MPhil, PGCert, PhD

Dept of Politics; www.gold.ac.uk/politics

art & politics, economics, politics & public policy, history, international studies, politics, sociology; BA(Hons), DPS, MA, MPhil, MRes, PhD

Dept of Professional and Community Education; www.gold.ac.uk/pace

social work, HE work, social & cultural studies, performing arts; music/drama & theatre, psychotherapeutic study, participatory & community arts, community & youth work; BA(Hons), DipHE, GradDip, PGCert

Dept of Psychology; www.gold.ac.uk/psychology

cognitive & clinical neuroscience, music, mind & brain, clinical/ occupational psychology, organizational behaviour, psychology, research methods; FoundCert, BSc(Hons), MPhil, MSc, PhD

Dept of Sociology; www.gold.ac.uk/sociology

critical & creative analysis, gender, media & culture, global networks & society, photography & urban cultures, social research, sociology & anthropology/history/media/cultural studies/politics, world cities & urban life; BA(Hons), MA, MPhil, PhD

Dept of Visual Cultures; www.gold.ac.uk/visual-cultures

aural & visual cultures, contemporary art theory/history, fine art, history of art, research architecture; BA(Hons), MA, MPhil, PGDip, PhD

UNIVERSITY OF LONDON; HEYTHROP COLLEGE
www.heythrop.ac.uk

Abrahamic religions, biblical studies, canon law, Christian spirituality/theology, Christianity & inter-religious relations, contemporary ethics, divinity, pastoral liturgy/mission/theology, philosophy, religion & ethics/theology, psychology & theology, study of religions, theology; BA, Certs, FD, GradDip, MA

UNIVERSITY OF LONDON; INSTITUTE IN PARIS
www.ulip.ac.uk

French/Paris studies – history & culture; BA, MA, MPhil, PhD

UNIVERSITY OF LONDON; INSTITUTE OF EDUCATION
www.ioe.ac.uk

teacher training; primary/secondary PGCE, post-compulsory , adult literacy/numeracy, working with children's education & wellbeing, lifelong learning, leadership, disabilities of sight/habilitation, advance educational pract special & inclusive education, mantoring & coaching, teaching English/in HE & professions, CPD adult literacy, language & numeracy, art & design in education, bilingual learners, child development, clinical education, comparative/development education, international development/gender/health promotion, assessment,developmental & educ psychology, early years, economics/planning of education, citizenship, history & RE, education, curriculum, pedagogy, assessment, effective learning, English/geography education, history of education, ICT in education, language & communication, literacy learning/difficulties, post-compulsory teaching, maths/science education, museums & galleries in education, music education, philosophy/psychology/sociology of education, policy studies, psychosocial studies, TESOL, world Englishes; BEd, Certs, DedPsy, EdD, GradDip, MA, MBA, MPhil, MRes, MSc, MTg, PGCE, PhD

UNIVERSITY OF LONDON; KING'S COLLEGE LONDON
www.kcl.ac.uk

The School of Arts & Humanities; www.kcl.ac.uk/humanities

ancient history, Byzantine/modern Greek studies, biblical studies, Chistianity & the arts, classical studies/archaeology, comparative literature, critical methodologies, conflict resolution, culture, media & creative industries, digital asset management/culture, early modern Eng lit/history, 18/19th-century studies, English/literature/language, European public policy, film studies, French, German, Turkish/modern Greek, Hispanic studies, history, war studies, humanities & academic English, Jewish studies, language studies, linguistics, medical humanities, medieval history, Middle East & Mediterranean studies, modern languages, music, philosophy/of medicine/mental disorder/psychology, Portuguese & Brazilian studies, Shakespeare studies, Spanish & Spanish American studies, religion, theology, ethics; BA(Hons), MA, MMus, MRes, MSc

School of Biomedical Sciences; www.kcl.ac.uk/biohealth

analytical science/toxicology, aviation medicine, biomedical science/& scientific English, drug discovery/ development, forensic science, healthcare, human sciences, molecular genetics/science/biophysics, neuroscience, pain science, clinical/pharmacology, pharmacy, pharmaceutics, physiology, space physiology & health, translational medicine; BSc, DHC, MB, MPharm, MRes, MSc, GradDip, PGDip/Cert, MPhil, PhD, MD

Dental Institute; www.kcl.ac.uk/dentistry

dentistry, general dental practice, aesthetic dentistry,-conscious sedation, dental public health, endodontology, maxillofacial technology, orthodontics, paediatric dentistry, periodontology, prosthdontics, sedation & special care dentistry; BDS, MClinDent, MOrth, MScDL, PGDip

Institute of Psychiatry; www.iop.kcl.ac.uk

addiction, advanced psychosocial practice, alcohol & drug use, child & adolescent mental health, clinical forensic psychiatry/psychology/neuroscience, cognitive behavioural therapies, epilepsy, forensic mental health, mental health studies, neuroscience, neuroimaging, mental health/learning disabilities/population research/social work with children & adults, organizational psychiatry & psychology, psychiatric research, psychology, social, genetic & developmental psychiatry, war & psychiatry; BSc, DClinPsy, Grad-Cert, MSc, PGDip,MPhil,PhD,MD

School of Law; www.kcl.ac.uk/law

construction law & dispute resolution, criminology & criminal justice, English law & French law/German law/American law, human values & contemporary globalization, medical ethics & law,tax/contract/criminal/European/trusts/property/public law; European legal studies, LlB, LLM, MA, MPhil, MSc, PhD

School of Medicine; www.kcl.ac.uk/schools/medicine

medicine, nutrition, dietetics, physiolology, cardiovascular res, immunology, translational cancer medicine, clinical pharmacology, drug development, clinical/medical imaging, medical engineering/physics, radiopharmaceutics, medical/vascular ultrasound, pain, palliative care, primary health care, public health, adv physiotherapy/paediatrics, clinical deramatology, imaging, rheumatology; MBBS, MPH, MSc, DDip/Cert,MD, MPhil, PhD

Florence Nightingale School of Nursing & Midwifery; www.kcl.ac.uk/schools/nursing

advanced practice – cancer care/child care/critical care/education/leadership/midwifery/primary care, gastrointestinal nursing, nursing studies – adult nursing/child nursing/mental health nursing, midwifery studies, public health/women's health; BSc(Hons), DipHE, DHC, DPhil, MRes, MSc

School of Natural & Mathematical Sciences; www.kcl.ac.uk /schools/school. of. natural.and mathematical. sciences

biomedical engineering, computer science/with management/mathematics/robotics/intelligent systems, adv computing, adv software engineering, bioinformatics, complex systems modelling, computing & internet systems/security/IT, law & management, mobile & personal communication, mobile internet research, telecommunications/& internet technology, web intelligence

mathematics: mathematics & philosophy/physics/ computer science/management & finance, financial mathematics

physics: physics & mathematics/philosophy/medical applications/ theoretical physics, robotics & intelligent systems electronic engineering/engineering with business management, robotics; BEng, BSc,MSc, MPhil, MSci,GradDip,PhD

School of Social Science and Public Policy; www.kcl.ac.uk/school/school_of social_science_and_public_policy

business management, accounting, accountability & financial management, HRM & organizational analysis, risk analysis,
education studies,assessment, child studies,creative arts, education – professional studies/management/social science/art & culture/English, ELT, teaching & learning, FE management, PGCE (various subjects), science/mathematics education, ICT education
bible & ministry, religious/Christian/Jewish education, contemporary ecclesiology/worship, English language & communication, youth ministry
International politics/studies/conflict studies/management/marketing/peace & security/relations/studies, air power, war studies & history/philosophy, European public policy, science & security,
geography, sustainable/cities, disasters, adaptation & development, environment & development/politics & globalization, environmental monitoring/modelling/management, geopolitics, territory & security, global environmental change, water, science & governance, acquatic resource management,
ageing & society, gerontology, health & society/promotion, medicine, science & society, public policy, public services,
English language & communication, French, applied linguistics, language – cultural diversity/ethnicity & education, 19th-century studies; BA, MA, MSc, MRes, GradDip, PGDip/Cert, FD, DThMin, DrPS, MPhil, PhD, EdD

UNIVERSITY OF LONDON; LONDON SCHOOL OF ECONOMICS & POLITICAL SCIENCE www.lse.ac.uk

Departments at LSE:

Accounting, Anthropology, Economics, Finance, Geography & Environment, Government, International History, International Relations, Law, Management, Mathematics, Media and Communications, Philosophy, Logic and Scientific Method, Social Policy, Sociology, Statistics

accounting/organizations & institutions, anthropology, applicable mathematics, biomedicine, bioscience & society, business management, city design, communications, criminal justice, policy, culture & society, decision science, development studies, economic history, econometrics, economics, economic history, employment relations, environment, European political economy/public & economic policy/social policy, finance, financial mathematics, gender, geography, global history/media/politics, health economics, human geography, HRM, human rights, information systems, international development/political economy/ relations, law, local economic development, logic & scientific method, management, managerial economics, mathematics, media, methodology, OR, organizational behaviour, philosophy, political science/economy/sociology/theory, logic & scientific method, politics, public policy, race & ethnicity, real estate economics, regulation, risk & stochastics, social anthropology/policy, social psychology, social research methodology, sociology/contemporary social thought/crime, statistics, urbanization & development; BA(Hons), BSc(Hons), Dips, EMBA, Ll, M, MBA, MPA, MPhil, MRes, MSc, PhD

UNIVERSITY OF LONDON; LONDON SCHOOL OF JEWISH STUDIES www.lsjs.ac.uk

ethics, Jewish ethics, Jewish studies; MA

UNIVERSITY OF LONDON; QUEEN MARY
www.qmul.ac.uk

Humanities & Social Sciences

School of Business & Management; www.busman.qmul.ac.uk

accounting, business/law/management/ethics, social media, consumer/occupational psychology, corporate social responsibility, theories of organization, economics, employment relations, financial accounting/ institutions/management, management, governance & business strategy, HRM, innovation/entrepreneurship, international business, marketing, microeconomics, operations management, social & political marketing, social networks, work & employment, global business, international business & politics/ financial management/HRM, management & organizational innovation; BA(Hons), BSc(Hons)

School of Economics & Finance; www.econ.qmul.ac.uk

banking, economics, finance, geography, law, management, mathematics, politics, financial economics, statistics; BSc, MPhil, MSc(Econ), PhD

Centre for Editing Lives and Letters; www.livesandletters.qmul.ac.uk

Centre for Renaissance and Early Modern Studies; www.qmul.ac.uk/renaissance

Renaissance and early modern studies; MA

Centre for the Study of Migration; www.politics.qmul.ac.uk/migration

migration, migration and law; MA, MRes, MSc

School of English and Drama; www.sed.qmul.ac.uk

Dept of Drama

drama, drama & English/French/German/Hispanic studies/Russian/film studies, historiography & archives, performance research, theatre & performance theory

Dept of English

English/& drama/film studies, history/modern language/French/German/Hispanic studies/Russian/linguistics, English literature in Renaissance & early modern studies, writing & society 1700–1820, writing in the modern age; BA(Hons), MA, MRes, PhD

School of Languages, Linguistics & Film; www.sllf.qmul.ac.uk

French/German/Hispanic studies/Russian, language with business management/film studies/linguistics, European studies, Anglo-German cultural relations, comparative literature; BA(Hons), MA, PhD

Dept of Geography; www.geog.qmul.ac.uk

cities, economies & social change, cities & cultures, community organizing, environmental geography/ science, business management, geography, global change: environment, economy/globalization & development, human geography, London studies, physical geography; BA(Hons), BSc(Econ), BSc(Hons), MA, MSc, PhD

Dept of History; www.history.qmul.ac.uk

contemporary/history, journalism, history & politics/ film studies/English/French, German language, crusader studies, Islam & the West, European Jewish history, medieval history, Paris studies & 20th-century history; BA(Hons), MA, PhD

School of Law; www.law.qmul.ac.uk law

banking & finance law, commercial & corporate law, comparative & international dispute resolution, competition law, computer & communications law, economic regulation, English and European law, environmental law, human rights law, intellectual property law, international business law, law & development/politics, legal theory & history, medical law, public international law, public law, tax law, media law; Dips, LlB, LlM, MPhil, MSc, PGDip, PhD

Dept of Philosophy; www.philosophy.qmul.ac.uk

philosophy; MPhil, PhD

School of Politics & International Relations; www.politics.qmul.ac.uk

international relations, politics, politics & economics/ law/geography/business management/French/German/Russian/Hispanic studies, public policy, global & comparative politics, globalization & development, international business, global & comparative politics, international relations, migration/& law, public policy, law with management/economics geography/ modern languages; BA(Hons), MA, MPhil, MRes, PhD

School of Medicine & Dentistry; www.smd.qmul.ac.uk

Barts and The London School of Medicine and Dentistry; www.smd-edu.qmul.ac.uk/medicine/

medicine, surgery, dentistry, dental surgery, biomedical engineering, clinical materials, experimental pathology, health science, infection & immunization, medical education, molecular medicine, neuroscience, oral biology, dental care professions, dental technology, sports & exercise science; also postgraduate taught courses in medicine & dentistry

Research Institutes

Barts Cancer Institute
Bizard Institute of Cell and Molecular Science
Institute of Dentistry
Institute of Health Science and Education
William Harvey Research Institute
Wolfson Institute of Preventative Medicine

BDS, BMedSci, FD, BDental Science, MBBS, MClinDent, MD, MRes, MPhil, MSc, NVQ, PGDip, PhD, MPrth, Certs, Dips

Department of Science & Engineering

School of Biological and Chemical Sciences; www.sbcs.qmul.ac.uk

aquatic biology, biochemistry, biology, biomedical sciences, freshwater & coastal sciences, genetics, marine ecology & environmental management, medical/genetics, pharmaceutical chemistry, psychology, zoology; BSc(Hons), FD, MPhil, MSci, PhD

School of Electronic Engineering & Computer Science; www.eecs.qmul.ac.uk

audio & music systems engineering, bioinformatics, business computing, communication engineering, computer engineering/science, digital music processing, digital signal processing, electrical engineering, electronic engineering, information/systems/management & communication technologies, interactive media design, internet, language & linguistics, multimedia computing, networks, security & surveillance, software engineering, telecommunications, web technologies, wireless networks; BEng, BSc(Eng), MEng, MSc, PhD

School of Engineering and Materials Science; www.sems.qmul.ac.uk

aerospace engineering, biomedical engineering, design & innovation, materials & design, materials science and engineering/research, dental materials, biomaterials, mechanical engineering, medical materials/electronics & physics/engineering, sustainable energy engineering/systems/materials; BEng, BSc, MEng, MPhil, MRes, PhD

Interdisciplinary Research Centre in Biomedical Materials; www.materials.qmul.ac.uk

forming & processing technology, hard tissue replacement & biology, interfaces & sensors, orthopaedic cell & tissue engineering; PhD

School of Mathematical Sciences; www.maths.qmul.ac.uk

mathematics, pure mathematics, statistics, astrophysics, financial economics, maths with business management, computing, physics, accountancy; BSc(Hons), MPhil, MSc, MSci, PGDip/Cert, PhD

Dept of Physics; www.phy.qmul.ac.uk

astrophysics, physics, theoretical physics & nanoscience, particle physics; BSc(Hons), MSc, MSci, PGDip, PhD

Research Centre in Psychology; www.psychology.sbcs.qmul.ac.uk

applied psychology, biological & experimental psychology, biology with psychology, computational psychology, language & communication, psychology; BSc(Hons), MPhil, PhD

UNIVERSITY OF LONDON; ROYAL HOLLOWAY
www.rhul.ac.uk

Faculty of Arts; www.rhul.ac.uk/departments/arts

Dept for Classics & Philosophy; www.rhul.ac.uk/classicsandphilosophy

ancient history, modern history & politics, late antique & Byzantine studies, Hellenic studies & poltical thought, crusader studies, medieval studies, public history; BA(Hons), MPhil, PhD

Dept of Drama & Theatre; www.rhul.ac.uk/drama

drama & theatre studies/music/English/classical studies/French/German/Italian/creative writing/

philosophy, theatre, applied drama(directing/performance/playwriting); BA(Hons), MPhil, PhD

Dept of English; www.rhul.ac.uk/english
English, English & philosophy/classics/comparative literature/modern languages, creative writing, English liteature, literature of modernity, medieval studies, poetic practice, Shakespeare, Victorian literature, art, culture

Dept of Media Arts; www.rhul.ac.uk/media-arts
documentary by practice, production, media arts, film & TV studies, screenwriting for TV & film; BA(Hons), MA, MPhil, PhD

Dept of Modern Languages, Literature & Culture; www.rghul.ac.uk/mllc
French, German, Italian, Spanish, modern literature & culture/film studies, critical theory, film, visual & performing arts. linguistics

Dept of Music; www.rhul.ac.uk/Music
advanced musical studies, music, composition, ethnomusicology, historical musicology, performance, music with performance studies; BA(Hons), BMus, MMus, MPhil, PhD

Faculty of History & Social Sciences; www.rhul.ac.uk/departments/hss

Centre for Criminology & Sociology; www.rhul.ac.uk/criminology & sociology
criminology, sociology, criminal justice systems, social policy, psychology of morality & behaviour

Dept of Economics; www.rhul.ac.uk/economics
economics, economics & management/politics/international relations/political studies/modern languages, financial & business economics/industrial economics, economics of public policy

Dept of European Studies; www.rhul.ac.uk/EuropeanStudies
European studies (French/Spanish/Italian/German), European international relations, issues in contemporary Europe, European parliament, EU budget, comparative parliamentary policy

Dept of Health and Social Care; www.rhul.ac.uk/healthandsocialcare
social work, work with children & families; BA(Hons), MA, MSc

Dept of History; www.rhul.ac.uk/history
history, public history, history/and French/German/Spanish/international relations, history of political thought & intellectual history, late antique & Byzantine studies, modern history & politics

School of Management; www.rhul.ac.uk/management
accounting, entrepreneurship, HR, business/information systems, marketing, international accounting/business/HRM/ management, leadership & management in health, Asia Pacific business, sustainability & management, sport management

Dept of Politics & International Relations; www.rhul.ac.uk/politics-and-IR
politics/with international relations/philosophy, economics, European studies/politics, geography, political theory, global politics, democracy, politics & governance, int relations theory, new political communication, transnational security studies; BA(Hons), BSc(Hons) MA, MBA, MSc, MPhil, PhD, PGCert, Grad Dip, PGDip

Faculty of Science; www.rhul.ac.uk/departments/science

School of Biological Sciences; www.rhul.ac.uk/biological-sciences
biochemistry, biology, biotechnology, ecology & environment, molecular biology, biomedical sciences, medical biochemistry; BA(Hons), BSc(Hons), MSc, PhD

Dept of Computer Science; www.cs.rhul.ac.uk
computer science (AI), bioinformatics, business information systems, machine learning, computing & business, information security; BSc(Hons), MPhil, MSc, PhD

Dept of Earth Sciences; www.gl.rhul.ac.uk
environmental geology/geoscience, geology and geography/biology, geoscience, petroleum geology/geoscience, environmental diagnosis & management; BSc, MSC, MSci, PhD

Dept of Geography; www.gg.rhul.ac.uk
cultural geography, geography, geology, human/physical geography, politics & international relations, practising sustainable development, sustainability & management, quarternary science; BA, BSc, MA, MSc, PhD

Dept of Mathematics; www.ma.rhul.ac.uk
information security, mathematics, mathematics for applications, maths of cryptology & communication, statistics; BSc(Hons), MSc, MSci, PhD

Dept of Physics; www.rhul.ac.uk/physics
physics, applied physics, astrophysics, low temperature physics, nanotechnology, particle physics, theoretical physics; BSc(Hons), MPhil, MPhys, MSc, PhD

Dept of Psychology; www.rhul.ac.uk/psychology
applied social psychology, cognitive behavioural theory, psychology; BSc(Hons), DClinPsych, MSc, PhD

UNIVERSITY OF LONDON; ROYAL VETERINARY COLLEGE www.rvc.ac.uk

bioveterinary sciences, control of infectious diseases in animals, livestock health & production, veterinary nursing/medicine, wild animal health, veterinary pathology/physiotherapy/education/epidemiology, wild animal biology, public health; BSc(Hons), BVetMed, FdSc, MPhil, PhD, MVMed, MRes, MSc, PGDip/Cert

UNIVERSITY OF LONDON; SCHOOL OF ORIENTAL AND AFRICAN STUDIES www.soas.ac.uk

African language and culture/literature/studies, ancient Near Eastern languages/studies, anthropological research, anthropology of food/media/tourism/travel, applied Japanese linguistics, applied linguistics and language pedagogy, Arabic cultural studies literature, Arabic/and Islamic studies, Asian politics, banking law, Chinese (modern and classical), Chinese law/literature/studies, comparative literature (Africa/Asia), critical media & cultural studies, development & globalization, development studies/central Asia, dispute & conflict resolution, economics, environmental law, ethnomusicology, finance & development/financial law, gender studies, geography, Bengali, Burmese (Myanmar), global cinemas & the transcultural, global media & postnational communication, Hausa, Hebrew & Israeli studies, Hindi, history of art/archaeology/Asia/Africa & Europe, history, history: Asia/Africa, human rights law, conflict & justice, Indonesian, international & comparative legal studies, international commercial/economic law, international management (China/Japan/Middle East and north Africa), international politics/development diplomacy, Islamic law/studies/literature, Japanese literature/studies, Japanese, Korean, Korean literature/studies, languages & cultures of south Asia, languages & literatures of south east Asia, law in the Middle East and north Africa, law, culture & society, development & governance, linguistics, medical anthropology, near /Middle East politics/ studies, migration & diaspora studies, migration mobility & development, music studies, Nepali, Pacific Asian studies, religions, performance, Persian, political economy of development, politics of China, Sanskrit, Sinology, social anthropology, south Asian area studies/law/studies, state, society and development, study of religions, sustainable development, Swahili, Taiwan studies, Thai, Tibetan, translation (Asian and African languages), Turkish, Vietmaneses, violence, conflict & development; BA(Hons), LlB, LlM, MMus, MPhil, MSc, PGDip, PhD

UNIVERSITY OF LONDON; THE SCHOOL OF PHARMACY www.pharmacy.ac.uk

clinical pharmacy, drug delivery/discovery, cell & molecular biology, medicine management, pharmacognosy, clinical pharmacy, pharmacy practice; Certs, MPharm, MSc, PGDip, PhD

UNIVERSITY OF LOUGHBOROUGH
www.lboro.ac.uk

Faculty of Engineering; www.lboro.ac.uk/eng

Aeronautical and Automotive Engineering; www.lboro.ac.uk/departments/tt/

advanced methods/aeronautical engineering, automotive engineering/systems engineering

Chemical Engineering; www.lboro.ac.uk/departments/cg

advanced /chemical engineering, advanced process engineering, chemical engineering/with environmental protection/management/IT pharmaceutical engineering

Civil and Building Engineering; www.lboro.ac.uk/departments/cv

air transport management, architectural engineering & design management, civil engineering, commercial management & quantity surveying, construction engineering management/ project management/construction business management, transport & business management, building surveying, low carbon building design, sustainable transport policy & travel building, infrastructure in emergencies,water & waste engineering/environmental management

Electronic and Electrical Engineering; www.lboro.ac.uk/departments/el

advanced/systems engineering, digital/mobile communication, electronic & electrical engineering, electronics & computer systems engineering/software engineering, media communications, networked communications, renewable energy systems technology, signal processing in communication systems

Materials; www.loboro.ac.uk/departments/materials

materials engineering, automotive materials, design with engineering materials, material science & technology, packaging/polymer technology; BEng, MEng, MSc Dip Cert

Mechanical and Manufacturing; www.lboro.ac.uk/departments/mm

advanced manufacturing engineering & management, engineering design, manufacture, innovative manufacturing engineering, mechanical engineering, mechatronics, product design engineering, sports technology, sustainable engineering

Systems Engineering; www.loboro.ac.uk/programmes/systems

BEng, BSc(Hons), MDes, MRes, MSc, PhD,Cert,Dip

Faculty of Science; www.lboro.ac.uk/sci

Faculty of Chemistry; www.lboro.ac.uk/departments/cm

analytical & pharmaceutical science, analytical chemistry, environmental science, chemistry, forensic analysis, sports science, chemistry & information technology, pharmaceutical chemistry, medicinal chemistry; BSc, MSc, PhD

Dept of Computer Science; www.lboro.ac.uk/departments/co

computer science, AI, IT management for business, computing & management/information management, internet computing & network security, digital imaging, computer graphics & vision, IT, networks, multimedia & internet computing, web development & design, factors in transport/inclusive design; BSc(Hons), MSc, PhD, Dip

Dept of Information Sciences; www.lboro.ac.uk/departments/is

information management & business studies/computing/ business technology, information & knowledge management, library management, publishing with English, web development & design; BSc(Hons), MPhil, PhD

Dept of Materials; www.lboro.ac.uk/departments/materials

automotive materials, design with engineering materials, materials engineering, materials for industry, packaging technology, polymer technology; BEng/MEng, BSc(Hons), Diploma in Industrial Studies, MSc, PGDip/Cert, PhD

School of Mathematics; www.lboro.ac.uk/departments/ma

financial mathematics, industrial mathematical modelling, mathematical finance, mathematics, mathematics & accounting & financial management/sports science/computer science/ mathematics; BSc(Hons), MSc, PhD

Dept of Physics; www.lboro.ac.uk/departments/ph

astrophysics & cosmology, engineering physics, materials physics & applications, nanoscience, physics, physics & maths/management/sports science/cosmology, psychophysics, quantum physics & applications, science of the internet, surface physics, experimental/theoretical condensed matter physics; BSc(Hons), MSc, PhD

Faculty of Social Sciences and Humanities; www.lboro.ac.uk/ssh

School of the Arts; www.loboro.ac.uk/departments/sota

3D design; fine art, graphic communication, illustration, textile innovation & design, 2D/3D vision, art & design, arts & the public sphere, studio ceramics, arts research by practice; BA(Hons), MA, MSc, MPhil, PhD

School of Business & Economics; www.loboro.ac.uk/departments/sbe

Business: accounting & financial maangement, banking, finance & management, international business/strategy, management science/& strategy/information systems, market research, retail management, retailing, marketing, HRM, organizational behaviour
Economics: economics, economics & finance/accounting, international economics. banking & finance/financial markets, international banking, money
Executive Education: management & leadership, HE administration, occupational health & safety management, healthcare emergency preparedness/governace, security management, fire safety management, automotive retail/dealership management; BSc, MA, MSc, MRes, MPhil, PhD, Cert, Dip, MBA

Loughborough Design School; www.loboro/departments/ds

design/ergonomics, ergonomics (human factors in design), product/industrial design & technology, product design in business, user-centred/virtual product design,road & vehicle safety; BA, MA, MSc, MDes, PGCE with QTS

Dept of English & Drama; www.lboro.ac.uk/departments/ea

creative writing, drama, English, film, history, North American literature, performance & multi-media, sports science; BA(Hons), MA, PhD

Dept of Politics, International Relations & European Studies; www.lboro.ac.uk/departments/eu

history & geography/English, international relations, politics; BSc(Hons), MPhil, MSc, PhD

Dept of Geography; www.lboro.ac.uk/departments/gy

environmental monitoring, geography, geography & management/economics/sport science, global transformations, globalization, human geography research, international financial & political relations, space & sport; BSc, MPhil, MSc, PhD

School of Sport, Exercise and Health Sciences; www.lboro.ac.uk/departments/ssehs

human biology, physical activity and health, physical education & QTS, psychology, sociology of sport, sport biomechanics, sport coaching, sport and exercise nutrition/psychology/science, exercise science/physiology, sport management/science; BSc(Hons), MPhil, MSc, PhD

Dept of Social Sciences; www.lboro.ac.uk/departments/ss

communications and media studies, criminology & criminal justice/social policy, global media & cultural analysis, social psychology, sociology; BSc(Hons), MPhil, MSc, PhD

Teacher Education Unit; www.lboro.ac.uk/departments/teu

design & technology, PE, science, initial teacher training; MSc, PGCE

UNIVERSITY OF MANCHESTER
www.manchester.ac.uk

Faculty of Engineering and Physical Sciences; www.eps.manchester.ac.uk

School of Chemical Engineering and Analytical Science; www.ceas.manchester.ac.uk

analytical & separation science, instrument & measurement science, biotechnology, biocatalysis, chemical engineering with chemistry/environmental technology/management, chemical process design, process design for energy & the environment, product formulation, refinery design & operation, systems biology; BEng, MEng, MSc, PhD

School of Chemistry; www.chemistry.manchester.ac.uk

biological, inorganic, materials, chemistry, forensic & analytical/medicinal chemistry, organic, physical & theoretical chemistry, patent law, polymer & materials science & engineering; BSc(Hons), EngD, MChem, MEnt, MPhil, MSc, PhD

School of Computer Science; www.cs.manchester.ac.uk

adv web technologies, AI, applications of NLP, computer science/security, computer systems engineering, computing for business applications, data & knowledge management, digital biology, distributed computing, internet computingy, multicore computing, semantic technology, software engineering BSc(Hons), MEng, MEnt, MPhil, MSc, PhD

School of Earth, Atmospheric & Environmental Sciences; www.seas.manchester.ac.uk

earth sciences, environmental sciences/policy & control, geochemistry, geography, geology, planetary science, environmental & resource geology, petroleum geoscience/engineering, pollution & environmental control; BSc(Hons), MEarthSci, MEng, MSc, PhD

School of Electrical and Electronic Engineering; www.eee.manchester.ac.uk

communication engineering, advanced control & systems engineering, digital image & signal processing, electrical & electronic engineering, electrical energy conversion systems, electrical power systems engineering, mechatronic engineering, nanoelectronics; BEng(Hons), Dip, BSc(Hons), EngD, MEng(Hons), MPhil, MSc, PhD

School of Materials; www.materials.manchester.ac.uk

advanced/engineering materials, biomaterials, biomedical materials science, composite materials, corrosion control engineering, design manufacture for fashion/& textile retailing, materials science & engineering, textile science & technology, textile design, marketing & management of fashion textiles; BSc, MEng, MPhil, PhD

School of Mathematics; www.maths.manchester.ac.uk

actuarial science, applied maths, biostatistics, computational science, financial mathematics, mathematical finance, mathematics, mathematical logic, pure maths, quantitative finance & financial engineering, statistics, theoretical & applied fluid dynamics; BSc, MMath, MPhil, MSc, PhD

School of Mechanical, Aerospace and Civil Engineering; www.mace.manchester.ac.uk

adv manufacturing technology & systems management, aerospace engineering, civil engineering, maintenance engineering & asset management, management of projects, mechanical engineering/design, structural engineering, thermal power & fluid engineering, theoretical & applied fluid dynamics; BEng, EngD, MEng, MEnt, MPhil, MSc, PhD

School of Physics & Astronomy; www.physics.manchester.ac.uk

physics, physics & astrophysics/mathematics/astrophysics/theoretical physics, biological physics, nuclear science & technology, photon science, radio imaging & sensing; BSc, EngD, MMath & Phys, MPhys, MSc, PhD

Faculty of Humanities; www.humanities.manchester.ac.uk

School of Arts, Histories and Cultures; www.arts.manchester.ac.uk

American studies, ancient history, applied theatre, art gallery & museum studies, archaeology (identity, complex societies, neolithic), art history, arts management, biblical studies, classical studies, classics, comparative religion, composition, the holy & the supernatural, contemporary literature & culture, creative writing, cultural history, drama, early modern history, economic & social history, economics, electroacoustic music composition, English literature, French, gender, sexuality & culture, Greek, history/& culture 1200-1700, humanitarianism & conflict response, Latin, linguistics, medieval studies, modern British/European history, music, musicology, performance, screen & visual cultures, politics, post-1900 literatures, post-colonial literatures & cultures, religion & political life/theology, screen studies, social anthropology, south Asian studies, Spanish, Jewish studies, theatre studies/& performance, theology, culture & society, Victorian times, war, culture & history, world history; BA(Hons), MA, MMus, PhD

School of Education; www.education.manchester.ac.uk

community & youth work studies, counselling, digital technology, communication & education, educational leadership & school improvement, TESOL, HE, inclusive education, language, literacy & communication, learning disability studies, management & leisure, PGCE primary, PGCE secondary (business education, design technology, English, mathematics, modern languages, science), profound & complex learning disability, psychology of education, supervision of counselling and the helping professions, TESOL; BA(Hons), DCons, DEd, EdD, MA, MEd, MPhil, MSc, PGCE, PGCert/Dip, PhD, UGCert/Dip

School of Environment and Development; www.sed.manchester.ac.uk

architecture, city & regional development, climate change, environment & development, conflict & reconstruction, development economics, international trade & global finance, environmental management, geography, geology, GIS, poverty, management & human resources in international development, ICT systems & information science, politics & welfare in international development, town & country planning, urban development, planning & sustainable cities, urbanism; BSc, MA, MPlan, MSc, MTCP, PGDip, PhD

School of Languages, Linguistics and Cultures; www.llc.manchester.ac.uk

Chinese studies, contemporary China, East Asian studies, Carribean studies, English language, European languages and cultures/studies, E.European studies, French/literature, Italian, German, Hebrew studies, history of art, Arabic, Italian studies, Japanese studies, Jewish studies, Latin American cultural/ studies, linguistics, Middle Eastern languages/studies, modern languages, Persian, Portuguese, Russian, screen studies, Spanish, translation & interpreting studies, Turkish; BA(Hons), MA, MML, MPhil, PhD

School of Law; www.law.manchester.ac.uk

law, bioethics and medical jurisprudence, corporate governance, crime/law & society, criminology/& socio-legal studies, health care ethics, intellectual property law, international business & commercial law, international financial law/trade transactions, law & economics/development, politics; BA, LlB, LlM, MA, MPhil, MRes, PGDip, PhD

Manchester Business School; www.mbs.manchester.ac.uk

accounting, American business studies, analytics/OR & risk analysis, business administration/(global), business economics, Chinese business, corporate communications & reputation management, economics, enterprise, finance, global business analysis, international business/management, international commercial & contract management, healthcare management/governance, HRM, industrial relations, information systems (business IT, e-business technology, organization & management), management, managerial psychology, marketing, operations, supply chain management, organizational psychology, quantitative finance (financial engineering, risk management, management (accounting & finance/HR/ innovation, sustainability & finance/international business economics/international studies/marketing/ information systems), management with compliance/ trusts & estates; BA, BSc, MBA, MBus, MDA, MEnt, MPA, MRes, MSc, PhD, DBA, PGCert

School of Social Sciences; www.socialsciences.manchester.ac.uk

accounting, anthropology, archaeology, business studies, criminology, development studies/economics, econometrics, economics, finance, financial economics, human rights, international development international business/finance/economics/politics/relations, law, political economy/science/ theory, philosophy, politics, social anthropology, social change/history, statistics, sociological research, sociology, visual anthropolgy; BAEcon, BSc, MA, MRes, MSc, PGDip, PhD

Centre for Continuing Education, Centre for Educational Leadership; www.cel.manchester.ac.uk
educational leadership, process consultancy; MEd, PGCert

Faculty of Life Sciences; www.lf.manchester.ac.uk
anatomical sciences, biochemistry, bioinformatics, & systems biology, biological sciences, biology, biomechanics, biomedical and forensic studies in Egyptology, biomedical sciences, biotechnology, cell biology, cancer research & molecular biomedicine, cognitive neuroscience and psychology, computational neuroscience, developmental biology, genetics, history of science, technology and medicine, immunology and immunogenetics, integrative biology. life sciences, medical biochemistry, microbiology, molecular biology/parasitology & vector biology, neuroscience, optometry, pharmacology, physiology, plant & microbiol sciences, zoology; BSc, MNeuroSci, MRes, MSc, PhD

Faculty of Medical & Human Sciences; www.mhs.manchester.ac.uk

School of Dentistry; www.dentistry.manchester.ac.uk
dental implantology, dental public health, dentistry, endodontics, prosthodontics, oral & maxillofacial surgery, oral health sciences, orthodontics, periodontology, restorative & aesthetic dentistry; BDS, BSc, MDen, MDPH, MSc, MSc(Clin), PGDip/Cert, PhD

School of Medicine; www.medicine.manchester.ac.uk
medicine, pathology, medical physics & clinical engineering, medical microbiology, clinical biochemistry, genetic medicine, psychiatry, forensic mental health; ChB, MB, MD/ChM, MPH, MPhil, MRes, MSc, PGCert, PGDip, PhD

School of Nursing and Midwifery & Social Work; www.nursing.manchester.ac.uk
advanced nursing/midwifery studies, adv audiology studies, health & social care, midwifery, adult/child/mental health nursing, adv professional health studies, cancer & palliative care, critical/surgical care, clinical care, maternal & child care, psychosocial interventions for psychosis, dementia, social work; BMidwif, BNurs, MA, MClinRes, MPhil, MRes, MSc, PGCert, PGD, PGDip, PhD

School of Pharmacy & Pharmaceutical Sciences; www.pharmacy.manchester.ac.uk
clinical & health services pharmacy, pharmaceutical industrial advanced training, pharmacy, modelling & simulation in pharmacokinetics/dynamics; MPharm, MPhil, MSc, PGCert/Dip, PhD

School of Psychological Sciences; www.psych-ci.manchester.ac.uk
audiology, clinical & health psychology, cognitive brain imaging, cognitive neuroscience & psychology, deaf education, pyschology, speech & language therapy, adv professional health studies; BSc, MPhil, MRes, MSc, PGDip, PhD, ClinPsyD

MANCHESTER METROPOLITAN UNIVERSITY
www.mmu.ac.uk

Faculty of Art & Design; www.artdes.mmu.ac.uk
acting, architecture, art & design, contemporary film & video/curating, creative practice, film & media studies, filmmaking, fine art, illustration, animation, graphic design, interior/3D design, international creative advertising, landscape architecture/design, media arts, movement/theatre, photography, urbanism, visual culture; BA(Hons), BArch, BL and Arch, MA, MEnterprise, MPhil, PGDip/Cert, PhD

Faculty of Health, Psychology & Social Care; www.hpsc.mmu.ac.uk

Health Professions; Nursing; Social Work & Social Change
acupuncture, adult nursing, community health, contemp health practice, counselling, criminology, disablement studies, health & social care, physiotherapy, psychology, speech pathology/therapy, practice development, social work/adv leadership, muscoskeletal/cardiorespiratory physiotherapy, public health/school nursing, emergency management/medicine, forensic psychology, health, health visiting

Faculty of Humanities, Law & Social Science; www2.hlss.mmu.ac.uk

criminology, sociology, digital media, communications, contemp European/ film & culture, critical theory, film, the Gothic, multimedia journalism, English, American literature, creative writing, French, German, Spanish, Italian, history, medieval / modern/political/social/local & regional history, European urban culture/philosophy, library & information management, informatics, law, law & society, legal practice, human rights law, European law, equality law, politics, public services, global change, web development; TEFL, BA(Hons), BSc(Hons), PGDip/Cert, MA, MPhil, PhD, LlB, LlM, MSc

Faculty of Science & Engineering; www.sci-eng.ac.uk

School of Healthcare Science; www.shs.mmuy.ac.uk

biological/ biomedical psychology, biomedical science, forensic biology, clinical physiology, dental technology, healthcare science, human biology, physical activity & health, physiology, pharamacology, human movement & health; BSc(Hons), MSc, PGCert/Dip

School of Computing, Mathematics, & Digital Technology; www.scmt.mmu.ac.uk;

computer games technology, computer science, adv/ forensic/internet computing, media technology, multimedia & web computing, software engineering, digital media computing, information systems, mobile application dev, post-prod technology film, TV, CGI, mathematics; FDSc, BSc(Hons), MSc PGDip/ Cert, PhD

School of Engineering; www.soe.mmu.ac.uk;

mechanical engineering, automation & control, automotive/computer-aided/communications/computer/ electrical/electronic engineering, engineering, electronic systems design, computer & network technolgy, mechanical/product/design & technology, computer networks, manufacture with management, sports technology; BSc(Hons), BEng(Hons), MSc, PGDip/ Cert, MPhil, PhD

School of Science & the Environment; www.ssty.mmu.ac.uk

Biology & Conservation Ecology:

animal behaviour, cell & molecular/conservation/ wildlife biology, conservation, tropical/ecology, microbiology, ornithology, human behaviour & ecology, environmental & climate change, GIS, zoo studies, countryside/env management, social & cultural geography, sustainable aviation; BSc(Hons), MSc, PGDip/Cert, MPhil, PhD

Chemistry & Environmental Science;

applied /chemistry, chemical & pharmaceutical science, environmental science, forensic/medicinal & biochemical/pharmaceutical chemistry; MChem, BSc(Hons)

Geography & Environmental Management;

climate change, environment & enterprise, environmental management & sustainability, human/physical geography, GIS & man magement/environment; BSc(Hons), PGCert/Dip, MSc, MPHil, PhD

Manchester Metropolitan University Business School; www.business.mmu.ac.uk

accounting, finance, financial planning & wealth management, advertising/brand management, PR, business/administration, management, HRM, marketing, business/economics, financial studies/services, planning & management, int business, management, retail marketing, sports marketing/ management, business IT, internet/retailing, regulated financial planning, leadership, digital /business management/marketing & communications, leadership in health, place management, project management, strategic financial mangement; BA(Hons), BSc(Hons), MA, MSc, MBA, DBA, PhD, FD,

Institute of Education; www.ioe.mmu.ac.uk

childhood studies, early childhood/years studies, education studies, primary education, professional studies (early years education/careers education and guidance/education/special educational needs), school administration/business management, secondary education, specific learning difficulties, teaching, youth & community work; BA(Hons), BA/BSc, Certs, EdD, FD, MA, MPhil, MSc, PGDip/Cert, PhD

Hollings Faculty; www.hollings.mmu.ac.uk

Department of Clothing Design & Technology

fashion materials & techn, clothing techn & product/ design, fashion buying, int fashion marketing, fashion design & technology

Department of Food & Tourism Management

consumer marketing, environmental health, events management, food management/marketing, hospitality/licensed retail management/business management/culinary arts/tourism, food and nutrition, food technology, human nutrition, hospitality/business management, events/ tourism management, trading standards, enviromental health, food management/ safety, BA(Hons), BSc(Hons), FdA, FdSc, HND, MA, MPhil, PhD, BTech, HND

MMU Cheshire; www.cheshire.mmu.ac.uk

Dept of Business & Management Studies; www.cheshire.mmu.ac.uk/bms

business, business management (financial management/HRM/ legal studies/marketing), HRM, marketing/management, strategic leadership & change, sport management; BA/BSc, BA(Hons), FD, HNC, HND, MBA, MSc, MPhil, PhD

Dept of Contemporary Arts; www.cheshire.mmu.ac.uk/dcu

contemporary arts, contemporary theatre & performance, creative music production, creative writing, dance, drama, music, popular music; BA(Hons), MA, MPhil, PhD

Dept of Exercise & Sports Science; www.cheshire.mmu.ac.uk/exspsci

coaching and sport development, coaching studies, leisure event management, PE, sport/ development/ science, sport & exercise science, psychology of sport and exercise; BA, BSc, Foundation degree, MA, MSc

MIDDLESEX UNIVERSITY
www.mdx.ac.uk

School of Arts and Education; www.mdx.ac.uk/schools/arts

Art & Design

animation, 3D animation & games, art /& design, creative technology, des for interactive media, digital product, fashion/design/ textiles, fine art, graphics des, des engineering & manufacture, interior architecture, jewellery & accessories, photography, product design, sonic arts; BA(Hons), FdA, MA, MSc

Dance, Music & the Theatre

dance performance/studies, music & arts management, jazz, music composition/performance, pop music, technical theatre design/performance/solo performance, theatre arts; BA(Hons), BMus, MA, MMus

English Literature & Language

English/English literature /& media, TEFL, English language

Film, Television & Media Arts

digital arts, film TV production/technical arts; BA(Hons)

Media, Culture & Communication

advertising, PR and media, communications management, creative and media writing, English literature, journalism, communication studies, magazine publishing, media and cultural studies, design for interactive media, moving image; BA(Hons), MA

Language & Translation Studies

international business & Arabic/Mandarin/Russian/ Spanish, TEFL, interpreting, theory & practice of translation; BA(Hons), MA

Teaching & Education

Early years, education studies, primary education, inclusive education, learning & teaching studies, professional studies; PGCE qualifications in range of subjects, supported learning, lifelong learning, TESOL/with applied linguistics; BA(Hons), FdA, MA, PGCE, PGCert

Middlesex University Business School; www.mdx.ac.uk/schools/bs

Accounting & Finance

accounting, business accounting, business economics, corporate accountability, finance, financial management, investment, statistics; BA(Hons), BSc(Hons), MSc

Business & Management

business administration/management, international business/ and Arabic/Mandarin/Russian/ Spanish, business enterprise & entrepreneurship, human rights, professional practice, management science &

operational research, professional practice, public works; BA(Hons), BSc(Hons), MSc, MBA

Economics & Statistics

banking, business economics, economics, finance, international finance, financial economics; BSc(Hons), MA, MBA, MSc, DBA, ProDoc

Human Resource Management

HRM, personal & professional development, employment law, recruitment practice; AdvDip, BA(Hons), FdA, PGCert, PGDip

Marketing & Enterprise

international /business/digital marketing, marketing, marketing communications/management, e-marketing & social media; BA(Hons), BSc(Hons), MA, MSc

Law

business/employment law, human rights & business, international business law, minorities, rights & the law; BA(Hons), GradDip, LlBHons, LlM, MA, PGDip

The School of Engineering and Information Sciences; www.mdx.ac.uk/schools/eis

Computing & Information Technology

biomedical modelling & informatics, business information/ systems/management/technology, computer & network security, computer networks/science/ communication, computing, graphics, games creative technology, data & knowledge engineering, digital inclusion, electronic security, enterprise management techn, forensic computing, interactive & social media, interactive system design, internet mobile/telecommunication engineering, interaction des/application, computing, IT, graphics and games, interactive systems design, internet application development, multimedia computing, networking, network eng/ management & security, software engineering; BSc, MSc

Product Design and Engineering

design engineering, engineering/management/ project management, manufacturing management, digital/product design, mobile telecommunication engineering, telecommunications; BA(Hons), BSc(Hons), MSc

School of Health & Social Sciences; www.mdx.ac.uk/schools/hssc

Biomedical and Biological Sciences

biomedical modelling & informatics, biomedical science, bioscience, haematology & transfusion science, obstetrics & gynaecological science, medical microbiology, molecular pathology, sports biomedicine; BSc(Hons), MSc

Complementary Health Sciences

Ayurvedic medicine, acupuncture, Chinese herbal med, Chinese medicine; AdvDip, BSc(Hons), MSc

Criminology & Sociology

criminal justice, criminology, psychology, sociology, forensic computing, policing, sociology with crime/ psychology, youth justice; BA(Hons), BSc(Hons), MA, MSc

Environment & Public Health

environmental health, public health, health promotion, occupational safety & health, food control, environmental pollution control/health, sustainable development, sustainable environmental management; BSc(Hons), MA, MSc

Nursing, Midwifery & Health

child, adolescent, nursing (child, adult, family/mental health/specialist practice), acute & critical care, children, drugs & alcohol, health promotion, dual diagnosis, mental health/young people, midwifery; AdvDip, BSc, BSc(Hons), Dip, MSc, PGCert

Social Science, Politics & Development

criminology, global government (public policy, housing), international politics, international relations/ development, psychology, social science; BA, BSc, CertHE, FdA, FdSc, MA

Social Work

social work; BA(Hons), MA

Psychology

applied psychology, criminology, counselling, forensic psychology, health psychology, psychology; BA(Hons), BSc(Hons), GradDip; MSc

Sport & Exercise Science

coaching and sports development, sport and exercise science, sport rehabilitation & injury prevention, strength & conditioning, performance analysis; BSc(Hons), FdSc, MSc

UNIVERSITY OF NEWCASTLE UPON TYNE
www.ncl.ac.uk

Faculty of Humanities and Social Sciences; www.ncl.ac.uk/hass

School of Architectural Planning and Landscape; www.ncl.ac.uk/apl

architecture & /practice/management/planning-design, digital architecture, geography, planning & environmental research, planning in developing countries/studies/practice, planning for sustainable & climate change, spatial planning, town planning, urban design; BA, BArch, Cert, Dip, MA, MPhil, MSc, PGCert, PhD

School of Arts and Cultures/music; www.ncl.ac.uk/sacs

Music

folk & traditional music, music, music & education, popular & contemporary music, theoretical & cultural musical origins, ethnomusicology, early & medieval music; BA, BMus, Diploma, MA, MLitt, MMus, MPhil, PhD

Fine Art

fine art, history of art; BA(Hons), MFA, MPhil, PhD

Digital Media

digital media/theoretical foundations/techniques, interactive media; Dip, MA, MRes

Museum, Gallery and Heritage Studies

art museum & gallery education/gallery studies, art as enterprise, heritage education & interpretation/ management, museum studies; MA, MPhil, MPrac, PGCert, PGDip, PhD

Media & Cultural Studies

media & jounalism/PR/cultural studies, international multimedia journalism, mass media, communication, culture; BA(Hons), MA, PhD

Business School; www.ncl.ac.uk/nubs

accounting, arts, business & creativity, banking, business accounting, business management, e-business (information systems/emarketing), economics, finance, e-marketing, financial & business economics, financial regulation, innovation, creativity and entrepreneurship, HRM, international business management/economics & finance/financial analysis/HR/ marketing, Islamic finance, law, management, marketing, operations management & logistics/supply chain management, strategic planning & investment, quantitative finance & marketing; BA, BSc, DBA, MA, MBA, MSc, PhD

School of Education, Communication and Language Sciences; www.ncl.ac.uk/ecls

applied linguistics & TESOL, cross-cultural communication & applied linguistics/education/international management/marketing/international relations/ media studies, education media & journalism, PR, PGCE primary/secondary, educational psychology, practictioner enquiry, education, speech & language science, languge pathology, international development/multimedia, journalism, language and linguistics, media, communication and cultural studies, PR; BA(Hons), BSc(Hons), DedPsych, EdD, MA, MEd, MSc, PGCE, PhD

Combined Studies Centre

combined studies; BS(Hons)

School of English Literature, Language, Linguistics; www.ncl.ac.uk/elll

English language/ literature, literary studies: writing, memory, culture, linguistics, creative writing, language acquisition, modern & contemporary studies; BA(Hons), MA, MLitt, MPhil, PGCert, PhD

Geography, Politics and Sociology; www.ncl.ac.uk/gps

applied policy research, geography(human, physical), European Union studies, international political economy, regional development, international politics (global justice & ethics/critical geopolitics/globalization, poverty, development), sociology, social research, world politics & popular culture; BA(Hons), BSc(Hons), MA, MSc, PhD

Global Urban Research Unit; www.ncl.ac.uk/guru

cities and international development, power, place & materiality, planning & environmental dynamics, cities, security & vulnerability; MPhil, PhD

Institute of Health and Society

public health & health services res; MSc, PGDip/Cert

School of Historical Studies; www.ncl.ac.uk/historical

ancient history, archaeology, archaeology of historic periods, British history, Byzantine & Roman archaeology, classical studies, classics, east Asian history, European history, Greek & Roman archaeology, history, politics, history of medicine, history of the Americas, neolithic & bronze age Europe, Roman frontier studies; BA(Hons), MA, MLitt, MPhil, PhD

Centre for History of Medicine; www.ncl.ac.uk/historical

history of medicine, medical history; BA(Hons), MLitt, MPhil, PhD

Centre for Knowledge, Innovation, Technology and Enterprise

innovation, creativity & enterprise, e-business & information science, arts, business & creativity; DBA, MSc, PhD

Newcastle Law School; www.ncl.ac.uk/nuls

environmental regulation & sustainanble development, criminology, international legal studies, international business law, law (complete range of legal areas taught at undergrad level); LlB, LlM, MPhil, PhD

Centre for Learning and Teaching; www.ncl.ac.uk/cflat

PGCE primary & secondary education, educational leadership and management, education & communication, graduate skills enhancement, information, communication and entertainment technology, inclusive education, international development & education, practitioner enquiry, pedagogy & learning, educational psychology; EdD, MA, MEd, PGCE

Newcastle Centre for he Literary arts/ www.ncl.ac.uk/ncla

creative writing; MA, PhD

School of Modern Languages; www.ncl.ac.uk/sml

Chinese, French, German, Japanese, Spanish, Portuguese & Latin American studies, Catalan, Dutch, Quecha, linguistics/for European languages, international film, Latin American interdisciplinary studies, translating for European languages, Spanish, translating and interpreting – Chinese strand; BA(Hons), MA, MLitt, PhD

Newcastle Institute for the Arts, Social Sciences and Humanities

Policy, Ethics and Life Sciences Research Centre; www.ncl.ac.uk/peals

ageing, biosecurity, bioinformation & security studies, clinical ethics, disability, fertility, genetics, human stem cell research, public participation; PhD

Centre for Research in Linguistics and Language Science; www.ncl.ac.uk/ linguistics

applied lingustics & TESOL, cross-cultural communication, education (TESOL), English language, human communication sciences, language acquisition/pathology, linguistics, European or Asian language, speech & language science; MA, MEd, MSc, PhD

Centre for Urban and Regional Development Studies; www.ncl.ac.uk/ curds

local /and regional development; MA

Faculty of Medical Sciences; www.ncl.ac.uk/aboutpeoplestudies academic/ biosciences

Biomedical and Biomolecular Sciences & Medicine; www.ncl.ac.uk/biomed

biochemistry, biomedical genetics/science, medical microbiology, biotechnology, medical science, pharmacology, psychological science, clinical education/ psychology, sociology

medicine, surgery, infection prevention & control, public health & health services, medical & molecular bioscience, minimal access surgery, oncology & palliative care, therapeutics

psychology, psychology & biology/mathematics/statistics, clinical psychology, neuroscience, pyschological therapies; BSc(Hons), DClinPsychol, MB, MClinEd, MClinRes, MD, MRes, MSc, MSci, PGCert/Dip, PhD, MClinRes, MBBS

Dental Sciences; www.ncl.ac.uk/dental

clinical dental implants, conscious sedation in dentistry, dental surgery, endodontics, orthodontics, restorative dentistry; BDS, DDS, MSc, PGDip, PhD

Faculty of Science, Agriculture & Engineering; www.ncl.ac.uk/ aboutpeoplestudies/academic/sage

School of Agriculture, Food and Rural Development; www.ncl.ac.uk/afrd

food marketing, agri-business management, agricultural & environmental science, agriculture, agronomy, animal production/science/behaviour & welfare, countryside management, ecological farming & food production systems, environmental resource assessment/science, farm business management, food & human nutrition, medicinal plants & functional foods, nutrition & pathology, rural social science/

studies, wildlife conservation & management; BSc(Hons), MPhil, MSc, PhD

School of Biology; www.ncl.ac.uk/biology

applied biology, biodiversity, conservation & ecotourism, biology, environmental consultancy, industrial & commercial biotechnology, zoology; BSc(Hons), MSC, PhD

School of Chemical Engineering and Advanced Materials

Biopharmaceutical Biprocess Technology Centre; www.ncl.ac.uk/ceam

applied process control, materials, design & engineering, chemical engineering, processing engineering, bioprocess automation, biopharmacological technology, clean technology, drug development, industrial quality technology, materials and process engineering, materials, design & engineering, process automation/ control, sustainable chemical engineering; BEng(Hons), MEng(Hons), MSc, PGDip

School of Chemistry; www.ncl.ac.uk/chemistry

chemistry, drug /medicinal chemistry, chemical nanoscience, molecular physics; BSc(Hons), MChem, MPhil, MSc, PhD

Civil Engineering and Geosciences; www.cegsncl.ac.uk

civil engineering, environmental engineering, geochemistry, geotechnical engineering, structural engineering, surveying & mapping science, physical geography, resources engineering, transport engineering, water environment; BEng, BSc(Hons), MEng, MPhil, MSc, PhD

Computing Science; www.cs.ncl.ac.uk/

computer game engineering, computer security and resilience, bioinformatics and computational systems biology, computing science, distributed systems/ games and virtual environments/software engineering, e-business & information systems, information systems, software engineering, internet technologies & enterprise computing; network systems & internet technology; BSc(Hons), MPhil, MSc, PhD

Electrical, Electronic and Computer Engineering; www.ncl.ac.uk/eece

adv sensor technology, automation and control, communications & signal processing, electrical & electronics engineering, electrical power, electronic communications, computer engineering, microelectronics, mobile & pervasive computing, power distribution; BEng, EngD, MEng, MPhil, PhD

Institute for Research on Environment and Sustainability; www.ncl.ac.uk/environment

agriculture, food & environment, biological sciences, biosciences, medicine & dentistry, engineering & science in the marine environment, environmental engineering, geography, rural development/social science, water resources engineering; MPhil, MRes, PhD

Informatics Research Institute; www.ncl.ac.uk/iri

research projects; PhD

Institute for Nanoscience and Technology; www.ncl.ac.uk/irisat

cellular medicine, chemical nanoscience, chemical energy systems, MEMS and smart materials, nano materials & electronics, nanoscience & nanotechnology, policy, ethics & life sciences, products and processes

Newcastle Centre for Railway Research; www.ncl.ac.uk/newrail

rail freight & logistics, rail infrastructure/systems/ vehicles

School of Marine Science and Technology; www.ncl.ac.uk/marine

aquaculture enterprise & technology, international marine environmental consultancy, marine & offshore power systems/technology, marine biology, marine engineering/structures & integrity/transport & management, marine zoology, marine electrical power technology, naval architecture, oceanography, offshore engineering, pipeline engineering, small craft technology/design, subsea engineering & management, tropical coastal management; BEng, BSc(Hons), MEng, MRes MSc

Mathematics and Statistics; www.ncl.ac.uk/math

applied/ financial mathematics, mathematics, pure mathematics, statistics; BSc(Hons), MMath, MMathStat, MPhil, PhD

School of Mechanical & Systems Engineering; www.ncl.ac.uk/mech

automotive engineering, bioengineering, design engineering, industrial quality technology, manufacturing engineering, materials engineering, mechanical engineering/design, mathematical modelling, mechatronics, microsystems, low carbon transport engineering, BEng, MEng, MSc

Centre for Rural Economy; www.ncl.ac.uk/cre

rural social science research; MPhil, MSc, PhD, MRes

Sir Joseph Swan Institute for Energy Research; www.ncl.ac.uk/energy

bioinformatics, environmental consultancy, industrial & commercial biotechnology, medical & molecular biosciences, medicinal plants & functional foods, renewable energy, rural science, wild life conservation; MRes, MSc, PhD

Centre for Software Reliability; www.csr.ncl.ac.uk

dependability of computer-based systems, dependable computing systems centre

UNIVERSITY OF NORTHAMPTON
www.northampton.ac.uk

School of Science & Technology; www.northampton.ac.uk/science-technology

Division of Computing; w.w.w2.northampton.ac.uk/computing

computing/internet technology/computer networks engineering/ security/software engineering/mobile technology, computer systems engineering/graphics & visualization; BA/BSc, BSc(Hons), HND, MSc, PhD

Division of Engineering; w.ww2.northampton.ac.uk/engineering

electrical and electronic engineering, engineering, lift (BSc(Hons), BTEC, FdSc, HNC, HND, MSc, ProfCert

Geographical & Environmental Science; w.ww2.northampton.ac.uk/geographical-and-environmental sciences

applied conservation biology, biology, biological conservation, environmental management/science, geography, international environmental conservation, physical geography; BA/B/Sc, BSc(Hons), FdSc, HNS, MBA, MSc, UnivCerts

Institute for Creative Leather Technologies; www2.leather technology

leather technology (international environmental management/leatherscience), environment, (marketing or business); BSc(Hons), BTEC NC, Leathersellers Cert, MSc, PhD/MPhil

The School of The Arts; www.northampton.ac.uk/info/20300/schol-of-the-arts

Division of Design; www2.northampton.ac.uk/arts/home/Design

architectural technology, creative advertising, graphic communication, illustration, interactive digital media, interior design, product design; BA(Hons), BSc(Hons)

Division of Fine Art; www2.northampton.ac.uk/arts/home/Fine Art

art and design, drawing, fine art, painting, photographic practice; BA(Hons), FDA, MA

Division of Media, English and Culture; www2.northampton.ac.uk/arts/home/Media English Culture

creative writing, English, film & TV studies, journalism, media production, digital filmaking; BA(Hons), MA, HND

Division of Performance Studies; www2.northampton.ac.uk/arts/home/Performance

acting, dance, drama, music production/practice, popular music, theatre; BA(Hons), HND, MA, PhD

Division of Fashion and Textiles; www2.northampton.ac.uk/arts/home/Division of Fashion

fashion, footware & accessories, printed textile fashion, surface design & printed textiles; BA(Hons)

School of Education; www.northampton.ac.uk/departments/education

education (early years & primary), graduate teacher programme (GTP), initial teacher training, learning & teaching, level teaching assistant status, early years education, childhood & youth, early years education, QTS early years/primary, professional studies, special education needs & inclusion, post-compulsory education & training, HE supporting learners; BA(Hons), GTP, PGCE; BA(Hons), CertHE, FD, PhD

School of Health; www.northampton.ac.uk/departments/health

adult/children's/dental nursing, health studies, community development, learning disability, mental health, human bioscience, midwifery, occupational therapy, paramedic science, podiatry, social care, social work, sport and exercise, work-based learning; BSc(Hons), MPhil, PGCert, PhD

Northampton Business School; www.northampton.ac.uk/departments/business

accounting, advertising, business, business computing/systems/entrepreneurship/studies, corporate governance, economics, EFL, fashion marketing, finance, French, German, Mandarin, HRM, information science, international accounting/HRM/logistics & trade finance/banking/development, IT service management, leadership, leisure & lifestyle management, management, marketing, sports marketing/marketing, travel & tourism management, web design; BA(Hons), BA/BscHons, CMS, DBA, DMS, FdA, HND, MA, MBA, MSc, PGDip (marketing), ProfDip

School of Social Sciences; www.northampton.ac.uk/departments/social sciences

History

history, social & cultural history; BA(Hons), MA, PhD

Law; www2.northampton.ac.uk/socialsciences/sshome/law-2

international business law/ criminal law & security, law, appl criminal justice, offender management, police & criminal justice; LlB, LlM, BSc, PhD, FdA

Psychology

child & adolescent mental health, development & educational/sport & exercise psychology, counselling, psychology, transpersonal psychology & consciousness; BA/BSc, BSc(Hons), PhD

Sociology

criminology, offender management, sociology; BA(Hons), MA

police & criminal justice service, probation & policing, urban affairs; BSc, FdA

geography (human, physical), media studies, philosophy, politics, media, philosophy, politics, international relations

UNIVERSITY OF NORTHUMBRIA AT NEWCASTLE
www.northumbria.ac.uk

Newcastle Business School; www.newcastlebusinessschool.ac.uk

accounting, advertising management, business administration, business creation/management/studies, corporate management, economics, finance, global financial management, global logistics & supply chain management, hospitality & tourism management, HRM, legal management, international business administration/business management/hospitality & tourism management/HRM/management, investment management, logistics & supply chain management, marketing management, multidisciplinary design innovation, tourism, travel & tourism management; BA, DBA, MA, MBA, MSc, PhD

School of Applied Sciences; www.northumbria.ac.uk/sd/academic/sac

Biosciences

applied biology, applied biomedical sciences, biology with forensic biology, biotechnology, human biosciences, medical biosciences/sciences, microbiology, molecular biology; BSc(Hons), MSc, PhD

Chemistry

analytical/applied chemistry, biomedical sciences, forensic/ pharmaceutical chemistry; BSc, BSc(Hons), MChem, MRes, MSc

Food and Nutritional Sciences

food science, human nutrition, nutritional science, nutrition & psychological science; BS(Hons), MSc

Forensic and Crime Sciences

biology, crime science, criminology, forensic biology/chemistry/science; BA(Hons), BSc(Hons), MSc, MSci

Geography and Environment

community wellbeing, environmental health/management, geography, human geography/geography

School of Arts & Social Sciences; www.northumbria.ac.uj./sd/academic/sass

Dept of Arts

arts, art & design, business with music management, promotion/arts & enterprise management, conservation of fine art, cultural management, dance, drama, performance,, film & TV studies, fine art, museum & heritage management, scriptwriting, contemporary photographic practice, preventive conservation; MA, MSc, MERes, BA(Hons)

Dept of Humanities

British sign language, French, German, Italian, Japanese, Mandarin Chinese, applied linguistics for TESOL, creative writing, English literature/& place, gender studies, history, language & cognition, linguistics, English language/literature; BA(Hons), MA, PGCert, MRes

Dept of Media

mass communication/management, media cultures/production, journalism, advertising, culture studies, BA(Hons), MA

Dept of Social Sciences

criminology & criminal justice, homeland security, international development, public administration/services, social sciences, politics, sociology, regeneration, media culture & society; psychology, Eng lit & history; BA(Hons), BSc(Hons), MA, MSc, MRes, MPA, PhD

School of Built & Natural Environment; www.northumbria.ac.uj./sd/academic/sobe

architectural technology, architecture, building design management/project management/services, crime science, engineering/surveying, commercial/quantity surveying, construction management, project management/for construction, crime science, disaster management & development, environmental health/management, geography, interior architecture, housing policy & management, international/real estate management, occupational safety & health, planning & development/quantity surveying, project management, surveying (minerals), sustainable development in the built environment; BA(Hons), BSc(Hons), FdSc, MA, MSc, PGDip/Cert, PhD, ProfDip

School of Computing, Engineering & Information Science: northumbria.ac.uj./sd/academic/ceis

Business Information Systems

business information management/systems/technology, IT management for business, information & communications technology; BSc(Hons), FdSc, MSc

Computing

applied computing, computer animation & digital SFX/forensics/games design & production/network technology/science/studies, computing and IT, digital forensics, ethical hacking for computer security, web design & development/computing; BSc(Hons), MSc

Engineering

communication & electronic engineering, computer network technology, electrical engineering, electrical power engineering, electronic design engineering, embedded computer systems engineering, information & communication technology, mobile communication engineering, engineering management, mechanical design/engineering, microelectronic engineering, product design technology, professional engineering; BEng(Hons), BSc(Hons), MSc

Information and Communications Management

communication & PR, computing and IT, information & library/web/communications management, librarianship, records management; BSc(Hons), MA, MSc

Mathematics & Statistics

mathematics/with business management; BSc(Hons)

School of Design; www.northumbria.ac.uk/sd/academic/scd

3D design, design for industry/management, professional practice, fashion, fashion communication/management /marketing, graphic design, interactive media design, interior design, motion graphics & animation, multidisciplinary design innovation, transportation design; BA(Hons), DocDesPract, BSc(Hons), MA, MSc, PhD

School of Health, Community & Education Studies; www.northumbria.ac.uj./sd/academic/shes

Health: midwifery studies, nursing studies/registered nurse/child/mental health/adult/learning disabilities, occupational therapy, operating dept practice, physiotherapy; AdvDipHE, BSc, MSc, PGDip

Education: early primary education, early years education, PGCE early years & primary/ secondary, education studies, professional practice, graduate teacher training, post-compulsory education & training, adult learners with learning difficulties, teaching assistants, lifelong learning /English/maths, autism, special educ needs & inclusion, dyslexia, mentoring; BA(Hons), MSc, MA, MTL, Cert/DipHE, PGDipCert

Social Work; social work/with chidren, young people & their families/in mental heath services; BSc(Hons), PGDip/Cert, ProfDoc

Northumbria Law School: northumbria.ac.uj./sd/academic/law

business/child/commercial property/commercial/employment law, information rights law and practice, international commercial/trade law, legal practice/management, medical law, mental health law, policy & practice, solicitors; GradCert, LlM, LlB, LPC, PGCert, MLaw, MSc, MBA

School of Life Sciences; www.northumbria.ac.uj./sd/academic/lifesciences

Biology, Food Science & Nutrition: applied biology/sciences, biology, forensic science, biotechnology, food science & nutrition, human nutrition, microbiology, nutrition science; BSc(Hons), MSc

Biomedical Sciences: biomedical science, chemistry, human bioscience, medical science, practical anatomy; BSc(Hons), MSc, ProfDoc, PGCert

Psychology: sport & exercise behaviour, criminology, sport science, business/health/occupational psychology, psychology of health & welbeing; BSc(Hons), MSc, MRes

Sport & Exercise Science: applied sport science/sport & exercise science, psychology of sport science/sport & exercise behaviour, sport exercise & nutrition, clinical exercise physiology

Sport Development; sport coaching, development/management/marketing, coaching, international sport management; BSc(Hons), MSc, ProfDoc

UNIVERSITY OF NOTTINGHAM
www.nottingham.ac.uk

Faculty of Arts; www.nottingham.ac.uk/arts

School of American and Canadian Studies; www.nottingham.ac.uk/american

American & Canadian studies (literature, history, culture), American studies (history, literature, Latin american, film & TV, visual culture, politics), Canadian literature/studies, American studies with European studies/English; BA(Hons), MA, MRes, PhD

Dept of Archaeology

archaeological materials, archaeology, ancient history, classical civilization, bioarchaeology, medieval archaeology, Mediterranean archaeology, Roman archaeology; BA(Hons), BSc(Hons), MA, MPhil

Art History; www.nottingham.ac.uk/art-history

art history, painting, sculpture, graphic arts, museum history, high art & popular culture, Renaissance to the present day modern art, criticism & display, art, photography & film; BA(Hons), MA

Dept of Classics; www.nottingham.ac.uk/classics

classical civilization, ancient history/drama, classical literature, classics, Greek, Latin, visual culture of classical antiquity, warrior societies; BA(Hons), MPhil/PhD

Dept of Culture, Film & Media; www.nottingham.ac.uk/cfm

cultural studies, entrepreneurship, international media & communications studies, critical theory, contemporary Middle East studies, film & TV studies, global Hollywood; BA(Hons), MA, MPhil

Centre for English Language Education; www.cele.nottingham.ac.uk
teacher training, arts & social sciences, business, teaching English for academic purposes; BA(Hons), FCert, PGCert

School of English Studies; www.nottingham.ac.uk/english
applied linguistics, communication & entrepreneurship, English studies/language teaching/language/literature, creative writing, literary linguistics, the 20th century & contemporary literature, Viking studies, world Englishes; BA(Hons), MA, MPhil, MSc, PGDip, PhD

Dept of French & Francophone Studies; www.nottingham.ac.uk/french
French, classical civilization, modern European studies, modern language studies, francophone & post-colonial studies, French culture & society, early modern French studies, 20th/21st-century French thought; BA(Hons), MA, MPhil, PhD

Dept of German Studies; www.nottingham.ac.uk/german
German, classical civilization, E European civilization, modern & contemporary German studies, modern language studies, modern languages & critical theory, comparative literature, English translation; BA(Hons), MA, MPhil, PhD

School of History; www.nottingham.ac.uk/history
history, ancient history, archaeology, British history, gender history, contemporary Chinese studies, art history, politics, medieval/ modern history, warrior societies; BA(Hons), MA, MPhil, PhD

School of Humanities; www.nottingham.ac.uk/humanities
archaeology, art history, classics, music, philosophy, theology & religious studies

School of Modern Languages & Cultures; www.nottingham.ac.uk/modern-languages
culture film & media, French & francophone studies, German studies, Language Centre, Russian & Slavonic studies, Spanish Portugese & Latin American studies; BA(Hons), MA, MPhil, PhD

Music; www.nottingham.ac.uk/music
music, early music, music on stage & screen, music theory & analysis; BA(Hons), MPhil, PhD

Dept of Philosophy; www.nottingham.ac.uk/philosophy
philosophy, metaphysics, mind & knowledge, ethics, philosophy of language, aesthetics; BA(Hons), MA, MPhil, PhD

Russian & Slavonic Studies; www.nottingham.ac.uk/slavonic
Russian studies, international media communications, south east European studies, Russian and East European civilizations, Slavonic studies; BA(Hons), MA, MPhil

Spanish, Portuguese and Latin American Studies; www.nottingham.ac.uk/splas
Hispanic studies, Portuguese/Spanish (beginners), Spanish & Latin American studies, Portuguese & Lusophone studies, modern language studies; BA(Hons), MA, MPhil, PhD

Department of Theology and Religious Studies; www.nottingham.ac.uk/theology
biblical interpretation, church history, philosophical theology, philosophy, philosophy & literary masters, systemic & philosophical theory, religious studies, theology; BA(Hons), MA, MPhil/PhD

Faculty of Science; www.nottingham.ac.uk/science

School of Biology; www.nottingham.ac.uk/biology
biology, zoology, human/genetics, biological photography & imaging; BSc(Hons), MSc, MRes, MSci, Phd

School of Biosciences; www.nottingham.ac.uk/biosciences
Agricultural and Environmental Sciences

agriculture, integrative systems biology, adv genomic & proteonomic science, environmental science

Plant and Crop Sciences

agriculture & biotechnology, applied biology, crop improvement/science, technology & entrepreneurship, environmental biology, genomic & proeonomic science, integrative systems biology, plant genetic manipulation, plant science

Animal Sciences

animal science, preveterinary science

Food Sciences

applied biomolecular technology, brewing science & food production management, food microbiology/science, industrial biochemistry, microbiology, nutrition & food science

Nutritional Sciences
advanced dietetic practice, food science, nutrition, nutritional biochemistry; BSc(Hons), Cert, Grad Dip, MRes, MSc, MNutrition, MPhil, PhD

School of Chemistry; www.nottingham.ac.uk/chemistry

biochemistry, biological chemistry, nanoscience chemistry/& entrepreneurship, molecular physics, medicinal chemistry; BSc(Hons), MChem, MPhil, MSc, MSci, PhD

School of Computer Science; www.nottingham.ac.uk/computerscience

artificial intelligence, computer science, computing & information systems, digital economy, human-computer interaction, interactive systems design, management of/information technology, scientific computation, software systems, BSc(Hons), MPhil, MSc

School of Mathematical Sciences; www.maths.nottingham.ac.uk/

financial mathematics, gravity, particles & fields, mathematics, numerical techniques for finance, pure mathematics, statistics, scientific computation/with industrial mathematics/mathematical medicine & biology, statistics with biomedical applications/ applied probability; BSc(Hons), MSc, PhD

School of Pharmacy; www.nottingham.ac.uk/pharmacy

medicinal & biological chemistry, pharmacy, nanoscience, stem cell technology; MPharm, MRes, MSc, MSci, PhD

School of Physics & Astronomy; www.nottingham.ac.uk/physics

astronomy, mathematical physics, medical physics, nanoscience, physics, physics & philosophy, theoretical astrophysics/physics, chemistry and molecular physics; BSc(Hons), MSc, MSci, PhD

School of Psychology; www.nottingham.ac.uk/psychology

cognitive neuroscience, neuroimaging, psychology / philosophy; BSc(Hons), MSc, PhD

Faculty of Engineering; www.nottingham.ac.uk/engineering

Dept of Architecture & Built Environment; www.nottingham.ac.uk/abe

architectural environment engineering, architecture, architecture & critical theory, design, energy conversion & management, environmental design, renewable energy, sustainable built environment/energy & entrepreneurship, sustainable tall buildings/building technology, technology, theory & design, urban design; BA(Hons), BArch (Hons), BEng (Hons), Dip Arch, MEng, MPhil, PhD

Dept of Chemical and Environmental Engineering; www.nottingham.ac.uk/scheme

chemical engineering, environmental engineering, environmental & resource engineering; BEng(Hons), MEng(Hons), MPhil, MRes, MSc, PhD

Dept of Electrical & Electronic Engineering; www.nottingham.ac.uk/eee

biophotonics, computer engineering/communications engineering, electrical engineering, electrical technology for sustainable & renewable energy systems, electromagnetics design, electronic computer & electronic engineering, electronic & ultrasonic instrumentation, photonic & optical engineering techniques, power electronics, machines & drives, renewable energy systems; BEng, MEng, MPhil, MRes, MSc, PGDip, PhD

Dept of Civil Engineering; www.nottingham.ac.uk/civil

civil engineering/mechanics, environmental engineering/fluid mechanics, geotechnical engineering, infrastructure, management & earth observation, pavement engineering, structural engineering, transportation, engineering surveying, survey & geodosy, positioning & navigation technology; BEng(Hons), MEng(Hons), MPhil, MSc, PhD

Dept of Mechanical, Materials and Manufacturing Engineering; www.nottingham.ac.uk/schoolm3

advanced materials/manufacture, applied ergonomics, design engineering, materials failure and analysis, healthcare, human factors, manufacturing engineering, materials, mechanical engineering, product design & manufacture; BEng, MEng, MSc, PGCert, PhD

Faculty of Medicine & Health Science; www.nottingham.ac.uk

School of Biology; www.nottingham.ac.uk/biology

biochemical genetics, biological photography & imaging, biology, human genetics; BSc, MSc, MSci, PhD

School of Biomedical Sciences; www.nottingham.ac.uk/biomedsci

biochemistry, biological chemistry, genetics, molecular medicine, surgery, anatomy, pharmacy, physiology, neuroscience, sports medicine, integrated physiology in health & disease; BSc(Hons), MPhil, MRes, MSc, PhD, BMBS, BMedSci

School for Clinical Sciences; www.nottingham.ac.uk/scs

assisted reproduction/stem cell technology, sports & exercise medicine; translational neuroimaging; DM, MSc, PhD

School of Community Health Sciences; www.nottingham.ac.uk/chs

epidemiology, applied/work & organization/rehabilitation/occupational/management/health/criminal psychology, mental health studies, psychology & health, workplace health, medical education, public health; MBBS, BMedSci, MMedSci, MPH, MSc, PGDip/Cert, PhD

School of Graduate Entry Medicine & Health; www.nottingham.ac.uk/gem

health care science; BSc, MRes, MPhil, PHD, DM

School of Molecular Medical Sciences; www.mol1.nottingham.ac.uk

human genetics, immunology, molecular & cellular bacteriology, translational cancer, virology; MSc, PhD

School of Nursing, Midwifery & Physiotherapy; www.nottingham.ac.uk/nursing

adult/critical care, advanced clinical practice/skills, advanced nursing, cognitive behaviour therapy, health and social care, health communication, health care sciences, midwifery, neurorehabilitation, physiotherapy, nursing – adult/mental health; BMid(-Hons), BSc(Hons), DHSci, MA, MNursSci, MPhil, MSc, PGDip/Cert, PhD

School of Veterinary Medicine & Science; www.nottingham.ac.uk/vet

laboratory animal medicine, veterinary medicine & surgery/science; BVMBVS, BVMedSci, MPhil, MRes, PhD, DVM, DVS

Institute of Work, Health & Organisations; www.nottingham.ac.uk/who

work/occupational/forensic/criminal/forensic/health/clinical psychology; MSc, DForPsych, DClinPsych

Faculty of Social Sciences, Law, & Education; www.nottingham.ac.uk

School of Contemporary Chinese Studies; www.nottingham.ac.uk/chinese

Chinese/English translation & interpreting, contemporary Chinese studies, corporate finance/banking & financial markets/management in contemporary China, global issues; BA, MSc, MSci, PhD

Economics; www.nottingham.ac.uk/economics

applied economics, behavioural economics, economic development & policy analysis, economics, economics with modern languages, international/development/inancial economics, econometrics, philosophy; BA(Hons), BSc(Hons), MPhil, PGDip, PhD

School of Education; www.nottingham.ac.uk/education

counselling/children & young people, initial teacher training (PGCE) – secondary (English, geography, history, mathematics, modern languages, science), primary, mentoring & coaching, educational leadership & management, special needs, international HE, trauma studies, TESOL, learning technology & education, special needs, TESOL, creative & professional writing, fine art, humanities; BA(Hons), MA, MPhil, MRes, PGCE, PGCert/Dip, PhD, SCITT, Edd

School of Geography; www.nottingham.ac.uk/geography

geography, environmental management/history, GIS, human geography, landscape & culture, contaminated land management, financial services & society, economy, space, society, geospatial intelligence; BA(Hons), PhD

School of Law; www.nottingham.ac.uk/law

law, French/German/Spanish/Euro/Chinese, Canadian/New Zealand/S. East Asian/Australian/American law

Master courses include: environmental law, human rights law, international commercial law/criminal justice and armed conflict, international law/and development, law & environmental science, maritime law, senior status; BA(Hons), LlB, LlM, MA, MSc, PhD

Nottingham University Business School; www.nottingham.ac.uk/business

business economics, corporate social responsibility/strategy and governance, entrepreneurship, finance accounting & management, finance & investment, industrial economics/with insurance, industrial engineering, international business, logistics & supply chain management, management studies, management with Asian studies/Chinese studies/French/German/Spanish, manufacturing systems, marketing, operations management, risk management, supply chain & operations management, strategic management, tourism and travel management; BA(Hons), ExecMBA, MA, MBA, MSc

Politics & International Relations; www.nottingham.ac.uk/politics

diplomacy, European & global politics, international relations & global issues, international security & terrorism, politics & economics/contemporary history/American studies/German/French, social and global justice; BA(Hons), MA, MPhil, MRes, PhD

School of Sociology and Social Policy; www.nottingham.ac.uk/sociology

administration, global citizenship, identities & human rights, health communication, cultural sociology, public administration/policy, social & cultural studies, international/social policy, social work, sociology, trauma studies; BA(Hons), MA, MPA, MPhil, MSWS, PhD, PGCert

NOTTINGHAM TRENT UNIVERSITY
www.ntu.ac.uk

School of Animal, Rural and Environmental Sciences; www.ntu.ac.uk/ares

animal biology/studies, biodiversity surveying, environmental design & management/science, equine health & welfare/sports science, geography, wildlife conservation, zoo biology; BSc(Hons), MSc/MRes/PGCert/PGDip, FdSc

School of Architecture, Design and Built Environment; www.ntu.ac.uk/adbe

adv project design engineering, architecture, architectural technology, interior architecture & design, civil engineering, furniture, product design, building/quantity surveying, planning & development, real estate, construction management, project management, structural engineering, smart design, creative tecnologies; BSc(Hons), MA, MSc, MArch,PGDip/Cert,PhD

School of Art & Design; www.ntu.ac.uk/art

art direction, branding & identity, computer-aided product design, costume design, decorative arts, design for film & TV, illustration, fashion & textile management/design/communication, promotion/knitwear design and knitted textiles/marketing and branding, film, fine art, graphic design, interaction design, motion graphic design, media creativity, multimedia, photography, product design, product design, puppetry and digital animation, textile design and innovation, theatre design; BA(Hons), GradDip, MA, MPhil, PhD

School of Arts & Humanities; www.ntu.ac.uk/hum

communication, English, broadcasting, creative writing, culture, history, heritage, international studies, journalism, language, linguistics, media, philosophy, politics, TESOl; BA(Hons), MA, PGDip/Cert, MPhil, PhD

Nottingham Business School; www.ntu.ac.uk/nbs

accounting & finance, business & management, economics, HRM, information management and systems, marketing,retail operations strategic management & international business; BA(Hons), DBA, MBA, MSc

School of Education; www.ntu.ac.uk/edu

business & education development, secondary design and technology education, early years, educational support, ICT & education, primary education, psychology & education/educational development, special & inclusive education, sport & leisure, teaching adult literacy, numerous PGCE courses, TESOL,teacher training; BA(Hons), MA, PGCE, PGCert, ProfCert, ProfDoc

Nottingham Law School; www.ntu.ac.uk/nls

corporate/commercial law, criminal justice, health law, human rights, insolvency law, intellectual property, international trade law, sports law, regulation, professional practice/business/criminology/psychology; GDL, GradDip, LlB, LlM, LPC, PhD

School of Science & Technology; www.ntu.ac.uk/sat

astrophysics, biological sciences, biomedical science, biosciences, biotechnology, chemical, forensics, coaching, computer science/systems (networks, forensics and security), computing & technology, digital media, environmental management, financial mathematics, forensic science, games technology, geonomic & proteonomic science, healthcare science, information & communication techn, information systems, materials science, mathematics, molecular cell biology, multimedia engineering, neuroscience, nutrition and health, pharmaceutical and medicinal chemistry, pharmacology, physics and mathematics, software engineering, sport sciences/& management/exercise science, technological physics; BSc, FdSc, MChem, MRes, MSc, MSci, PhD

School of Social Sciences; www.ntu.ac.uk/soc

applied child psychology, career /guidance, child care practice, criminology, forensic mental health/psychology, health & social care, health & safety risk management, psychological well-being & mental health, psychology with criminology/sociology/sports science, public health, safety & environment, social work, sociology, youth studies /work; BA(Hons), MA, MRes, MSc, Pfdip/Cert, PGDip/Cert, PhD, ProfDoc

Degrees validated by Nottingham Trent University offered at:

SOUTHAMPTON SOLENT UNIVERSITY
www.solent.ac.uk

Faculty of Media, Arts, & Society; www.solent.ac.uk/fmas www.solent.ac.uk/courses/artsandmedia

Communications & Writing: creative/advertising, PR, media/writing, creative writing, fashion/multimedia journalism, sports/radio & TV broadcasting, screenwriting
Human Sciences: psychology, politics & international relations, criminology, criminal justice, crime investigation & analysis, social work, housing & public health, health promotion
Media: film, media, film performance, PR, pop music, TV
Visual & Interactive Arts: illustration, photography, digital media production, computer animation, interactive games; BA(Hons), HND, MA, MPhil, PhD

Faculty of Business, Sport & Enterprise; www.solent.ac.uk/fbse

Business School: accountancy, business, business IT/management/administration/studies, law, commercial law, criminology, entrepreneurship, finance, HRM, international, international business/management & English, management, marketing, advertising management, entrepreneurship, event management, public service management, Sport, Tourism
Languages: sports coaching, health, physical activity & exercise, fitness training, tourism, international business management & English; BA(Hons), Cert, CIM, FdA, GradDip, HND/C, LLM, MA, MBA, MProf, PGDip, ProfCert/Dip

Technology; www.solent.ac.uk/Technology

Computing & Communication Engineering

computing, computer games development, computer network management, computer systems, networks, business information technology, music studio technology, audio, film & TV, communications technology, software engineering, web design, internet technology

Engineering, Construction & Maritime

Built Environment

interior design, architecture, construction management, surveying, property development, civil engineering.

Design Engineering;

mechanical engineering, production, manufacture & design technology.

Environment & Geography;

environmental, marine, sustainability

Shipping;

ship & port management, maritime business & enterprise

Yacht Engineering;

design & surveing, yacht & powercraft technology

Engineering;
electrical/electronic engineering, engineering (general), engineering with business (manufacture/service), mechanical/manufacturiing engineering, mechanical design

Design;
digital music, fashion/graphics/styling, live performance make up design, media styling, graphic design, interior design, 3D design, product design, fashion merchandise management, industrial design, BA(Hons), BEng(Hons), BSc(Hons), FdSc, HNC, HND, MPhil, MSc, PhD

UNIVERSITY FOR THE CREATIVE ARTS
www.ucreative.ac.uk (at Canterbury, Epsom, Farnham, Maidstone and Rochester)

art & design, illustration, animation, architecture, computer games arts, jewellery, ceramics & glass, design for theatre, management, fashion/design & textiles, film & video, fine art, graphic design, interior design, journalism, marketing, performance & events, photography, product design, media arts, 3D & product design; BA(Hons), FD, Grad Dip, MA, MPhil, PGCert, PhD

THE OPEN UNIVERSITY
www.open.ac.uk

Arts and Humanities Studies; www3.open.ac.uk/study/undergraduate/arts-and-humanities/index.htm
art history, classical studies, English language & literature, history, humanities, literature, music, politics, philosophy, economics, psychological studies, religious studies; BA(Hons), MA, PGDip

Business and Management; www3.open.ac.uk/study/undergraduate/business.and.management/index.htm
accounting, business management/administration/studies, public services, financial services, leadership and management, global development management, retail management, knowledge management, clinical leadership, HRM, international finance; BA/BSc, Diplomas, DipHE, FD, MA, MSc, PGDip

Childhood and Youth; www3.open.ac.uk/study/undergraduate/childhood-and-youth/index.htm
childhood practice, childhood & youth studies, early years, primary teaching & learning, youth justice, effective practice youth work, youth: BA(Hons), Diplomas, DipHE, Certificates

Computing and ICT; www3.open.ac.uk/study/undergraduate/computing-and-ICT/index.htm
advanced networking, computing/for commerce and industry, information systems, management of software, software development, strategic management of IT systems; BSc(Hons), Certs, Diplomas, DipHE, FD, MSc, PGDip

Education; www3.open.ac.uk/study/undergraduate/education/index.htm
academic practice, child development, childhood practice, childhood & youth studies, early years, education, mathematics & its learning, online & distance education, primary teaching & learning, professional practice, QTS,secondary education in physics, working together for children, working with young people, youth work; BA/BSc, Certs, DipHE, FD, MA, PGCE

Engineering and Technology; www3.open.ac.uk/study/undergraduate/engineering.and-technology/index.htm
adv networking, computing and IT/practice, design & innovation, ECT practice, engineering, information & communications technology, information systems, materials fabrication & engineering, systems & technology, technology management; BEng, FD, MBA, MEng, MSc, PGDip,DipHE

Environment, Development and International Studies; www3.open.ac.uk/study/undergraduate/environment-development-and-international-studies/index.htm
environment & development, development management, environment science/studies, environmental policy/decision making, international studies, human rights, international development and business innovation, pollution control; BSc(Hons), MSc, PGDip/Cert

Health and Social Care; www3.open.ac.uk/study/undergraduate/health-and-social-care/index.htm
adult nursing, childhood & youth studies, childhood practice, counselling, CPD courses, early years, health studies/science, health & social care, health-care practice, managing care, mental health nursing, promoting public health, social work studies, sport & fitness, working with young people, youth justice, youth work; BA(Hons), BA/BSc, CertHE, DipHE, FD

Language Studies; www3.open.ac.uk/study/undergraduate/language-studies/index.htm
French, German, modern language studies, Spanish, English language & literature, humanities; BA(Hons), Dip/CertHE

Law; www3.open.ac.uk/study/undergraduate/law/index.htm
agreements, ownership & trusts, legal system, criminal justice, business, human rights & corporate responsibility, company law, employment law, English law; Certs, Dips, LlB(Hons), PGDip

Mathematics and Statistics; www3.open.ac.uk/study/undergraduate/mathematics_and_statistics/index.htm
computing/economics & mathematical sciences, statistics, mathematics; BA/BSc, BSc(Hons), MMath, MSc, UGCert

Psychology; www3.open.ac.uk/study/undergraduate/psychology/index.htm
counselling, forensic psychology & criminology, forensic psychological studies, psychological studies & criminology; BA/BSc, MSc, PGDip, UGDip

Science; www3.open.ac.uk/study/undergraduate/science/index.htm
analytical sciences, astronomy, planetary science/studies, contemporary science, earth science, environmental studies/science, health sciences, medical physics, medicinal chemistry, natural sciences, operating department practice, paramedic sciences, physics, secondary education in physics; BSc(Hons), DipHE, FD, MSc

Social Sciences; www3.open.ac.uk/study/undergraduate/social_sciencess/index.htm
counselling, economics, environmental science, forensic psychology, criminology, politics, psychological studies, social policy, philosophy, social sciences; BA(Hons), BA/BSc, FD, MA, PGDip

Postgraduate subjects

arts & humanities, business & management, childhood & youth, computing & ICT, education, engineering & technology, environment, development & international studies, health & social care, languages, law, mathematics & statistics, psychology, science, social sciences

UNIVERSITY OF OXFORD
www.ox.ac.uk

Division of Humanities; www.ox.ac.uk/divisions/humanities

Rothermere American Institute; www.rai.ox.ac.uk/
English and American studies; MSt

Faculty of Classics; www.classics.ox.ac.uk
ancient & modern history, classical archaeology & ancient history, classical languages & literature, modern languages, Greek and/or Latin language & literature; BA(Hons), MPhil, MSt

Ruskin School of Drawing and Fine Art; www.ruskin-sc.ox.ac.uk
art history & theory, drawing, fine art, theoretical & practice-led research; BFA, MLitt, DPhil

Faculty of English; www.english.ox.ac.uk,
English language and literature (650–1550; 1550–1700; 1600–1830; 1800–1914; 1900–present day), English & American studies, film aesthetics, history & English, medieval studies, women's

studies, Shakespeare; BA(Hons), DPhil, MLitt, MPhil, MSt

History of Art Department; www.hoa.ox.ac.uk
history of art, authenticity & replication in art and visual culture, media & modernity: Gothic; artistic originality & transmission of style & mass culture, 1880–2000, theories of vision; BA(Hons), DPhil, MLitt, MSt

Faculty of History; www.history.ox.ac.uk
ancient & modern history, economic & social history, international global & imperial history, Gothic, history of science, medicine,, technology, media & modernity: art & mass culture, medieval history/ studies, modern British & European history, US history, women, art & culture in early modern Europe; BA(Hons), DPhil, MPhil, MSc, MSt, MLetters

Faculty of Linguistics, Philology and Phonetics; www.ling-phil.ox.ac.uk
comparative philology & comparative linguistics, philology & phonetics, modern languages & linguistics; BA, MPhil, PhD

Faculty of Medieval & Modern Languages; www.mod-langs.ox.uk
Celtic, comparative literature or medieval literature, cultural studies, Czech, French, German, linguistics, literature, modern Greek, Italian, medieval literature, language history, medieval & modern languages, European enlightenment, Polish, Portuguese, Russian, Russian, Spanish, Slavonic languages, Yiddish; BA(Hons), DPhil, MPhil, MSt

Faculty of Music; www.music.ox.ac.uk
aesthetics & criticism, chamber music, choral studies/ conducting performance, composition & analysis, dance music, ethnomusicology, historical musicology, jazz, musical history/theory, orchestration, performance & interpretation, theory & analysis, source studies Western music theory; BMus, DPhil, MA(Hons), MPhil, MSt, MLitt

Faculty of Oriental Studies; www.orinst.ox.ac.uk
Arabic, Persian, Turkish, Sanskrit, Buddhist studies, Chinese studies, eastern Christianity, Egyptology & ancient Near East, south and inner Asia & East Asian studies, Hebrew & Jewish studies, Islamic world, Japanese studies, Korean studies; BA(Hons), DPhil, MPhil, MSt

Faculty of Philosophy; www.philosophy.ox.ac.uk
aesthetics, Aquinas, Aristotle, ethics, formal logic, Frege, history of philosophy Descartes to Kant, knowledge & reality, post-Kant, logic & language, medieval philosophy, philosophy of mind/ physics/ religion/language & linguistics, Plato, post-Kantian philosophy, Russell, Wittgenstein; BA(Hons), BPhil, MPhil, PhD

Faculty of Theology; www.theology.ox.ac.uk
theology, oriental studies, pastoral studies, the Old Testament, the New Testament, biblical interpretation, patristics, scholastic/modern/reformation theology, ecclestiastical history, christian ethics, science & religion, philosophy & theology, early Christian studies, Judaism in Graeco-Roman world, applied theology; BA(Hons), BTh, MTh, MSt, MLitt, MPhil, DPhil, PGDip/Cert

Division of Mathematical, Physical and Life Sciences; www.ox.ac.uk/divisions/mpls

Dept of Chemistry; www.chemistry.ox.ac.uk
chemical biology, inorganic chemistry, mathematical techniques, medical chemistry, organic and chemical biology, organic reactions/synthesis, organometallic chemistry, physical & theoretical chemistry, quantum mechanics, reaction mechanisms, solid state chemistry, spectroscopy, theoretical chemistry, thermodynamics; DPhil, MChem, MSc

Oxford University Computing Laboratory; www.comlab.ox.ac.uk
computer science/& mathematics, mathematics & scientific computation, systems security, object technology, languages, software engineering; BA(Hons), MSc, DPhil

Dept of Engineering Science; www.eng.ox.ac.uk
biomedical engineering, chemical engineering, computer engineering, process engineering, civil & offshore engineering, electrical & opto-electronic engineering, electronic engineering, information/control & vision engineering, materials engineering, mechanical/civil/structural engineering; DPhil, MEng, MSc

Doctoral Training Centre
biological physics, computational biology, medical imaging & signals, bioinformatics, evolution & genetics; DPhil

Division of Materials; www.materials.ox.ac.uk
materials science, materials structures & mechanical properties of metals, electrical/mechanical properties, nanoelectronics, non-metallic materials; composites, polymers, packaging/superconducting/semiconducting materials, etc; DPhil, MEng, MSc, MS, MEm

Mathematical Institute; www.maths.ox.ac.uk
algebra, analysis, applied maths, statistics, geometry, pure maths, differential equations, probability; BA(Hons), DPhil, MCF, MFoCS, MS, MSc, MMath

Dept of Physics; www.physics.ox.ac.uk
atmospheric oceanic & planetary physics, astrophysics, condensed matter physics, particle physics, physics, atomic & laser/theoretical physics; BA(Hons), DPhil, MPhys, MPhysPhil

Dept of Plant Science; www.lps.plants.ox.ac.uk/plants
biochemistry & cell biology/physiology, biological science, biology, comparative developmental genetics, evolution, ecology & systematics, plant science; BA(Hons), DPhil, MRes, MSc

Dept of Statistics; www.stats.ox.ac.uk
applied statistics, bioinformatics, mathematics & statistics, probability; BA(Hons), DPhil, MMath, MSc, PGDip

Dept of Zoology; www.zoo.ox.ac.uk
animal behaviour, biological science, biology, molecular biology & bioinformatics, ornithology, integrative bioscience, wildlife conservation; BA(Hons), DPhil, MRes, MSc

Division of Medical Science; www.oc.ac.uk/divisions/ medicalscience

Medical Science; www.medschool.oc.ac.uk
pre-clinical/post-clinical meducine, neuroscience, global health, immunology, athletic performance, psychological research, pharmacology, diagnostic imaging, neuroradiology, musculoskeletal sciences, clinical embryology, medicinal chemistry for cancer, health care, therapeutics; MB, BCh, MSc, DPhil, PhD

Dept of Biochemistry; www.bioch.ox.ac.uk
biochemistry (molecular & cellular), bioenergetics, cell biology, chromosome & developmental biology, genetics & molecular biology, infection, immunity & translational medicine, macromolecular structure, medical sciences, molecular biochemistry & chemical biology, neuroscience, structural biology; DPhil, MBiochem, MSc, PhD

Dept of Cardiovascular Medicine; www.cardiov.ox.ac.uk
cardiovascular science; DPhil

Nuffield Dept of Clinical Laboratory Siences; www.ndcls.ox.ac.uk
microbiology, cellular pathology, genetics, haematology, clinical biology; DPhil, MSc

Dept of Clinical Neurology; www.clneuro.ox.ac.uk
clinical imunology, biochemistry, structural biology, genetics, bioinformatics, infectious disease, developmental biology, cancer. endocrinology, metabolic medicine, epidemiology; integrated immunology, global health science; DPhil, MSc

Nuffield Dept of Clinical Medicine; www.ndm.ac.uk
acute general medicine, clinical immunology, dermatology, gastroenterology, genito-urinary med, gerantology, infectious diseases, intensive care, muscoskeletal med, palliative care, radiology, renal med, respiratory med, tropical med; PhD

Dept of Clinical Pharmacology; www.clinpharm.ox.ac.uk
clinical pharmacology, experimental therapeutics, practical drug therapy; MSc, DPhil

Dept of Experimental Psychology; www.psy.ox.ac.uk
clinical/ experimental psychology, philosophy & psychology, psychological research; BA(Hons), DPhil, MSc

Wellcome Trust Centre for Human Genetics; www.well.ox.ac.uk
human/statistical genetics, functional genomics, bioinformatics, structural biology; PhD

Wetherall Institute of Molecular Medicine; www.imw.ox.ac.uk
clinical genetics,, haematopoistic stem cell biology, human immunology, molecular immunology/oncology/parasitology/haematology; DPhil

Nuffield Dept of Obstetrics & Gynaecology; www.obs-gyn.ox.ac.uk
clinical embryology, human reproduction, obstetrics, gynaecology labour, antenatal care, sexual health; MSc, DPhil

Nuffield Laboratory of Ophthalmology; www.eye.ox.ac.uk
retinal genetics, artificial vision, ocular biology, vision & disease, gene theory, circadian biology, photoreceptors, opthalmology, neuroscience, sleep; DPhil, MSc

Nuffield Department of Orthopaedics, Rheumatology and Musculoskeletal Sciences; www.ndorms.ox.ac.uk
orthopaedics, rheumatology, musculoskeletal sciences; MSc, DPhil

Dept of Paediatrics; www.paediatrics.ox.ac.uk
paediatric infection & immunity/gastroenterological & nutrition/neurology/vaccine.endocrine & diabetes, childhood care; PhD, MSc

Dept of Pharmacology; www.pharm.ox.ac.uk
pharmacology & drug discovery, neuroscience, medicinal chemistry for cancer; DPhil, MSc

Dept of Physiology, Anatomy, and Genetics; www.dpag.ox.ac.uk
ion channels, transporters & signalling, myoccardial, vascular & respiratory science, functional genomics, neuroscience, development and reproduction; MPhil, MSc, DPhil

Dept of Psychiatry; www.pschiatry.ox.ac.uk
adolescent psychiatry, autism, eating disorders, evidence-based mental health, experimental psychopathology and cognitive therapy, forensic psychiatry, molecular neuropathology, neurobiology of ageing, neuroimaging, psychopharmacology, suicide research; DPhil, MRCPsych

Division of Public Health & Primary Health Care; www.dphpc.ox.ac.uk
global health science, perinatal epidiomology, health economics/services, offender health; DPhil, MSc

Nuffield Dept of Surgery; www.surgery.ox.ac.uk
endovascular neurosurgery, diagnostic imaging, integrated immunology, surgical science & practice; DPhil, MCh, MSc

Divison of Social Sciences; www.socsci.ox.ac.uk

School of Anthropology and Museum Ethnography, www.anthro.ox.ac.uk
museum ethnography, material/medical/ social/ visual/ecological anthropology, migration studies; BA, BSc, DPhil, MSc, MPhil

Institute of Cognitive & Evolutionary Anthropology; www.iceq.ox.ac.uk
anthropology, cognitive evolutionary anthropology; DPhil, MSc

Institute of Human Sciences; www.ihs.ox.ac.uk
human sciences; BA(Hons)

Centre for Anthropology and Mind, Centre on Migration, Policy & Society
civil society & everyday life, dynamics of migration, migrants/& labour markets, migration; DPhil, MPhil

PittRivers Museum; www.prm.ox.ac.uk
material anthropology, museum ethnography; DPhil, MPhil, MSc

School of Archaeology; www.arch.ox.ac.uk
archaeology & anthropology, classical archaeology & ancient history, European landscape archaeology, visual cultures, world/environmental/palaeothic/ maritime archaeology; BA(Hons), DPhil, MLitt, MSc, MSt

SAID Business School; www.sbs.ox.ac.uk
accounting, engineering/materials/economics & management, major project management, finance, financial strategy, global business, law management science, marketing, organizational behaviour/leadership, operational management, public policy, science & technology, strategy & entrepreneurship; BA(Hons), DPhil, MBA, MEng, MSc, Oxford Dip

Dept of Economics; www.economics.ox.ac.uk
economics/development, engineering/materials/economics & management, history & economics, financial economics, philosophy, politics & economics; BA(Hons), DPhil, MEng, MSc

Dept of Education; www.education.ox.ac.uk
applied linguistics, child development and education, comparative & international education, e-learning, educational research methodology, HE, learning and teaching/technology, teaching English in university setting; DPhil, MSc, PGCE, PGDip

School of Geography & the Environment; www.geog.ox.ac.uk
biodiversity, biogeography, conservation & management, earth systems, environmental change & management, human/forensic/finance/environmental geography, nature, society & environmental policy, water science, policy & management; BA(Hons), DPhil, MSc

School of Interdisciplinary Area Studies; www.area-studies.ox.ac.uk
Africa/modern Japan/Chinese/Russian & east European studies, contemporay India, public polcy/Latin America; MSc, MPhil, DPhil

Dept of International Development; www.qeh.ox.ac.uk
development studies, economics for development, refugee & forced migration studies, global governance, diplomacy; Cert/Dip, DPhil, MPhil, MSc

Oxford Internet Institute; www.oil.ox.ac.uk
social science of the internet, information, comunication & the internet; DPhil, MSc

Faculty of Law; www.law.ox.ac.uk
common/company/competition law, constitutional & administration, criminal law, criminology, environmental law, EU/ family, human rights, intellectual property, law, judicial process, jurisprudence, media, law, property & trusts, public interest, Roman law, social legal studies, tax; BA(Hons), BCL, Dip, DPhil, MJur, MLitt, MPhil, MSc, MSt, PGDip

Oxford Martin School; www.oxfordmartin.ox.ac.uk
research in health & medicine, energy & environment, technology & society, ethics & governance

Oxford-Man Institute of Quatitative Finance; www.oxford-man.ox.ac.uk
research in quantitative finance, alternative investment

Dept of Politics & International Relations; www.politics.ox.ac.uk
comparative government, history and politics, international relations, philosophy, political theory, politics and economics, politics (comparative government/European politics and society/political theory); BA(Hons), DPhil, MLitt, MPhil, MSc

Dept of Social Policy & Intervention; www.spi.ox.ac.uk
comparative social policy, evidence-based social intervention, family policy, ageing, poverty, inequality, health & social policy. housing & homelessness, social policy & the environment, labour markets; BA, MPhil, MSc

Dept of Sociology; www.sociology.ox.ac.uk
political sociology, quantitative methods in politics and sociology, sociological theory, sociology, sociology of industrial societies; BA(Hons), DPhil, MPhil, MSc

OXFORD BROOKES UNIVERSITY
www.brookes.ac.uk

School of Arts & Humanities; www.ah.brookes.ac.uk

English and Drama:
English/literature, modern & contemporary literature, 19th-century literature & culture, creative writing, drama, modern & contemporary writing/ culture

Fine Art:
fine art, composition & sonic art, contemporary art, & music, social sculpture

History:
history, history of medicine; history of art

Modern Languages:
European business, culture and language, French, Japanese studies, Spanish; BA(Hons), MA

Music:
composition, music/interdisciplinary art/sonic music, performance, pop culture, 19th-century music; BA(/ BSc(Hons), MA

Oxford International Centre for Publishing Studies; www.ah.brookes.ac.uk/publishing
digital publishing, publishing – magazines, journals, books, language, publishing media, book history & publishing culture; BA(Hons), European Master in Publishing; MA

School of Built Environment; www.brookes.ac.uk/schools/be

Architecture:
adv architectural design, architecture, development & architectural practice, interior architecture, regeneration & building, sustainable building

Planning:
environmental impact assessment, spatial planning, transport planning, construction project management, development & emergency planning, environmental management & technology assessment, historic conservation, city & regional planning, planning & property development

Real Estate & Construction:
construction, quantity surveying & commercial management, real estate, spatial planning, surveying & commercial management, project management

Development & Emergency Practice, shelter after disaster;
BA(Hons)/BSc(Hons), Cert, FBE, FdSc, MArch, MPhil, MPlan, MRes, MSc, PGCert, PGDip, PhD

Business School; www.business.brookes.ac.uk

accounting, business analysis/business management, business and marketing, e-business, e-marketing, enterprise, international business/economics, international business, finance, information technology managment for business, HRM, international trade & logistics, international hospitality & tourism management, international hospitality management, politics, international relations; BA(Hons), BSc(Hons), Certs, DCaM, DBA, Dips, MA, MBA, MRes, MSc, PhD

School of Health and Social Care; htp:/ shsc.brookes.ac.uk

adult nursing, cancer care, children & families, children' s nursing, emergency care, health and social care, group pychotherapy, learning disability/mental health nursing, midwifery, occupational therapy, operating department practice, osteopathy, physiotherapy, palliative care, rehabilitation, public health, social work; BScHons, DipHE, FD, MPhil, PhD

School of Life Sciences; www.brookes.ac.uk/lifesci

animal & conservation biology, applied human biology/nutrition, biological sciences, biomedical science, biotechnology, conservation ecology, environmental management/science, human biology, bio science, exercise, nutrition & health, medical science, nutrition, sport & exercise science; BA(Hons)/ BSc(Hons), MSc, PGDip, PhD, BMedSci

School of Technology; http:/ tech.brookes.ac.uk

advanced engineering design, automotive engineering, broadband networks, business informatics communication & network engineering, computer science, computing, digital media production, e-business, information systems, mathematics & statistics, media technology, medical statistics, high speed networks, mobile computing, network computing, motorsport engineering, racing engine design, software engineering, web technologies, wireless computing/communication systems; BEng/MEng, FdSc, HNC, MPhil, MSc, PhD

Westminster Institute of Education; www.brookes.ac.uk/wie

advanced educational practice, communication, media and culture, early PGCE primary/secondary/ post-compulsory education, primary teacher education, religion, & theology, culture secondary teacher training, sport and coaching studies, support for learning, ESOL; BA(Hons), BA/BSSc(Hons), CertEd, FdA, MA, MPhil, PGCE, PGDip, PhD

UNIVERSITY OF WEST OF SCOTLAND
www.uws.ac.uk

Faculty of Business & Creative Industries:

Business School; www.uws.ac.uk/ schoolsdepts/business
accounting, business analysis/studies/administration, hospitality management, international/event management/HRM/banking & financial management/business management/operations & logistics, marketing, tourism, economics/financial management/marketing, law, logistics & supply chain management, management; BA, BSc, MSc, MBA

School of Creative and Cultural Industries; www.uws.ac.uk/schoolsdepts/mlm

broadcast journalism/production, commercial music/ sound pdn, contemporary art practice/screen acting, creative media practice, digital art, film-making & screen writing, innovation & entrepreneurship, journalism, languages, music theatre, performance, sports journalism; BA, BA(Hons), BAcc, ExecMBA, MA, MSc, PGDip, PhD

Biological Science; www.uws.ac.uk/ schoolsdepts/science/biology

applied bioscience and psychology/zoology/forensic investigation/immunology/microbiology/multimedia/environmental science, biology, biomedical science, earth science, environment, environmental biology, forensic science, health & lifestyle; BSc(Hons), CertHE, DipHE, MSc, PhD

Centre for Environment & Waste Management; www.uws.ac.uk/ schoolsdepts/science/cewm

managing/working with environmental responsibilities, occupational safety & health, waste/environmental management; BSc, IOSHCert, MSc, PGDip

Chemistry & Chemical Engineering; www.uws.ac.uk/schoolsdepts/es/ chemistry

chemical engineering, chemistry, forensic science, health science, drug design & discovery; BEng(Hons), BSc(Hons), MSc, PhD

Earth Science ; www.uws.ac.uk/ schoolsdepts/es/environment/earth-science

earth science, climate change, construction & environment/human health, soils, sedimernts & waste, water environment; BSc(Hons),MSc,PhD

Mathematics & Statistics; www.uws.ac.uk/ schoolsdepts/science/maths

pure/applied maths, statistics, operational research simulation, statistics; BA(Hons), BSc(Hons), MSc, PhD

Sports, Health & Exercise; www.paisley.ac.uk/schoolsdepts/science/ sports-studies

sport coaching/development, exercise & health, physical activity & health, sports industries; BSc, BA, DipHE, PhD

Design & Engineering; www.uws.ac.uk/ schools/dept/es/eng

civil/chemical/mechanical/aircraft/motorsport engineering, computer-aided design, product design & development, engineering management, product design & development, mechatronics; BEng(Hons), GradDip, MSc

Physics; www.uws.ac.uk/schoolsdepts/es/ physics

physics, microscale/sensor design, thin films, nuclear physics; BSc(Hons), MSc, PGD, PhD

School of Computing; www.uws.ac.uk/ schools/depts/computing

advanced computer systems development, business technology, computer animation/ games development/ technology/networking, computing, information technology, web authoring/technology, multimedia technology; BA(Hons), BSc(Hons), MSc, PGDip

Faculty of Education, Health & Social Science;

School of Education; www.uws.ac.uk/ schoolsdepts/education

chartered teacher, childhood studies, curriculum education, initial teacher education, inclusive education, primary education, PE, teaching for learning; BA, BEd MEd, PGCert/Dip

School of Health, Nursing & Midwifery; www.uws.ac.uk/schoolsdepts/hnm

adv clinical practice, child protection, health studies, non-medical prescribing, midwifery, adult/mental health/public health nursing, maternal & health care occupational health, non-medical prescribing, public services, cancer & palliative care, vulnerability, health & social care; BSc(Hons), MSc, PGCert/Dip, DipHE

School of Social Sciences; www.uws.ac.uk/ schoolsdepts/socialsciences

alcohol & drug studies, criminal justice, police studies politics, psychology, social policy, social sciences, social work, sociology; BA(Hons), MSc, PGDip/Cert

UNIVERSITY OF PLYMOUTH
www.plymouth.ac.uk

Faculty of Arts; www.plymouth.ac.uk/arts

School of Architecture, Design, Environment

architecture, architectural technology & the environment, architectural conservation; 3D designer maker/furniture & interior design/product design, design(-design thinking/service design/spatial practice/sustainable futures), environment; building surveying & the environment, sustainable construction, construction management /environment, landscape; BA(Hons), MA, MRes, MArch

School of Art & Media

digital art & techn/media & animation, graphic communication with typography, illustration, publishing, multimedia production & technology, fine art, media arts, communication design contemporary art/film practice, photography, TV arts; BA(Hons), MA, MArch, BA(Hons), GradDip, MA, MRes, PhD, MSc, BSc

School of Humanities & Performing Arts

art history, dance, theatre, 18th-century: art, literature, identity, English & creative writing/history/media arts/French/literature/Spanish, art history, fine art, art history, history with international relations/politics, music, sound & music production, performance practice, social history, theatre & performance; BA(Hons), MA, PGDip, MRes, PhD

Faculty of Health; www.plymouth.ac.uk/faculties/health

School of Social Science & Social Work

health & social care studies, mental health, social work, sociology with criminal justice studies, cognitive behavioural therapy, social & market/educational research, social research & evaluation; BA(Hons), BSc(Hons), MA, MSc, PGDip

School of Nursing & Midwifery

midwifery, adult/child health/mental health nursing, adv practice in education for health professionals/healthcare/service improvement, genetic healthcare, surgical care practitioner; BSc(Hons), DipHE, MSc,PGDip

School of Health Professions

paediatric/dietetics, mental health, neurological rehabilitation, occupational therapy, optometry, paramedic practitioner/studies, physiotherapy, podiatry, women's health, work & wellbeing; BSc(Hons), DipHE, MSc, PGCert, PGDip

Plymouth Business School; www.plymouth.ac.uk/faculties/pbs

Plymouth Law School

criminology & criminal justice studies, law, law with business studies, legal practice, maritime & marine law; BA(Hons), BSc(Hons), LlB, LlM,MSc, PGDip
accounting, business admin/economics/management/studies, finance, marketing, economics, entrepreneurship, regional development, HR, leadership,management information systems & operations, politics, international business/economics/finance/logistics/trade & operations management/supply chain management, maritime business & logistics, shipping & logistics, leadership & management, port management, organizational leadership, personnel & development, public administration/management/services; BA(Hons), BSc(Hons), MA, DBA, MSc, PGCert/Dip, DMS, DPA

School of Tourism & Hospitality

business & tourism, cruise management, event management, international/hospitality management, marketing, tourism & hospitality management; BSc(Hons), BA(Hons), MSc, PGDip

Faculty of Education; www.plymouth.ac.uk/education

School of Early Years & Primary Education Studies

early childhood studies, humanities, primary art & design/English/information & communication/maths/science, special ed needs; BA(Hons), BEd, PGCE, MA,PGCert

School of Secondary & Further Education Studies

secondary art and design/science/ drama/English/geography/mathematics/music, teaching in the lifelong learning sector, children's workforce, learning for sustainabilty; CertEd, BA(Hons), FdA, PGCE, MSc, PGCert, ProfDoc,

Faculty of Science & Technology; www.plymouth.ac.uk/faculties/scitech

School of Biomedical & Biological Sciences

animal behaviour/welfare, appl bioscience(agriculture & environment/aquaculture/food & nutrition/ plant science), biomedical/biological science/diversity, healthcare science, human bioscience, environmental biology, marine biology, sustainable aquaculture,wildlife/botanical conservation, zoo conservation; BSc(Hons), MRes, PGDip,NSSc

School of Computing & Mathematics

applied statistics, computing, computer science/systems & networks, civil engineering, communications, computing for business application/ games development/software/web technologies, electrical & electronic engineering, information technology/systems, information security, mathematics, network systems engineering, robotics, signal processing, web applications dev; BSc, MSc, MRes

School of Electronics & Communication

electrical & electronic engineering, electronic communication engineering, signals processing, network systems engineering; BSc(Hons), BEng, MEng, MRes, MSc

School of Mathematics & Statistics

mathematics, mathematics with statistics/education/ finance/computing, applied/statistics, management sci; BSc(Hons), MMath, MStat

Robotics

robotics/technology; BSc(Hons), BEng, MSc, MEng, MRes

School of Geography, Earth, & Environmental Science

analytical chemistry, applied/geology, environmental science/consultancy, geography, ocean science, physical geography, geosciences, holistic science, marine geosciences,planning, sustainable environmental management; BA(Hons), BSc(Hons), MGeol, MSc, MRes, MSc, PGDip

School of Marine Science & Engineering

applied marine sports science/technology, civil & coastal engineering, marine & composites technology, marine biology & coastal ecology/oceanography, marine studies (merchant shipping/navigation/ocean yachting), marine technology, mechanical design & manufacture, mechanical engineering & composites, ocean exploration/science, surf science & technology, coastal engineering, geomatics, hydrography, marine policy & planning, marine renewable energy, water & coastal management; BSc(Hons), BA(Hons), MEng, MRes, MSc

School of Psychology

psychological studies, psychology/with law, human biology/sociology, criminology & criminal justice studies, psychology research methods; BSc(Hons), MSc, PGDip

Peninsula College of Medicine and Dentistry; www.pcmd.ac.uk

Peninsula Dental School; Pensinsula School of Medicine

medicine, surgery, dentistry, clinical science/education, infection prevention & control, remote treatment, environmental & human health, diabetes, cardiovascular risk & ageing, neuroscience, health services; MB, BS, BDS, MD, MS, MPhil, PhD

Degrees validated by the University of Plymouth offered at:

SOUTH DEVON COLLEGE
www.southdevon.ac.uk

animal science, automotive master technician, biosciences, building services engineering, business, computing, construction & building services, creative digital media, teaching in the lifelong learning sector, law, early years care & education, electrical & electronics engineering, events & conference management, healthcare practice, hospitality management, mechanical, electrical & electronic engineering, outdoor education, performance practice & events management, 3D design, tourism & hospitality management, visual studies, yacht operations, young people & community services; BA/BSc, BSc(Hons), FD, HNC, HND, PGCE

TRURO COLLEGE
www.trurocollege.ac.uk

action photography, archaeology, children & young people's workforce, commercial fashion/music, contemporary world jazz, community studies, complementary body therapies, counselling, dance, digital visualization, early childhood education, education/ and training, English studies, environmental & public health/nutrition, hairdressing & salon management, history heritage, HRM, information, advice & guidance, interior design, law, libraries, museums & archives, media advertising, post-compulsory education & training, music performance, outdoor education, personal trainer, photography & digital imaging, popular music, biology, biomedical studies, services, silversmithing & jewellery, sound engineering, sports coaching & therapy, sports science & injury management, web technology; BA(Hons), BSc, FdA, FdSc, HNC, HND, PCET, PGCE, UnivCert/Dip

UNIVERSITY OF PORTSMOUTH
www.port.ac.uk

Portsmouth Business School; www.port.ac.uk/departments/faculties/portsmouthbusinessschool

Department of Accounting and Finance; www.port.ac.uk/departments/academic/accountingandfinance

accountancy, business, business English/communication, finance, financial decision analysis/management, forensic accounting, international finance & trade; BA(Hons), BSc(Hons), MSc

Department of Economics; www.port.ac.uk/departments/academic/economics

applied economics, business law, banking, business economics, cultural & tourism management, international/economics, finance; BA(Hons), BScEcon(Hons), MA, MSc, PGDip

Department of Human Resource and Marketing Management; www.port.ac.uk/departments/academic/hrmm

business administration/studies/communication, coaching & development, hospitality management/ with tourism, HRD, international/HRM, marketing/ with digital media/psychology, sales management, training management & consultancy; BA(Hons), MA, MPhil, PGCert/Dip, PhD

School of Law; www.port.ac.uk/departments/academic/law

law with European studies/international relations/ business/bus communications/criminology, corporate governance, employment law, forensic accounting, international business law; BA(Hons), LlB, LlM

Department of Strategy and Business Systems; www.port.ac.uk/academic/sbs

business/administration/enterprise development/systems, European business, international business studies, leadership & management, leadership in health wellbeing, management, project management & leadership, risk management, strategic quality management; BA(Hons), FdA, HND, MBA, MSc, PGDip/Cert

Faculty of Creative and Cultural Industries; www.port.ac.uk/departments/faculties/facultyofcreativeartsandindustries

Portsmouth School of Architecture; www.port.ac.uk/departments/academic/architecture/

architecture, interior design, professional practice, sustainable architecture, urban design, historic building conservation; BA(Hons), MA, MArch

School of Art, Design and Media; www.port.ac.uk/departments/academic/adm

design for digital media, art, contemporary fine art fashion & textile design with enterprise, fine art, graphic design, illustration, photography; BA(Hons), MA

School of Creative Arts, Film and Media; www.port.ac.uk/departments/academic/scafm

creative & performing arts, creative writing, drama, English, entertainment technology, film/TV studies, media studies; BA(Hons), MA

School of Creative Technologies; www.port.ac.uk/departments/academic/ct

animation, computational sound, computer animation/games enterprise/technology, creative technologies & enterprise, digital media, entertainment technology, music & sound technology, TV & film production, video & games technology; BA(Hons), BSc(Hons), FdSc, MSc

Institute for Industrial Research; www.port.ac.uk/departments/academic/iir

data analysis, image processing, monitoring systems & ambient, intelligent robotics, traffic analysis & resource management

Faculty of Humanities and Social Science; www.port.ac.uk/departments/faculties/facultyofhumanities

Institute of Criminal Justice Studies; www.port.ac.uk/departments/academic/icjs

counter fraud & corruption studies, crime & criminology/community safety/criminal justice/criminal psychology/crime culture/forensic studies/law, investigation & evidence, law, sociology & criminality, police studies, policing, policy & leadership, risk & security management; BSc(Hons), FdA, LlB, MSc

School of Education and Continuing Studies; www.port.ac.uk/departments/academic/iecs

childhood & youth studies, early childhood studies, early years care & education, education administration, education & training/management, PGCE in numerous subject courses/post-compulsory education, practice & pedagogy in education, learning & teaching/in HE; BA(Hons), CertEd, FdA, MA, MSc, PGCE, PGCert,EYPS

School of Languages & Area Studies; www.port.ac.uk/departments/academic/slas

American studies & history, applied languages/linguistics & TESOL, combined modern languages, communication & English studies/language skills, English language, European studies, francophone Africa, French studies, German studies, international business/English/development studies/languages/international relations/trade & business communication/logistics, languages & law, linguistics & business English, Spanish & Latin American studies, technical communication, translation; BA(Hons), MA

School of Social, Historical and Literary Studies; www.port.ac.uk/departments/academic/sshls

criminology/media studies/psychology, English & history/media studies/languages & literature, English literature, psychology, European law & policy/studies, government, history/& politics, history of war, culture & society, international relations & history/politics, journalism, media studies, local government, politics, sociology/& crime, literature, culture & identity, public administration; BA(Hons), BSc(Hons), FdA, MPA, MSc

Faculty of Science; www.port.ac.uk/departments/faculties/faculty of science

School of Biological Sciences; www.port.ac.uk/departments/academic/biology

applied aquatic biology, cells/& biochemistry, biology, forensic biology, genome science, molecular genetics & forensics, organisms & ecosystems; BSc(Hons), MSc,MPhil, PhD

School of Earth and Environmental Sciences; www.port.ac.uk/departments/academic/isees

applied physics, contaminated land, crisis & disaster management, engineering geology & geotechnics, environmental science, geological & environmental hazards, geology, marine environmental science, palaeobiology & evolution; BSc(Hons), MEng(Hons), MSc

Department of Geography; www.port.ac.uk/departments/academic/geography

environmental geography, geography, GIS, human geography, physical geography; BA(Hons), BSc(Hons), MSc

The Dental Academy; www.port.ac.uk/departments/academic/dentalacademy

dental hygiene/therapy nursing, science & dental therapy; BSc (Hons), CertHE, FdSc

School of Health Sciences and Social Work; www.port.ac.uk/departments/academic/shssw

applied clinical healthcare, child care social work, design & health, diagnostic radiography, medical imaging, operating department practice, paramedic science, social work, speech, language; DipHE, FdSc, GradDip, MSc, PGDip

Pharmacy & Biomedical sciences
applied/biomedical science, pharmacy/practice, medicines management, pharmacology, biomedicine; FdSc, BSc(Hons), MSc

Psychology
forensic/psychology, applied psychology of intellectual disabilities, child forensic studies; BSc(Hons), MSc, PGCert, MPhil, PhD

Sport & Exercise Science
sport & exercise science, sports development/business management/performance, clinical exercise science; BSc(Hons), MSc

Faculty of Technology www.port.ac.uk/departments/faculties/facultyoftechnology

Civil Engineering & Surveying; www.port.ac.uk/departments/academic/sces
civil engineering, construction engineering management, property development, environmental/geotechnical/ structural engineering, construction project management, quantity surveying; BSc(Hons), BEng(Hons), MEng, MSc

Computing; www.port.ac.uk/departments/academic/comp
business information systems, computer science, computing & information systems/society/digital image, digital forensics, information systems/technology, software engineering, web technologies, forensic/IT; BSc(Hons), MSc

Electronic & Computer Engineering; www.port.ac.uk/departments/academic/ece
commmunication systems/engineering, computer engineering, computer network management & design, electronic engineering/systems engineering, communication network planning & management/administration, internet engineering/technology,network apps & services/design & simulation/management & administration; BSc(Hons), BEng(Hons), MEng, MSc

Mathematics; www.port.ac.uk/departments/academic/maths
mathematics for finance & management/with statistics, logistics & transportation/optimisation; BSc(Hons) MSc,PgCert/Dip, MPhil, PhD

Mechanical & Design Engineering; www.port.ac.uk/departments/academic/mde
computer-aided product design, engineering & technology, engineering, marine sports/mechanical & manufacturing engineering, petroleum engineering, product design & modern materials/innovation, adv manufacturing technology, technology management; BSc(Hons), BEng(Hons), MEng, MSc, PgCert

QUEEN MARGARET UNIVERSITY COLLEGE
www.qmuc.ac.uk

School of Business, Enterprise and Management; www.qmuc.ac.uk/be
business management, consumer studies, cultural management, entrepreneurship, events/golf and country club management, international hospitality, hospitality and tourism management, marketing, public service management, retail business; BA/BA(Hons), MBA, PhD

The School of Media, Communication & Performing Arts; www.qmuc.ac.uk/mcpa
acting for stage & screen, costume design & construction,, drama and performance, film, media, PR, marketing, cultural management, psychology, sociology; BA/BA(Hons), MA, MBA

The School of Health Sciences; www.qmuc.ac.uk/hs
applied pharmacology, human biology, dietetics, nursing, nutrition, occupational & arts therapies, palliative/primary nursing, public health practice, physiotherapy, podiatry, radiography,speech & hearing sciences, care; BSc(Hons), MSc, HECert

Institute for International Health and Development; www.qmuc.ac.uk/iild
health systems, human resources for health, international health, sexual & reproductive health, social justice, development & health; PgDipCert, MSc,PhD

UNIVERSITY OF READING
www.reading.ac.uk

Faculty of Arts & Humanities; www.reading.ac.uk/fah

School of Arts & Communication Design; www.reading.ac.uk/sacd

Art: art, fine art, history of art, art & phillosophy/film & theatre/psychology, history of art & ancient history/classics/English/architecture
Film, Theatre and Television: film & theatre, TV/ theatre/film studies,theatre & history of art/German/ italian, English literature
Typography & Graphic Communication: graphic communication & English/history/history of art, book/information typeface design, typography & graphic communication; BA(Hons), MA, MA(R-es),MFA, MPhil, PhD

School of Continuing Education; www.reading.ac.uk/conted

archaeology & combined studies, English literature, history, history of art & architecture; HE Cert

School of Humanities; www.reading.ac.uk/ humanities

Classics: ancient history, & history/history of art, the city of Rome, classical & medieval studies, classical studies & English/English literature/history of art, the classical tradition, classics
History of Art: history of art & architecture/art/ English/history/ancient history/ classics
History: history, modern history, history & economics/English/European literature & culture/international relations/moderrn European langauge
Philosophy: philosophy & ethics value/politics/modern European language; BA(Hons)MA,MPhil,PhD

School of Linguistics & Applied Languages; www.reading.ac.uk/slas

applied/English language/eaching, applied linguistics, ELT, linguistic research; BA(Hons), MA, PhD

French Studies; www.reading.ac.uk/ languages/about/les-aboutfrench.aspx

French, French and Franco-British history, French studies; BA(Hons), MA, MPhil, PhD

Italian; www.reading.ac.uk/languages/ about/les-aboutitalian

Italian, Italian & classical studies, Italian studies, modern Italian history; BA(Hons), MA, MPhil, PhD

Faculty of Social Sciences; www.reading.ac.uk/internal/fss

Institute of Education; www.reading.ac.uk/ education

children's development & learning, early years, education (art/English/music specialism), theatre art, education & deaf studies, PGCE (secondary, primary, graduate teacher profession, subject knowledge enhancement), instrument teaching, teaching & learning,education for sustainable global future; BA(Hons), FdA, PGCE, PhD

School of Law; www.reading.ac.uk/law

law, advanced legal studies, European union law, international law & world order/commercial law/ corporate finance/financial regulation, law & society, legal history; DPhil, LlB,LLM, MARes, MRes, PhD

School of Politics & International Relations; www.reading.ac.uk/spirs

international relations & politics/English literature/ hisory/philosophy/modern European language, international relations (diplomacy/international law & order/international security/strategy), war, peace & international relations, military history & strategy; BA(Hons), MA, MPhil, MRes, PhD

School of Health & Social Care; www.reading.ac.uk/hsc

advanced professional practice, counselling, leadership & management, primary care/public health nursing, social work (bursary/employment)/with children & young people, their families & carers/ adults, social work practice education; BSc(Hons), MA, PgDip, MSc/PG, PhD

The School of Economics; www.reading.ac.uk/economics

banking and finance/business & management in emerging economies, business economics, econometrics; economics & accounting/politics/international rels/IT/history/geography/foreign Euro language, economic development in emerging markets, international banking & financial services/ business & economic development/finance; BA(Hons), BSc(Hons), MSc, PhD

Henley Business School; www.henley.ac.uk as at School of Economics

Faculty of Life Sciences; www.reading.ac.uk/internal/lifesci

School of Agriculture, Policy & Development; www.reading.ac.uk/apd

agriculture, agricultural business management/development economics, applied development studies, animal science, consumer behaviour & marketing, development finance/policy, environment & development, environmental & countryside management, food economics & marketing, research agricultural & food economics, social development & sustainable livelihoods; BA(Hons), BSc(Hons), MPhil, PhD

School of Biological Sciences; www.reading.ac.uk/biologicalsciences

applied ecology & conservation, biochemistry, biological sciences, biomedical sciences, horticulture, microbiology, plant diversity, species identification & survey skills, wildlife management & conservation, zoology; BSc(Hons), MPhil, MSc, PhD

School of Chemistry, Food & Pharmacy; www.reading.ac.uk/fcfp

chemistry, food science/technology, forensic analysis, medical chemistry, nutrition, pharmacy; BSc(Hons), MPharm, MSc, PhD

School of Psychology & Clinical Language Science; www.reading.ac.uk/pcls

psychology of childhood and ageing, neuroscience of language, psychology & maths/biology/philosophy/art, speech & language therapy, cognitive neuroscience, development & psychopathology; BSc(Hons), MSc, PhD

Faculty of Science; www.reading.ac.uk/internal/facsci

School of Systems Engineering; www.reading.ac.uk/sse

artificial intelligence, computer science and informatics, cybernetics, digital signal processing & communications, electronic engineering, IT, network & e-business-centered computing, robotics, software engineering, systems engineering; BEng, BSc(Hons), FdSc, MEng, MPhil, MRes, MSc, PhD

School of Construction Management and Engineering; www.reading.ac.uk/CME

building/quantity surveying, construction management, built environment /project management, renewable energy: technology & sustainability; BSc(Hons), MPhil, MSc, PGDip, PhD

School of Mathematical & Physical Sciences;

applied/meteorology, atmosphere, oceans & climate, computational mathematics, mathematics, mathematics and economics/meterology/psychology, statistics/applied statistics, mathematics of scientific and industrial computation, meteorology, biometrics; BSc(Hons), MMath, MPhil, MSc, PhD

School of Human & Environmental Science; www.reading.ac.uk/shes

archaeology/ with ancient history/classics/history/italian/environmental science, medieval archaeology, geoarchaeology, geography/physical/human, economics, environmental management, soils & environmental pollution; BSc(Hons), MSc, MA, MPhil, PhD

ROBERT GORDON UNIVERSITY
www.rgu.ac.uk

Faculty of Health and Social Care

School of Applied Social Studies; www.rgu.ac.uk/social

applied social sciences, mental health, practice learning, psychology, social care/work, sociology; BA(Hons), HNC, MSc, PGDip, PhD

School of Health Sciences; www.rgu.ac.uk/health

diagnostic radiography, health improvement & health promotion, occupational therapy, physiotherapy, radiography, sport & exercise science, sports nutrition; BSc(Hons), CertHE, MPhil, MSc, PhD

School of Nursing & Midwifery; www.rgu.ac.uk/nursing

acute/adult/children's/mental health/community nursing occupational health, midwifery; BN, DipHE, MPhil, MSc, PhD, MMid, MNurs

School of Pharmacy & Life Sciences; www.rgu.ac.uk/pharmacy-life

applied /biomedical science, bioscience, nutrition, dietetics, pharmacy, prescribing science, clinical pharmacy, forensic & analytical science; MPharm, MSc, PGDip, PhD

Aberdeen Business School; www.rgu.ac.uk/abs

Accounting & Finance: accounting, finance
Management: int/business/management, HRM, marketing
Communication & Media: communication, PR, journalism, media studies, publishing,
Events & Fashion Management: event /fashion management
Hospitality & Tourism: international hospitality/ tourism management
Law: law, law & management; information/management studies, project management, business admin, oil & gas management/accounting, financial management, health & safety & risk management, international business, international marketing management, quality management, corporate management & public affairs, politics, information science/management, information & library science, construction law & arbitration, employment law, international commercial/ oil & gas law; BA/ BA(Hons), DBA, DInfSc, LlB, LlM, MBA, MPA, MPhil, MSc, PGDip/Cert, PhD

Faculty of Design & Technology

School of Computing; www.rgu.ac.uk/ computing

business information systems, computer science, computing for graphics and animation/internet and multimedia, information systems technology, computing/ information engineering/with network management with design/software technology/network management, IT management, multimedia development; BSc(Hons), MSc, PGCert/Dip

School of Engineering; www.rgu.ac.uk/eng

electrical/electronic/mechanical/offshore engineering, asset integrity management, oil & gas /drilling & well/ petroleum production engineering, subsea engineering, communications engineering, intelligent biometric security systems, offshore engineering; BSc, BSc(Hons), MPhil, MSc, PhD

Gray's School of Art, Design & Craft; www.rgu.ac.uk/grays

art & design, commercial photography, design for digital media, fashion/product/graphic design, fine art, painting, photographic & electronic media, printmaking, visual communication, 3D/textiles & surface design; BA/BA(Hons), BDes/BDes(Hons), MDes, MRes, PGDip/MA

The Scott Sunderland School of Architecture and Built Environment; www.rgu.ac.uk/sss

advanced architecture studies, design management, construction project management, property development, surveying; GradDip, MArch, MSc, PhD,BSc(Hons)

ROEHAMPTON UNIVERSITY
www.roehampton.ac.uk

Dept of Dance; www.roehampton.ac.uk/ dance

ballet studies, dance anthropology/choreography/ studies, SE Asia dance studies, community dancing, teaching dance; BA, MA, PGDip/Cert, MRes

Dept of Drama, Theatre & Performance; www/roehampton.ac.uk/ drama.theatre.and.performance

drama, theatre & perfomance studies, performance & creative research; BA(Hons), MPhil, MRes, PhD

Dept of English & Creative Writing; www.roehampton.ac.uk/ english.and.creative.writing;

creative/professional writing, modern literature & culture, English
literature, children's literature; BA, MA, MPhil, PhD

Dept of Humanities; www.roehampton.ac.uk/humanities;

classical civilization; history, philosophy, Christian ministry, theology & religious studies; ministerial theology; BA, MTh, PGDip, MPhil, PhD

Department of Education; www.roehampton.ac.uk/education

applied music education, art, craft and design education, education leadership & management, early child studies, English education, primary education, secondary education, social research methods, special education needs; BA(Hons), BA/BSc, EdD, FdA, Froebel Cert and Grad Cert, MA, MPhil, PGCE Primary/Secondary, PhD

Dept of Life Sciences; www.roehampton.ac.uklif-sciences

Biological Sciences; www.roehampton.ac.uk/hals/subjectareas/biologicalsciences

Anthropology: animal ecology, anthropology, biological/social anthropology, primate biology, behaviour & conservation

Biosciences & Health Sciences: biological/biomedical sciences, biology, conservation biology, health & social care, health studies/sciences, health & human sciences, human bioscience, nutrition, zoology, animal ecology, clinical neuroscience/nutrition, health & community, obesity, primate biology, behaviour & conservation, stress & health

Sport & Exercise Sciences: sport psychology, sport & exercise physiology/science; BA, BSc, MRes, PhD

Dept of Media, Culture & Language; www.roehampton.ac.uk/media-culture-and language

English language & linguistics, jounalism & news media, film, media & culture, modern languages, photography, Spanish, TESOL, translation and interpreting, audiovisual translation, documentary practice, media, culture & identity; BSc, BA, MA, MRes, MPhil, PGDip, PhD

Dept of Psychology; www.roehampton.ac.uk/psychology

applied music psychology, counselling, counselling psychology, integrative counselling, psychotherapy, play/music/drama/dance therapy, music psychology, attachment studies; BSc, PsychD, MA, MPhil, PhD

Dept of Social Sciences; www.roehampton.ac.uk/social-sciences

childhood & society, criminology, human rights & society/international relations, sociology; BA, MA, PGDip/Cert, PhD

London Business School; www.roehampton/business-school

business management/HRM/retail management/marketing, international business/management, marketing, multimedia, business information systems, information management, web & creative technologies, finance, international supply chain & logistics management; MBA, PGDip/Cert, BA, BSc, MSc, MPhil, PhD

THE ROYAL ACADEMY OF DANCE
www.rad.org.uk

ballet education, dance education, professional dancer's teaching diploma; BA, PGCert

ROYAL ACADEMY OF DRAMATIC ART
www.rada.org

acting, technical theatre & stage management, property making, scenic art/construction, stage electrics & lighting design, theatre costume/ design/directing, text & performance; BA, MA, PGDip

ROYAL BALLET SCHOOL
www.royalballetschool.co.uk

classical ballet training, performance dancing/arts, professional dance, Irish, Morris and Scottish dancing; BTEC, NatDip

ROYAL COLLEGE OF ART
www.rca.ac.uk

Departments

animation, architecture, communication art & design, ceramics & glass, conservation, critical writing in art & design, curating contemporary art, critical and historical studies, design interactions/products, drawing studio, fashion menswear/ womenswear, goldsmithing, history of design, innovation design engineering, metalwork & jewellery, painting, photography, printmaking, sculpture, silversmithing, textiles, vehicle design; MA, MPhil, PGCert, PhD

ROYAL COLLEGE OF MUSIC
www.rcm.ac.uk

advanced vocal performance, composition, conducting, opera, performance, historical/orchestral performance, vocal studies; DipRCM, BMus, BSc, PGDip, MMus,DMus, GradDip, MPerf

THE ROYAL COLLEGE OF ORGANISTS
www.rco.org.uk

CertRCO, DipCHD, ARCO, FRCO, LTRCO

ROYAL NORTHERN COLLEGE OF MUSIC
www.rncm.ac.uk

chamber music, composition, musicology, opera studies, orchestral studies, keyboard studies, strings, vocal studies, wind, brass & percussion, period performance, instrumental teaching, performing arts leadership, popular music practice, solo performance; PGCert, PGCE, PGDip, MMus, PhD

ROYAL SCOTTISH ACADEMY OF MUSIC & DRAMA
www.rsmad.ac.uk

acting, arts in social contexts, classical and contemporary text, composition, conducting, contemporary performance practice, digital film and television, modern ballet, musical theatre, opera, technical and production, performance, Scottish music; BA (Hons), BEd(Hons), BMus(Hons), MA, MA(Musical Theatre), MMus, MOpera, MPhil, PGDip, PhD

UNIVERSITY OF ST ANDREWS
www.st-andrews.ac.uk

Faculty of Arts

School of Art History; www-ah.st-andrews.ac.uk

art history, history of photography, medieval studies, museum & gallery studies: GradCert, GradDip, MA, MLitt, MPhil, PhD

School of Classics; www.st-andrews.ac.uk/classics

ancient history & archaeology, classical studies, Greek, Latin; MA, MLitt, MPhil, PGDip, PhD

School of Economics & Finance; www.st-andrews.ac.uk/economics

analytical finance, applied economics/quantitative finance, economics, international finance/strategy & economics, money, banking & finance, microeconomics, macroeconomics, sustainable development; BSc, MA, MSc, MPhil, PhD

School of English; www.st-andrews.ac.uk/english

creative writing, English, medieval English, Romantic/Victorian studies, Shakespeare & Renaissance literature, women, writing & gender; GradDip, MA, MLitt, MPhil, PhD

School of History; www.st-andrews.ac.uk/history

Arabic, book history, central & Eastern European studies, environmental history, history, Iranian studies, medieval history, Middle East studies/history, modern history, Reformation studies, Scottish historical studies/history; GradDip, MA, DLitt, MPhil, PhD

School of International Relations; www.st-andrews.ac.uk/intrel

international relations (numerous jt hons degrees), Middle East & Central Asian security studies, peace & conflict, sustainable development; MA, MLitt, MPhil, MRes, PhD

School of Management; www.st-andrews.ac.uk/management

corporate social responsibility/finance, finance & accounting/management, dynamic strategic management, entrepreneurship, global business management, HRM, information technology, dynamic strategic management, international business/marketing/banking, management, managing in the creative industries, marketing, organizational studies, sustainable development; BSc, DipRes, MA, MLitt, MSc, MRes, PhD

School of Modern Languages; www.st-andrews.ac.uk/modlang

Arabic, comparative literature, cultural identity studies, French/German/Italian studies, language/& linguistics, modern Hispanic literature & film, Russian, Central & Eastern European studies, Spanish, Spanish & Latin American studies, medieval studies; DLang, MA, MLitt, MPhil, PGDip, PhD

School of Philosophical, Anthropological & Film Studies; www.st-andrews.ac.uk/philosophy

Philosophy: analytical/classical philosophy, logic & philosophy of science, philosophy of Scottish enlightenment, Kant, metaphysics

Social Anthropology: social anthropology & Pacific studies

Film Studies: film studies, film theory & history, world cinema

Music: opera, keyboard performance, Scottish/bagpipe/electronic music; BSc, MA, MLitt, MPhil, MRes, PhD

Faculty of Divinity

School of Divinity; www.st-andrews,.ac.uk/divinity

bible & the contemporary world, divinity, New Testament, theological studies/interpretation of scripture, biblical language & literature, scripture & theology, systematic & historical theology; BD, MA, MLitt, MPhil, MTheol, PGDip, PhD

Faculty of Medicine

Bute Medical School; www.medicine.st-andrews.ac.uk

health psychology, medicine, surgery, community health, molecular medicine; BSc, MD, MPhil, MSc, PhD, MRes

Faculty of Science

School of Biology; www.biology.st-andrews.ac.uk

behavioural/cell/environmental/evolutionary/marine/molecular biology, biochemistry, biology, ecology &

conservation, marine mammal sci/systems sci, behavioural & neural sci, neuroscience, zoology; BSc, MPhil, MRes, PhD

School of Chemistry; www.ch.st-andrews.ac.uk

biomolecular/chemical sciences, chemistry, materials science; BSc, MChem, MSci, PGDip, PhD

School of Computer Science; www.cs.st-andrews.ac.uk

advanced/computer science, AI, computer information technology/coding/graphics/architecture/security, databases, data communications & networks, distributed systems, human computer interaction, programming language design, operating systems, multimedia, component technology, internet programming, computer management & IT, networks & distributed systems, software engineering; BSc, MPhil, MSc, PhD

School of Geography & Geosciences; www.st-andrews.ac.uk/gg

environmental geoscience/history, geography, geoscience, geology, earth sciences, managing environmental change, physical geography, sustainable development; BSc, MA, MLitt, MPhil, MRes, MSc, PGCert, PGDip, PhD

School of Mathematics & Statistics; www-maths.mcs.st-andrews.ac.uk

applied mathematics/statistics & data mining, mathematics, pure mathematics, statistics; BSc, GradDip, MA, MLitt, MMath, MPhil, MSc, PhD

School of Physics & Astronomy; www.st-andrews.ac.uk/physics

astrophysics, physics, theoretical physics, photonics & optoelectronic devices; BSc, EngDoc, MPhys, MSc, PhD,MSci

School of Psychology; www.psy.st-andrews.ac.uk

behavioural & neurosciences, evolutionary & comparative psychology, human cognition, learning disabilities, neuroscience, perception, psychology, social/health/psychology; BSc, MA, MPhil, MRes, MSc, PhD

UNIVERSITY OF SALFORD
www.salford.ac.uk

College of Arts, Social Sciences; www.famss.salford.ac.uk

School of Art & Design; www.artdes.salford.ac.uk

advertising design, animation, art & design, arts & museum management, communication design, computer & video games, contemporary fine art, creative games/technology, design for digital media/management/for the creative industries, design futures, fashion, graphic design, heritage studies, interior design, journalism & design studies, museum & heritage exhibition design, photography, product design, visual arts; BA(Hons), BSc(Hons), HND, MA, PGDip, PhD

School of English, Sociology, Politics & Contemporary History; www.espach.salford.ac.uk

English: creative writing: innovation & experiment, drama & performance studies film studies/creative writing/linguistics/cultural studies/journalism, English language/literature, literature, culture & modernity

Sociology & Criminology:
crime and criminal justice, criminology, cultural studies, human rights & ethics, journalism, law, politics, psychology, social sciences, sociology, regeneration & social inclusion

Politics & Contemporary History: contemporary history, contemporary military & international history, intelligence & security studies, international relations & globalization/politics, politics/& contemporary history, terrorism & security, war studies; BA(Hons), MA, PGDip/Cert.PhD

School of Languages; www.languages.salford.ac.uk

Arabic/English translation & interpreting/security studs/politics, Chinese/English, translation & interpreting, French, German, Italian, Portugese, Spanish with law, linguistics, modern language studies/with TESOL, translating for international business; BA(Hons), MA, PGDip/Cert,

Salford Law School; www.law.salford.ac.uk

construction law & practice, environmental/health care law, health & safety law, international business law & regulation, law/ & criminology/finance/Spanish; LlB, LLM, MA, MSc, PGCert, PGDip

School of Media, Music & Performance; www.smmp.salford.ac.uk

animation, Asian cinema, broadcasting, childrens' digital media, computer & video games, contemporary theatre practice, critical/popular musicology, English, film & TV production, film screenwriting/ studies, journalism, media & performance, media production/technology, mobile & internet TV, music/ performance, physical & dance theatre, pop music & production/& recording, pop/musicology, radio production, social media, TV & radio/scriptwriting, TV documentary production, wildlife documentary production; BA(Hons), BSc(Hons), HND, MA, MPhil, MSc, PgCert, PgDip, PhD

Salford Business School; www.business.salford.ac.uk

accounting, business & management studies/with law, business information technology/management/ studies with financial management corporate finance, economics, design/events management, finance, financial services management, hospitality management, HRM & D, international banking & finance/ business management/marketing, managing IT, marketing, procurement, media asset management, quantitative business management, logistics & supply chain management, project management, sport & leisure management, tourism management; BA(Hons), BSc(Hons), CertHE, DipHE, FD, GradCert, HNC, HND, MA, MBA, MPhil, ProfDip, ProfPGDip, PhD

Faculty of Business, Law & the Built Environment; www.flbe.salford.ac.uk

College of Health & Social Care; www.fhsc.salford.ac.uk

School of Social Work, Psychology & Public Health; www.swpph.salford.ac.uk

adult care, applied psychology (therapies), child care, cognitive behavioural therapy, complementary medicine/ therapy, counselling & psychotherapy, counselling, learning disabilities, psychology, criminology & social justice, media psychology, public health, social policy, social work, nursing, sociology; BA, MA, MPhil, MSc, PgCert, PgDip, PhD

School of Health, Sport & Rehabilitation Sciences; www.healthcare.salford.ac.uk

prosthetics & orthotics, physiotherapy, podiatry, occupational therapy, radiography, advanced medical imaging, nuclear medicine, dental implantology, diagnostic radiography, exercise, physical activity & health, sport and exercise; surgical practice, applied sports science, sports development/rehabilitation/ strength & conditioning rehabilitation, trauma & orthopaedics; BSc(Hons), MSc, PGDip/Cert

School of Nursing & Midwifery; www.nursing.salford.ac.uk

adult/children's/mental health/children & young people/learning disability, advanced practice (health & social care/neonatal), contemporary healthcare practice, mental health, health & social care, leadership & management for health care practice, midwifery, non-medical prescribing, social work (learning disabilities), public health, therapeutic intervention; BSc, BSc(Hons), DipHE, DProfMed & Social Care, MSc, PGDip/Cert

College of Science & Technology; www.fsee.salford.ac.uk

School of the Built Environment; www.sobe.salford.ac.uk

adv manufacturing in construction, building surveying, construction & property, construction law & practice/ management/project management, corporate real estate, digital architectural design, facilities management, project management in construction, property management & investment, quantity surveying, real estate development/management, urban design; BSc(Hons), DBEnv, DConstMangt, DRealEst, MSc, PGDip/Cert, PhD

School of Computing, Science & Engineering; www.cse.salford.ac.uk

acoustics, advanced control systems, aeronautical engineering, aerospace design & manufacture/engineering, aircraft engineering, animation, audio & video systems, audio production, aviation technology, civil engineering, computer networks/science, data telecommunications & networks, databases and web-based systems, gas engineering & management, industrial & commercial combustion engineering, information security, internet computing, interactive media, physics, pilot studies, professional sound & video technology, robotics & automation, software engineering, space technology, sound & video technology, structural engineering, transport engineering

& planning, vacuum engineering & applications; BEng, BSc(Hons), HND, MEng, MEnt(Tech), MPhys, MSc, PGDip, PG(Tech)

School of Environmental & Life Sciences; www.els.salford.ac.uk

Biosciences:
analytical biosciences & drug design, biochemistry, biology, biomedical science, pharmaceutical science, molecular parasitology & vector biology, biotechnology,

Geography:
GIS, biogeography, environmental geography, geography,

Environmental Studies:
environmental assessment & management, environmental management/studies

Environmental Health/Management;
environmental & public health, occupational safety & health, safety, health & environment, environment management & assessment

Housing & Regeneration;
housing practice, housing, regeneration & sustainability, sustainable communities

Wildlife & Zoo Biology;
wildlife documentary production, drug design, wildlife & practical conservation, zoo biology, zoology; BSc(Hons), FD, MA, MSc, PhD

Degrees validated by University of Salford offered at:

RIVERSIDE COLLEGE, HALTON
www.riversidecollege.ac.uk

business & management, counselling, early years & young people, manufacturing technology/technology, teaching in the lifelong learning sector; Dip, FD, FdSc, PGDip

UNIVERSITY OF SHEFFIELD
www.sheffield.ac.uk

Faculty of Arts & Humanities; www.sheffield.ac.uk/faculties/arts-and-humanities

Dept of Archaeology
archaeology, archaeological materials, archaeology, bible and ancient cultures, Aegean/classical and historical archaeology, cognitive studies, environmental archaeology & palaeoeconomy, European historical archaeology/prehistory, experimental archaeology, geoarchaeology, human osteology and funerary archaeology, landscape archaeology, material culture studies, palaeoanthropology; BA(Hons), BSc(Hons), MA, MPhil, MSc, PhD

School of English Literature, Language and Linguistics
18th/19th-century studies, applied linguistics with TESOL, creative writing, culture of the British Isles, English literature, language & linguistics, language acquisition, theatre/& performance studies; BA(Hons), MA, MPhil, PhD

Dept of History
18th/19th-century studies, American history, early/modern history, historical research, history, international/medieval/ modern European history; BA(Hons), MA, MPhil, PhD

School of Modern Languages & Linguistics
Catalan, Czech, Dutch, French, German, Hispanic studies, European gender studies, intercultural communication, Latin American studies, Luxembourgish, modern languages, multilingual information management, Polish, Russian, Russian and Slavonic studies, screen translation, translation studies; BA(Hons), MA, MPhil, PhD

Department of Music
ethnomusicology, music, music management/performance, music psychology in education, psychology of music/for musicians sonic arts, world music; BA(Hons), BMus(Hons), DPhil, MA, MMus, PhD

Dept of Philosophy
philosophy, metaphysics, epistemology, logic, philosphy of language & the mind, ethics, political philosophy, aesthetics, history of philosophy

Dept of Bible Studies

bible studies, society & culture, postcolonialism, archaeology, bible & ancient culture, religion, conflict & the media; BA(Hons), MA, MPhil, PhD

Faculty of Engineering; www.sheffield.ac.uk/faculties/engineering

Dept of Aerospace Engineering

aerospace materials/engineering, aerospace engineering with private pilot instruction, aerostructures & aerodynamics, avionics. control systems; BEng, MEng, MPhil, MSc, PhD, PGDip

Dept of Automatic Control & Systems Engineering

control systems, gas turbine control, computer systems engineering, electronic/mechanical systems engineering, mechatronics, systems & control engineering; BEng, MEng, MPhil, MSc, PhD

Dept of Bioengineering

bioengineering, biomedical engineering, biomaterioals science with tissue engineering, biological systems bioprocessing, medical devices & systems; BEng, MEng

Dept of Chemical & Process Engineering

biological and bioprocessing engineering, chemical engineering, chemical & process engineering, environmental & energy engineering, fuel technology, process safety & loss prevention; BEng, MEng, MPhil, MSc, MSc(Eng), PhD

Dept of Civil & Structural Engineering

architectural engineering design, civil/structural engineering, civil structures, contaminant hydrogeology, earthquake & civil engineering dynamics, environmental management of urban land & water, groundwater & water engineering, steel construction, structural & concrete engineering, structural engineering, urban water engineering & management; BEng, MEng, MPhil, MSc, PGDip/Cert, PhD

Dept of Computer Science

advanced computer science, advanced software engineering, computer science with speech & language processing, enterprise computing, software engineering, AI, data communications, information systems, information technology management for business, software systems & internet technology; BEng, BSc, MComp, MEng, MPhil, MSc, MSc(Eng), PhD

Dept of Electrical & Electronic Engineering

avionic systems, computer vision & photonics, data communications, electrical/communications/electronic engineering, wireless commuinications, microelectronics; Eng, MEng, MPhil, MSc, PhD

Dept of Materials Science & Engineering

aerospace materials, materials science & engineering, biomaterials, metallurgy, ceramic science & engineering, polymers & polymer composites, adv solid state chemistry, nuclear environmental science/science, nanomaterials for nanoengineering, bionantechnology; BEng, EngD, MEng, MPhil, MSc, MRes, PhD

Dept of Mechanical Engineering

advanced mechanical engineering, advanced manufacturing technology, aerodynamics & aerostructures, automotive engineering, mechanical engineering/ with Spanish/industrial management; BEng, MEng, MPhil, MSc, MSc(Res), PhD

Faculty of Medicine, Dentistry & Health; www.sheffield.ac.uk/faculties/medicine-dentistry-health

The Medical School

cardiovascular science, endocrinology & reproduction, human metabolism/nutrition, infection & immunity, medicine, molecular medicine, musculoskeletal science, nephrology, neuroscience, orthoptics, surgery, vision & strabismus, pharmacokinetics/ dynamics; BMedSci, MBChB, MD, PhD, PGCert/Dip

Dept of Cardiovascular Science

cell biology, coronary artery disease, haemostasis, medical physics, non-mammalian models, pulmonary vascular, platelets, inflammatory signals, vascular biology; MPhil, PhD

School of Clinical Dentistry

adult dental care, dental hygiene and therapy, dental implantology, dental public health, dentistry, oral pathology, oral health, orthodontics, paediatric dentistry, periodontics, restorative dentistry; BDS, ClinDent, Diploma, MDPH, MMedSci, MPhil, PhD

Health & Related Research; www.sheffield.ac.uk/scherr

clinical research, health services, public health (management & leadership, international development), health economics & decision modelling, psychotherapy studies, statistics appl to medicine; MSc, PGDip/ Cert

Dept of Human Communication Sciences

cleft palate studies, clinical/human communication sciences, language & communication impairment in children, speech/difficulties; AdvCert, BMedSci(-Hons), BSc(Hons), MMedSci, MPhil, MSc, PGCert/Dip, PhD

Dept of Human Metabolism

Dept of Infection & Immunity

Dept of Neuroscience

molecular medicine neuroscience; BMedSci, MSc, MRCPsych

School of Nursing & Midwifery

advanced nursing studies, advancing practice, health & social care studies, infection control, maternity care, midwifery/ nursing studies, occupational health nursing, orthoptics, palliative care, public health, primary/critical/cancer/neonatal intensive care; BMedSci, MMedSci, MMid, MPhil, PGCert, PhD

The Faculty of Science; www.sheffield.ac.uk/faculties/science

Dept of Animal & Plant Science

animal behaviour, biology, conservation & biodiversity, ecology, plant sciences; evolution & behaviour, eology & environment, plant & microbiol biology, molecular science, population & community ecology, zoology; MBiolSci, PhD, MPhil

Dept of Biomedical Science

biomedical science, molecular & cellular basis of human disease, integrative physiology & pharmacology, stem cell & regenerative medicine; BSc(Hons), MSc, PhD

Dept of Chemistry

chemistry, polymers for advanced technologies, science commuunication; BSc, MChem, MPhil, MPhys, PhD

Dept of Molecular Biology & Biotechnology

biochemistry, biology, genetics, medical genetics/microbiology, microbiology, molecular cell/cell biology/microbiology/biologymechanistic biology, structural biology; BSc(Hons), MBiolSci, PhD

Dept of Physics & Astronomy

astronomy, astrophysics, medical physics, nanoscale science and technology, nanoelectronics & nanomechanics, physics, theoretical physics; BS(Hons), MPhys, MSc, PhD

Dept of Psychology

cognitive studies, cognitive & computational neuroscience, human neuroimaging, science communication, psychology, psychological research; BA(Hons), BSc(Hons), DClinPsych, MA, MPhil, MSc, PhD

School of Mathematics & Statistics; www.math.dept.sheac.uk/maths

mathematics, financial maths, statistics/with medical applications; BSc, MSc, PhD, MMath, MComp

Faculty of Social Science; www.sheffield.ac.uk/faculty/social-science

School of Architecture

architectural design, architecture/& landscape, computer-aided environmental design, conservation & regeneration, designing learning environments, structural engineering, sustainable architectural studies, urban design; BA(Hons), MArch, MPhil, MSc, PhD

School of East Asian Studies

Chinese studies, East Asian studies, Japanese studies, Korean studies; BA(Hons), MA, PhD

Dept of Economics

development economics & policy, accounting, business finance, economics, economics & mathematics/politics/philosophy, finance/management, financial economics, health economics, international finance and economics, money, banking & finance; Adv Cert, BA(Hons), BSc(Hons), MSc, PhD

Sheffield Law School

biotechnological law and ethics, commercial law, European law/health law, criminology, international law/commercial law & practice, law, law international law; LlB, LlM, MAPhil, PhD

Sheffield Management School

accounting, financial management, economics, HRM, information systems/management, business management & economics/information management/sociology/social policy/variuos foreign language studies, international business/marketing & management, leadership & management, logistics & supply chain management, creative & cultural industries, marketing, occupational/workplace psychology; MSc, MPhil, PhD, Sheffield MBA, ExecMBA

Dept of Politics

politics, economics, European law, governance & politics, international politics/relations/history/political economy, sociology, public administration &

management, global politics and law/security, globalization & development, governance & public policy, philosophy, political theory, politics; BA, MA, MPhil, PhD

Dept of Sociological Studies

childhood studies, children and their families, criminology, global & international/social policy, social work, sociology; BA(Hons), MA, MPhil, PhD

Dept of Town & Regional Planning

architecture/ & town & regional planning, commercial property, geography, international development & planning, landscape architecture, planning /& development, planning research, urban studies; BA(Hons), MA, MPlan, PhD

The School of Education

applied professional studies in education, early childhood education, educational psychology, education, culture & children, globalization & education, PGCE, English, geography, history, mathematics, modern languages & science; initial teacher education, psychology & education, teaching and learning in HE, working with communities: identities, regeneration and change; EdD, MA, MEd, MPhil, PhD, PCHE

Dept of Geography

arid land studies, environmental science, human geography, international development, social & cultural geography, environmental analysis of terrestial systems, physical geography, social & cultural geographies; BA(Hons), BSc(Hons), MEnvSci, PhD

School of Information

accounting & financial management, business management, electronic & digital library management, health informatics, information literacy, information management/in business, information systems/management, librarianship, multilingual information management; MA, MChem, MSc, MSc(Res), PhD/MPhil

Dept of Journalism Studies

global/magazine/journalism studies, international political communication, broadcast/print/web journalism; BA, MPhil, PhD

Dept of Landscape

landscape architecture/with ecology/planning, landscape management, architecture & landscape, landscape studies; BA(Hons), BSc(Hons), MA, PGDip, PhD, MLA

SHEFFIELD HALLAM UNIVERSITY
www.shu.ac.uk

Faculty of Arts, Computing, Engineering & Science; www.shu.ac.uk/art/faculties.aces

Business Systems and IT

applied computing, business information systems, business & ICT, computer & information security, computer networks/science, computer security with forensics; BSc(Hons), FdSc

Media, PR & Journalism

corporate/communication, international broadcast journalism, PR, film & media production, media, professional communication, journalism, technical communication, cultural policy & management; BA(Hons), MA, MPhil, PhD, PGCert/Dip

Computing, Computer & Electronic Systems

animation for computer games, business & ICT, computer & information security/network engineering, computer-aided design technology, computer networks, information systems, databases, forensic & security technologies, information technology, interactive media, multimedia technologies, network management, software engineering, web & cloud technology; BEng, BSc(Hons), FDSc, GradDip, HND, MComp, MSc

Engineering & Technology

aeronautical/aerospace/aerospace electronic engineering, advanced design engineering/aeronautical engineering/engineering materials/mechanical engineering, aerospace electronic systems/engineering, automotive des engineering, computer-aided engineering, electical & electronic engineering, electronics, information technology, forensic engineering, industrial management, logistics & supply chain management, mechanical/ engineering, engineering materials & product design, software engineering, sports technology, telecommunication engineering; BSc(Hons), BEng FdSc, MBA, MSc, PhD

Mathematics & Statistics; www.shu.ac.uk/mathematics

statistics, specialist teaching, QTS, secondary mathematics, mathematics; BSc(Hons), MSc, PhD

Sheffield Institute of the Arts; www.shu.ac.uk/prospectus/subject/1

creative art practice, design – graphics/industrial/metalwork & jewellery/fashion/packaging; BA(Hons), MA, MArt, MDes, PhD

Faculty of Development & Society; www.shu.ac.uk/faculties/ds

Built Environment

architectural technology, architecture, environmental design, building surveying/studies, built environment, construction/management & real estate, planning & property development, project management, quantity surveying, real estate management, technical architecture, sustainable communities & environment; BSc(Hons), HNC, HND, MPhil, MSc, PGDip/Cert, PhD

Criminology & Community Justice

criminology & psychology/sociology/politics, forensic criminology, international criminal justice; BEng, BSc(Hons), FdSc, MA/PgDip/PgCert, MSc

Education

Asperger' s syndrome, autism, early/childhood studies, early years/education with QTS, design & technology, education & disability studies/specialist learning, education for international students, TESOL/psychology & counselling/education studies, learning & skills, education & training, primary ed with QTS, design & technology/science with education & QTS, PGCE, early years education, learning & skills, secondary (broad range of taught subjects), inclusion, teaching & learning in HE, mentoring, TESOL, TESOL or numeracy learning and skills, inclusion, business education/citizenship/design and technology/English/information and communication technology/mathematics/modern foreign languages/physical education/religious education/science, integrated working, learning & skills, young people' s services, youth work; BA(Hons), CertE, EdD, FdA, MA, MPhil, MSc, PGCert/Dip, PhD

Environment

environmental management (business/international resource & climate management/wildlife & landscape conservation, sustainable communities & environment, environmental conservation/science/studies; BA(Hons), BSc(Hons), MPlan, MSc/PGDip/PGCert

English

creative writing, history, English language/literature, Shakespeare & Renaissance literature, writing; BA(Hons), MA, PgDip, MPhil, PhD

History

history, criminology, politics, local & global, history, imperialism & culture; BA(Hons), MA, PGDip, MPhil, PhD

Film, Theatre, & Performance

animation & special effects, film studies, film and media, performance & professional practice, screen studies, scenewriting, visual effects; BA(Hons), FdA, MA, MA/PGDip/PGCert

Geography

geography/with planning, GIS, human geography; BA(Hons), BSc(Hons), MSc, PGDip/Cert

Forensics

forensic accounting, & analytical criminology/engineering/ psychology, intelligence & forensics management, forensic & security technologies; BSc(Hons), FdSc, MSc

Law

business law, international commercial law, forensic accounting/criminology/psychology/science, law, law and criminology, maîtrise en droit Français; LlB, LLM, MSc, PGCert/Dip

Planning, Regeneration & Housing

geography & planning, GIS, housing for environmental health, housing policy and practice, int real estate, sustainable communities/and environments, transport/planning and management, urban and regional/environmental planning, urban regeneration, local & regional economic planning; BA(Hons), BSc(Hons), MPlanning and Transport, MSc/PGDip

Psychology

pyschology, applied cognitive neuroscience, cognitive analytic therapy, developmental/forensic/organizational, health psychology; BSc(Hons), MRes/PGDip/PGCert, MSc

Sociology & Politics

applied social science, business, cultural studies, criminology, sociology, education, health & society, history, international relations, politics, psychology, public health, social sciences, social work, planning and policy, youth & community work, working with children, young people & families; BA(Hons), Grad-Dip, MA, MPhil/PhD, MRes/PgDip/PgCert

Faculty of Health & Wellbeing; www.shu.ac.uk/faculties/hwb

Sport and Active Lifestyles

PE, youth sport, performance/coaching, sport injury management and therapy, sport business management, physical ed & youth sport, sport & community development/exercise psychology, sport & active lifestyles, leading & managing PE & youth sport/sport development; BA(Hons), BSc(Hons), MA, MSc, PgDip/Cert, PRofDoc

Biosciences

biochemistry, biology, biomedical laboratory science, biosciences, biotechnology, forensic & analytical science, forensic biosciences, human biology, medical sci, pathological sciences, pharmaceutical analysis/sciences, pharmacology and biotechnology; BSc(Hons), MSc/PGDip/PGCert, ProfDocBiomedSci

Diagnostic Radiography

breast imaging & diagnosis, diagnostic radiography, medical imaging, medical ultrasound radiological studies; DocProf Studies (Health and Social Care), BA(Hons), BSc(Hons), MSc/PGDip/PGCert

Management and Leadership

health & social care, leadership/management/services management; BA(Hons), DipHE, MSc, PhD

Nursing & Midwifery

acute and critical care, advancing paediatric practice, health and social care, learning disability, maternal health care, midwifery, adult, child or mental health nursing, supportive and palliative care, primary care nursing/district nursing, public health, health visiting and school nursing, social work; AdvDip, AdvProf-Dev, BA(Hons), BSc(Hons), DocProfStud, Foundation degree, MSc/PGDip/PGCert

Occupational Therapy; www.shu.ac.uk/occupational

occupational therapy, paediatric practice, vocational rehabilitation, occupational social care practice; BSc(Hons), DocProf, MSc/PGDip/PGCert

Operating Department Practice

operating dept practice; BA(Hons), BSc(Hons), DipHE, DocProfStud, MSc/PGDip/Cert

Paramedic Studies

paramedic practice, BSc(Hons), DipHE

Physiotherapy

advancing/applying paediatric practice, physiotherapy, sport injury management and therapy; BA(Hons), BSc(Hons), MSc, PGCert, PGDip

Radiotherapy and Oncology

radiotherapy planning, radiotherapy & oncology practice, supportive and palliative care; BA(Hons), BSc(Hons), DipHE, MSc/PGDip/PGCert

Social Work

applied nursing & social work (learning disability), caring for children & young people, social work, specialist mental health practice/practitioner, working with children, young people & families, youth & community work; BA(Hons), GradDip, MScPgDip, MSW, PGCert, Doc SocWork

Sheffield Business School; www.shu.ac.uk/faculties/sbs

Accounting, Banking & Finance

accounting & finance, audit management & consultancy, banking, business accounting/economics/financial management, forensic accounting, risk management, international finance/banking/economics/stockbroking; BA(Hons), MA, MSc, PGDip/Cert

Business & Management

business and management, business admin/economics/studies, enterprise management, finance, financial management, ICT, international business studies, global marketing/business/strategic marketing, HRM/HR development, leadership, industrial management, international business & management/HRM/marketing/business studies, marketing, tourism; BSc(Hons), DBA, FD, GradDip, HNC, HND, MBA, MPhil, MSc, PGCert, PGDip, PhD

Facilities Management

food management, events management, tourism, hospitality & facilities management; BA(Hons), BSc(Hons), Cert, FD, MA, MPhil, MSc, PGCert, PGDip, PhD

Languages

business & English, English language teaching, educational studies & TESOL, int business studies & languages, teaching English for academic purposes; GradDip/Cert, MPhil, PGCert, PhD

Tourism, Hospitality & Events Management

events & leisure management, international events and conference management, international hospitality and tourism management, hospitality business management; BSc(Hons), FdSc, HND, MA, MPhil, MSc, PGCert, PGDip, PhD

UNIVERSITY OF SOUTHAMPTON
www.soton.ac.uk

*Faculty of Business and Law; www.soton.ac.uk/about/faculties/faculty_*

School of Law; www.soton.ac.uk/law
commercial & corporate law, European & comparative property law, European law/legal studies, IT & commerce/telecommunications. international law/business law/legal studies, maritime law; LlB, LlM, MPhil, PhD

Management Business School; www.southampton.ac.uk/management
accounting, business & administration, business analytics & management studies, corporate risk & security management, digital marketing, enterepreneurship, finance, HRM/strategies, international banking, financial studies/markets/marketing, knowledge & information systems management, marketing analytics, management, risk management; BSc(Hons), MSc, PhD, MBA, DBA

Winchester School of Art; www.wsa.soton.ac.uk
advertising design, design/fashion management, graphic/communications design, illustration, luxury brand management, photography, motion graphics, luxury illustration & digital animation, fine art, fashion & fibre, fashion promotion & marketing, new media, painting, printmaking, sculpture, textile design; BA(Hons), MA, MPhil, PhD

Faculty of Engineering & the Environment; www.soton.ac.uk/about/faculties/faculty_engineering_environment

Civil Engineering & the Environment; www.civil.soton.ac.uk
civil/environmental engineering, environmental sciences/management, energy & sustainability, engineering in coastal environment, transportation planning; BEng, MEng, MSc, PhD, EngD

School of Engineering Sciences; www.southampton.ac.uk/ses

Aeronautics & Astronautics:
adv materials/aerodynamics/air vehicle design/spacecraft engineering/structural design/engineering management, space sytems engineering, aerodynamics & computation, race aerodynamics

Mechanical Engineering:
advanced materials/aerospace/automotive/bioengineering/mechatronics/naval engineering/sustainable energy systems, energy management, computational engineering design, electromechanical engineering, bioengineering design, energy technology, engineering materials & surface engineering;

Ship Science:
(advanced materials/naval architecture/naval engineering/yacht & small craft engineering), maritime engineering science, marine technology; BEng, MEng, MSc, MPhil, PhD, EngD

Institute of Sound & Vibration Research; www.isvr.soton.ac.uk
acoustics/& music, applied digital signal processing, audiology, biomedical signal processing, engineering acoustics, sound & vibration studies, structural dynamics; DClinPract, MSc, PhD

Faculty of Health Sciences; www.soton.ac.uk/about/faculties/faculty_healthsciences

nursing (adult, children, mental health), midwifery, occupational therapy, phsyiotherapy, podiatry, leadership & management in/health & social care, clinical/public health practice, mental health practitioner, health & rehabiltation; BSc(Hons), MSc, PGDip, MPhil, PhD, MRes, DocClinPract

Faculty of Humanities; www.soton.ac.uk/about/faculties/faculty_humanities

Archaeology:
archaeology & history/geography, archaeological computing, Rome & provinces, ceramic & Lithic/maritime/social archeology, osteoarchaeology,

English;

English, English literature studies, 18th-century studies, 20th/21st century literature, creative writing

Film;

film/ film & culture

History;

history, modern history, jt hons incl archaeology, English, foreign language, philosophy, Jewish history studies, 18th century studies

Modern Languages:

European studies, French/German/Portugese/Spanish/ Latin American studies, applied/linguistics studies/for language teaching, English language teaching, transnational studies

Music:

performance, composition, music technology, commercial muisic, music therapy, musicology, electronic/media music

Philosophy:

philosophy: jt hons degrees incl sociology, politics, mathematics, foreign language, aesthetics
BA(Hons), MA, MRes, MPhil, PhD, CetHE, MMus

*Faculty of Medicine; www.soton.ac.uk/about/faculties/faculty_*

Medicine

adv clinical practice, allergy, biomedical sciences, cancer sciences, origins of health & disease, human genetics, medicine, mental health practitioner, public health/nutrition; BM, MSc, BMedSci, PGDip/Cert, PhD, DM

Faculty of Natural and Environmental Sciences; www.soton.ac.uk/about/faculties/faculty_natural_environmental-sciences

Biological Sciences; www.soton.ac.uk/biosc

biochemistry, biology, cellular & molecular sciences, molecular biosciences, neurosciences, pharmacology, zoolology, ecology & the environment; BSc(Hons), Cert/DipHE, MPhil, PhD

Chemistry; www.soton.ac.uk/chemistry

chemistry/with medical science, electrochemistry, complex systems chemistry, molecular diagnostics & therapeutics, magnetic resonance, molecular assembly, function & structure

National Oceanography Centre, Southampton; www.noc.soton.ac.uk

geology, geography, oceanography, marine science, policy & law, marine resource management, engineering in the coastal environment, marine environment & resources

School of Ocean and Earth Science; www.soton.ac.uk/soes

geology, geophysics, oceanography, ocean, earth & climate science, marine biology/science, policy & law, engineering in coastal environment, marine environment & resources, marine geology & geophysics, ocean remote sensing

Faculty of Physical and Applied Sciences; www.soton.ac.uk/about/faculties/faculty_physical-applied_sciences

Electronics and Computer Science; www.ecs.soton.ac.uk

computer science, AI, distributed networks, image & multimedia systems, mobile & secure systems, software/electrical/elelectronic/electromechanical engineering, nanotechnology, optical communication, power systems, wireless communications

Optoelectronics Research Centre; www.orc.soton.ac.uk

photonics; PhD

Physics & Astronomy; www.phy.soton.ac.uk

astronomy, theoretical particle physics, physics with astronomy/nanotechnology/space science/photonics/mathematics, quantum, light & matter

Faculty of Social and Human Sciences; www.soton.ac.uk/about/faculties/facultysocial_human-sciences

Centre for Contemporary China; www.soton.ac.uk/ccc

international comparative studies; MSc

School of Education; www.southampton.ac.uk/education

educational studies, education & training (primary), educational studies with psychology, education (management & leadership/practice & innovation/specific learning difficulties, PGCE (English/geography/history/IT/mathematics/modern languages/PE/Physics/science/secondary/primary/RE, PCET; BSc(Hons), BA(Hons), MSc, MA(Ed), CertEd, MPhil, PhD, EdD

Geography & Environment; www.soton.ac.uk/geography

geography, geology, physical geography, oceanography, applied GIS & remote sensing, city & regional development, river science & management, palaeoecology, geo-information science; BSc(Hons), BA(Hons), MA, MSc, MPhil, PhD

School of Mathematics; www.soton.ac.uk/maths

mathematical studies, mathematics with actuarial science/astronomy/biology/computer science/economics/finance/management science/music/OR/physics/statistsics, applications in medicine; BSc(Hons), MMath, MSc, PGDip, PhD

School of Psychology; www.southampton.ac.uk/psychology

psychology/& educational studies, companion animal behaviour counselling, health psychology, human animal behaviour; BSc(Hons), MSc, MPhil, PhD

School of Social Sciences; www.southampton.ac.uk/socsci

applied social sciences (anthropology/criminology/psychological studies/accounting, economics, actuarial science, finance, management sciences, politics, contemporary Europe, international relations, sociology, population & geography, philosophy & sociology, social policy, gerontology, international comparative studies, econometrics, citizenship & democracy, intrnational political economy, global politics, governance & policy, demographics, official/social statistics, social work, social policy/research; BSc(Hons)BA(Hons), MEcon, MSc, MPhil, PhD

Southampton Statistical Sciences Research Institute; www.southampton.ac.uk/s3ri;

PhD

STAFFORDSHIRE UNIVERSITY
www.staffs.ac.uk

Staffordshire University Business School; www.staffs.ac.uk/business

accounting, business, business analysis/economics/information systems/management/start-ups/administration/studies, e-business, events management, economics/for business analysis/of international trade & European/international marketing, post-compulsory education, lifelong learning, mentoring & coaching, international supply chain management, entrepreneurship, events management, finance, forensic accounting, strategic/HRM, international business/management marketing/supply chain /management, multimedia marketing, personnel practice, tourism management; BA, BSc, HNC, HND, MA, MBA, MPhil, MSc, PGCert, PGDip, PhD

Faculty of Arts, Media & Design; www.staffs.ac.uk/faculties/art_and_design

advertising/brand design management, animation, 3D design (ceramics, jewellery, interior products), arts media & design, community & participatory arts, design management/product innovation, publication design, surface pattern/product/transport design, comic arts, fine art (digital media, photography, video, theory), illustration, interior design, visual effects, journalism, product innovation/publication/transport design, international history/policy & diplomacy/relations, regeneration, media management, transnational organized crime

film, TV & radio studies/documentary, film production/practice & theory/visual cultures, media studies, leisure industries, scriptwriting, sports PR, children & family work, creative writing, crime, deviance & society/security

drama, performance & theatre arts, English/literature, history, international history/relations/diplomacy, literature & contemporary culture, philiosophy, school, youth & community work, practical theology, sociology, theatre studies & tech stage production/design, digital media production, drama, performance & theatre arts; BA, FdA, MA, MFA, MPhil, MSc, PhD

Faculty of Computing, Engineering & Technology; www.staffs.ac.uk/faculties/comp_eng_tech

3D games modelling, aeronautical technology, automotive electronics/engineering, autosport engineering, broadcast engineering, business computing, information technology, computer game design/development, digital feature film production,3D games technology, electrical/electronic/electronic & broadcast engineering, environmental engineering, film production technology, mathematics & applied statistics, mechanical engineering, mechatronics, medical engineering/devices, motorsport technology, music technology, network computing/engineering/ systems management, product design engineering/ technology, robotics,telecommunications engineering; BA, BEng, BSc, FdSc, HND, MEng, MSc, MPhil, MRes, PGCE, PGCert, PGDip, PhD

Faculty of Health; www.staffs.ac.uk/ faculties/health

ageing/dementia, mental health, clinical practice/ biomechanics, diabetes, pain management, health management & policy/social care, hypnosis & stress, major incident medical management, medical education, midwifery practice, nursing practice: adult / children's /district nursing/mental health/specialist / clinical practice (public health – health visiting) nursing, leadership, operating dept practice, palliative & end of life care, paramedic science, perioperative care, professional practice specialist community public health nursing, social care/work; BSc, MA, MPhil, MSc, PGCE, PGCert, PGDip, PhD

Faculty of Sciences; www.staffs.ac.uk/ faculties/sciences

animal biology & conservation, applied sport & exercise psychology, biochemistry & microbiology, biology, biomedical science, clinical psychology, counselling, child development, criminology, early childhood studies, environment & sustainability, environmental conservation/forensics/management & protection, forensic biology/investigation/psychology/science, geography, governanace, habitat creation & management, health psychology, human biology, molecular biology, policing & criminal investigation, psychology, sport & exercise psychology, sustainable communities dev, teaching psychology, BA, BSc, DClinPsy, DHealthPsy, FdSc, MA, MSc, MPhil, PGCert, PGDip, PhD

Law School; www.staffs.ac.u/faculties/ law

business law, criminology, environmental/family/ employment/international trade & commerce law, human rights law, law, legal practice, international/ sports law, healthcare & ethics; LLB, LLM, MPhil, PhD

UNIVERSITY OF STIRLING
www.external.stir.ac.uk

Schoool of Applied Social Science; www.dass.stir.ac.uk

child welfare & protection, criminology, crime & justice, dementia & gerontology, governance, participation, inclusion, social policy/work, adult services support & protection, social surveys/statistics, Scottish addiction surveys, sociology; BA, GradCert, MSc, PGCert, PGDip, PhD

School of Arts & Humanities; www.stir.ac.uk/schools/arts-and-humanities

Dept of English Studies; www.english.stir.ac.uk

English studies, creative writing, the Gothic imagination, humanities, modern Scottish writing, postcolonial studies, international publishing management, publishing studies, Renaissance studies; BA, MLitt, MPhil, MRes, MSc, PhD

Dept of Film, Media & Journalism; www.fmj.stir.ac.uk

film & media studies, financial journalism, global cinema, journalism studies, media & culture/management, public communications management, PR; BA, MLitt, MPhil, MSc, PGDip, PhD

History & Politics; www.historyandpolitics.stir.ac.uk

History: environmental history, Scottish/medieval/ history, American revolution, 18th-century British/ European/African/urban history, history of medicine; Politics; international conflict & cooperation, European social democracy & public policy, Eurasian geopolitics, modern British party politics, devolution & Scottish politics; BA(Hons), MSc, MRes, MA, Dphil, PhD

School of Languages, Culture and Regions; www.slcr.stir.ac.uk

hermeneutics, humanities, French/Spanish & Latin American, translation studies, TESOL, film studies, global cinema, religion; BA, MLitt, MRes, PhD

Dept of Philosophy; www.philosophy.stir.ac.uk

philosophy, logic & language, legal, moral & social, epistemology & philiosophy of mind, history of early analytics; BA, MLitt, MPhil, PhD

Stirling Law School; www.law.stir.ac.uk

business/commercial law, law; BA, LLB, LLM, PhD

School of Education; www.ioe.stir.ac.uk

Initial teacher education (primary), tertiary education (TQFE/TQAE), sports studies, PE, professional education, English language teaching, EFL, creativity/ leadership, applied linguistics, computer-assisted language learning, international policing, professional enquiry, TESOL; BA, BSc, EdD, MEd, MPhil, MRes, MSc, PGCert/Dip, PhD,UnivCert

School of Natural Sciences; www.stir/ schools/natural-sciences

Institute of Aquaculture; www.aqua.stir.ac.uk

aquaculture & the environment/development/business management/nutrition/systems, aquatic veterinary studies/pathobiology/biotechnology, marine biology, sustainable aquaculture; BSc, MPhil, MSc, PGCert, PGDip, PhD

School of Biological & Environmental Sciences; www.sbes.stir.ac.uk

animal/cell/conservation biology, conservation biology & management, ecology, environmental geography/history/ management/science & outdoor education, river basin management, sports & exercise science; BSc, MPhil, MRes, MSc, PGCert, PGDip, PhD

Dept of Computing Science & Mathematics; www.cs.stir.ac.uk

advanced/business, computing for financial markets, IT, mathematics & its applications; BSc, MSc, PhD, MBA

Dept of Psychology; www.psychology.stir.ac.uk

child development: evolution & behaviour, health psychology, psychology, psychological research, therapy in primary care, measuring perception, psychology of faces; BA, BSc, MSc, PGDip, PhD

School of Nursing & Midwifery & Health; www.nm.stir.ac.uk

advanced/professional practice, dermatology, non-medical prescribing, health studies/research, midwifery, nursing (adult, mental health), supporting self-care; BM, BN, BSc, DAHP, DM, DN, MPhil, MRes, MSc, PGDip, PhD, DipHE

School of Sport; www.sports.stir.ac.uk

sport & exercise science, sports coaching/management/studies, physical education & professional education;BA,BSc,MPjhil,MSc, PGDip,PhD

Stirling Management School; www.management.stir.ac.uk

Accounting & Finance Division

accountancy, finance, international accounting & finance, investment analysis

Business & Marketing Division

business & management, business studies, HRM, international business, marketing, management science

Division of Economics

money, banking & finance, economics, energy management; BA, BSc, MBA, MSc, PhD, BAcc, MPhil, PGDip, MBA, MRes

Institute for People-centred Healthcare Management;

PhD

Institute for Retail Studies;

retail studies; PhD

Institute for Social Marketing;

PhD

Institute for Socio-management;

PhD

STOCKPORT COLLEGE
www.stockport.ac.uk

access to HE, art, design, media, building/ services/ constructions & civil eng, business & IT technology/ management/marketing, childcare, early childhood studies, photography, computing, illustration, surface design, graphic design/illustration/moving image/ surface design, engineering, forensic science, graphic communication, photography, social work/counselling, health & social care; BA, FdA, FDSc

UNIVERSITY OF STRATHCLYDE
www.strath.ac.uk

Strathclyde Business School; www.strath.ac.uk/business

Undergraduate Courses:
accounting, business, international business/& moderrn languages, business enterprise, business technology, economics, finance, hospitality & tourism, HRM, management, marketing, business law
Postgraduate Courses:
business information technology systems, business analysis & consulting, business & management, economic management & policy, finance, HRM, international accounting & finance/banking/hospitality & management tourist management/management/marketing, investement, marketing, business administration, operational research, procurement management
BA, MSc, MBA, DBA, MPhil, PhD, MRes, PGCert/ Dip, MBM

Faculty of Engineering; www.strath.ac.uk/engineering

Dept of Architecture; www.strath.ac.uk/ architecture

architecture, adv architectural design/studies, lean design practice & management, urban design; MArch, MRes, MSc, PGCert, PGDip

Bioengineering Unit; www.strath.ac.uk/ bioeng

bioengineering, medical devices, biomedical engineering, medical technology; EngD, MPhil, MRes, MSc, PGCert, PGDip, PhD

Dept of Chemical & Process Engineering; www.strath.ac.uk/chemeng

chemical engineering, chemical processing, chemical/ process & technology management; BEng, MEng, MSc, PGCert, PGDip

Dept of Civil Engineering; www.strath.ac.uk/civeng

architectural/civil/environmental engineering, forensics/health/science/studies, environmental management/health forensics, geotechnics, global water sustainability, hydrogeology; BEng, BSc, MEng, MPhil, MRes, MSc, PhD

Dept of Design, Manufacture & Engineering Management; www.strath.ac.uk/dmen

computer-aided engineering design, digital creativity, engineering design, global innovation management, integrated product development, management of competitive manufacturing, mechatronics & automation, operations management in engineering, product design engineering/design & innovation, production engineering & management, sports engineering, supply chain & ops management, management; BEng, BSc, MEng, MSc, PGCert, PGDip

Dept of Electronic & Electrical Engineering; www.strath.ac.uk/eee

communications, computer & electronic systems, control & digital processing systems, digital multimedia & communication systems, electrical energy systems, electrical & mechanical/ electrical power/ electronic engineering, electronic & digital systems; BEng, MEng, MSc, PGCert, PGDip

Dept of Mechanical Engineering; www.strath.ac.uk/mecheng

aero-mechanical/enviro-mechanical/mechanical engineering, power plant engineering/technologies, sustainable engineering: renewable energy systems & the environment, materials engineering; BEng, MEng, MPhil, PGCert, PGDip, PhD

Dept of Naval Architectural & Marine Engineering; www.strath.ac.uk/na-me

marine engineering/technology, naval architecture, with marine engineering/ocean engineering/small craft engineering, subsea engineering, offshore renewable energy/floating systems, technical ship management; BEng, MEng, MPhil, MSc, PGCert, PGDip, PhD

National Centre for Prosthetics & Orthotics; www.strath.ac.uk/prosthetics

prosthetics & orthotics, rehabilitation studies; BSc, MPhil, MSc, PGCert, PGDip, PhD

Faculty of Humanities & Social Sciences; www.strath.ac.uk/humanities

School of Applied Social Sciences; www.strath.ac.uk/humanities/school of appliedsocialsciences

community education, adv professional studies, human/ geography, social work/management, residential child/community care, mental health officer social work, sociology, social research, refugee & migration studies, investigatory journalism, media & communication; BA(Hons), Cert,MPhil,PhD,MSc,MRes,MLitt

School of Education; www.strath.ac.uk/humanities/schoolofeducation

autism, childhood practice, early childhood studies, education & social services, maths recovery, applied educational research, educational support, management & leadership in education, philosophy with children, school leadership & management, PGCE(-primary,secondary), supporting bilingual learners; BA, BSc, EdD, BEd, MSc, PGCE,PGCert, MEd, MPhil, PGDE, PGDip, PhD

School of Government & Public Policy; www.strath.ac.uk/humanities/schoolofgovermentand publicpolicy

European/international public policy, political research, politics, public policy; BA, MSc, PhD

School of Humanities; www.strath.ac.uk/humanities/schoolofhumanities

creative writing, English language teaching, English studies, history (Scottish, British, international, history of health & medicine), French, Spanish, Italian, journalism, music, teacher training; MA, MLitt, MPhil, MRes, PGDip/Cert, PhD

School of Law; www.strath.ac.uk/humanities/lawschool

law, construction law, criminology & criminal justice, human rights law, international economic law, international law & sustainable development, IT & telecommunications law, mediation & conflict resolution, Scots law; BA, LLB, LLM, PGCert, PGDip

School of Psychological Science & Health; www.strath.ac.uk/humanities/schoolofpsychologicalsciencehealth

psychology,sport & physical activity, speech & language pathology, educational psychology, counselling; BA,BSc, MRes, DEdPsy, PGCert/Dip, MCounselling

Faculty of Science; www.strath.ac.uk/science

Dept of Pure & Applied Chemistry; www.chem.strath.ac.uk

applied chemistry, analytical/organic/inorganic/physical/bioorganic chemistry, chemical engineering, chemistry, drug discovery, forensic chemistry/science; BSc, MChem, MSc, PGDip, PhD

Dept of Pure & Applied Chemistry; www.chem.strath.ac.uk

applied chemistry, analytical/organic/inorganic/physical/bioorganic chemistry, chemical engineering, drug discovery, forensic chemistry/science; BSc, MChem, MSc, PGDip, PhD

Dept of Computer & Information Sciences; www.strath.ac.uk/cis

automated planning for autonomous systems, business information systems, computer & electronic systems, adv/computer science, information & library studies, software engineering; BEng, BSc, MEng, MPhil, MRes, MSc, PGCert, PGDip

Dept of Mathematics & Statistics; www.mathstat.strath.ac.uk

mathematics (business/science/engineering based), mathematics & computer science/physics/statistics, acccounting/economics/finance/management science/teaching; BSc, MSc, PhD

Dept of Physics; www.strath.ac.uk/physics
nano science, optics, plasma, physics, physics with teaching; BSc, MPhys, MSc, PhD

Strathclyde Institute of Pharmacy & Biomedical Sciences; www.strath.ac.uk/sipbs
biochemistry, immunology, formulation & drug delivery, microbiology, biological/biomedical sciences,medicinal chemistry, microbiology, forensic biology, clinical pharamacy, physiology/& pharmacology, pharmaceutical analysis/practice/quality; BSc, MPharm, MPhil, MSc, PGCert, PGDip, PhD

UNIVERSITY CAMPUS SUFFOLK
www.ucs.ac.uk

School of Arts & Humanities; www.ucs.ac.uk/study/SchoolsAndCentres/SchoolOfArtsAndHumanities
computer games design, creative music, dance, graphic & typographic design, English, history, local & community history, fashion & textiles, film, fine art, football development & coaching, graphic communication/design/illustration/motion graphics, history, interior architectural design, landscape & garden design, music production, photographic & digital media, visual media ; BA, FdA, MA, PGCert, PGDip

School of Health, Science & Social Care; www.ucs.ac.uk/study/SchoolsAndCentres/SchoolOfHealthScienceAndSocialCare
animal science & welfare, applied computing, architectural technology, building control/services engineering/surveying, civil engineering, clinical practice, computing, construction management, counselling, English, event management, electrical/electronic/mechanical/operations engineering, holistic therapies, hospitality, health & social care, nutrition & human health, photography, operating department practice, person-centred counselling, personal training, sports massage therapy, social care practice, social work, specialist community public health nursing; FdA, FdSc, MA, PGCert, PGDip

School of Nursing & Midwifery; www.ucs.ac.uk/study/SchoolsAndCentres/SchoolOfArtsAndHumanities/events/events
adult/child health/mental health nursing, health administration, health & wellbeing, health care practice, diagnostic imaging, radiotherapy, oncology, public health practice; BSc, DipHE, FdA, FdSc

School of Social Science & Business; www.ucs.ac.uk/study/SchoolsAndCentres/SchoolOfSocialScienceAndBusiness
business administration/management, children's care, criminology, youth studies, employment law, event management, HR strategy, leadership, leisure/tourism management, network & communication technologies, personnel management, psychology & business management/sociology BA, BSc, CertEd, FdA, FdSc, GradCert, MA, MBA, PGCert, PGDip

UNIVERSITY OF SUNDERLAND
www.sunderland.ac.uk

Faculty of Applied Sciences; www.sunderland.ac.uk/faculties/apsc

Dept of Computing, Engineering & Technology; www.sunderland.ac.uk/faculties/apsc/ourfaculty/ourdeparts/cet
applied business/network computing, mechanical/manufacturing eng, automotive/electronic & electrical/ manufacturing/mechanical engineering, business computing, telecommunications engineering, computer systems engineering/forensics/science, games software development, health information management, information & communications management, IT management, network systems/computing, performance improvement/management, operations management, project management, renewable energy

eng, software engineering/enterprise, telecommunications engineering; BA, BEng, BSc, FdSc, MSc

Dept of Pharmacy, Health & Well-being; www.sunderland.ac.uk/faculties/apsc/ourfaculty/ourdepartments/phw

advanced clinical practice, biomedical sciences, biotechnology, biopharmaceutical science, changing health behaviour, community health, clinical pharmacy/prescribing sciences/physiology, cognitive behavioural therapy, diabetes management, environmental/health & safety management/technology/training/drug & alcohol studies, substance misuse, hea lth & social care, health promotion, independant prescribing, mentorship, public health, nursing, pharmacological science, medicines management, pharmacy; BA, BSc, FdA, MPharm, MSc, PGCE, Univ Dip, PGDip

Dept of Psychology; www.sunderland.ac.uk/faculties/apsc/ourfaculty/ourdepartments/psychology

counselling, psychology, sport & exercise psychology; BA, FdA, MA, MSc

Dept of Sport & Exercise Sciences; www.sunderland.ac.uk/faculties/apsc/ourfaculty/ourdepartments/sport

exercise, health & fitness, sport & exercise development/sciences, sport studies, sports coaching; BA, BSc, FdA MSc

Faculty of Arts, Design & Media; www.sunderland.ac.uk/faculties/adm/

Dept of Arts & Design; www.sunderland.ac.uk/faculties/adm/ourfaculty/ourdepartments/departmentofartsdesign

dance, drama, music,design, fine art, glass & ceramics, photography; BA, BSc, FdA, MA

Dept of Media; www.sunderland.ac.uk/faculties/adm/ourfaculty/ourdepartments/departmentofmedia

media & cultural studies, film, media, & cultural studies, journalism & PR, TV, video & news media; BA, BSc, FdA, MA

Faculty of Business & Law; www.sunderland.ac.uk/faculties/bl

Business & Management: accounting, accountancy, finance, financial management, applied investment/professional pract, business & management/enterprise, HRM, coaching, events/travel management, health & safety man, business admin, sports management/education

Law: law, criminology, business law, legal practice, criminal law, human rights, magazine/news journalism

Tourism, Hospitality & Events: international hospitality & tourism management, tourism, events, hospitality, travel; BA,(Hons), BA/BSc, CertHE, FdA, GradDip, LLB, LLM, MA, MBS, MSc, PGDip,MBA

Faculty of Education & Society

Dept of Education; www.sunderland.ac.uk/faculties/es/ourfaculty/ourdepartments/departmentofeducation

advanced professional practice (secondary, advanced pedagogy, children's literature, independant distance learning, primary education, professional learning & guidance/teaching & education, PGCE secondary (various subjects)/primary (5-11), special needs & inclusive education, teaching & learning in HE/ with ICT, TESOL; BA, BSc, MA, PGCE

Dept of Culture; www.sunderland.ac.uk/faculties/es/ourfaculty/ourdepartments/departmentofculture

contemporary history & politics, British politics, political theory & international affairs, English/creative writing, religious studies, French, German, Spanish, EFL, world literatures; BA, BSc, MA, PGCE

Dept of Social Sciences; www.sunderland.ac.uk/faculties/es/ourfaculty/ourdepartments/departmentofsocialsciences/

family studies, career guidance, childhood studies, community & youth studies, criminology, education & care/curriculum studies, health & social care, interprofessional practice education, social work, sociology, understanding community development; BA, FdA, MA, BA(Hons), BEng(Hons), BSc(Hons), EdEng, FdA, FdSc, LLM, MA, MBA, MSc, PGCE, PGCert

Degrees validated by University of Sunderland offered at:

CITY OF SUNDERLAND COLLEGE
www.citysun.ac.uk

accountancy, art and design, beauty therapy, business administration, business & management, care, catering & hairdressing, childcare, construction, planning & the built environment, counselling & health, education, training & teaching assistants, engineering & motor vehicle, English courses, horticulture, ICT & computing, media & performing arts, science & mathematics

UNIVERSITY OF SURREY
www.surrey.ac.uk

Faculty of Arts & Human Sciences; www2.surrey.ac.uk/fahs/

Dept of Dance, Film & Theatre; www.surrey.ac.uk/dance
dance, cultures, film/theatre studies, creative writing; BA, MA, MPhil, PGDip, PhD

Dept of Economics; www.econ,surrey.ac.uk
finance, economics, energy economics & policy, business/international economics, finance & development; BSc, MSc, PhD

Dept of English; wwwr.english.surrey.ac.uk
communication & international marketing, English literature, creative writing, intercultural communication with international business; BA, MA, MPhil, PGDip, PhD

Dept of Languages & Translation Studies; www.surrey.ac.uk/languages
audiovisual translation, French/German/Spanish, business translation, international communication, interpreting, monolingual subtitles & audio description, public service translation; BA, BSc, MA, MSc, PGDip

Dept of Music & Sound Recording; www.surrey.ac.uk/music
creative music technology, music, music & sound recording, musicology; BMus, BSc, MMus, MPhil, MRes, PGDip, PhD

Dept of Political, International & Policy Studies; www2.surrey.ac.uk/politics
European politics/business & law, international politics & languages, international intervention; BA, LLB, MA, MPhil, PhD

Dept of Psychology; www.psy.surrey.ac.uk
applied psychology & sociology, clinical/environmental/forensic/health/occupational & organizational/social psychology, psychology, subversion & consultation, psychological intervention; BSc, MSc, PhD, PsychD

Dept of Sociology; www.soc.surrey.ac.uk
criminology, criminal justice & social research, media studies, social research methods, sociology; BSc, MSc, PhD

Faculty of Engineering & Physical Sciences; www.surrey.ac.uk/feps

Dept of Computing; www2,surrey.ac.uk/computing
computer science/& engineering, computing & information technology, information systems, internet computing, security technologies & applications; BSc, MSc, PhD

Dept of Electronic Engineering; www.ee.surrey.ac.uk
communications/satellite communications engineering/networks & software, electronics/& computer engineering, satellite engineering, media engineering, medical imaging, microwave engineering, & wireless subsystems, mobile & satellite communication, mobile communication systems, multimedia technology & systems, nanotechnology & nanoelectronic devices, signal processing & machine intelligence, space technology & planetary exploration; BEng, MEng, MPhil, MSc, PhD

Dept of Mathematics; www.maths.surrey.ac.uk
financial mathematics, statistics, mathematics; BSc, MMath, MSc, PhD

Dept of Physics; www.surrey.ac.uk/physics
medical physics/imaging, physics, nuclear astrophysics, satellite technology, radiation detection & instrumentation, radiation & environmental protection; BSc, MSc, MPhys

Division of Civil, Chemical & Environmental Engineering; www.surrey.ac.uk/cce
chemical engineering, bio-systems engineering, civil engineering, information & process/business systems engineering, process & environmental systems engineering, renewable energy, petroleum refining, bridge engineering, structural engineering, water & environmental engineering, corporate environmental management, enviromental strategy, sustainable development, transport planning & practice, water regulation & management; BEng, MEng, MSc, PGCert, PGDip

Division of Mechanical, Medical, & Aerospace Engineering; www.surrey.ac.uk/mma
advanced materials, aerospace/mechanical engineering, biomedical/medical engineering; BEng, MEng, MSc, PGCert, PGDip

Faculty of Health & Medical Sciences; www2.surrey.ac.uk/fhms

Division of Biochemical Sciences; www2.surrey.ac.uk/biochem
applied/genetic toxicology, biochemistry, clinical biochemistry/pharmacology, toxicology; BSc, MSc

Division of Chemical Sciences; www2.surrey.ac.uk/chemistry
chemistry/with forensic investigation, medicinal chemistry, drug discovery; BSc, MChem, MRes, MSc, PGDip, PhD

Division of Health & Social Care; www2.surrey.ac.uk/healthandsocialcare
advanced/clinical practice, health & social care, learning & teaching for professional practice, mental health (primary care), midwifery studies, nursing studies: adult/child/mental health nursing, operating department practice, paramedic practice, public health practice; BSc, DipHE, MSc, PGCert/Dip, PhD,DClinPract

Division of Microbial Sciences; www2.surrey.ac.uk/microbial
applied toxicology, biomedical science, clinical/biochemistry, food science, medical/microbiology, veterinary biosciences; BSc, MSc

Division of Nutritional Sciences; www.surrey.ac.uk/nutrition
nutrition, food science, dietetics, nutritional medicine; BSc, MSc, PGCert, PGDip

Faculty of Management & Law; www.surrey.ac.uk/fml

School of Management; www.som.surrey.ac.uk
accounting & finance, business & retail management, entrepreneurship, finance, food management, HRM, international business/financial management event/tourism management, hotel operations & logistics management, international retail management/hospitality & tourism, tourism development/management/marketing; BSc, DBA, MBA, MSc, PhD

School of Law; www2.surrey.ac.uk/law
employment/environmental law, health/European/international/international commercial law, justice, criminology, international studies; LLB, LLM, MA, PhD

Degrees validated by the University of Surrey offered at:

FARNBOROUGH COLLEGE OF TECHNOLOGY
www.farn-ct.ac.uk

accounting, aeronautical engineering, business management, childcare, complementary medicine, computing with gaming/networking, education early childhood/years/learning support/lifelong learning, electrical/electronic engineering, graphic design, holistic therapies, hospitality management, media/music prodn, motorsport engineering, multimedia, photography, public service (uniformed), software engineering, sports tourism & event management; BA, BSc, FdA, FdSc

NESCOT (NORTH EAST SURREY COLLEGE OF TECHNOLOGY)
www.nescot.ac.uk

acoustics & noise control, biomedical science, business management, counselling, health & social care, computing & IT, complementary therapies, early years, music technology, osteopathy, performing arts, photography, perfusion sci, sports therapy, teachier training, travel & tourism management; BA(Hons), BSc(Hons), DipHE, FdA, FdSc, HNC, HND, MSc, PGDip

ST MARY'S COLLEGE
www.smuc.ac.uk

applied linguistics, ELT, sport & exercise physiology, sport psychology, bioethics & medical law, business law, Catholic school leadership, charity management, clinical hypnosis, creative & professional writing, drama, applied theatre, drama & physical theatre, education leading innovation & change/pedagogy & professional values & practice, education & social science, English, employment & corporate law, film, geography, health & exercise, history, culture & belief, international business practice, Irish studies, management studies, media arts, mentoring & coaching, sports/nutrition, physical activity for public health, pastoral theology, philosophy, PE, sport education, physical theatre, PGCE (primary, secondary), psychology, sociology, sport & exercise rehabilitation, sport science/coaching science/journalism, strength & conditioning science, theatre directing, theology & religious studies, tourism; BA, BSc, FdA, LLM, MA, MPhil, MSc, PGCE, PGCert, PGDip, PhD

UNIVERSITY OF SUSSEX
www.sussex.ac.uk

Brighton & Sussex Medical School; www.bsms.sussex.ac.uk

cardiology, clinical education, global health, health or social care, diabetes, leadership & management in health care, medical education, medicine, nephrology, psychiatry, psychopharmacology, public health, surgery, trauma & orthopaedics; MA, MD, MPhil, PGCert, PGDip, PhD

School of Business, Management & Economics; www.sussex.ac.uk/aboutus/schoolsdepartments/bmec

Dept of Business & Management; www.sussex.ac.uk/Units/spru/bams

business admin/finance, international finance/management/marketing/corporate governance, business/economics & management studies, economics, finance, corporate & financial risk management, financial mathematics, HRM, international accounting/finance/management, management & entrepreneurship/finance, managing innovation & projects, marketing & management; BA, BSc, MSc, PGDip, LlB, Mphil, DPhil

Dept of Economics; www.sussex.ac.uk/economics

economics, development economics, international economics, international finance; BA, BSc, GradDip, MSc, MPhil, DPhil

Dept of Science & Technology Policy Research (SPRU); www.sussex.ac.uk/spru

public policies for science, technology & innovation, science & technology policy/for sustainability, technology & innovation management; DPhil, MPhil, MSc

School of Education & Social Work; www.sussex.ac.uk/aboutus/schoolsdepartments/esw

Dept of Education; www.sussex.ac.uk/education

education, working with children & young people, initial teacher education; PGCE 11-18/7-14, international education & development, social research, CPD; BA, MA, PGCE, PGCert/ Dip, EdD, MPhil, DPhil, MSc

Dept of Social Work; www.sussex.ac.uk/socialwork
leadership & management/practice/social work with children, their families & carers, working with children & young people, effective practice/leadership & management in integrated children's services; BA, DPhil, MA, MPhil, MSc, PGCert

School of Engineering & Design; www.sussex.ac.uk/aboutus/schoolsdepartments/engdes
advanced mechanical engineering, aerospace technology, automotive/mechanical engineering, biomedical instrumentation, electrical/electronic/computer engineering, digital communications & embedded systems, product design, satellite communications & space systems; BEng, BSc, DPhil, MEng, MPhil, MSc

School of English; www.sussex.ac.uk/aboutus/schoolsdepartments/english
English language/literature/studies, American studies/literature:critical reading/theatre, drama studies, early modern literature & culture, English literature & culture 1700-1900, literature, film & visual culture, modern & contemporary cuture, sexual dissidence & culture, creative & critical writing, colonial & postcolonial culture, critical thought, literature & philosophy, applied/linguistics; BA, DPhil, MA, MPhil

School of Global Studies; www.sussex.ac.uk/aboutus/schoolsdepartments/global

Dept of Anthropology; www.sussex.ac.uk/anthroplogy
anthropology & cultural studies/ history/modern languages, anthropology & international development/geography/relations, anthropology of development/social transformation; BA, DPhil, MA, MSc

Dept of Geography; www.sussex.ac.uk/geography
geography & international relations/development/modern languages, applied geomorphology, climate change/environment & policy/development, human geography, migration studies, comparative & cross-culture; BA, BSc, DPhil, MA, MPhil, MSc

International Development; www.sussex.ac.uk/devlopment
international development, anthopology, development & social transformation, environmental development & policy, gender & development, globalization, ethnicity and culture, social development, human rights; BA, MA, MPhil, DPhil

Dept of International Relations; www.sussex.ac.uk/ir
conflict, security & development, geopolitics & grand strategy, global political economy, international relations & anthroplogy/ contemporary European studies/modern languages/law/politics/sociology/economics/geograpphy/development, international security; BA, DPhil, MA

School of History, Art History & Philosophy; www.sussex.ac.uk/aboutus/schoolsdepartments/hahp

Dept of American Studies; www.sussex.ac.uk/americanstudies
American literature: critical reading, American studies; BA, MA, MPhil, DPhil

Dept of Art History; www.sussex.ac.uk/arthistory
art history & musem curating/philosophy, cultural studies, film studies; BA, MA, MPhil, DPhil

Dept of History; www.sussex.ac.uk/history
contemporary history, history/& American studies/English/philosophy/sociology, intellectual history, modern European history; BA, MPhil, DPhil, MA

Dept of Philosophy; www.sussex.ac.uk/philosophy:
philosophy, philosophy & cognitive science, aesthetics, analytical/continental philosophy, social & political thought; BA, MA, MPhil, DPhil

School of Informatics; www.sussex.ac.uk/aboutus/schoolsdepartments/informatics
computer science, adv/computing & AI, computing for business & managememt/digital media, evolutionary & adaptive systems, games & multimedia environments, human-centred computer systems, IT with business & management, intelligent systems, music informatics; BA, BSc, DPhil, MA, MComp, MPhil, MSc, PGCert

School of Law, Politics & Sociology; www.sussex.ac.uk/aboutus/schoolsdepartments/lps

Dept of Politics & Contemporary European Studies; www.sussex.ac.uk/polces

contemporary European studies, European politics, politics & international relations/languages/history/law/sociologyphilosophy; BA, DPhil, MPhil

Sussex Law School; www.sussex.ac.uk/law

law, European/family & child /international criminal law, international law/trade law; DPhil, GradDip, LLB, LLM, MPhil, MSc

Dept of Sociology; www.sussex.ac.uk/sociology

sociology with cultural studies/politics/psychology/media studies, gender studies, social sciences; BA, DPhil, MA, MPhil, MSc

School of Mathematical & Physical Sciences; www.sussex.ac.uk/aboutus/schoolsdepartments/mps

Dept of Mathematics; www.sussex.ac.uk/maths

mathematics, corporate & financial risk management, financial mathematics with computer science/economics, scientific computation; BSc, DPhil, MMath, MPhil, MSc

Dept of Physics & Astronomy; www.sussex.ac.uk/physics

astronomy, astrophysics, cosmology, physics, astrophysics, theoretical/particle physics; BSc, DPhil, MPhil, MPhys

School of Life Sciences; www.sussex.ac.uk/aboutus/schoolsdepartments/lifesci

Dept of Biology & Environmental Science; www.sussex.ac.uk/biology

biology, biosciences, cellular & molecular neuroscience, cognitive neuroscience, developmental cell biology, ecology & conservation; BSc, DPhil, MPhil, MSc, PGDip

Dept of Chemistry & Biochemistry; www.sussex.ac.uk/biochemistry

biochemistry, bioinformatics, biological sciences, biomedical science, genetic manipulation & molecular cell biology, molecular genetics, molecular medicine, chemistry, inorganic & bio/organic chemistry, physical & computational chemistry, chemical biology, forensic science; BSc, DPhil, MPhil, MChem, MSc

School of Media, Film & Music; www.sussex.ac.uk/aboutus/schoolsdepartments/mfm

creative media practice, cultural studies, digital documentary/media, film studies, gender & media/cultural studies, media practice/studies, journalism, music, music & sonic media; BA, BSc, DPhil, MA, MPhil, PGDip

School of Psychology; www.sussex.ac.uk/aboutus/schoolsdepartments/psychology

applied social psychology, experimental psychology, clinical psychology & mental health, health psychology, cognitive/ neoroscience, psychological methods, psychology, substance misuse; BSc, MRes, MSc, PGDip

SWANSEA UNIVERSITY
www.swansea.ac.uk

School of Arts & Humanities; www.swansea.ac.uk/artsandhumanities

applied linguistics, classics, English language studies, English literature, finance, French, German, Italian, Spanish, language & communication, Latin, media studies, public & media relations, screen studies, TEFL, translation, Welsh, American studies, ancient Egyptian culture/history, ancient & medieval history, child welfare, childhood studies, classical archaeology/civilization, classics, ancient/economic/social / European history, global politics & intercultural studies, Greek, international communication/relations/security, early modern history, maritime & imperial medieval studies, modern Celtic studies/history, philosophy, politics & economics (PPE), political communications/theory, politics, social history & social policy, social research, war & society; BA, MA, MPhil, MSc, MScEcon, PhD

School of Business & Economics; www.swansea.ac.uk/business

accounting & finance, actuarial studies, business economics/management/with law, economics, finance, financial economics, international business management/management science, management theory & practice/finance/marketing, marketing/management, strategic management; BA, BSc, MBA, MPhil, MSc, MScEcon, PhD

School of Engineering; www.swansea.ac.uk/engineering

aerospace engineering/ chemical engineering, biochemical engineering/bioprocess engineering, computationai engineering/modelling/mechanics, civil engineering, communication systems, electronic & electrical engineering, electronic systems design engineering, environmental engineering/management, information, communication & computer technology, materials engineering/science, mechanical engineering, medical engineering, medical radiation physics, product design, sports science, steel technology, nanomedicine/technology/electronics eng/science, structural materials for gas turbines; BEng, EngD, MEng, MPhil, MRes, MSc

School of the Environment & Society; www.swansea.ac.uk/ environmentsociety

aquatic ecology & conservation, biology, biological sciences, geography, environmental dynamics & climate change,European studies, human/physical geography, geoinformatics, marine biology, physical earth sciences, global migration, sustainable aquaculture & fisheries, zoology; BA, BSc, MA, MPhil, MSc, PhD

School of Health & Human Sciences; www.swansea.ac.uk/ HumanandHealthSciences

adult nursing, audiology, advanced clinical practice/ (infection control/), chronic condition management, clinical physiology with cardiology/respiratory physiology, clinical technology (medical physics), ageing studies, community health studies, applied social studies, health & social care, health care law & ethics/ science/management/informatics, public health/promotion/care, infection prevention & control, medical sciences & humanities, mental health nursing, midwifery, nursing (adult/child/mental health), partnerships in care/specialist community public health nursing, abnormal & clinical psychology, paramedic science, osteopathy, ageing studies, early childhood, developmental & therapeutic play, applied criminal justice & criminology, childhood studies, abnormal & clinical/psychology, social policy/work/studies/history, developmental & therapeutic play, law & criminology; BA, BSc,BMid, BN, DipHE, HND, LLB, MA, MPhil, MSc, MScEcon, PGCert/Dip,PhD

School of Law; www.swansea.ac.uk/law

global legal orders & law, international commercial/ maritime/ trade law, law, law & globalization; GradDip, LLB, LLM, MA, MPhil, PGDip, PhD

School of Medicine; www.swansea.ac.uk/medicine

medical/genetics, medical/biochemistry, trauma surgery, separation science; BSc, MBBCh, MD, MPhil, MSc, PhD

School of Physical Sciences; www.swansea.ac.uk/physical.sciences

applied/pure mathematics, computer science, computer graphics, computing, communications, future interaction technologies, software technology, computing with finance, geoinformatics, logic & computation, information & communications technology), modelling, physics, nanotechnology, particle physics & cosmology, stochastic processes, sports science, theoretical physics, visual computation; BSc, MEng, MMath, MPhil, MPhys, MRes, MSc, PhD

UNIVERSITY OF TEESSIDE
www.tees.ac.uk

School of Arts & Media; www.tees.ac.uk/ schools/sam

broadcast media production, creative writing, dance, design, digital arts, creating theatre, English & cultural studies, European history, fine art, future design, graphic arts/advertising/illustration/multimedia & web publishing), graphical image, history, interior architecture/design, journalism, local &

regional /social & cultural history, mass communication, media studies, modern & contemporary European history, motion graphics, multimedia PA/ journalism/PR, performance & events production, product design, social & cultural history, TV & film production; BA(Hons),BSc(Hons), FdA, MA, MPhil, MSc, PhD

School of Computing; www.tees.ac.uk/ schools/scm

applied/computing, adv computer science, adv management systems, international business IT, IT project management, computer games design/programming/ art, concept art, information & communication technology, animation & games, computer animation/graphics/art, network systems, web & multimedia design, digital animation,creating digital media, digital animation, computing networking, ICT, software development, networks & communication, graphic design (multimedia & web publishing), music technology, web multimedia design/design/ development; BA, BSc, DProf, FdSc, HNC, HND, MA, MPhil, MProf, MSc, PGDip, PhD

School of Health & Social Care; www.tees.ac.uk/schools/soh

adv clinical practice, neurological rehabilitation/ manipulative therapy, muscoskeletal studies, behavioural analysis, cardiac care, clinical psychology, dental hygiene/therapy/nurse practice, diagnostic radiography, evidence-based medicine/practice, forensic radiography, leadership in/managing/health & social care, long-term health conditions, midwifery, public health, nursing studies (adult, child, learning disabilities, mental health,surgery), manipulative therapy, medical ultrasound, occupational therapy, operating dept practice, orthopaedics, physiotherapy, primary care, public health, surgical care, social work; BA, BSc, DipHE, FdSc, HND, MA, MPhil, MSc, PGCert

Science & Engineering; www.tees.ac.uk/ schools/sse

adv manufacturing systems, chemistry, biological sciences, biotechnology, chemical/civil engineering, computer & digital forensics, control & electronics, crime & investigation, crime scene science, disaster management, electrical & electronic engineering, electronics & communications, engineering/management, environmental science/sustainability/technology, food & consumer safety/nutrition & health science, forensic biology/science, instrumentation & control engineering, mechanical engineering, petroleum technology, project management, trading standards & consumer protection; BEng, BSc, FdEng, HNC, HND, MPhil, MRes, MSc, PGDip, PhD

School of Social Sciences & Law; www.tees.ac.uk/schools/ss

counselling & psychology, childhood & youth studies, clinical psychology,criminal investigation/law, criminology with sociology/law/psychology/youth studies/investigation, drug use, early childhood studies, education, forensic psychology, global development, health psychology, human rights, international/criminal law, law, social research methods, social sciences, sociology, sport & exercise (exercise science/sport science/coaching psychology/development/therapy & rehabilitation), teaching in lifelong learning, youth & community studies/criminology/ pychology; BA, BSc, DProf, FdA, FdSc, FdSocSc, GradCert, HNC,CertEd, HND, LLB, LLM, MA, MPhil, MProf, MSc, PhD

Teeside Business School; www.tees.ac.uk/ schools/tubs/

accounting & finance, advertising, applied accountancy, business administration/finance/management,, business with law,coaching for transformational change, financial investigation & crime, fraud management, HRM, international/management, marketing, public services, transport & logistics, travel & tourism/management, leadership & change; BA, BSc, DBA, FdA, FdSc, HND, MA, MBA, MSc, PGDip

THAMES VALLEY UNIVERSITY
www.tvu.ac.uk

Faculty of the Arts; www.tvu.ac.uk/the_university/faculties_and_schools/Faculty_of_the_Arts

London College of Music; www.tvu.ac.uk/music/london college of music

audio technology,ballet, music theatre, theatre production, music (performance & composition), management & artist development, performance/technology, composing concert music, music industry management, record production, pop music; BA, BMus, BSc, DipHE, FdA, FdMus, MA, MMus, PGCert, PGDip

School of Art Design, & Media; www.tvu.ac.uk/artdesign/school_of_art_and_design

digital animation/media production, fashion & textiles, games development (games art/games design), graphic design, new media art & design, photography, digital imaging, web design, advertising, broadcast journalism, broadcasting, media studies, PR, video production & film studies; BA, FdA, MA, DipHE

Faculty of Health & Human Studies; www.tvu.ac.uk/the_university/faculties_and_schools/Faculty_of_Health_and_Human_Sciences

School of Psychology, Social Care & Human Sciences

substance use & misuse studies, nutrition, nutitional therapeutics, counselling theory, food & consumer health, criminology, enhancing professional practice, forensic sciences, health promotion & public health, end of life care, leadership for health & care, psychology & health, nutritional therapeutics, primary health care, psychology, strategic workforce planning, social work/care; BSc, CertHE, DipHE, FdSc, MA, MPhil, MSc, PGCert, PGDip, PhD

School of Nursing & Midwifery

learning disability/adult/child nursing, midwifery, operating dept practice, public health, primary care; BSc, DipHE, MA, MM, MPhil, PGDip, PhD

Faculty of Professional Studies

Business School; www.tvu.ac.uk/businessschool/Business_School.jsp

accounting & finance, business studies, HRM, marketing, management, HRM, international business management/marketing/culinary arts management, corporate communications, logistics management, management studies (health & social care), music management, personnel practice, project management, PR, public service management, purchasing & supply, tourism management; DMS, FdA, GradCert, GradDip, HND, MA, MBA, MPhil, MSc, PGDip, PhD

Ealing Law School; www.tvu.ac.uk/law/Ealing_Law_School.jsp

law, criminology, forensic science/psychology, substance use & misuse, international /business & commercial /banking law, finance law, policing, legal practice; GradDip, LLB, LLM

London School of Hospitality & Tourism; www.tvu.ac.uk/hospitality/London_School_of_Hospitality_and_tourism.jsp

airline & airport management, business travel & tourism, cruise ship management, events management, food & professional cookery, hospitality management, international culinary arts/hotel management, tourism, licensed hospitality, travel & tourism/management; BA, DipHE, FdA, GradCert, HND, MA, MPhil, PGDip, PhD

School of Computing & Technology; www.tvu.ac.uk/computing/School_of_Computing_and_Technology.jsp

computing /science, network & mobile computing, information systems/for business, software engineering, computer interaction design/systems management, library/information management, electronic/electrical engineering, mechanical engineering, mechatronics, microelectronics, power & control, power eng, communications, civil & environmental engineering, construction management, architectural technology, interior architecture, quantity surveying, sustainable design; BSc, FdSc, HND, MSc

TRINITY COLLEGE LONDON
www.trinitycollege.co.uk

dance, drama & speech, music, performing arts, English language, teaching English; PGDip, SfL, TESOL

UNIVERSITY OF ULSTER
www.ulster.ac.uk

Faculty of Art, Design & the Built Environment; www.adbe.ulster.ac.uk

School of Architecture & Design; www.adbe.ulster.ac.uk/schools/archi.design

3D design (interior, product & furniture design), architectural studies/technology & management, architecture, interior design, landscape architecture; BA, BDes, BSc, CertHE, MArch, MLA, MSc

School of Art & Design; www.adbe.ulster.ac.uk/schools/art.design

art & design, art in public, design for visual communication, fine & applied arts, fine art, interactive multimedia design, photography, textile material product, textiles & fashion design; BA, BDes, BSc, MA, MDes, MFA, PGDip

School of the Built Environment; www.adbe.ulster.ac.uk/schools/built.environment

building engineering & materials, building services & energy engineering, building surveying, civil engineering, construction engineering/business project management, energy & building services engineering, environmental health, fire safety engineering, housing management/studies, hydrogen safety engineering, infrastructure engineering, occupational therapy, property investment & development/ planning, quantity surveying & commercial management, renewable engineering & energy management, transportation; BEng, BSc, MEng, MPhil, MSc, PGCert, PGDip, PhD

Faculty of Arts; www.arts.ulster.ac.uk

dance, design & communication, drama, music, American studies, English, history, Irish/history & politics, international politics, Irish literature in English, European studies, film studies, French, German, Spanish, Irish, Chinese, documentary practice, film & TV management & policy, interactive media arts, design/communication, journalism,media studies/& production, photo-imaging; BA, MA, MPhil, PGDip, PhD, MRes, BMus, MMus, MDes, CertHE

Faculty of Computing & Engineering; www.compeng.ulster.ac.uk

School of Computing & Information Engineering; www.compeng.ulster.ac.uk/cie

computing, computing artificial intelligence/digital games development/internet systems, financial engineering, telecommunications & internet systems; jt degrees; BSc, MSc, PGDip, PhD

School of Computing & Intelligent Systems; www.scis.ulster.ac.uk

computer games development/science, computing & creative technologies/e-business/intelligent systems/financial services, electronics & computer systems, mobile robotics, multimedia computing & design/computer games; BEng, BSc, MSc, PGDip, PhD

School of Computing & Mathematics; www.infj.ulst.ac.uk/cm/

computing & information systems, computing science/ & mathematics, computing/web technology/health informatics/communication/artificial intelligence, information & communication technologies, industrial practice, interactive multimedia design, interactive teaching technologies, software engineering; BSc, MSc, PGCert, PGDip, PhD

School of Engineering; www.seng.ulster.ac.uk/eme

biomedical engineering, clean technology, electronic engineering, communications & software, engineering management, mechanical engineering, mechatronics, sports technology, technology/design, adv composites & polymers, medical electronics, manufacturing management, nanotechnology, sports technology; BSc, BEng, MEng, MSc, PGDip, PhD

Faculty of Life & Health Sciences; www.science.ulster.ac.uk

School of Biomedical Sciences; www.biomed.science.ulster.ac.uk

biology, biomedical science, biotechnology, cataract & refractory studies, dietetics, food regulatory affairs, food & nutrition, forensic & legal medicine, food biotechnology, forensic studies, human nutrition, medical science, optometry, pharmaceutical sciences, pharmacy, veterinary public health; BSc, DMedSc, GradCert, MPharm, MSc, PGCert, PGDip

School of Environmental Sciences; www.science.uster.ac.uk/envsci

coastal zone management, environmental management/science/studies/toxicology & pollution monitoring, GIS, geography, marine science; AB, BSc, DEnvSci, MPhil, MRes, MSc, PGCert, PGDip, PhD

School of Health Sciences; www.science.uster.ac.uk/health

advanced practice, clinical physiology/research, health science, occupational therapy, physiotherapy, podiatry, radiography (diagnostic/therapeutic), speech & language therapy; BSc, MClinRes, MSc

School of Nursing; www.science.ulster.ac.uk/nursing

community & public health nursing, dementia studies, health promotion & population health, health & social care/wellbeing, independent & supplementary prescribing, midwifery, specialist midwifery/nursing practice; BSc, CertHE, MSc, PGCert, PGDip,MPhil,PhD

School of Psychology; www.science.ulster.ac.uk/psychology

applied behaviour analysis, applied psychology (mental health), careers guidance, social/health psychology, psychology; BSc, MSc, PGDip

School of Sports Studies; www.science.ulsportsster.ac.uk

physical activity & population health, sport & exercise sciences, applied sport & exercise psychology, sports management/coaching/studies/technology/development; BSc, FdSc, MPhil, MSc, DPhil, PGDip, PhD

Faculty of Social Sciences; www.socsci.ulster.ac.uk

School of Communication; www.comms.ulster.ac.uk

communication, advertising & marketing, PR, counselling, therapeutic communication, political lobbying, public affairs, language & linguistics, linguistics/ in advertising; BSc, MPhil, MSc, PGCert, PGDip, PhD

School of Economics; www.socsci.ulster.ac.uk/ecompolitics

applied/ business economics, economics, economics with accounting/marketing/politics; BSc, MSc, PGDip

School of Education; www.socsci.ulster.ac.uk/education

PGCE (post-primary, primary, in numerous school subjects), Certificate in Teaching, educational leadership & management, ICT, inclusive & special education, teaching & learning, library & information management, TESOL further & Higher Education; MA, MEd, PGCE, PGCert, PGDip

School of Law; www.socsci.ulster.ac.uk/law

law, human rights law, criminology, human rights & transitional justice; LLB, LLM

School of Criminology, Politics & Social Policy; www.socsci.ulster.ac.uk/policy

criminology & criminal justice, health & social care policy, politics, public administration, social policy, executive development, international studies, procurement executive development; BSc, MPA, PGCert, PGDip

School of Sociology & Applied Social Studies; www.socsci.ulster.ac.uk/sociology

community development/youth work, restorative practices, profession development in /social work, sociology, international politics; BSc, MSc, PGCert, PGDip

Graduate School of Professional Legal Education; www.socsci.ulster.ac.uk/gsple

legal practice; PGDip

Ulster Business School; www.business.ulster.ac.uk

accounting, advertising, agrifood business development, computing, business & management, business administration/development & innovation/improvement/studies, consumer studies, cultural management, executive leadership, event management, financial services, HRM, international business/hospitality management/hotel & tourism management/

travel & tourism management, leisure & events management, management & corporate governance/ leadership, marketing, retail studies, sport management, social enterprise; BSc, CertHE, HND, MBA, MBS, MSc, PGDip

UNIVERSITY OF WALES INSTITUTE, CARDIFF
www.uwic.ac.uk

Cardiff School of Art & Design; www.csad.uwic.ac.uk

advanced/product design, architectural design & technology, art & design/communication, ceramics, environmental change & practice: building, fine art, textiles, graphic communication, illustration, interior architecture, product design, music production & technology, photographic practice, sonic arts; BA, BSc, HNC, HND, MA, MFA, MPhil, MSc, MDes,PG-Cert, PhD

Cardiff School of Education; www3.uwic.ac.uk/English/education

Dept of Humanities; www3.uwic.ac.uk/ English/education/humanities

educational studies, early childhood studies, English, psychology, sport & physical activity, Welsh, creative writing, drama, contemporary media; BA, MA, PGCert, PGDip

Dept of Professional Development; www3.uwic.ac.uk/English/education/ profdevelopment

education, management in the community professions, youth & community education, preparing to teach, learning support; BA, MA, MPhil, MSc, PhD, CertEd, FdD,PGCE

Dept of Teacher Education & Training; www3.uwic.ac.uk/English/education/ teachedu

initial teacher training, PGCE (primary, secondary), music, Welsh, French; BA, PGCE

Cardiff School of Health Sciences; www3.uwic.ac.uk/English/health

Centre for Applied Social Sciences; www3.uwic.ac.uk/English/health/ass

health & social care, housing: policy & practice/ supported housing, youth & communities, management in the community professions, health & social science res/science, social work; BA, BSc, FdSc, GradCert, GradDip, HNC, HND, MRes, MSc PGCert, PGDip

Centre for Biomedical Science; www3.uwic.ac.uk/English/health/cbs

, applied/biomedical sciences, sports biomedicine & nutrition; BSc, FdSc, HNC, HND, MSc, PGCert/Dip

Centre for Complementary Therapies; www3.uwic.ac.uk/English/health/cct

complementary therapies, aromatherapy, reflexology, holistic massage; BSc, Dip/Cert

Centre for Dental Technology; www3.uwic.ac.uk/English/health/cdt

dental technology; BSc, FdSc, MSc, PGCert, PGDip

Centre for Nutrition, Dietetics & Food Sciences; www3.uwic.ac.uk/English/ health/cnfc

applied public health, dietetics, food science & technology, human nutrition, public health nutrition, sports biomedicine & management/nutrition, food science & technology/safety management; BSc, FdSc, HNC, MSc, PGDip

Dept of Applied Psychology; www3.uwic.ac.uk/English/health/cp

forensic/health psychology, psychology, BSc, FdSc, MSc

Centre for Public Protection; www3.uwic.ac.uk/English/health/cpp

applied public health, environmental health/risk management, health science, consumer & trading standards, occupational health & safety, waste management; BSc, FdSc, HNC, MSc, PGDip

Centre for Speech & Language Therapy; www3.uwic.ac.uk/English/health/cslt

speech & language therapy; BSc

Wales Centre for Podiatric Studies; www3.uwic.ac.uk/English/health/wcps

musculoskeletal studies, podiatry, therapeutic footware; BSc, MSc, PGCert, PGDip

Cardiff School of Management; www3.uwic.ac.uk/English/management

Business & Management

business administration/studies, business & management, management studies, health sector management, international business management/administration, marketing, product design, project management; BA, HND, MBA, MSc

Accounting, Economics & Finance

accounting, finance, business/economics, financial management, information management, international economics & finance; BA, BSc, FdA, MSc

Computing & Information Systems/& International Studies

business information systems/ technology, software development, information & communication technology management, computing, mobile technology, technology project management, international business management/adminstrtaion; BSc, HNC, HND, MSc

Tourism, Hospitality & Events Management

events management/marketing, international tourism/events hospitality marketing/sports tourism management; BA, FdA, HNC, HND, MSc, PGCert, PGDip

Cardiff School of Sport; www3.uwic.ac.uk/English/sport

dance, performance analysis, physical activity & health, sports coaching/development, sport & exercise science/medicine, sport psychology, PE, sport management/conditioning, rehabilitation & massage; BA(Hons), BSc(Hons), MA, MSc, PGDip/Cert

UNIVERSITY OF WALES: GLYNDWR UNIVERSITY www.newi.ac.uk

Institute forArts, Science & Technology; www.glyndwr.ac.uk/en/UniversityInstitutes/ArtsSienceandTechnology

Institute for Health, Medical Science & Society; www.glyndwr.ac.uk/en/UniversityInstitutes/HealthMedicalScienceandSociety

Creative Industries, Media & Performance

Applied Art: design, applied arts, garden design, art/design practice. Communications Technology; music technology, studio recording & performance technology, TV. Design, Communication & Digital Art; design communication/creative media, digital media design & production. Fine Art. creative computing; computer game development, creative media computing. Journalism & Media; broadcasting, journalism, media communications, screen studies, English, print jouranalism, Theatre, TV & Performance; BA(Hons), BSc(Hons), FdSA, FdSc, CertHE, MA, MPhil, PhD

Natural & Built Environment

residential surveying; ProfCert, MPhil, Phd

Early Childhood Studies

education/families & childhood studies, childhood care & education, learning & development of babies & young children; BA(Hons), FdA

Education

post-compulsory/professional education & training, learning & teaching support, e-learning, theory & practice, professional development in education/HE, teaching of psychology, professional education; BA(Hons), FdA, PGCert, GradCert, ProDoc, MPhil, PhD, MA, MSc

Electrical Engineering

aeronautical & electronic engineering (avionics), automotive electronic technology, electrical & electronic engineering/technology, sound & broadcast engineering, automation, instrumentation & control, renewable energy systems, digital & RF communication systems, adv electronic technology; BEng(Hons), FdEng, HNC/D, MSc, PhD, MPhil, MRes

Computing

applied/computing, computer game development, computer network management & security, creative media computing/technology, information technology support, library & information practice, computer networking/science, creative & digital technology; BSc(Hons), FdEng, MSc, MRes, PhD

Aeronautical & Mechanical Engineering
Aeronautical Engineering: aeronautical & electronic engineering (avionics)/mechanical engineering, aeronautical engineering (manufacture/logistics), aircraft maintenance. Mechanical Engineering: mechanical technology. Performance Car Technology; BEng(Hons), FdEng, HNC/D, MPhil, PhD, MSc, MRes

Health & Medical Sciences
Complementary Medicine; acupuncture, complementary therapies for healthcare. Occupational Health & Safety; occupational health, safety & environmental management, public health, occupational employment risk management. Nursing & Health Care studies (pre reg); nursing (adult/mental health), health & care studies (post reg); community practice, community specialist practice (community children's/district/general practice nursing), health studies, healthcare/& social care leadership & management, specialist community professions, palliative care, pub health nursing (health visiting/occupational health/school nursing), clinical/community practice. counselling/with children & young people, occupational therapy. psychology; psychology/of religion, teaching of psychology; BSc(Hons), FdSc, BN(Hons), Dip/CertHE, MSc, MPhil, PhD, MA, ProfDoc

Humanities & Theology
English: creative writing, history, media communications, screen studies, history, broadcasting, journalism, media communications. history, Welsh language studies, local history. information management; library & information practice, information management. languages; history & Welsh language studies, Welsh translation, languages & language education, English for speakers of other languages. Screen Studies; broadcasting, journalism, screen studies, media communication. Theology; religion & education, psychology of religion; BA(Hons); FdA, FdSc, PhD, MA, DMin, MSc, MPhil

Materials & Analytical Science
forensic science, criminal justice, environmental science; BSc(Hons), FdSc

Management
business accounting/management/marketing/administration, financial management, market, festival & events marketing, accounting, marketing, logistics & operations management, HRM, marketing management; BA(Hons), FdA, HNC, PhD, MPhil, MA, MBA, MSc, ProfDoc

Natural & Built Environment
Built environment; architectural design technology, building studies (construction/maintenance management), estate agency/management, housing studies, sustainable development, housing & sustainable communities, supported housing, regeneration & sustainability, environmental science, horticulture / production management, landscape management/design. Animal Studies & Equestrian Psychology; animal studies, equestrian psychology; BSc(Hons), FdSc

Science & the Environment
polymer science & technology; MRes, MPhil, PhD

Society & Community
Counselling: counselling studies, person-centred & experiential counselling & psychotherapy. Criminal Justice. Social Care; social work, therapeutic childcare, counselling & psychotherapy, counselling children & young people. Social Policy; Social Science. public & social policy. Youth & Community; youth & community work/studies, youth studies; Cer/DiptHE, BA(Hons), FdA, MPhil, PhD, MA, ProfDoc

Social Sciences
MRes, MPhil, PhD

Sport & Exercise Sciences

sport & exercise sciences, sports coaching; BSc(Hons), MRes, MPhil, PhD

Welsh; Welsh translation, history & Welsh language studies, BA(Hons)FdA

UNIVERSITY OF WALES: NEWPORT
www.newport.ac.uk

Newport Business School; www.nbs.newport.ac.uk
accounting & economics/finance/financial management/law/business, building studies, energy management, HRM, law, management, marketing, business leadership/enterprise development/studies, construction engineering, civil engineering, computing, electrical engineering, electronic &

communication engineering, energy management, engineering, fire safety engineering, forensic computing, information security, IT management, mechanical & manufacturing engineering, project management, robotic & intelligent systems engineering, public sector management, strategic management/ marketing, telecommunications with management; BA, BSc, BEng, FdSc, HNC, HND, MBA, MSc

School of Art, Media & Design; www.amd.newport.ac.uk

advertising design, animation, computer games design, creative music practice/sound & music, design by practice, development disorders, documentary film & television/photography, fashion design, film, video, fine art, graphic design, interactive media, performing arts, photographic art, for fashion & advertising, printmaking; BA, MA, MFA

School of Education; www.education.newport.ac.uk

adult literacy/numeracy, applied drama, art psychotherapy, music therapy, autism, child & adolescent mental health, childhood studies, creative & therapeutic arts, creative writing, development disorders, early years, education & ICT, education leadership & management(PCET/health education), history, inclusive education, education studies, English, secondary teaching, learning support (secondary & further education), learning technology, mobility & orientation, post-compulsory education & training(PGCE/adult numeracy/literacy, primary studies with QTS, RE,regional history, rehabilitation (visual impairment), returning & supply teachers, secondary teaching design & technology(QTS)/mathematics/ science, secondary design & technology, SEN specific learning difficulties/ teaching English as an additional language, special educational needs, TESOL,;-TAEL; BA, BSc, FdA, MA, PGCE, PGCert, PGDip, CertHE,Univ Cert

School of Health & Social Sciences; www.hss.newport.ac.uk

business psychology, community health studies, consultative supervision, cognitive behavioural therapy, counselling/studies, criminology & criminal justice, social work, social studies, sports coaching, sports studies/management, working with young people, youth & community work, youth justice; BA, BSc, MA, PGCert, PGDip

UNIVERSITY OF WALES: SWANSEA METROPOLITAN UNIVERSITY www.smu.ac.uk

Faculty of Applied Design & Engineering; www.smu.ac.uk/index.php/potential-students/faculty-of-applied-design-and-engineering

School of Applied Computing; www.smu.ac.uk/index.php/potential-students/faculty-of-applied-design-and-engineering/school-ofapplied-computing

business information technology, computer games development, networks/systems & electronics, computing & information systems/technology, e-commerce, electronic/software engineering, web development; BEng, BSc, HND, MSc

School of Automotive Engineering; www.smu.ac.uk/index.php/potential-students/faculty-of-applied-design-and-engineering/school of automotive engineering

automotive engineering, motorcycle engineering, motorsport engineering & design/technology; BEng, BSc, HND

School of Built & Natural Environment; www.smu.ac.uk/index.php/potential-students/faculty-of-applied-design-and-engineering/school- of-natural-environment

building studies, environmental management, facilities management, project & construction management, quantity surveying; BSc, HNC, HND, MSc

School of Digital Media; www.smu.ac.uk/index.php/potential-students/faculty-of-applied-design-and-engineering/school-of digital-media

3D/computer animation, creative computer games design, interactive digital media, multimedia, music technology; BA, BSc, HND, MA, MSc

School of Industrial Design; www.smu.ac.uk/index.php/potential-students/faculty-of-applied-design-and-engineering/school-of-industrial-design

automotive design, industrial design, product design/& innovation, transportation design; BA, BSc, MA, MSc

School of Logistics & Manufacturing Engineering; www.smu.ac.uk/index.php/potential-students/faculty-of-applied-design-and-engineering/school-of-logistics-a-manufacturing

logistics, lean & agile manufacturing, mechanical & manufacturing engineering, food logistics, motor-sport management, non-destructive testing & evaluation; BSc, BEng, HND, MA, MSc

Welsh School of Architectural Glass; www.smu.ac.uk/index.php/faculty-of-applied-design-a-engineering/welsh-school-of-architectural-glass

architectural glass, stained glass; BA, MA

Faculty of Art & Design; www.smu.ac.uk/index.php/potential-students/faculty-of-art-and-design

School of Contextual Studies & Visual Communication; www.smu.ac.uk/index.php/potential-students/faculty-of-art-and-design/csvc

graphic/design for advertising, general illustration; BA, HND

School of Fine & Applied Arts; www.smu.ac.uk/index.php/potential-students/faculty-of-art-and-design/school-of-fine-a-applied-arts

fine art: ceramics/combined media/painting & drawing/3D & sculpture, contemporary dialogue
photography & video: photography in the arts, photojournalism, documentary video, video,
surface pattern (textiles); surface pattern design (contemporay arts practice/textiles for fashion/for interiors},
visual communication: graphic design, design for-advertising, general illustration; BA, FdA,MA

Faculty of Humanities

Swansea School of Education; www.smu.ac.uk/index.php/faculty-of-humanities/swansea-school-of-education

educational studies, English studies, post-compulsory education & training, primary education, professional development (education & training), learning support, intro to teaching, maths education, PGCE primary/secondary (in numerous subjects), secondary education; BA, MA, FD, MRes,MA,GradDip

School of Performance & Literature; www.smu.ac.uk/index.php/faculty-of-humanities/school-of-performance-a-literatuture

performing arts, drama & counselling, educational studies/psychology,technical theatre; BA, HNC, HND,MPhil,PhD

School of Psychology & Counselling; www.smu.ac.uk/index.php/faculty-of-humanities/school-of-psychology-a-counselling

counselling & educational studies/psychology counselling practice; BA, MPhil, PhD,Dip,PGDip, MA

Faculty of Business & Management; www.smu.ac.uk/faculty-of-businss-and-management

Swansea Business School; www.smu.ac.uk/index.php/faculty-of-humanities/swansea-business-schools

accounting, business & finance, business admin, HRM, financial services, management & leaderhip, marketing management, international business; BA, FdA, GradDip, HND, MA, MA(Ed), MRes, PGCE, MBA

Leisure, Tourism & Sport; events management/sports managementt; BA, HND, MBA, MSc

School of Public Service Leadership; www.smu.ac.uk/index.php/faculty-of-humanities/school-of-public-service-leadership

health & social care, public services; BA, MPhil, PhD

UNIVERSITY OF WALES: TRINITY COLLEGE, CARMARTHEN
www.trinity-cm.ac.uk

Faculty of Arts & Social Sciences; www.trinity-cm.ac.uk/en/facarts

School of Computing, Business & Tourism; www.trinity-cm.ac.uk/en/facarts/schcbt
business information technology, business & management, community development, computing, heritage tourism, information systems management, local history, management (heritage), management/& sustainability, tourism management; BA, BSc, FdA, FdSc, MA, MBA

School of Creative Arts & Humanities; www.trinity-cm.ac.uk/en/facarts/schcah
arts management, creative writing, educational studies, English, film studies, fine art, media studies; BA, MBA

School of Sport, Health & Outdoor Education; www.trinity-cm.ac.uk/en/facarts/schshoe
health & exercise, sports studies, health, nutrition & lifestyle, outdoor/physical education, adventure/outdoor education; BA, MA

School of Theatre & Performance; www.trinity-cm.ac.uk/en/facarts/schtp
acting, drama & education, educational drama, theatre design & production, context & practice, theatre & society; BA, MA

Faculty of Education & Training; www.trinity-cm.ac.uk/en/facedu

School of Education Studies & Social Inclusion; www.trinity-cm.ac.uk/en/facedu/essi
adolescent psychology, additional learning needs, health & social care, social justice, youth, teaching assts, community support, early years education & social inclusion, education studies & English, inclusive studies, primary education studies, psychology, religious studies & social inclusion; BA, BSc, CertHE, DipHE, FdA, GradCert, MA

School of Initial Teacher Education Training; www.trinity-cm.ac.uk/en/facedu/tet
education, primary education, professional development; BA, GradCert, GradDip, MA, PGCEBA

School of Early Years Education; www.trinity-cm.ac.uk/en/facedu/eye
early years education, nursery management, Welsh & bilingual practice, foundation practice; BA, CertHE, MA, PGDip

School of Theology and Religious Studies; www.trinity-cm.ac.uk/en/facedu/trs
religious studies, religion in society, religious education, Christianity & community studies; education studies/social inclusion; BA

UNIVERSITY OF WALES: TRINITY SAINT DAVID
www.trinitysaintdavid..ac.uk

Faculty of Humanities; www.trinitysaintdavid.ac.uk/en/facultyof humanities

School of Archaeology, History & Anthropology
anthropology, applied/archaeology, history, medieval studies, modern historical studies, landscape management & environmental archaeology, ancient history/civilizations, cultural astronomy & astrology, environmental anthropology, social anthropology/archaeology; BA, MA, PhD

School of Cultural Studies
Chinese Studies; creative writing; creative writing & English, creative & script writing; English & creative writing/TEFL, word & the visual imagination; applied philosophy, European philosophy

School of Classics
ancient history/civilizations, classical studies, medieval history, ancient myth & society/narrative literature, classical language & literature, classics, Greek, Latin; BA, MA, MPhil, PhD

Dept of Theology & Religious Studies & Islamic Studies

Arthurian studies, Biblical interpretation, Celtic christianity, church history, divinity, Indian religions, Islamic studies, monastic studies, religious history/studies, systematic & philosophical theology, theology, the world's religions; BA, DMin, DPT, LTh, MA, MMin, MTh

Faculty of Arts & Social Studies; www.trinitysaintdavid.ac.uk/en/facultyofartsand social studies

School of Business

business information technology/management, internet/computing, management & information technology, managing civil society organizations, prof practice, tourism/management, banking finance, social/entrepreneurship, HRM, information security/management, leadership, marketing, professional arts management, heritage tourism, management, technology enhanced learning; BA, MBA, MA, MSc, MPhil, PhD, GradCert, GradDip

School of Creative Arts

art & design, 3D designer maker-craft product, ceramics & jewellery, digital illustration, apparel design & construction, fine art, graphic communication, photography, textiles – art, design, Britsih cinema history, genre film-making; BA(Hons), MPhil, PhD

School of Sport, Health & Outdoor Education

health, nutrition & lifestyle, PE, health & exercise/& sport studies, outdoor education; BA, BSc, MA

School of Theatre & Performance

acting, theatre design & production, drama & education- context & practices, theatre & society; BA, MA

Faculty of Education & Training; www.trinitysaintdavid.ac.uk/en/faculty of educationand training

School of Early Childhood

early years education, nursery management, Welsh & bilingual practice in early years, foundation phase; MA, BA, CertHE, PGDip

School of Initial Training & Education

primary education with QTS, professional development, education; MA, BA, GradDip

School of Welsh & Bilingual Studies

bilingual studies, bilingualism & multilingualism; BA, MA, MPhil, PhD

UNIVERSITY OF WARWICK
www.warwick.ac.uk

Faculty of Arts; www2.warwick.ac.uk/fac/arts

Dept of Classics & Ancient History; www2.warwick.ac.uk/fac/arts/classics

ancient history & classical archaeology, ancient visual & material culture, visual & material culture in ancient Rome, classical civilization/with philosophy, classics, English & Latin literature; BA, MA, MPhil, PhD

Dept of English & Comparative Literary Studies; www2.warwick.ac.uk/fac/arts/english

English literature, creative writing, English & theatre studies, pan-romanticisms, philosophy & literature, writing, translation & transcultural studies; BA, MA, MPhil, PhD

Dept of Film & TV Studies; www2.warwick.ac.uk/fac/arts/film

film & literature/TV studies; BA, MA, MPhil, PhD

Dept of French Studies; www2.warwick.ac.uk/fac/arts/french

English & French, French studies with German/history/international studies/Italian/politics/film/sociology, film, French culture & thought, French & francophone studies; BA, MA, MPhil, PGDip, PhD

Dept of German Studies; www2.warwick.ac.uk/fac/arts/german

English & German literature, German cultural studies, German/German studies with business studies/French/international studies/Italian/Spanish, pan-romanticism, translation,writing & cultural differences; BA, MA, MPhil, PGDip, PhD

Dept of History; www2.warwick.ac.uk/fac/arts/history

history, 18th-century studies, global history, history & culture/politics/sociology, modern European, renaissance & early modern, medieval world, histiography, history of medicine, history, religious & social history, 1500-1700; BA, MA, MPhil, PhD

Dept of History of Art; www2.warwick.ac.uk/fac/arts/arthistory

art history with Italian, history of art/& French, history & business of art & collecting; BA, MA, MPhil, PGDip, PhD

Dept of Italian; www2.warwick.ac.uk/fac/arts/italian

English & Italian literature, Italian/& theatre studies/film studies/international studies Italian culture & communication, Italian studies; BA, MA, MPhil, PGDip, PhD

School of Comparative American Studies; www2.warwick.ac.uk/fac/arts/cas

history, literature & culture of the Americas, history of race in the Americas; BA, MA, PhD

School of Theatre, Performance & Cultural Policy Studies; www2.warwick.ac.uk/fac/arts/Theatre.s

theatre consultancy, international cultural policy & management, creative & media enterprise, global media & communication, theatre & performance studies; BA, MA, MPhil, PhD

Faculty of Medicine; www2.warwick.ac.uk/fac/med

Warwick Medical School

child health, clinical systems improvement, diabetes, emergency care, health sciences, health services management, medical education/leadership, medicine & surgery, occupational health, orthopaedics & trauma, orthodontics, palliative care, philosophy & ethics of/mental health, pre-hospital critical care, primary care, public health, & epidemiology, sexual & reproductive health care, dentistry, implant dentistry, otho/endodontics, restorative dentistry; MBChB, MD, MMedSci, MPhil, MSc, PhD

Faculty of Science; www2.warwick.ac.uk/fac/sci

Dept of Life Sciences; www2.warwick.ac.uk/fac/sci/lifesci

biochemistry, biomedical science, biological sciences, biotechnology, bioprocessing, food science, environmental bioscience in a changing climate, plant bioscience for crop production, sustainable crop production environmental biology, microbiology; BSc, MD, MPhil, MSc, PhD

Dept of Chemistry; www2.warwick.ac.uk/fac/sci/chemistry

analytical science, chemical biology, chemistry, molecular/physical chemistry, chemical physics, materials chemistry, synthetics, theoretical & computational chemistry; BSc, MChem, MSc, PhD

Dept of Computer Science; www2.warwick.ac.uk/fac/sci/dcs

computer & management sciences, cognitive science, computer science/& applications, computing systems, discrete mathematics; BSc, MEng, MPhil, MSc, PhD

School of Engineering; www2.warwick.ac.uk/fac/sci/eng

automotive engineering, biomedical engineering, civil engineering, computer & information engineering, electronic engineering/systems, electronic systems with communications/sensor technology, energy & power electronic systems, engineering/ & business, engineering business management, manufacturing & mechanical engineering/systems, systems engineering, tunnellng & underground space; BEng, BSc, EngD, MPhil, MSc, PhD

Dept of Mathematics/Warwick Mathematics Institute; www2.warwick.ac.uk/fac/sci/maths

financial/interdisciplinary mathematics, mathematics, mathematics & business studies/economics/philosophy/physics/statistics,discrete mathematics; BSc, MMath, MSc, PhD

Dept of Physics; www2.warwick.ac.uk/fac/sci/physics

mathematics & physics, physics/& business studies, Master project options; BSc, MPhys, MSc, PhD

Dept of Psychology; www2.warwick.ac.uk/fac/sci/psych

philosophy with psychology, behavioural, economic & psychological science, clinical applications of psychology, psychology; BSc, MPhil, MSc, PhD

Dept of Statistics; www2.warwick.ac.uk/fac/sci/statistics

statistics, mathematics, financial mathematics; MMathStat, MPhil, MSc, PgDip, PhD

Faculty of Social Studies; www2.warwick.ac.uk/fac/soc

Centre for Applied Linguistics; www2.warwick.ac.uk/fac/soc/al

English language teaching/for young learners/studies & methods, intercultural communication/for business & the professions; EdD, MA, MPhil, PGCert, PGDip, PhD

Dept of Economics; www2.warwick.ac.uk/fac/soc/economics

economics, economics & industrial organization, international financial economics, economics, economics & psychological science, behavioural & economic science; BA, BSc, MSc, PGDip, PhD

Dept of Philosophy; www2.warwick.ac.uk/fac/soc/philosophy

continental philosophy, philosophy, philosophy & literature/maths, philosophy of mind, philosophy, politics & economics; BA, BSc, MA, MPhil, PGDip, PhD

Dept of Politics & International Studies; www2.warwick.ac.uk/fac/soc/pais

politics & international studies/ French/ sociology/ history/economics/international studies, globalization & development, international political economy/politics & East Asia/Europe, international relations/security, politics; BA, MA, MPhil, PhD

Dept of Sociology; www2.warwick.ac.uk/fac/soc/sociology

gender & international development, science, media & public policy, social & political thought, sociology; BA, MA, MPhil, PGDip, PhD

School of Health & Social Studies; www2.warwick.ac.uk/fac/soc/shss

applied social research with health studies, health & social studies, nursing, health care, ethnic relations, social work; MA, MPhil, PGDip, PhD

Warwick Business School; www2.wbs.warwick.ac.uk/fac/soc/

accounting & finance, business & consulting, finance & behavioural science, industrial relations & managing human resources, information systems & management, international business, international & European employment relations, international management, management, organizational analysis, management science & operational research, marketing & strategy, public leadership & management; BA, BSc, MA, MBA, MPA, MPhil, MSc, PGDip, PhD

Warwick Institute of Education; www2.warwick.ac.uk/fac/soc/wie

applied education & training, business & enterprise education,childhood, education & society, early childhood studies, drama & theatre education, educational assessment/leadership & innovation research methods/studies, learning & teaching, mathematics education/subject leadership, religious education, multiagency leadership, teaching advanced mathematics; BA, EdD, FdA, MA, MPhil, MSc, PGCE, PhD

Warwick School of Law; www2.warwick.ac.uk/fac/soc/law

advanced legal studies, European law, international corporate governance & financial regulation, international economic/ development law & human rights, law & business/sociology, socio-legal studies; BA, LLB, LLM, MPhil, PhD, PGCert, PGDip

THE UNIVERSITY OF WESTMINSTER
www.wmin.ac.uk

School of Architecture & the Built Environment; www.westminster.ac.uk/schools/architecture

architectural technology, interior/design architecture, prof practice, global identity & globalization, anti-social behaviour, air transport planning, building engineering/surveying, business management & urban development, business with property, project management, construction project/management, domestic violence studies, housing law & policy/practice, interior design, international planning & sustainability, logistics & supply chain management, property with business/urban development, quantity surveying, real estate development, tourism &

planning, transport planning & management, travel & tourism, conference & events management, urban design/estate management/regeneration, urban & regional planning/sustainable development; BA, BSc, MA, MPhil, MSc, PGCert, PGDip, PhD

School of Electronics & Computer Science; www.westminster.ac.uk/schools/computing

business & information systems, computer games development/science computer software/systems engineering, computer network security, networks & communications, electronic, network & computer engineering, interactive systems, multimedia communications, e-commerce with online databases, electronic engineering, embedded systems, information & knowledge management/quality/systems, interactive multimedia, IT security, media technology, mobile & web computing, software engineering; BEng, BSc, MEng, MPhil, MSc, PhD

School of Law; www.westminster.ac.uk/schools/law

law, commercial/corporate finance law, dispute prevention & resolution, entertainment law, EU law, European legal studies, international & commercial dispute resolution, international commercial/banking /law, legal practice; GradDip, LLB, LLM, LPC

School of Life Sciences; www.westminster.ac.uk/schools/science

applied biomedical science/microbiology & biotechnology, biochemistry, biochemical engineering, biological/biomedical sciences, biotechnology, cellular pathology, Chinese medicine/acupuncture, clinical chemistry, complementary therapies, drug discovery & development, environmental biotechnology, forensic biology, nutritional therapy, public health nutrition, herbal medicine, haematology, human nutrition/micobiology, medical biotechnology/microbiology/molecular biology, genetics, nutrition & exercise science, physiology & pharmacology; BSc, FdSc, MA, MPhil, MSc, PGCert, PhD

School of Media, Arts & Design; www.westminster.ac.uk/schools/media

animation, art & media practice, audio production, ceramics, clinical photography, commercial music, communication/policy, contemporary media practice, fashion /buying/business management/design/merchandise management, film & TV directing/production/theory, global media, graphic information design, illustration, journalism, media, mixed media, fine art, music business management, photography, digital imaging, photojournalism, PR, TV, screenwriting/producing; BA, BMus, BSc, FdA, GradDip, MA, PGDip

School of Social Sciences, Humanities & Languages; www.westminster.ac.uk/schools/humanities

creative writing, cultural studies, English language/literature, linguistics, international relations/global change/security/Europolitics, London studies, TESOL, visual culture, Arabic/studies, bilingual translation, Chinese, conference interpreting, French, German, Russian, Spanish, Asian studies, museums, galleries, translation interpreting, visual culture, politics, global culture, contemporary political theory, cognitive neuroscience, business/health psychology, applied market & social research, modern/history, globalization, criminology, criminal justice, sociology; BA, MA, MPhil, PhD

Westminster Business School; www.westminster.ac.uk/schools/business

accounting, business, business administration/ economics/management/studies, economics. entrepreneurship, finance, health & social care, law, project management, financial management/services, global marketing, HRM/D, information management & finance, international business/marketing/management/development/finance, investment & risk finance, management, marketing communications/management/strategy, purchasing & supply chain management, social work; BA, MA, MBA, MPhil, MSc, PGCert, PhD

THE UNIVERSITY OF WINCHESTER
www.winchester.ac.uk

Faculty of Arts; www.winchester.ac.uk/aboutus/universitystructure/

American studies/literature, creative/critical writing,, English language studies/literature, contemporary literature, digital media, film & cinema technniques, film studies, journalism, media, cultural studies, choreography, dance, contemporary performance,-drama, performance management, popular/devised performance, street arts, theatre & media for development, vocal & choral studies; BA, FdA, MA, PGCert/Dip, PhD

Faculty of Humanities and Social Sciences; www.winchester.ac.uk/aboutus/universitystructure/hss

Dept of Archaeology

archaeology, archaeological practics, ancient & medieval archaeology & art, cultural & heritage & resource management regional and local archaeology

Dept of Theology and Religious Studies

ethics & spirituality, theology & religious studies, Christian theology & ministry, practical theology, rhetoric & rituals of death, orthodox studies

Dept of History

history, regional and local history &/or archaeology, modern, medieval, world history, historical studies

Dept of Psychology

psychological science, child development, cognition, psychology; BA, BSc, MA, MPhil, MRes, MSc, PGCert, PGDip, PhD

Faculty of Education, Health & Social Care; www.winchester.ac.uk/aboutus/universitystructure/Educationhealthsocialcare

educational studies, modern liberal arts, early childhood, learning & teacher education, children's health, social work & community studies, childhood studies, youth & community studies, primary education practice; PGCE secondary (RE), primary ed,with QTS; BA, FdA, MA(Ed), MPhil, PGCE, PhD

Faculty of Business, Law & Sport; www.winchester.ac.uk/?page=9734

Winchester Business School

accounting, finance, enterprise & innovation, economics, logistics, retail, business administration/management, event management, HRM, management, managing contemporary global issues, marketing, politics & global studies, sport, sustainable business; BA, FdA, MBA, MSc, PGCert, PGDip

Dept of Law

law; BA/LLB, LLB

Dept of Sports Studies

sports coaching & development/management/science/studies; BA, BSc, FdA

UNIVERSITY OF WOLVERHAMPTON
www.wlv.ac.uk

School of Applied Sciences; www.wlv.ac.uk/default.aspx?page=6878

animal behaviour & wildlife conservation, applied bioscience/microbiology/biotechnology, biochemistry, biological science, bioinformation, biotechnology, cognitive behaviour therapy, counselling psychology, environmental health/management/technology, forensic science/human identification, genetics, healthcare, human physiology, medical sciences/biotechnology, molecular biology, pharmaceutical science, pharmacology, pharmacy, occupational/psychology; BA, BSc, DBMS, FdSc, GradDip, HND, MPharm, MSc, PGDip

School of Art & Design; www.wlv.ac.uk/default.aspx?page=6963

animation, applied arts, art & design, computer games design, computer science (digital media tech/games development/software engineering), commercial video production, design & applied arts, digital & visual communication, fashion & textiles, film production & studies, fine art, graphic communication, illustration, interior design, photography, product design, video & film production; BA, FdA, HND, MA

School of Education; www.wlv.ac.uk/default.aspx?page=6965

adult numeracy/literacy, childhood & family studies, conductive education, counselling psychology, early years services, primary ed, education studies, learning assistants, TESOL, post-compulsory education, secondary/medical education, PGCE (numerous secondary subjects), early/ primary education, special needs & inclusion studies; BA, EdD, FdA, MA, PGCert, PGDip, PhD

School of Technology; www.wlv.ac.uk/default.aspx?page=24367

advanced technology management, architectural studies, auctioneering & valuation, automotive systems engineering, building surveying/studies, civil engineering, computer science/computing/digital media/games development/software development, environmental engineering, commercial management & quantity surveying, computer-aided design & construction, construction, construction law/management/project management, design technology, engineering design & management, electronics & communications engineering, engineering design management, information technology/management/security/systems, interior architecture & property development, mathematics, mechanical engineering, mechatronics, polymer engineering, product design & innovation, property management, rapid production, sustainable design & manufacture, advanced development & manufacture, real estate, transport & environmental management/infrastructure management; BDes, BEng, BSc, FdSc, HNC, MEng, MSc, PGCert

School of Health & Wellbeing; www.wlv.ac.uk/default.aspx?page=6067

adult /children's/mental health nursing, emergency practitioner, health & social care practice/& well-being, midwifery, specialist community nursing (district/general practice/health/school), nursing studies (acute/cancer/cardiac/older person/critical diabetes/emergency/lymphoedema/mental health/neonatal intensive/opthalmic/ortopaedicpalliative/renal/stroke), specialist social work(adults/children, young people & families), non-medical prescribing, primary healthcare practice, public health nursing (visiting/school nursing), social care & criminology & social justice/deaf studies/social policy/sociology, district nursing; BA, BSc, DipHE, FdA, GradDip, MA, MPH, MSc, PGCert, PGDip

School of Law, Social Sciences & Communications

armed forces, broadcasting & journalism, conflict studies, consumer protection, contemporary media, corporate & financial law, creative & professional writing, criminology & criminal justice, deaf studies, English/language, film studies, French, German, history, international corporate & financial law, interpreting, law, linguistics, media & communication/cultural studies, philosophy, policing, politics, popular culture, practice management, PR, public sector, religious studies, social policy, sociology, voluntary & public sectors: policy & practice, uniformed public services, war studies, world & sign language; BA, FdA, LLB, LLM, MA

School of Sport, Performing Arts & Leisure; www.wlv.ac.uk/default.aspx?page=6970

creative music production/writing, dance science, drama & performance, event & venue management, international hospitality management, music/theatre, popular music/technology/industry practice, sound production, sport & exercise science, sport/tourism management, sports coaching, travel operations management; BA, BSc, FdA, FdSc, MA, MSc

University of Wolverhampton Business School; www.wlv.ac.uk/default.aspx?page=6971

finance, healthcare leadership, HRD/M, information systems & networking, marketing/management, management studies, organizational change, international/ business management; BA, FdA, HND, MA, MBA, PGDip/Cert, MSC

UNIVERSITY COLLEGE WORCESTER
www.worc.ac.uk

Institute of Education; www.worc.ac.uk/departments/661.html

early childhood, education (early years/children/in service), educational management & leadership, HE, improving practice in education, integrated children's service, ICT in education, ITT for teachers in lifelong learning, learning support, teaching & learning English/PGCE (primary, secondary, graduate teacher), retraining to teach, special needs & inclusive education, mentoring & coaching, teaching primary languages; BA, CertHE, FdA, MA, MSc, PGCE, PGCert, PGDip

Institute of Health & Safety; www.worc.ac.uk/departments/659.html

advanced social & health care practice, applied health sciences, business psychology, child & adolescent mental health, dance & movement therapy, drama therapy, health & complementary therapies/social care, learning disabilities, midwifery, nursing studies, nutritional therapy, psycho therapies/intervention, applied/psychology, social welfare/work, sports therapy, substance misuse, young people services, youth & community services; BSc, DipHE, FdA, FdSc, GradDip, MA, MSc, PGCert, PGDip

Institute of Humanities & Creative Arts; www.worc.ac.uk/departments/663.html

American studies, art & design/professional practice, digital media, dance, drama & performance, English language studies/literary studies/literature, politics, film making/studies, fine art practice, history(local, Irish,modern), journalism, media & cultural studies, performance (costume & make-up), politics, sociology, theatre studies, urban & electronic music production, visual arts; BA, HND, MA, MSc

Science & the Environment; www.worc.ac.uk/departments/652.html

animal biology/care science/welfare & management, arboriculture, archaeology & heritage studies, landscape studies/construction, forensic/human biology, garden design,conservation/biology/ecology, environmental conservation/ management/science, human/physical/geography, organic & sustainable/ horticulture, plant science, professional practice, sustainable woodland management, water & environmental management; BSc, FdSc, HNC, HND, MSc, PGCert, PGDip

Institute of Sport & Exercise Science; www.worc.ac.uk/departments/652.html

applied sport science, outdoor adventure leadership & management/education, PE, sport & exercise psychology/science, sports coaching/management/ performance & coaching/therapy/business management; BSc, HND, MSc

Worcester Business School; www.worc.ac.uk/departments/655.html

accountancy, accounting, advertising, business IT/ management, computing, computer game design, economics, entrepreneurship, finance, financial management, hospitality, HRM, innovation, international business, IT for education , leadership, management/ studies, marketing, networks & information security, retail, travel & tourism, service sector management, PR, public services, web design/development; BA, BSc, DMS, GradCert, MBA, MSc

UNIVERSITY OF YORK
www.york.ac.uk

Dept of Archaeology; www.york.ac.uk/depts/arch

archaeology, archaeology of buildings, archaeological information systems, bioarchaeology, coastal & marine/digital/field/landscape/medieval archaeology, conservation studies, cultural heritage management, early prehistory, historic landscape studies, historical archaeology, mesolithic studies, zoo archaeology; BA, BSc, MA, MPhil, MSc, PhD

Dept of Biology; www.york.ac.uk/depts/biol

biology, bioscience technology, biotechnology & microbiology, computational biology, ecology & environmental management, post-genomic biology, genetics, molecular cell biology; BSc, MPhil, MRes, MSc, PhD

Dept of Chemistry; www.york.ac.uk/depts/chemistry

chemistry, chemistry with biological & medicinal chemistry/management & industry/resources & the environment, chemoinformatics, computational biology, green chemistry & sustainable industrial technology; BSc, MChem, MPhil, MSc, PhD

Dept of Computer Science & Engineering; www.cs.york.ac.uk/depts

computer science/with AI/mathematics, computer systems & engineering/embedded systems/business enterprise systems/software engineering, natural computation, gas turbine control, human-centred interactive technologies, information technology, safety critical systems engineering, social media & interactive technology; BEng, BSc, MEng, MMath, MPhil, MSc, PGCert, PGDip

Dept of Economics & Related Studies; www.york.ac.uk/depts/econ

economics, econometrics & finance/economic history/sociology/philosophy/politics, development economics & emerging markets, econometrics, project analysis, finance & investment, health/public/ economics, economic & social policy analysis, finance & investment; BA, BSc, MSc, PGCert, PGDip, PhD

Dept of Educational; www.york.ac.uk/depts/educ

educational studies, language & literature in education, teaching English(young learners/TESOL), PGCE (English, history, maths, foreign languages), global & international citizenship, education for sustainable development, equity issues, language learning & education, science education & learning, sociology & education, teaching studies; BA, MA, MPhil, PhD

Dept of Electronics; www.york.ac.uk/depts/elec

avionics, communications engineering, digital systems engineering/signal processing, digital media systems, electronic engineering, internet & wireless technology, music technology/systems, nanotechnology, communications engineering, computer engineering; BEng, MEng, MSc, MPhil, PhD

Dept of English & Related Literature; www.york.ac.uk/depts/engl

English, English & history/history of art/linguistics/philosophy/politics, English literary studies, film & literature, medieval English/Renaissance literature, modern & contemporary/19th century literature & culture, romantic & sentimental literature 1770 -1830; BA, MA, MPhil, PhD

Dept of Environment; www.york.ac.uk/depts/eeem

environmental economics, marine/environmental management, environmental geography/science, ecology, corporate social responsibilty; BSc, MPhil, MSc, PGDip, PhD

Dept of Health Sciences; www.york.ac.uk/depts/healthsciences

haematopathology, cancer epidemiology, health sciences, public health, cognitive behavioural therapy, midwifery practice, nursing studies (adult/child/learning disability/mental health); BA, BSc, DipHE, MPhil, MSc, PGCert, PGDip, PhD

Dept of History; www.york.ac.uk/depts/hist

history, history with archaeology/economics/English, medieval history, railway studies & transport history, early/modern history, public history; BA, GradCert, MA, MPhil, PhD

Dept of History of Art; www.york.ac.uk/depts/histart

history of art, stained glass conservation & heritage management; BA, MA, MPhil, PhD

Dept of Language & Linguistic Science; www.york.ac.uk/depts/lang

modern languages, linguistics, phonetics & phonology, psycholinguistics, sociolinguistics, French, German, Spanish, syntax & semantics, phonological development, forensic speech science; BA, MA, MPhil, MSc, PhD

York Law School; www.york.ac.uk/depts/law

law, law & society, international corporate & commercial law, international human rights & practice; LLB, LLM, MPhil, PhD

Dept of Mathematics; www.york.ac.uk/depts/maths

mathematics, mathematics with computer science/economics/physics/statistics/modern applications, financial mathematics, mathematical finance; BA, BSc, MMath, MPhil, MRes, MSc, PGCert, PGDip, PhD

Dept of Music; www.york.ac.uk/depts/music

music, community music, music technology; BA, MA, MPhil, PhD

Dept of Philosophy; www.york.ac.uk/depts/phil
philosophy, philosophy of art & literature, practical ethics, PPE, theology & ethics; BA, BSc, GradDip, MA, MPhil, PGCert, PGDip, PhD

Dept of Physics; www.york.ac.uk/depts/physics
physics, physics with astrophysics, theoretical physics, fusion energy; BA, BSc, MMath, MPhil, MPhys, MSc, PhD

Dept of Politics; www.york.ac.uk/depts/poli
conflict, governance & development, history & politics, international political economy/relations, political philosophy, public administration & public policy, PPE, politics/with English/history/international relations/social & political sciences/economics & philosophy, postwar recovery; BA, MA, PGDip, PhD

Dept of Psychology; www.york.ac.uk/depts/psych
cognitive neuroscience, forensic psychology, development disorders of language & cognition, psychology; BSc, MPhil, MRes, MSc, PhD

Dept of Social Policy & Social Work; www.york.ac.uk/depts/spsw
applied social science (children/crime), international development, public administration, public policy & management, social policy, social work, comparative & international social policy; BA, MA, MPhil, MRes, PGCert, PhD,MPA

Dept of Sociology; www.york.ac.uk/depts/soci
sociology /with criminology/economics/education/philosophy/politics/social psychology, social research, social media & management/ interactive technology; BA, MA, MPhil, MSc, PhD

Dept of Theatre, Film & Television; www.york.ac.uk/depts/tft
cinema, TV & society, post-production with visual effects/sound design, theatre, film & TV production, theatre writing, directing & performance; BA, MA, MPhil, MSc, PhD

Hull York Medical School; www.hyma.york.ac.uk
medicine, medical education; BMBS, MD, MPhil, MSc, PGCert, PhD

School of Politics, Economics & Philosophy; www.york.ac.uk/depts/pep
economics, philosophy, politics, development, political economy, public affairs; BA, MA, MRes, PGCert, PhD

York Management School; www.york.ac.uk/depts/management
accounting, business finance & management, management, international business & strategic management, financial management, corporate social responsibilty & environmental management; HRM; BA, BSc, MA, MPhil, MRes, MSc, PhD

YORKSHIRE COAST COLLEGE
www.yorkshirecoastcollege.ac.uk

Higher education
applied digital media, costume, fine art, teacher education; BA, FdA

Part 5

Qualifications Awarded by Professional and Trade Associations

THE FUNCTIONS OF PROFESSIONAL ASSOCIATIONS

Qualifications

Some associations qualify individuals to act in a certain professional capacity. They also try to safeguard high standards of professional conduct. Few associations have complete control over the profession with which they are concerned. Some professions are regulated by the law, and their associations act as the central registration authority. Entry to others is directly controlled by associations that alone award the requisite qualifications. If a profession is required to be registered by the law and is controlled by the representative council, a practitioner found guilty by his or her council of misconduct may be suspended from practice or completely debarred by the removal of his or her name from the register of qualified practitioners. In other professions the consequence of misdemeanour may not be so serious, because the profession does not exercise the same degree of control. The professions registered by statute, and therefore subject to restrictions on entry and loss of either privileges or the right to practise on erasure, are listed in Table 5.1. Certain other professions are closed.

Table 5.1 Professions registered by statute

Profession	Statutory committee controlling professional conduct
Architects	Architects Registration Board
Dentists	General Dental Council
Doctors	General Medical Council
Professions supplementary to medicine: chiropodists; dieticians; medical laboratory technicians; occupational therapists; orthoptists, physiotherapists; radiographers	Health Professions Council
Nurses and midwives	Nursing and Midwifery Council
Opticians	General Optical Council
Patent agents	Chartered Institute of Patent Attorneys
Social workers	General Social Care Council
Teachers	General Teaching Councils for England, Wales, Scotland and Northern Ireland

Study

Some associations give their members an opportunity to keep abreast of a particular discipline or to undertake further study in it. Such associations are especially numerous in medicine, science and applied science. Many qualifying associations also provide an information and study service for their members. Some of the more famous learned societies confer added status upon distinguished practitioners by electing them to membership or honorary membership.

Protection of Members' Interests

Some associations exist mainly to look after the interests of individual practitioners and the group. A small number are directly concerned with negotiations over salary and working conditions.

Qualifying Associations

The principal function of qualifying associations is to examine and qualify people who wish to become practitioners in the field with which they are concerned. As already indicated, some regulate professional conduct and many offer opportunities for further study. Membership is divided into grades, usually classified as corporate and non-corporate. Non-corporate members are those not yet admitted to full membership, mainly students; they are divided from corporate membership by barriers of age and levels of responsibility and experience. The principal requirement for admission to membership is the knowledge and ability to pass the association's exams; candidates may be exempted from the association's exams if they have acceptable alternative qualifications.

Non-Corporate or Affiliated Members

Non-corporate members are those who are as yet unqualified or only partly qualified. They are accorded limited rights and privileges, but may not vote at meetings of the corporate body. Most associations have a student membership grade. Students are those who are preparing for the exams that qualify them for admission to corporate membership. Some associations have licentiate and graduate membership grades, which are senior to the student grade. Graduates are those who have passed the qualifying exams but lack other requirements, such as age and experience, for admission to corporate membership.

Corporate or Full Members

Corporate members are the fully qualified constituent members of incorporated associations. They are accorded full rights and privileges and may vote at meetings of the corporate body. Corporate membership is often divided into two grades: a senior grade of members or fellows and a general grade of associate members or associates.

Honorary Members

Some associations have a special class of honorary members or fellows for distinguished members or individuals who have made an outstanding contribution to the profession in question.

Examinations and Requirements

Professionals normally become corporate members by exam or exemption, with or without additional requirements. Many final professional exams are of degree standard, and a number of professional qualifications are accepted by employers as evidence of competence at operational level. Ongoing professional development is encouraged by most associations to ensure members' skills and knowledge are up to date and relevant.

The transition from the general grade of membership to the senior can be automatic in some associations (for instance, on reaching a prescribed age), but in others the higher grade is reached only after the submission of evidence of research or progress in the profession.

Qualifying exams are usually conducted in two or more stages. The first stage leads to an Intermediate or Part I qualification, the second leads to a Final or Part II or Part III qualification, which is about the standard of a degree.

Gaining Professional Qualifications

Prospective students can study by any of the following means:

- correspondence courses (distance learning and/or online support);
- personal attendance at the schools maintained by some associations (eg the Architectural Association School of Architecture);
- further and higher education institutions.

ACCOUNTANCY

Membership of Professional Institutions and Associations

ASSOCIATION OF ACCOUNTING TECHNICIANS

140 Aldersgate Street
London EC1A 4HY
Tel: 0845 863 0802
Fax: 020 7397 3009
E-mail: aat@aat.org.uk
Website: www.aat.org.uk

AAT is the UK's leading qualification and membership body for accounting professionals. We have over 120,000 members including students, people working in accountancy and self-employed business owners, in more than 90 countries worldwide. Established in 1980 to ensure consistent training and regulation for accounting staff, our qualifications provide a progression route to CIMA, CIPFA, ICAS, ICAEW and ACCA.

MEMBERSHIP
Student Member
Affiliate Member
Full Member (MAAT)
Fellow Member (FMAAT)

QUALIFICATION/EXAMINATIONS
AAT Accounting Qualification
AAT Access Level 1 in accounting
AAT Level 2 Award in Bookkeeping

DESIGNATORY LETTERS
MAAT and FMAAT

ASSOCIATION OF CHARITY INDEPENDENT EXAMINERS

The Gatehouse
White Cross
South Road
Lancaster
Lancashire LA1 4XQ
Tel: 01524 34892
Fax: 01524 34892
E-mail: info@acie.org.uk
Website: www.acie.org.uk

ACIE provides support, training, conferences, resources and qualifications for independent examiners of charity accounts throughout the UK (*subscriptions apply*). Further information at the website; www.acie.org.uk

Registered charity in E&W 1139609 & SC039066. Registered company limited by guarantee 7461134; registered in England at 4-6 Grimshaw St, Burnley BB11 2AZ.

MEMBERSHIP
Associate
Full Member (with category of Licentiate, Member or Fellow)

QUALIFICATION/EXAMINATIONS
Licentiate (Receipts & Payments Accounts only): LCIE
Licentiate (All Accounts): LCIE
Member: MCIE
Fellow: FCIE

DESIGNATORY LETTERS
LCIE, MCIE, FCIE

CHARTERED INSTITUTE OF INTERNAL AUDITORS

13 Abbeville Mews
88 Clapham Park Road
London SW4 7BX
Tel: 020 7498 0101
Fax: 020 7978 2492
E-mail: info@iia.org.uk
Website: www.iia.org.uk

The Chartered Institute of Internal Auditors (IIA) is the only professional body in the UK and Ireland focused exclusively on internal auditing and we are passionate about supporting, promoting and training the professionals who work in it. Every year we help internal auditors at every stage of their career with training, qualifications and technical resources.

MEMBERSHIP
Student Member
Affiliate Member
Voting Member (PIIA, CMIIA)
Head of Internal Audit Service Member
Fellow (FIIA, CFIIA)

QUALIFICATION/EXAMINATIONS
IIA Certificate in Internal Audit and Business Risk (IA Cert)
IIA Diploma in Internal Audit Practice (PIIA)
IIA Advanced Diploma in Internal Auditing and Management (CMIIA)
IT Auditing Certificate

DESIGNATORY LETTERS
IA Cert, PIIA, CMIIA, FIIA, CFIIA

CIMA – THE CHARTERED INSTITUTE OF MANAGEMENT ACCOUNTANTS

26 Chapter Street
London SW1P 4NP
Tel: 020 8849 2251
Fax: 020 8849 2450
E-mail: cima.contact@cimaglobal.com
Website: www.cimaglobal.com

CIMA is the employers' choice when recruiting financially qualified business leaders.

The Chartered Institute of Management Accountants, founded in 1919, is the world's leading and largest professional body of Management Accountants, with 183,000 members and students operating at the heart of business in 168 countries. CIMA works closely with employers and sponsors leading-edge research, constantly updating its qualification, professional experience requirements and continuing professional development to ensure it remains the most relevant international accountancy qualification for business.

MEMBERSHIP
Member
Associate (ACMA)
Fellow (FCMA)

QUALIFICATION/EXAMINATIONS
Certificate in Business Accounting
Chartered Management Accounting Qualification
Certificate in Islamic FInance
Diploma in Islamic Finance

DESIGNATORY LETTERS
ACMA, FCMA

ICAEW (THE INSTITUTE OF CHARTERED ACCOUNTANTS IN ENGLAND AND WALES)

Metropolitan House
321 Avebury Boulevard
Milton Keynes MK9 2FZ
Tel: 01908 248 250
Fax: 01908 248 260
E-mail: careers@icaew.com
Website: icaew.com/careers

ICAEW is a world leader of the accountancy profession, with more than 136,000 members in over 160 countries. Our members work at the highest levels of business, across all industry sectors around the world. Our professional qualification, the ACA, delivers essential knowledge, skills and technical expertise in accountancy and business.

MEMBERSHIP
ACA (Associate of the Institute of Chartered Accountants in England and Wales) FCA (Fellow Chartered Accountant)

QUALIFICATION/EXAMINATIONS
The ACA qualification consists of 15 examined modules in the Professional and Advanced Stages, 450 days of technical work experience, structured training in ethics and initial professional development. It takes between three and five years to complete depending on your entry route to starting your training and students undertake the ACA with an ICAEW authorized training employer. Find out more information at icaew.com/careers
The Certificate in Finance, Accounting and Business (CFAB) consists of the knowledge modules of the ACA qualification. There are no entry requirements in order to start CFAB and it can be studied via distance learning or self-study. Students do not need to be in an ICAEW training agreement in order to study CFAB. Find out more information at icaew.com/cfab

DESIGNATORY LETTERS
ACA, FCA

ICAS

CA House
21 Haymarket Yards
Edinburgh EH12 5BH
Tel: 01313470166
E-mail: catraining@icas.org.uk
Website: www.icas.org.uk

ICAS is the world's first professional accountancy body. It was also the first to adopt the designation 'Chartered Accountant'. We've been training CAs for over 150 years, and are highly regarded throughout the world for the high calibre of our members.

MEMBERSHIP
To qualify as a Chartered Accountant (CA) students must enter into a training contract with an ICAS authorized employer. The CA qualification provides students with a solid grounding in all aspects of business and financial management. Both ICAS and the employer will give the student all the help and

support they need to study and work during training. For further information please see the ICAS website.

QUALIFICATION/EXAMINATIONS

Test of Competence (TC): Financial Accounting, Principles of Auditing and Reporting, Finance, Business Management, Business Law.

Test of Professional Skills (TPS): Taxation, Advanced Finance, Financial Reporting, Assurance and Business Systems.

Test of Professional Expertise (TPE): One multi-disciplinary case study designed to test candidates' ability to apply their theoretical knowledge and practical skills to problems likely to be encountered by the newly qualified accountant. Additional material includes Corporate Planning, Corporate Strategies and Management, Business Improvement, Management of Financial Structures, and Ethics.

DESIGNATORY LETTERS

CA

INSTITUTE OF FINANCIAL ACCOUNTANTS

Burford House
44 London Road
Sevenoaks
Kent TN13 1AS
Tel: 01732 458080
Fax: 01732 455848
E-mail: mail@ifa.org.uk
Website: www.ifa.org.uk

The IFA was established in 1916 and is the oldest body of non-Chartered Accountants in the world. We represent members and students in more than 80 countries, providing qualifications for those wishing to work in financial management and accountancy, and CPD for qualified Financial Accountants, particularly in SMEs.

MEMBERSHIP

Affiliate
Financial Accounting Executive
Associate (AFA)
Fellow (FFA)

QUALIFICATION/EXAMINATIONS

Financial Accounting Diploma
Professional Financial Accountant

DESIGNATORY LETTERS

AFA, FFA

INTERNATIONAL ASSOCIATION OF BOOK-KEEPERS

Suite 30
40 Churchill Square
Kings Hill
West Malling
Kent ME19 4YU
Tel: 01732 897750
Fax: 01732 897751
E-mail: mail@iab.org.uk
Website: www.iab.org.uk

The IAB specializes in providing high-quality, accredited and regulated financial and business qualifications. We continue to be the leading international membership body for professional book-keepers. Established in 1973, we now have many thousands of students and members worldwide.

MEMBERSHIP
Associate (AIAB)
Member (MIAB)
Fellow (FIAB)

QUALIFICATION/EXAMINATIONS
Award in Bookkeeping (Level 1)
Award in Manual Bookkeeping (Level 1)
Award in Computerized Bookkeeping (Level 1)
Certificate in Bookkeeping (Level 2)
Award in Manual Book-keeping (Level 2)
Award in Computerized Bookkeeping (Level 2)
Certificate in Applied Bookkeeping (Level 2)
Certificate in Bookkeeping (Level 3)
Certificate in Manual Bookkeeping (Level 3)
Award in Computerized Bookkeeping (Level 3)
Certificate in Applied Bookkeeping (Level 3)
Diploma in Accounting to International Standards (Level 4)
Award in Payroll (Level 1)
Certificate in Payroll (Level 2)
Award in Practical Payroll (Level 2)
Award in Computerized Payroll (Level 2)
Award in Applied Payroll (Level 2)
Certificate in Payroll (Level 3)
Award in Computerized Payroll (Level 3)

DESIGNATORY LETTERS
AIAB, MIAB, FIAB,

THE ASSOCIATION OF CHARTERED CERTIFIED ACCOUNTANTS

London WC2A 3EE
Tel: 020 7059 5000
Fax: 020 7059 5050
E-mail: info@accaglobal.com
Website: www.accaglobal.com

ACCA is the largest and fastest-growing international accountancy body, with over 424,000 students and 147,000 members in 170 countries. The ACCA Qualification is an established route to professional status, and we offer continued support to our members throughout their careers.

MEMBERSHIP
Associate (ACCA)
Fellow (FCCA)

QUALIFICATION/EXAMINATIONS
Foundations in Accountancy
Certified Accounting Technician (CAT) qualification
The ACCA Qualification
BSc in Applied Accounting (awarded by Oxford Brookes University)
MBA (awarded by Oxford Brookes University; accredited by the Association of MBAs)

DESIGNATORY LETTERS
ACCA, FCCA

THE ASSOCIATION OF CORPORATE TREASURERS

51 Moorgate
London EC2R 6BH
Tel: 020 7847 2540
Fax: 020 7374 8744
E-mail: enquiries@treasurers.co.uk
Website: www.treasurers.org

The ACT is the international body for professionals working in treasury, risk and corporate finance. We are the leading examining body for international treasury, providing the widest scope of benchmark qualifications and continuing development through training, conferences and publications – including *The Treasurer* magazine.

MEMBERSHIP
Student Member
Faculty Member

Associate Member (AMCT)
Member (MCT)
Fellow (FCT)
Corporate Member
International Affiliate

QUALIFICATION/EXAMINATIONS
Advanced Diploma in Treasury, Risk and Corporate Finance (MCT)
Diploma in Treasury (AMCT)
Certificate in Financial Fundamentals for Business (CertFin)
Certificate in International Treasury Management (CertITM)
Certificate in International Treasury Management – Public Finance (CertITM-PF)
Certificate in Corporate Finance and Funding (CertCFF)
Certificate in Financial Maths and Modelling (CertFMM)
Certificate in International Cash Management (CertICM)
Certificate in Risk Management (CertRM)

DESIGNATORY LETTERS
AMCT, MCT, FCT

THE ASSOCIATION OF INTERNATIONAL ACCOUNTANTS

Staithes 3
The Watermark
Metro Riverside
Newcastle upon Tyne
Tyne & Wear NE11 9SN
Tel: 0191 493 0277
Fax: 0191 493 0278
E-mail: aia@aiaworldwide.com
Website: www.aiaworldwide.com

AIA was founded in the UK in 1928 as a professional accountancy body and from conception has promoted the concept of 'international accounting' to create a global network of accountants in over 85 countries worldwide. AIA is recognized by the UK government as a Recognized Qualifying Body (RQB) for statutory auditors.

MEMBERSHIP
Student Member
Graduate Member
Affiliate Member (AMIA)
Academic Member
Associate (AAIA)
Fellow (FAIA)
Honorary Member
Retired Member

QUALIFICATION/EXAMINATIONS
Professional Accountancy Qualification
Statutory Audit Qualification
Audit Diploma
Corporate Finance Diploma
IFRS Diploma
Management Accounting & Costing Diploma

DESIGNATORY LETTERS
AMIA, AAIA, FAIA

THE CHARTERED INSTITUTE OF PUBLIC FINANCE AND ACCOUNTANCY

3 Robert Street
London WC2N 6RL
Tel: 020 7543 5656
Fax: 020 7543 5700
E-mail: students@cipfa.org.uk
Website: www.cipfa.org.uk

The CIPFA is the professional body for people in public finance. Our 14,000 members work throughout the public services and as the only UK professional accountancy body to specialize in public services, CIPFA's qualifications are the foundation for a career in public finance.

MEMBERSHIP
Student Member
Affiliate
Associate
Full Member

QUALIFICATION/EXAMINATIONS
CIPFA Professional Qualification
Certificate in Charity Finance and Accountancy
Certificate in International Treasury Management – Public Finance

THE INSTITUTE OF CERTIFIED BOOKKEEPERS

1 Northumberland Avenue
Trafalgar Square
London WC2N 5BW
Tel: 0845 060 2345
Fax: 01635 298960
E-mail: info@bookkeepers.org.uk
Website: www.bookkeepers.org.uk

The ICB is the largest bookkeeping institute in the world. Our aims are to promote bookkeeping as a profession, to improve training in the principles of bookkeeping, and to establish qualifications and the award of grades of membership that recognize academic attainment, work experience and professional competence, and thereby enable qualified bookkeepers to gain recognition as an integral part of the financial world.

MEMBERSHIP
Registered Student
Affiliate
Associate Member (AICB)
Member (MICB)
Fellow (FICB)

QUALIFICATION/EXAMINATIONS
Level 1: Certificate in Basic Bookkeeping
Level 2: (Intermediate): Certificate in Computerized Bookkeeping
Level 2: (Intermediate): Certificate in Manual Bookkeeping
Level 3: (Advanced): Diploma in Computerized Bookkeeping
Level 3: (Advanced): Diploma in Manual Bookkeeping
Level 3: (Advanced): Diploma in Payroll Management
Level 3: (Advanced): Diploma in Self-Assessment Tax Returns
Level 4: (Advanced) Diploma in Drafting Financial Statements, Management Accounts, Personal and Business Taxation.

DESIGNATORY LETTERS
AICB, MICB, FICB

ACOUSTICS

Membership of Professional Institutions and Associations

INSTITUTE OF ACOUSTICS

77A St Peter's Street
St Albans
Hertfordshire AL1 3BN
Tel: 01727 848195
Fax: 01727 850553
E-mail: ioa@ioa.org.uk
Website: www.ioa.org.uk

The IOA is the UK's professional body for those working in acoustics, noise and vibration, and has more than 3,000 members in research, educational, environmental, government and industrial organizations. We offer a range of professionally recognized courses and are licensed by the Engineering Research Council to offer registration at Chartered and Incorporated Engineer levels.

MEMBERSHIP
Student
Affiliate
Technician Member (TechIOA)
Associate Member (AMIOA)
Member (MIOA)
Fellow (FIOA)
Honorary Fellow (HonFIOA)
Incorporated Engineer (IEng)
Chartered Engineer (CEng)
Sponsor

QUALIFICATION/EXAMINATIONS
Certificate of Competence in Environmental Noise Measurement
Certificate of Competence in Workplace Noise Risk Assessment
Certificate Course in the Management of Occupational Exposure to Hand–Arm Vibration
Diploma in Acoustics and Noise Control

DESIGNATORY LETTERS
TechIOA, AMIOA, MIOA, FIOA, HonFIOA, IEng, CEng

ADVERTISING AND PUBLIC RELATIONS

Membership of Professional Institutions and Associations

CHARTERED INSTITUTE OF PUBLIC RELATIONS

52–53 Russell Square
London WC1B 4HP
Tel: 020 7631 6900
Fax: 020 7631 6944
E-mail: info@cipr.co.uk
Website: www.cipr.co.uk

The CIPR, founded in 1948, is the professional body for PR practitioners and has more than 9,000 members, to whom it offers information, advice, support and training. Our aim is to raise standards within the profession through the promotion of best practice and our members abide by our strict code of professional conduct.

MEMBERSHIP
Student
Affiliate
Associate (ACIPR)
Member (MCIPR)
Fellow (FCIPR)
Honorary Fellow (Hon FCIPR)

QUALIFICATION/EXAMINATIONS
Foundation Award in Public Relations
Advanced Certificate
Diploma

DESIGNATORY LETTERS
ACIPR, MCIPR, FCIPR

INSTITUTE OF PRACTITIONERS IN ADVERTISING

44 Belgrave Square
London SW1X 8QS
Tel: 020 7235 7020
Fax: 020 7245 9904
E-mail: training@ipa.co.uk
Website: www.ipa.co.uk

The IPA is the UK's leading professional body for advertising, media and marketing communications agencies. We promote the services of our member agencies, which have access to a range of services and benefits, including a Legal Department, Information Centre and training courses provided by our Professional Development Department.

MEMBERSHIP
Personal Member (MIPA)
Fellow/Honorary Fellow (FIPA)
Member Agency

QUALIFICATION/EXAMINATIONS
Foundation Certificate
Advanced Certificate
LegRes Certificate
Excellence Diploma

DESIGNATORY LETTERS
MIPA, FIPA

INSTITUTE OF PROMOTIONAL MARKETING

70 Margaret Street
London W1W 8SS
Tel: 020 7291 7733
E-mail: enquiries@theipm.co.uk
Website: www.theipm.org.uk

The Institute of Promotional Marketing represents promoters, agencies and service partners engaged in promotional marketing in the UK by protecting, promoting and progressing effective sales promotion across all media channels through its education, legal advice, awards, and other products and services.

MEMBERSHIP
Personal Member (MISP)
Corporate Member

QUALIFICATION/EXAMINATIONS
Certificate in Digital Promotions
Certificate in Experiential Marketing
Diploma in Motivation
Certificate in Promotional & Interactive Marketing
Diploma in Promotional & Interactive Marketing

DESIGNATORY LETTERS
MISP

LONDON SCHOOL OF PUBLIC RELATIONS

David Game House
69 Notting Hill Gate
London W11 3JS
Tel: 020 7221 3399
Fax: 020 7243 1730
E-mail: info@lspr-education.com
Website: www.pr-school-london.com

The LSPR provides up-to-date training for those wishing to enter public relations as a career or for those already in PR or an information/communications job who require some formal training. Our Diploma, *An Integrated Approach to Public Relations for the 21st Century,* is awarded to students upon successful completion of a 2-week full-time intensive course or 3-month part-time evening course.

QUALIFICATION/EXAMINATIONS
Diploma

AGRICULTURE AND HORTICULTURE

Membership of Professional Institutions and Associations

INSTITUTE OF HORTICULTURE

Capel Manor College
Bullsmoor Lane
Enfield
Middlesex EN1 4RQ
Tel: 01992 707025
E-mail: ioh@horticulture.org.uk
Website: www.horticulture.org.uk

The IoH represents all those professionally engaged in horticulture in the UK and the Republic of Ireland. Our main aim is to promote the profession and its importance in food and ornamental plant production, improving the environment, providing employment and as the leisure pursuit of gardening. We are also developing CPD and mentoring schemes for our members and liaise with government and other bodies on matters of interest or concern.

MEMBERSHIP
Student Member, Affiliate, Associate (AI Hort), Member (MI Hort), Fellow (FI Hort), Group Membership

DESIGNATORY LETTERS
AI Hort, MI Hort, FI Hort

ROYAL HORTICULTURAL SOCIETY

RHS Qualifications
RHS Garden Wisley
Woking
Surrey GU23 6QB
Tel: 0845 260 9000
E-mail: qualifications@rhs.org.uk
Website: www.rhs.org.uk

RHS Qualifications is a recognized awarding body offering a range of qualifications in horticultural knowledge and skills. Part-time courses leading to RHS qualifications are offered by approved centres throughout the UK and Ireland, and by distance-learning providers. The RHS School of Horticulture provides courses in practical horticultural skills.

QUALIFICATION/EXAMINATIONS
RHS Level 1 Award in Practical Horticulture
RHS Level 2 Certificate in the Principles of Plant Growth, Propagation and Development
RHS Level 2 Certificate in the Principles of Garden Planning, Establishment and Maintenance
RHS Level 2 Certificate in the Principles of Horticulture
RHS Level 2 Certificate in Practical Horticulture
RHS Level 2 Diploma in the Principles and Practices of Horticulture
RHS Level 3 Certificate in the Principles of Plant Growth, Health and Applied Propagation
RHS Level 3 Certificate in the Principles of Garden Planning, Construction and Planting
RHS Level 3 Certificate in Practical Horticulture
RHS Level 3 Diploma in the Principles and Practices of Horticulture
Master of Horticulture (RHS)
Wisley Diploma in Practical Horticulture
Certificate in Practical Horticulture
Specialist Option Certificates in:
Ornamental Horticulture
Fruit Cultivation
Rock and Alpine Gardening
Orchid Culture and Glasshouse Technique
Estate Management with Arboriculture
Plant Centre Management Skills

THE ROYAL BOTANIC GARDEN EDINBURGH

20A Inverleith Row
Edinburgh EH3 5LR
Tel: 01312 482825
Fax: 01312 482901
E-mail: education@rbge.org.uk
Website: www.rbge.org.uk

The RBGE was founded in the 17th century as a physic garden, growing medicinal plants. Now it extends over four gardens boasting a rich living collection of plants, and is a world-renowned centre for plant science and education.

QUALIFICATION/EXAMINATIONS
Certificate in Practical Field Botany
Certificate in Practical Horticulture
Diploma in Botanical Illustration
Diploma in Garden Design
Diploma in Herbology
HND/BSc in Horticulture with Plantsmanship
MSc in The Biodiversity and Taxonomy of Plants

AMBULANCE SERVICE

Membership of Professional Institutions and Associations

AMBULANCE SERVICE INSTITUTE

Suite 183
Maddison House
226 High Street
Croydon CR9 1DF
E-mail: enquiries@asi-international.com
Website: www.asi-international.com

The ASI is a non-union, non-political, independent institute whose membership is dedicated to raising the standards and quality of ambulance provision and thereby improving the professionalism and quality of care available to patients. Membership is open to non-NHS personnel as well as to employees of NHS Ambulance Services.

MEMBERSHIP
Student
Member (MASI)
Licentiate (LASI)
Associate (AASI)
Graduate (GASI)
Fellow (FASI)

QUALIFICATION/EXAMINATIONS
The Institute offers professional examinations and qualifications in the areas of Pre-Hospital Care, Control and Communications, and Management, for those who desire a career in the ambulance service.

DESIGNATORY LETTERS
MASI, LASI, AASI, GASI, FASI

ARBITRATION

Membership of Professional Institutions and Associations

THE CHARTERED INSTITUTE OF ARBITRATORS

12 Bloomsbury Square
London WC1A 2LP
Tel: 020 7421 7444
Fax: 020 7404 4023
E-mail: info@ciarb.org
Website: www.ciarb.org

The CIArb is a not-for-profit, UK-registered charity with 12,000 members worldwide that exists to promote and facilitate the settlement of private disputes by arbitration and alternative dispute resolution. We provide training for arbitrators, mediators and adjudicators and act as an international centre for practitioners, policy-makers, academics and those in business concerned with the cost-effective and early settlement of disputes.

MEMBERSHIP
Associate (ACIArb)
Member (MCIArb)
Fellow (FCIArb)

QUALIFICATION/EXAMINATIONS
Introductory Certificate
Advanced Certificate
Diploma

DESIGNATORY LETTERS
ACIArb, MCIArb, FCIArb

ARCHAEOLOGY

Membership of Professional Institutions and Associations

THE INSTITUTE FOR ARCHAEOLOGISTS

SHES
University of Reading
Whiteknights
PO Box 227
Reading RG6 6AB
Tel: 0118 378 6446
Fax: 0118 378 6448
E-mail: admin@archaeologists.net
Website: www.archaeologists.net

The IfA is a professional organization for all archaeologists and others involved in protecting and understanding the historic environment, with more than 2, 700 members. We advance the practice of archaeology and allied disciplines by promoting professional standards and ethics for conserving, managing, understanding and enjoying our heritage.

MEMBERSHIP
Student
Affiliate
Practitioner (PIfA)
Associate (AIfA)
Member (MIfA)
Registered Organization

ARCHITECTURE

Membership of Professional Institutions and Associations

ARCHITECTS REGISTRATION BOARD

8 Weymouth Street
London W1W 5BU
Tel: 020 7580 5861
Fax: 020 7436 5269
E-mail: info@arb.org.uk
Website: www.arb.org.uk

The ARB is the regulatory body for architects in the UK. Only individuals registered with the Board can use the title 'architect'. Applicants must have passed the recognized exams at a school of architecture in the UK (or have an equivalent non-UK professional qualification) and have at least 2 years' practical experience working under the supervision of an architect.

CHARTERED INSTITUTE OF ARCHITECTURAL TECHNOLOGISTS (CIAT)

397 City Road
London EC1V 1NH
Tel: 020 7278 2206
Fax: 020 7837 3194
E-mail: info@ciat.org.uk
Website: www.ciat.org.uk

CIAT represents professionals working and studying in the field of Architectural Technology. We are internationally recognised as the qualifying body for Chartered Architectural Technologists (MCIAT) and Architectural Technicians (TCIAT).

MEMBERSHIP

Student member
Profile candidate
Associate (ACIAT)
Architectural Technician (TCIAT)
Chartered Architectural Technologist (MCIAT)
Honorary Member (HonMCIAT)

DESIGNATORY LETTERS

ACIAT, TCIAT, MCIAT

ROYAL INSTITUTE OF BRITISH ARCHITECTS

60 Portland Place
London W1B 1AD
Tel: 020 7580 5533
Fax: 020 7255 1541
E-mail: info@inst.riba.org
Website: www.architecture.com

The Royal Institute of British Architects is the UK body for architecture and the architectural profession. We provide support for our 40, 500 members worldwide in the form of training, technical services, publications and events, and set standards for the education of architects, both in the UK and overseas. We also work with government to improve the design quality of public buildings, new homes and new communities.

MEMBERSHIP

Student Member
Affiliate Member
Associate Member
Chartered Member
Chartered Practice

ART AND DESIGN

Membership of Professional Institutions and Associations

BRITISH ASSOCIATION OF ART THERAPISTS

Claremont
24–27 White Lion Street
London N1 9PD
Tel: 020 7686 4216
E-mail: info@baat.org
Website: www.baat.org

The BAAT is the professional organization for art therapists in the UK and has its own Code of Ethics of Professional Practice. We maintain a comprehensive directory of qualified art therapists and work to promote art therapy in the UK through 20 regional groups. We also have a European section and an international section.

MEMBERSHIP
Trainee Member
Associate Member
Full Member
Honorary Member
Fellow
Corporate Member

QUALIFICATION/EXAMINATIONS
The BAAT organizes a programme of CPD courses for Art Therapists. For details see the website.

BRITISH ASSOCIATION OF PAINTINGS CONSERVATOR-RESTORERS

PO Box 258
Norwich NR13 4WY
Tel: 01603 516237
Fax: 01603 510985
E-mail: office@bapcr.org.uk
Website: www.bapcr.org.uk

The BAPCR (founded in 1943 as the Association of British Picture Restorers) is the professional association for conservator-restorers of paintings and has more than 400 members worldwide. Our aims are to advance the profession by providing means for CPD to our members and thereby a service to the public.

MEMBERSHIP
Associate (Student)
Associate
Fellow

D&AD (BRITISH DESIGN & ART DIRECTION)

9 Graphite Square
Vauxhall Walk
London SE11 5EE
Tel: 020 7840 1111
Fax: 020 7840 0840
E-mail: info@dandad.co.uk
Website: www.dandad.org

Founded in 1962, D&AD is a professional association and educational charity with a membership of more than 2,000, working on behalf of the design and advertising communities. Our mission is to set creative standards, educate and inspire the next creative generation, and promote the importance of good design and advertising to business as a whole.

MEMBERSHIP
Student
New Creative
Elected Associate
Associate
Member

SOCIETY OF DESIGNER CRAFTSMEN (SDC)

24 Rivington Street
London EC2A 3DU
Tel: 07531 798983
E-mail: info@societyofdesignercrafstmen.org.uk
Website: www.societyofdesignercraftsmen.org.uk

The Society, which was founded in 1887 as the Arts and Crafts Exhibition Society, is the largest and oldest multi-craft society in the UK. Our aim is to emphasize designer-making where innovation, originality and quality are important; we provide promotional services and exhibiting opportunities to members.

MEMBERSHIP
Associate
Licentiate (LSDC)
Member (MSDC)
Fellow (FSDC)

DESIGNATORY LETTERS
LSDC, MSDC, FSDC

THE CHARTERED SOCIETY OF DESIGNERS

1 Cedar Court
Royal Oak Yard
Bermondsey Street
London SE1 3GA
Tel: 020 7357 8088
Fax: 020 7407 9878
E-mail: info@csd.org.uk
Website: www.csd.org.uk

The CSD, which was founded in 1930, is the professional body for designers and has more than 3,000 members. We promote sound principles of design in all areas in which design considerations apply, further design practice and encourage the study of design techniques for the benefit of the community.

MEMBERSHIP
Student Member

Graduate Member
Member (MCSD)
Fellow (FCSD)

DESIGNATORY LETTERS
MCSD, FCSD

THE INDEX OF PROFESSIONAL MASTER DESIGNERS

Kensington House
33 Imperial Square
Cheltenham Spa
Gloucestershire GL50 1QZ
Tel: 08701 161823
Fax: 08702 626146
E-mail: masterdesigners@kensington-house.com

The Index was formed to provide a register of designers practising in all areas of design. Our objectives are to enable designers to achieve recognition and attain qualifications and also to accredit schools and training organizations offering suitable courses.

MEMBERSHIP
Student
Professional Designer (IPMD (DIP))
Master Designer (IPMD (MAS))

QUALIFICATION/EXAMINATIONS
Certificate of Excellence – Interior Design Students

DESIGNATORY LETTERS
IPMD (DIP), IPMD (MAS)

ASTRONOMY AND SPACE SCIENCE

Membership of Professional Institutions and Associations

THE BRITISH INTERPLANETARY SOCIETY

27/29 South Lambeth Road
London SW8 1SZ
Tel: 020 7735 3160
Fax: 020 7587 5118
E-mail: mail@bis-spaceflight.com
Website: www.bis-spacef.com

The BIS was formed in 1933 and has been at the forefront of actively promoting new ideas on space exploration at technical, educational and popular levels for over 70 years. We serve the interests of those professionally involved with space, promote fundamental space research, technology and applications, encourage technical and scientific space studies, and undertake educational activities on space topics.

MEMBERSHIP
Member
Fellow (FBIS)

DESIGNATORY LETTERS
FBIS

AVIATION

Membership of Professional Institutions and Associations

THE GUILD OF AIR PILOTS AND AIR NAVIGATORS

Cobham House
9 Warwick Court
London WC1R 5DJ
Tel: 020 7404 4032
Fax: 020 7404 4035
E-mail: gapan@gapan.org
Website: www.gapan.org

The Guild, an active Livery Company of the City of London, represents pilot and navigator interests within all areas of aviation. Most of our members are, or have been, professional licence holders, or hold a private licence. Our aims include promoting the highest standards of air safety, liaising with all authorities connected with licensing, training and legislation, providing advice and facilitating exchange of information.

MEMBERSHIP
Associate
Freeman
Upper Freeman

QUALIFICATION/EXAMINATIONS
Master Air Pilot Certificate
Master Air Navigator Certificate

THE GUILD OF AIR TRAFFIC CONTROL OFFICERS

4 St Mary's Road
Bingham
Nottingham
Nottinghamshire NG13 8DW
Tel: 01949 876405
Fax: 01949 876405
E-mail: caf@gatco.org
Website: www.gatco.org

Founded in 1954, GATCO is an independent professional organization that exists to promote honourable practice and the highest standards in all aspects of aviation. It is dedicated to the safety of all who seek their livelihood or pleasure in the air.

MEMBERSHIP
Student Member
Associate Non-Operational Member
Associate Operational Member
Full Member
Corporate Member

QUALIFICATION/EXAMINATIONS
Qualifying criteria apply to all memberships categories. Further information should be sought from GATCO Ltd, Central Administrative Facility (CAF).

BANKING

Membership of Professional Institutions and Associations

IFS SCHOOL OF FINANCE

8th Floor
Peninsular House
36 Monument Street
London EC3R 8LJ
Tel: 01227 818609
Fax: 01227 784331/786030
E-mail: customerservices@ifslearning.ac.uk
Website: www.ifslearning.ac.uk

The ifs School of Finance is a world-class provider of financial learning, and has more than 50,000 students in over 90 countries. Having built a reputation for excellence in learning, all the qualifications it provides combine innovation and quality, and draw from over 130 years of educational experience.

MEMBERSHIP
Member
Affiliate
Associate
Fellow
Chartered Associate
Adviser Membership (for financial and mortgage advisers)

QUALIFICATION/EXAMINATIONS
The ifs offers a wide range of qualifications for those employed or aspiring to a career in the financial services industry, and for consumers. For details see; www.ifslearning.ac.uk

THE CHARTERED INSTITUTE OF BANKERS IN SCOTLAND

Drumsheugh House
38B Drumsheugh Gardens
Edinburgh EH3 7SW
Tel: 0131 473 7777
Fax: 0131 473 7788
E-mail: info@charteredbanker.com
Website: www.charteredbanker.com

The Chartered Institute of Bankers in Scotland provides world-class professional qualifications for both the UK and international markets. Our vision for the financial services industry is one of professionalism. We are the only organization in the world entitled to award the designation 'Chartered Banker' to its members.

MEMBERSHIP
Student
Affiliate
Associate (ACIBS)
Member (MCIBS)
Fellow (FCIBS)

QUALIFICATION/EXAMINATIONS
Certificate
Diploma
Advanced Diploma
Chartered Banker

DESIGNATORY LETTERS
ACIBS, MCIBS, FCIBS

BEAUTY THERAPY AND BEAUTY CULTURE

Membership of Professional Institutions and Associations

ASSOCIATION OF THERAPY LECTURERS

18 Shakespeare Business Centre
Hathaway Close
Eastleigh
Hampshire SO50 4SR
Tel: 0844 875 2022
Fax: 023 8062 4399
E-mail: info@fht.org.uk
Website: www.fht.org.uk

(Part of the Federation of Holistic Therapists)

The ATL began in 1963 as the Society of Beauty Teachers, when Beauty Therapy teaching was still in its infancy. In the 1990s it amalgamated with the National Beauty Teachers and Lecturers Association (NBTLA) and today it represents Lecturers in a wide range of therapies.

MEMBERSHIP
Member

QUALIFICATION/EXAMINATIONS
Please see www.fht.org.uk for details.

BRITISH ASSOCIATION OF BEAUTY THERAPY AND COSMETOLOGY LTD

BABTAC Limited
Ambrose House, Meteor Court
Barnett Way
Barnwood
Gloucester GL4 3GG
Tel: 0845 065 9000
Fax: 0845 065 9001
E-mail: enquiries@babtac.com
Website: www.babtac.com

BABTAC was formed in 1977 and is a non-profit-making organization for beauticians and therapists in the UK. Members work to a rigorous code of ethics and good practice, both in terms of the treatments and therapies they offer and the way they conduct their relationships with their clients. CIBTAC, an international, educational awarding body that works closely with BABTAC, offers over 30 internationally recognized diplomas in beauty and complementary therapies to accredited colleges and students in the UK and abroad.

MEMBERSHIP
Student Member
Associate Member
Nail Technician
Full Member
Overseas Member
Salon Plan Member

QUALIFICATION/EXAMINATIONS
BABTAC offers a programme of short courses. For details see the BABTAC website. For CIBTAC diplomas see www.cibtac.com/courses_home.htm

BRITISH INSTITUTE AND ASSOCIATION OF ELECTROLYSIS LTD

40 Parkfield Road
Ickenham
Middlesex UB10 BLW
Tel: 08445 441373
E-mail: sec@electrolysis.co.uk
Website: www.electrolysis.co.uk

The BIAE is a non-profit-making organization that demands a high standard of skill and ethical conduct from its members, who are spread throughout the UK and overseas. Candidate Electrolysists must complete the rigorous assessments, both theoretical and practical, of the BIAE Examining Board before being accepted onto the Register.

MEMBERSHIP
Member

QUALIFICATION/EXAMINATIONS
Certificate in Remedial Electrolysis (CRE)

FEDERATION OF HOLISTIC THERAPISTS

18 Shakespeare Business Centre
Hathaway Close
Eastleigh
Hampshire SO50 4SR
Tel: 0844 875 2022
Fax: 023 8062 4396
E-mail: info@fht.org.uk
Website: www.fht.org.uk

The FHT is the leading and largest professional beauty, sports and complementary therapist association in the UK, which has been representing the interests of holistic therapists since 1962. The FHT leads the industry by offering its members a Code of Ethics, public liability insurance, access to regulation, a robust CPD programme with auditing, class-leading journal, local therapist network, and comprehensive business and public affairs updates.

MEMBERSHIP
Student
Affiliate
Associate
Member
Fellow
International

QUALIFICATION/EXAMINATIONS
Please see the FHT's website.

DESIGNATORY LETTERS
MFHT, FFHT, AFHT, AfFHT

ITEC

2nd Floor, Chiswick Gate
598–608 Chiswick High Road
London W4 5RT
Tel: 020 8994 4141
Fax: 020 8994 7880
E-mail: info@itecworld.co.uk
Website: www.itecworld.co.uk

ITEC is an international examination board offering a variety of qualifications in the beauty therapy, complementary therapy and sports therapy sectors worldwide. We also offer teacher training courses in: Skincare; Make-up; Manicure and Pedicure; Waxing; Holistic Massage; Aromatherapy; Reflexology; Body Treatments; and other areas as required.

QUALIFICATION/EXAMINATIONS
Please see the ITEC website.

BIOLOGICAL SCIENCES

Membership of Professional Institutions and Associations

INSTITUTE OF BIOMEDICAL SCIENCE

12 Coldbath Square
London EC1R 5HL
Tel: 020 7713 0214
Fax: 020 7837 9658
E-mail: mail@ibms.org
Website: www.ibms.org

The IBMS is the professional body for biomedical scientists in the UK. We aim to promote and develop the role of biomedical science within healthcare to deliver the best possible service for patient care and safety.

MEMBERSHIP
Associate
Licentiate (LIBMS)
Member (MIBMS)
Fellow (FIBMS)
Company member

QUALIFICATION/EXAMINATIONS
Certificate of Competence (also required for registration with the Health Professions Council (HPC))
Specialist Diploma in:
Cellular Pathology, Clinical Biochemistry, Clinical Immunology, Cytopathology, Haematology & Transfusion Science, Histocompatibility & Immunogenetics (developed in conjunction with BSHI), Medical Microbiology, Transfusion Science, Virology.
Diploma of Specialist Practice
Higher Specialist Diploma in:
Cellular Pathology, Clinical Chemistry, Cytopathology, Haematology, Immunology, Histocompatibility & Immunogenetics (developed in conjunction with BSHI), Medical Microbiology, Transfusion Science, Virology.
Diploma of Higher Specialist Practice
Complementary qualifications/examinations related to areas of scientific expertise (available to Members and/or Fellows)
Certificates and Diplomas of Expert Practice
Advanced Specialist Diplomas

DESIGNATORY LETTERS
LIBMS, MIBMS, FIBMS

SOCIETY OF BIOLOGY

9 Red Lion Court
London EC4A 3EF
Tel: 020 7936 5900
Fax: 020 7936 5901
E-mail: info@societyofbiology.org
Website: www.societyofbiology.org

The Society of Biology aims to be a single unified voice for biology: advising government and influencing policy; advancing education and professional development; supporting members; and engaging and encouraging public interest in the life sciences.

MEMBERSHIP
Associate Member (AMSB)
Member (MSB)
Fellow (FSB)
Chartered Biologist (CBiol)

DESIGNATORY LETTERS
AMSB, MSB, FSB, CBiol

BREWING

Membership of Professional Institutions and Associations

INSTITUTE OF BREWING & DISTILLING

33 Clarges Street
Mayfair
London W1J 7EE
Tel: 020 7499 8144
Fax: 020 7499 1156
E-mail: enquiries@ibd.org.uk
Website: www.ibd.org.uk

The IBD is a members' organization dedicated to the education and training needs of brewers and distillers and those in related industries. We do this by offering a range of internationally recognized qualifications and the training to support them, through either direct instruction or distance learning.

MEMBERSHIP
Member
Honorary Member
Senior Member
Fellow (FIBD)
Honorary Fellow
Corporate Member

QUALIFICATION/EXAMINATIONS
Certificate in the Fundamentals of Brewing and Packaging of Beer (FBPB) (City & Guilds Level 2)
Certificate in the Fundamentals of Distilling (FD) (City & Guilds Level 2)
General Certificate in Brewing (GCB) (City & Guilds Level 3)
General Certificate in Distilling (GCD) (City & Guilds Level 3)
General Certificate in Packaging (GCP) (City & Guilds Level 3)
Diploma in Packaging (Dipl.Pack) (City & Guilds Level 4)
Diploma in Brewing (Dipl.Brew) (City & Guilds Level 4)
Diploma in Distilling (Dipl.Distill) (City & Guilds Level 4)
Master Brewer (MBrew)

DESIGNATORY LETTERS
Dipl.Brew, Dipl.Distil, Dipl.Pack, MBrew, FIBD, Hon FIBD

BUILDING

Membership of Professional Institutions and Associations

INSTITUTE OF ASPHALT TECHNOLOGY

Paper Mews Place
280 High Street
Dorking
Surrey RH4 1QT
Tel: 01306 742792
Fax: 01306 888902
E-mail: secretary@instofasphalt.org
Website: www.instofasphalt.org

The IAT is the UK's professional body for persons working in asphalt technology and those interested in aspects of the manufacture, placing, technology and uses of materials containing asphalt or bitumen. A fully audited CPD system for members has been available since 1994 and is now also offered in computerized format for ease of data entry and auditing, via members' own PCs.

MEMBERSHIP
Student
Technician (Tech IAT)
Affiliate (AIAT)
Member (MIAT)
Fellow (FIAT)

DESIGNATORY LETTERS
Tech IAT, AIAT, MIAT, FIAT

THE CHARTERED INSTITUTE OF BUILDING

Englemere
Kings Ride
Ascot
Berkshire SL5 7TB
Tel: 01344 630700
Fax: 01344 630777
E-mail: educationadmin@ciob.org.uk
Website: www.ciob.org

The CIOB is the international voice of the construction industry. CIOB members are largely Construction Managers engaged in managing the development, conservation and improvement of the built environment, with a common commitment to achieving and maintaining the highest possible standards.

MEMBERSHIP
Student Member
Associate (ACIOB)
Incorporate (ICIOB)
Member (MCIOB)
Fellow (FCIOB)
Chartered Environmentalist (CENV)

QUALIFICATION/EXAMINATIONS
The CIOB has routes to membership to suit a range of professionals from those with degrees or vocational qualifications to those with experience but no formal qualifications. All our members have a strong commitment to improve and develop themselves in a challenging and exciting career.

Chartered Member status is recognized internationally as the mark of a skilled professional in the construction industry. CIOB members are from a wide range of professions in the construction industry.

To find out more about our membership qualifications and joining the CIOB just visit our website www.ciob.org

The CIOB Awarding Body offers a suite of qualifications to enable site operatives to progress into management roles.
Level 3 Diploma in Site Supervisory Studies
Level 4 Certificate in Site Management
Level 4 Diploma in Site Management
The CIOB qualifications develop the skills and confidence to manage and coordinate all types of construction projects. The site management qualifications are nationally recognized and allow the learner to progress to higher education and National Vocational Qualifications (NVQs).
For more information on the Site Management Qualifications visit the website at www.ciob.org.uk/education/courseinfo/sitemanagement

DESIGNATORY LETTERS
ACIOB, ICIOB, MCIOB, FCIOB, CENV

THE INSTITUTE OF CARPENTERS

32 High Street
Wendover
Buckinghamshire HP22 6EA
Tel: 0844-879-7696
Fax: 01296-620981
E-mail: info@instituteofcarpenters.com
Website: www.instituteofcarpenters.com

The IOC was founded in 1890 to oversee training for carpenters and joiners and maintain high professional standards at a time when many feared that traditional skills were being lost. Today, while remaining committed to our original aims, we embrace many other wood craftsmen, such as shopfitters, furniture and cabinetmakers, boat builders (woodworking skills), structural post & beam carpenters (heavy structural timber framers), wheelwrights, wood carvers and wood turners, and offer professional status to those holding recognized qualifications.

MEMBERSHIP
Student
Mature Student
Affiliate
Licentiate (LIOC)
Member (MIOC)
Fellow (FIOC)
College Member
Corporate Member
Corporate Associate

QUALIFICATION/EXAMINATIONS
Certificate of Competence in Joinery & Shopfitting Setting-Out
Foundation Certificate in Carpentry and Joinery
Intermediate Examination
Advanced Craft Examination
Fellowship Examination

DESIGNATORY LETTERS
LIOC, MIOC, FIOC

THE INSTITUTE OF CLERKS OF WORKS AND CONSTRUCTION INSPECTORATE OF GREAT BRITAIN INC

28 Commerce Road
Lynch Wood
Peterborough PE2 6LR
Tel: 01733 405160
Fax: 01733 405161
E-mail: info@icwgb.co.uk
Website: www.icwgb.org

The ICWCI is the professional body that supports quality construction through inspection. As a membership organization, we provide a support network of meeting centres, technical advice, publications and events to help keep our members up to date with the ever-changing construction industry.

MEMBERSHIP
Student
Licentiate (LICWCI)
Member (MICWCI)
Fellow (FICWCI)

DESIGNATORY LETTERS
LICWCI, MICWCI, FICWCI

BUSINESS STUDIES

Membership of Professional Institutions and Associations

ASSOCIATION OF BUSINESS RECOVERY PROFESSIONALS (R3)

8th Floor
120 Aldersgate Street
London EC1A 4JQ
Tel: 020 7566 4200
Fax: 020 7566 4224
E-mail: association@r3.org.uk
Website: www.r3.org.uk

The Association of Business Recovery Professionals (known by its brand name 'R3') is the leading professional association for insolvency, business recovery and turnaround specialists in the UK. A not-for-profit organization, it promotes best practice for professionals working with financially troubled individuals and businesses, and provides a forum for debate on key issues facing the profession.

MEMBERSHIP
Student Member
Networking Member
Associate Member (AABRP)
Full Member (MABRP)
Fellow (FABRP)

QUALIFICATION/EXAMINATIONS
R3 provides comprehensive Continuing Professional Education in the field of Insolvency and Restructuring. For details of courses see R3's website.

DESIGNATORY LETTERS
AABRP, MABRP, FABRP

INSTITUTE OF ASSESSORS AND INTERNAL VERIFIERS

PO Box 148
Wirral CH62 7WB
Tel: 01925 485 786
E-mail: office@iavltd.co.uk

The IAV is the professional organization representing assessors and internal verifiers in the UK in vocational training and assessment.

MEMBERSHIP
Affiliate Member
Associate Member
Licentiate Member

THE ACADEMY OF EXECUTIVES & ADMINISTRATORS

Head Office
Warwick Corner
42 Warwick Road
Kenilworth
Warwickshire CV8 1HE
Tel: 01926 259342
E-mail: info@academyofexecutivesandadministrators.org.uk
Website: www.academyofexecutivesandadministrators.org.uk

The Academy of Executives & Administrators was founded in 2002 to give professional status and recognition to the knowledge and skills of executives and administrators. We encourage excellence and flexibility in the changing environment of executive and administrative roles, and support lifelong learning to help members fulfil their career ambitions.

MEMBERSHIP
Student Member (StudAEA)
Associate Member (AMAEA)
Member (MAEA)
Fellow (FAEA)
Companion (CAEA)

QUALIFICATION/EXAMINATIONS
Certified Business Economist
Certified Financial Analyst
Certified Accounting Assistant
Certified Corporate Accountant
Certified Trainer

THE ACADEMY OF MULTI-SKILLS

Head Office
219 Bow Road
London
Middlesex E3 2SJ
Tel: 00 44 (0)709 201 291
E-mail: The MSAcademy@yahoo.co.uk
Website: www.academyofmultiskills.org.uk

The Academy of Multi-Skills was founded in 1995 to give professional recognition to multi-skilled personnel, skilled trades, crafts and professions. The Academy encourages a positive and energetic attitude to the challenges of careers that require diversity, creativity and intellect, and recognizes the valuable contribution that these skills provide to society.

MEMBERSHIP
Student Member (StudAMS)
Affiliate Member (AffAMS)
Associate Member (AMAMS)
Member (MAMS)
Fellow (FAMS)
Companion (CAMS)

THE FACULTY OF SECRETARIES AND ADMINISTRATORS (1930) WITH THE ASSOCIATION OF CORPORATE SECRETARIES

Brightstowe
Catteshall Lane
Godalming
Surrey GU7 1LL
Tel: 01483 427323

The Faculty and Association is a professional body for company and corporate secretaries whose prime qualified designation is that of Certified Public or Corporate Secretary.

MEMBERSHIP
Membership Fellows (FFCS)
Associates (AFCS)
Member (MACS)
Ordinary Member
Student Member

QUALIFICATION/EXAMINATIONS
Part 1 The Generic Business Assessment to ONC/D Level
Part 2 Professional Papers in Company Secretarial Practice, Company Law and Management, Secretarial and Administrative Practice, Commercial Law
Part 3 Professional Meetings Law and Procedure, Company Taxation, Accountancy and Finance, Company Law

DESIGNATORY LETTERS
FFCS, AFCS, MACS

THE INSTITUTE OF CHARTERED SECRETARIES AND ADMINISTRATORS

16 Park Crescent
London W1B 1AH
Tel: 020 7580 4741
Fax: 020 7323 1132
E-mail: studentsupport@icsaglobal.com
Website: www.icsaglobal.com

The Institute of Chartered Secretaries and Administrators is the international qualifying and membership body for the Chartered Secretary profession. With a global community of 37,000 members we provide Chartered Membership, training and a professional qualifying scheme to set you on the path to a diverse, challenging and rewarding career.

MEMBERSHIP
Affiliate
Graduate (GradICSA)
Associate (ACIS)
Fellow (FCIS)

QUALIFICATION/EXAMINATIONS
Chartered Secretaries Qualifying Scheme (CSQS)
Certificate in Offshore Finance and Administration
Diploma in Offshore Finance and Administration
Certificate in Company Secretarial Practice and Share Registration Practice
Certificate in Irish Company Secretarial Practice and Share Registration Practice
Certificate in Employee Share Plans
Postgraduate Certificate in Charity Management
ICSA Certificate in Further Education Governance

DESIGNATORY LETTERS
GradICSA, ACIS, FCIS

CATERING AND INSTITUTIONAL MANAGEMENT

Membership of Professional Institutions and Associations

BII

Wessex House
80 Park Street
Camberley
Surrey GU15 3PT
Tel: 01276 684449
E-mail: info@bii.org
Website: www.bii.org

Founded in 1981, BII is the professional body for the licensed retail sector with a remit to raise standards throughout the industry. BIIAB, the wholly owned awarding body of BII, does this through offering qualifications specifically tailored to, and designed in conjunction with, the industry.

MEMBERSHIP
There is a wide range of membership grades available, from those who have just started their careers in licensed retailing to those who have been in the industry for many years. The grade of membership awarded depends on both experience and qualifications and is determined by a points system. Member of the Hotel Catering and Management Association, HCIMA.

QUALIFICATION/EXAMINATIONS
Qualifications for licensing
National Certificate for Personal Licence Holders (Level 2)
Scottish Certificate for Personal Licence Holders
Scottish Certificate for Licensed Premises Staff
National Certificate for Door Supervisors (Level 2)
National Certificate for Door Supervisors (Scotland)
National Certificate for Door Supervisors (Northern Ireland) (Level 2)
Certificate in Physical Interventions (in conjunction with Maybo)
National Certificate for CCTV Operators (Public Space Surveillance) (Level 2)
National Certificate for Security Guards (Level 2)
National Certificate for Security Guards (Scotland)
National Certificate for Licensees (Drugs Awareness) (Level 2)
Scottish Licensee's Certificate in Drug Awareness
National Certificate for Designated Premises Supervisors (Level 2)

Qualifications for new licensed retail managers
National Certificate in Licensed Retailing (Level 2)
Award in Beer and Cellar Quality

Qualifications for staff development
Award in Responsible Alcohol Retailing (Level 1)
Award in Conflict Management
Award in Essentials of Catering (Level 1)
Award in Cooking Theory and Practice (Level 2)
Certificate in Kitchen Management (Level 3)
Award in Customer and Drinks Service (Licensed Hospitality) (Level 1)
Scottish Award in Customer and Drinks Service (Licensed Hospitality)
Qualifications for management development
Profitable Business Portfolio (professional development programme)
Advanced Certificate in Licensed Hospitality (Level 3)
Diploma in Licensed Hospitality (Level 3)
Qualifications for personal and social responsibility
Certificate in Alcohol Awareness (Level 1)
Scottish Certificate in Alcohol Awareness
Award for Music Promoters (Level 2)

CONFEDERATION OF TOURISM AND HOSPITALITY

13–16 Manchester Street
London W1U 4DJ
Tel: 020 7258 9850
Fax: 020 7258 9869
E-mail: info@cthawards.com
Website: www.cthawards.com

The CTH was established in 1982 to provide recognized standards of management and vocational training appropriate to the needs of the hotel and travel industries, via its syllabuses, examinations and awards. We work with approved centres worldwide and are acknowledged by leading hotel and travel industry organizations.

MEMBERSHIP
Student Member
Associate Member (AMCTH)
Member (MCTH)
Fellow (FCTH)

QUALIFICATION/EXAMINATIONS
Diploma in Hotel Management
Advanced Diploma in Hotel Management
Diploma in Hotel and Casino Management
Diploma in Tourism Management
Advanced Diploma in Tourism Management
Diploma in Travel Agency Management

DESIGNATORY LETTERS
AMCTH, MCTH, FCTH

GUILD OF INTERNATIONAL PROFESSIONAL TOASTMASTERS

Life President: Ivor Spencer
12 Little Bornes
Alleyn Park
London SE21 8SE
Tel: 020 8670 5585
Fax: 020 8670 0055
Website: www.guildoftoastmasters.co.uk

The Guild of Professional Toastmasters was established over 30 years ago to improve standards in the profession and support its members. A 5-day course is offered to prospective members, who may apply for membership upon successful completion of the course. Applications are considered by the Fellows of the Guild.

MEMBERSHIP
Fellow (FGIntPT)

DESIGNATORY LETTERS
FGIntPT

INSTITUTE OF HOSPITALITY

Trinity Court
34 West Street
Sutton
Surrey SM1 1SH
Tel: 020 8661 4900
Fax: 020 8661 4901
E-mail: awardingbody@instituteofhospitality.org
Website: www.instituteofhospitality.org

The Institute of Hospitality is the professional body for managers and aspiring managers in the hospitality, leisure and tourism industries. We are an accredited awarding body in the UK and have more than 10,000 members worldwide, whose professional and career development we promote to ensure the highest standards.

MEMBERSHIP
Student Member
Affiliate
Associate (AIH)
Member (MIH)
Fellow (FIH)

DESIGNATORY LETTERS
AIH, MIH, FIH

CHEMISTRY

Membership of Professional Institutions and Associations

SOCIETY OF COSMETIC SCIENTISTS

Suite 6
Langham House East
Mill Street
Luton
Bedfordshire LU1 2NA
Tel: 01582 726661
Fax: 01582 405217
E-mail: ifscc.scs@btinternet.com
Website: www.scs.org.uk

The main object of the Society, which was formed in 1948, is to advance the science of cosmetics. We endeavour to do this by attracting highly qualified scientists with both academic and industrial experience in cosmetics or a related science to our membership of around 900 members, and by means of our publications, educational programmes and scientific meetings.

MEMBERSHIP
Student
Affiliate
Associate Member
Member – B Grade
Member – A Grade
Honorary Member

QUALIFICATION/EXAMINATIONS
Diploma in Cosmetic Science (validated by De Montfort University)

THE OIL AND COLOUR CHEMISTS' ASSOCIATION

1st Floor
3 Eden Court
Eden Way
Leighton Buzzard
Bedfordshire LU7 4FY
Tel: 01525 372530
Fax: 01525 372600
E-mail: membership@occa.org.uk
Website: www.occa.org.uk

OCCA, founded in 1918, is a learned society comprising individual qualified persons employed in, or associated with, the worldwide surface coatings industries. Most of our members work in a technical capacity, but there are senior personnel from throughout the surface coating industries. The word 'oil' in our title refers to vegetable oils, which once formed a major part of surface coatings' formulations.

MEMBERSHIP
Student Member
Ordinary Member
Honorary Member
Licentiate (LTSC)
Associate (ATSC)
Fellow (FTSC)

DESIGNATORY LETTERS
LTSC, ATSC, FTSC

THE ROYAL SOCIETY OF CHEMISTRY

Thomas Graham House
Science Park
Milton Road
Cambridge CB4 0WF
Tel: 01223 420066
Fax: 01223 423623
E-mail: membership@rsc.org
Website: www.rsc.org

The RSC is the UK professional body for chemical scientists and an international learned society for advancing the chemical sciences. With over 46,000 members worldwide and an internationally acclaimed publishing business, our activities span education and training, conferences, science policy and the promotion of the chemical sciences to the public.

MEMBERSHIP
Affiliate
Associate Member (AMRSC)
Member (MRSC)
Fellow (FRSC)

QUALIFICATION/EXAMINATIONS
NVQ Analytical Chemistry (Level 5)
Qualified Person (QP) for the Pharmaceutical Industry
Mastership in Chemical Analysis (MChemA)
Chartered Chemist (CChem)
Chartered Scientist (CSci)

DESIGNATORY LETTERS
AMRSC, MRSC, FRSC, CChem

CHIROPODY

Membership of Professional Institutions and Associations

BRITISH CHIROPODY AND PODIATRY ASSOCIATION

The New Hall
149 Bath Road
Maidenhead
Berkshire SL6 4LA
Tel: 01628 632440
Fax: 01628 674483
E-mail: membership@bcha-uk.org
Website: www.bcha-uk.org

The BChA, formed in 1959, is the largest professional organization in the UK representing the interests of independent private chiropodists / podiatrists. Since 2005 we have added foothealth practitioners to include our 7,000 members, most of whom work mainly in private practice. Those who are registered with the Health Professions Council may work in the NHS or in education.

MEMBERSHIP
Member (MSSCh & MBChA) – Podiatrists
Fellow (FSSCh) – Podiatrist
Associate members are foothealth practitioners trained by The SMAE Institute.

QUALIFICATION/EXAMINATIONS
Diploma in Podiatric Medicine (DipPodMed)
Foothealth practitioners carry the qualification – MAFHP

DESIGNATORY LETTERS
MSSCh, MBChA, FSSCh and MAFHP

THE INSTITUTE OF CHIROPODISTS AND PODIATRISTS

27 Wright Street
Southport
Merseyside PR9 0TL
Tel: 01704 546141
Fax: 01704 500477
E-mail: secretary@iocp.org.uk
Website: www.inst-chiropodist.org.uk

The IOCP represents all levels of the profession and our CPD is open to both members and non-members, as by elevating professional standards we aim to improve public safety. We have branches throughout the UK and the Republic of Ireland, and members overseas, and hold lectures, seminars and workshops to enable members to keep up to date.

MEMBERSHIP
Full Member
Fellow

THE SOCIETY OF CHIROPODISTS AND PODIATRISTS

1 Fellmongers Path
Tower Bridge Road
London SE1 3LY
Tel: 020 7234 8620
Fax: 0845 450 3721
E-mail: enq@scpod.org
Website: www.feetforlife.org

The SCP is the professional body and trade union for registered podiatrists. Membership is restricted to those qualified for registration and the Society represents around 10,000 NHS podiatrists, private practitioners and students. We monitor standards of undergraduate education and provide opportunities for CPD for our members.

MEMBERSHIP
Member (MChS)
Fellow (FChS)

DESIGNATORY LETTERS
MChS, FChS

CHIROPRACTIC

Membership of Professional Institutions and Associations

MCTIMONEY CHIROPRACTIC ASSOCIATION

Crowmarsh Gifford
Wallingford
Oxfordshire OX10 8DJ
Tel: 01491 829211
Fax: 01491 829494
E-mail: admin@mctimoney-chiropractic.org
Website: www.mctimoneychiropractic.org

The McTimoney Chiropractic Association is the professional association for McTimoney chiropractors, who in the UK are registered with the General Chiropractic Council.

MEMBERSHIP
Provisional Member
Full Member
Fellow

DESIGNATORY LETTERS
MMCA

SCOTTISH CHIROPRACTIC ASSOCIATION

1 Chisholm Avenue
Bishopton
Renfrewshire PA7 5JH
Tel: 0141 404 0260
Fax: 0)141 404 0260
E-mail: admin@sca-chiropractic.org
Website: www.sca-chiropractic.org

The SCA was formed in 1979 and now has more than 60 members practising in Scotland and over 120 associated members elsewhere in the UK and abroad. Our aims are to enhance the chiropractic profession in the UK, maintain high standards of professional practice, and provide advice and support to our members.

MEMBERSHIP
Member

UNITED CHIROPRACTIC ASSOCIATION

1st Floor
45 North Hill
Plymouth
Devon PL4 8EZ
Tel: 01752 658785
Fax: 01752 658786
E-mail: admin@united-chiropractic.org
Website: www.united-chiropractic.org

The UCA is a UK-based organization for qualified, professional, principal-based chiropractors, associates and students. Full membership is open to qualified, GCC-registered chiropractors from any recognized school of chiropractic.

MEMBERSHIP
Student
Associate
Affiliate
1st Year Graduate
2nd Year Graduate
Full Member
Overseas Member

THE CHURCHES

Membership of Professional Institutions and Associations

BAPTIST UNION OF SCOTLAND

Baptist House
14 Aytoun Road
Glasgow G41 5RT
Tel: 0141 423 6169
Fax: 0141 424 1422
E-mail: admin@scottishbaptist.org.uk
Website: www.scottishbaptist.org.uk

The Baptist Union of Scotland was formed in 1869, when 51 churches with a total congregation of about 3, 500 united. Today, with 142 churches and about 14,000 members, the Union strives for simplicity in organizational structure and promotes increasing contact between the local churches and Council-appointed Core Leaders, who function under the overall direction of the General Director.

QUALIFICATION/EXAMINATIONS
Certificate/Diploma of Higher Learning in Theology
BD in Theology & Pastoral Studies
Graduate Diploma in Applied Theology through Work Based Learning
Graduate Diploma in Pastoral Studies
(awarded by the Scottish Baptist College, Paisley, and validated by the University of Paisley)

BRISTOL BAPTIST COLLEGE

The Promenade
Clifton Down
Clifton
Bristol BS8 3NJ
Tel: 0117 946 7050
Fax: 0117 946 7787
E-mail: admin@bristol-baptist.ac.uk
Website: www.bristol-baptist.ac.uk

The central aim of the College is to train men and women for ministry in the Church and in the world. We do this by enabling critical reflection upon the Bible and Christian theological tradition and on the contexts from which we come and within which we are placed.

QUALIFICATION/EXAMINATIONS
Certificate in Theological Studies
Diploma in Theological Studies
BA in Theological Studies
MA in Biblical Studies
MA in Mission Studies
(all validated by the University of Bristol)

METHODIST CHURCH IN IRELAND

Board of Examiners
Secretary: Rev Peter D Murray, BA, BD
28 Windermere Drive
Bangor
Co Down BT20 4QF

MEMBERSHIP
Candidates for training must normally have the standard of general education for university entrance. They must be accredited Local Preachers of the Methodist Church, and are examined by written papers in Biblical Studies and Theology and by oral aptitude and personality tests. After admission to training, candidates normally spend 3 years at Edgehill Theological College, Belfast, studying for a diploma or degree of Queen's University, Belfast, in New Testament Greek, Hebrew, the English Bible, Theology, Church History, Pastoral Psychology, or Homiletics. This is followed by 3 years as a probationer Minister working under a superintendent Minister. During probation the candidate continues study within a tutorial system and is examined by continuous assessment.

THE CHURCH OF ENGLAND

Ministry Division of The Archbishops' Council
Church House
Great Smith Street
London SW1P 3AZ
Tel: 020 7898 1404
Fax: 020 7898 1421
E-mail: david.way@churchofengland.org (ordination training)
susan.hart@churchofengland.org (Reader training)
Website: www.cofe.anglican.org www.archbishopofcanterbury.org/1027

The Church of England's Ministry Division oversees training for ordination and issues certificates for successful completion for Reader ministry. Enquiries about entry into training should be directed to the candidate's own diocese. In addition, The Archbishop's Examination in Theology offers means of study at three postgraduate levels.

QUALIFICATION/EXAMINATIONS
Archbishop's Examination:
PG Diploma of Student of Theology
Master of Philosophy
Doctor of Philosophy

THE CHURCH OF SCOTLAND

Church of Scotland Offices
121 George Street
Edinburgh EH2 4YN
Tel: 0131 225 5722
Fax: 0131 220 3113
Website: www.churchofscotland.org.uk

The Ministries Council runs an enquiry process to help those who sense a call to any of the ministries within the Church of Scotland to consider it in a supportive environment. Attendance at one of our enquirers' conferences, which are held twice each year, is the first stage of the enquiry process. For more information see; www.churchofscotland.org.uk/councils/ministries/mintraining.htm

THE METHODIST CHURCH

Formation in Ministry Office (Initial Development of Ministries)
25 Marylebone Road
London NW1 5JR
Tel: 020 7486 5502

Candidates for Diaconal or Presbyteral Ministry in the Methodist Church must have been members of the Methodist Church at least 2 years and are expected to offer at least 10 years of ministerial service. The first stage of preparation is Foundation Training, which requires 1 year (FT) or 2 years (PT) to complete, during which a person may apply to become a candidate for ordained ministry. The process of selection takes 6 months. To enter into training for Presbyteral Ministry, a candidate must be a trained Local Preacher, which involves taking the Methodist Local Preachers' Training Course, Faith & Worship. Deacons become members of the Methodist Diaconal and are not required to be preachers. Accepted candidates for either order receive 1 or 2 years of further theological training, which in most cases leads to a degree or diploma in Theology or Ministry. Upon completion of training, a candidate serves as a Methodist Minister for 2 years on probation before ordination. For Presbyters, the appointment may be to an itinerant appointment (stipendiary) or to a local appointment (usually non-stipendiary) or as licensed to minister in secular employment. Deacons are always itinerant.

THE MORAVIAN CHURCH IN GREAT BRITAIN AND IRELAND

Moravian Church House
5–7 Muswell Hill
London N10 3TJ
Tel: 020 8883 3409
Fax: 020 8365 3371
E-mail: moravianchurchhouse@btinternet.com
Website: www.moravian.org.uk

Candidates for Moravian Church Service must be members of the Moravian Church and would normally have completed the Lay Training Course and have the support of their local church committee. They should make an initial application to the Provincial Board of the Moravian Church. Their qualifications are examined by the Church Service Advisory Board, which reports on them to the Provincial Board, with whom the final decision rests. Normally the standard of education required for the work of the Ministry is a university Divinity degree or Certificate together with a thorough acquaintance with the history, principles and methods of the Moravian Church. Candidates receive guidance for the Ministry during a period of supervised service under the direction of experienced Ministers. A class of non-stipendiary Ministers has been established for those who wish to serve on a non-maintained basis. Training varies according to candidates' needs. In all cases applications should be made to the address given above.

THE PRESBYTERIAN CHURCH IN IRELAND

The Director of Ministerial Studies
Union Theological College
108 Botanic Avenue
Belfast BT7 1JT
Tel: 02890 205088
Fax: 02890 205099

Qualifications required: Under 30 – a non-theological degree; over 30 but under 40 (as reckoned on 1 October following application) – either a non-theological degree or 2 years, non-graduating Arts or 4 modules of PT BD study or 6 modules of PT study in Humanities acceptable to the Board of Studies; over 40 – not normally accepted, except in exceptional circumstances, where candidate is already possessed of good educational background and/or professional experience.

THE PRESBYTERIAN CHURCH OF WALES

Tabernacle Chapel
81 Merthyr Road
Whitchurch
Cardiff CF14 1DD
Tel: 02920 627465
Fax: 02920 616188
E-mail: swyddfa.office@ebcpcw.org.uk
Website: www.ebcpw.org.uk

The Presbyterian Church of Wales (PCW) is a Protestant non-conformist denomination. Ordination is dependent on successful application through the local church and Presbytery to the Candidates and Training Department.

MEMBERSHIP
Ministers are ordained to the full-time, part-time or non-stipendary ministry.

QUALIFICATION/EXAMINATIONS
Pastoral Studies course

THE ROMAN CATHOLIC CHURCH

Candidates for the priesthood in the RC Church attend a residential seminary course of at least 6 years. Among subjects studied are Philosophy, Psychology, Dogmatic and Moral Theology, Scripture, Church History, Canon Law, Liturgy, Catechetics, Communications and Pastoral Theology. Each college/seminary has its own arrangements for the university education of its students. Those who do not attend university take a final internal exam.

THE SALVATION ARMY

UK Headquarters
101 Newington Causeway
London SE1 6BN
Tel: 020 7367 4500
E-mail: thq@salvationarmy.org.uk
Website: www.salvationarmy.org.uk

Salvation Army officers engaged in FT service are ordained ministers of religion, and are commissioned following a 2-year period of residential training at the William Booth College, Denmark Hill, London SE5 8BQ. This course – an HE Diploma in Salvation Army Officer Training – may now be undertaken by distance learning, or a mixture of residential and distance learning. Officers may be appointed to corps (church) work, to social services centres (for which additional professional qualifications are required) or to administrative posts.

THE SCOTTISH EPISCOPAL CHURCH

Theological Institute of the Scottish Episcopal Church
Forbes House
21 Grosvenor Crescent
Edinburgh EH12 5EE
Tel: 0131 225 6357
Fax: 0131 346 7247
E-mail: tisec@scotland.anglican.org
Website: www.scotland.anglican.org

Candidates are trained for lay and ordained, stipendiary and non-stipendiary ministries in the Scottish Episcopal Church, Methodist Church and the United Reformed Church.

The curriculum is delivered centrally through residential sessions and regionally through diocesan groups. The Diploma in Theology for Ministry course run by the Institute is validated by York St John's University. Some students undertake further studies through universities, leading to degree qualifications.

THE SCOTTISH UNITED REFORMED AND CONGREGATIONAL COLLEGE

The Principal
Glasgow G1 2BQ
Tel: 0141 332 7667
E-mail: Scottishcollege@urcscotland.org.uk
Website: www.scotland.urc.org.uk

The College is recognized as a resource centre for learning by the General Assembly of the United Reformed Church and is one of the institutions charged with responsibility for initial ministerial education.

QUALIFICATION/EXAMINATIONS

The College awards only its own certificate, which is part of the process of accreditation of ordinands as ministers of the United Reformed Church. Students, however, are normally concurrently matriculated for a degree, normally in Theology or Religious Studies, at a university.

THE UNITARIAN AND FREE CHRISTIAN CHURCHES

Essex Hall
London WC2R 3HY
Tel: 020 7240 2384
Fax: 020 7240 3089
E-mail: info@unitarian.org.uk
Website: www.unitarian.org.uk

Candidates accepted for training for the ministry in the Unitarian and Free Christian Churches take courses of training either at Manchester Academy & Harris College, Oxford (2 to 4 years' study for an Oxford degree in Theology/or Theology & Philosophy or an Oxford Certificate in Theology/Religious Studies), or at the Unitarian College (Luther King House, Brighton Grove, Rusholme, Manchester; an individually designed contextual theology course of the Partnership for Theological Education which may lead to a degree or other academic qualification validated by Chester or Manchester University). Alternative arrangements can be made for candidates wishing to study through the Welsh language. Placement work and Unitarian studies are also integral to ministerial preparation. Training normally takes 2 or more years.

THE UNITED REFORMED CHURCH

Church House
86 Tavistock Place
London WC1H 9RT
Tel: 020 7916 2020
Fax: 020 7916 2021
E-mail: training@urc.org.uk
Website: www.urc.org.uk

Stipendiary Ministry: URC Ministers are usually trained in the Church's theological colleges. All training is ecumenical. Candidates must been a member of the URC for at least 2 years and go through a candidating process in the other Councils of the Church to decide whether they should be sponsored for training. Most then take a 3- or 4-year degree in Theology or a diploma of the university to which their college is attached. In certain cases it is possible to train PT on an ecumenical course. The minimum requirement on training completion is a Theology diploma and 800 hours placement in a church.

Non-Stipendiary: A training programme of PT study usually over 4 years is open to committed members of the URC. Candidates must be recommended by their local church and go though the process indicated above. A Director of Training guides the student. Most students study PT on a recognized ecumenical course, with an additional programme to study Reformed History Ethics and Worship, but some train FT in a college. A Leaving Certificate for a call to the ordained ministry is granted. Training is arranged by the Board of Studies of the Training Committee.

Church-related Community Workers: They help lead and strengthen the local church's mission through community development in an area where specialist help is required to meet unusual needs. Candidates must be members of the URC and show capabilities for leadership. They are required to obtain at least a Diploma in Theology and a Diploma in Community Work before being commissioned.

Lay Preacher's Certificate: Training for Learning & Serving is the qualifying course for this. The course takes 3 years. Work is done in local groups and there are five residential weekend courses each year. Candidates are also expected to undertake some practical work in churches.

THE WESLEYAN REFORM UNION

Wesleyan Reform Church House
123 Queen Street
Sheffield S1 2DU
Tel: 0114 272 1938
E-mail: admin@thewru.co.uk
Website: www.thewru.com

The Wesleyan Reform Union has no training college of its own and encourages candidates for its Ministry to enter a Bible College for 2 or 3 years. All candidates are, however, under the personal supervision of a Union Tutor, who directs a Biblical Studies & Training Department offering fairly extensive courses. Candidates attend Headquarters once a year for an oral exam in Theology conducted by the Tutor in the presence of the Union Examination Committee; they also take written exams.

UNITED FREE CHURCH OF SCOTLAND

11 Newton Place
Glasgow G3 7PR
Tel: 01413 323435
Fax: 01413 331973
E-mail: office@ufcos.org.uk
Website: www.ufcos.org.uk

The United Free Church of Scotland is a small presbyterian denomination which came into being in 1929. Those seeking to become candidates for the ministry should normally have been members of the denomination for at least a year. They will require to undertake a degree course in theology.

THE CHURCH IN WALES

St Michael's College
Llandaff
Cardiff CF5 2YJ
Tel: 029 205 63379
Fax: 029 208 38088

The Church in Wales expects candidates for ordination to satisfy the requirements of recognized theological courses. University graduates usually spend at least 2 years at a theological college, and if they are non-theological graduates, they are encouraged to study for a university degree or diploma in Theology. Non-graduate candidates must have at least 5 passes at GCSE and normally study for a university diploma in Theology or a degree in Theology if they have obtained the necessary grades at A level. These requirements may be modified in the case of older candidates.

CINEMA, FILM AND TELEVISION

Membership of Professional Institutions and Associations

BRITISH KINEMATOGRAPH SOUND AND TELEVISION SOCIETY (BKSTS)

Pinewood Studios
Pinewood Road
Iver Heath
Buckinghamshire SL0 0NH
Tel: 01753 656656
E-mail: info@bksts.com
Website: www.bksts.com

The BKSTS was founded in 1931 to serve the growing film industry and today arranges meetings, presentations, seminars, international exhibitions and conferences, as well as organizing an extensive programme of training courses, lectures, workshops and special events. We ensure that our members remain up to date with the latest techniques through master classes and our print and electronic publications.

MEMBERSHIP
Student Member
Intermediate Member
Associate Member
Full Member (MBKS)
Retired Member
Fellow (FBKS)

DESIGNATORY LETTERS
MBKS, FBKS

THE LONDON FILM SCHOOL

24 Shelton Street
Covent Garden
London WC2H 9UB
Tel: 020 7836 9642
Fax: 020 7497 3718
E-mail: info@lfs.org.uk
Website: www.lfs.org.uk

The LFS is one of the foremost independent film schools in Europe and is recognized by Skillset as a Centre of Excellence. It is a registered charity and a non-profit-making company, limited by guarantee. Since 1956 we have trained thousands of directors, cinematographers, editors and other film professionals from around the world.

QUALIFICATION/EXAMINATIONS
MA in Filmmaking (validated by London Metropolitan University)
MA in Screenwriting (validated by London Metropolitan University)

THE NATIONAL FILM AND TELEVISION SCHOOL

Beaconsfield Studios
Station Road
Beaconsfield
Buckinghamshire HP9 1LG
Tel: 01494 671234
Fax: 01494 674042
E-mail: info@nfts.co.uk
Website: www.nfts.co.uk

A Skillset Screen & Media Academy, the UK's leading film and television school offers full-time MA and Diploma courses in all the key film and television disciplines, from Animation to VFX. Purpose-built studios include two film stages, a large television studio, and post-production facilities rivalling those of many professional companies.

QUALIFICATION/EXAMINATIONS
Diploma (in 1 of 3 disciplines)
MA in Film and Television (specializing in 1 of 13 disciplines)

CLEANING, LAUNDRY AND DRY CLEANING

Membership of Professional Institutions and Associations

BRITISH INSTITUTE OF CLEANING SCIENCE

9 Premier Court
Boarden Close
Moulton Park
Northampton NN3 6LF
Tel: 01604 678710
Fax: 01604 645988
E-mail: info@bics.org.uk
Website: www.bics.org.uk

The BICSc is the largest independent professional and educational body within the cleaning industry. Our aim is to raise the status and standards of the cleaning industry through training and education. We offer our 5,000 members a range of assessment schemes and training courses, together with a telephone and e-mail helpline.

MEMBERSHIP
Practitioner
Associate
Member
Corporate Member

THE GUILD OF CLEANERS AND LAUNDERERS

5 Portland Place
London W1B 1PW
Tel: 0845 600 1838
E-mail: enquiries@gcl.org.uk
Website: www.gcl.org.uk

The Guild, formed in 1949, is a technical and professional society whose aim is to further knowledge and skill in all branches of the industry. We keep out members up to date through lectures, seminars and written reports, exchange information of mutual benefit with other organizations in the industry, and voice our opinion in relevant forums.

MEMBERSHIP
Young Guilder
Member
Associate (AGCL)
Advanced Member (AdGCL)
Licentiate (LGCL)
Fellow (FGCL)

DESIGNATORY LETTERS
AGCL, AdGCL, LGCL, FGCL

COLOUR TECHNOLOGY

Membership of Professional Institutions and Associations

PAINTING AND DECORATING ASSOCIATION

32 Coton Road
Nuneaton
Warwickshire CV11 5TW
Tel: 024 7635 3776
Fax: 024 7635 4513
E-mail: info@paintingdecoratingassociation.co.uk
Website: www.paintingdecoratingassociation.co.uk

The PDA is a registered trade and employers' organization, catering exclusively for the needs of professional painting and decorating trade employers. The Association conducts no examinations, but all membership applications are scrutinized at branch level to ensure that only bona fide firms that agree to abide by our code of conduct are admitted.

MEMBERSHIP
Full Member
Associate

THE SOCIETY OF DYERS AND COLOURISTS

Perkin House
82 Grattan Road
Bradford BD1 2JB
Tel: 01274 761792
Fax: 01274 392888
E-mail: members@sdc.org.uk
Website: www.sdc.org.uk

An educational charity, professional body and chartered society, serving globally all aspects of the coloration industries including the textile supply chain through the knowledgeable and enthusiastic involvement of its professional members and industry partners.
Recognized as the authority for colour science and technology, delivering high-quality international qualifications and training programmes.

MEMBERSHIP
Professional Voting Member (FSDC, ASDC, LSDC, CCol)
Ordinary Voting Member
Individual Member
Individual Student Member
Educational Institute Member
Corporate (Company) Member

QUALIFICATION/EXAMINATIONS
Diploma of Fellowship (FSDC)
Diploma of Associateship (ASDC)
Diploma of Licentiateship (LSDC)
Chartered Colourist (CCol)

DESIGNATORY LETTERS
FSDC, ASDC, LSDC, CCol.

COMMUNICATIONS AND MEDIA

Membership of Professional Institutions and Associations

THE PICTURE RESEARCH ASSOCIATION

Box 105 Hampstead House
176 Finchley Road
London NW3 6BP
Tel: 07771 982308
Website: www.picture-research.org.uk

The PRA, founded in 1977, is a professional organization for picture researchers, picture editors and anyone specifically involved in the research, management and supply of visual material to the media industry. Our aims are to provide information and give support to our members, and to promote their interests and specific skills to potential employers.

MEMBERSHIP
Introductory Member
Associate Member
Full Member

COMPUTING AND INFORMATION TECHNOLOGY

Membership of Professional Institutions and Associations

ASSOCIATION OF COMPUTER PROFESSIONALS

ACP
Chilverbridge House
Arlington
East Sussex BN26 6SB
Tel: 01323 871874
Fax: 01323 871875
E-mail: admin@acpexamboard.com
Website: www.acpexamboard.com

The ACP is an independent professional examining body, founded in 1984 to set and maintain standards of education that reflect the constantly changing requirements of the computer industry, both in the UK and overseas. We do so through the provision of course syllabuses and examinations to our carefully vetted training centres around the world.

MEMBERSHIP
Student
Practitioner
Graduate (GradACP)
Licentiate (LACP)
Associate (AACP)
Member (MACP)
Fellow (FACP)

QUALIFICATION/EXAMINATIONS
Please see the ACP's website for details of certificates and diplomas.

DESIGNATORY LETTERS
GradACP, LACP, AACP, MACP, FACP

BRITISH COMPUTER SOCIETY

1st Floor, Block D
North Star House
North Star Avenue
Swindon
Wiltshire SN2 1FA
Tel: 01793 417417
Fax: 01793 417444
E-mail: customerservices@hq.bcs.org.uk
Website: www.bcs.org.uk

The BCS is the professional membership and accreditation body for IT and has more than 70,000 members, including practitioners, businesses, academics and students, in the UK and internationally. Our aim is to promote the academic study and professional practice of computing and to show the public that IT is about far more than simply using a PC.

MEMBERSHIP
Student
Affiliate
Associate Member (AMBCS)
Professional Fellow (FBCS)
Honorary Fellow
Distinguished Fellow
Incorporated Engineer (IEng)
Chartered Engineer (CEng)
Chartered IT Professional (MBCS CITP)
Chartered Fellow (FBCS CITP)
Chartered Scientist (CSci)
Education Affiliate (institutional member)

QUALIFICATION/EXAMINATIONS
Certificate in IT
Certificate in IT for Insurance Professionals (developed jointly with The Chartered Insurance Institute)
Diploma in IT
Professional GradDip in IT

See the BCS website for details of other qualifications.

INSTITUTE FOR THE MANAGEMENT OF INFORMATION SYSTEMS

Suite A, (Part) 2nd Floor
3 White Oak Square
London Road
Swanley
Kent BR8 7AG
Tel: 0845 850 0006
Fax: 0845 850 0007
E-mail: central@imis.org.uk
Website: www.imis.org.uk

IMIS is one of the leading professional associations in the IT sector. A registered charity, it plays a prominent role in fostering greater understanding of IS management, in working to enhance the status of those engaged in the profession, and in promoting higher standards through better education and training worldwide.

MEMBERSHIP
Student Member
Practitioner Member
Licentiate Member (LIMIS)
Associate Member (AIMIS)
Full Member (MIMIS)
Fellow (FIMIS)

QUALIFICATION/EXAMINATIONS
Foundation
Diploma
Higher Diploma

DESIGNATORY LETTERS
LIMIS, AIMIS, MIMIS, FIMIS

INSTITUTION OF ANALYSTS AND PROGRAMMERS

Charles House
36 Culmington Road
London W13 9NH
Tel: 020 8567 2118
Fax: 020 8567 4379
E-mail: dg@iap.org.uk
Website: www.iap.org.uk

The IAP is a professional organization for people who work in the development, installation and testing of business systems and computer software. Our aim is to promote high standards of competence and conduct among our members, to encourage them to develop their skills and progress their career, and to facilitate the advancement and spreading of knowledge within the profession.

MEMBERSHIP
Licentiate
Graduate (GradIAP)
Associate Member (AIAP)
Member (MIAP)
Fellow (FIAP)

DESIGNATORY LETTERS
GradIAP, AIAP, MIAP, FIAP

COUNSELLING

Membership of Professional Institutions and Associations

COUNSELLING LTD

Registered Office
5 Pear Tree Walk
Wakefield
West Yorkshire WF2 0HW
E-mail: E-mail via the website
Website: www.counselling.ltd.uk

Counselling, a registered charity founded in 1998, is a membership organization for counsellors and psychotherapists in the UK that has established a network of about 2,700 affiliated CCC-registered counsellors, many of whom are able to provide occasional free or discounted face-to-face counselling with clients on low incomes.

MEMBERSHIP
Affiliate

COUNSELLORS AND PSYCHOTHERAPISTS IN PRIMARY CARE

Queensway House
Queensway
Bognor Regis
West Sussex PO21 1QT
Tel: 01243 870701
Fax: 01243 870702
E-mail: cpc@cpc-online.co.uk
Website: www.cpc-online.co.uk

CPC is a professional membership association for individual practitioners, whose names are entered in a Register of Members. The aims of the Association are to represent counsellors and psychotherapists working in an NHS setting and to lead the way in establishing national standards and guidelines for further development of professional and effective counselling throughout the NHS.

MEMBERSHIP
Student
Subscriber
Intermediate Member
Registered Member
Supervisor
Organizational Member

QUALIFICATION/EXAMINATIONS
PGDip in Supervision for the Primary Care Setting

CSCT COUNSELLING TRAINING

13 Coleshill Street
Sutton Coldfield
West Midlands B72 1SD
Tel: 0121 321 1396/0870 1
Fax: 0121 355 5581
E-mail: info@counsellingtraining.com
Website: www.counsellingtraining.com

CSCT has been producing counselling training courses for over 25 years, during which time we have trained over 50,000 students. Our courses are offered PT via a network of colleges and private providers throughout the UK. Our training materials are written to the specifications of the appropriate awarding body and we provide 24-hour e-mail and telephone support from Client Services and the Academic Team.

QUALIFICATION/EXAMINATIONS
Please see the CSCT's website.

CREDIT MANAGEMENT

Membership of Professional Institutions and Associations

INSTITUTE OF CREDIT MANAGEMENT

The Water Mill
Station Road
South Luffenham
Oakham
Leicestershire LE15 8NB
Tel: 01780 722900
Fax: 01780 721333
E-mail: info@icm.org.uk
Website: www.icm.org.uk

The ICM is the largest professional credit management organization in Europe and the only one accredited by Ofqual as an awarding body. We represent the credit profession across trade, consumer and export credit, as well as in related activities such as collections, credit reporting, credit insurance and insolvency, promote excellence in credit management and raise awareness of its vital role in business and the community.

MEMBERSHIP
Affiliate
Asociate Member (AICM)
Graduate Member (MICM(Grad))
Member (MICM)
Fellow (FICM)

QUALIFICATION/EXAMINATIONS
Diploma in Credit Management (Level 2)
Diploma in Credit Management (Level 3)
Diploma in Credit Management (Level 5)

DESIGNATORY LETTERS
AICM, MICM (Grad), MICM, FICM

DANCING

Membership of Professional Institutions and Associations

BRITISH BALLET ORGANIZATION

Woolborough House
39 Lonsdale Road
Barnes
London SW13 9JP
Tel: 020 8748 1241
Fax: 020 8748 1301
E-mail: info@bbo.org.uk
Website: www.bbo.org.uk

The BBO, founded in 1930, is an awarding body offering teacher training and examinations in classical ballet, tap, modern dance and jazz. We have schools throughout the UK and in several other countries.

MEMBERSHIP
Student Member
Senior Student Member
Affiliated Member
Student Teacher Member
Teacher Member

QUALIFICATION/EXAMINATIONS
Please see the BBO website for details.

IMPERIAL SOCIETY OF TEACHERS OF DANCING

Imperial House
22/26 Paul Street
London EC2A 4QE
Tel: +44 (0)20 7377 1577
Fax: +44 (0)20 7247 8309
E-mail: education@istd.org
Website: www.istd.org

The ISTD is a registered educational charity and examinations board. We aim to promote knowledge of dance, to maintain and improve teaching standards, and to qualify (by examination) teachers of dancing. Our dance techniques cover more than 12 different genres and are taught by more than 7,500 members by our members worldwide.

MEMBERSHIP
A range of 9 categories from Student to Life Membership.

QUALIFICATION/EXAMINATIONS
Please see our website www.istd.org or www.dance-teachers.org.

DESIGNATORY LETTERS
ISTD

INTERNATIONAL DANCE TEACHERS' ASSOCIATION LIMITED

International House
76 Bennett Road
Brighton BN2 5JL
Tel: 01273 685652
Fax: 01273 674388
E-mail: info@idta.co.uk
Website: www.idta.co.uk

The IDTA is one of the world's largest dance examination boards, with more than 7,000 members in 55 countries. Our aims are to promote knowledge and foster the art of dance in all its forms, to maintain and improve dancing standards, and to offer a comprehensive range of professional qualifications in all dance genres.

MEMBERSHIP
Associate (AIDTA)
Licentiate (LIDTA)
Fellow (FIDTA)

DESIGNATORY LETTERS
AIDTA, LIDTA, FIDTA

THE BENESH INSTITUTE

36 Battersea Square
London SW11 3RA
Tel: 020 7326 8031
Fax: 020 7924 3129
E-mail: beneshinstitute@rad.org.uk
Website: www.benesh.org

The Benesh Institute is the international centre for Benesh Movement Notation (BMN) founded in 1962 to promote, develop and offer education in BMN. We also function as an examining body and professional centre, and are responsible for coordinating technical developments. Since 1997 The Benesh Institute has been incorporated within the Royal Academy of Dance.

MEMBERSHIP
Fellow (FI Chor)

QUALIFICATION/EXAMINATIONS
Certificate in Benesh Movement Notation (CBMN) (validated by the Royal Academy of Dance)
Diploma for Professional Benesh Movement Notators (DPBMN) (validated by the Royal Academy of Dance)
Associate of the Institute of Choreology (AI Chor)

DESIGNATORY LETTERS
FI Chor

DENTISTRY

Membership of Professional Institutions and Associations

GENERAL DENTAL COUNCIL

37 Wimpole Street
London W1G 8DQ
Tel: 0845 222 4141
Fax: 020 7224 3294
E-mail: information@gdc-uk.org
Website: www.gdc-uk.org

The GDC regulates dental professionals in the UK. All dentists, clinical dental technicians, dental hygienists, dental nurses, dental technicians, dental therapists and orthodontic therapists must be registered with the GDC in order to work in the UK.

THE BRITISH DENTAL ASSOCIATION

64 Wimpole Street
London W1G 8YS
Tel: 020 7935 0875
Fax: 020 7487 5232
E-mail: enquiries@bda.org
Website: www.bda.org

The BDA, which was founded in 1880, is the professional association and trade union for dentists in the UK. Our aims are to advance the science, arts and ethics of dentistry, improve in UK's oral health, and promote the interests of our members. Membership, which is voluntary, stands at around 23,000, mostly in general practice.

MEMBERSHIP
Student Member
(Recently) Qualified Member
Ordinary Member
Retired Member
Overseas Member

BRITISH SOCIETY OF DENTAL HYGIENE AND THERAPY

3 Kestrel Court
Waterwells Business Park
Gloucester GL2 2AT
Tel: 01452 886365
Fax: 01452 886468
E-mail: enquiries@bsdht.org.uk
Website: www.bsdht.org.uk

The BSDHT is the only nationally recognized body that represents dental hygienists, dental hygienist-therapists and students of dental hygiene. We have a membership of more than 3,500 in the UK and beyond, and look after their interests through liaising with the Department of Health, General Dental Council, British Dental Association and other organizations.

MEMBERSHIP
Member

BRITISH ASSOCIATION OF DENTAL NURSES

PO Box 4, Room 200
Hillhouse International Business Centre
Thornton-Cleveleys
Lancashire FY5 4QD
Tel: 01253 338360
Fax: 01253 773266
E-mail: admin@badn.org.uk
Website: www.badn.org.uk

The BADN represents dental nurses, whether qualified or unqualified, working in general practice, hospital, the community, the armed forces, industry, practice management or reception, and has representation on the National Examining Board, the Dental Nurses Standards and Training Advisory Board and its Registration Committee, the Joint Consultative Committee, and other bodies.

MEMBERSHIP
Associate Member
Full Member

CLINICAL DENTAL TECHNICIANS ASSOCIATION

Room 3b, Ground Floor
Tower House Business Centre
Fishergate
York YO10 4UA
Tel: 01904 625130
Fax: 01904 658361
Website: www.cdta.org.uk

The CDTA provides political and educational representation for its members, who are registered with the General Dental Council and trained in designing, creating, constructing, repairing and rebasing removable appliances to ensure optimal fit, maximum comfort and general wellbeing of patients. We are committed to team dentistry and ensure that our members work to the highest professional standards.

MEMBERSHIP
Member

DENTAL TECHNOLOGISTS ASSOCIATION

3 Kestral Court
Waterwells Drive
Waterwells Business Park
Gloucester GL2 2AT
Tel: 0870 243 0753
E-mail: sueadams@dta-uk.org
Website: www.dta-uk.org/

The DTA is an organization that supports the development of the dental technology profession by encouraging and promoting education, including CPD, and for the exchange of views between dental technicians. We advise, develop and support dental technicians and maintain links with the government, other dental organizations, service providers and the public.

MEMBERSHIP
Member

DIETETICS

Membership of Professional Institutions and Associations

THE BRITISH DIETETIC ASSOCIATION

5th Floor
Charles House
Queensway
Birmingham B3 3HT
Tel: 0121 200 8080
Fax: 0121 200 8081
E-mail: info@bda.uk.com
Website: www.bda.uk.com

The BDA, established in 1936, is the professional association and trade union for dietitians. Our aims are to advance the science and practice of dietetics and associated subjects, to promote education and training in the science and practice of dietetics and associated subjects, and to regulate relations betweens our more than 6,700 members and their employers.

MEMBERSHIP
Student Member
Associate Member
Affiliate Member
Full Member

DISTRIBUTION

Membership of Professional Institutions and Associations

THE CHARTERED INSTITUTE OF LOGISTICS AND TRANSPORT (UK)

Earlstrees Court
Earlstrees Road
Corby
Northamptonshire NN17 4AX
Tel: 01536 740104
Fax: 01536 740101
E-mail: membership@ciltuk.org.uk
Website: www.ciltuk.org.uk

The CILT(UK) is the professional body for transport, logistics and integrated supply chain management and has more than 20,000 members in manufacturing, distribution, passenger transport, retail, import and export, national and local government, purchase and supply, warehousing, education, research and the armed forces. Our aim is to promote professional excellence and the development of modern techniques, and to encourage the adoption of efficient and sustainable policies.

MEMBERSHIP
Part-time Student
Full-time Student
Affiliate
Member (MILT)
Chartered Member (CMILT)
Chartered Fellow (CFILT)

QUALIFICATION/EXAMINATIONS
Certificate (Level 2)
Certificate (Level 3)
Professional Diploma (Level 5)
Advanced Diploma in Logistics and Transport (Level 6)

MSc in International Transport and Logistics *or* International Logistics and Supply Chain Management

DESIGNATORY LETTERS
MILT, CMILT, CFILT

DIVING

Membership of Professional Institutions and Associations

DIVING CERTIFICATES

Health & Safety Executive, Diving Operations Strategy Team
Wren House, Hedgerows Business Park
Colchester Road, Springfield
Chelmsford
Essex CM2 5PF
Tel: 01245 706256
Fax: 01245 706222
E-mail: cathy.uprichard@hse.gsi.gov.uk
Website: www.hse.gov.uk/diving

The Health and Safety Executive (HSE) issues diver competence certificates to divers who have been assessed as competent by an HSE-recognized diver-training organization (a list of which can be obtained from the HSE) for the following competencies: SCUBA, Surface Supplied, Surface Supplied (top-up) and Closed Bell.

DRAMATIC AND PERFORMING ARTS

Membership of Professional Institutions and Associations

EQUITY

Guild House
Upper St Martins Lane
London WC2H 9EG
Tel: 020 7379 6000
Fax: 020 7379 7001
E-mail: info@equity.org.uk
Website: www.equity.org.uk

Equity is the UK trade union representing professional performers and other creative workers from across the entertainment, creative and cultural industries. The main function of Equity is to negotiate minimum terms and conditions of employment for its members and to represent its members' interests to the government and other bodies.

MEMBERSHIP
Youth Member
Student Member
Graduate Member
Full Member

NATIONAL COUNCIL FOR DRAMA TRAINING

249 Tooley Street
London SE1 2JX
Tel: 020 7407 3686
Fax: 020 7387 3860
E-mail: info@ncdt.co.uk
Website: www.ncdt.co.uk

The NCDT is a partnership of employers in the theatre, broadcast and media industries, employee representatives and training providers. We accredit vocational courses, act as a champion for the sector and work to optimize support for professional drama training and education in acting, stage management and technical theatre, embracing change and development.

THE BRITISH (THEATRICAL) ARTS

12 Deveron Way
Rise Park
Romford
Essex RM1 4UL
Tel: 01708 756263
Website: www.britisharts.org

The British Arts is a non-profit-making organization dedicated to maintaining and where necessary raising the standard of the teaching of Performing Arts subjects. We work to encourage a strong technical foundation combined with an understanding of professional theatrical presentation and conduct exams in Dramatic Art, Classical, Stage Ballet, Mime, Tap, Musical Theatre and Modern Dance.

MEMBERSHIP
Student Member
Companion
Associate (Teaching and Non-teaching)
Member (Teaching and Non-teaching)
Advanced Teacher Member
Fellow

QUALIFICATION/EXAMINATIONS
Please see the British Arts website.

DRIVING INSTRUCTORS

Membership of Professional Institutions and Associations

REGISTER OF APPROVED DRIVING INSTRUCTORS

The Axis Building
112 Upper Parliament Street
Nottingham NG1 6LP
Tel: 0300 200 1122
E-mail: ADIReg@dsa.gsi.gov.uk

The Register of Approved Driving Instructors (ADI) and the licensing scheme for trainee instructors (PDI) are administered under the provisions of the Road Traffic Act 1988 by the Department for Transport (DfT). It is an offence for anyone to give professional instruction (that is instruction paid for by or in respect of the pupil) in driving a motor car unless: (a) his or her name is on the Register of Approved Driving Instructors; or (b) he or she holds a 'trainee's licence to give instruction' issued by the Registrar.

QUALIFICATION/EXAMINATIONS

Please see the Business Link website (www.businesslink.gov.uk) for details of the qualifying examinations.

EMBALMING

Membership of Professional Institutions and Associations

INTERNATIONAL EXAMINATIONS BOARD OF EMBALMERS

39 Poplar Grove
Kennington
Oxford OX1 5QN
Tel: 01865 735788
Fax: 01865 730941

The Board examines candidates who wish to become qualified members of the British Institute of Embalmers (qv), which is not itself an examining body but can provide information packs (also available from the above address) that contain lists of approved schools and accredited tutors.

THE BRITISH INSTITUTE OF EMBALMERS

Anubis House
21c Station Road
Knowle
Solihull
West Midlands B93 0HL
Tel: 01564 778991
Fax: 01564 770812
E-mail: enquiries@bioe.co.uk
Website: www.bioe.co.uk

The BIE, founded in 1927, is an organization for professional embalmers. Its objectives include supporting and protecting the status, character and interests of embalmers, promoting the efficient tuition of persons seeking to become embalmers, and encouraging the study and practice of improved methods of embalming.

MEMBERSHIP

Member (MBIE)
Fellow (FBIE)

DESIGNATORY LETTERS

MBIE, FBIE

EMPLOYMENT AND CAREERS SERVICES

Membership of Professional Institutions and Associations

RECRUITMENT AND EMPLOYMENT CONFEDERATION

4th Floor
Albion House
Chertsey Road
Woking
Surrey GU21 6BT
Tel: 020 7009 2100
Fax: 01483 714979
E-mail: info@rec.uk.com
Website: www.rec.uk.com

The REC is the representative body for the UK's £27 billion private recruitment and staffing industry, with a membership of more than 8,000 Corporate Members comprising agencies and businesses from all sectors, and 6,000 members of the Institute of Recruitment Professionals (IRP) made up of recruitment consultants and other industry professionals.

MEMBERSHIP
Affiliate (AIRP)
Member (MIRP)
Fellow (FIRP)

QUALIFICATION/EXAMINATIONS
Certificate in Recruitment Practice (CertRP)
Diploma in Recruitment Practice (DipRP)
BA in Recruitment Practice (run jointly with Middlesex University Business School)
MA in Recruitment Practice (run jointly with Middlesex University Business School)

DESIGNATORY LETTERS
AIRP, MIRP, FIRP

THE INSTITUTE OF CAREER GUIDANCE

Ground Floor
Copthall House
1 New Road
Stourbridge
West Midlands DY8 1PH
Tel: 01384 376464
Fax: 01384 440830
E-mail: hq@icg-uk.org
Website: www.icg-uk.org

The ICG is the oldest and largest professional association for career guidance practitioners in the UK. Our aim is to promote access to high-quality guidance services, delivered by professionally qualified staff working within an appropriate ethical framework, and to underpin this our members adhere to a strict code of ethics.

MEMBERSHIP
Student Member
Full Member
Fellow
Honorary Fellow
School Member
Organizational Member

QUALIFICATION/EXAMINATIONS
Qualification in Career Guidance (QCG)

ENGINEERING, AERONAUTICAL

Membership of Professional Institutions and Associations

ROYAL AERONAUTICAL SOCIETY

4 Hamilton Place
Hyde Park Corner
London W1J 7BQ
Tel: 020 7670 4300
Fax: 020 7670 4309
E-mail: raes@aerosociety.com
Website: www.aerosociety.com

The RAeS, founded in 1866 to further the science of aeronautics, is a multidisciplinary professional institution dedicated to the global aerospace community. We work on our members' behalf to promote the highest professional standards in all aerospace disciplines, to provide specialist information and act as a central forum for the exchange of ideas, and to play a leading role in influencing opinion on aviation matters.

MEMBERSHIP
Student Affiliate
Affiliate
Associate (ARAeS)
Associate Member (AMRAeS)
Member (MRAeS)
Companion (CRAeS)
Fellow (FRAeS)
Engineering Technician (EngTech)
Incorporated Engineer (IEng)
Chartered Engineer (CEng)

ENGINEERING, AGRICULTURAL

Membership of Professional Institutions and Associations

BRITISH AGRICULTURAL AND GARDEN MACHINERY ASSOCIATION

Middleton House
2 Main Road
Middleton Cheney
Oxfordshire OX17 2TN
Tel: 01295 713344
Fax: 01295 711665
E-mail: info@bagma.com
Website: www.bagma.com

BAGMA is the trade association representing agricultural and garden machinery dealers in the UK. We have some 850 dealer members and 75 affiliated suppliers and allied industry companies. We offer a range of training and assessment courses through our online learning package and at approved Training and Assessment Centres.

QUALIFICATION/EXAMINATIONS
Please see the BAGMA website.

THE INSTITUTION OF AGRICULTURAL ENGINEERS

The Bullock Building
University Way
Cranfield
Bedford
Bedfordshire MK43 0GH
Tel: 01234 750876
Fax: 01234 751319
E-mail: secretary@iagre.org
Website: www.iagre.org

The IAgrE is the professional body for engineers, scientists, technologists and managers in agricultural and allied land-based industries, including forestry, food engineering and technology, amenity, renewable energy, horticulture and the environment. The IAgrE also administers the Landbased Engineering Technician Accreditation schemes (LTA) for the industry.

MEMBERSHIP
Student
Associate (AIAgrE)
Associate Member (AMIAgrE)
Member (MIAgrE)
Fellow (FIAgrE)
Honorary Fellow

QUALIFICATION/EXAMINATIONS
Chartered Engineer (CEng), Chartered Environmentalist (CEnv), Incorporated Engineer (IEng), Engineering Technician (EngTech)

DESIGNATORY LETTERS
AIAgrE, AMIAgrE, MIAgrE, FIAgrE

ENGINEERING, AUTOMOBILE

Membership of Professional Institutions and Associations

INSTITUTE OF AUTOMOTIVE ENGINEER ASSESSORS

Brooke House
24 Dam Street
Lichfield
Staffordshire WS13 6AA
Tel: 01543 266906
Fax: 01543 257848
E-mail: secretary@iaea-online.co.uk
Website: www.iaea-online.org

The IAEA, a Professional Affiliate of the Engineering Council, was founded in 1932 and now represents more than 1,500 automotive engineer assessors responsible for activities such as vehicle damage assessment, accident reconstruction, investigation of mechanical failures, electrical failures and vehicle fires, providing expert witness testimony, repair assessment, car fleet surveys, and conciliation and arbitration.

MEMBERSHIP
Student
Graduate
Associate
Licensed Estimator
Incorporated Member (IMInstAEA)
Member (MInstAEA)
Fellow (FInstAEA)

QUALIFICATION/EXAMINATIONS
Basic Principles of Maths & Physics Application to Accident Reconstruction
Motor Vehicle Legislation as related to Insurance Principles

Principles and Practice of Vehicle Damage Assessment
Motor Insurance

DESIGNATORY LETTERS
IMInstAEA, MInstAEA, FInstAEA

SOCIETY OF AUTOMOTIVE ENGINEERS

PO Box 13312
Birmingham B28 1BG
E-mail: info@sae-uk.org
Website: www.sae-uk.org

SAE-UK is the only professional society dedicated solely to the vehicle and component manufacturing industries and has more than 2,000 members. Our aims are to improve the standards of design, use of materials, methods of manufacturing and safety, to encourage the development and continuous updating of automotive technology, and to improve the status of our members.

MEMBERSHIP
Personal Member
Corporate Member

THE INSTITUTE OF THE MOTOR INDUSTRY

Fanshaws
Brickendon
Hertford SG13 8PQ
Tel: 01992 511521
Fax: 01992 511548
E-mail: imi@motor.org.uk
Website: www.motor.org.uk and www.automotivetechnician.org.uk

The IMI is the professional association for individuals working in the motor industry and exists to help individuals and employers improve professional standards and performance by qualifying, recognizing and developing people. We are the Sector Skills Council for the automotive retail industry, a Licensed Member of the Engineering Council and the governing body for Automotive Technician Accreditation (ATA) – the UK's first national voluntary assessment system for vehicle technicians.

MEMBERSHIP
Affiliate (AffIMI)
Licentiate (LIMI)
Associate (AMIMI)
Member (MIMI)
Fellow (FIMI)
For technicians only, there are two special IMI awards recognizing technical qualifications and experience:
AAE (Advanced Automotive Engineer)
CAE (Certificated Automotive Engineer)

DESIGNATORY LETTERS
AffIMI, LIMI, AMIMI, MIMI, FIMI, AAE, CAE

ENGINEERING, BUILDING SERVICES

Membership of Professional Institutions and Associations

THE CHARTERED INSTITUTION OF BUILDING SERVICES ENGINEERS

222 Balham High Road
London SW12 9BS
Tel: 020 8675 5211
Fax: 020 8675 5449
Website: www.cibse.org

CIBSE is the professional body for people involved in the design, construction, operation and maintenance of the engineering elements of a building other than its structure and enables it to operate efficently by saving energy and contributing to a low carbon built environment. This includes heating, ventilation, air conditioning, electrical services, lighting etc.

MEMBERSHIP
Student Affiliate
Affiliate
Graduate
Companion
Licentiate (LCIBSE)
Associate (ACIBSE)
Member (MCIBSE)
Fellow (FCIBSE)

QUALIFICATION/EXAMINATIONS
Please see the CIBSE website.

DESIGNATORY LETTERS
LCIBSE, ACIBSE, MCIBSE, FCIBSE

ENGINEERING, CHEMICAL

Membership of Professional Institutions and Associations

THE INSTITUTION OF CHEMICAL ENGINEERS

Davis Building
Railway Terrace
Rugby
Warwickshire CV21 3HQ
Tel: 01788 578214
Fax: 01788 560833
E-mail: onlineassistance@icheme.org
Website: www.icheme.org

The IChemE, founded in 1922, is an international professional membership organization for chemical, biochemical and process engineers, and we have some 30,000 members in more than 113 countries. We promote competence and a commitment to sustainable development, advance the discipline for the benefit of society, and support the professional development of our members.

MEMBERSHIP
Student
Affiliate
Associate Member (AMIChemE)
Member (MIChemE)
Fellow {FIChemE)
Chartered Chemical Engineer (CEng MIChemE)
Chartered Engineer (CEng)
Chartered Scientist (CSci)
Chartered Environmentalist (CEnv)

DESIGNATORY LETTERS
AMIChemE, MIChemE, FIChemE, CEng MIChemE, CEng, CSci, CEnv

ENGINEERING, CIVIL

Membership of Professional Institutions and Associations

INSTITUTION OF CIVIL ENGINEERS

1 Great George Street
Westminster
London SW1P 3AA
Tel: 020 7222 7722
Fax: 020 7233 0515
E-mail: membership@ice.org.uk
Website: www.ice.org.uk

The ICE is a UK-based international organization with 80,000 members that strives to promote and progress civil engineering around the world. Our purpose is to quality professionals engaged in civil engineering, exchange knowledge and best practice, and support our members, and in the UK we liaise with government and publish reports on civil engineering issues.

MEMBERSHIP
Student
Graduate
Affiliate
Technician Member
Associate Member (AMICE)
Member (MICE)
Companion
Fellow (FICE)

ENGINEERING, ELECTRICAL, ELECTRONIC AND MANUFACTURING

Membership of Professional Institutions and Associations

INSTITUTION OF LIGHTING PROFESSIONALS

Regent House
Regent Place
Rugby
Warwickshire CV21 2PN
Tel: 01788 576492
Fax: 01788 540145
E-mail: info@theilp.org.uk
Website: www.theilp.org.uk

The ILP is a professional lighting association with about 2,200 members, including lighting designers, consultants and engineers. We are dedicated to excellence in lighting and to raising awareness about the important contribution of lighting in road safety, crime prevention and the environment. We support members by providing technical advice and encourage their CPD through our bimonthly journal and by holding a wide range of conferences, regional meetings, seminars and courses.

MEMBERSHIP
Student
Affiliate
Associate Member (AMILP)
Member (MILP)
Fellow (FILP)
Siver Group Member
Gold Group Member
Engineering Technician (EngTech)
Incorporated Engineer (IEng)
Chartered Engineer (CEng)

QUALIFICATION/EXAMINATIONS
Exterior Lighting Diploma

DESIGNATORY LETTERS
AMILP, MILP, FILP, EngTech, IEng, CEng

THE INSTITUTION OF ENGINEERING AND TECHNOLOGY

Michael Faraday House
Stevenage
Hertfordshire SG1 2AY
Tel: 01438 313311
Fax: 01438 765526
E-mail: postmaster@theiet.org
Website: www.theiet.org

The IET was formed in 2006 by the amalgamation of the Institution of Electrical Engineers and the Institution of Incorporated Engineers and has more than 150,000 members in 127 countries worldwide. We provide a global knowledge network to facilitate the exchange of ideas and promote the positive role of science, engineering and technology in the world.

MEMBERSHIP
Student
Associate
Member (MIET)
Fellow (FIET)
Honorary Fellow
ICT Technician (ICTTech)
Engineering Technician (EngTech)
Incorporated Engineer (IEng)
Chartered Engineer (CEng)

DESIGNATORY LETTERS
FIET, ICTech, EngTech, IEng, CEng, MIET

ENGINEERING, ENERGY

Membership of Professional Institutions and Associations

ENERGY INSTITUTE

61 New Cavendish Street
London W1G 7AR
Tel: 020 7467 7100
Fax: 020 7255 1472
E-mail: info@energyinst.org.uk
Website: www.energyinst.org.uk

The EI is the leading professional body for the energy industries, supporting almost 13,500 professionals internationally. A Royal Charter membership organization, we are licensed to offer Chartered, Incorporated and Engineering Technician status to engineers, and to award Chartered Scientist and Chartered Environmentalist status.

MEMBERSHIP
Student Member
Affiliate
Graduate Member (Grad EI)
Member (MEI)
Fellow (FEI)
Engineering Technician (EngTech)
Incorporated Engineer (IEng)
Chartered Engineer (CEng)
Chartered Scientist (CSci)
Chartered Environmentalist (CEnv)

DESIGNATORY LETTERS
GradEI, MEI, FEI, EngTech, IEng, CEng

ENGINEERING, ENVIRONMENTAL

Membership of Professional Institutions and Associations

INSTITUTE OF ENVIRONMENTAL MANAGEMENT AND ASSESSMENT

St Nicholas House
Lincoln LN1 3DP
Tel: 01522 540069
Fax: 01522 540090
E-mail: info@iema.net
Website: www.iema.net

The IEMA is a not-for-profit membership organization that provides recognition and support to environmental professionals and promotes sustainable development through improved environmental practice and performance. We have about 15,000 individual and corporate members in 87 countries, in the public, private and non-governmental sectors.

MEMBERSHIP
Student Member
Affiliate Member
Graduate Member
Associate (AIEMA)
Full Member (MIEMA)
Fellow (FIEMA)
Chartered Environmentalist (CEnv)
Corporate Member

QUALIFICATION/EXAMINATIONS
Foundation Certificate in Environmental Management
Associate Certificate in Environmental Management
Diploma

DESIGNATORY LETTERS
AIEMA, MIEMA, FIEMA, CEnv

THE CHARTERED INSTITUTION OF WATER AND ENVIRONMENTAL MANAGEMENT

15 John Street
London WC1N 2EB
Tel: 020 7831 3110
Fax: 020 7405 4967
E-mail: admin@ciwem.org
Website: www.ciwem.org

Founded in 1895, CIWEM is an independent professional body and registered charity with 12,000 members that advances the science and practice of water and environmental management for a clean, green and sustainable world by promoting environmental excellence and professional development and training, supplying independent advice and evidence-based opinion, and providing a forum for debate through conferences, technical meetings and its publications.

MEMBERSHIP
Student
Associate ACIWEM
Graduate
Member MCIWEM C.WEM
Fellow FCIWEM C.WEM
Environmental Partner
Chartered Engineer (CEng)
Chartered Environmentalist (CEnv)
Chartered Scientist (CSci)

QUALIFICATION/EXAMINATIONS
Online training courses in partnership with Staffordshire University, accredited university courses at 12 leading institutions, CPD modules and Rural Environmental Management Programme

DESIGNATORY LETTERS
CEng, CEnv, CSi. C.WEM

THE SOCIETY OF ENVIRONMENTAL ENGINEERS

The Manor House
High Street
Buntingford
Buntingford
Hertfordshire SG9 9AB
Tel: 01763 271209
Fax: 01763 273255
E-mail: office@environmental.org.uk
Website: www.environmental.org.uk

The SEE, founded in 1959, is a professional society that promotes awareness of the discipline of environmental engineering (the measurement, modelling, control and simulation of all types of environment). We provide members with information, training and representation within this field and encourage communication and good practice in quality, reliability, and cost-effective product development and manufacture.

MEMBERSHIP
Student
Member
Corporate Member
Engineering Technician (EngTech)
Incorporated Engineer (IEng)
Chartered Engineer (CEng)

DESIGNATORY LETTERS
EngTech, IEng, CEng

ENGINEERING, FIRE

Membership of Professional Institutions and Associations

ASSOCIATION OF PRINCIPAL FIRE OFFICERS

10/11 Pebble Close
Amington
Tamworth
Staffordshire B77 4RD
Tel: 01827 302300
Fax: 01827 302399
E-mail: enquiries@apfo.org.uk
Website: www.apfo.org.uk

The APFO is the staff association of the most senior Fire Officers in the UK. Our objectives are: to represent and promote the interests of members in conditions of service and legal and employment matters; to negotiate and promote the settlement of disputes involving members; to provide assistance to members and their dependants in exceptional circumstances; and to provide support to members in matters concerning employment or a work-related injury.

MEMBERSHIP
Associate Member
Lifetime Past Member

CHIEF FIRE OFFICERS' ASSOCIATION

9–11 Pebble Close
Amington
Tamworth
Staffordshire B77 4RD
Tel: 01827 302300
Fax: 01827 302399
Website: www.cfoa.org.uk

The CFOA is a professional membership association of the most senior fire officers in the UK. We provide independent advice to the government, local authorities and others. Our aim is to reduce loss of life, personal injury and damage to property by improving the quality of fire fighting, rescue, fire protection and fire prevention in the UK.

MEMBERSHIP
Member

THE INSTITUTION OF FIRE ENGINEERS

London Road
Moreton-in-March
Gloucestershire GL56 0RH
Tel: 01608 812580
Fax: 01608 812581
E-mail: info@ife.org.uk
Website: www.ife.org.uk

The IFE, founded in 1918, is a non-profit-making professional body for fire professionals and has more than 12,000 members worldwide. Our aim is to encourage and improve the science and practice of fire extinction, fire prevention and fire engineering, to enhance technical networks, and to give advice and support to our members for the benefit of the community at large.

MEMBERSHIP
Student
Affiliate Member
Technician (TIFireE)
Graduate (GIFireE)
Associate (AIFireE)
Member (MIFireE)
Fellow (FIFireE)
Engineering Technician (EngTech)
Incorporated Engineer (IEng)
Chartered Engineer (CEng) Affiliate Organization

QUALIFICATION/EXAMINATIONS
Level 2 Certificate Level 3 Certificate
Level 3 Diploma Level 4 Certificate

DESIGNATORY LETTERS
TIFireE, GIFireE, AIFireE, MIFireE, FIFireE, EngTech, IEng, CEng

ENGINEERING, GAS

Membership of Professional Institutions and Associations

THE INSTITUTION OF GAS ENGINEERS AND MANAGERS

IGEM House
High Street
Kegworth
Derbyshire DE74 2DA
Tel: 0844 375 4436
Fax: 01509 678198
Website: www.igem.org.uk

IGEM is licensed by EC(UK) and serves a wide range of professionals in the UK and international gas industry through membership and technical standards, having a diverse membership ranging from university students to qualified professionals. Anyone working or interested in the gas industry can form positive connections to enhance their career through IGEM.

MEMBERSHIP
Student Member
Associate (AIGEM)
Associate Member (AMIGEM)
Graduate Member (GradIGEM)
Member Manager (MIGEM)
Technician Member (Eng Tech (MIGEM))
Incorporated Member (I Eng (MIGEM))
Chartered Member (C Eng (MIGEM))
Fellow (C Eng (FIGEM))
Industrial Affiliate (company membership)

DESIGNATORY LETTERS
MIGEM, Eng Tech (MIGEM), I Eng (MIGEM), C ENG (MIGEM), C Eng (FIGEM)

ENGINEERING, GENERAL

Membership of Professional Institutions and Associations

ASSOCIATION OF COST ENGINEERS

Lea House
Sandbach
Cheshire CW11 1XL
Tel: 01270 764798
Fax: 01270 766180
E-mail: enquiries@acoste.org.uk
Website: www.acoste.org.uk

The ACostE represents the professional interests of those with responsibility for the prediction, planning and control of resources for engineering, manufacturing and construction. As a Professional Affiliate of The Engineering Council, we can propose suitably qualified members for the award of the titles of Chartered Engineer (CEng) and Incorporated Engineer (IEng).

MEMBERSHIP
Student
Associate (AA Cost E)
Companion (Companion A Cost E)
Graduate (Grad A Cost E)
Member (MA Cost E)
Fellow (FA Cost E)
Honorary Fellow (Hon FA Cost E)
Certified Cost Engineer (CCE)
Engineering Technician (EngTech)
Incorporated Engineer (IEng)
Chartered Engineer (CEng)

DESIGNATORY LETTERS
AA Cost E, Companion A Cost E, Grad A Cost E, MA Cost E, FA Cost E, CCE, EngTech, IEng, CEng

INSTITUTE OF MEASUREMENT AND CONTROL

87 Gower Street
London WC1E 6AF
Tel: 020 7387 4949
Fax: 020 7388 8431
E-mail: membership@instmc.org.uk
Website: www.instmc.org.uk

The IMC is a multidisciplinary body that brings together thinkers and practitioners from the many disciplines that have a common interest in measurement and control. Our object is to promote for the public benefit, by all available means, the general advancement of the science and practice of measurement and control technology and its application.

MEMBERSHIP
Student Member
Affiliate Member
Associate Member
Member (MemInstMC)
Fellow (FInstMC)
Honorary Fellow (HonFInstMC)

SEMTA – THE SECTOR SKILLS COUNCIL FOR SCIENCE, ENGINEERING AND MANUFACTURING TECHNOLOGIES

14 Upton Road
Watford
Hertfordshire WD18 0JT
Tel: 01923 238441
Fax: 01923 256086
E-mail: customerservices@semta.org.uk
Website: www.semta.org.uk

Semta is part of the Skills for Business network of 25 employer-led Sector Skills Councils in the UK and works with employers in the aerospace, automotive, electrical, electronics, marine, mechanical, metals and science & bioscience sectors to ascertain their current and future skills needs and provide short- and long-term solutions to meet those needs.

THE ENGINEERING COUNCIL

2nd Floor
246 High Holborn
London WC1V 7EX
Tel: 020 3206 0500
Fax: 020 3206 0501
Website: www.engc.org.uk

The Engineering Council holds the national registers of Chartered Engineers (CEng), Incorporated Engineers (IEng), Engineering Technicians (EngTech) and Information and Communications Technology Technicians (ICTTech). We set and maintain internationally recognized standards of competence and ethics, ensuring that employers, government and society can have confidence in registrants' skills and commitment.

DESIGNATORY LETTERS
ICTTech, EngTech, IEng, CEng

THE INSTITUTION OF BRITISH ENGINEERS

Clifford Hill Court
Clifford Chambers
Stratford upon Avon
Warwickshire CV37 8AA
Tel: 01789 298739
Fax: 01789 294442
E-mail: info@britishengineers.com
Website: www.britishengineers.com

MEMBERSHIP
Vice President
Fellow (FIBE)
Member (MIBE)
Associate Member (AMIBE)
Graduate Member (GradIBE)
Qualified Sales Engineer (SEng)
Bi-Lingual Engineer (BLEng)
Diploma in Business Engineering (DBE)
Certificate of Competence in Engineering

DESIGNATORY LETTERS
FIBE, MIBE, AMIBE, GradIBE, SEng, BLEng, DBE

WOMEN'S ENGINEERING SOCIETY

Michael Faraday House
Six Hills Way
Stevenage
Herts SG1 2AY
Tel: 01438 765506
E-mail: info@wes.org.uk
Website: www.wes.org.uk

The WES, founded in 1919, is a professional, not-for-profit network of women engineers, scientists and technologists, who offer inspiration, support and professional development. Working in partnership, we campaign to encourage women to participate and achieve as engineers, scientists and as leaders.

MEMBERSHIP
Student Member
Associate
Member (MWES)
Group Member
Corporate Member

DESIGNATORY LETTERS
MWES

ENGINEERING, MARINE

Membership of Professional Institutions and Associations

THE INSTITUTE OF MARINE ENGINEERING, SCIENCE AND TECHNOLOGY

80 Coleman Street
London EC2R 5BJ
Tel: +44 (0)20 7382 2600
Fax: +44 (0)20 7382 2670
E-mail: membership@imarest.org
Website: www.imarest.org

The IMarEST, established in 1889, is the leading international membership body and learned society for marine professionals and has more than 15,000 members worldwide. We have a strong international presence, with a network of 50 international branches, affiliations with major marine societies around the world, representation on the key marine technical committees and non-governmental status at the International Maritime Organization.

MEMBERSHIP

Membership Categories

IMarEST membership is open to everyone with an interest in the marine world across scientific, engineering and technological disciplines and applications.

Categories of membership are available to those who are seeking professional recognition, those who are currently studying or just starting out in their careers, or those who simply have a general interest in the IMarEST and its activities. There are no academic requirements for Non-corporate Membership of the IMarEST. However, professionals seeking Corporate Membership will require certain academic qualifications according to the type of membership being sought.

Corporate Membership Categories

Fellow (FIMarEST)

Fellows are those who qualify for the category of Member and have demonstrated to the satisfaction of Council a level of knowledge and understanding, competence and commitment involving superior responsibility for the conceptual design, management or the execution of important work in a marine related profession, and have given a commitment to abide by the Institute's Code of Professional Conduct.

Member (MIMarEST)

Members are those who qualify for the category of Associate Member and have demonstrated to the satisfaction of Council that they have achieved a position of professional standing having normally been professionally engaged in the marine sector for a period of 5 years that includes significant responsibility and have given a commitment to abide by the Institute's Code of Professional Conduct.

Associate Member (AMIMarEST)

Associate Members are those demonstrating to the satisfaction of Council that they have achieved a position as a technician, or are professionally engaged in Initial Professional Development or occupy an occupational role in the marine sector, and have given a commitment to abide by the Institute's Code of Professional Conduct.

Non-corporate Membership Categories

Affiliate

Affiliates may either be those with an interest in, or who may contribute to, the activities of the Institute; or persons who, in the opinion of Council, can contribute to, or wish to have access to, the technical services of the Institute, being resident in a recognized overseas territory and also members of a professional society with which the Institute has a reciprocal arrangement.

Student (SIMarEST)

Student members are those enrolled on a programme of further or higher education accredited or recognized by the IMarEST.

Professional Registration

In addition to membership, the IMarEST is licensed to provide a range of registers covering the fields of engineering, science and technology. In addition, the IMarEST's Royal Charter empowers the Institute to offer registers designed to meet the specific needs of the marine profession. Corporate members can become registered (chartered) as follows:

Engineers

Chartered Engineer (CEng)
Chartered Marine Engineer (CMarEng)

Incorporated Engineer (IEng)
Incorporated Marine Engineer (IMarEng)
Engineering Technician (EngTech)
Marine Engineering Technician (MarEngTech)
Scientists
Chartered Scientist (CSci)
Chartered Marine Scientist (CMarSci)
Registered Marine Scientist (RMarSci)
Marine Technician (MarTech)
Technologists
Chartered Marine Technologist (CMarTech)
Registered Marine Technologist (RMarTech)
Marine Technician (MarTech)

DESIGNATORY LETTERS
SIMarEST, AMIMarEST, MIMarEST, FIMarEST

ENGINEERING, MECHANICAL

Membership of Professional Institutions and Associations

INSTITUTION OF MECHANICAL ENGINEERS

1 Birdcage Walk
Westminster
London SW1H 9JJ
Tel: 020 7304 6999
E-mail: membership@imeche.org
Website: www.imeche.org

The IMechE is a professional engineering body with about 80,000 members. Our aims are to promote sustainable energy and engineering sustainable supply, economic growth while mitigating and adapting to climate change and the depletion of natural resources, and safe, efficient transport systems to ensure less congestion and emissions, and to inspire, prepare and support tomorrow's engineers so we can respond to society's changes.

MEMBERSHIP
Affiliate
Associate Member (AMIMechE)
Member (MIMechE)
Fellow (FIMechE)
Engineering Technician (EngTech)
Incorporated Engineer (IEng)
Chartered Engineer (CEng)

DESIGNATORY LETTERS
AMIMechE, MIMechE, FIMechE, EngTech, IEng, CEng

ENGINEERING, MINING

Membership of Professional Institutions and Associations

INSTITUTE OF EXPLOSIVES ENGINEERS

Wellington Hall 289
Cranfield University
Defence Academy of the UK
Shrivenham, Swindon
Wiltshire SN6 8LA
Tel: 01793 785322
Fax: 01793 785772
E-mail: iexpe@cranfield.ac.uk
Website: www.iexpe.org

The Insitute of Explosives Engineers promotes the occupational competency, education and professional standing of those who work with explosives and provides consultative facilities for organizations and government departments within the explosives field.

MEMBERSHIP
Student
Associate (AIExpE)
Member (MIExpE)
Fellow (FIExpE)
Company

DESIGNATORY LETTERS
AIExpE, MIExpE, FIExpE

THE INSTITUTE OF MATERIALS, MINERALS AND MINING (IOM^3)

1 Carlton House Terrace
London SW1Y 5DB
Tel: 020 7451 7300
Fax: 020 7839 1702
Website: www.iom3.org

IOM^3 is a major UK engineering institution whose activities encompass the whole materials cycle, from exploration and extraction, through characterization, processing, forming, finishing and application, to product recycling and land reuse. We promote and develop all aspects of materials science and engineering, geology, mining and associated technologies, mineral and petroleum engineering and extraction metallurgy, as a leading authority in the worldwide materials and mining community.

MEMBERSHIP
Student
Graduate
Affiliate
Member (MIMMM)
Fellow (FIMMM)

DESIGNATORY LETTERS
MIMMM, FIMMM

THE INSTITUTE OF QUARRYING

7 Regent Street
Nottingham NG1 5BS
Tel: 0115 945 3880
Fax: 0115 948 4035
E-mail: mail@quarrying.org
Website: www.quarrying.org

The Institute of Quarrying, which dates from 1917, is the international professional body for quarrying, construction materials and related extractive and processing industries, and has 6,000 members in some 50 countries. Our aim is to improve all aspects of operational performance through education and training at supervisory and management level.

MEMBERSHIP
Student
Associate
Member (MIQ)
Fellow (FIQ)

QUALIFICATION/EXAMINATIONS
Professional Examination

DESIGNATORY LETTERS
MIQ, FIQ

ENGINEERING, NUCLEAR

Membership of Professional Institutions and Associations

THE NUCLEAR INSTITUTE

Allan House
1 Penerley Road
London SE6 2LQ
Tel: 020 8695 8220
Fax: 020 8695 8229
E-mail: admin@nuclearinst.com
Website: www.nuclearinst.com

The NI (a Nominated Body of the Engineering Council) is a registered charity established to support the nuclear sector. We organize lectures, seminars and events at a regional and national level, and can award EngTech, IEng and CEng to suitably qualified individuals.

MEMBERSHIP
Student Member
Learned Member
Graduate Member
Technician Member (TNucI)
Associate Member (AMNucI)
Member (MNucI)
Fellow (FNucI)
Honorary Fellow

DESIGNATORY LETTERS
TNucI, AMNucI, MNucI, FNucI

ENGINEERING, PRODUCTION

Membership of Professional Institutions and Associations

THE INSTITUTE OF OPERATIONS MANAGEMENT

CILT(UK)
Earlstrees Court
Earlstrees Road
Corby
Northamptonshire NN17 4AX
Tel: 01536 740105
E-mail: info@iomnet.org.uk
Website: www.iomnet.org.uk

The IOM is the professional body for persons involved in operations and production management in the manufacturing and service industries and in the public sector in the UK. Our objective is to equip operations professionals with the skills and resources they need to maximize individual potential and organizational success.

MEMBERSHIP
Student
Associate
Member (MIOM)
Fellow (FIOM)
Group Member
Corporate Member

QUALIFICATION/EXAMINATIONS
Certificate in Operations Management (COM)
Diploma in Operations Management (DOM)
Advanced Diploma in Operations Management
IOM now offer APICS certifications

DESIGNATORY LETTERS
MIOM, FIOM

ENGINEERING, REFRACTORIES

Membership of Professional Institutions and Associations

INSTITUTE OF REFRACTORIES ENGINEERING

25 Woodland Way
Long Newton
Stockton-on-Tees
Co Durham TS21 1DJ
Tel: 01642 583840
Fax: 01642 589397
E-mail: secretary@ireng.org
Website: www.ireng.org

The IRE is a non-profit-making organization dedicated to fostering the science, technology and skills of refractories engineering and to serving the needs of refractories engineers worldwide. Our members have a background in R&D, design, engineering, manufacturing and installation contracting in the iron & steel, cement, non-ferrous, glass, chemical/petrochemical incineration, power generation, ceramics/bricks and similar industries.

MEMBERSHIP
Student
Associate Member (AMI Ref Eng)
Member (MI Ref Eng)
Fellow (FI Ref Eng)

DESIGNATORY LETTERS
AMI Ref Eng, MI Ref Eng, FI Ref Eng

ENGINEERING, REFRIGERATION

Membership of Professional Institutions and Associations

THE INSTITUTE OF REFRIGERATION

Kelvin House
76 Mill Lane
76 Mill Lane
Carshalton
Surrey SM5 2JR
Tel: 020 8647 7033
Fax: 020 8773 0165
E-mail: ior@ior.org.uk
Website: www.ior.org.uk

The IOR is the professional body for the refrigeration and air conditioning industries. We promote the technical advancement and perfection of refrigeration, and the minimization of its effects on the environment, encourage the extension of refrigeration, air conditioning and heat pump services for the benefit of the community, and provide advice, CPD and support to our members.

MEMBERSHIP
Student
Affiliate
Associate Member (AMInstR)
Member (MInstR)
Fellow (FInstR)
Engineering Technician (EngTech)
Incorporated Engineer (IEng)
Chartered Engineer (CEng)

DESIGNATORY LETTERS
AMInstR, MInstR, FInstR

ENGINEERING, ROAD, RAIL AND TRANSPORT

Membership of Professional Institutions and Associations

INSTITUTE OF HIGHWAY ENGINEERS

De Morgan House
58 Russell Square
London WC1B 4HS
Tel: 020 7436 7487
Fax: 020 7436 7488
E-mail: secretary@theihe.org
Website: www.theihe.org

The IHE is the professional body for highway and traffic professionals. We are run by engineers for engineers and technicians, and work to keep the standards of the profession high, to safeguard the interests of our members, and to ensure that their contribution is recognized.

MEMBERSHIP
Student Member
Graduate Member
Associate Member (AMIHE)
Member (MIHE)
Fellow (FIHE)
Engineering Technician (EngTech)
Incorporated Engineer (IEng)
Chartered Engineer (CEng)

QUALIFICATION/EXAMINATIONS
Prof Cert in Traffic Sign Design
Prof Cert in Traffic Signal Control

Prof Cert in Transport Development Management

DESIGNATORY LETTERS
AMIHE, MIHE, FIHE, EngTech, IEng, CEng

INSTITUTION OF RAILWAY SIGNAL ENGINEERS

4th Floor
1 Birdcage Walk
Westminster
London SW1H 9JJ
Tel: 020 7808 1180
Fax: 020 7808 1196
E-mail: hq@irse.org
Website: www.irse.org

The Institution of Railway Signal Engineers, known more usually as the IRSE, is an international organization, active throughout the world. It is the professional institution for all those engaged or interested in railway signalling and telecommunications and allied disciplines. Membership is open to anyone engaged or interested in the management, planning, design, installation, telecommunications or associated equipment.

MEMBERSHIP
Student
Associate
Accredited Technician
Associate Member
Member
Fellow
Companion

QUALIFICATION/EXAMINATIONS
Professional Examination

DESIGNATORY LETTERS
AMIRSE, MIRSE, FIRSE, CompIRSE

SOCIETY OF OPERATIONS ENGINEERS

22 Greencoat Place
London SW1P 1PR
Tel: 020 7630 1111
Fax: 020 7630 6677
E-mail: soe@soe.org.uk
Website: www.soe.org.uk

The SOE is a professional membership organization that represents more than 18,000 individuals and companies in the engineering industry. It was formed in 2000 by the merger of the Institute of Road Transport Engineers (IRTE) and the Institution of Plant Engineers (IPlantE). The Society's third professional sector, the Bureau of Engineer Surveyors (BES), joined us in 2004.

MEMBERSHIP
Associate Member (AMSOE)
Member (MSOE)
Fellow (FSOE)
Honorary Fellow (HonFSOE)
Companion (CompanionSOE)
Engineering Technician (EngTech)
Incorporated Engineer (IEng)
Chartered Engineer (CEng)

THE CHARTERED INSTITUTION OF HIGHWAYS AND TRANSPORTATION

119 Britannia Walk
London N1 7JE
Tel: 020 7336 1555
Fax: 020 7336 1556
E-mail: info@ciht.org.uk
Website: www.ciht.org.uk

The CIHT is a learned society and membership organization concerned with the planning, design, construction, maintenance and operation of land-based transport systems and infrastructure. CIHT provides professional development and networking opportunities to members, with routes to qualifications, cutting-edge technical conferences and exciting social events.

MEMBERSHIP

Student
Associate Member (AMCIHT)
Member (MCIHT)
Fellow (FCIHT)
Incorporated Engineer (IEng)
Chartered Engineer (CEng)

QUALIFICATION/EXAMINATIONS

Transport Planning Professional (TPP) status (awarded jointly with the Transport Planning Society (TPS))

DESIGNATORY LETTERS

AMCIHT, MCIHT, FCIHT, IEng, CEng

ENGINEERING, SHEET METAL

Membership of Professional Institutions and Associations

INSTITUTE OF SHEET METAL ENGINEERING

102 Richmond Drive
Perton
Wolverhampton
West Midlands WV6 7UQ
Tel: 07891499146
E-mail: ismesec@googlemail.com
Website: www.isme.org.uk

The ISME is a learned body with individual membership open to those employed in the sheet metal and associated industries and corporate membership open to relevant companies. Our aims are to promote the science of working and using sheet metal by providing opportunities for the exchange of ideas and information, and to encourage the professional development of our members.

MEMBERSHIP

Student Member
Member (MISME)
Fellow (FISME)
Corporate Member

DESIGNATORY LETTERS

MISME, FISME

ENGINEERING, STRUCTURAL

Membership of Professional Institutions and Associations

THE INSTITUTION OF STRUCTURAL ENGINEERS

11 Upper Belgrave Street
London SW1X 8BH
Tel: 020 7235 4535
Fax: 020 7235 4294
E-mail: membership@istructe.org
Website: www.istructe.org

The Institution of Structural Engineers, founded in 1908, is the world's largest membership organization dedicated to the art and science of structural engineering. Our aims include: maintaining professional standards for structural engineering; ensuring continued technical excellence; advancing safety, creativity and innovation; and promoting a sustainable approach to both the structural engineering profession and the built environment.

MEMBERSHIP
Student
Affiliate
Graduate
Technician (TIStructE)
Associate Member (AMIStructE)
Associate (AIStructE)
Chartered Member (MIStructE)
Fellow (FIStructE)
Engineering Technician (EngTech)
Incorporated Engineer (IEng)
Chartered Engineer (CEng)

DESIGNATORY LETTERS
TIStructE, AMIStructE, AIStructE. MIStructE, FIStructE, EngTech, IEng, CEng

ENGINEERING, WATER

Membership of Professional Institutions and Associations

INSTITUTE OF WATER

4 Carlton Court
Team Valley
Gateshead
Tyne and Wear NE11 0AZ
Tel: 0191 422 0088
Fax: 0191 422 0087
E-mail: info@instituteofwater.org.uk
Website: www.instituteofwater.org.uk

The IW is the only institute concerned with the UK water industry. Our aim is to promote high standards of integrity, conduct and ethics, and to provide our members with an opportunity for CPD and growth through sharing knowledge, experience and networking opportunities.

MEMBERSHIP
Student Member
Associate Member
Full Member
Fellow
Honorary Member
Engineering Technician (EngTech)
Incorporated Engineer (IEng)
Chartered Engineer (CEng)
Chartered Environmentalist (CEnv)
Company Member

DESIGNATORY LETTERS
EngTech, IEng, CEng, CEnv

ENGINEERING DESIGN

Membership of Professional Institutions and Associations

THE INSTITUTION OF ENGINEERING DESIGNERS

Courtleigh
Westbury Leigh
Westbury
Wiltshire BA13 3TA
Tel: 01373 822801
Fax: 01373 858085
E-mail: ied@ied.org.uk
Website: www.ied.org.uk

Established in 1945, the IED represents 4,000 members worldwide working in engineering design, product design and CAD. Benefits include a bimonthly journal, access to an extensive library, legal advice helpline, local branch activities, and guidance and support to registration with the EC(UK) for suitably qualified members.

MEMBERSHIP
IED membership has two divisions: Engineering Design, and Product Design and Technology.

Each division has a range of membership grades: Student Member (StudIED), Graduate/Diplomate Member (GradIED/DipIED), Competent Draughting Associate (CDAIED), Associate (AIED), Member (MIED), Fellow (FIED).

QUALIFICATION/EXAMINATIONS
Registration with EC(UK) for suitably qualified members

DESIGNATORY LETTERS
AIED, MIED, FIED

ENVIRONMENTAL SCIENCES

Membership of Professional Institutions and Associations

INSTITUTE OF ECOLOGY AND ENVIRONMENTAL MANAGEMENT

43 Southgate Street
Winchester
Hampshire SO23 9EH
Tel: 01962 868626
Fax: 01962 868625
E-mail: enquiries@ieem.net
Website: www.ieem.net

Founded in 1991 to advance the science, technology and practice of ecology, environmental management and sustainable development to further conservation and the enhancement of biodiversity through education, training, study and research. IEEM now has more than 4,000 members drawn from local authorities, government agencies, industry, environmental consultancy, teaching/research and NGOs.

MEMBERSHIP
Student Member
Affiliate Member
Graduate Member (Grad IEEM)

Associate Member (AIEEM)
Full Member (MIEEM)
Fellow (FIEEM)

DESIGNATORY LETTERS
Grad IEEM, AIEEM, MIEEM, FIEEM

EXPORT

Membership of Professional Institutions and Associations

THE INSTITUTE OF EXPORT

Export House
Minerva Business Park
Lynch Wood
Peterborough PE2 6FT
Tel: 01733 404400
E-mail: info@export.org.uk
Website: www.export.org.uk

Established since 1935 offering training and professional qualifications to those working within international trade. We are the only professional institute in the UK offering qualifications ranging from the new 14–19 Diploma up to a level 5 Diploma as well as standard and bespoke training courses for individuals and companies.

MEMBERSHIP
Affiliate
Student
Associate
Member MIEx (Grad)
Member MIEx
Fellow
Business
Corporate

QUALIFICATION/EXAMINATIONS
Diploma in International Trade (DIT)
Certified International Trade Advisor (CIT)
Advanced Certificate in International Trade (ACIT)

FISHERIES MANAGEMENT

Membership of Professional Institutions and Associations

INSTITUTE OF FISHERIES MANAGEMENT

22 Rushworth Avenue
West Bridgford
Nottingham NG2 7LF
Tel: 01159 822317
Fax: 01159 826150
E-mail: info@ifm.org.uk
Website: www.ifm.org.uk

The Institute of Fisheries Management is an international organization of persons sharing a common interest in the modern and sustainable management of recreational and commercial fisheries. It is a non-profit-making body and is a constituent body of the Society for the Environment.

MEMBERSHIP
Subscriber
Student Member
Associate Member (AMIFM)
Registered Member (MIFM)
Fellow (FIFM)
Honorary Fellow (Hon FIFM)

Corporate Member

QUALIFICATION/EXAMINATIONS
Certificate
Diploma (accredited by The Open University)

DESIGNATORY LETTERS
AMIRM, MIFM, FIFM, Hon FIFM

FLORISTRY

Membership of Professional Institutions and Associations

SOCIETY OF FLORISTRY LTD

Tel: 07896 639520
E-mail: info@societyoffloristry.org
Website: www.societyoffloristry.org

The SOF, founded in 1951, is an awarding body that promotes the highest standards in professional floristry. We are responsible for preparing and setting the highest floristry qualifications and for designing programmes for the training of SOF judges and examiners. We provide help, advice and information to our more than 1,000 members, who include business owners, florists, training providers, and students.

MEMBERSHIP
Member
Corporate Member

QUALIFICATION/EXAMINATIONS
Level 4 Higher Diploma in Floristry (ICSF)
Level 5 Master Diploma in Professional Floristry (NDSF)

FOOD SCIENCE AND NUTRITION

Membership of Professional Institutions and Associations

INSTITUTE OF FOOD SCIENCE AND TECHNOLOGY

5 Cambridge Court
210 Shepherd's Bush Road
London W6 7NJ
Tel: 020 7603 6316
Fax: 020 7602 9936
E-mail: info@ifst.org
Website: www.ifst.org

IFST is the leading independent qualifying body for food professionals in Europe and the only professional body in the UK concerned with all aspects of food science and technology. As a registered charity we are independent of government, industry, lobby or special interest groups.

MEMBERSHIP
Associate
Member (MIFST)
Fellow (FIFST)
Chartered Scientist (CSci)

DESIGNATORY LETTERS
MIFST, FIFST, CSci

FORESTRY AND ARBORICULTURE

Membership of Professional Institutions and Associations

INSTITUTE OF CHARTERED FORESTERS

59 George Street
Edinburgh EH2 2JG
Tel: 0131 240 1425
Fax: 0131 240 1424
E-mail: icf@charteredforesters.org
Website: www.charteredforesters.org

The ICF is the Royal Chartered body for foresters and arboriculturists in the UK. We have over 1,000 members, to whom we offer advice, guidance and support. We also strive to foster a greater public understanding and awareness of the profession, as the environment and its management become more relevant to everyone.

MEMBERSHIP
Student Member
Supporter
Associate Member
Professional Member (MICFor)
Fellow (FICFor)

QUALIFICATION/EXAMINATIONS
Professional Membership Entry (PME) exam

DESIGNATORY LETTERS
MICFor, FICFor

THE ARBORICULTURAL ASSOCIATION

Ullenwood Court
Ullenwood
Cheltenham
Gloucestershire GL53 9QS
Tel: 01242 522152
Fax: 01242 577766
E-mail: admin@trees.org.uk
Website: www.trees.org.uk

The Arboricultural Association, founded in 1964, is the leading body in the UK for the amenity tree care professional in either civic or commercial employment at craft, technical, supervisory, managerial or consultancy level. There are currently over 2,000 members of The Arboricultural Association in a variety of membership classes.

MEMBERSHIP
Individual Membership
Student Member
Ordinary Member
Associate Member
Technician Member
Professional Member
Fellow
Corporate Membership
Corporate Member

QUALIFICATION/EXAMINATIONS
Arboricultural Association Approved Contractor
Arboricultural Association Registered Consultant

DESIGNATORY LETTERS
TechArborA; MArborA; FArborA

THE ROYAL FORESTRY SOCIETY

102 High Street
Tring
Hertfordshire HP23 4AF
Tel: 01442 822028
Fax: 01442 890395
E-mail: rfshq@rfs.org.uk
Website: www.rfs.org.uk

The RFS was founded in 1882 and now has over 3, 600 members. We are dedicated to promoting the wise management of trees and woodlands, and to increasing people's understanding of forestry. We publish a popular magazine, the *Quarterly Journal of Forestry,* arrange outdoor meetings, organize woodland study tours in the UK and overseas, run exams in arboriculture and manage model woodlands.

MEMBERSHIP
Member

FOUNDRY TECHNOLOGY AND PATTERN MAKING

Membership of Professional Institutions and Associations

THE INSTITUTE OF CAST METALS ENGINEERS

National Metalforming Centre
47 Birmingham Road
West Bromwich
West Midlands B70 6PY
Tel: 01216 016979
Fax: 01216 016981
E-mail: info@icme.org.uk
Website: www.icme.org.uk

The ICME is the professional body for those in the castings and associated industry. It was formed in 1904, granted its first Royal Charter in 1921, a Third Supplemental Charter in 1994 and changed its name in 2001. The granting of the Third Supplemental Charter aligned its membership requirements with those of the EC(UK).

MEMBERSHIP
Student
Member (MICME)
Professional Member (Prof MICME)
Fellow (FICME)
Engineering Technician (EngTech)
Incorporated Engineer (IEng)
Chartered Engineer (CEng)
European Engineer (EurIng)

DESIGNATORY LETTERS
MICME, Prof MICME, FICME, EngTech, IEng, CEng, EurIng

FREIGHT FORWARDING

Membership of Professional Institutions and Associations

BRITISH INTERNATIONAL FREIGHT ASSOCIATION (BIFA)

Redfern House
Browells Lane
Feltham
Middlesex TW13 7EP
Tel: 020 8844 2266
Fax: 020 8890 5546
E-mail: bifa@bifa.org
Website: www.bifa.org

BIFA is the principal trade association providing representation and support to British companies engaged in the international movement of freight to and from the UK by air, rail, road and sea. It is a not-for-profit organization. Members are encouraged to contribute to the running of the Association.

MEMBERSHIP
Associate Member
Trade Member

FUNDRAISING

Membership of Professional Institutions and Associations

INSTITUTE OF FUNDRAISING

Park Place
12 Lawn Lane
London SW8 1UD
Tel: 020 7840 1000
Fax: 020 7840 1001
E-mail: info@institute-of-fundraising.org.uk
Website: www.institute-of-fundraising.org.uk

The Institute of Fundraising is the professional body for fundraisers in the UK. We offer professional support, act as a voice for fundraisers and promote best practice. We also offer professional qualifications, training and our annual IoF National Convention is the largest fundraising conference of its type in Europe.

MEMBERSHIP
Associate
Full Member (MInstF)
Fully Certificated Member MInstF(Cert)
Diploma Qualified Member MInstF(Dip)
Organizational Member
Corporate Member

QUALIFICATION/EXAMINATIONS
Introductory Certificate in Fundraising
Certificate in Fundraising
Diploma in Fundraising
Certificate in Direct Marketing

DESIGNATORY LETTERS
MInstF, MInstF(Cert), MInstF(Dip), FInstF

FUNERAL DIRECTING, BURIAL AND CREMATION ADMINISTRATION

Membership of Professional Institutions and Associations

NATIONAL ASSOCIATION OF FUNERAL DIRECTORS

618 Warwick Road
Solihull
West Midlands B91 1AA
Tel: 0845 230 1343
Fax: 0121 711 1351
E-mail: info@nafd.org.uk
Website: www.nafd.org.uk

The NAFD, founded in 1905, is an independent trade association whose members include more than 3, 200 funeral homes throughout the UK, suppliers to the profession, and overseas funeral directing businesses. We provide support to our members and offer informed opinion to government.

MEMBERSHIP
Funeral Director (Category A) Member
Supplier (Category B) Member
Overseas Member

QUALIFICATION/EXAMINATIONS
Foundation Certificate in Funeral Service
Advanced Certificate in Funeral Services
Diploma in Funeral Directing (DipFD)
Diploma in Funeral Service Management (DipFSM)
Advanced Diploma in Funeral Arranging and Administration

NATIONAL ASSOCIATION OF MEMORIAL MASONS

1 Castle Mews
Rugby
Warwickshire CV21 2AL
Tel: 01788 542264
Fax: 01788 542276
E-mail: enquiries@namm.org.uk
Website: www.namm.org.uk

The NAMM was formed in 1907 to promote excellence and craftsmanship within the memorial masonry trade. Our services to members include training, business advice, technical advice, promotion, a legal helpline, a conciliation and arbitration service, trade exhibitions and a conference. We protect members' interests through representation to the British Standards Institution (BSI) and the Burial & Cemeteries Advisory Group (BCAG).

MEMBERSHIP
Individual Associate Member
Affiliate Retail Member
Full Retail and Wholesale Members
Company Associate Member
Corporate Associate Member

THE INSTITUTE OF BURIAL AND CREMATION ADMINISTRATION

Kelham Hall
Newark
Nottinghamshire NG23 5QX
Tel: 01636 708311
Fax: 01636 706311

MEMBERSHIP
Student
Registered Licentiate (LInstBCA)
Associate Member (AInstBCA)
Member (MInstBCA)
Fellow (FInstBCA)

QUALIFICATION/EXAMINATIONS
Diploma
Final Diploma

DESIGNATORY LETTERS
LInstBCA, AInstBCA, MInstBCA, FInstBCA

FURNISHING AND FURNITURE

Membership of Professional Institutions and Associations

FLOORING INDUSTRY TRAINING ASSOCIATION

4c St Marys Place
The Lace Market
Nottingham NG1 1PH
Tel: 0115 9506836
E-mail: info@fita.co.uk
Website: www.fita.co.uk

FITA was set up and is fully supported by the CFA and the NICF to provide training for the floor-covering industry. We have a fully equipped training centre at Loughborough, where the majority of our courses are run. We also offer tailor-made courses to suit individual specifications and requirements.

QUALIFICATION/EXAMINATIONS
FITA standard courses are:
Carpet Fitting – Basic (4 days)
Carpet Fitting – Intermediate (4 days)
Carpet Fitting – Advanced (3 days)
Commercial Vinyl Fitting – Basic (2 days)
Commercial Vinyl Fitting– Intermediate (2 days)
Commercial Vinyl Fitting – Advanced (2 days)
Domestic Sheet Vinyl Fitting (2 days)
Estimating, Planning and Quantification (2 days)
Resilient/Luxury Vinyl Tile Fitting – Basic (2 days)
Resilient/Luxury Vinyl Tile Fitting – Advanced (2 days)
Laminate and Wood Fitting – Basic (2 days)
Wood Fitting – Intermediate (3 days)
Wood Fitting – Advanced
Subfloor Preparation – Commercial (1 day)
Subfloor Preparation – Domestic (1 day)
Wood Sanding and Finishing - (2 days)
Understanding Moisture (1 day)
Tailor-made courses are available upon request. Content and course length tailored to your requirements.

NATIONAL INSTITUTE OF CARPET AND FLOORLAYERS

4c St Marys Place
The Lace Market
Nottingham NG1 1PH
Tel: 0115 9583077
Fax: 0115 9412238
E-mail: info@nicfltd.org.uk
Website: www.nicfltd.org.uk

The NICF furthers the interests of its members by promoting excellence in the field of carpet and floorlaying and providing a range of benefits, products and services.

MEMBERSHIP
Master Fitter Member
Fitter Member
Trainee Fitter Member
Retailer Member
Associate Member
Patron Member

QUALIFICATION/EXAMINATIONS
Master Fitter qualification assessment

GEMMOLOGY AND JEWELLERY

Membership of Professional Institutions and Associations

THE GEMMOLOGICAL ASSOCIATION OF GREAT BRITAIN

27 Greville Street
London EC1N 8TN
Tel: 020 7404 3334
Fax: 020 7404 8843
E-mail: edu@gem-a.com
Website: www.gem-a.com

The Gemmological Association of Great Britain (Gem-A), a UK-registered charity, is the world's longest established provider of gem and jewellery education, our first diploma having been awarded in 1913. We are committed to promoting the study of gemmology and to providing CPD to our members – an international community of gem professionals and enthusiasts.

MEMBERSHIP
Member
Fellow (FGA)
Diamond Member (DGA)
Corporate Member

QUALIFICATION/EXAMINATIONS
Foundation Certificate in Gemmology
Diploma in Gemmology
Gem Diamond Diploma

DESIGNATORY LETTERS
FGA, DGA

THE NATIONAL ASSOCIATION OF GOLDSMITHS

78A Luke Street
London EC2A 4XG
Tel: 020 7613 4445
Fax: 020 7613 4450
E-mail: nag@jewellers-online.org
Website: www.jewellers-online.org

The NAG, established in 1894, serves and supports the jewellery industry of Great Britain and Ireland. We promote high professional standards among our members, who must adhere to a code of professional practice. In return, we offer them advice, support and CPD in the form of distance learning courses, seminars and tutorials.

MEMBERSHIP
Alumni Member
Allied Member
Affiliate Member
Ordinary Member

QUALIFICATION/EXAMINATIONS
Professional Jewellers' Diploma
Professional Jewellers' Gemstone Diploma
Professional Jewellers' Management Diploma
Professional Jewellers' Valuation Diploma

GENEALOGY

Membership of Professional Institutions and Associations

SOCIETY OF GENEALOGISTS

14 Charterhouse Buildings
Goswell Road
London EC1M 7BA
Tel: 020 7251 8799
Fax: 020 7250 1800
E-mail: info@sog.org.uk
Website: www.sog.org.uk

The Society (founded 1911) is the National Library and Education Centre for Family History. A registered educational charity, it was founded to encourage and foster the study, science and knowledge of genealogy. This it does chiefly through its library, publications and extensive education programme of courses and events. It currently does not hold exams.

MEMBERSHIP
Member
Fellow (FSG)
Honorary Fellow (FSG Hon)

DESIGNATORY LETTERS
FSG, FSG Hon

THE HERALDRY SOCIETY

PO Box 772
Guildford GU3 3ZX
Tel: 01438 237373
Fax: 01483 237375
Website: www.theheraldrysociety.com

The Heraldry Society is a registered charity that aims to encourage interest in heraldry through publications, lectures, visits and related activities. Members receive *The Heraldry Gazette*, which contains heraldic news and comment, and Society information quarterly. We maintain contact with heraldic societies in many parts of the UK and abroad.

MEMBERSHIP
Associate Member
Ordinary Member
Fellow (FHS)
Honorary Fellow (Hon FHS)
Institutional Member

QUALIFICATION/EXAMINATIONS
Elementary Certificate
Intermediate Certificate
Advanced Certificate
Diploma (DipHS)

DESIGNATORY LETTERS
FHS, Hon FHS

THE INSTITUTE OF HERALDIC AND GENEALOGICAL STUDIES

79–82 Northgate
Canterbury
Kent CT1 1BA
Tel: 01227 768664
Fax: 01227 765617
E-mail: registrar@ihgs.ac.uk
Website: www.ihgs.ac.uk

The IHGS, founded in 1961, is an independent educational charitable trust that offers a wide range of courses on family history, heraldry and related historical subjects, and has an extensive library, archive and research facilities. We also publish a monthly e-mail newsletter and a quarterly journal, *Family History*.

MEMBERSHIP
Associate Member
Graduate Member
Licentiate (LHG)
Fellow (FHG)

QUALIFICATION/EXAMINATIONS
Correspondence Course in Genealogy
Higher Certificate in Genealogy
Diploma in Genealogy

DESIGNATORY LETTERS
LHG, FHG

GEOGRAPHY

Membership of Professional Institutions and Associations

ROYAL GEOGRAPHICAL SOCIETY (WITH THE INSTITUTE OF BRITISH GEOGRAPHERS)

1 Kensington Gore
London SW7 2AR
Tel: 020 7591 3000
Fax: 020 7591 3001
E-mail: info@rgs.org
Website: www.rgs.org

The RGS-IBG is the learned society and professional body for geography. We aim to foster an understanding and informed enjoyment of our world: developing, supporting and promoting geographical research, expeditions and fieldwork, education, public engagement, and providing geography input to policy.

MEMBERSHIP
Young Geographer
Member
Postgraduate Fellow
Fellow
Chartered Geographer (CGeog)
Corporate Member

DESIGNATORY LETTERS
FRGS, CGeog

GEOLOGY

Membership of Professional Institutions and Associations

THE GEOLOGICAL SOCIETY

Burlington House
Piccadilly
London W1J 0BG
Tel: 020 7434 9944
Fax: 020 7439 8975
E-mail: enquiries@geolsoc.org.uk
Website: www.geolsoc.org.uk

The Geological Society, founded in 1807, is the UK's national organization for professional Earth scientists. The normal grade of membership is Fellow. Students may become Candidate Fellows. Members of the public not eligible for any other status may join as Friends.

MEMBERSHIP
Friend
Candidate Fellow
Fellow
Chartered Geologist

DESIGNATORY LETTERS
FGS, CGeol

GLASS TECHNOLOGY

Membership of Professional Institutions and Associations

BRITISH SOCIETY OF SCIENTIFIC GLASSBLOWERS

Unit W1, MK2 Business Centre
Barton Road
Bletchley
Milton Keynes
Buckinghamshire MK2 3HU
Tel: 01908 821191
Fax: 01908 821195
E-mail: bssg@biochemglass.co.uk
Website: www.bssg.co.uk

The Society was founded in 1960 for the benefit of those engaged in Scientific Glassblowing and its associated professions, and to uphold and further the status of Scientific Glassblowers. We welcome written submissions to our quarterly journal, which is circulated to members.

MEMBERSHIP
Associate
Student Member
Fellow
Full Member
Master
Honorary Member
Retired Member
Overseas Member

SOCIETY OF GLASS TECHNOLOGY

9 Churchill Way
Chapeltown
Sheffield
South Yorkshire S35 2PY
Tel: 01142 634455
Fax: 01142 634411
E-mail: info@sgt.org
Website: www.sgt.org

The objects of the Society of Glass Technology are to encourage and advance the study of the history, art, science, design, manufacture, after treatment, distribution and end use of glass of any and every kind.

MEMBERSHIP
Personal Member
Fellow (FSGT)
Fellow Emeritus
Honorary Fellow (HonFSGT)
Corporate Member

QUALIFICATION/EXAMINATIONS
Peer review by the Board of Fellows

DESIGNATORY LETTERS
FSGT, HonFSGT

HAIRDRESSING

Membership of Professional Institutions and Associations

HABIA

Oxford House
Sixth Avenue
Sky Business Park, Robin Hood Airport
Doncaster
South Yorkshire DN9 3GG
Tel: 0845 2 306080
Fax: 01302 774949
E-mail: info@habia.org
Website: www.habia.org

Habia is the government-appointed standards-setting body for hair, beauty, nails, spa therapy, barbering and African-type hair, and creates the standards that form the basis of all qualifications, including NVQs, SVQs, apprenticeships, diplomas and foundation degrees, as well as industry codes of practice.

MEMBERSHIP

Habia offers a membership programme for training providers (Habia Members) and a wider, free membership for industry professionals and educators.

THE GUILD OF HAIRDRESSERS

Archway House
Barnsley S71 1AQ
Tel: 01226 786555
Fax: 01226 786555

The Guild of Hairdressers dates back to 1340, when it was part of the Guild of Barbers and Surgeons. Then in the late 16th century, when the surgeons split off, it became the Guild of Hairdressers, Wigmakers and Perfumers. Today it still exists for the benefit of its members, who adhere to a code of ethics and to whom it provides help and advice.

HEALTH AND HEALTH SERVICES

Membership of Professional Institutions and Associations

BRITISH OCCUPATIONAL HYGIENE SOCIETY – FACULTY OF OCCUPATIONAL HYGIENE

5/6 Melbourne Business Court
Millennium Way
Pride Park
Derby DE24 8LZ
Tel: 01332 298101
Fax: 01332 298099
E-mail: admin@bohs.org
Website: www.bohs.org

BOHS is a professional membership organization and learned society, promoting public and professional awareness, good practice and high standards of occuaptional hygiene, to help reduce work-related ill-health. The Faculty is our professional arm and examining board, and administers examinations and awards qualifications in Occupational Hygiene and allied subjects.

MEMBERSHIP
Individual
Student
Affiliate (corporate)
Retired
Associate (AFOH)
Licentiate (LFOH)
Member (MFOH)
Specialist Member (MFOH(S))
Fellow (FFOH)

QUALIFICATION/EXAMINATIONS
A range of UK and international qualifications in occupational hygiene and related subjects, which include stand-alone modules covering general principles and practical applications at the technician level, through to BOHS's own professional level Certificate and Diploma qualifications.

The Occupational Hygiene Modules are aimed at those who want to gain a qualification in a particular topic of occupational hygiene to demonstrate technical expertise in that area or, grouped together, to gain exemption from the Faculty's professional level Certificate Core examination.

The International Occupational Hygiene Modules are based on the Occupational Hygiene Modules, without specific reference to UK or other legislation. The Proficiency Modules cover both theory and practical training in a specific subject, and are aimed at those needing to demonstrate a level of proficiency to carry out the area of work covered by the Module.

Our professional qualifications are as follows: The Certificate of Competence in an individual subject is for candidates wanting to establish their competence in a specific field, and follows on from successful completion of one of the Occupational Hygiene Modules. This is an oral examination, supported by submission of a written report. The Certificate of Operational Competence in Occupational Hygiene is the entry level qualification required to join the Faculty of Occupational Hygiene as a Licentiate, and demonstrates knowledge and competence in the broad principles and practice of occupational hygiene. This is a two-part written and oral examination. The Diploma of Professional Competence in Occupational Hygiene is the highest professional occupational hygiene qualification. Candidates must already hold the Certificate of Operational Competence, and be able to demonstrate 5 years' experience in the field of occupational hygiene. Award of the Diploma qualifies the holder to become a Member of the Faculty, and demonstrates knowledge of, and competence in, assessment of health hazards and the extent of risk in various workplace circumstances, and an ability to advise on suitable control procedures. This is also a two-part, written and oral, examination.

For further information see; www.bohs.org/education/examinations/

DESIGNATORY LETTERS
AFOH, LFOH, MFOH, FFOH, MFOH(S)

CHARTERED INSTITUTE OF ENVIRONMENTAL HEALTH

Chadwick Court
15 Hatfields
London SE1 8DJ
Tel: 020 7827 5800
Fax: 020 7827 5832
E-mail: customerservices@cieh.org
Website: www.cieh.org

The CIEH is a professional, awarding and campaigning body at the forefront of environmental and public health and safety.

MEMBERSHIP
Student member
Associate
Accredited Associate
Graduate Member
Fellow

QUALIFICATION/EXAMINATIONS
The CIEH offers a range of Ofqual-regulated qualifications at four levels in health and safety, food safety, environmental protection and train the trainer.

ERGONOMICS SOCIETY

Elms Court
Elms Grove
Loughborough
Leicestershire LE11 1RG
Tel: 01509 234904
Fax: 01509 235666
E-mail: ergsoc@ergonomics.org.uk
Website: www.ergonomics.org.uk

The Ergonomics Society, founded in 1949, is a UK-based professional society for ergonomists worldwide. We encourage and maintain high standards of professional practice through education, accreditation and development, promote the interests of our members across government, academia, business and industry, and raise awareness of ergonomics in general.

MEMBERSHIP
Student Member
Associate Member
Graduate Member
Registered Member (MErgS)
Fellow (FErgS)

INSTITUTE OF HEALTH PROMOTION AND EDUCATION

c/o Helen Draper
School of Dentistry, University of Manchester
Coupland 3, Oxford Road
Manchester M13 9PL
Tel: 01612 756610
E-mail: honsec@ihpe.org.uk
Website: www.ihpe.org.uk

The IHPE was established 40 years ago to bring together professionals with a common interest in health education and promotion to share their experience, ideas and information. Our members come from a diverse range of backgrounds, including nursing, midwifery, health visiting, medicine, dentistry, public health, stress management, psychology and teaching.

MEMBERSHIP
Student Member
Associate Member (AIHPE)
Full Member (MIHPE)
Fellow (FIHPE)
Corporate Member

DESIGNATORY LETTERS
MIHPE, AIHPE, FIHPE

INSTITUTE OF HEALTH RECORDS AND INFORMATION MANAGEMENT

744a Manchester Road
Rochdale
Lancashire OL11 3AQ
Tel: 01706 868481
Fax: 01706 868481
E-mail: ihrim@zen.co.uk
Website: www.ihrim.co.uk

IHRIM was founded in 1948, primarily as an educational body, to provide qualifications as well as career and professional assistance to members. We encourage professionalism and high standards among our members who work in the fields of health records, information management, clinical coding and information governance.

MEMBERSHIP
Student
Affiliate
Licentiate
Certificated Member (CHRIM)
Accredited Clinical Coder (ACC)
Associate (AHRIM)
Fellow (FHRIM)
Corporate Affiliate

QUALIFICATION/EXAMINATIONS
Certificate of Technical Competence
Foundation exam
Certificate
Diploma
National Clinical Coding Qualification

DESIGNATORY LETTERS
CHRIM, ACC, AHRIM, FHRIM

INSTITUTE OF HEALTHCARE ENGINEERING AND ESTATE MANAGEMENT

2 Abingdon House
Cumberland Business Centre
Northumberland Road
Portsmouth PO5 1DS
Tel: 023 92 823186
Fax: 023 92 815927
E-mail: office@iheem.org.uk
Website: www.iheem.org.uk

IHEEM is the learned society and professional body for those working in the Healthcare Estates sector. Our members are architects, builders, engineers, estate managers, surveyors, medical engineers and other related professionals. We provide benefits to members to keep them up to date with developing technology and changing regulations.

MEMBERSHIP
Graduate (GIHEEM)
Associate Member (AMIHEEM)
Member (MIHEEM)
Fellow (FIHEEM)

DESIGNATORY LETTERS
GIHEEM, AMIHEEM, MIHEEM, FIHEEM

INSTITUTE OF HEALTHCARE MANAGEMENT

18–21 Morely Street
London SE1 7QZ
Tel: 020 7620 1030
Fax: 020 7620 1040
E-mail: enquiries@ihm.org.uk
Website: www.ihm.org.uk

The IHM is the professional organization for managers throughout healthcare, including the NHS, independent providers, healthcare consultants and the armed forces. Our focus is on improving patient/user care by publishing standards of management practice, promoting the IHM Code (which covers behavioural and ethical aspects of management practice) and establishing a CPD framework for our members.

MEMBERSHIP
Associate Member
Full Member (MIHM)
Fellow (FIHM)
Companion (CIHM)

QUALIFICATION/EXAMINATIONS
Certificate in Health Management Studies (CertHMS)
Certificate in Health Services Management (CertHSM)
Certificate in Managing Health Services (CertMHS)
Certificate in Managing Health & Social Care (CertMHSC)
Diploma in Health Services Management (DipHSM)

DESIGNATORY LETTERS
MIHM, FIHM, CIHM

THE ROYAL SOCIETY FOR PUBLIC HEALTH

3rd Floor
Market Towers
1 Nine Elms Lane
London SW8 5NQ
Tel: 020 3177 1600
Fax: 020 3177 1601
E-mail: info@rsph.org.uk
Website: www.rsph.org.uk

The RSPH was formed in October 2008 by the merger of the Royal Society for the Promotion of Health (RSPH/RSH) and the Royal Institute of Public Health (RIPH). We offer a wide range of vocationally related qualifications in the fields of food safety and nutrition, hygiene, health and safety, pest control, health promotion and the built environment.

MEMBERSHIP
Associate (ARSPH)
Licentiate (LRSPH)
Member (MRSPH)
Fellow (FRSPH)

QUALIFICATION/EXAMINATIONS
Please see the RSPH's website.

DESIGNATORY LETTERS
ARSPH, LRSPH, MRSPH, FRSPH

HORSES AND HORSE RIDING

Membership of Professional Institutions and Associations

THE BRITISH HORSE SOCIETY

Contact: Equestrian Qualifications GB Limited
c/o The British Horse Society
Abbey Park
Kenilworth
Warwickshire CV8 2XZ
Tel: 02476 840500
Fax: 02476 840501
E-mail: exams@bhs.org.uk
Website: www.bhs.org.uk

The British Horse Society offers vocational and work-based examinations for grooms, stable managers, riding instructors and coaches. Founded in 1947, the BHS exams system is world renowned as credible and rigorous, producing competent, practical people who follow safe practices. We also offer competency certificates for the recreational rider.

MEMBERSHIP
Individual Member
Trade Member
Corporate Member

QUALIFICATION/EXAMINATIONS
Equestrian Qualifications GB Limited awards examinations and qualifications for grooms, stable managers, riding instructors and coaches on behalf of The British Horse Society and British Equestrian Federation. Please see the EQL website, www.equestrian-qualifications.org.uk, for details.

HOUSING

Membership of Professional Institutions and Associations

THE CHARTERED INSTITUTE OF HOUSING

Octavia House
Westwood Way
Coventry CV4 8JP
Tel: 02476 851700
Fax: 02476 695110
E-mail: customer.services@cih.org
Website: www.cih.org

The CIH is the professional body for people involved in housing and communities. We are a registered charity and not-for-profit organization. We have a diverse and growing membership of over 22,000 people – both in the public and private sectors – living and working in over 20 countries on five continents across the world.

MEMBERSHIP

From January 2012 the two new grades of membership will be introduced and replace the existing six grades of membership.
CIH Member (formerly Student, Affiliate, Practitioner, Associate)
CIH Chartered Member (formerly Corporate and Fellow).
Visit www.cih.org to find out more about changes to CIH membership.

QUALIFICATION/EXAMINATIONS

Certificate Courses
The CIH offers a range of certificated courses at Levels 2, 3 and 4 delivered at various centres across the UK. They are also available by distance learning. We also offer a suite of certificated courses in repairs and maintenance, also at Levels 2, 3 and 4, developed in partnership with the Chartered Institute of Building (CIOB).
Professional Qualifications
The CIH Professional Qualification can be achieved at either undergraduate or postgraduate level, FT or PT.
Please see the CIH's website for details.

DESIGNATORY LETTERS

CIH Members: CIH Member or CIHM, CIH Chartered Members: CIH Chartered Member or CIHCM (existing Fellows can continue to use FCIH and Honorary Members can use (Hon).

INDEXING

Membership of Professional Institutions and Associations

SOCIETY OF INDEXERS

Woodbourn Business Centre
10 Jessell Street
Sheffield S9 3HY
Tel: 01142 449561
E-mail: admin@indexers.org.uk
Website: www.indexers.org.uk

The Society of Indexers is the professional body for indexing in the UK and Ireland, and exists to promote indexing, the quality of indexes and the profession of indexing. We offer information to publishers and other organizations on commissioning indexes and our online directory 'Indexers

Available' provides an up-to-date guide to indexers currently working in a wide range of fields.

MEMBERSHIP
Student Member
Member
Professional Member (MSocInd)
Advanced Professional Member (MSocInd(Adv))
Fellow (FSocInd)
Corporate Member

QUALIFICATION/EXAMINATIONS
Training in Indexing course
Advanced Test
Fellowship index submission

DESIGNATORY LETTERS
MSocInd, MSocInd(Adv), FSocInd

INDUSTRIAL SAFETY

Membership of Professional Institutions and Associations

BRITISH SAFETY COUNCIL

70 Chancellors Road
London W6 9RS
Tel: 020 8741 1231
Fax: 020 8741 4555
E-mail: mail@britsafe.org
Website: www.britsafe.org

The BSC is one of the world's leading health and safety organizations. Our mission is to keep people healthy and safe at work. Our range of charitable initiatives, such as free health and safety qualifications for school children, is supported by a broad mix of commercial activities centred on membership, training, auditing and qualifications.

MEMBERSHIP
UK Member
International Member

QUALIFICATION/EXAMINATIONS
Certificate in Process Safety
Certificate in COSHH Risk Assessment (Level 2)
Certificate in DSE Risk Assessment (Level 2)
Certificate in Fire Risk Assessment (Level 2)
Certificate in Manual Handling Risk Assessment (Level 2)
Certificate in Risk Assessment (Level 2)
Certificate in Supervising Staff Safely (Level 2)
Certificate in Occupational Health and Safety (Level 3)
Diploma in Occupational Health and Safety (Level 6)
Diploma in Environmental Management (DipEM)
International Certificate in Occupational Health and Safety
International Diploma in Environmental Management
International Diploma in Occupational Health and Safety

HEALTH & SAFETY EXECUTIVE APPROVED MINING QUALIFICATIONS

Mining Qualifications, The Health & Safety Executive
2nd Floor, Foundry House
3 Millsands, Riverside Exchange
Sheffield
South Yorkshire S3 8NH
Tel: 0114 291 2394
Fax: 0114 291 2399
E-mail: sarah.johnson@hse.gsi.gov.uk
Website: www.hse.gov.uk/mining

The HSE issues First and Second Class Certificates of Qualification as required under the Management and Administration of Safety and Health at Mines Regulations (MASHAM) 1993 for the appointment of a manager and undermanager respectively, in mines of coal, shale and fireclay in the UK. It also issues certificates to Mining Mechanical and Mining Electrical Engineers, Mechanics and Electricians Class I and Class II, Mines Surveyor, and Mines Deputy. For details see; www.hse.gov.uk/mining

INTERNATIONAL INSTITUTE OF RISK AND SAFETY MANAGEMENT

Suite 7a
77 Fulham Palace Road
London W6 8JA
Tel: 020 8741 9100
Fax: 020 8741 1349
E-mail: info@iirsm.org
Website: www.iirsm.org

The IIRSM is a professional body for health & safety practitioners and specialists in associated professions. Our aim is to advance professional standards in accident prevention and occupational health throughout the world. We have more than 8, 100 members, in the UK and over 70 other countries, to whom we provide support and offer advice via a technical helpline.

MEMBERSHIP
Student
Affiliate
Associate (AIIRSM)
Member (MIIRSM)
Specialist Member (SIIRSM)
Fellow (FIIRSM)

DESIGNATORY LETTERS
AIIRSM, MIIRSM, SIIRSM, FIIRSM

NEBOSH (THE NATIONAL EXAMINATION BOARD IN OCCUPATIONAL SAFETY AND HEALTH)

Dominus Way
Meridian Business Park
Leicester LE19 1QW
Tel: 0116 263 4700
Fax: 0116 282 4000
E-mail: info@nebosh.org.uk
Website: www.nebosh.org.uk

NEBOSH offers globally recognized qualifications designed to meet the health, safety, environmental and risk management needs of all places of work. Courses leading to NEBOSH qualifications attract over 30,000 candidates annually in nearly 80 countries around the world. NEBOSH also offers qualifications in Oil and Gas, and Health and Well-being.

MEMBERSHIP

NEBOSH's National General Certificate, National Certificate in Fire Safety and Risk Management, National Certificate in Construction Health and Safety, and the International General Certificate are all accepted as meeting the academic requirements to apply for Technician Membership (Tech IOSH) of the Institution of Occupational Safety and Health (IOSH), and Associate Membership (AIIRSM) of the International Institute of Risk and Safety Management (IIRSM).

NEBOSH's National Diploma and International Diploma are accepted as meeting the requirements to apply for Graduate Membership (Grad IOSH) of the Institution of Occupational Safety and Health (IOSH). Diplomates may also apply to become full Members (MIIRSM) of the International Institute of Risk and Safety Management (IIRSM). The National Diploma provides a sound basis for progression to MSc level: a number of UK universities offer MSc programmes that accept the National Diploma as a full or partial entry requirement.

The NEBOSH Environmental Diploma fulfils the academic requirements for both Associate Membership (AIEMA) of the Institute of Environmental Management and Assessment (IEMA) and Associate Membership (AIIRSM) of the International Institute of Risk and Safety Management (IIRSM).

QUALIFICATION/EXAMINATIONS

Award in Health and Safety at Work
National Certificate in Construction Health and Safety (Level 3)
National Certificate in Environmental Management
National Certificate in Fire Safety and Risk Management (Level 3)
NEBOSH National General Certificate in Occupational Health and Safety (Level 3)
International General Certificate in Occupational Health and Safety
NEBOSH International Technical Certificate in Oil and Gas Operational Safety
NEBOSH National Certificate in the Management of Health and Well-being at Work
NEBOSH International Certificate in Construction Health and Safety
NEBOSH National Diploma in Environmental Management (Level 6) (EnvDipNEBOSH)
NEBOSH National Diploma in Occupational Health and Safety (Level 6) (DipNEBOSH)
International Diploma in Occupational Health and Safety (IDipNEBOSH)

THE INSTITUTION OF OCCUPATIONAL SAFETY AND HEALTH

The Grange
Highfield Drive
Wigston
Leicestershire LE18 1NN
Tel: 0116 257 3100
Fax: 0116 257 3101
E-mail: membership@iosh.co.uk
Website: www.iosh.co.uk

IOSH is the world's largest organization for health and safety professionals, with more than 36,000 members worldwide, including 13,000 Chartered Safety and Health Practitioners. The Institution was founded in 1945 and is an independent, not-for-profit organization that sets professional standards, supports and develops members, and provides authoritative advice and guidance on health and safety issues.

MEMBERSHIP
Affiliate Member
Technician Member (Tech IOSH)
Graduate Member (Grad IOSH)
Chartered Member (CMIOSH)
Chartered Fellow (CFIOSH)

DESIGNATORY LETTERS
Tech IOSH, Grad IOSH, CMIOSH, CFIOSH

INSURANCE AND ACTUARIAL WORK

Membership of Professional Institutions and Associations

ASSOCIATION OF AVERAGE ADJUSTERS

Secretariat: The Baltic Exchange
St Mary Axe
London EC3A 8BH
Tel: 020 7623 5501
Fax: 020 7369 1623
E-mail: aaa@balticexchange.com
Website: www.average-adjusters.com

The AAA was founded in 1869 to promote correct principles in the adjustment of marine insurance claims and general average, uniformity of practice among average adjusters and the maintenance of good professional conduct. It ensures the independence and impartiality of its members by imposing a strict code of conduct and has close links with other international associations and insurance markets.

MEMBERSHIP
Subscriber
Associate
Fellow

QUALIFICATION/EXAMINATIONS
The Association's examination consists of 6 modules. Passes in Modules 1 & 2 are required for Associateship, passes in Modules 3–6 for Fellowship. For details see the Association's website.

THE CHARTERED INSTITUTE OF LOSS ADJUSTERS

Warwick House
65/66 Queen Street
London EC4R 1EB
Tel: 020 7337 9960
Fax: 020 7929 3082
E-mail: info@cila.co.uk
Website: www.cila.co.uk

The CILA, which was founded in 1941, is the professional body representing the claims specialists who investigate, negotiate and agree the conclusion of insurance and other claims on behalf of insurers and policyholders. We safeguard the interests of our members and maintain the high standards of the profession by requiring them to abide by our code of professional conduct.

MEMBERSHIP
Student Member
Ordinary Member
Associate (ACILA)
Fellow (FCILA)
Honorary Member

QUALIFICATION/EXAMINATIONS
CILA examination

DESIGNATORY LETTERS
ACILA, FCILA

THE CHARTERED INSURANCE INSTITUTE

42–48 High Road
South Woodford
London E18 2JP
Tel: 020 8989 8464
Fax: 020 8530 3052
E-mail: customer.serv@cii.co.uk
Website: www.cii.co.uk

The CII is the premier professional body for those working in the insurance and financial services industry. We are dedicated to promoting higher standards of competence and integrity through the provision of relevant qualifications for employees at all levels across all sectors of the industry.

MEMBERSHIP
Ordinary Member
Qualified Member
Associate Member (ACII)
Fellow (FCII)

QUALIFICATION/EXAMINATIONS
Award in Financial Planning
Award in Insurance
Certificate in Equity Release
Certificate in Financial Administration
Certificate in Financial Planning
Certificate in Insurance
Certificate in Life and Pensions
Certificate in Mortgage Advice
Diploma in Financial Planning
Diploma in Insurance
Advanced Diploma in Financial Planning
Advanced Diploma in Insurance
MSc in Insurance and Risk Planning (in association with Cass Business School)

DESIGNATORY LETTERS
ACII, FCII

THE FACULTY AND INSTITUTE OF ACTUARIES

Faculty of Actuaries
Maclaurin House
18 Dublin Street
Edinburgh EH1 3PP
Tel: 0131 240 1313
E-mail: faculty@actuaries.org.uk
Website: www.actuaries.org.uk

Institute of Actuaries
Staple Inn Hall
High Holborn
London WC1V 7QJ
Tel: 020 7632 2111
E-mail: institute@actuaries.org.uk

Napier House
4 Worcester Street
Oxford OX1 2AW
Tel: 01865 268211
E-mail: institute@actuaries.org.uk

Actuaries are experts in assessing the financial impact of tomorrow's uncertain events. They enable financial decisions to be made with more confidence by analysing the past, modelling the future, assessing the risks involved, and communicating what the results mean in financial terms.

MEMBERSHIP
Student Member
Affiliate Member
Associate (AFA or AIA)
Fellow (FFA or FIA)
Honorary Fellow

QUALIFICATION/EXAMINATIONS
Certificate in Financial Mathematics

DESIGNATORY LETTERS
AFA, AIA, FFA, FIA

JOURNALISM

Membership of Professional Institutions and Associations

NATIONAL COUNCIL FOR THE TRAINING OF JOURNALISTS

NCTJ Training Ltd
The New Granary
Newport
Saffron Walden
Essex CB11 3PL
Tel: 01799 544014
Fax: 01799 544015
E-mail: info@nctj.com
Website: www.nctj.com

The NCTJ provides a range of journalism training products and services in the UK, including: accredited courses; qualifications and examinations; awards; careers information; distance learning; short courses and CPD; information and research;

publications and events. We play an influential role in all areas of journalism education and training.

QUALIFICATION/EXAMINATIONS
Diploma in Journalism
National Certificate Examination (NCE) for Press photographers and photo-journalists
National Certificate Examination (NCE) for Reporters
National Certificate Examination (NCE) for Sub-editors
National Certificate Examination (NCE) for Sports Reporters

THE CHARTERED INSTITUTE OF JOURNALISTS

2 Dock Offices
Surrey Quays Road
London SE16 2XU
Tel: 020 7252 1187
Fax: 020 7232 2302
E-mail: memberservices@cioj.co.uk
Website: www.cioj.co.uk

The CIoJ, which dates back to 1884, is a professional body and trade union for journalists. We expect our members to uphold high standards in the way they work and to adhere to a strict code of conduct, and in return we champion journalistic freedom, protect their interests in the workplace and campaign for better working conditions.

MEMBERSHIP
Student Member
Affiliate Member
Trainee Member
Full Member
International Member

DESIGNATORY LETTERS
MCIJ – Member, FCIJ – Fellow

LAND AND PROPERTY

Membership of Professional Institutions and Associations

RICS (ROYAL INSTITUTION OF CHARTERED SURVEYORS)

Parliament Square
London SW1P 3AD
Tel: 0870 333 1600
Fax: 020 7334 3811
E-mail: contactrics@rics.org
Website: www.rics.org/careers

RICS, an independent, not-for-profit organization, has around 100,000 qualified members and more than 50,000 students and trainees in some 140 countries, and provides the world's leading professional qualification in land, property, construction and associated environmental issues. We accredit over 600 courses at leading universities worldwide and provide impartial, authoritative advice on key issues for business, society and governments.

MEMBERSHIP
Student
Associate (AssocRICS)
Member (MRICS)
Fellow (FRICS)

DESIGNATORY LETTERS
AssocRICS, MRICS, FRICS

THE COLLEGE OF ESTATE MANAGEMENT

Whiteknights
Reading
Berkshire RG6 6AW
Tel: 0118 921 4696
Fax: 01189 921 4620
E-mail: courses@cem.ac.uk
Website: www.cem.ac.uk

The College of Estate Management is the leading provider of supported distance learning for real estate and construction professionals. We have been playing a key role in the property world for over 90 years. At any one time we have over 4,000 students based all over the world.

QUALIFICATION/EXAMINATIONS
Diploma in Construction Practice
BCSC Diploma in Shopping Centre Management
Diploma in Surveying Practice
BSc in Building Services Quantity Surveying
BSc in Building Surveying
BSc in Construction Management
BSC in Estate Management
BSc in Property Management
BSc in Quantity Surveying
Postgraduate Diploma/MSc in Conservation of the Historic Environment
Postgraduate Diploma/MSC in Surveying
MBA in Real Estate and Construction Management
MSc in Real Estate
Postgraduate Diploma in Adjudication
Postgraduate Diploma in Arbitration
RICS Postgraduate Diploma in Project Management
Postgraduate Diploma/MSc in Conservation of the Historic Environment
Postgraduate Diploma/MSc in Facilities Management
Postgraduate Diploma/MSc in Property Investment
RICS Professional Membership Graduate Route – Adaptation 1

THE INSTITUTE OF REVENUES, RATING AND VALUATION

Northumberland House
5th Floor
303-306 High Holborn
London WC1V 7JZ
Tel: 020 7831 3505
Fax: 020 7831 2048
E-mail: education@irrv.org.uk
Website: www.irrv.org.uk

The Institute offers professional and technical qualifications for all those whose professional work is concerned with local authority revenues and benefits, valuation for rating, property taxation and the appeals procedure. Our qualifications are widely recognized throughout the profession.

MEMBERSHIP
Student Member
Affiliate Member
Graduate Member
Technician Member (Tech IRRV)
Diploma Member (Dip IRRV)
Honours Member (IRRV Hons)
Honorary Member
Fellow (FIRRV)

QUALIFICATION/EXAMINATIONS
Level 3 Certificate
Level 3 Local Taxation & Benefits (QCF) / SVQ
Professional Diploma in Local Taxation and Benefits Honours

DESIGNATORY LETTERS
Tech IRRV, IRRV (Dip), IRRV (Hons), FIRRV

THE NATIONAL FEDERATION OF PROPERTY PROFESSIONALS

Arbon House
6 Tournament Court
Edgehill Drive
Warwick CV34 6LG
Tel: 01926 417794
Fax: 01926 417789
E-mail: quals@nfopp.co.uk
Website: www.nfopp.co.uk

The NFOPP Awarding Body is committed to raising standards within agency through the provision of accredited, nationally recognized qualifications. We are recognized by the Qualifications and Examinations Regulator (Ofqual) and have to follow strict guidelines and maintain quality standards in the provision of all our qualifications.

MEMBERSHIP
For membership details of the following organizations please refer to the relevant website:
APIP; www.apip.co.uk
ARLA; www.arla.co.uk
ICBA; www.icba.uk.com
NAEA; www.naea.co.uk
NAVA; www.nava.org.uk

QUALIFICATION/EXAMINATIONS
Technical Award in Commercial Property Agency (Level 3)
Technical Award in Real Property Auctioneering (Level 3)
Technical Award in Residential Letting and Property Management (Level 3)
Technical Award in Sale of Residential Property (Level 3)
Diploma in Commercial Property Agency (DipCPA) (Level 5)
Diploma in Commercial Property Agency (DipREA) (Level 5)
Diploma in Residential Letting and Management (DipRLM) (Level 5)

THE PROPERTY CONSULTANTS SOCIETY

Basement Office
Surrey Court
1 Surrey Street
Arundel
West Sussex BN18 9DT
Tel: 01903 883787
E-mail: info@propertyconsultantssociety.org
Website: www.propertyconsultantssociety.org

The Property Consultants Society is a non-profit-making organization that offers advice to qualified surveyors, architects, valuers, auctioneers, land and estate agents, master builders, construction engineers, accountants and members of the legal profession to help them to undertake their property consultancy in a competent, legitimate and publicly acceptable way.

MEMBERSHIP
Student (SPCS)
Licentiate (LPCS)
Associate (APCS)
Fellow (FPCS)
Honorary Member

DESIGNATORY LETTERS
SPCS, LPCS, APCS, FPCS

LANDSCAPE ARCHITECTURE

Membership of Professional Institutions and Associations

LANDSCAPE INSTITUTE

Charles Darwin House
12 Roger Street
London WC1N 2JU
Tel: 020 7685 2640
E-mail: membership@landscapeinstitute.org
Website: www.landscapeinstitute.org

The LI is an educational charity and chartered body responsible for protecting, conserving and enhancing the natural and built environment for the benefit of the public. We champion well-designed and well-managed urban and rural landscape. Our 6,000 members include chartered landscape architects, academics and scientists working for local authorities, government agencies and in private practice, and students.

MEMBERSHIP
Student Member
Affiliate Member
Licentiate Member
Chartered Member (CMLI)
Fellow (FLI)
Academic
Academic Fellow

QUALIFICATION/EXAMINATIONS
Pathway to Chartership oral examination conferring chartered professional status (CMLI).

DESIGNATORY LETTERS
CMLI, FLI

LANGUAGES, LINGUISTICS AND TRANSLATION

Membership of Professional Institutions and Associations

INSTITUTE OF TRANSLATION & INTERPRETING

Fortuna House
South Fifth Street
Milton Keynes MK9 2PQ
Tel: 01908 325250
Fax: 01908 325259
E-mail: info@iti.org.uk
Website: www.iti.org.uk

The Institute of Translation & Interpreting is one of the primary sources of information on these services to government, industry, the media and the general public. We promote the highest standards, providing guidance to those entering the profession and advice to those who offer language services and to their customers.

MEMBERSHIP
Student Associate
Associate
Academic
Qualified Member (MITI)
Corporate Member

QUALIFICATION/EXAMINATIONS
Applicants for qualified membership must take an exam (translators) or attend an interview (interpreters).

THE CHARTERED INSTITUTE OF LINGUISTS

Saxon House
48 Southwark Street
London SE1 1UN
Tel: 020 7940 3100
Fax: 020 7940 3101
E-mail: info@iol.org.uk
Website: www.iol.org.uk

The Chartered Institute of Linguistics, founded in 1910, is a respected language assessment and accredited awarding body, with about 6, 500 members. Our aims include promoting the learning and use of modern languages, improving the status of all professional linguistics, and ensuring the maintenance of high professional standards through adherence to our code of conduct.

MEMBERSHIP
Registered Student
Associate Member (ACIL)
Member (MCIL)
Fellow (FCIL)
Chartered Linguist (CL)

QUALIFICATION/EXAMINATIONS
Certificate in Bilingual Skills (CBS)
Diploma in Public Service Interpreting (DPSI)
International Diploma in Bilingual Translation (IDBT)
Diploma in Translation (DipTrans)

DESIGNATORY LETTERS
ACIL, MCIL, FCIL, CL

THE GREEK INSTITUTE

34 Bush Hill Road
London N21 2DS
Tel: 020 8360 7968
Fax: 020 8360 7968
E-mail: info@greekinstitute.co.uk
Website: www.greekinstitute.co.uk

The Greek Institute, which was founded in 1969, is a non-profit-making cultural organization that promotes Modern Greek studies and culture through lectures, publications, literary competitions, Greek cultural evenings and the award of Certificates and a Diploma which are recognized by many UK universities as equivalent to GCSE and GCE A level Modern Greek.

MEMBERSHIP
Member
Associate (AGI)
Fellow (FGI)

QUALIFICATION/EXAMINATIONS
Certificate in Greek Conversation – Basic Stage: Levels 1 and 2
Certificate in Greek Conversation – Intermediate Stage: Levels 3 and 4
Certificate in Greek Conversation – Higher Stage: Levels 5 and 6
Preliminary Certificate
Intermediate Certificate
Advanced Certificate
Diploma in Greek Translation (DipGrTrans)

DESIGNATORY LETTERS
AGI, FGI

LAW

ENGLAND AND WALES

MAGISTRATES

Following the Constitutional Reform Act 2005, which came into force in April 2006, the Lord Chief Justice has become head of the Judiciary. He is responsible for the welfare, training and deployment of magistrates, for approving the names of the candidates recommended for appointment and for disciplinary action, short of removal. The Lord Chancellor also has responsibility for the protection of judicial independence and for working to ensure that the magistracy reflects the diversity of society as a whole.

There are six key qualities that a magistrate must possess: good character, social awareness, maturity and sound temperament, sound judgement, commitment and reliability. Political views are no longer sought and considered.

Before sitting in court, magistrates must undertake some basic training, which includes structured observations in court. This covers practice and procedure in court, structured decision making, sentencing, etc. New magistrates are assigned a mentor for their first two years. Consolidation training takes place about 18 months to two years after appointment, followed by appraisals. Magistrates only sit in adult courts when first appointed. Having got that experience they may apply to sit in youth courts and family courts and have to undertake more training before they can sit.

JUDGES

All judicial office holders are Her Majesty's Judges and as such all appointments are made by the Queen or her Ministers. Since 2006 all candidates for judicial appointment in England and Wales have been selected by the independent Judicial Appointments Commission (JAC), which passes its recommendations to the Lord Chancellor for approval. Once the JAC's selections have been received, the actual appointments are made in slightly different ways depending on the type of post. The Lord Chancellor himself appoints Deputy District Judges and most members of tribunals. He also appoints the 30,000 unpaid magistrates (who are selected by local Advisory Committees, not by the JAC). The Queen appoints High Court and Circuit Judges, Masters, Registrars and District Judges, District Judges (Magistrates' Courts) and Recorders on the advice of the Lord Chancellor. The most senior appointments – the Lord Chief Justice and other Heads of Division, and the Lords Justices who are the judges of the Court of Appeal – are approved by the Lord Chancellor and then passed to the Queen via the Prime Minister. Scotland and Northern Ireland have their own separate court systems, with their own arrangements for appointing members of the judiciary. The Supreme Court has jurisdiction over the whole of the UK, so its Justices are not selected by the JAC, which is an England and Wales body. Rather, a special committee is set up, which is made up of the three judicial appointments bodies from around the UK (England and Wales, Scotland and Northern Ireland), who recommend a name to Ministers. The Queen appoints the Justices on the basis of advice from the Prime Minister.

Appointments to salaried or fee-paid judicial posts are made from among judges or practising lawyers. In general the requirement for appointment is that the candidate must have been a practising barrister or solicitor for at least 10 years (for appointment to the Circuit Bench or above) or for five years (appointments to the District Bench and to most tribunal posts). Certain posts are also open to legal executives, patent agents and trade mark agents of the required seniority. Candidates for appointment as Justices of the Supreme Court must be existing holders of high judicial office or must have been practising barristers or solicitors of the senior courts for at least 15 years.

OFFICERS OF THE COURT

Officers of the Court include judicial and administrative staff; the former include Masters and Registrars, the latter secretaries and clerks to the judges and the staff who administer the court service. Details are given in The English Legal System 2011–2012 (Routledge). Qualifications for the judicial offices vary somewhat, but most appointments are limited to established barristers and solicitors.

THE LEGAL PROFESSION

The legal profession consists of two branches. Each performs distinct duties, although there is a degree of overlap in some aspects of their work.

Solicitors undertake all ordinary legal business for their clients (with whom they are in direct contact). They may also appear on behalf of a client in the magistrates' and county courts and tribunals, and with specialist training are able to represent them in the higher courts (Crown Court, High Court and Court of Appeal).

Barristers (known collectively as the 'Bar' and collectively and individually as 'Counsel') advise on legal problems submitted by solicitors and conduct cases in court when instructed by a solicitor; only barristers or qualified solicitor advocates may represent clients in the higher courts.

LEGAL EXECUTIVES

Both graduates and non-graduates can work in a legal office with the option of qualifying as a solicitor through further vocational training.

CORONERS

Coroners must be barristers, solicitors or legally qualified medical practitioners of not less than five years' standing. They are appointed by local authorities. There are approximately 110 coroners' jurisdictions in England and Wales. Coroners are independent judicial officers. When not engaged in coronal duties, coroners (apart from 'whole-time' coroners) continue in their legal or medical practices. Further information from the Coroners' Society of England and Wales, website; www.coronersociety.org.uk

Qualification as a Barrister at the Bar of England and Wales

There are three stages that must be completed in order to qualify as a barrister. The academic stage consists of an undergraduate degree in law or an undergraduate degree in any other subject with a minimum of a 2ii. For those with an undergraduate degree in a subject other than law a one-year conversion course (CPE/GDL) must be completed. Before commencing the vocational stage candidates must join one of the four Inns and then undertake the Bar Professional Training, which is either one year full-time or two years part-time, as well as undertaking 12 qualifying sessions. Once these have been successfully completed candidates are 'Called to the Bar' by their Inn. The Pupillage Stage consists of one year spent in an authorized pupillage training organization.

To find out more about all three stages of qualification as a barrister visit www.barcouncil.org.uk.

Qualification as a Solicitor in England and Wales

To practise as a solicitor in England and Wales a person must have been admitted as a solicitor, his or her name having been entered on the Roll of Solicitors, and must hold a practising certificate issued by The Solicitors Regulation Authority (SRA) (Ipsley Court, Berrington Close, Redditch, Worcestershire B98 0TD, Tel: 0870 606 2555). The SRA is the independent regulatory body of the Law Society of England and Wales. People will be admitted as solicitors only if they have passed the appropriate academic and vocational course and have completed a training contract and professional skills course, or have transferred from another jurisdiction or the Bar. The SRA controls the training of solicitors. Most solicitors become members of the Law Society, but membership is not compulsory. Intending solicitors other than Fellows of the Institute of Legal Executives and Justices' Clerk's Assistants, and qualified lawyers from other jurisdictions, are required to serve a period of training with a practising solicitor after they have completed the legal practice course.

All new entrants to the profession are required to complete a Criminal Records Bureau standard disclosure prior to admission. Candidates wishing to start training must enrol as a student with the SRA and satisfy it that they have successfully completed the academic stage of training and have no issues that may call their character and suitability into question.

The Common Professional Exam/Postgraduate Diploma in Law

Subjects: the foundations of legal knowledge: Public Law, including Constitutional Law, Administrative Law and Human Rights, Law of the European Union, Criminal Law, Obligations including Contract, Restitution and Tort, Property Law, and Equity and the Law of Trusts. For an up-to-date list of course providers for the CPE, see the SRA website; www.sra.org.uk/students/conversion-courses.

The Legal Practice course

Stage 1 covers Core Practice Areas: Litigation, Property Law and Practice (PLP), Business Law and Practice (BLP); Course Skills: Research, Writing, Drafting, Interviewing and Advising, and Advocacy – these skills form an integral part of the compulsory and elective subjects; Professional Conduct and Regulation; Taxation, and Wills and Administration of Estates. Stage 2 covers three Vocational Electives: from a range of corporate client or private client topics (the range of elective available can differ from institution to institution). An up-to-date list of course providers for the LPC is available from the SRA website; www.sra.org.uk/students/lpc.page.

Training contract

The training contract to be served by all intending solicitors, other than Fellows of the Institute of Legal Executives and Justices' Clerk's Assistants, is two years full-time or a maximum of four years part-time. The training contract can also be a part-time-study training contract that normally lasts between three and four years. During this period the trainee works and is studying the last two years of a part-time qualifying law degree, the part-time Common Professional Examination course and/or the part-time Legal Practice course.

The law graduate who holds a qualifying law degree must complete the Legal Practice course at a recognized institution, and then serve under the training contract for two years. The non-law graduate must first pass the Common Professional Exam (CPE) or the Postgraduate Diploma in Law, having attended either a one-year full-time or two-year part-time preparatory course. He or she may then serve under the training contract for two years after completion of a Legal Practice course. A Professional Skills course must be attended and successfully completed during the training contract.

Fellows of the Institute of Legal Executives may obtain partial or full exemptions from the CPE and Justices' Clerk's Assistants partial exemptions by virtue of similar subjects passed in their Fellowship exams or the Diploma in Magisterial Law. After passing or being exempted from the CPE, the Fellow/Justices' Clerk's Assistant may be exempt from serving under a training contract following successful completion of an LPC. A Professional Skills course must be taken prior to application for admission.

The Professional Skills course

The aim of the Professional Skills course is to build on the foundations laid in the LPC so as to develop a trainee's professional skills. Providers of the course, trainees and their employers are encouraged to regard the course as the first stage of a trainee's lifetime professional development.

Built upon the LPC, the course provides training in three subject areas: financial and business skills; advocacy and communication skills; client care and professional standards. Elective topics will also be chosen, which fall within one or more of these three core areas. All trainees have to complete all sections of the course satisfactorily before being admitted. The course consists of eight days of face-to-face instruction on the core subjects and 24 hours on the elective subjects, and must be completed during the training contract. The PSC is offered by accredited external course providers.

QUALIFIED LAWYERS FROM OTHER JURISDICTIONS

UK lawyers together with lawyers from certain foreign jurisdictions and EU lawyers can apply for admission under the Qualified Lawyers Transfer Scheme Regulations 2010. They need to obtain a QLTS Certificate of Eligibility.

Under the European Communities Directive No 2005/36/EC, lawyers from EU jurisdictions may apply for admission if they can prove they have met the requirements of the Directive and implementing legislation. Any lawyer applying for admission under the Directive may be required to pass one or more QLTS Assessments. All international applicants must satisfy the requirements and pass all of the QLTS Assessments. The Assessments are in three parts. Part 1 is a multiple-choice test; Part 2 is a practical examination that will test interviewing and advocacy skills in the context of three areas of practice – business, civil and criminal litigation, and property and probate; Part 3 is a technical legal skills test that will test the skills of legal research, drafting and writing. The Solicitors Regulation Authority has appointed Kaplan QLTS as the sole assessment organization for the first three years of the operation of the assessments. All transferees are required to prove their character and suitability to be a solicitor.

Prospective candidates wanting more information on QLTS can consult the website www.sra.org.uk/solicitors/qlts/key-features.page for guidance, or contact the SRA on 0870 606 2555.

SCOTLAND

The Court of Session, High Court of Justiciary, Sherriff Courts and Justice of the Peace Courts are administered by the Scottish Court service, an Executive Agency of the Scottish Government. For further information on Scottish Courts go to www.scotcourts.gov.uk.

THE LEGAL PROFESSION

The profession consists of Solicitors and Advocates.

Qualification as a Solicitor in Scotland

Solicitors in Scotland have their names inserted in a Roll of Solicitors and are granted annual Certificates entitling them to practise by The Law Society of Scotland (26 Drumsheugh Gardens, Edinburgh EH3 7YR, Tel: 01312 267411; Fax: 01312 252934; e-mail: lawscot@lawscot.org.uk; website; www.lawscot.org.uk). A Certificate is granted to candidates who have passed approved exams, completed a term of practical training and been admitted as solicitors. (The Law Society will be happy to provide copies of its Careers Information leaflet on request.)

The qualifying examinations

In academic session 2011/12, the LLB will be replaced by a new Foundation Programme, which will be offered at the same level as the LLB but with some changes to the programme itself, including changes to the professional subjects.

The Diploma in Legal Practice will become professional education and training stage 1 (PEAT 1) and the traineeship will become professional education and training stage 2 (PEAT 2). The vocational stage (PEAT 1) is the stage of legal education where knowledge, skills, attitudes and values are learnt in a simulated environment. The work-based element (PEAT 2) is the stage of legal education where the knowledge, skills, attitudes and values are built on and honed in a live environment. A major change is the introduction of outcomes, which apply across both PEAT 1 and PEAT 2, in 'professionalism, professional ethics and standards', 'professional communication' and 'business, commercial, financial and practice awareness'.

The structured learning element of the traineeship (ie, PEAT 2) will also change. Trainee CPD will replace the Professional Competence course. All trainees starting on or after 1 September 2011 will be required to undertake Trainee Continuing Professional Development (although to aid transition, the PCC can be deemed as TCPD up until 31 August 2013).

There will also be changes to CPD requirements for all solicitors. The new framework, in force from 1 November 2011, retains the existing requirement of a minimum of 20 hours each year. To support solicitors in their CPD activities, from 2011 the Society introduced basic templates, which will be capable of being completed online, to assist with identifying training needs, recording CPD undertaken and evaluating the outcome of the training. In addition, from 2011 a wider range of activities are acceptable as CPD. These will include activities such as structured and formalized one-to-one training, coaching and online training, rather than the present narrow definition of group study.

The alternative route to qualification has also been reviewed and there is a commitment to retain it until a replacement can be found. However, it is likely that within the next few years details will emerge on how this route is to be phased out, with other flexible options for qualifying being phased in.

An alternate route to qualifying as a solicitor in Scotland is by a combination of the Law Society's own examinations and three years' pre-Diploma training. To be eligible to sit the Law Society's examinations, non-law graduates must find full-time employment as a pre-Diploma trainee with a qualified solicitor practising in Scotland. A pre-Diploma training contract lasts for three years and during that time training must be given in the three prescribed areas of conveyancing, litigation, and either trusts and executries or the legal work of a public authority. To be eligible to enter into a pre-Diploma training contract, non-law graduates must fulfil certain educational requirements as outlined in Appendix 1 of the leaflet Pre-Diploma training found on the Law Society of Scotland website (www.lawscot.org.uk/media/196398/103_pre-diploma training.pdf). During the period of the training contract, a pre-Diploma trainee will study for the Law Society's examinations, having four years from commencement of the first examination in which to complete the core subjects (Public Law and the Legal System, Conveyancing, Scots Private Law, Evidence, Scots Criminal Law, Taxation, and Scots Commercial Law (I). European Community Law must be passed prior to admission as a solicitor, but can be obtained during post-Diploma training. The two routes to qualification (degree and law society exams) merge at this point as all intending solicitors are required to complete the Diploma in Legal Practice. Upon successful completion of the Diploma the graduate will enter into a two year post-Diploma training contract with a qualified solicitor practicing in Scotland.

Qualification as an Advocate in Scotland

Barristers in Scotland are called Advocates. Scottish Advocates are not only members of the Faculty of Advocates, but also members of the College of Justice and officers of the Court. The procedure for the admission of 'Intrants' is subject in part to the control of the Court and in part to the control of the Faculty;

the Court is responsible for most of the formal procedures and the Faculty for the exams and periods of professional training. To become an Intrant, applicants must produce evidence that they hold one of the following standard of degree: a degree with Honours, Second Class (Division 2) or above, in Scottish Law at a Scottish university, or a degree in Scottish Law at a Scottish university together with a degree with Honours, Second Class (Division 2) or above, in another subject at a UK university or an ordinary degree with distinction in Scottish Law at a Scottish university. A Diploma in Legal Practice from a Scottish University is also required, although in exceptional cases this requirement may be waived.

Once this evidence is provided and the relevant references obtained, a notice is posted outside Parliament House for a period of 21 days declaring the candidate's intention to present a Petition. At the end of this period the Petition is presented to the Court. After the Petition has been remitted by the Court to the Faculty and it is signed off by the Clerk of Faculty and Dean of Faculty the candidate is considered to have matriculated as an Intrant.

An Intrant must also comply with the professional training required by the Faculty, which consists of a period of 21 months' training in a Solicitors office (in some cases 12 months). The Faculty Exams in Legal Scholarship are conducted on the standard known as the 'LLB standard' at the Scottish universities. Subject-for-subject exemptions are granted to Intrants who have passed exams at this standard in the course of a curriculum for a law degree at a Scottish university. Every Intrant must pass or be exempted from exams in nine compulsory subjects and two optional subjects. The compulsory subjects include Roman Law of Property and Obligations, Jurisprudence, Constitutional and Administrative Law, Scottish Criminal Law, Scottish Private Law, Commercial Law and Business Institutions, Evidence, International Private Law and European Law and Institutions. In addition, and prior to the commencement of pupillage (also known as 'devilling') every Intrant must sit the Faculty's entrant examination in Evidence, Practice and Procedure. If successfully passed, the Intrant can then commence his or her pupillage.

During the first five or six weeks of pupillage pupils undertake the Foundation course. After about three months of work with their 'devil master', the pupils will participate in the February Skills course, comprising a series of performance workshops involving the use of documents in evidence, the conduct of a procedure roll discussion, workshops on judicial review, section 275 applications and working with expert evidence. Shortly before admission, the pupils attend the May Preparation for Practice course, covering workshops on vulnerable witnesses, longer motions, reclaiming motions, negotiation and mediation, as well as carrying out civil and criminal appeals before a serving judge.

Intrants who have passed all the necessary exams and undergone the necessary professional training as well as successfully completing their pupillage may apply to be admitted to membership of the Faculty and are admitted at a public meeting of the Faculty. Once admitted, Intrants are introduced to the Court by the Dean of Faculty, make a Declaration of Allegiance to the Sovereign in open Court and are then admitted by the Court to the public office of Advocate. For further information on becoming an advocate contact Dean's Secretariat, Faculty of Advocates, Parliament House, Edinburgh EH1 1RF, Tel: 0131 260 5765; e-mail: admissions@advocates.org.uk; website; www.advocates.org.uk.

NORTHERN IRELAND

As in England and Wales, the superior courts are the Court of Appeal, the High Court and the Crown Court. The latter is an exclusively criminal court. The Court of Appeal hears appeals in civil cases from the High Court and in criminal cases from the Crown Court and cases stated on a point of law from, inter alia, the County Court and the Magistrates' Courts. Appeals lie from the Court of Appeal to the House of Lords.

Inferior Courts: As in England and Wales, the county courts are principally civil courts, but in Northern Ireland they also hear appeals from conviction in the Magistrates' Courts for summary offences.

Magistrates' Courts: these deal principally with minor criminal offences (summary offences) and are presided over by Resident Magistrates (stipendiaries). Resident Magistrates are appointed by the Crown on the advice of the Lord Chancellor.

Coroners: Coroners must be barristers or solicitors of not less than years standing practising in Northern Ireland.

THE LEGAL PROFESSION

The legal profession in Northern Ireland consists of barristers and solicitors belonging to professional bodies organized on similar lines to those in England and Wales.

Qualification as a barrister in Northern Ireland

To qualify for practice as a barrister in Northern Ireland a candidate must be admitted to the degree of Barrister-at-Law by the Honourable Society of the Inn of Court of Northern Ireland (enquiries to Under Treasurer, Bar Council Office, The Bar Library, 91 Chichester Street, Belfast BT1 3JQ, Tel: Belfast 028 9056 2349; e-mail: chief.executive@barlibrary.com; website; www.barlibrary.com).

A candidate must be at least 21, hold a recognized law degree (the list of recognized law degrees can be found at www.qub.ac.uk/schools/InstituteofProfessionalLegalStudies/FileStore/) of not lower than second class honours and have obtained his or her Certificate of Professional Legal Studies or otherwise be qualified to Call to the Bar of Northern Ireland.

Qualification as a Solicitor in Northern Ireland

The solicitors' professional body in Northern Ireland is the Law Society of Northern Ireland (Law Society House, 96 Victoria Street, Belfast BT1 3GN; Tel: 028 9023 1614; website; www.lawsoc-ni.org.uk). It has overall responsibility for education and admission to the profession.

Admission to training is generally dependent upon possession of a recognized law degree from a university. Details of the recognized law degrees are available on the website of the Institute of Professional Legal Studies (www.qub.ac.uk/schools/InstituteofProfessionalLegalStudies/Admissions/RecognisedLawDegrees/). Details are also available on the Graduate School website (see Information Booklet for Applicants; www.socsci.ulster.ac.uk/gsple/info_-booklet.pdf). Law graduates must attend a two-year vocational apprenticeship course at the Institute of Professional Legal Studies, The Queen's University of Belfast, or the Graduate School of Professional Legal Education at the University of Ulster's Magee Campus, after which they may be admitted as solicitors, but they are restricted from practising on their own account until they have served for three years as the qualified assistant of a practising solicitor.

Non-law graduates must satisfy the Society that they possess an acceptable degree in a discipline other than law and have attained a satisfactory level of knowledge of the following subjects: Constitutional Law, Law of Tort, Law of Contract, Criminal Law, Equity, European Law, Land Law, Law of Evidence; that they have been offered a place in the Institute; and that they have obtained a Master (a solicitor with whom the applicant proposes to serve his or her apprenticeship). It is also possible to be accepted as a student of the Law Society if the applicant is 29 years or over and can demonstrate the required experience, knowledge or relevant qualifications (see the Law Society of Northern Ireland website; www.lawsoc-ni.org/joining-the-legal-profession/).

Membership of Professional Institutions and Associations

COUNCIL FOR LICENSED CONVEYANCERS

16 Glebe Road
Chelmsford
Chelmsford
Essex CM1 1QG
Tel: 01245 349599
Fax: 01245 341300
E-mail: clc@clc-uk.org
Website: www.conveyancer.org.uk/

The CLC was established under the provisions of the Administration of Justice Act 1985 as the Regulatory Body for Licensed Conveyancers. Our purpose is to set entry standards and regulate the profession of Licensed Conveyancers effectively.

MEMBERSHIP
Student
Licensed Conveyancer
Probate Practitioner

QUALIFICATION/EXAMINATIONS
Foundation
Finals
Practical Training

THE LAW SOCIETY OF SCOTLAND

26 Drumsheugh Gardens
Edinburgh EH3 7YR
Tel: 0131 226 7411
Fax: 0131 225 2934
E-mail: lawscot@lawscot.org.uk
Website: www.lawscot.org.uk

The Law Society of Scotland is the membership organization of Scottish solicitors. We promote the interests of the profession and of the public in relation to the profession. Our services include providing initial career advice, overseeing legal education in Scotland, handling admissions to the profession, monitoring trainees, providing post-qualifying legal education, and administering courses and examinations for the Society of Law Accountants in Scotland.

MEMBERSHIP
All practising solicitors in Scotland must be members of the Society and must hold a current Practising Certificate which is issued by the Society.

QUALIFICATION/EXAMINATIONS
Please see the Law Society of Scotland's website.

INSTITUTE OF LEGAL EXECUTIVES

Kempston Manor
Kempston
Bedford MK42 7AB
Tel: 01234 841000
E-mail: info@ilex.org.uk
Website: www.ilex.org.uk

ILEX, founded in 1892, is a professional body representing around 22,000 practising and trainee legal executives (qualified lawyers who specialize in a particular area of law). Our objectives are to provide for the education, training and development of our Fellows, to advance and protect their interests, and to promote cooperation among everyone engaged in legal work.

MEMBERSHIP
Student Member
Affiliate Member
Associate Member (AInstLEX)
Graduate Member (GInstLEX)
Fellow (FInstLEX)

QUALIFICATION/EXAMINATIONS
Level 3 Certificate in Law and Practice
Level 3 Professional Diploma in Law and Practice
Level 6 Certificate in Law
Level 6 Professional Higher Diploma in Law and Practice
Graduate Fast Track Diploma (Level 6)

DESIGNATORY LETTERS
AInstLEX, GInstLEX, FInstLEX

THE ACADEMY OF EXPERTS

3 Gray's Inn Square
Gray's Inn
London WC1R 5AH
Tel: 020 7430 0333
Fax: 020 7430 0666
E-mail: admin@academy-experts.org
Website: www.academy-experts.org

The Academy of Experts is a multidisciplinary body established in 1987 to establish and promote high objective standards for those acting as expert witnesses. We act as an accrediting and professional body, offering training, technical guidance and representation. In addition we promote cost-efficient dispute resolution, maintaining a register of qualified dispute resolvers.

MEMBERSHIP
Non-Practising Subscriber
Associate Member
Associate Member (AMAE)
Full Member (MAE)
Fellow (FAE)
Practising Corporate Member
Dispute Resolver Member

QUALIFICATION/EXAMINATIONS
There are examinations for upgrade.

DESIGNATORY LETTERS
AMAE, MAE, FAE, QDR

THE INSTITUTE OF LEGAL CASHIERS AND ADMINISTRATORS (ILCA)

2nd Floor
Marlowe House
109 Station Road
Sidcup
Kent DA15 7ET
Tel: 020 8302 2867
Fax: 020 8302 7481
E-mail: info@ilca.org.uk
Website: www.ilca.org.uk

The ILCA, which was founded in 1978, is a non-profit-making professional body dedicated to the education and support of specialist financial and administrative personnel working within the legal community. We encourage the development of our members' skills through educational courses, training workshops, seminars, conferences and our bimonthly magazine, *Legal Abacus*.

MEMBERSHIP
Ordinary Member
Diploma Member (ILCA (Dip))
Associate Member (AILCA)
Fellow Member (FILCA)
Affiliated Professional Member

QUALIFICATION/EXAMINATIONS
Diploma
Associateship examination

DESIGNATORY LETTERS
ILCA (Dip), AILCA, FILCA

LEISURE AND RECREATION MANAGEMENT

Membership of Professional Institutions and Associations

INSTITUTE FOR SPORT, PARKS AND LEISURE

Abbey Business Centre
1650 Arlington Business Park
Theale
Reading RG7 4SA
Tel: 0844 418 0077
Fax: 0118 929 8001
E-mail: infocentre@ispal.org.uk
Website: www.ispal.org.uk

ISPAL is the membership body for sport, parks and leisure industry professionals. We promote high standards and provide CPD as well as a wide range of training courses to our members in-house and at venues across the UK. We also work hard to influence government policy on behalf of our members.

MEMBERSHIP
Student
Studying Member
Full Member
Retiree
Local Authority Member
Corporate Member

INSTITUTE OF GROUNDSMANSHIP

28 Stratford Office Village
Walker Avenue
Wolverton Mill East
Milton Keynes MK12 5TW
Tel: 01908 312511
Fax: 01908 311140
E-mail: iog@iog.org
Website: www.iog.org

The Institute of Groundsmanship is the only membership organization supporting the whole of the grounds care industry. Serving the industry for 75 years, we provide a range of quality products, services and events including education, training and membership services, exhibitions, local information days, an annual conference and awards programme.

MEMBERSHIP
Junior Member
Student Member
Amateur Associate
Professional Associate
Full Individual Member
Affiliate Member
Corporate Member

QUALIFICATION/EXAMINATIONS
For details see; www.iog.org/training-training-courses.asp

INSTITUTE OF SPORT AND RECREATION MANAGEMENT (ISRM)

Sir John Beckwith Centre for Sport
Loughborough University
Loughborough
Leicestershire LE11 3TU
Tel: 01509 226474
Fax: 01509 226475
E-mail: info@isrm.co.uk
Website: www.isrm.co.uk

ISRM is the only national professional body for those involved exclusively in providing, managing, operating and developing sport and recreation services in the UK. Our aim is to ensure that the benefits of sport and physical activity are delivered effectively through the professional, safe and efficient management and development of facilities and services.

MEMBERSHIP
Associate Member
Member
Diploma Member
Companion (CInstSRM)
Fellow (FInstSRM/FInstSRM(Hons))
Corporate Affiliate
Further & Higher Education Corporate Affiliate
Commercial Affiliate

QUALIFICATION/EXAMINATIONS
National Pool Plant Operators Foundation Certificate
National Spa Pool Foundation Certificate
National Spa Pool Operators Certificate
National Pool Carers Certificate (Level 2)
Operations Certificate (Level 2)
Events Management Certificate (Level 3)
Fitness Management Certificate (Level 3)
Food and Beverage Management Certificate (Level 3)
Health & Safety Management Certificate (Level 3)
National Pool Plant Operators Certificate (Level 3)
Supervisory Management Certificate (Level 3)
National Pool Lifeguard Qualification (NPLQ)
Pool Technical Management Diploma

DESIGNATORY LETTERS
CInstSRM, FInstSRM, FInstSRM(Hons)

LIBRARIANSHIP AND INFORMATION WORK

Membership of Professional Institutions and Associations

CHARTERED INSTITUTE OF LIBRARY AND INFORMATION PROFESSIONALS

7 Ridgmount Street
London WC1E 7AE
Tel: 020 7255 0500
Fax: 020 7255 0501
E-mail: quals@cilip.org.uk
Website: www.cilip.org.uk

CILIP is the professional body representing those working within libraries and the information profession in the UK.

MEMBERSHIP
Certified Affiliate (ACLIP)
Chartered Member (MCLIP)
Chartered Fellow (FCLIP)
Revalidated Chartered Member or Fellow
Student Membership

QUALIFICATION/EXAMINATIONS
Application for membership qualifications is through the submission of a portfolio of evidence meeting published criteria. Please contact the Institute for further information.

DESIGNATORY LETTERS
ACLIP, MCLIP, FCLIP

MANAGEMENT

Membership of Professional Institutions and Associations

ASSOCIATION FOR PROJECT MANAGEMENT

Ibis House, Regent Park
Summerleys Road
Princes Risborough
Buckinghamshire HP27 9LE
Tel: 0845 458 1944
Fax: 0845 458 8807
E-mail: info@apm.org.uk
Website: www.apm.org.uk

APM is the largest independent professional body of its kind in Europe. We have over 18, 500 individual and 450 corporate members throughout the UK and abroad. Our aim is to develop and promote project management across all sectors of industry and beyond.

MEMBERSHIP
Student
Associate
Full Member (MAPM)
Fellow (FAPM)
Corporate Member

QUALIFICATION/EXAMINATIONS
Introductory Certificate in Project Management
APMP
APM Practitioner
Certified Project Manager
Registered Project Professional

DESIGNATORY LETTERS
MAPM, FAPM, RPP

ASSOCIATION OF CERTIFIED COMMERCIAL DIPLOMATS (ACCD)

Commercial Diplomats Regulation Authority
ACCD Global Headquarters
Central Administration Office
PO Box 50561, Canary Wharf,
London E16 3WY
Tel: +44(0)8445 864249
Fax: +44(0)8445 864252
E-mail: enquiries@commercialdiplomats.eu or enquiries@chartereddiplomats.org
Website: www.commercialdiplomats.eu

Association of Certified Commercial Diplomats is the first independent regulation authority, and global professional awarding body for commercial diplomats. The umbrella of ACCD covers ambassadors, representatives of government, trade commissioners, advisors and negotiators, arbitrators, negotiators of IIAs, policy-makers & government officials involved in trade, commercial and or investment issues, commercial counselors, IIA experts, academia, private sector & NGO representatives, officials in government ministries, parastatals, corporations, academic, public and private institutions worldwide. Its principal objectives are to provide accreditation and regulation, and to advance the interests of its members as qualified, certified and competent commercial diplomats. As the global voice, ACCD has overall responsibility, including the setting of policy and guidelines, as well as the qualification and accreditation procedures for the commercial diplomatic profession. ACCD is non-partisan, not-for-profit, independent of government, and uniquely the professional regulatory body for commercial diplomats, and institutions of higher learning providing advanced postgraduate, doctoral, and postdoctoral programmes on commercial diplomacy.

MEMBERSHIP
Associate
Member
Fellow
Academic Institutional Member

QUALIFICATION/EXAMINATIONS
ACCD QUALIFICATIONS/EXAMINATIONS:
Advanced Certificate of Competency (ACDipl)
Master of Commercial Diplomacy (M.CD or MCDipl)
Doctorate in Commercial Diplomacy (D.CD)
ACCD ACCREDITATIONS:
Qualified Policy Advocate (QA)
Qualified Certified Diplomat (QCD)
Chartered Diplomat (C. Dipl)

DESIGNATORY LETTERS
ACDipl, M.CDipl, M.CD, FCDipl. D.CDipl, D.CD, QA. QCD, C. Dipl

AUA

AUA National Office
University of Manchester
Oxford Road
Manchester M13 9PL
Tel: 0161 275 2063
Fax: 0161 275 2036
E-mail: aua@aua.ac.uk
Website: www.aua.ac.uk

As a member-led organization with over 4,000 members, AUA promotes best practice in higher education management and exists to advance and promote professional recognition and development of those who work in higher and further education by encouraging and fostering sound methods of leadership, management and administration, through a range of professional development initiatives.

AUA members are individually and collectively committed to:

- the continuous development of their own and others' professional knowledge, skills and practices
- actively championing equality of educational and professional opportunity
- the advancement of higher education through the robust application of professional knowledge, skills and practices
- the highest standards of fair, ethical and transparent professional behaviors

AUA is at the forefront of professional development in higher education and has developed a sector-wide framework to support the development of professional services colleagues. Through continuing professional development, individuals, teams and institutions can foster skills and behaviours associated with the profession. AUA also holds the largest professional development annual conference in the UK higher education calendar.

MEMBERSHIP
Member (MAUA)
Associate Member (AUA (A))
International Associate Member (AUA (A))
Fellow (FAUA)

QUALIFICATION/EXAMINATIONS
Postgraduate Certificate in Professional Practice (PG Cert)
This programme is validated by The Open University and credits from the course can be used on a number of MA courses.

BRITISH INSTITUTE OF FACILITIES MANAGEMENT

Number One Building
The Causeway
Bishop's Stortford
Hertfordshire CM23 2ER
Tel: 0845 058 1356
Fax: 01279 712669
E-mail: info@bifm.org.uk
Website: www.bifm.org.uk

The BIFM is the 'natural home' of facilities management (FM) in the UK. Founded in 1993, the Institute provides information, education, training and networking services for nearly 13,000 members – both individual professionals and organizations. The BIFM's mission is to advance the profession – to consolidate FM as a vital management discipline.

MEMBERSHIP
Affiliate
Associate (ABIFM)
Member (MBIFM)
Certified Member (CBIFM)
Fellow (FBIFM)
Corporate Member

QUALIFICATION/EXAMINATIONS
BIFM Level 4 Award in Facilities Mangement
BIFM Level 4 Certificate in Facilities Management
BIFM Level 4 Diploma in Facilities Management
BIFM Level 5 Award in Facilities Management
BIFM Level 5 Certificate in Facilities Management
BIFM Level 5 Diploma in Facilities Management
BIFM Level 6 Award in Facilities Management
BIFM Level 6 Certificate in Facilities Management
BIFM Level 6 Diploma in Facilities Management

DESIGNATORY LETTERS
ABIFM, MBIFM, CBIFM, FBIFM

BUSINESS MANAGEMENT ASSOCIATION

1 High Oak House
Collett Road
Ware
Hertfordshire SG12 7LY
Tel: 01920 898156
Fax: 01920 823261
E-mail: enquiries@businessmanagement.org.uk
Website: www.businessmanagement.org.uk

The Business Management Association is a professional body for businesses owners and managers. We promote the aims and interests of the small business sector internationally, provide information and advice to our members, encourage networking between members, and seek to provide members with advanced knowledge, skill and qualifications in several aspects of management.

MEMBERSHIP
Affiliate (AffBMA)
Associate (ABMA)
Member (MBMA)
Fellow (FBMA)
Companion (CBMA)
Certified Manager (CertMgr)
Certified Master of Management (CMMgt)
Certified Master of Business Administration (CMBA)
Certified Doctor of Business Administration (CDBA)
Member Certified Business Management Accountant (MCBMA)
Fellow Certified Business Management Accountant (FCBMA)

QUALIFICATION/EXAMINATIONS
Entrepreneurs Award (EA)
Diploma In Business Management (DipBMA)

DESIGNATORY LETTERS
AffBMA, ABMA, MBMA, FBMA, CBMA, CertMgr, CMMgt, CMBA, CDBA, MCBMA, FCBMA

DIPLOMATIC ACADEMY OF EUROPE AND THE ATLANTIC

Research, Development and Training Division
ACCD Global Headquarters
P.O Box 50561, Canary Wharf
Greater London E16 3WY
Tel: 08445 857027
Fax: 08445 857077
E-mail: enquiries@eatcd.org
Website: www.eatcd.org

Diplomatic Academy of Europe is a key professional diplomatic institution that enjoys global reputation for excellence in advanced specialized commercial diplomatic education. A Member of the Global Community (UN Global Compact), DAe offers complete portfolio of commercial diplomatic training, including the Mandatory Commercial Diplomat Qualifying Programme; the Qualified Policy Advocate Mandatory Qualifying Programme; and the Post-qualification Qualified Certified Diplomat Mandatory Qualifying Programme. Its advanced projects offer commercial diplomatic practitioners the opportunity to excel in their diplomatic careers as qualified commercial diplomats. The renowned diplomatic academy is a professional regulatory body, and the world's leading provider of advanced specialized programmes on commercial diplomatic education and practice.

MEMBERSHIP
Fellow of the Diplomatic Academy – FDAe
Doctoral Fellow of the Diplomatic Academy
Honorary Fellow of the Diplomatic Academy – FDAe (Hons)
Distinguished Fellow of the Diplomatic Academy

QUALIFICATION/EXAMINATIONS
EXAMINATIONS:
Master of Commercial Diplomacy
Doctorate in Commercial Diplomacy

DESIGNATORY LETTERS
ACDipl, M.CD (MCDipl), D.CD, FDAe, FDAe (Hons)

FACULTY OF PROFESSIONAL BUSINESS AND TECHNICAL MANAGEMENT

Head Office
Warwick Corner
42 Warwick Road
Kenilworth
Warwickshire CV8 1HE
Tel: 01926 259342
E-mail: info@pbtm.org.uk
Website: www.pbtm.org.uk

PBTM was founded in 1983 to forge the link between business and technology. We give professional recognition to the knowledge and skills of managers in business and technology, supporting lifelong learning to help members fulfil their career ambitions and develop their potential.

MEMBERSHIP
Student Member (StudProfBTM)
Associate Member (AMProfBTM)
Member (MProfBTM)
Fellow (FProfBTM)
Companion (CProfBTM)

INSTITUTE OF ADMINISTRATIVE MANAGEMENT

6 Graphite Square
Vauxhall Walk
London SE11 5EE
Tel: 020 7091 9620
Fax: 020 7091 7340
E-mail: info@instam.org
Website: www.instam.org

The IAM is the leading professional body and UK government-recognized awarding body for those involved in the administration and management of business. We offer a range of qualifications, from an introduction to the subject up to a full BA Hons degree.

MEMBERSHIP
Student Member
Associate (AInstAM)
Member (MInstAM)
Fellow (FInstAM)

QUALIFICATION/EXAMINATIONS
Introductory Award in Administrative Management (Level 2)
Certificate in Administrative Management (Level 3)
Diploma in Administrative Management (Level 4)
Advanced Diploma in Administrative Management (Level 5)
BA Hons degree in Business Management, from The Open University, Sheffield Hallam University or The University of Teeside

DESIGNATORY LETTERS
AInstAM, MInstAM, FInstAM

INSTITUTE OF BUSINESS CONSULTING

4th Floor
2 Savoy Court
Strand
London WC2R 0EZ
Tel: 020 7497 0580
Fax: 020 7497 0463
E-mail: ibc@ibconsulting.org.uk
Website: www.ibconsulting.org.uk

The Institute of Business Consulting was formed in 2007 by the merger of the Institute of Business Advisers and the Institute of Management Consultancy, and we are the professional body for business consultants and advisers. Our aim is to raise the standards of professional practice in support of better business performance.

MEMBERSHIP
Student
Affiliate
Associate (AIBC)
Member (MIBC)
Fellow (FIBC)
Certified Business Advisor (CBA)
Certified Management Consultant (CMC)
Practice Member (corporate membership)

QUALIFICATION/EXAMINATIONS
Certificate in Business Support
Certificate in Management Consulting Essentials
Diploma in Business Support
Diploma in Management Consultancy (in conjunction with the Chartered Management Institute)

DESIGNATORY LETTERS
AIBC, MIBC, FIBC

INSTITUTE OF DIRECTORS

116 Pall Mall
London SW1Y 5ED
Tel: 020 7766 2601
Fax: 020 7930 1949
E-mail: professionaldev@iod.com
Website: www.iod.com/development

The IoD is the UK's largest organization representing professional leaders, with individual members ranging from entrepreneurs of start-up companies to CEOs of multinational organizations. The Institute's principal objectives are to advance the interests of its members as company directors, and to provide them with business facilities and a variety of services.

MEMBERSHIP
Associate Member
Member (MIoD)
Fellow (FIoD)
Chartered Director (C Dir)

QUALIFICATION/EXAMINATIONS
Certificate in Company Direction (CertIoD)
Diploma in Company Direction (DipIoD)

DESIGNATORY LETTERS
MIoD, FIoD, C Dir

INSTITUTE OF LEADERSHIP & MANAGEMENT

Stowe House
Netherstowe
Lichfield
Staffordshire WS13 6TJ
Tel: 01543 266867
Fax: 01543 266893
E-mail: customer@i-l-m.com
Website: www.i-l-m.com

The ILM supports, develops and informs leaders and managers at every stage of their career. With our broad range of industry-leading qualifications, membership services and learning resources, the ILM provides flexible development solutions that can be blended to meet the specific needs of employers and learners.

MEMBERSHIP
Studying Member
Professional Member

QUALIFICATION/EXAMINATIONS
Management
Award in Effective Team Skills (Level 2)
Award and Certificate in Team Leading (Level 2)
Award, Certificate and Diploma in First Line Management (Level 3)
Award, Certificate and Diploma in Management (Level 4)
Award, Certificate and Diploma in Management (Level 5)
Award in Management (Level 6)
Award, Certificate and Diploma in Executive Management (Level 7)
Leadership
Award and Certificate in Leadership (Level 3)
Award in Leadership (Level 4)
Award and Certificate in Leadership (Level 5)
Award, Certificate and Diploma in Strategic Leadership (Level 7)
Leadership and management
Award, Certificate and Diploma in Leadership and Management (Level 3)
Award, Certificate and Diploma in Leadership and Management (Level 5)
Award, Certificate and Diploma in Strategic Leadership and Executive Management (Level 7)
Coaching and mentoring

Award and Certificate in Workplace Coaching for Team Leaders and First Line Managers (Level 3)
Certificate in Workplace Coaching and Mentoring (Level 3)
Certificate in Coaching and Mentoring in Management (Level 5)
Diploma for Professional Management Coaches and Mentors (Level 5)
Certificate in Executive Coaching and Leadership Mentoring (Level 7)
Diploma for Professional Executive Coaches and Leadership Mentors (Level 7)

Specialist management qualifications
Environmental Management
Facilities Management
Managing Equality and Diversity
Managing Volunteers
Sales Management
Site Waste Management

INSTITUTE OF MANAGEMENT SERVICES

Brooke House
Lichfield
Staffordshire WS13 6AA
Tel: 01543 266909
Fax: 01543 257848
E-mail: admin@ims-stowe.fsnet.co.uk
Website: www.ims-productivity.com

The IMS is the primary body in the UK concerned with the promotion, practice and development of methods and techniques for the improvement of productivity and quality. We act as the qualifying body for the management services profession in the UK, focusing developments in practice and knowledge and acting as a forum for information exchange.

MEMBERSHIP
Affiliate
Associate (AMS)
Member (MMS)
Fellow (FMS)

QUALIFICATION/EXAMINATIONS
Management Services Certificate
Management Services Diploma

DESIGNATORY LETTERS
AMS, MMS, FMS

INSTITUTE OF VALUE MANAGEMENT

Westminster
London SW1H 9JJ
Tel: 08709 020905
E-mail: secretary@irm.org.uk
Website: www.ivm.org.uk

The Institute aims to establish Value Management as a process for achieving value in every sector of the economy and to provide support in the innovative use of value management techniques.

MEMBERSHIP
Corporate Membership: Open to any company or organization practising or promoting value techniques. Each corporate member may nominate up to 10 members of their organization as representatives to the Institute. A member nominated by a corporate body can hold executive office and has full voting rights.
Ordinary Membership: Open to any professional person who has an interest in and can demonstrate an involvement in practising value techniques.
Student Membership: Open to students who have an interest in value management and who are registered FT students possessing a valid student card.
Fellow: Awarded to a member as a special honour for outstanding contribution to the field of value management.

QUALIFICATION/EXAMINATIONS

Certificate and Training: The Institute has worked closely with the Commission of the European Communities to establish a European Training System and Certification Procedure.

Roll of Practitioners: The Institute maintains an authorized list of value practitioners who are members of the Institute.

It launched its European Training and Certification System in 1998. This European Commission funded initiative offers, through the IVM's Certification Board, certification in the following categories: Certificated Value Analyst (CVA); Professional in Value Management (PVM); Certificated Value Manager (CVM); Trainer in Value Management (TVM). The Certification Board also approves basic and advanced courses in value management that have been designed by trainers in value management. The Institute provides a list of trainers.

INTERNATIONAL PROFESSIONAL MANAGERS ASSOCIATION

5 Starnes Court
Union Street
Maidstone
Kent ME14 1EB
Tel: 01622 672867
Fax: 01622 755149
E-mail: admin@ipma.co.uk
Website: www.ipma.co.uk

The IPMA is an international examining, licensing and regulatory professional body, which, through its qualifying examinations, enables practising managers to participate in and be part of the process of improving managerial performance and effectiveness in all areas of business, industry and public administration.

MEMBERSHIP

Student member
Graduate Member (GRD PMA)
Licentiate Member (LMPMA)
Certified Associate (AMPMA)
Certified Member (MPMA)
Certified Fellow (FPMA)
Honorary Member (MPMA)
Honorary Fellow (FPMA)

QUALIFICATION/EXAMINATIONS

Certified International Professional Manager (CIPM) examinations

DESIGNATORY LETTERS

GRD PMA, LMPMA, AMPMA, MPMA, FPMA, CIPM

THE ASSOCIATION OF BUSINESS EXECUTIVES

5th Floor, CI Tower
St Georges Square
New Malden
Surrey KT3 4TE
Tel: 020 8329 2930
Fax: 020 8329 2945
E-mail: info@abeuk.com
Website: www.abeuk.com

ABE is a professional membership body and examination board. We develop business and management qualifications at Diploma Level 4, Higher Diploma Level 5, Graduate Diploma Level 6 and Postgraduate Diploma Level 7. ABE qualifications provide progression routes to degree and Master's programmes worldwide.

MEMBERSHIP
Student Member
Associate Member (AMABE)
Member (MABE)
Fellow (FABE)

QUALIFICATION/EXAMINATIONS
Diploma Levels 4, 5 and 6 in:
Business Management
Management of Information Systems (Pathway)
Financial Management (Pathway)
Human Resource Management
Marketing Management
Travel, Tourism and Hospitality Management
and Postgraduate Diploma (Level 7) in Business Management

DESIGNATORY LETTERS
AMABE, MABE, FABE

THE CAMBRIDGE ACADEMY OF MANAGEMENT

Wellington House
Cambridge CB1 1BH
E-mail: info@cambridge-uk.org
Website: www.businessmanagcmcnt.org.uk

The Cambridge Academy of Management (CAM) is a professional, autonomous, not-for-profit institution established to foster the concept of UK management education made available to all internationally. CAM is built on the foundation of promoting state-of-the-art knowledge and expertise in all facets of management education, training and development for the global educational arena.

MEMBERSHIP
Associate Category (ACAM)
Member Category (MCAM)
Fellowship Category (FCAM)

QUALIFICATION/EXAMINATIONS
All programmes offered by Cambridge Academy of Management are accredited by Quality Assurance Commission UK. Programmes offered:
CAM International Foundation Diploma CAM International Certificate in Restaurant & Catering Management
CAM International Diploma in Business Management CAM International
Diploma in Business (Restaurant & Catering Management)
CAM International Diploma in Business (Tourism Management)
CAM International Advanced Diploma in Business Management
CAM International Advanced Diploma in Business (Restaurant & Catering Management)
CAM International Advanced Diploma in Business (Tourism Management)
CAM International Postgraduate Diploma in Hospitality Management
CAM International Postgraduate Diploma in Business
CAM International Postgraduate Diploma in Business with Specialization in: Marketing, Finance, Human Resource

THE CHARTERED MANAGEMENT INSTITUTE

Membership Department
Management House
Cottingham Road
Corby
Northants NN17 1TT
Tel: 01536 207307
Fax: 01536 400388
E-mail: membership@managers.org.uk
Website: www.managers.org.uk

The CMI is the only chartered professional body dedicated to managers and leaders, and to the organizations they work in. As founders of the National Occupational Standards for Management and Leadership excellence, we set the standards that others follow. As a membership organization we give our members the tools they need to make a genuine impact on business in the UK.

MEMBERSHIP
Associate (ACMI)
Member (MCMI)
Fellow (FCMI)
Chartered Manager (CMgr)

DESIGNATORY LETTERS
ACMI, MCMI, FCMI, CMgr

THE INSTITUTE OF COMMERCIAL MANAGEMENT

ICM House
Castleman Way
Ringwood
Hampshire BH24 3BA
Tel: 01202 490555
Fax: 01202 490666
E-mail: info@icm.ac.uk
Website: www.icm.ac.uk

The Institute is the leading professional body for Commercial and Business Development Managers. It is a fully accredited QCA/Ofqual UK Examining and Awarding Body for those undertaking business and management studies and offers in excess of 200 programmes. ICM is authorized to offer awards from HNDs to doctorates and works with public and private sector education and training providers in more than 100 countries.

MEMBERSHIP
Student Membership

QUALIFICATION/EXAMINATIONS
ICM Awards cover the following areas: Accounting & Finance; Business Studies; Commercial Management; Hospitality Management; Human Resource Development; Journalism; Legal Studies; Management Studies; Maritime Management; Marketing Management; Sales Management; Travel & Tourism.

THE INSTITUTE OF MANAGEMENT SPECIALISTS

Head Office
Warwick Corner
42 Warwick Road
Kenilworth
Warwickshire CV8 1HE
Tel: 01926 259342
E-mail: info@instituteofmanagementspecialists.org.uk
Website: www.instituteofmanagementspecialists.org.uk

The Institute of Management Specialists was founded in 1971 to give professional recognition to the knowledge and skills of managers and specialists. The Institute encourages management excellence and specialist expertise, and supports lifelong learning to help members fulfil their career ambitions.

MEMBERSHIP
Student Member (StudIMS)
Associate Member (AMIMS)
Member (MIMS)
Fellow (FIMS)
Companion (CompIMS)

QUALIFICATION/EXAMINATIONS
Diploma in Management

THE SOCIETY OF BUSINESS PRACTITIONERS

PO Box 11
Sandbach
Cheshire CW11 3GE
Tel: 01270 526339
Fax: 01270 526339
E-mail: info@mamsasbp.org.uk
Website: www.mamsasbp.org.uk

The SBP is an international organization formed by experienced educationalists and executives to fulfil a need to set standards in business practice to be achieved by examinations/assessments. Both inexperienced and mature students should be able to follow careers in further education and/or be proficient in employment and receive the benefits of membership.

MEMBERSHIP
Student (StuSBP)
Member (MSBP)
Certified Professional Manager (CPMSBP)
Professional Memberships *(Senior Professional Qualifications)*
Associateship (ASBP)
Licentiateship (LSBP)
Graduateship (GSBP)
Fellowship (FSBP)
These are certified competency-based Membership Awards open to persons occupied in business practice who are considered suitable by the Membership Committee.
CPD programmes are also offered for the Asia region.

QUALIFICATION/EXAMINATIONS
Diploma in Business Administration
Advanced Diploma in Business Administration
PGDip in Business Administration
PGDip in International Marketing
Diploma in Computer Studies
Advanced Diploma in Computer Studies
GradDip in IT & E-Commerce
GradDip in Entrepreneurship
Advanced Diploma in Accounting
Diploma & Advanced Diploma in Marketing Management (Joint Award with the Managing & Marketing Sales Association)

DESIGNATORY LETTERS
StuSBP, MSBP, CPMSBP, ASBP. LSBP. GSBP. FSBP

MANUFACTURING

Membership of Professional Institutions and Associations

THE INSTITUTE OF MANUFACTURING

Head Office
Warwick Corner
42 Warwick Road
Kenilworth
Warwickshire CV8 1HE
Tel: 01926 259342
E-mail: info@instituteofmanufacturing.org.uk
Website: www.instituteofmanufacturing.org.uk

The Institute of Manufacturing was founded in 1978 to give professional recognition to the knowledge and skills of people in all aspects of manufacturing. The Institute supports lifelong learning to help members fulfil their career ambitions and develop their potential.

MEMBERSHIP
Student Member (StudIManf)
Associate Member (AMIManf)
Member (MIManf)
Fellow (FIManf)
Companion (CompIManf)

MARKETING AND SALES

Membership of Professional Institutions and Associations

LONDON CENTRE OF MARKETING

Buckingham House East
Stanmore
London HA7 4EB
Tel: 020 8385 7766
Fax: 020 8385 7755
E-mail: info@lcmuk.com
Website: www.lcmuk.com

The London Centre of Marketing is an accredited, non-political, non-profit-making institution based in London, which exists with the sole aim of providing internationally recognized professional qualifications in marketing and marketing management.

QUALIFICATION/EXAMINATIONS
Diploma, Higher Diploma, Professional Diploma, Graduate Diploma and Postgraduate Dipolma in:

Business Management & Marketing
Human Resource Development & Marketing
Sales & Marketing Management
Travel & Tourism Marketing
Public Relations & Marketing
Entrepreneurship & Marketing

MANAGING AND MARKETING SALES ASSOCIATION EXAMINATION BOARD

PO Box 11
Sandbach
Cheshire CW11 3GE
Tel: 01270 526339
Fax: 01270 526339
E-mail: info@mamsasbp.org.uk
Website: www.mamsasbp.org.uk

MAMSA is an international organization offering qualifications in Sales, Marketing and Management and its senior specialist Stategic Marketing Diploma. The importance of 'Customer Service' is emphasized throughout all the programmes.

MEMBERSHIP
Graduate (GradMAMSA)
Graduate Affiliate (GradAfMAMSA)
Professional (MMAMSA)
Fellow (FMAMSA)

QUALIFICATION/EXAMINATIONS
Standard Diploma in Salesmanship
Certificate in Sales Marketing
Higher Diploma in Marketing
Advanced Diploma in Sales Management
Certificate in Marketing Strategy
Diploma in Marketing Strategy & Management (Hypothesis/Thesis)
Diploma in Sales and Marketing Practices (Joint Award with the Society of Business Practitioners)
A CPD programme is also offered.

DESIGNATORY LETTERS
GradMAMSA, GradAfMAMSA, MMAMSA, FMAMSA

MRS (THE MARKET RESEARCH SOCIETY)

15 Northburgh Street
London EC1V 0JR
Tel: 020 7490 4911
Fax: 020 7490 0608
E-mail: profdevelopment@mrs.org.uk
Website: www.mrs.org.uk

With members in more than 70 countries, MRS is the world's largest association serving those with professional equity in the provision or use of market, social and opinion research. We offer various qualifications and membership grades, and are an awarding body for vocationally related qualifications in market and social research.

MEMBERSHIP
Affiliate
Studying Affiliate
Associate Member (AMRS)
Full Member (MMRS)
Fellow (FMRS)
Honorary Member

QUALIFICATION/EXAMINATIONS
Certificate in Market and Social Reseach
Certificate in Interviewing Skills in Market and Social Research
Advanced Certificate in Market and Social Research Practice
Diploma in Market and Social Research Practice

DESIGNATORY LETTERS
AMRS, MMRS, FMRS

THE CHARTERED INSTITUTE OF MARKETING

Moor Hall
Maidenhead
Berkshire SL6 9QH
Tel: 01628 427120
Fax: 01628 427158
E-mail: qualifications@cim.co.uk
Website: www.cim.co.uk/learningzone

The Chartered Institute of Marketing is the leading international professional marketing body, with 47,000 members worldwide. We aim to improve the skills of marketing practitioners, enabling them to deliver exceptional results for their organization. Qualifications from Introductory to Chartered postgraduate level are offered to anyone wanting to develop their career in marketing.

MEMBERSHIP
Affiliate (Studying/Professional)
Associate (ACIM)
Member (MCIM)
Fellow (FCIM)
Chartered Marketer

QUALIFICATION/EXAMINATIONS
Introductory Certificate in Marketing
Professional Certificate in Marketing
Professional Diploma in Marketing
Chartered Postgraduate Diploma in Marketing
Diploma in Marketing Communications
Diploma in Managing Digital Media
Diploma in Digital Marketing
Diploma in Hospitality and Tourism Marketing

DESIGNATORY LETTERS
ACIM, MCIM, FCIM

THE INSTITUTE OF DIRECT MARKETING

1 Park Road
Teddington
Middlesex TW11 0AR
Tel: 020 8977 5705
Fax: 020 8943 2535
E-mail: enquiries@theidm.com
Website: www.theidm.com

The IDM is Europe's leading professional development body for direct, data and digital marketing. Founded in 1987, we are an educational trust and registered charity. We advocate lifelong learning and maintain an up-to-date education portfolio designed to meet the needs of marketing practitioners throughout their career.

MEMBERSHIP
Affiliate Member
Associate Member
Member
Fellow
Corporate Member

QUALIFICATION/EXAMINATIONS
Certificate in B2B Marketing (Cert BusM)
Certificate in Digital Marketing (Cert DigM)
Certificate in Direct and Interactive Marketing (Cert IDM)
Diploma in B2B Marketing (Dip BusM)
Diploma in Digital Marketing (Dip DigM)
Diploma in Direct and Interactive Marketing (Dip IDM)
Diploma in Integrated Marketing Communications (Dip IMC)

THE INSTITUTE OF SALES AND MARKETING MANAGEMENT

Harrier Court
Woodside Road
Lower Woodside
Bedfordshire LU1 4DQ
Tel: 01582 843260
Fax: 01582 849142
E-mail: education@ismm.co.uk
Website: www.ismm.co.uk

The ISMM offers professional qualifications in sales and marketing. The qualifications are accredited by the Qualification and Curriculum Authority, the body set up by the government to regulate qualifications. The programmes are available through ISMM-accredited centres.

MEMBERSHIP
Student
Associate (AInstSMM)
Member
Fellow

QUALIFICATION/EXAMINATIONS
Award in Basic Sales Skills (Level 1)
Award and Certificate in Sales and Marketing (Level 2)
Award, Certificate and Diploma in Advanced Sales and Marketing (Level 3)
Award, Certificate and Diploma in Operational Sales and Marketing (Level 4)
Award, Certificate and Diploma in Account Management/Sales Management (Level 5)
Diploma in Sales and Account Management (Level 5)
Executive Award, Executive Certificate and Executive Diploma in Strategic Sales and Account Management (Level 6)

DESIGNATORY LETTERS
AInstSMM, MInstSMM, FInstSMM

THE SOCIETY OF SALES & MARKETING

40 Archdale Road
East Dulwich
London SE22 9HJ
Tel: 0845 643 6832
Fax: 0845 643 6834
E-mail: info@ssm.org.uk
Website: www.ssm.org.uk

The Society is the only professional examining body that awards Certificates and Diplomas in all the four areas of selling, namely selling and sales management, marketing, retail management, and international trade and services. The Society celebrated its Silver Jubilee in style in 2005 at Imperial College London.

MEMBERSHIP
Graduate (GSSM)
Associate (ASSM)
Fellow (FSSM)

QUALIFICATION/EXAMINATIONS
Candidates for the Certificate, Advanced Certificate or Diploma choose any one of the following: (A) Selling & Sales Management, (B) Marketing, (C) Retail Management and (D) International Trade & Services.
(A) Selling & Sales Management subjects:
Certificate: (1) Business Communication, (2) Book-keeping & Accounts, (3) Selling & Sales Management, (4) Fundamentals of Marketing
Advanced Certificate: (5) Marketing Research Management, (6) Consumer Behaviour, (7) Principles of Selling, (8) Consumer Law

Diploma: (9) Management Information Systems, (10) Consumerism, Ethics & Social Responsibility, (11) Marketing Planning & Control, (12) Marketing Communication
(B) Marketing subjects:
Certificate: (1) Business Communication, (2) Bookkeeping & Accounts, (3) Selling & Sales Management, (4) Fundamentals of Marketing
Advanced Certificate: (5) Marketing Research Management, (6) Consumer Behaviour, (7) Principles of Selling, (8) Consumer Law
Diploma: (9) Management Information Systems, (10) Consumerism, Ethics & Social Responsibility, (11) Marketing Planning & Control, (12) Marketing Communication
(C) Retail Management subjects:
Certificate: (1) Business Communication, (2) Bookkeeping & Accounts, (3) Selling & Sales Management, (4) Retail Management
Advanced Certificate: (5) Marketing Research Management, (6) Consumer Behaviour, (7) Principles of Selling, (8) Consumer Law
Diploma: (9) Management Information Systems, (10) Consumerism, Ethics & Social Responsibility, (11) Fundamentals of Marketing, (12) Marketing Communication
(D) International Trade & Services:
Certificate: (1) Business Communication, (2) Bookkeeping & Accounts, (3) International Trade & Services, (4) Fundamentals of Marketing
Advanced Certificate: (5) Marketing Research Management, (6) Import & Export Management, (7) Finance for Export, (8) Consumer Law
Diploma: (9) Management Information Systems, (10) Consumerism, Ethics & Social Responsibility, (11) Marketing Planning & Control, (12) Marketing Communication

DESIGNATORY LETTERS
GSSM, ASSM, FSSM

MARTIAL ARTS

Membership of Professional Institutions and Associations

INSTITUTE OF MARTIAL ARTS AND SCIENCES

1 Henrietta Street
Bolton
Lancashire BL3 4HL
Tel: 01942 212378
Fax: 01942 211650
E-mail: admin@institute-of-martialarts-and-sciences.com
Website: www.institute-of-martialarts-and-sciences.com

The IMAS was formed by a group of high-ranking martial arts instructors, educators, researchers and academics to encourage education and research in martial arts, promote professionalism among martial arts instructors, afford martial artists the opportunity of obtaining recognized and accredited qualifications, and to act as a platform to encourage academic debate.

MEMBERSHIP
Associate (AIMAS)
Member (MIMAS)
Fellow (FIMAS)

QUALIFICATION/EXAMINATIONS
Bachelors, Masters and Doctoral in Martial Arts and Sciences

DESIGNATORY LETTERS
Grad.IMAS, MSc, PhD

MASSAGE AND ALLIED THERAPIES

Membership of Professional Institutions and Associations

BRITISH MEDICAL ACUPUNCTURE SOCIETY

BMAS House
3 Winnington Court
Winnington Street
Northwich
Cheshire CW8 1AQ
Tel: 01606 786782
Fax: 01606 786783
E-mail: admin@medical-acupuncture.co.uk
Website: www.medical-acupuncture.co.uk

The BMAS was formed in 1980 as an association of medical practitioners interested in acupuncture and we now have a membership of more than 2, 500 registered doctors and allied health professionals who practise acupuncture alongside more conventional techniques. We believe that acupuncture has an important role to play in healthcare and promote its use as a therapy following orthodox medical diagnosis by suitably trained practitioners. We run training programmes in the UK for doctors, dentists and other healthcare professionals.

MEMBERSHIP
Member
Accredited Member
Dental/Veterinary Member
Retired Member
Honorary Member
Overseas Member

QUALIFICATION/EXAMINATIONS
Certificate of Basic Competence (CoBC)
Diploma of Medical Acupuncture (DipMedAc)
University of Hertfordshire MSc in Western Medical Acupuncture

LCSP REGISTER OF REMEDIAL MASSEURS AND MANIPULATIVE THERAPISTS

38A High Street
Lowestoft
Suffolk NR32 1HY
Tel: 01502 563344
Fax: 01502 582220
E-mail: lcsp@btconnect.com
Website: www.lcsp.uk.com

The Register accepts practitioners who currently work in Massage, Remedial Massage or Manipulative Therapy. Applicants must have completed a course of education at an establishment whose training meets or exceeds the National Occupational Standards. The Register offers heavily discounted comprehensive medical malpractice insurance, business support, regular communications and CPD opportunities.

MEMBERSHIP
Student Member
Associate Member (LCSP (Assoc))
Full Member (LSCP (Phys))
Affiliate
Fellow (FLCSP)
Honorary Member

DESIGNATORY LETTERS
LCSP (Assoc), LCSP (Phys), FLCSP

NORTHERN INSTITUTE OF MASSAGE LTD

14–16 St Mary's Place
Bury
Greater Manchester BL9 0DZ
Tel: 0161 797 1800
E-mail: information@nim.co.uk
Website: www.nim.co.uk

The NIM was founded in 1924 and offers professional training in Remedial Massage, Advanced Remedial Massage, and Manipulative Therapy. We also offer a number of CPD seminars and short courses to supplement our main training programme. Research is carried out mostly by therapists on patients from their own clinics or by students completing university courses.

QUALIFICATION/EXAMINATIONS

Diploma in Remedial Massage
Advanced Remedial Massage Diploma
Manipulative Therapy Diploma

SOCIETY OF HOMEOPATHS

11 Brookfield Duncan Close
Moulton Park
Northampton NN3 6WL
Tel: 0845 450 6611
Fax: 0845 450 6622
E-mail: info@homeopathy-soh.org
Website: www.homeopathy-soh.org

The Society of Homeopaths was established in 1978 and is now the largest organization registering professional homeopaths in Europe. Our vision is 'homeopathy for all' and we aim to achieve this both by supporting our members and by raising the profile of homeopathy in general.

MEMBERSHIP

Subscriber
Student Member
Student Clinical Member
Registered Member (RSHom)

DESIGNATORY LETTERS

RSHom

MATHEMATICS

Membership of Professional Institutions and Associations

EDINBURGH MATHEMATICAL SOCIETY

School of Mathematics, Edinburgh University
James Clerk Maxwell Building
Mayfield Road
Edinburgh EH9 3JZ
Tel: 01316 505040
Fax: 01316 506553
E-mail: edmathsoc@maths.ed.ac.uk
Website: www.maths.ed.ac.uk

The EMS, founded in 1883, is the principal mathematical society for the academic community in Scotland as well as mathematicians in industry and commerce. We organize meetings, publish a journal and support mathematical activities through various funds.

MEMBERSHIP
Ordinary Member
Reciprocal Member
Honorary Member

THE INSTITUTE OF MATHEMATICS AND ITS APPLICATIONS

Catherine Richards House
16 Nelson Street
Southend-on-Sea
Essex SS1 1EF
Tel: 01702 354020
Fax: 01702 354111
E-mail: post@ima.org.uk
Website: www.ima.org.uk

The IMA, founded in 1964, is the UK's learned society for mathematics and its applications. We promote mathematical research, education and careers, and the use of mathematics in business, industry and commerce. In 1990 the Institute was incorporated by Royal Charter and subsequently granted the right to award the status of Chartered Mathematician, Chartered Scientist and Chartered Mathematics Teacher.

MEMBERSHIP
Student
Affiliate
Associate Member (AMIMA)
Member (MIMA)
Fellow (FIMA)
Chartered Mathematician (CMath)
Chartered Mathematics Teacher (CMathTeach)
Chartered Scientist (CSci)

DESIGNATORY LETTERS
AMIMA, MIMA, FIMA, CMath, CMathTeach, CSci

THE MATHEMATICAL ASSOCIATION

259 London Road
Leicester LE2 3BE
Tel: 01162 210013
Fax: 01162 122835
E-mail: office@m-a.org.uk
Website: www.m-a.org.uk

The MA dates from 1871 and supports and improves the teaching and learning of mathematics and its applications, and provides opportunities for communication and collaboration between teachers and students of mathematics. We publish a number of books, journals and magazines, hold an annual conference and regional meetings, and organize CPD events for our members. We also confer with government re the curriculum and assessment.

MEMBERSHIP
Student Member
Personal Member
Institutional Member

MEDICAL HERBALISM

Membership of Professional Institutions and Associations

THE NATIONAL INSTITUTE OF MEDICAL HERBALISTS

Clover House
James Court
South Street
Exeter
Devon EX1 1EE
Tel: 01392 426022
Fax: 01392 498963
E-mail: info@nimh.org.uk
Website: www.nimh.org.uk

The NIMH is the UK's leading professional organization of qualified medical herbal practitioners. We maintain high standards of practice and patient care, and work to promote the benefits of western herbal medicine. We provide codes of conduct, ethics and practice, and represent the profession, patients and the public through participation in external processes.

MEMBERSHIP
Member (MNIMH) Membership is open to graduates holding a BSc(Hons) degree in Herbal Medicine from: the Scottish School of Herbal Medicine, Edinburgh Napier University, University of Central Lancashire, Leeds Metropolitan University, Middlesex University, University of East London, University of Lincoln or University of Westminster. There is also a student affiliate membership scheme for those who are undergraduates of any of the above schools.
Fellow (FNIMH)

QUALIFICATION/EXAMINATIONS
The NIMH has historically managed its own accreditation process, with universities currently offering a BSc(Hons) degree in Herbal Medicine at Middlesex University, University of Lincoln, University of Westminster and University of East London. The programme at the University of East London is delivered by blended learning.
From 2011 accreditation of the above courses will transfer to The European Herbal and Traditional Medicine Practitioners Association (EHTPA), as an umbrella body of Professional Herbal Medicine Associations, although graduates will continue to be eligible to apply for NIMH membership.

DESIGNATORY LETTERS
MNIMH, FNIMH

MEDICAL SECRETARIES

Membership of Professional Institutions and Associations

ASSOCIATION OF MEDICAL SECRETARIES, PRACTICE MANAGERS, ADMINISTRATORS AND RECEPTIONISTS

Tavistock House North
Tavistock Square
London WC1H 9LN
Tel: 020 7387 6005
Fax: 020 7388 2648
E-mail: info@amspar.co.uk
Website: www.amspar.com

AMSPAR is a professional membership and educational organization. We work with City & Guilds to provide non-clinical qualifications for health administration within the UK qualification frameworks. We aim to promote quality and coherence in the delivery of qualifications, and encourage and support standards of excellence in the pursuit of continuous professional development and lifelong learning.

MEMBERSHIP
Associate Member (AAMS)
Member (MAMS)
Fellow (FAMS)

QUALIFICATION/EXAMINATIONS
The Level 5 Diploma in Primary Care & Health Management
The Level 5 Certificate in Primary Care & Health Management
The Level 3 Diploma for Medical Secretaries
The Level 3 Certificate in Medical Administration
The Level 3 Certificate in Medical Terminology
Diploma in Medical Administration
The Level 2 Certificate in Medical Administration
The Level 2 Award in Medical Terminology

DESIGNATORY LETTERS
AAMS, MAMS, FAMS

MEDICINE

Membership of Professional Institutions and Associations

COLLEGE OF OPERATING DEPARTMENT PRACTITIONERS

197–199 City Road
London EC1V 1JN
Tel: 0870 746 0984
Fax: 0870 746 0985
E-mail: office@codp.org
Website: www.codp.org

The CODP is the professional body for Operating Department Practitioners. It is a membership, not-for-profit organization that sets standards of education for the pre-registration aspect of the profession and promotes the enhancement of knowledge and skills, in the context of the multidisciplinary team, through regional, national and international networks.

MEMBERSHIP
Student Member
Association Member
Full College Member

ROYAL COLLEGE OF GENERAL PRACTITIONERS

1 Bow Churchyard
London EC4M 9DQ
E-mail: info@rcgp.org.uk
Website: www.rcgp.org.uk

The aims of the College are to encourage, foster and maintain the highest possible standards in general medical practice. Full entry to the College is by exam undertaken whilst in training for General Practice, or assessment as a qualified GP.

MEMBERSHIP
Associate in Training
Associate
Member (MRCGP)
Fellow (FRCGP)

Undergraduate medical students and Foundation programme students may register with the College's Student Forum, which exposes the students to life in general practice.

QUALIFICATION/EXAMINATIONS
Assessment for Membership of the RCGP (MRGGP)

DESIGNATORY LETTERS
MRCGP, FRCGP

ROYAL COLLEGE OF OBSTETRICIANS AND GYNAECOLOGISTS

27 Sussex Place
London NW1 4RG
Tel: 020 7772 6200
Fax: 020 7723 0575
E-mail: library@rcog.org.uk
Website: www.rcog.org.uk

The RCOG encourages the study and advancement of the science and practice of obstetrics and gynaecology. We do this through postgraduate medical education and training development, and the publication of clinical guidelines and reports on aspects of the specialty and service provision. The RCOG International Office works with other international organizations to help lower maternal morbidity and mortality in under-resourced countries.

MEMBERSHIP
Junior Affiliate
Affiliate
Associate
Diplomate
Trainee – pre-membership
Member without Examination (MRCOG)
Member (MRCOG)
Fellow (FRCOG)
Fellow *honoris causa*
Fellow *ad eumdem* (FRCOG)
Honorary Fellow (FRCOG)

QUALIFICATION/EXAMINATIONS
MRCOG
DRCOG

DESIGNATORY LETTERS
MRCOG, FRCOG

ROYAL SOCIETY OF MEDICINE

1 Wimpole Street
London W1G 0AE
Tel: 020 7290 2900
Fax: 020 7290 2989
E-mail: membership@rsm.ac.uk
Website: www.rsm.ac.uk

The RSM, founded in 1805, is a medical charity that promotes the exchange of information and ideas in medical science. We provide a broad range of educational activities and opportunities for doctors, dentists, veterinary surgeons, students of these disciplines and allied healthcare professionals, organize conferences, and publish books and journals through our publishing division, RSM Press.

MEMBERSHIP
Student
Associate
Fellow

THE FEDERATION OF ROYAL COLLEGES OF PHYSICIANS OF THE UNITED KINGDOM

MRCP(UK)
11 St Andrews Place
Regent's Park
London NW1 4LE
Tel: +44 (0)20 7935 1174
Fax: +44 (0)20 7935 4143
E-mail: part1@mrcpuk.org
Website: www.mrcpuk.org

The Federation is a partnership between the Royal College of Physicians of Edinburgh, the Royal College of Physicians and Surgeons of Glasgow and the Royal College of Physicians of London. Working together, the colleges develop and deliver membership and specialty examinations that are recognized around the world as quality benchmarks.

MEMBERSHIP
Membership of the Royal Colleges of Physicians (MRCP(UK)): Once candidates have successfully completed their final Part of the examination they must then submit and complete the Form of Faith and a testimonial for election to membership. The testimonial must be completed by a Fellow or Member of the Royal Colleges of Physicians of the United Kingdom. The latter should have worked with the candidate within the previous 3 years and must be a holder of MRCP(UK) for at least 8 years.

QUALIFICATION/EXAMINATIONS
The Federation is responsible for a portfolio of examinations: MRCP(UK) Diploma (Membership of the Royal Colleges of Physicians of the United Kingdom): Candidates for the MRCP(UK) Diploma may enter through the Royal College of Physicians of Edinburgh, the Royal College of Physicians and Surgeons of Glasgow, the Royal College of Physicians of London, or through the online application system. There are three components to the MRCP(UK) Diploma. The part 1 examination has a two-paper format. Each paper is 3 hours in duration and contains 100 multiple choice questions in one from five (best of five) format, where a candidate chooses the best answer from five possible answers. The part 2 written examination has a three-paper format. All papers in the MRCP(UK) part 2 written examination are 3 hours in duration and contain up to 100 multiple choice questions. The questions will usually have a clinical scenario, may include the results of investigations and may be illustrated. The Part 2 clinical examination (PACES) consists of five clinical stations, each assessed by two independent examiners. Candidates will start at any one of the five stations, and then move round the carousel of

stations at 20-minute intervals until they have completed the cycle. There is a 5-minute period between each station. Candidates may apply to sit the MRCP(UK) part 1 examination provided they graduated at least 12 months in advance of the examinations date (and have had at least 12 months' experience in medical employment). Candidates who have passed the part 1 examination can proceed to complete the remaining components. The Specialty Certificate Examinations (SCEs): The Federation of Royal Colleges of Physicians of the UK, in association with the Specialist Societies, has developed a programme to deliver Specialty Certificate Examinations within the new specialist training structure. The aim of these national assessments is to ensure that trainees have sufficient knowledge of their specialty to practise safely and competently as consultants. The Specialty Certificate Examination comprises two 3-hour multiple choice tests of 100 items each and is delivered in computer-based format (referred to as CBT) at a Pearson VUE test centre. Each paper is based on the MRCP(UK) written paper format and contains 100 multiple choice questions in 'best of five' format.

THE INSTITUTE OF CLINICAL RESEARCH

Institute House
Boston Drive
Bourne End
Buckinghamshire SL8 5YS
Tel: 0845 521 0056/01628
Fax: 01628 530641
E-mail: info@icr-global.org
Website: www.icr-global.org

The ICR was founded in 1978 and is now the largest professional clinical research body in Europe and India. Our aim is to promote knowledge and understanding by engaging with the healthcare community and the general public, to support and facilitate communication between our members, and to provide opportunities for learning and development to enhance professional competence.

MEMBERSHIP
Affiliate
Registered Member (RICR)
Professional Member (MICR)
Fellow (FICR)
Honorary Fellow (Hon FICR)

QUALIFICATION/EXAMINATIONS
Please see the ICR's website.

DESIGNATORY LETTERS
RICR, MICR, FICR, HonFICR

THE ROYAL COLLEGE OF ANAESTHETISTS

Churchill House
35 Red Lion Square
London WC1R 4SG
Tel: 020 7092 1500
Fax: 020 7092 1730
E-mail: info@rcoa.ac.uk
Website: www.rcoa.ac.uk

The RCA, which dates from 1948, is the professional body responsible for the specialty of anaesthesia throughout the UK. Our principal responsibility is to ensure the quality of patient care through the maintenance of standards in anaesthesia, pain management and intensive care. We set and run examinations, and provide CPD for all practising anaesthetists.

MEMBERSHIP
Trainee
Affiliate
Associate Member
Member (MRCA)
Associate Fellow
Fellow *ad eundem* (FRCA)
Fellow (FRCA)
Honorary Fellow (FRCA)

QUALIFICATION/EXAMINATIONS
FRCA Examinations

DESIGNATORY LETTERS
MRCA, FRCA

THE ROYAL COLLEGE OF PATHOLOGISTS

2 Carlton House Terrace
London SW1Y 5AF
Tel: 020 7451 6700
Fax: 020 7451 6701
E-mail: info@rcpath.org
Website: www.rcpath.org

The College aims to advance the science and practice of pathology, to provide public education, to promote research in pathology and to disseminate the results.

MEMBERSHIP
Affiliate Member
Associate
Diplomate Member (DipRCPath)
Fellow (FRCPath)

QUALIFICATION/EXAMINATIONS
Training programmes are approved for all pathology specialities and sub-specialities. The exact examination arrangements vary for each speciality but they will all involve a Part 1 and a Part 2 which include, inter alia, written, practical and oral components. In addition the College offers a Diploma in Cytopathology, a Diploma in Dermatopathology and a Diploma in Forensic Pathology. Further details may be obtained from the Examinations Department or the College's website.

DESIGNATORY LETTERS
DipRCPath, FRCPath

THE ROYAL COLLEGE OF PHYSICIANS AND SURGEONS OF GLASGOW

232–242 St Vincent Street
Glasgow G2 5RJ
Tel: 0141 2216072
Fax: 0141 2211804
Website: www.rcpsg.ac.uk

The Royal College of Physicians and Surgeons of Glasgow (RCPSG) welcomes professionals from a diverse range of disciplines. At present, our collegiate body includes Physicians, Surgeons, professionals in Dentistry and Travel Medicine, and other professionals allied to medicine. The College aims to provide career support to our membership through education, training, professional development, examinations and assessment, whilst acting as a charity and leading voice on health issues in order to set the highest standards of health care.

MEMBERSHIP
Member (MRCPS(Glasg)/MFDS RCPS(Glasg)/MRCS(Glasg))/MFTM RCPS(Glasg)
Fellow (FRCP(Glasg)/FRCS(Glasg)/FDS RCPS(Glasg))/FFTM RCPS(Glasg)
Associate Member
Affiliate Member
Associate in Training
Introductory Member

QUALIFICATION/EXAMINATIONS
Diploma in Child Health (DCH)
Diploma in Dermatology (Dip Derm)
Diploma in Geriatric Medicine (DGM)
Diploma in Otolaryngology – Head and Neck Surgey (DOHNS)
Diploma in Travel Medicine (DipTravMed)
Diploma of Membership of the Royal College of Physicians of the United Kingdom (MRCP(UK)) (see RCP(UK) website)
Diploma of Membership of the Royal College of Surgeons (MRCS (Glasg))
Diploma of Membership of the Faculty of Dental Surgery (MFDS RCPS(Glasg))
Diploma of Membership in Oral and Maxillofacial Surgery (MOMS RCPS(Glasg))
Diploma of Membership of the Faculty of Travel Medicine (MFTM RCPS(Glasg))
Diploma of Fellowship of the Royal College of Physicians and Surgeons of Glasgow in Ophthalmology (FRCS (Glasg))
Diploma of Fellowship of the Royal College of Physicians and Surgeons of Glasgow (FDS (dental speciality)RCPS(Glasg)
Diploma of Fellowship of the Royal College of Physicians and Surgeons of Glasgow (FRCSGlasg(-surgical speciality))

DESIGNATORY LETTERS
MFDS RCPS(Glasg), MFTM RCPS(Glasg), MRCP(UK), MRCPS(Glasg), FRCP(Glasg)/FRCS(Glasg)/FDS RCPS(Glasg)/FRCS(Urol)(Glasg)

THE ROYAL COLLEGE OF PHYSICIANS OF EDINBURGH

9 Queen Street
Edinburgh EH2 1JQ
Tel: 01312 257324
Fax: 01312 266124
E-mail: l.tedford@rcpe.ac.uk
Website: www.rcpe.ac.uk

The RCPE promotes the highest standards in internal medicine internationally. Along with our sister Colleges in Glasgow and London we oversee the Member of the Royal College of Physicians (MRCP(UK)) examination enabling doctors to enter higher specialist training, leading eventually to a Certificate of Completion of Specialist Training (CCST).

MEMBERSHIP
e-Associate
Associate
Collegiate Member (MRCPE)
Fellow (FRCPE)

QUALIFICATION/EXAMINATIONS
MRCP(UK)
Specialty Certificate Examinations

DESIGNATORY LETTERS
MRCPE, FRCPE

THE ROYAL COLLEGE OF PHYSICIANS OF LONDON

11 St Andrews Place
Regent's Park
London NW1 4LE
Tel: +44 (0)20 7935 1174
Fax: +44 (0)20 7935 4143
E-mail: DGM@rcplondon.ac.uk; DTMH@rcplondon.ac.uk
Website: www.rcplondon.ac.uk

The Royal College of Physicians of London offers a Diploma in Geriatric Medicine (DGM) Examination and a Diploma in Tropical Medicine and Hygiene, run in conjunction with the London School of Tropical Medicine and Hygiene.

MEMBERSHIP

The Royal College of Physicians of London runs the MRCP(UK) Examination which is the MRCP(UK) membership examination. As the examination is run in conjunction with two other Royal Colleges of Physicians, this examination and the membership qualification MRCP(UK) are listed in this directory under ***The Federation of Royal Colleges of Physicians***

QUALIFICATION/EXAMINATIONS

Diploma in Geriatric Medicine The Diploma in Geriatric Medicine is designed to give recognition of competence in the provision of care of older people to General Practitioner vocational trainees, staff physicians and others working in non-consultant career posts in Departments of Geriatric Medicine, and other doctors with interests in or responsibilities for the care of older people.

The Diploma in Geriatric Medicine is available to all registered doctors. It is not primarily directed towards career geriatricians, but is generally to family doctors, psycho-geriatricians and indeed any doctor involved in the care of older people.

The Diploma in Geriatric Medicine is in two parts, the first of which is a written examination of multiple choice (best of 5) questions, lasting 2 1/2 hours normally held twice a year at the Royal College of Physicians of London.

The second part is a Clinical Examination also held twice a year at various clinical centres in England and Wales. The clinical examination is a four-station standardized examination similar to an Objective Standard Clinical Examination (OSCE).

Diploma in Tropical Medicine and Hygiene The Diploma in Tropical Medicine and Hygiene is intended to test the knowledge required of physicians who wish to practise medicine effectively in developing countries.

Candidates for the Diploma in Tropical Medicine & Hygiene must hold a primary medical qualification recognized by the Royal College of Physicians of London.

The Royal College of Physicians of London will accept applications from candidates who are in the process of completing, or have completed within the last 5 years, the Tropical Medicine courses in London, Liverpool, Sheffield and Glasgow, which are recognized as appropriate training centres for the examination. The examination is held once a year over 2 days (unless required for a viva) and is conducted in the following sections: A **Practical Section** lasting 2 hours and 30 minutes consists of a mixture of microscopy specimens, including 20 'spot' questions that are set up on a microscope for identification. Other specimens require the candidate to use the microscopes themself. They are mainly parasitological and may include faecal, blood and haematological preparations together with some entomological specimens. A **Written Section** (3 hours and 20 minutes in total) consists of three papers. The **Clinical Paper** (1 hour) contains 18 compulsory questions. The first 16 are based on clinical pictures – usually of patients with abnormal physical signs; but occasionally laboratory slides, X-rays, or epidemiological data may be shown. There will be two or three questions on each, asking (for example) identification, diagnosis, further investigation, treatment etc. Each of these 16 questions is worth a maximum of 5 marks. The last 2 questions (17 and 18) are brief clinical cases, with 2 or 3 questions (again concentrating on diagnosis or differential diagnosis, investigation and treatment). The **Multiple Choice Question Paper** (1 hour and 20 minutes) consists of 40 multiple choice questions designed to test the knowledge of tropical medicine and hygiene over a wide area. The **Preventative Medicine Paper** (1 hour including 5 minutes reading time) consists of 10 questions of which the candidate must choose 5. Each question may have several parts, covering all aspects of preventative medicine and international community health in a tropical context.

There is also an **Oral ('Viva') Examination** for borderline candidates. The examination is conducted by two examiners. The first part of the examination (10 minutes) is a discussion of an illustrated clinical case history, which candidates are allowed to study for 10 minutes before the examination. The second part of the examination (10 minutes) consists of more general questions.

THE ROYAL COLLEGE OF PSYCHIATRISTS

17 Belgrave Square
London SW1X 8PG
Tel: 020 7235 2351
Fax: 020 7245 1231
E-mail: latkinson@rcpsych.ac.uk
Website: www.rcpsych.ac.uk

The RCPsych is the professional and educational body for psychiatrists in the UK and Ireland. We are committed to improving the understanding of psychiatry and mental health, and are at the forefront in setting and achieving the highest standards through education, training and research. We actively promote psychiatry as a career, and provide guidance and support to our members and associates.

MEMBERSHIP
Pre-Membership Psychiatric Trainee
New Associate
Corresponding Associate
Affiliate
Specialist Associate
Member (MRCPsych)
Fellow (FRCPsych)
Honorary Fellow
International Associate

QUALIFICATION/EXAMINATIONS
MRCPsych qualifying exams
FRCPsych qualifying exams

DESIGNATORY LETTERS
MRCPsych, FRCPsych

THE ROYAL COLLEGE OF RADIOLOGISTS

38 Portland Place
London W1B 1JQ
Tel: 020 7636 4432
Fax: 020 7323 3100
E-mail: enquiries@rcr.ac.uk
Website: www.rcr.ac.uk

The RCR is a professional body representing over 8,000 medical and dental practitioners worldwide that aims to advance the science and practice of clinical radiology and clinical oncology. We promote the highest standards of professional competence, undertake regular audits of training and practice, conduct examinations for Certificates and Diplomas, encourage CPD among our members, and provide information for the public.

MEMBERSHIP
Junior Member
Associate
Member
Fellow (FRCR)
Honorary Member/Fellow (Hon MRCR/Hon FRCR)

QUALIFICATION/EXAMINATIONS
First FRCR Examination
Final FRCR Examination
Diploma in Dental and Maxillofacial Radiology (DDMFR)

DESIGNATORY LETTERS
FRCR, Hon MRCR, Hon FRCR

THE ROYAL COLLEGE OF SURGEONS OF EDINBURGH

Nicolson Street
Edinburgh EH8 9DW
Tel: 0131 527 1600
Fax: 0131 557 6406
E-mail: information@rcsed.ac.uk
Website: www.rcsed.ac.uk

The Royal College of Surgeons of Edinburgh, which dates from 1505, is dedicated to the maintenance and promotion of the highest standards of surgical practice, through education, training and rigorous examination, and its liaison with external medical bodies. Today, with more than 17,000 Fellows and Members, we pride ourselves also on our innovation and adaptability.

MEMBERSHIP
Affiliate
Surgical Associate Member
Member (MRCSEd)
Fellow (FRCSEd)

QUALIFICATION/EXAMINATIONS
Please see the Royal College of Surgeons of Edinburgh website.

DESIGNATORY LETTERS
MRCSEd, FRCSEd

THE ROYAL COLLEGE OF SURGEONS OF ENGLAND

35–43 Lincoln's Inn Fields
London WC2A 3PE
Tel: 020 7405 3474
Fax: 020 7831 9438
E-mail: exams@rcseng.ac.uk
Website: www.rcseng.ac.uk

The Royal College of Surgeons of England is committed to enabling surgeons to achieve and maintain the highest standards of surgical practice and patient care. We examine trainees, supervise the training of and provide support and advice for surgeons, promote and support surgical research in the UK, and liaise with the DoH, health authorities, Trusts and hospitals in the UK and other medical and academic organizations worldwide.

MEMBERSHIP
Intercollegiate Member

QUALIFICATION/EXAMINATIONS
Please see the Royal College of Surgeons of England website.

THE SOCIETY OF APOTHECARIES OF LONDON

Black Friars Lane
London EC4V 6EJ
Tel: 020 7236 1180
Fax: 020 7329 3177
E-mail: registrar@apothecaries.org
Website: www.apothecaries.org

The Society of Apothecaries of London was incorporated by Royal Charter in 1617 and allowed to prepare and sell drugs for medicinal purposes, laying the foundations of the British pharmaceutical industry. Later, apothecaries were permitted to prescribe and dispense medicines, becoming the forerunners of today's GPs. Now the Society is primarily an examining body.

QUALIFICATION/EXAMINATIONS

PGDip in the Forensic and Clinical Aspects of Sexual Assault (DFCASA)
PGDip in Forensic Medical Sciences (DFMS)
PGDip in Genitourinary Medicine (DGUM)
PGDip in the History of Medicine (DHMSA)
PGDip in HIV Medicine (DHIV)
PGDip in the Medical Care of Catastrophes (DMCC)
PGDip in Medical Jurisprudence (Pathology) (DMJ[Path])
PGDip in the Philosophy of Medicine (DPMSA)

METALLURGY

Membership of Professional Institutions and Associations

INSTITUTE OF CORROSION

7B High Street Mews
High Street
Vimy Road
Leighton Buzzard
Bedfordshire LU7 1EA
Tel: 01525 851771
Fax: 01525 376690
E-mail: admin@icorr.org
Website: www.icorr.org

The Institute of Corrosion has since 1959 been serving the corrosion science, technology and engineering community in the fight against corrosion, which costs the UK around 4 per cent of GNP per annum. We promote the establishment and promotion of sound corrosion management practice, the advancement of cost-effective corrosion control measures, and a sustained effort to raise corrosion awareness at all stages of design, fabrication and operation.

MEMBERSHIP

Student Member
Ordinary Member
Technical Member (TICorr)
Professional Member (MICorr)
Engineering Technician (EngTech)
Incorporated Engineer (IEng)
Chartered Engineer (CEng)
Chartered Scientist (CSci)

QUALIFICATION/EXAMINATIONS

Please see the Institute of Corrosion website.

DESIGNATORY LETTERS

TICorr, MICorr, EngTech, IEng, CEng

THE INSTITUTE OF METAL FINISHING

Exeter House
48 Holloway Head
Birmingham B1 1NQ
Tel: 01216 227387
Fax: 01216 666316
E-mail: exeterhouse@instituteofmetalfinishing.org
Website: www.uk-finishing.org.uk

The IMF, founded in 1925, provides a focus for surface engineering and finishing activities worldwide through the fulfilment of technical, educational and professional needs at all levels for individuals and companies involved in the coatings industry. We promote R&D within the industry and CPD for our members, cooperate with other institutes, and liaise with legislative bodies to influence decision-making.

MEMBERSHIP
Student
Affiliate
Associate (AssocIMF)
Technician (TechIMF)
Licentiate (LIMF)
Member (MIMF)
Fellow (FIMF)
Engineering Technician (EngTech)
Sustaining Member (company)

QUALIFICATION/EXAMINATIONS
Foundation Certificate
Technician Certificate
Advanced Technician Certificate

DESIGNATORY LETTERS
AssocIMF, TechIMF, LIMF, MIMF, FIMF, EngTech

METEOROLOGY AND CLIMATOLOGY

Membership of Professional Institutions and Associations

MET OFFICE COLLEGE

Met Office
Fitzroy Road
Exeter
Devon EX1 3PB
Tel: 01392 885680
Fax: 01392 885681
E-mail: met-training@metoffice.gov.uk
Website: www.metoffice.gov.uk

The Meteorological Office College is part of the Met Office and is located in Exeter, Devon. We provide meteorological training for our own staff and to meteorological services worldwide, as places become available on a fee-paying basis.

QUALIFICATION/EXAMINATIONS
NVQ in Meteorological Observing (Level 3)
NVQ in Meteorological Weather Forecasting (Level 4)
Forecaster Foundation Training Programme
Professional Development Programme
Specialist Forecaster Programme

ROYAL METEOROLOGICAL SOCIETY

104 Oxford Road
Reading RG1 7LL
Tel: 0118 956 8500
Fax: 0118 956 8571
E-mail: info@rmets.org
Website: www.rmets.org

The RMetS is the learned and professional society for anyone whose profession or interests are connected with weather and climate. It administers the NVQs of the profession and is the accreditation body for the status of Chartered Meteorologist. Its principal aim is the advancement of the understanding of weather and climate for the benefit of everyone.

MEMBERSHIP
Student
Associate Fellow
Fellow (FRMetS)
Honorary Member
Chartered Meteorologist (CMet)
Chartered Environmentalist (CEnv)
School Member
Corporate Member

DESIGNATORY LETTERS
FRMetS, CMet, CEnv

MICROSCOPY

Membership of Professional Institutions and Associations

THE ROYAL MICROSCOPICAL SOCIETY

Oxford OX4 1AJ
Tel: 01865 254760
Fax: 01865 791237
E-mail: info@rms.org.uk
Website: www.rms.org.uk

The RMS, which dates from 1839, is an international scientific society dedicated to advancing the science of microscopy and the interests of its 1, 400 members, who range from individuals interested in microscopy to scientists and company members representing manufacturers and suppliers of microscopes, other equipment and services.

MEMBERSHIP
Ordinary Member
Fellow (FRMS)
Corporate Member

DESIGNATORY LETTERS
FRMS

MUSEUM AND RELATED WORK

Membership of Professional Institutions and Associations

MUSEUMS ASSOCIATION

24 Calvin Street
London E1 6NW
Tel: 020 7426 6955
Fax: 020 7426 6962
E-mail: cpd@museumsassociation.org
Website: www.museumsassociation.org

The MA is the oldest museums association in the world, set up in 1889 to guard the interests of museums and galleries. Today, we have 5, 200 individual members, 600 institutional members and 250 corporate members. Our aim is to enhance the value of museums to society by sharing knowledge, developing skills, inspiring innovation and providing leadership.

MEMBERSHIP
Student
Volunteer
Professional Member
Associate (AMA)
Commercial Member
Institutional Member

DESIGNATORY LETTERS
AMA

MUSIC

Membership of Professional Institutions and Associations

ABRSM (ASSOCIATED BOARD OF THE ROYAL SCHOOLS OF MUSIC)

24 Portland Place
London W1B 1LU
Tel: 020 7636 5400
Fax: 020 7637 0234
E-mail: abrsm@abrsm.org
Website: www.abrsm.org

ABRSM's mission is to motivate musical achievement. We aim to support the development of learners and teachers in music education worldwide and to celebrate their achievements. We do this through authoritative and internationally recognized assessments, publications and professional development support for teachers, and through charitable donations.

MEMBERSHIP
Licentiate (LRSM)
Fellow (FRSM)

QUALIFICATION/EXAMINATIONS
Certificate of Teaching (CT ABRSM)
Diploma in Instrumental/Vocal Teaching (DipABRSM)
Diploma in Music Direction (DipABRSM)
Diploma in Music Performance (DipABRSM)

Please see the ABRSM website for details of other examinations and awards.

DESIGNATORY LETTERS
CT ABRSM, DipABRSM, LRSM, FRSM

INCORPORATED SOCIETY OF MUSICIANS

10 Stratford Place
London WIC 1AA
Tel: 020 7629 4413
Fax: 020 7408 1538
E-mail: membership@ism.org
Website: www.ism.org

The ISM, a non-profit-making organization founded in 1882, is the UK's professional body for musicians. We promote the art of music and the interests of musicians through campaigns, support and practical advice. Members also receive our monthly in-house magazine, *Music Journal,* which includes news and information on CPD.

MEMBERSHIP
Student Member
Associate Member
Full Member
Corporate Member

MUSICAL INSTRUMENT TECHNOLOGY

Membership of Professional Institutions and Associations

INCORPORATED SOCIETY OF ORGAN BUILDERS

Smithy Steads
Cragg Vale
Hebden Bridge
West Yorkshire HX7 5SQ
Fax: 0870 139 3645
E-mail: admin1@isob.co.uk
Website: www.isob.co.uk/

The ISOB was founded in 1947 to advance the science and practice of organ building, to provide a central organization for organ builders, and to provide for the better definition and protection of the profession by a system of examinations and the issue of certificates and distinctions. We hold regular meetings and conferences around the UK and overseas.

MEMBERSHIP
Student Member
Ordinary Member (MISOB)
Associate Member (AISOB)
Fellow (FISOB)
Councillor (CISOB)

DESIGNATORY LETTERS
MISOB, AISOB, FISOB, CISOB

PIANOFORTE TUNERS' ASSOCIATION

PO Box 1312
Lightwater
Woking
Surrey GU18 5UB
Tel: 0845 602 8796
E-mail: secretary@pianotuner.org.uk
Website: www.pianotuner.org.uk

The PTA is a professional body committed to improving standards, and applicants for membership must pass a theoretical and practical examination to prove their ability as a qualified piano tuner or technician. We publish a regular newsletter and hold an Annual Convention and General Meeting in different towns around Britain, to which members and aspiring non-members are invited.

MEMBERSHIP
Student
Patron
Associate
Technician Member
Member

NAVAL ARCHITECTURE

Membership of Professional Institutions and Associations

THE ROYAL INSTITUTION OF NAVAL ARCHITECTS

10 Upper Belgrave Street
London SW1X 8BQ
Tel: 020 7235 4622
Fax: 020 7259 5912
E-mail: membership@rina.org.uk
Website: www.rina.org.uk

The RINA is an internationally renowned professional institution whose members are involved at all levels in the design, construction, maintenance and operation of marine vessels and structures. Our members are widely represented in industry, universities and colleges, and maritime organizations in over 90 countries.

MEMBERSHIP
Student Member
Associate (AssocRINA)
Associate Member (AMRINA)
Member (MRINA)
Fellow (FRINA)

DESIGNATORY LETTERS
AssocRINA, AMRINA, MRINA. FRINA

NAVIGATION, SEAMANSHIP AND MARINE QUALIFICATIONS

Membership of Professional Institutions and Associations

THE NAUTICAL INSTITUTE

202 Lambeth Road
London SE1 7LQ
Tel: 020 7928 1351
Fax: 020 7401 2817
E-mail: sec@nautinst.org
Website: www.nautinst.org

The Nautical Institute is an international professional body for maritime professionals and others with an interest in maritime sciences, with 40 branches worldwide and more than 6, 500 members in over 100 countries. It provides the strongest possible professional focus, dedicated to improving standards of those in control of seagoing craft while maintaining the Institute as an international centre of nautical excellence.

MEMBERSHIP
Honorary Fellow
Fellow
Associate Fellow (AFNI)
Member (MNI)
Associate Member (AMNI)

QUALIFICATION/EXAMINATIONS
Harbour Master's Certificate
Pilotage Certificate
Command Diploma

DESIGNATORY LETTERS
FNI, AFNI, MNI, AMNI

THE ROYAL INSTITUTE OF NAVIGATION

1 Kensington Gore
London SW7 2AT
Tel: 020 7591 3130
Fax: 020 7591 3131
E-mail: info@rin.org.uk
Website: www.rin.org.uk

The RIN is a learned society with charitable status. Our aims are: to unite those with a professional or personal interest in any aspect of navigation in one unique body; to further the development of navigation in every sphere; and to increase public awareness of both the art and science of navigation, how it has shaped the past, how it impacts our world today, and how it will affect the future.

MEMBERSHIP
Junior Associate Member
Student
Associate
Member (MRIN)
Associate Fellow (AFRIN)
Fellow (FRIN)
Affiliate Club
Affiliate College or University
Corporate Member

DESIGNATORY LETTERS
MRIN, AFRIN, FRIN

NON-DESTRUCTIVE TESTING

Membership of Professional Institutions and Associations

THE BRITISH INSTITUTE OF NON-DESTRUCTIVE TESTING

Newton Building
St George's Avenue
Northampton NN2 6JB
Tel: 01604 89 3811
Fax: 01604 89 3861
E-mail: info@bindt.org
Website: www.bindt.org

The BINDT was formed in 1976 from the merger of the Society of Non-Destructive Examination (SONDE) and the Society of Industrial Radiology and Allied Methods of Non-Destructive Testing, later renamed the NDT Society of Great Britain (NDTS), both formed in 1954. Our aim is to promote and advance the science and practice of non-destructive testing, condition monitoring, diagnostic engineering and all other materials and quality testing disciplines.

MEMBERSHIP
Student Member
Affiliate
Practitioner Member (PInstNDT)
Graduate Member (GInstNDT)
Member (MInstNDT)
Fellow (FInstNDT)
Engineering Technician (EngTech)
Incorporated Engineer (IEng)
Chartered Engineer (CEng)
Licensed Engineering Practitioner
Associate Member (corporate)

DESIGNATORY LETTERS
PInstNDT, GInstNDT, MInstNDT, FInstNDT, EngTech, IEng, CEng

NURSERY NURSING

Membership of Professional Institutions and Associations

COUNCIL FOR AWARDS IN CHILDREN'S CARE AND EDUCATION

Apex House
81 Camp Road
St Albans
Hertfordshire AL1 5GB
Tel: 0845 347 2123
Fax: 01727 818618
E-mail: info@cache.org.uk
Website: www.cache.org.uk

CACHE is an Awarding Body that designs courses and qualifications in the care and education of children and young people. Our courses, which are widely available, range from entry level to advanced qualifications for sector professionals. We regularly lobby the government and other agencies to raise the quality and professionalism of child care.

QUALIFICATION/EXAMINATIONS
Please see the CACHE website.

NURSING AND MIDWIFERY

Membership of Professional Institutions and Associations

THE NURSING & MIDWIFERY COUNCIL

23 Portland Place
London W1B 1PZ
Tel: 020 7333 9333
E-mail: advice@nmc-uk.org
Website: www.nmc-uk.org

We are the nursing and midwifery regulator for England, Wales, Scotland, Northern Ireland and the Islands. We exist to safeguard the health and well-being of the public.

OCCUPATIONAL THERAPY

Membership of Professional Institutions and Associations

BRITISH ASSOCIATION OF OCCUPATIONAL THERAPISTS

106–114 Borough High Street
Southwark
London SE1 1LB
Tel: 020 7357 6480
Fax: 020 7450 2299
E-mail: membership@cot.co.uk
Website: www.cot.org.uk

The British Association and College of Occupational Therapists is the professional body for occupational therapy in the UK. The College has 28,000 members and represents the profession nationally and internationally.

MEMBERSHIP
Student Member
Associate
Discounted Associate
Professional Member
Discounted Professional Member
Self-employed Member
Retired Member
Overseas Member

QUALIFICATION/EXAMINATIONS
Diploma (DipCOT)

OPTICIANS (DISPENSING)

Dispensing opticians need to be registered with the General Optical Council (GOC; 41 Harley Street, London W1G 8DJ E-mail: goc@optical.org Website: www.optical.org). Qualification takes three years in total, and can be completed by combining a distance learning course or day release while working as a trainee under the supervision of a qualified and GOC-registered optician. Alternatively students can do a two-year full-time course followed by one year of supervised practice with a qualified and registered optician. In the UK you can study at six GOC-approved training establishments: Association of British Dispensing Opticians (ABDO), Anglia Ruskin University, Bradford College, City and Islington College, City University and Glasgow Caledonian University. All routes are assessed by final ABDO examinations. On successful completion of training you must register with the GOC in order to practise in the UK. Once qualified, you will need to undertake a minimum amount of continuing education and training to remain on the register. If you qualify as a dispensing optician and have completed training to fit contact lenses, the University of Bradford offers a career progression course that enables you to graduate with a degree in optometry in one calendar year.

ENTRY REQUIREMENTS

You will normally need to have 5 GCSEs (or equivalent) at grades C or above, including English, maths and science. For mature students and overseas, alternative and vocational courses, admission requirements will vary and may be more flexible. For further details contact the admissions tutor at the university you wish to apply to.

Membership of Professional Institutions and Associations

ASSOCIATION OF BRITISH DISPENSING OPTICIANS

199 Gloucester Terrace
London W2 6LD
Tel: 020 7298 5100
Fax: 020 7298 5111
E-mail: general@abdolondon.org.uk
Website: www.abdo.org.uk

The ABDO is the qualifying body for dispensing opticians in the UK. Our aims are to advance the science and art of dispensing optics, to further the education and training of dispensing opticians, and to support and promote the interests of the profession.

MEMBERSHIP

Student Member
Associate Member
Full Member
Fellow (FBDO)

QUALIFICATION/EXAMINATIONS

Certificate in Contact Lens Practice (Level 6)
Diploma in The Assessment & Management of Low Vision (Level 6)
Diploma in Ophthalmic Dispensing (Level 6)
Diploma in Advanced Contact Lens Practice (Level 7)
Diploma in Spectacle Lens Design (Level 7)

DESIGNATORY LETTERS

FBDO

ASSOCIATION OF CONTACT LENS MANUFACTURERS

PO Box 735
Devizes
Wiltshire SN10 3TQ
Tel: 01380 860418
Fax: 01380 860863
E-mail: secgen@aclm.org.uk
Website: www.aclm.org.uk

The ACLM was founded in 1962 to publicize the work of UK contact lens manufacturers, to develop new products and to raise standards. Today we represent the manufacturers of over 95 per cent of prescription contact lenses and lens care products in the UK, and provide a cohesive voice for our members.

MEMBERSHIP

Member

BRITISH CONTACT LENS ASSOCIATION

Walmar House
288/292 Regent Street
London W1B 3AL
Tel: 020 7580 6661
Fax: 020 7580 6669
Website: www.bcla.org.uk

The BCLA is the UK's leading supplier of information and education on contact lenses and the anterior eye, with a membership of around 1, 800 in more than 40 countries. Our mission is to promote excellence in the research, manufacture and clinical practice of contact lenses and related areas. Our annual Clinical Conference and Exhibition, the world's largest, attracts more than 1,000 visitors.

MEMBERSHIP
Student Member
Member
Fellow (FBCLA)

QUALIFICATION/EXAMINATIONS
Educational activities include approved Continuing Education and Training courses and evening meetings. For details see the website.

DESIGNATORY LETTERS
FBCLA

OPTOMETRY

Careers in optometry are overseen by the General Optical Council (41 Harley Street, London W1G 8DJ E-mail: goc@optical.org Website: www.optical.org). You can study for an undergraduate optometry degree from one of eight GOC-approved institutions in the UK: Anglia Ruskin University, Aston University, the University of Bradford, Cardiff University, City University, Glasgow Caledonian University, the University of Manchester and the University of Ulster.

LENGTH OF COURSE
Usually four years in total (five in Scotland): a full-time three-year (four-year in Scotland) degree course, followed by one year's salaried pre-registration training with a practice under the guidance of a GOC-registered optometrist. This includes a series of assessments, set by the College of Optometrists, throughout the placement.

ENTRY REQUIREMENTS
You will normally need 5 GCSEs (or equivalent) at grade C or above, one of which should be in English. You will normally be required to have 3 A Level passes/approximately 320 UCAS tariff points from the following subjects: physics, biology, chemistry or mathematics. Requirements vary between universities, so be sure to check the university's prospectus and/or consult the relevant admission tutors.

Membership of Professional Institutions and Associations

ASSOCIATION OF OPTOMETRISTS

61 Southwark Street
London SE1 0HL
Tel: 020 7261 9661
Fax: 020 7261 0228
E-mail: postbox@aop.org.uk
Website: www.aop.org.uk

The AOP serves its members by promoting and protecting them, providing them with relevant services, representing and supporting them, enhancing their professional and business effectiveness, and expanding the role of optometry in primary and secondary eyecare.

MEMBERSHIP
Student Member
Honorary Member
Dispensing Associate
Full Member

ORTHOPTICS

Membership of Professional Institutions and Associations

BRITISH AND IRISH ORTHOPTIC SOCIETY

4th Floor
14 Bedford Row
London WC1R 4ED
Tel: 0207 306 1135
E-mail: bios@orthoptics.org.uk
Website: www.orthoptics.org.uk

Orthoptists are AHPs, who diagnose and treat problems with visual development and binocular vision (how the eyes work together as a pair), and eye movement disorders. They are experts in childhood vision screening. Extended roles include stroke, glaucoma, reading difficulties, neurological disorders, low vision.

MEMBERSHIP
Student Members
Members

QUALIFICATION/EXAMINATIONS
Degrees in orthoptics are offered by Liverpool University (www.liv.ac.uk) and Sheffield University (www.sheffield.ac.uk)

OSTEOPATHY AND NATUROPATHY

Membership of Professional Institutions and Associations

BRITISH OSTEOPATHIC ASSOCIATION

3 Park Terrace
Manor Road
Luton
Bedfordshire LU1 3HN
Tel: 01582 488455
Fax: 01582 481533
E-mail: enquiries@osteopathy.org
Website: www.osteopathy.org

The BOA was formed in 1998 as a result of the merger of the British Osteopathic Association, the Osteopathic Association of Great Britain and the Guild of Osteopaths. We provide opportunities for individual and professional development in osteopathic practice and promote the highest standards of osteopathic education and research.

MEMBERSHIP
Student Member
1st/2nd/3rd Year Graduate Member
Full Member
Overseas Member

PATENT AGENCY

Membership of Professional Institutions and Associations

THE CHARTERED INSTITUTE OF PATENT ATTORNEYS

95 Chancery Lane
London WC2A 1DT
Tel: 020 7405 9450
Fax: 020 7430 0471
E-mail: mail@cipa.org.uk
Website: www.cipa.org.uk

CIPA is the professional, training and examining body for patent attorneys in the UK. From 2010 the IP Regulation Board, an independent body within the CIPA, sets the standards for regulation of the profession. Trainees, all technical graduates, also study for the qualification to practise before the European Patent Office.

MEMBERSHIP
Student Member
Associate
Fellow
Registered Patent Attorney (RPA)
Chartered Patent Attorney (CPA)

QUALIFICATION/EXAMINATIONS
Qualifying examination for registration as a Patent Attorney

DESIGNATORY LETTERS
RPA, CPA

PENSION MANAGEMENT

Membership of Professional Institutions and Associations

THE PENSIONS MANAGEMENT INSTITUTE

PMI House
4–10 Artillery Lane
London E1 7LS
Tel: 020 7247 1452
Fax: 020 7375 0603
E-mail: education@pensions-pmi.org.uk
Website: www.pensions-pmi.org.uk

The Pensions Management Institute is the professional body that promotes standards of excellence and lifetime learning for pensions professionals and trustees through its qualifications, membership and ongoing support services. For further details please visit our website.

MEMBERSHIP
Student Member
Ordinary Member (MPMI)
Associate Member (APMI)
Fellow (FPMI)

QUALIFICATION/EXAMINATIONS
Retirement Provision Certificate (RPC)
Advanced Diploma in Retirement Provision
Qualification in Pensions Administration (QPA)
Diploma in Pension Calculations (DPC)
Qualification in Public Sector Pensions Administration (QPSPA)
Diploma in Member Directed Pension Scheme Administration (MDPSA)
Diploma in International Employee Benefits (Dip. IEB)
The Awards in Pensions Trusteeship

DESIGNATORY LETTERS
MPMI, APMI, FPMI

PERSONNEL MANAGEMENT

Membership of Professional Institutions and Associations

CHARTERED INSTITUTE OF PERSONNEL AND DEVELOPMENT

151 The Broadway
London SW19 1JQ
Tel: 020 8612 6208
Fax: 020 8612 6201
E-mail: membershipenquiry@cipd.co.uk
Website: www.cipd.co.uk

The CIPD is Europe's largest HR and development professional body. As a globally recognized brand with over 135,000 members, we pride ourselves on supporting and developing those responsible for the management and development of people within organizations.

MEMBERSHIP
Affiliate Member
Studying Affiliate Member
Associate Member
Licentiate Member
Graduate Member
Chartered Member (MCIPD)
Chartered Fellow (FCIPD)
Chartered Companion (CCIPD)
For further information see; www.cipd.co.uk/membership

QUALIFICATION/EXAMINATIONS
We are launching a new qualifications structure in January 2010. For details of current courses see; www.cipd.co.uk/qualifications

DESIGNATORY LETTERS
MCIPD, FCIPD, CCIPD

THE INSTITUTE OF CONTINUING PROFESSIONAL DEVELOPMENT

Grosvenor Gardens House
35/37 Grosvenor Gardens
London SW1W 0BS
Tel: 020 7828 1965
Fax: 020 7828 1967
E-mail: info@cpdinstitute.org
Website: www.cpdinstitute.org

The Institute of Continuing Professional Development is part of the Continuing Professional Development Foundation, an educational charitable trust providing high-quality and broad-ranging CPD since 1981. We serve the public interest by helping to raise the effectiveness of professionals through the promotion of CPD as an important and integral element of lifelong learning.

MEMBERSHIP
Member (MInstCPD)
Fellow (FInstCPD)

DESIGNATORY LETTERS
MInstCPD, FInstCPD

UK EMPLOYEES ASSISTANCE PROFESSIONALS ASSOCIATION

3 Moors Close
Ducklington
Witney
Oxfordshire OX29 7TW
Tel: 07770 924615
Fax: 01993 772765
E-mail: info@eapa.org.uk
Website: www.eapa.org.uk

The EAPA is the professional body for Employee Assistance Programmes (EAPs). It represents the interests of professionals concerned with employee assistance, psychological health and well-being in the UK. EAPA members include external and internal EAP providers, purchasers, counsellors, consultants and trainers.

MEMBERSHIP
Individual Member
Associate Member
Retiree Member
Organizational Member
Registered External/Internal Provider

PHARMACY

Membership of Professional Institutions and Associations

ROYAL PHARMACEUTICAL SOCIETY OF GREAT BRITAIN

1 Lambeth High Street
London SE1 7JN
Tel: 020 7735 9141
Fax: 020 7735 7629
E-mail: enquiries@rpsgb.org
Website: www.rpsgb.org

The RPSGB, which dates from 1841, is the professional body for pharmacists and pharmacy technicians in England, Scotland and Wales. Our primary objectives are to lead, regulate, develop and represent the profession. We promote advancement of the science and practice of pharmacy, and pharmaceutical education and knowledge, and liaise with government and other bodies in the interests of our members.

MEMBERSHIP
Pharmacy Technician
Member (MRPharmS)
Fellow (FRPharmS)

DESIGNATORY LETTERS
MRPharmS, FRPharmS

THE COLLEGE OF PHARMACY PRACTICE

28 Warwick Row
Coventry CV1 1EY
Tel: 024 762 21359
Fax: 024 765 21110
E-mail: info@collpharm.org.uk
Website: www.collpharm.org.uk

The College of Pharmacy Practice, set up in 1981 by the Pharmaceutical Society of Great Britain, is an organization of pharmacists who share the aim of promoting and maintaining a high standard of pharmacy practice. Its mission is to promote professional and personal development through education, examination, practice and research, benefiting both patients and healthcare provision.

MEMBERSHIP
Student Member
Associate (ACPP)
Member (MCPP)
Fellow (FCPP)
Member Emeritus

DESIGNATORY LETTERS
ACPP, MCPP, FCPP

THE PHARMACEUTICAL SOCIETY OF NORTHERN IRELAND

73 University Street
Belfast BT7 1HL
Tel: 028 9032 6927
Fax: 028 9043 9919
Website: www.psni.org.uk

The Pharmaceutical Society of Northern Ireland, founded in 1925, is the regulatory and professional body for pharmacists in Northern Ireland. It maintains a register of more than 2,000 pharmacists and over 500 pharmacy premises, and sets and promotes the standards for pharmacists' admission to and remaining on the register, thereby protecting public safety.

MEMBERSHIP
Trainee
Member

QUALIFICATION/EXAMINATIONS
Registration Examination

PHOTOGRAPHY

Membership of Professional Institutions and Associations

ASSOCIATION OF PHOTOGRAPHERS (AOP)

81 Leonard Street
London EC2A 4QS
Tel: 020 7739 6669
Fax: 020 7739 8707
E-mail: general@aophoto.co.uk
Website: www.the-aop.org

The AOP was founded in 1968 to promote the highest standards throughout the industry and to improve the rights of all professional photographers based in the UK. Our membership currently comprises 1, 800 photographers and photographic assistants, and we are supported by photographers' agents, printers, and manufacturers and suppliers of photographic equipment.

MEMBERSHIP
Student Member
Assistant Member
Provisional Member
Photographer (full) Member
Agent Member
College Member
Affiliated Company

BRITISH INSTITUTE OF PROFESSIONAL PHOTOGRAPHY

The Coach House
The Firs, High Street
Whitchurch
Aylesbury
Buckinghamshire HP22 4SJ
Tel: 01296 642020
Fax: 01296 641553
E-mail: info@bipp.com
Website: www.bipp.com

The BIPP is the qualifying body for professional photographers in the UK. We provide support, training and qualifications for photographers across all types of photography, and organize a number of regional activities and events. A not-for-profit organization, we ensure that professional standards are met and maintained.

MEMBERSHIP
Open to full- or part-time professional photographers. Join as a Qualifying member (maximum of 1 year) and work towards gaining a professional qualification. Student membership is also available.

QUALIFICATION/EXAMINATIONS
Three tiers of qualification:
Licentiateship (LBIPP)
Associateship (ABIPP)
Fellowship (FBIPP)
Full details of the qualifications criteria can be found at www.bipp.com

DESIGNATORY LETTERS
LBIPP, ABIPP, FBIPP

MASTER PHOTOGRAPHERS ASSOCIATION

Jubilee House
1 Chancery Lane
Darlington
Co Durham DL1 5QP
Tel: 01325 356555
Fax: 01325 357813
E-mail: general@mpauk.com
Website: www.mpauk.com

The MPA was founded in 1952 and is now the UK's only organization for FT, qualified professional photographers. We have more than 2,000 members, who enjoy a range of benefits, including education, qualifications, informative regional meetings, business building promotions and marketing support, and abide by the Association's Code of Conduct.

MEMBERSHIP
Licentiate (LMPA)

Associate (AMPA)
Fellow (FMPA)

QUALIFICATION/EXAMINATIONS
The Diploma in Photographic Practice (Dip.PP) is recognised by SkillSet, as a benchmark competence mapped to the Photo Imaging National Standards: it is available to all qualified members and is an assessment process of professional photographic business and personal skills.

DESIGNATORY LETTERS
LMPA, AMPA, FMPA, DipPP

THE ROYAL PHOTOGRAPHIC SOCIETY

Fenton House
122 Wells Road
Bath BA2 3AH
Tel: 01225 325733
Fax: 01225 448688
E-mail: reception@rps.org
Website: www.rps.org

The RPS, which dates from 1853, is an educational charity whose aim is to promote the art and science of photography. Membership is open to anyone and we provide information, training and advice, hold workshops on a variety of photographic topics and stage three major touring exhibitions, as well as a monthly exhibition of members' work at our headquarters in Bath.

MEMBERSHIP
Student Member
Member
Licentiate (LRPS)
Associate (ARPS)
Fellow (FRPS)

QUALIFICATION/EXAMINATIONS
Qualified Imaging Scientist and Licentiate (QIS LRPS)
Graduate Imaging Scientist and Associate (GIS ARPS)
Accredited Imaging Scientist and Associate (AIS ARPS)
Accredited Senior Imaging Scientist and Fellow (ASIS FRPS)

DESIGNATORY LETTERS
LRPS, ARPS, FRPS

PHYSICS

Membership of Professional Institutions and Associations

INSTITUTE OF PHYSICS AND ENGINEERING IN MEDICINE

Fairmount House
230 Tadcaster Road
York YO24 1ES
Tel: 01904 610821
Fax: 01904 612279
E-mail: office@ipem.org.uk
Website: www.ipem.ac.uk

The IPEM is dedicated to bringing together physical science, engineering and clinical professionals in academia, healthcare services and industry to share knowledge, advance science and technology, and inform and educate the public, with the purpose of improving the understanding, detection and treatment of disease and the management of patients.

MEMBERSHIP
Student Member
Affiliate
Associate
Medical Member (MedMIPEM)
Medical Fellow (MedFIPEM)
Incorporated Member (IIPEM)
Corporate Member (MIPEM)
Fellow (FIPEM)
Overseas Affiliate
Company Member

DESIGNATORY LETTERS
MedMIPEM, MedFIPEM, IIPEM, MIPEM, FIPEM

THE INSTITUTE OF PHYSICS

76 Portland Place
London W1B 1NT
Tel: 020 7470 4800
Fax: 020 7470 4848
E-mail: physics@iop.org
Website: www.iop.org

The IOP is a scientific charity devoted to increasing the practice, understanding and application of physics. We have a worldwide membership of over 36,000 and are a leading communicator of physics-related science to all audiences, from specialists through to government and the general public. Our publishing company, IOP Publishing, is a world leader in scientific publishing and the electronic dissemination of physics.

MEMBERSHIP
Student Member
Affiliate
Associate Member (AMInstP)
Member (MInstP)
Fellow (FInstP)
Chartered Physicist (CPhys)

DESIGNATORY LETTERS
AMInstP, MInstP, FInstP, CPhys

PHYSIOTHERAPY

Membership of Professional Institutions and Associations

THE CHARTERED SOCIETY OF PHYSIOTHERAPY

14 Bedford Row
London WC1R 4ED
Tel: 0207 306 6666
Fax: 0207 306 6611
E-mail: enquiries@csp.org.uk
Website: www.csp.org.uk

The CSP is the professional, educational and trade union body for the UK's 50,000 chartered physiotherapists, physiotherapy students and assistants. In order to become a member of the CSP it is necessary to have undertaken a qualification recognized by the Health Professions Council (HPC) – see; www.hpc-uk.org.

MEMBERSHIP
Student Member
Associate
Member (MCSP)
Fellow (FCSP)

DESIGNATORY LETTERS
MCSP, FCSP

PLASTICS AND RUBBER

Membership of Professional Institutions and Associations

LONDON METROPOLITAN POLYMER CENTRE

London Metropolitan University
166–220 Holloway Road
London N7 8DB
Tel: 020 7133 2248
Fax: 020 7133 2184
E-mail: polymers@londonmet.ac.uk
Website: www.londonmet.ac.uk/depts/polymers/

The London Metropolitan Polymer Centre is a leading UK centre for education, research and consultancy in polymer engineering, science and technology. We have a comprehensive range of modern equipment for polymer processing, testing, characterization, etc, offer courses from technician to postgraduate level, and work closely with industry, contributing to its continuing technical and commercial success.

QUALIFICATION/EXAMINATIONS
NC in Polymer Technology
HNC in Polymer Engineering
HND in Polymer Science and Engineering
BEng in Polymer Engineering
BSc in Sports Product Design
MSc in Manufacture and Design for Polymer Products
MSc in Plastics Product Design
MSc in Plastics Product Design with Management
MSc in Plastics Product Design with Marketing
MSc in Polymer Science and Engineering
MRes in Polymer Technology

PLUMBING

Membership of Professional Institutions and Associations

CHARTERED INSTITUTE OF PLUMBING AND HEATING ENGINEERING

64 Station Lane
Hornchurch
Essex RM12 6NB
Tel: 01708 472791
Fax: 01708 448987
E-mail: linfo@ciphe.org.uk
Website: www.ciphe.org.uk

The CIPHE, founded in 1906, is the professional body for the UK plumbing and heating industry. Our membership of around 12,000 is made up of individuals from a wide range of backgrounds and includes consultants, specifiers, designers, public health engineers, lecturers, trainers, trainees and practitioners, as well as manufacturers and distributors.

MEMBERSHIP
Trainee
Affiliate
Companion (CompCIPHE)
Associate (ACIPHE)
Member (MCIPHE)
Fellow (FCIPHE)

QUALIFICATION/EXAMINATIONS
Master Plumber Certificate (awarded jointly with the Worshipful Company of Plumbers and the City & Guilds of London Institute)

DESIGNATORY LETTERS
CompCIPHE, ACIPHE, MCIPHE, FCIPHE

PRINTING

Membership of Professional Institutions and Associations

PROSKILLS UK

Centurion Court
85b Milton Park
Abingdon
Oxfordshire OX14 4RY
Tel: 01235 833844
E-mail: info@proskills.co.uk
Website: www.proskills.co.uk

Proskills UK is the bridge between employers and government on skills and training. Employer-led representing nine key industries, Building Products, Coatings, Extractive and Mineral Processing, Furniture, Furnishings & Interiors, Glass & Related Industries, Glazed Ceramics, Paper, Printing and Wood industries, which make up a third of UK manufacturing sector. We help to raise the profile of the sector, set the skills standards and qualifications and ensure that the skills and funding system delivers against the current and future needs of the industries.

QUALIFICATION/EXAMINATIONS
Please see the Proskills UK website.

THE INSTITUTE OF PAPER, PRINTING AND PUBLISHING (IP3)

Runnymede Malthouse
off Hummer Road
Egham
Surrey TW20 9BD
Tel: 0870 330 8625
Fax: 0870 330 8615
E-mail: info@ip3.org.uk
Website: www.ip3.org.uk

IP3 is the professional body representing the interests of individuals within the paper, printing and publishing sector. It was formed in 2005 from the merger of the Institute of Paper, the Institute of Printing and the Institute of Publishing, and brought together more than 2,000 members and a wealth of knowledge.

MEMBERSHIP
Student
Associate (AIP3)
Member (MIP3)
Fellow (FIP3)

QUALIFICATION/EXAMINATIONS
Certificate

DESIGNATORY LETTERS
AIP3, MIP3, FIP3

PROFESSIONAL INVESTIGATION

Membership of Professional Institutions and Associations

THE INSTITUTE OF PROFESSIONAL INVESTIGATORS

Claremont House
70-72 Alma Road
Windsor
BERKS., SL4 3EZ
Tel: 0870 330 8622
Fax: 0870 330 8612
E-mail: admin@ipi.org.uk
Website: www.ipi.org.uk

The IPI was founded in 1976 as a professional body, catering primarily for the work and educational needs of professional investigators of all types and all specializations. We encourage members' CPD and require them to adhere to the Institute's strict code of ethics, and we promote the recognition of professional investigation as a profession by government, legislative bodies and the public.

MEMBERSHIP
Associate
Member (MIPI)
Fellow (FIPI)

QUALIFICATION/EXAMINATIONS
The Institute provides an interactive online Foundation Course for students and others interested in becoming part of the investigative industry; this course also provides a refresher course for those who need to update their specialization and/or interest in other areas of investigative work.

DESIGNATORY LETTERS
MIPI, FIPI

PSYCHOANALYSIS

Membership of Professional Institutions and Associations

THE BRITISH PSYCHOANALYTICAL SOCIETY

Byron House
112a Shirland Road
London W9 2EQ
Tel: 020 7563 5000
Fax: 020 7563 5001
Website: www.psychoanalysis.org.uk

The British Psychoanalytical Society was founded in 1913 and now has 438 members and 46 candidates for membership. Our aims include: to support the development of psychoanalytical knowledge as a general theory of mind, to further the clinical and scientific standards of psychoanalysis, and to train high-quality psychoanalytical professionals in sufficient numbers to develop the profession.

MEMBERSHIP
Associate Member
Full Member

PSYCHOLOGY

Membership of Professional Institutions and Associations

BRITISH PSYCHOLOGICAL SOCIETY

St Andrews House
48 Princess Road East
Leicester LE1 7DR
Tel: 0116 254 9568
Fax: 0116 227 1314
E-mail: enquiries@bps.org.uk
Website: www.bps.org.uk

The British Psychological Society is the representative body for psychology and psychologists in the UK. Formed in 1901, it has more than 48,000 members. Through its Royal Charter, the Society has responsibility for the development, promotion and application of pure and applied psychology for the public good.

MEMBERSHIP
Student Member
Graduate Member
Associate Fellow (AFBPsS)
Fellow (FBPsS)
Honorary Fellow
Affiliate
Chartered Membership (CPsychol)
Subscriber
e-Subscriber

QUALIFICATION/EXAMINATIONS
Qualification in Educational Psychology (Scotland) (Stage 2)
Qualification in Forensic Psychology (Stage 2) (QFP)
Qualification in Clinical Neuropsychology (QiCN)
Qualification in Counselling Psychology (QCoP)
Qualification in Health Psychology (Stage 2)
Qualification in Occupational Psychology (QOccPsych)
Qualification in Sport & Exercise Psychology (QSEP)

DESIGNATORY LETTERS
AFBPsS, FBPsS, CPsychol

PSYCHOTHERAPY

Membership of Professional Institutions and Associations

ASSOCIATION OF CHILD PSYCHOTHERAPISTS

120 West Heath Road
London NW3 7TU
Tel: 020 8458 1609
Fax: 020 8458 1482
E-mail: contactus@childpsychotherapy.org.uk
Website: www.childpsychotherapy.org.uk

The ACP is the main professional body for psychoanalytic child and adolescent psychotherapists in the UK. Our members work with children and young people as well as their parents, families and wider networks, treating a wide range of difficulties ranging from problems with sleeping and bedwetting to eating disorders, self-harm, depression and anxiety.

MEMBERSHIP
Member

BRITISH ASSOCIATION FOR COUNSELLING AND PSYCHOTHERAPY

BACP House
15 St John's Business Park
Lutterworth
Leicestershire LE17 4HB
Tel: 01455 883300
Fax: 01455 550243
E-mail: bacp@bacp.co.uk
Website: www.bacp.co.uk

BACP is the largest and broadest body within the sector and participates in the development of counselling and psychotherapy at an international level. Our work with large and small organizations ranges from advising schools on how to set up a counselling service to assisting the NHS on service provision, working with voluntary agencies and supporting independent practitioners.

MEMBERSHIP
Student Member
Affiliate Member
Associate Member
Member (MBACP)
Accredited Member (MBACP Accred)
Fellow (FBACP)

QUALIFICATION/EXAMINATIONS
We run workshops for members and accredit individual counsellors/psychotherapists, supervisors, counselling services and training courses. For details see our website.

DESIGNATORY LETTERS
MBACP, MBACP (Accred). FBACP

BRITISH ASSOCIATION FOR COUNSELLING AND PSYCHOTHERAPY

15 St John's Business Park
Lutterworth
Leicestershire LE17 4HB
Tel: 01455 883300
Fax: 01455 550243
E-mail: bacp@bacp.co.uk
Website: www.bacp.co.uk

The British Association for Counselling and Psychotherapy welcomes applications from qualified and experienced counsellors who wish to become BACP Accredited. BACP Accreditation as a counsellor offers a direct route to Registration as an independent practitioner with the United Kingdom Register of Counsellors.

MEMBERSHIP
Student
Associate
Member (MBACP)
Fellow (FBACP)

QUALIFICATION/EXAMINATIONS
SEAs Certificate
SEAs Diploma
SEAs Professional Qualification

DESIGNATORY LETTERS
MBACP, MBACP(Accred), FBACP

BRITISH ASSOCIATION FOR THE PERSON CENTRED APPROACH

BAPCA
PO Box 143
Ross-on-Wye
Herefordshire HR9 9AH
Tel: 01989 763863
E-mail: enquires@bapca.org.uk
Website: www.bapca.org.uk

The BAPCA was founded in 1989 as a non-religious, non-profit-making organization with the aim of advancing education in Client-Centred Psychotherapy and Counselling and the Person-Centred Approach through its publications and website, and cooperation with other national and international organizations with similar goals.

MEMBERSHIP
Individual Member
Joint Member
International Member
Institutional Member

BRITISH ASSOCIATION OF PSYCHOTHERAPISTS

37 Mapesbury Road
London NW2 4HJ
Tel: 020 8452 9823
Fax: 020 8452 5182
E-mail: mail@bap-psychotherapy.org
Website: www.bap-psychotherapy.org

The BAP is one of the longest established and largest independent providers of Jungian analytic and psychoanalytic psychotherapy for adults and children in the UK. We have been training psychoanalytic and Jungian psychotherapists for nearly 60 years, and our members work in the NHS, the corporate and voluntary sectors and as private practitioners.

MEMBERSHIP
Member

QUALIFICATION/EXAMINATIONS
Certificate/Diploma/MSc in Psychodynamics of Human Development (jointly with Birkbeck College, University of London)
DPsych in Child and Adolescent Psychotherapy (jointly with Birkbeck College, University of London)

CAMBRIDGE COLLEGE OF HYPNOTHERAPY

24 Milton Road
Impington
Cambridge CB24 9NF
Tel: 01223 235127
E-mail: j.teague@ntlworld.com
Website: www.hypnotherapytraining.org.uk

The CCH offers training to become a professional hypntherapist The course is accredited by the NCH, HA, APHP, NGH and NRAH. No formal qualifications are required to enrol on the course. What is required is a willingness to learn, a sense of humour and a genuine compassion and liking for people from all paths in life. This can be a very rewarding new or second career or a supplement to your current work / lifestyle. In addition to the College Diploma, it is possible to gain the HPD (Hypnotherapy Practitioner

Diploma) which is awarded by ncfe and also possible to gain a Diploma awarded by the National Guild of Hypnotists in the USA. The HPD is at NVQ level 4/5 and has transferable credits of 45 for a first year degree with the Open University.

MEMBERSHIP
RSM, HA, NCH, NRAH, NSHP, APHP, HS

QUALIFICATION/EXAMINATIONS
Diploma in Hypnotherapy

DESIGNATORY LETTERS
DipTHP

NATIONAL COLLEGE OF HYPNOSIS AND PSYCHOTHERAPY

PO Box 5779
Loughborough
Leicestershire LE12 5ZF
Tel: 0845 257 8735
E-mail: enquiries@nchp, org, uk
Website: www.hypnotherapyuk.net

The NCHP is a not-for-profit organization founded in 1977 and now offers accredited hypnotherapy training, hypnosis training and psychotherapy training at weekends in Leeds, Leicester, Liverpool, London, Manchester, Newcastle, Oxford, Glasgow and South Wales. We also provide a programme of 1- and 2-day workshops and seminars, and (where appropriate) distance-learning courses.

QUALIFICATION/EXAMINATIONS
Foundation Course
Certificate in Hypno-Psychotherapy (CHP(NC))
Diploma in Hypno-Psychotherapy (DHP(NC))
Advanced Diploma in Hypno-Psychotherapy (ADHP(NC))
European Certificate of Clinical Hypnosis (through the European Association for Hypno-Psychotherapy)
Hypnotherapy Practitioner Diploma

NATIONAL COUNCIL OF PSYCHOTHERAPISTS

PO Box 7219
Heanor
Derbyshire DE75 9AG
Tel: 08452 306072
Fax: 01773 711031
E-mail: ncphq@btinternet.com
Website: www.ncphq.co.uk

The National Council is a registering and accrediting body for psychotherapists, counsellors and coaches within the UK and also, through the International Council, the rest of the world.

Members can join the Council regardless of which discipline and where they completed their training.

MEMBERSHIP
Affiliate (ANCP)
Licentiate (LNCP)
Full Member (MNCP)
Fellow (FNCP)

DESIGNATORY LETTERS
ANCP, LNCP, MNCP, FNCP

THE FOUNDATION FOR PSYCHOTHERAPY AND COUNSELLING

Tel: 020 7378 2090
E-mail: office@thefoundation-uk.org
Website: www.thefoundation-uk.org

The Foundation for Psychotherapy and Counselling was formed during the 1970s as the graduate body of WPF Therapy (the largest charitable provider of counselling and psychotherapy in England) and now has some 700 fully trained and qualified members, most of whom are in private practice.

MEMBERSHIP
Member

THE NATIONAL REGISTER OF HYPNOTHERAPISTS AND PSYCHOTHERAPISTS

1st Floor
18 Carr Road
Nelson
Lancashire BB9 7JS
Tel: 01282 716839
E-mail: admin@nrhp.co.uk
Website: www.nrhp.co.uk

NRHP (est 1985) – a professional association of qualified hypno-psychotherapists who trained with a UKCP-accredited training organization. Members are required to adhere to a code of ethics and carry appropriate insurance. We publish a Directory of Practitioners and offer a public referral service via our website and office. Member of the UKCP.

MEMBERSHIP
Student
Associate 1 (NRHP(Assoc 1))
Associate 2 (NRHP(Assoc 2))
Associate 3 (NRHP(Assoc 3))
Full Member (MNRHP)
Fellow (FNRHP)

DESIGNATORY LETTERS
NRHP(Assoc 1), NRHP(Assoc 2), NRHP(Assoc 3), MNRHP, FNRHP

UK COUNCIL FOR PSYCHOTHERAPY

2nd Floor Edward House
2 Wakley Street
London EC1V 7LT
Tel: 020 7014 9955
Fax: 020 7014 9977
E-mail: info@ukcp.org.uk
Website: www.psychotherapy.org.uk

The purpose of the UK Council for Psychotherapy (UKCP) is to promote the art and science of psychotherapy for the public benefit; to promote research and education in psychotherapy and disseminate the results of any such research; and to promote (or assist in the promotion, preservation and protection of public health) by encouraging high standards of training and practice in psychotherapy and the wider provision of psychotherapy for the public. UKCP offers a free public listing of UKCP member psychotherapists and psychotherapeutic counsellors who are on the UKCP register, available on the website. Only psychotherapists and psychotherapeutic counsellors who meet the requirements of UKCP and abide by its ethical guidelines are included.

PUBLIC ADMINISTRATION

Membership of Professional Institutions and Associations

THE INSTITUTE OF PUBLIC SECTOR MANAGEMENT

45 Cherry Tree Road
Axminster
Devon EX13 5GG
Tel: 01297 35423
Fax: 01297 35423
E-mail: info@ipsm.org.uk
Website: www.ipsm.org.uk

The IPSM is the only membership body exclusively dedicated to managers working in the public, voluntary and not-for-profit sectors. We encourage the sharing of knowledge, skills and experience between our members, provide advice and support ourselves, and as a campaigning body seek to raise public awareness and respect for public services and the role of the manager in those services.

MEMBERSHIP
Student Member
Individual (Full) Member (MIPSM)
Fellow (FIPSM)
Corporate Member

PURCHASING AND SUPPLY

Membership of Professional Institutions and Associations

THE CHARTERED INSTITUTE OF PURCHASING & SUPPLY

Easton House
Easton on the Hill
Stamford
Lincolnshire PE9 3NZ
Tel: 01780 756777
Fax: 01780 751610
E-mail: info@cips.org
Website: www.cips.org

The Chartered Institute of Purchasing & Supply (CIPS) is the leading international body representing purchasing and supply management professionals. It is the worldwide centre of excellence on purchasing and supply management issues. CIPS has 65,000 members in 150 different countries, including senior business people, high-ranking civil servants and leading academics. The activities of purchasing and supply chain professionals can have a major impact on the profitability and efficiency of all types of organization. CIPS also offers business solutions to companies, public and third sector.

MEMBERSHIP
Student Member
Affiliate
Certificate Member
Diploma Member
Associate Member
Full Member (MCIPS)
Fellow (FCIPS)

QUALIFICATION/EXAMINATIONS
Please see website; www.cips.org

DESIGNATORY LETTERS
MCIPS, FCIPS

QUALITY ASSURANCE

Membership of Professional Institutions and Associations

THE CHARTERED QUALITY INSTITUTE

12 Grosvenor Crescent
London SW1X 7EE
Tel: 020 7245 6722
Fax: 020 7245 6788
E-mail: info@thecqi.org
Website: www.thecqi.org

The CQI is the chartered body for quality management professionals. Established in 1919, we gained a Royal Charter in 2006 and became the CQI shortly afterwards. Our vision is to place quality at the heart of every organization; we promote the benefits of quality management to industry, disseminate quality knowledge and resources, provide qualifications and training, and assess quality competence.

MEMBERSHIP
Student
Associate Member (ACQI)
Member, Chartered Quality Professional (MCQI, CQP)
Fellow, Chartered Quality Professional (FCQI, CQP)
Company Member

QUALIFICATION/EXAMINATIONS
Certificate in Quality
Diploma in Quality

DESIGNATORY LETTERS
MCQI, CQP; FCQI, CQP

RADIOGRAPHY

Membership of Professional Institutions and Associations

THE SOCIETY OF RADIOGRAPHERS

207 Providence Square
Mill Street
London SE1 2EW
Tel: 020 7740 7200
Fax: 020 7740 7204
E-mail: info@sor.org
Website: www.sor.org

The Society of Radiographers, founded in 1920, represents more than 90 per cent of the diagnostic and therapeutic radiographers in the UK. It is responsible for their professional, educational, public and workplace interests. Together with the College of Radiographers, our charitable subsidiary, our efforts are directed towards education, research and other activities in support of the science and practice of radiography.

MEMBERSHIP
Student Member
Radiographic Assistant
Assistant Practitioner
Member

RETAIL

Membership of Professional Institutions and Associations

IGD

Grange Lane
Letchmore Heath
Watford
Hertfordshire WD25 8GD
Tel: 01923 857141
Fax: 01923 852531
E-mail: igd@igd.com
Website: www.igd.com

IGD (the Institute of Grocery Distribution) was formed in 1972 from the merger of the Institute of Charted Grocers and the Institute of Food Distribution. We provide information and practical training to the industry and now have more than 700 corporate members, covering a broad spectrum of companies and organizations across the world.

MEMBERSHIP
Corporate Member

QUALIFICATION/EXAMINATIONS
PG Cert in Food & Grocery Industry Management (validated by the University of Edinburgh)

INSTITUTE OF MASTERS OF WINE

2/3 Philpot Lane
London EC3M 8AN
Tel: 020 7621 2830
Fax: 020 7929 2302
Website: www.mastersofwine.org

The Institute of Masters of Wine is a membership body that represents the interests of its members (Masters of Wine), administers the MW Examination, and runs an education programme in preparation for the examination. We also hold a number of events throughout the year, including seminars and tastings, master classes, discussions, and, every 4 years, a symposium, most of which are open to the public.

MEMBERSHIP
Master of Wine (MW)

QUALIFICATION/EXAMINATIONS
Master of Wine Examination

DESIGNATORY LETTERS
MW

MEAT TRAINING COUNCIL

PO Box 141
Winterhill House
Snowdon Drive
Milton Keynes MK6 1YY
Tel: 01908 231062
Fax: 01908 231063
E-mail: info@meattraining.org.uk
Website: www.meattraining.org.uk

The MTC is a registered charity, limited by guarantee, working for, and with, the UK meat industry. We provide information about jobs, careers and the qualifications required to work in the red meat and poultry sector of the food business. Professional membership is administered by the Worshipful Company of Butchers via its Guild of Freemen. The qualifications awarding body is now the Food and Drink Qualifications Awarding Body (FDQ Ltd) (www.fdq.org.uk).

MEMBERSHIP
Affiliate (AffInstM)
Associate (AInstM)
Graduate Member (GMInstM)

QUALIFICATION/EXAMINATIONS
Please see the Meat Training Council's website.

DESIGNATORY LETTERS
AffInstM, AInstM, GMInstM

THE BRITISH ANTIQUE DEALERS' ASSOCIATION

20 Rutland Gate
London SW7 1BD
Tel: 020 7589 4128
Fax: 020 7581 9083
E-mail: info@bada.org
Website: www.bada.org

BADA, which was founded in 1918, is the trade association for antique dealers in Britain. Our vetted members are elected for their high business standards and expertise, and adhere to a strict code of practice; we provide safeguards for members of the public who deal with our members, including independent arbitration if a dispute arises.

MEMBERSHIP
Member

THE GUILD OF ARCHITECTURAL IRONMONGERS

8 Stepney Green
London E1 3JU
Tel: 020 7790 3431
Fax: 020 7790 8517
E-mail: info@gai.org.uk
Website: www.gai.org.uk

The GAI represents the interests of architectural ironmongers and manufacturers of architectural ironmongery. We develop, promote and protect standards of integrity and excellence, and encourage academic study relating to the industry, operating an Institute for individual members to facilitate their continuous professional development. We liaise with various bodies on matters affecting the industry.

MEMBERSHIP
Affiliate Member
Associate Member
Full Member
Registered Architectural Ironmonger (Reg AI)

QUALIFICATION/EXAMINATIONS
The GAI provides a 3-year incremental training programme. Students are examined each year and must pass each year in turn before progressing to the next. A Certificate is awarded to successful students each year, culminating in the GAI Diploma (Dip GAI) on successful completion of year 3.

DESIGNATORY LETTERS
Reg AI

THE INSTITUTE OF BUILDERS MERCHANTS

Touchwood
Oak View Rise
Harlow Wood
Mansfield
Nottinghamshire NG18 4UT
Tel: 01623 427693
E-mail: admin@instbm.co.uk
Website: www.instbm.co.uk

To improve through seminars and website articles, the technical and general knowledge of persons engaged in builders' merchants; to verify management training courses with providers; to acknowledge personal achievements and award diplomas, certificates and other distinctions; to encourage the need for knowledge, integrity and efficiency in the builders' merchants industry.

MEMBERSHIP
Student
Associate
Member
Fellow
Corporate Supporter

QUALIFICATION/EXAMINATIONS
University Degree
The Institute of Builders Merchants Business Studies Course
The Builders Merchants Federation Diploma in Merchanting
Higher National Certificate (HNC) in Business Studies
Higher National Diploma (HND) in Business Studies
NVQ Level 4
Company management programmes as approved by the Board of Governors

THE SOCIETY OF SHOE FITTERS

c/o The Anchorage
28 Admirals Walk
Hingham
Norfolk NR9 4JL
Tel: 01953 851171
Fax: 01953 851190
E-mail: secretary@shoefitters-uk.org
Website: www.shoefitters-uk.org

The Society of Shoe Fitters is a not-for-profit organization in our 50th year, set up to assist the trade and public. We disseminate shoe fitting/ footwear knowledge via courses and an examination, and in turn endeavour to keep shoe fitting advice available via our website, leaflets and a helpline.

MEMBERSHIP
Student Member
Member (MSSF)
Fellow (FSSF)
Associate Member (corporate membership)

QUALIFICATION/EXAMINATIONS
One-day on-site courses – certificate only
Five- or 10-month course leading to membership qualification
Entrance examination for experienced shoe fitters leading to qualification

DESIGNATORY LETTERS
MSSF, FSSF

SECRETARIAL AND OFFICE WORK

Membership of Professional Institutions and Associations

INSTITUTE OF PROFESSIONAL ADMINISTRATORS

6 Graphite Square
Vauxhall Walk
London SE11 5EE
Tel: 020 7091 2606
Fax: 020 7091 7340
E-mail: info@inprad.org
Website: www.inprad.org

The IPA was founded in 1957 as the Institute of Qualified Professional Secretaries and is today the leading membership body for administration and office professionals. We provide our members with information, advice and guidance on suitable training and development to advance their career as well as a CPD scheme designed to meet their individual needs.

MEMBERSHIP
Student Member
Affiliate (AffIPA)
Member (MIPA)
Fellow (FIPA)
Corporate Member

DESIGNATORY LETTERS
AffIPA, MIPA, FIPA

SECURITY

Membership of Professional Institutions and Associations

THE SECURITY INSTITUTE

1 The Courtyard
Caldecote
Warwickshire CV10 0AS
E-mail: info@security-institute.org
Website: www.security-institute.org

The Institute promotes professionalism in the security world and encourages a proper understanding of the value of the security function by management. The Institute has declared its intention to progress towards chartered status. Membership of the Institute is now recognized as an employment prerequisite by many companies and government departments.

MEMBERSHIP
Affiliate/Student
Graduate
Associate

Member
Fellow (FSyI)

QUALIFICATION/EXAMINATIONS
Certificate in Security Management
Diploma in Security Management

DESIGNATORY LETTERS
FSyI

SOCIAL WORK AND PROBATION

SOCIAL WORK
The General Social Care Council (GSCC) is responsible for regulating and supporting social work education and training in England. The GSCC accredits universities who offer social work qualifications at both qualifying and post-qualifying levels, and quality-assures all social work courses. In 2003, professional qualifying training for social workers in the United Kingdom changed to a degree in social work. The diploma in social work (DipSW) and all other 'predecessor' social work qualifications will continue to be recognized as valid social work qualifications. To find GSCC approved degree courses visit www.gscc.org.uk/courseSearchSwd.php. For further details contact the General Social Care Council, Myson House, Railway Terrace, Rugby CV21 3HT; Tel: 0845 070 0630; website; www.gscc.org.uk.

For information about social work training in Scotland, contact Scottish Social Services Council, Compass House, 11 Riverside Drive, Dundee DD1 4NY; Tel: 08456 030891; e-mail: enquiries@sssc.uk.com; website; www.sssc.uk.com.

For information about social work training in Wales, contact Care Council for Wales, South Gate House, Wood Street, Cardiff CV10 1EW; Tel: 02920 226257; e-mail: info@ccwales.org.uk; website; www.ccwales.org.uk.

For information about social work training in Northern Ireland, contact Northern Ireland Social Care Council, 7th Floor, Millennium House, 19–25 Great Victoria Street, Belfast BT2 7AQ; Tel: 02890 417600; e-mail: info@nisocialcarecouncil.org.uk; website; www.niscc.info.

Membership of Professional Institutions and Associations

THE BRITISH ASSOCIATION OF SOCIAL WORKERS

16 Kent Street
Birmingham B5 6RD
Tel: 0121 6223911
Fax: 0121 6224860
Website: www.basw.co.uk

The BASW is the largest professional association representing social work and social workers in the UK. Whether you are qualified or not, experienced or just entering the profession, we are here to help, support, advise and campaign on your behalf.

MEMBERSHIP
Student Member
Affiliate
Member (4 categories)
Retired Member
Overseas Member

SOCIOLOGY

Membership of Professional Institutions and Associations

BRITISH SOCIOLOGICAL ASSOCIATION

Bailey Suite, Palatine House
Belmont Business Park
Belmont
Durham DH1 1TW
Tel: 0191 383 0839
Fax: 0191 383 0782
E-mail: enquiries@britsoc.org.uk
Website: www.britsoc.co.uk

The BSA was founded in 1951 to represent the intellectual and sociological interests of sociologists in the UK. Our members include researchers, teachers, students and practitioners in a variety of fields. We provide a network of communication to all who are concerned with the promotion and use of sociology and sociological research.

SPEECH AND LANGUAGE THERAPY

Membership of Professional Institutions and Associations

ROYAL COLLEGE OF SPEECH AND LANGUAGE THERAPISTS

2 White Hart Yard
London SE1 1NX
Tel: 020 7378 1200
Fax: 020 7378 7254
E-mail: postmaster@rcslt.org
Website: www.rcslt.org

The RCSLT is the professional body for speech and language therapists and support workers. We set, promote and maintain high standards in education, clinical practice and ethical conduct. Our national campaigning work aims to improve services for people with speech, language, communication and swallowing needs and to influence health, education and social care policies.

MEMBERSHIP
Student Member
Newly Qualified Member
Full Member
Fellow (FRCSLT)
Honorary Fellow (Hon FRCSLT)

DESIGNATORY LETTERS
FRCSLT, Hon FRCSLT

SPORTS SCIENCE

Membership of Professional Institutions and Associations

LONDON SCHOOL OF SPORTS MASSAGE

28 Station Parade
Willesden Green
London NW2 4NX
Tel: 020 8452 8855
Fax: 020 8452 4524
E-mail: admin@lssm.com
Website: www.lssm.com

The LSSM, founded in 1989, was the first to provide specialist training in Sport & Remedial Massage. We offer vocational training for those who want to develop a professional career in massage therapy and were instrumental in setting up the Institute of Sport & Remedial Massage (ISRM), which is the professional body promoting our needs and aspirations as clinical therapists.

MEMBERSHIP
Member

QUALIFICATION/EXAMINATIONS
Introductory Massage Workshop
Professional Diploma in Clinical Sport & Remedial Massage Therapy (Level 5)

STATISTICS

Membership of Professional Institutions and Associations

THE ROYAL STATISTICAL SOCIETY

12 Errol Street
London EC1Y 8LX
Tel: 020 7638 8998
Fax: 020 7614 3905
E-mail: rss@rss.org.uk
Website: www.rss.org.uk

The RSS is the learned society and professional body for statistics and statisticians in the UK. We have over 7,000 members worldwide, and are active in a wide range of areas both directly and indirectly relating to the study and application of statistics.

MEMBERSHIP
Student Member
Fellow
Graduate Statistician (GradStat)
Chartered Statistician (CStat)

QUALIFICATION/EXAMINATIONS
Ordinary Certificate in Statistics
Higher Certificate in Statistics
Graduate Diploma in Statistics

DESIGNATORY LETTERS
GradStat, CStat

STOCKBROKING AND SECURITIES

Membership of Professional Institutions and Associations

CFA SOCIETY OF THE UK

2nd Floor
135 Canon Street
London EC4N 5BP
Tel: 020 7280 9620
Fax: 020 7280 9636
E-mail: info@cfauk.org
Website: www.cfauk.org

The CFA Society of the UK was formerly the UK Society of Investment Professionals (UKSIP) and was renamed in 2007. Our aim is to promote the development of the investment profession in the UK through the promotion of the highest standards of ethical behaviour and the provision of education, professional development, information, career support and advocacy to our members.

MEMBERSHIP
IMC Member
Candidate Member
Affiliate Member
Regular Member

QUALIFICATION/EXAMINATIONS
Investment Management Certificate (IMC)

THE CHARTERED INSTITUTE FOR SECURITIES & INVESTMENT

8 Eastcheap
London EC3M 1AE
Tel: 020 7645 0600
Fax: 020 7645 0601
Website: www.cisi.org.uk

The Chartered Institute for Securities & Investment is the largest professional body for practitioners in stockbroking, derivatives markets, investment management, corporate finance, operations and related activities, having over 44,000 members.

MEMBERSHIP
Student Member
Affiliate
Associate (ACSI)
Member (MCSI)
Chartered Member (Ch. MCSI)
Fellow (FCSI)
Chartered Fellow (Ch. FCSI)

QUALIFICATION/EXAMINATIONS
Introduction to Investment
Islamic Finance Qualification
IT in Investment Operations
Risk in Financial Services
Combating Financial Crime
Global Financial Compliance
Investment Operations Certificate (IOC) also known as Investment Administration Qualification (IAQ)
Certificate in Corporate Finance
Certificate in Investments
Certificate in Investment Management (CertIM)
Certificate in Private Client Investment Advice & Management
International Certificate in Wealth Management
Investment Advice Diploma
Advanced Certificate in Global Securities Operations
Advanced Certificate in Operational Risk
Diploma in Investment Compliance
Diploma in Investment Operations
CISI Diploma
CISI Masters in Wealth Management

DESIGNATORY LETTERS
ACSI, MCSI, Ch. MCSI, FCSI, Ch.FCSI

SURGICAL, DENTAL AND CARDIOLOGICAL TECHNICIANS

Membership of Professional Institutions and Associations

THE BRITISH INSTITUTE OF DENTAL AND SURGICAL TECHNOLOGISTS

4 Thompson Green
Shipley
West Yorkshire BD17 7PR
Tel: 0845 644 3726
E-mail: secretary@bidst.org
Website: www.bidst.org

The BIDST has been established for over 70 years and exists to provide a vehicle for the continuing education of technicians within the spheres of dental and surgical technology. It is our aim to make membership of the Institute an aspiration for all technicians, raising standards and portraying an image of professionalism which professional technicians deserve.

MEMBERSHIP
Student Associate
Associate
Licentiate (LBIDST)
Life Member
Fellow (FBIDST)

DESIGNATORY LETTERS
LBIDST, FBIDST

SURVEYING

Membership of Professional Institutions and Associations

ASSOCIATION OF BUILDING ENGINEERS

Lutyens House
Billing Brook Road
Weston Favell
Northampton NN3 8NW
Tel: 0845 126 1058
Fax: 01604 784220
E-mail: building.engineers@abe.org.uk
Website: www.abe.org.uk

The ABE is the professional body for those specializing in the technology of building and the management processes by which buildings are designed, constructed, renewed and maintained. Our objectives are to promote and advance the planning, design, construction, maintenance and repair of the built environment; to maintain a high standard of professional practice; and to encourage co-operation between professionals.

MEMBERSHIP
Student
Technician
Associate Member (ABEng)
Graduate Member (GradBEng)
Member (MBEng)
Fellow (FBEng)
Honorary Fellow (HonFBEng)

QUALIFICATION/EXAMINATIONS
2011 EDEXCEL Edexcel Level 3 NVQ Diploma in Construction Site Supervision (QCF)
Edexcel Level 3 NVQ Diploma in Construction Contracting Operations (QCF)
Edexcel Level 6 NVQ Diploma in Construction Contracting Operations Management (QCF)
Edexcel Level 6 NVQ Diploma in Construction Site Management (QCF)

Edexcel Level 7 NVQ Diploma in Construction Senior Management (QCF)

ABBE ABBE Level 3 NVQ Diploma in Built Environment and control Technical Support (QCF)
ABBE Level 6 NVQ Diploma in Built Environment and Control (QCF)
ABBE Level 3 Certificate Fire Risk Assessment

DESIGNATORY LETTERS
ABEng, GradBEng, MBEng, FBEng

SWIMMING INSTRUCTION

Membership of Professional Institutions and Associations

THE SWIMMING TEACHERS' ASSOCIATION

Anchor House
Birch Street
Walsall
West Midlands WS2 8HZ
Tel: 01922 645097
Fax: 01922 720628
E-mail: sta@sta.co.uk
Website: www.sta.co.uk

The STA is dedicated to the preservation of human life by the teaching of swimming, lifesaving and survival techniques to as many people as possible, both in the UK and internationally. We offer a range of specialist training programmes and qualifications, which are used in more than 25 countries worldwide, and liaise with other organizations concerned with swimming teaching and water safety.

MEMBERSHIP
Junior Member
Associate Member (ASTA)
Qualified Member (MSTA)
Corporate Member

QUALIFICATION/EXAMINATIONS
STA Certificate in Teaching Swimming – Beginners
STA Certificate in Teaching Swimming – Full
STA Certificate in Teaching Swimming – Primary Teacher
STA Certificate in Aquatic Teaching – Baby & Pre-School
STA Certificate in Aquatic Teaching – Special Needs (Teacher)
STA Foundation Certificate in Swimming Pool and Spa Water Treatment
STA Certificate in Swimming Pool and Spa Water Treatment
STA Certificate for the National Rescue Standard – Pool Lifeguard
STA Certificate for the National Rescue Standard – Pool Attendant
STA Certificate for the National Rescue Standard – Poolside Helper
STA Award in Emergency First Aid at Work
STA Award in Emergency First Aid for Sport

DESIGNATORY LETTERS
ASTA, MSTA

TAXATION

Membership of Professional Institutions and Associations

SOCIETY OF TRUST & ESTATE PRACTITIONERS

Artillery House (South)
11–19 Artillery Row
London SW1P 1RT
Tel: +44 (0)20 7340 0500
Fax: +44 (0)20 7340 0501
E-mail: step@step.org
Website: www.step.org

The Society of Trust and Estate Practitioners (STEP) is a unique professional body providing members with a local, national and international learning and business network focusing on the responsible stewardship of assets today and across the generations.

MEMBERSHIP
Full members of STEP are the most experienced and senior practitioners in the field of trusts and estates.

QUALIFICATION/EXAMINATIONS
STEP Diplomas and Foundation Certificates are recognized as essential qualifications and TEP's are sought after by employers. A portfolio of courses have been designed to enhance your career. STEP qualifications include the STEP Diploma for England & Wales (Trusts and Estates), STEP Diploma for Ireland, STEP Diploma for Scotland, STEP Diploma in International Trust Management, STEP Certificate for Financial Services (Trusts and Estate Planning) and many more.

DESIGNATORY LETTERS
TEP

THE ASSOCIATION OF TAXATION TECHNICIANS

1st Floor
Artillery House
11–19 Artillery Row
London SW1P 1RT
Tel: 0844 251 0830
Fax: 0844 251 0831
E-mail: info@att.org.uk
Website: www.att.org.uk

The ATT was founded in 1989 in recognition of the increasing demand for tax services and the development of tax practice as a professional activity in its own right. Our primary aim is to provide an appropriate qualification for individuals who undertake such work, and we now have more than 10, 500 members, affiliates and registered students.

MEMBERSHIP
Student
Affiliate
Member

QUALIFICATION/EXAMINATIONS
Certificate of Competency in Business Compliance
Certificate of Competency in Business Taxation and Accounting Principles

DESIGNATORY LETTERS
ATT

THE CHARTERED INSTITUTE OF TAXATION

First Floor
11–19 Artillery Row
London SW1P 1RT
Tel: 020 7340 0550
Fax: 0844 579 6701
E-mail: post@tax.org.uk
Website: www.tax.org.uk

The CIOT, which dates from 1930, is the professional body for Chartered Tax Advisers and has 14, 300 members. Our aims are to promote education in and the study of the administration and practice of taxation, and to achieve a better, more efficient, tax system for all affected by it – taxpayers, advisers and the authorities.

MEMBERSHIP
Associate (CTA or ATII)
Fellow (CTA or FTII)

QUALIFICATION/EXAMINATIONS
Chartered Tax Adviser (CTA) examination
Advanced Diploma in International Taxation (ADIT)

DESIGNATORY LETTERS
CTA, ATII, FTII

THE INSTITUTE OF INDIRECT TAXATION

The Stables
Station Road West
Oxted
Surrey RH8 9EE
Tel: 01883 730658
Fax: 01883 717778
E-mail: enquiries@theiit.org.uk
Website: www.theiit.org.uk

The Institute was founded in 1991 to establish a professional body of indirect tax practitioners to regulate and support its members. Membership is worldwide and includes barristers, solicitors, accountants, sole practitioners and tax specialists in commerce, the professions and government. The Institute is a member of the Confederation Fiscale Europeenne.

MEMBERSHIP
Student
Affiliate
Associate (AIIT)
Honorary Associate (AIIT(Hon))
Fellow (FIIT)
Honorary Fellow (FIIT(Hon)

QUALIFICATION/EXAMINATIONS
Associate Examination
VAT Compliance Diploma (IIT (Dip))

DESIGNATORY LETTERS
AIIT, AIIT (Hon), FIIT, FIIT (Hon)

TAXI DRIVERS

Membership of Professional Institutions and Associations

TAXI DRIVERS (LONDON)

Cab drivers and cab proprietors in the Metropolitan Police District and City of London are licensed by an Assistant Commissioner of the Metropolitan Police, through the Public Carriage Office at 15 Penton Street, Islington N1 9PU. A cab driver's licence is valid for 3 years and a cab proprietor's licence for 1 year.

TEACHING/EDUCATION

Initial qualifications in the UK

Qualified Teacher Status

To obtain a teaching appointment as a qualified teacher in maintained schools in England and Wales, it is necessary to have **Qualified Teacher Status (QTS)**. To be qualified, teachers must have satisfactorily completed an approved course of initial teacher training (ITT), and to be able to teach in maintained schools in England must have successfully completed their induction period (there are similar arrangements for teaching in Scotland, Wales and Northern Ireland).

Teacher training courses

Initial teacher training courses in England and Wales are provided by accredited training providers mainly through University Departments of Education. Courses available include Bachelor of Arts with QTS and Bachelor of Science with QTS for undergraduates, and Postgraduate Certificates of Education (PGCEs) for graduates.

Undergraduate training typically lasts three years, and a PGCE generally lasts one year full time. There are also some employment-based routes into teaching. The Graduate Teacher Programme is for graduates who wish to earn money while they train and are able to take on responsibilities quickly. The Registered Teacher Programme is for those without a degree but with at least two years of higher education. In addition, Teach First is a programme enabling graduates to spend two years working in challenging secondary schools in London, the North-West, the Midlands, or Yorkshire and the Humber. The programme enables trainees to qualify as a teacher while also completing leadership training.

The qualification of Professional Graduate Diploma in Education is a one-year postgraduate degree course leading to registration as a primary or secondary school teacher in Scotland (see www.teachinginscotland.com). The Postgraduate Certificate of Education course, approved by the Department of Education Northern Ireland, leads to recognition as a school teacher in Northern Ireland (see www.deni.gov.uk).

Qualifications for admission to training

Higher Education Institutions offering undergraduate Initial Teacher Training courses will set admissions criteria; typically two good A levels (or equivalent qualifications). Entrants to PGCE and other graduate training courses will require a relevant UK Bachelors degree or a recognized equivalent and be expected to demonstrate a standard equivalent to GCSE grade C in English and mathematics, and additionally a standard equivalent to GCSE grade C in a science subject for those wishing to train to teach primary school children. Trainees who have undertaken their initial teacher training in England must pass professional skills tests in numeracy, literacy and ICT. These tests cover core skills that teachers need in their jobs and QTS cannot be awarded until they are passed. If you are undertaking initial teacher training in Wales, you are not required to complete the skills tests in order to be awarded QTS.

The General Teaching Councils of the UK

At the time of writing, the General Teaching Council for England (GTCE) is an independent professional council for teachers in England. The Government is working towards a closure date of the General Teaching Council for England of March 2012. In the interim, teachers must continue to register with the Council. Similar councils exist in Wales (GTCW), Scotland (GTCS) and Northern Ireland (GTCNI). These councils hold registers of qualified teachers and also act as disciplinary bodies. You can find out more from their respective websites: GTCE; www.gtce.org.uk; GTCW; www.gtcw.org.uk; GTCS; www.gtcs.org.uk; GTCNI; www.gtcni.org.uk.

Applications

Applications for undergraduate courses are made through the University and Colleges Admission Services (UCAS) and postgraduate applications through the Graduate Teacher Training Registry (GTTR). You cannot apply for courses in Northern Ireland through GTTR, but must visit the Department for Education in Northern Ireland's website for information about these courses (www.deni.gov.uk).

You can find out more about training to teach from the following websites: GTTR; www.gttr.ac.uk; UCAS; www.ucas.ac.uk; Training and Development Agency for Schools (TDA); www.tda.gov.uk. You can also call the TDA's Teaching Information Line on 0800 389 2500 (English speakers) and 0800 085 0971 (Welsh speakers), (minicom 0117 915 8161).

TECHNICAL COMMUNICATIONS

Membership of Professional Institutions and Associations

THE INSTITUTE OF SCIENTIFIC AND TECHNICAL COMMUNICATORS (ISTC LTD)

Airport House
Purley Way
Croydon CR0 0XZ
Tel: 020 8253 4506
Fax: 020 8253 4510
E-mail: istc@istc.org.uk
Website: www.istc.org.uk

The ISTC is a non-profit-making organization and the largest UK body representing professional communicators and information designers. Our aims include improving standards of scientific and technical communication, promoting scientific and technical communication as a career, supporting our members, and consulting, cooperating and collaborating with other bodies that share out ideals.

MEMBERSHIP
Student
Associate
Junior
Member (MISTC)
Fellow (FISTC)
Business Affiliate

DESIGNATORY LETTERS
MISTC, FISTC

TEXTILES

Membership of Professional Institutions and Associations

THE TEXTILE INSTITUTE

1st Floor St James' Buildings
79 Oxford Street
Manchester
UK M1 6FQ
Tel: 0161 2371188
Fax: 0161 2361991
E-mail: tiihq@textileinst.org.uk
Website: www.textileinstitute.org

The Textile Institute covers all disciplines – from technology and production to design, development and marketing – relating to fibres, fabrics, clothing, footwear, and interior and technical textiles.

MEMBERSHIP
Student
Individual
Licentiate (LTI)
Associate (CText ATI)
Fellow (CText FTI)
Companion
Honorary Fellow
Corporate

DESIGNATORY LETTERS
LTI, CText ATI, CText FTI

TIMBER TECHNOLOGY

Membership of Professional Institutions and Associations

WOOD TECHNOLOGY SOCIETY

The Boilerhouse
Springfield Business Park
Caunt Road
Grantham
Lincs NG31 7FZ
Tel: 01476-513880
Fax: 01476-513899
E-mail: emily.drury@iom3.org
Website: www.iom3.org/content/wood-technology

The Wood Technology Society (IWSc – a Division of the Institute of Materials, Minerals and Mining), formerly the Institute of Wood Science, is the professional body for the timber and allied industries. We promote and encourage a better understanding of timber, wood-based materials and associated timber processes, and are the UK examining body, awarding qualifications at Foundation, Certificate and Diploma level.

MEMBERSHIP
Student Member
Affiliate Member
Technician (TIWSc)
Licentiate (LIWSc)
Member (MIWSc)
Fellow (FIWSc)
Corporate Member

QUALIFICATION/EXAMINATIONS
Timber Studies Award (Foundation course)

Certificate
Diploma

DESIGNATORY LETTERS
TIWSc, LIWSc, MIWSc, FIWSc

TOWN AND COUNTRY PLANNING

Membership of Professional Institutions and Associations

ROYAL TOWN PLANNING INSTITUTE

41 Botolph Lane
London EC3R 8DL
Tel: 020 7929 9494
E-mail: membership@rtpi.org.uk
Website: www.rtpi.org.uk

The RTPI is the largest professional institute for planners in Europe, with over 22,000 members. As well as promoting spatial planning, we develop and shape policy affecting the built environment, work to raise professional standards and support members through continuous education, training and development.

MEMBERSHIP
Student Member
Licentiate Member
Associate Member
Legal Associate Member (LARTPI)
Technical Member (TechRTPI)
Retired Member
Honorary Member (HonMRTPI)
Chartered Member (MRTPI)
Chartered Fellow (FRTPI)

QUALIFICATION/EXAMINATIONS
Please see www.rtpi.org.uk/item/178/23/5/3 for a list of accredited training providers

DESIGNATORY LETTERS
LARTPI, TechRTPI, HonMRTPI, MRTPI, FRTPI

TRADING STANDARDS

Membership of Professional Institutions and Associations

THE TRADING STANDARDS INSTITUTE

1 Sylvan Court
Sylvan Way
Southfields Business Park
Basildon
Essex SS15 6TH
Tel: 0845 608 9400
Fax: 0845 608 9425
E-mail: institute@tsi.org.uk
Website: www.tradingstandards.gov.uk

The TSI, formed in 1881, is a not-for-profit membership association representing trading standards professionals in both the public and private sectors in the UK and overseas. TSI encourages honest enterprise and business, and helps safeguard the economic, environmental, health and social well-being of consumers.

MEMBERSHIP
Student Member
Affiliate Member

Associate Member (ASTI)
Full Member (MSTI)
Fellow (FSTI)
Corporate Affiliate

QUALIFICATION/EXAMINATIONS
The Trading Standards Qualification Framework consists of:
Certificate of Competence
Foundation Certificate in Consumer Affairs and Trading Standards
Core Skills Certificate in Consumer Affairs and Trading StandardsModule Certificate in Consumer Affairs and Trading Standards
Diploma in Consumer Affairs and Trading Standards
Higher Diploma in Consumer Affairs and Trading Standards

DESIGNATORY LETTERS
ATSI, MTSI, FTSI

TRANSPORT

Membership of Professional Institutions and Associations

INSTITUTE OF TRANSPORT ADMINISTRATION

The Old Studio
25 Greenfield Road
Westoning
Bedfordshire MK45 5JD
Tel: 01525 634940
Fax: 01525 750016
E-mail: director@iota.org.uk
Website: www.iota.org.uk

The primary aim of IoTA is to broaden and improve the knowledge, skills and experience of its members in the practice of efficient road, rail, air and sea transport. We are one of the few professional bodies still recognized within the terms of the Road Traffic 1968 (Statutory Instrument 78), wherein it is permitted to proffer qualified opinion as to the professional competence of its members. IoTA has applied for awarding body status to offer the CPC in its new format from December 2011.

MEMBERSHIP
Student
Associate (AInstTA)
Honorary Member

Associate Member (AMInstTA)
Member (MInstTA)
Fellow (FInstTA)
Patron Scheme for Companies

DESIGNATORY LETTERS
AInstTA, AMInstTA, MInstTA, FInstTA

THE INSTITUTE OF TRAFFIC ACCIDENT INVESTIGATORS

Column House
London Road
Shrewsbury
Shropshire SY2 6NN
Tel: 08456 212066
Fax: 08456 212077
E-mail: gensec@itai.org
Website: www.itai.org

The Institute provides a means of communication, education, representation and regulation in the field of Traffic Accident Investigation. Our main aim is to provide a forum for spreading knowledge and enhancing expertise among those engaged in the discipline. Members include police officers, lecturers in higher education and private practitioners.

MEMBERSHIP
Affiliate
Associate (AITAI)
Member (MITAI)

DESIGNATORY LETTERS
AITAI, MITAI

TRAVEL AND TOURISM

Membership of Professional Institutions and Associations

CONFEDERATION OF TOURISM AND HOSPITALITY

37 Duke Street
London W1U 1LN
Tel: 020 7258 9850
Fax: 020 7258 9869
E-mail: info@cthawards.com
Website: www.cthawards.com

The Confederation of Tourism and Hospitality is an awarding body approved by Ofqual, and registered on the QCA's National Qualifications Framework. We were established in 1982 to provide recognized standards of management and vocational training appropriate to the needs of the hotel and travel industries, via our syllabuses, examinations and awards.

MEMBERSHIP
Student Member
Associate Member (AMCTH)
Professional Member (PMCTH)
Fellow (FCTH)

QUALIFICATION/EXAMINATIONS
Diploma in Hospitality and Tourism Management
Diploma in Hotel Management
Diploms in Hotel and Casino Management
Diploma in Tourism Management
Diploma in Travel Agency Management
Advanced Diploma in Hotel and Event Management
Advanced Diploma in Tourism Management
Advanced Diploma in Travel Agency Management
Graduate Diploma in Hospitality and Tourism Management
Postgraduate Diploma in Hotel Management

DESIGNATORY LETTERS
AMCTH, PMCTH, FCTH

INSTITUTE OF TRAVEL AND TOURISM

PO Box 217
Ware
Hertfordshire SG12 8WY
Tel: 0844 4995 653
Fax: 0844 4995 654
E-mail: enquiries@itt.co.uk
Website: www.itt.co.uk

The ITT, founded in 1956, is a professional membership body for individuals employed in the travel and tourism industry. We provide support and guidance for our members throughout their career and offer them CPD and training to maintain standards for the benefit of the industry as a whole.

MEMBERSHIP
Student Member
Introductory Member
Affiliate Member
Member
Member (MInstTT)
Fellow
Fellow (FInstTT)
University/College Member
Group Member
Corporate Member

DESIGNATORY LETTERS
MInstTT, FInstTT

THE TOURISM MANAGEMENT INSTITUTE

c/o Hon. Secretary, Dr. Cathy Guthrie, FTMI, FTS
18 Cuninghill Avenue
Inverurie
Aberdeenshire AB51 3TZ
Tel: 01467 620769
E-mail: secretary@tmi.org.uk
Website: www.tmi.org.uk

Part of the Tourism Society, the TMI is the professional body for tourism destination managers. Its network of over 300 professionals shares information via website, conferences, seminars, working groups, e-mails and newsletters. Committed to excellence, the TMI/Tourism Society Continuing Professional Development programme aims to support destination management and tourism professionals.

MEMBERSHIP
Student
Associate (ATMI)
Member (MTMI)
Fellow (FTMI)

DESIGNATORY LETTERS
ATMI, MTMI, FTMI

THE TOURISM SOCIETY

Trinity Court
34 West Street
Sutton
Surrey SM1 1SH
Tel: 0208 661 4636
Fax: 0208 661 4637
E-mail: admin@tourismsociety.org
Website: www.tourismsociety.org

The Tourism Society, founded in 1977, is the professional membership body for people working in all sectors of tourism. We strive to drive up standards of professionalism and act as an advocate of tourism to the government and the public and private sectors, and liaise with other tourism professionals worldwide. We also provide advice, support and networking opportunities to our 1, 200 or so members.

MEMBERSHIP
Student
Full Member (MTS)
Fellow (FTS)
Overseas/Retired Member
Group Member
Corporate Member

DESIGNATORY LETTERS
MTS, FTS

VETERINARY SCIENCE

Membership of Professional Institutions and Associations

BRITISH VETERINARY ASSOCIATION

7 Mansfield Street
London W1G 9NQ
Tel: 020 7636 6541
Fax: 020 7908 6349
E-mail: bvahq@bva.co.uk
Website: www.bva.co.uk

The BVA is the representative body for the veterinary profession in the UK and has more than 11,500 members. We promote and support the interests of our members and the animals under their care, liaise with the government and are the leading provider of veterinary information to the media and general public.

MEMBERSHIP
Student Member
Associate Member
Full Member
Overseas Member
Organizational Member

SOCIETY OF PRACTISING VETERINARY SURGEONS

The Governor's House
Cape Road
Warwick CV34 5DJ
Tel: 01926 410454
Fax: 01926 411350
E-mail: office@spvs.org.uk
Website: www.spvs.org.uk

The SPVS was founded in 1933 with the aim of promoting the interests of veterinary surgeons in private practice. We are a non-territorial division of the British Veterinary Association. Our remit is to advise on all aspects of managing the business of a clinical veterinary practice, and we hold one-day, weekend and week-long courses and an annual congress.

MEMBERSHIP
Student Member
Associate Member
Full Member
Retired Member

THE ROYAL COLLEGE OF VETERINARY SURGEONS

Belgravia House
62–64 Horseferry Road
London SW1P 2AF
Tel: 020 7222 2001
Fax: 020 7222 2004
E-mail: admin@rcvs.org.uk
Website: www.rcvs.org.uk

The RCVS is the regulatory body for veterinary surgeons in the UK. Its role is to safeguard the health and welfare of animals committed to veterinary care, through the regulation of the educational, ethical and clinical standards of the veterinary profession, and to act as an impartial source of informed opinion on animal health and welfare issues and their interaction with human health.

MEMBERSHIP
Member (MRCVS)
Fellow (FRCVS)

QUALIFICATION/EXAMINATIONS
Certificate in Advanced Veterinary Practice (CertAVP)
Diploma (various titles, eg Small Animal Surgery; Animal Welfare Science Ethics & Law; Equine Internal Medicine; Cattle Health & Production etc)
RCVS Recognised Specialist
Diploma in Advanced Veterinary Nursing
Diploma of Fellowship (FRCVS)

DESIGNATORY LETTERS
MRCVS, FRCVS

WASTES MANAGEMENT

Membership of Professional Institutions and Associations

CHARTERED INSTITUTION OF WASTES MANAGEMENT

9 Saxon Court
St Peter's Gardens
Marefair
Northampton NN1 1SX
Tel: 01604 620426
Fax: 01604 621339
E-mail: education@ciwm.co.uk
Website: www.ciwm.co.uk

The CIWM represents more than 7,000 waste management professionals – predominantly in the UK but also overseas. We promote education, training and research in the scientific, technical and practical aspects of waste management for the safeguarding of the environment, and set and strive to maintain high standards for individuals working in the waste management industry.

MEMBERSHIP
Student Member
Technician Member (TechMCIWM)
Associate Member (AssocMCIWM)
Graduate Member (GradMCIWM)
Licentiate (LCIWM)
Member (MCIWM)
Fellow (FCIWM)
Affiliated Organization

QUALIFICATION/EXAMINATIONS
CIWM Training Services specializes in developing and providing waste management training for individuals & organizations. Each year we organize more than 70 courses. For details see the website.

DESIGNATORY LETTERS
TechMCIWM, AssocMCIWM, GradMCIWM, LCIWM, MCIWM, FCIWM

WATCH AND CLOCK MAKING AND REPAIRING

Membership of Professional Institutions and Associations

THE BRITISH HOROLOGICAL INSTITUTE LIMITED

Upton Hall
Upton
Newark
Nottinghamshire NG23 5TE
Tel: 01636 813795
Fax: 01636 812258
E-mail: clock@bhi.co.uk
Website: www.bhi.co.uk

The BHI, which was formed in 1858 to promote horology, is a professional body with about 3,000 members worldwide. We provide education and specialist training, set recognized standards of excellence in workmanship and professional conduct, and support our members in their work, making, repairing and servicing clocks and watches.

MEMBERSHIP
Associate
Member (MBHI)
Fellow (FBHI)

QUALIFICATION/EXAMINATIONS
Certificate in Clock and Watch Servicing (Level 2) – final registration January 2012
Certificate in the Repair, Restoration and Conservation of Clocks/Watches (Level 3) – anticipated final registration, January 2012
Diploma in Clock and Watch Servicing (Level 3)
Diploma in the Servicing and Repair of Clocks / Watches (Level 4) – awaiting confirmation of accreditation – August 2011
Diploma in the Repair, Restoration and Conservation of Clocks / Watches (Level 5) – awaiting confirmation of accreditation – August 2011

DESIGNATORY LETTERS
MBHI, FBHI

WELDING

Membership of Professional Institutions and Associations

THE WELDING INSTITUTE

Granta Park
Great Abington
Cambridge CB21 6AL
Tel: 01223 899000
Fax: 01223 894219
E-mail: professional@twi.co.uk
Website: www.twiprofessional.com

The Welding Institute is the engineering institution for welding and joining professionals. We are committed to promoting the importance of welding/materials joining technology, given its importance as a key industrial technology governing the reliability and safety of many products, and to the advancement of education, training and CPD for our members.

MEMBERSHIP
Graduate (GradWeldI)
Technician (TechWeldI)
Senior Associate (SenAWeldI)
Incorporated Member (IncMWeldI)
Member (MWeldI)
Senior Member (SenMWeldI)
Fellow (FWeldI)
Honorary Fellow (HonFWeldI)
Engineering Technician (EngTech)
Incorporated Engineer (IEng)
Chartered Engineer (CEng)

QUALIFICATION/EXAMINATIONS
Certificate in Welding and Joining Technology for Students in Materials and Engineering

DESIGNATORY LETTERS
GradWeldI, TechWeldI, SenAWeldI, IncMWeldI, MWeldI, SenMWeldI, FWeldI, HonFWeldI, EngTech, IEng, CEng

WELFARE

Membership of Professional Institutions and Associations

INSTITUTE OF WELFARE

PO Box 5570
Stourbridge
West Midlands DY8 9BA
Tel: 01214 548883
Fax: 01214 547873
E-mail: info@instituteofwelfare.co.uk
Website: www.instituteofwelfare.co.uk

The Institute of Welfare was founded in 1945 and exists to promote the highest possible standards in the delivery of welfare to those who need it. We make representations to government, undertake research on welfare issues, encourage and facilitate the exchange of information, and provide opportunities for those engaged in welfare work to pursue CPD.

MEMBERSHIP
Associate Member (AMIW)
Member (MIW)
Fellow (FIW)
Companion (CIW)

DESIGNATORY LETTERS
AMIW, MIW, FIW, CIW

Part 6

Bodies Accrediting Independent Institutions

THE BRITISH ACCREDITATION COUNCIL FOR INDEPENDENT FURTHER AND HIGHER EDUCATION (BAC)

BAC is a registered charity that was established in 1984 to act as the national accrediting body for independent further and higher education. It is independent both of government and of the colleges it accredits.

A college that is accredited by BAC undergoes a thorough inspection every four years, with an interim visit after two years. Until 2000, BAC accreditation was only available to colleges in the United Kingdom, but there are now accredited colleges in Bulgaria, the Czech Republic, France, Germany, Greece, India, Lebanon, Mauritius, South Africa and Switzerland. At present BAC accredits 525 colleges in the United Kingdom and 29 overseas. Lists of accredited colleges are published each year; full details can be viewed on the BAC website.

BAC maintains close links with all the major bodies concerned with the maintenance of standards in British education, including The British Council, Open and Distance Learning Quality Council (ODL QC), the Council of Validating Universities (CVU), National Recognition Information Centre (UK NARIC), the Quality Assurance Agency for Higher Education (QAA), Association of Colleges (AoC), GuildHE and the United Kingdom Council for International Student Affairs (UKCISA.

Accreditation by BAC is recognized by the UK Border Agency (UKBA) of the Home Office as a qualifying requirement for institutions to enrol visa students.

Further details of the work of the BAC and a current list of accredited institutions may be obtained from The Chief Executive, BAC, 44 Bedford Row, London WC1R 4LL; Tel: 020 7447 2584; Fax: 020 7447 2585; e-mail: info@the-bac.org; website: www.the-bac.org

THE BRITISH COUNCIL

The British Council runs the Accreditation UK scheme in partnership with English UK for the inspection and accreditation of organizations that provide courses in English as a Foreign Language (EFL) in Britain. One of its aims is to effectively promote accredited UK English Language Teaching (ELT) through the British Council's network of overseas offices.

Under the terms of the scheme, institutions are inspected rigorously every four years in the areas of management, resources and environment, teaching and learning, and welfare and student services. The scheme also includes a system of random spot-checking. The management and policy of the scheme are conducted by an independent board while a separate independent committee reviews inspectors' reports.

The majority of recognized schools are also members of English UK, which insists on British Council accreditation as a criterion for membership. In addition, all English UK members, of which there are around 450, are required to abide by the Association's Code of Practice and Regulations. English UK exists to raise the high standards of its members even further through conferences, training courses and publications. The association also represents the interests of members and students to government bodies, and promotes international student mobility through membership of the UKVisas User Panel

Further information on the Accreditation UK scheme may be obtained from the Accreditation Unit, British Council, Bridgewater House, 58 Whitworth Street, Manchester M1 6BB; Tel:

01619 577692; e-mail: accreditation.unit@britishcouncil.org; website: www. britishcouncil.org/ accreditation. Further information on English UK may be obtained from English UK, 219 St John Street, London EC1V 4LY; Tel: 020 7608 7960; Fax: 020 7608 7961; e-mail: info@englishuk.com; website: www.englishuk.com

THE OPEN AND DISTANCE LEARNING QUALITY COUNCIL (ODLQC)

ODL QC was established in 1968 as the Council for the Accreditation of Correspondence Colleges, a joint initiative of the then Labour government and representatives of the sector. It is the principal accrediting body for a wide variety of providers of open and distance learning in the UK, from commercial colleges to professional and public-sector institutions. Now independent, it nevertheless continues to have the informal support of government.

ODL QC promotes quality by:

- establishing standards of education and training in open and distance learning;
- recognizing good quality provision, wherever it occurs;
- supporting and protecting the interests of learners;
- encouraging the improvement of existing methods and the development of new ones;
- linking open and distance learning with other forms of education and training;
- promoting wider recognition of the value of open and distance learning.

Accreditation includes a rigorous assessment of educational provision, including materials, tutorial support, publicity, contractual arrangements with learners and general administrative procedures, each of which is measured against the Council's published benchmark standards. If accredited, the provider is monitored on a regular basis and reassessed at least once every three years.

The Council promotes those colleges that it accredits, which are by definition quality providers of ODL, and acts as honest broker in matching accredited colleges to potential markets. A list of courses offered by accredited providers is circulated widely, both in the UK and abroad, and is included on the Council's website, www.odlqc.org.uk. The Council also seeks to protect the interests of learners by promoting the importance of accreditation, and by offering advice and support directly to learners. At the same time, knowledge of good practice is disseminated more widely, and quality encouraged wherever open and distance learning occurs.

The Council consists of members nominated by professional and public bodies involved in education, as well as representatives of accredited providers, and has strong links with other bodies in the sector, both in the UK and abroad.

All enquiries should be addressed to ODL QC, 79 Barnfield Wood Road, Beckenham, Kent BR3 6ST; Tel: 020 8658 8377; e-mail: info@odlqc.org.uk; website: www.odlqc.org.uk

THE COUNCIL FOR INDEPENDENT EDUCATION (CIFE)

CIFE was founded in 1973 to promote strict adherence by independent sixth-form and tutorial colleges to the highest standards of academic and professional integrity. All member colleges must be accredited by the British Accreditation Council for Independent Further and Higher Education (BAC), and/or the Independent Schools Inspectorate (ISI) if they are registered by the

Department for Education (DfE) as schools. Candidate membership is available for up to three years for colleges that are seeking BAC or ISI accreditation and otherwise satisfy CIFE's own exacting membership criteria. All colleges must also abide by stringent codes of conduct and practice, the character and presentation of their published exam results are subject to regulation, and the accuracy of the information must be validated by BAC as academic auditor to CIFE. Full members are subject to re-inspection by their accrediting bodies. There are 17 colleges in full or candidate membership of CIFE at present, spread throughout England but with concentrations in London, Oxford and Cambridge.

CIFE colleges offer a wide range of GCSE, A and AS level courses. In addition some CIFE colleges offer English language tuition for students from overseas, and degree-level tuition. A number of the colleges offer summer holiday academic courses, and most of them also provide A level and GCSE revision courses during the Christmas and/or Easter holidays. Further information on CIFE may be obtained from the CIFE website: www.cife.org.uk; Tel: 020 8767 8666; e-mail: enquiries@cife.org.uk

Part 7

Study Associations and the 'Learned Societies'

Study associations consist of people who wish to increase their knowledge of a particular subject or range of subjects; they may be professionals or amateurs. Some associations consist almost entirely of specialists (eg the Royal Statistical Society); others (eg the Royal Geographical Society and the Zoological Society of London) have a more general membership. The learned societies usually have two grades of membership: fellows or members. Some also admit group members (such as schools or libraries), which are known as corporate members, and junior associate, corresponding and overseas members, who pay lower subscriptions. Some also elect honorary fellows or members. The members of some societies may use designatory letters, but this does not mean that the holder is 'qualified' in the same sense as a doctor or a chartered accountant.

Membership of some learned societies is by election, and is commonly accepted as distinguishing the candidate by admission to an exclusive group. Candidates may be selected in respect of pre-eminence in their subject or in the public service. The chief associations of this type are the Royal Society (founded 1660 and granted Royal Charters in 1662 and 1663), the Royal Academy of Arts (founded 1768) and the British Academy (granted the Royal Charter in 1902).

The **Royal Society** was established to improve 'natural knowledge' and is mainly concerned with pure and applied science and technology. Election to Fellowship (FRS) is regarded as one of the highest distinctions. The society elects Fellows, Foreign Members and Royal Fellows (www.royalsociety.org).

The **Royal Academy** was established to cultivate and improve the arts of painting, sculpture and architecture. There are two main grades of membership: Academicians (RA), including Senior Academicians, and Associates (ARA); there are also a small number of Honorary Academicians (www.royalacademy.org.uk).

The **British Academy** is the UK's national academy for the humanities and the social sciences. It is the counterpart to the Royal Society that exists to serve the natural sciences. The Academy has Fellows (FBA), Corresponding Fellows and a small number of Honorary Fellows.

A list of learned societies and study associations can be found below.

OCCUPATIONAL ASSOCIATIONS

The occupational associations do not qualify practitioners but organize them. Some coordinate the activities of specialists (eg the Society of Medical Officers of Health) and others promote the individual and collective interests of professionals working in a wider area. Both types also seek to safeguard the public interest and to offer an educational service to their members. The latter type of association is especially numerous among teachers, who have over 20 associations (eg the National Union of Teachers, the Educational Institute of Scotland, the National Association of Schoolmasters/Union of Women Teachers and the National Association of Head Teachers), and is represented in the medical profession by the British Medical Association.

LIST OF STUDY ASSOCIATIONS AND LEARNED SOCIETIES

This list largely excludes qualifying bodies, which are covered in Part 5. The date on the left is that of foundation or adoption of title.

Agriculture and related subjects

1926	Agricultural Economics Society
1952	British Agricultural History Society
1945	British Grassland Society
1944	British Society of Animal Science
1947	British Society of Soil Science
1921	Commonwealth Forestry Association
1927	Herb Society of Great Britain
1925	Institute of Chartered Foresters
1938	Institution of Agricultural Engineers
1947	International Fertiliser Society
1839	Royal Agricultural Society of England
1882	Royal Forestry Society of England, Wales and N Ireland
1784	Royal Highland and Agricultural Society of Scotland
1804	Royal Horticultural Society
1854	Royal Scottish Forestry Society
1904	Royal Welsh Agricultural Society
1943	Society of Dairy Technology
1945	The Soil Association

Anthropology and related subjects

1963	African Studies Association of the UK
1979	Association for the Study of Modern and Contemporary France
1982	Association for the Study of Modern Italy
1946	Association of Social Anthropologists of the UK and Commonwealth
1985	British Association for Irish Studies
1974	British Association for Japanese Studies
1972	British Association for South Asian Studies
1961	British Institute of Persian Studies
1973	British Society for Middle Eastern Studies
1981	European Association for Jewish Studies
1878	Folklore Society
1943	Hispanic and Luso Brazilian Council
1974	International Association for the Study of German Politics
1972	Japan Foundation
1891	Japan Society
1843	Royal Anthropological Institute of Great Britain and Ireland
1823	Royal Asiatic Society of Great Britain and Ireland
1868	Royal Commonwealth Society
1901	Royal Society for Asian Affairs
1936	Saltire Society
1977	Society for Caribbean Studies
1964	Society for Latin American Studies
1969	Society for Libyan Studies
1983	Society for the Promotion of Byzantine Studies
1879	Society for the Promotion of Hellenic Studies
1910	Society for the Promotion of Roman Studies
1969	University Association for Contemporary European Studies
1892	Viking Society for Northern Research

Archaeology and related subjects

1924	Ancient Monuments Society
1979	Association for Environmental Archaeology
1843	British Archaeological Association
1996	British Epigraphy Society
1948	British Institute at Ankara
1846	Cambrian Archaeological Association
1944	Council for British Archaeology
1838	Eccleriological Society
1882	Egypt Exploration Society
1855	London and Middlesex Archaeological Society
1865	Palestine Exploration Fund
1908	Prehistoric Society
1843	Royal Archaeological Institute
1967	Society for Post-Medieval Archaeology

Art and Design

1974	Association of Art Historians
1910	Contemporary Art Society
1915	Design and Industries Association
1950	International Institute for Conservation of Historic and Artistic Works
1888	National Society for Education in Art and Design
1899	Pastel Society
1768	Royal Academy of Arts
1814	Royal Birmingham Society of Artists
1883	Royal Institute of Oil-Painters
1831	Royal Institute of Painters in Watercolours
1826	Royal Scottish Academy of Art and Architecture
1754	Royal Society for the Encouragement of Arts, Manufactures and Commerce
1904	Royal Society of British Sculptors
1904	Royal Society of Marine Artists
1895	Royal Society of Miniature Painters, Sculptors and Gravers
1884	Royal Society of Painter/Printmakers
1891	Royal Society of Portrait Painters
1804	Royal Watercolours Society
1919	Society of Graphic Fine Art
1952	Society of Portrait Sculptors
1952	United Society of Artists
1955	William Morris Society

Biology and related subjects

1936	Association for the Study of Animal Behaviour
1904	Association of Applied Biologists
1968	Biomedical Engineering Society
1836	Botanical Society of Scotland
1836	Botanical Society of the British Isles
1896	British Bryological Society
1929	Freshwater Biological Association
1889	Marine Biological Association
1833	Royal Entomological Society
1931	Society for Applied Microbiology
1911	The Biochemical Society
1913	The British Ecological Society
1896	The British Mycological Society
1858	The British Ornithologists' Union
1959	The British Society for Cell Biology
1933	The British Trust for Ornithology
1937	The Systematics Association
1826	Zoological Society of London

Chemistry

1918	Oil and Colour Chemists' Association
1980	Royal Society of Chemistry
1881	Society of Chemical Industry
1897	Society of Leather Technologists and Chemists

Economics, Statistics and related subjects

1992	Association of Business Schools
1927	Economic History Society
2003	Economic Research Institute of Northern Ireland
1955	Institute of Economic Affairs
1902	Royal Economic Society
1834	Royal Statistical Society
1897	Scottish Economic Society

Engineering and related subjects

1847	Architectural Association
1966	Concrete Society
1946	Faculty of Building
1978	Institute of Concrete Technology
1997	Institute of Ergonomics and Human Factors
1976	Royal Academy of Engineering
1866	Royal Aeronautical Society

1916	Royal Incorporation of Architects in Scotland
1860	Royal Institution of Naval Architects
1916	Society of Automotive Engineers
1958	Society of Environmental Engineers
2003	The Energy Institute
1899	Town and Country Planning Association

Geography, Geology and related subjects

1963	British Cartographic Society
1949	British Geotechnical Society
1940	British Society of Rheology
1968	Council for Environmental Education
1923	English Place-Name Society
1931	Gemmological Association of Great Britain
1893	Geographical Association
1807	Geological Society of London
1858	Geologists Association
1846	Hakluyt Society
1971	Institution of Environmental Sciences
1876	Mineralogical Society of Great Britain and Ireland
1847	Palaeontographical Society
1957	Paleontological Association
1830	Royal Geographical Society
1997	Royal Institute of Navigation
1884	Royal Scottish Geographical Society

History and related subjects

1902	British Academy
1952	British Agricultural History Society
1888	British Record Society
1932	British Records Association
1947	British Society for the History of Science
1988	Centre for Metropolitan History
1864	Early English Texts Society
1964	Furniture History Society
1869	Harleian Society
1885	Huguenot Society of Great Britain and Ireland
1961	Institute of Heraldic and Genealogical Studies
1921	Institute of Historical Research
1893	Jewish Historical Society of England
1964	London Record Society
2000	Museums, Libraries and Archives Council
1920	Newcomen Society for the Study of the History of Engineering and Technology
1921	Oriental Ceramic Society
1868	Royal Historical Society
1836	Royal Numismatic Society
1869	Royal Philatelic Society, London
1953	Scottish Genealogy Society
1886	Scottish History Society
1897	Scottish Record Society
1976	Social History Society
1921	Society for Army Historical Research
1910	Society for Nautical Research
1967	Society for Renaissance Studies
1970	Society for the Social History of Medicine
1707	Society of Antiquaries of London
1780	Society of Antiquaries of Scotland
1956	Society of Architectural Historians in Great Britain
1947	Society of Archivists
1911	Society of Genealogists
1906	The Historical Association
1958	Victorian Society

Languages

1883	Alliance Française
1891	An Comunn Gaidhealach
1981	Association for French Language Studies
1932	Association for German Studies in Great Britain and Ireland
1990	Association for Language Learning
1910	Chartered Institute of Linguists
1991	Instituto Cervantes

1964	National Association for the Teaching of English	1993	University Council of Modern Languages
2003	National Centre for Languages	1988	Women in German Studies

Law

1958	British Institute of International and Comparative Law	1949	Law Society of Scotland
		1920	Royal Institute of International Affairs
1972	Intellectual Property Bar Association	1965	Scottish Law Commission
1922	Law Society of Northern Ireland	1887	Selden Society

Literature and Arts

1959	Academi – Yr Academi Gymreig	1906	English Association
1973	Alliance of Literary Societies	1886	Francis Bacon Society Inc
1969	Art Libraries Society	1960	H. G. Wells Society
1970	Association for Scottish Literary Studies	1997	Historical Novel Society
		1973	Joseph Conrad Society
1989	Association of Independent Libraries	1997	Leeds Philosophical and Literary Society
1892	Bibliographical Society		
1992	British Association for Information and Library Education and Research	1906	Malone Society
		1781	Manchester Literary and Philosophical Society
1975	British Comparative Literature Association	1995	Philip Larkin Society
		1842	Philological Society
1933	British Film Institute	1909	Poetry Society
1960	British Society of Aesthetics	1820	Royal Society of Literature
1893	Bronte Society	1884	Society of Authors
1949	Cambridge Bibliographical Society	2004	Society of College, National and University Libraries
1935	Charles Lamb Society		
1904	Classical Association	1984	Standing Conference for the Arts and Social Sciences
1902	Dickens Fellowship		
1890	Edinburgh Bibliographical Society	1968	Thomas Hardy Society

Management

1986	British Academy of Management

Mathematics and Physics

1924	Astronomical Society of Edinburgh	1930	Institution of Electronics
1890	British Astronomical Association	1871	Mathematical Association
1966	British Biophysical Society	1820	Royal Astronomical Society
1927	British Institute of Radiology	1850	Royal Meteorological Society
1933	British Interplanetary Society		

Medicine (including Psychology)

1887 Anatomical Society of GB and Ireland
1957 Association for Child and Adolescent Mental Health
1957 Association for the Study of Medical Education
1932 Association of Anaesthetists of GB and Ireland
1933 Association of British Neurologists
1953 Association of Clinical Biochemistry
1927 Association of Clinical Pathologists
1920 Association of Surgeons of GB and Ireland
1959 British Academy for Forensic Science
2003 British Association for Sexual Health and HIV
1977 British Association of Clinical Anatomists
1950 British Association of Forensic Medicine
1962 British Association of Oral Surgeons
1943 British Association of Otolaryngologists
1954 British Association of Paediatric Surgeons
1973 British Association of Surgical Oncology
1945 British Association of Urological Surgeons
1934 British Diabetic Association
1948 British Geriatrics Society
1832 British Medical Association
1950 British Neuropathological Society
1953 British Occupational Hygiene Society
1965 British Orthodontic Society
1918 British Orthopaedic Association
1925 British Osteopathic Association
1913 British Psychoanalytical Society
1901 British Psychological Society
1948 British Society for Allergy and Clinical Immunology
1962 British Society for Clinical Cytology
1937 British Society of Gastroenterology
1960 British Society for Haematology
1947 British Society for Research on Ageing
1945 British Thoracic Society
1947 Ergonomics Society
1946 Experimental Psychology Society
1950 Faculty of Homeopathy
1959 Forensic Science Society
1819 Hunterian Society
1969 Institute of Occupational Medicine
1964 Institute of Pharmacy Management
1773 Medical Society of London
1901 Medico-Legal Society
1941 Nutrition Society
1906 Pathological Society of Great Britain and Ireland
1875 Royal Environmental Health Institute of Scotland
1734 Royal Medical Society
1931 Royal Pharmaceutical Society of Great Britain
2008 Royal Society for Public Health
1805 Royal Society of Medicine
1907 Royal Society of Tropical Medicine and Hygiene
1946 Society for Endocrinology
1950 Society for Reproduction and Fertility
1884 Society for the Study of Addiction
1926 Society of British Neurological Surgeons

Music

1977 Alkan Society
1979 British Music Society
1971 Chopin Society
1932 English Folk Dance and Song Society
1882 Incorporated Society of Musicians
1888 Plainsong and Medieval Music Society
1874 Royal Musical Association
1955 Welsh Music Guild

Philosophy

1880 Aristotelian Society
2003 British Philosophical Association
1984 British Society for the History of Philosophy
1819 Cambridge Philosophical Society

1990	Friedrich Nietzsche Society
1979	Hegel Society of Great Britain
1781	Manchester Literary and Philosophical Society
1913	Philosophical Society of England
1925	Royal Institute of Philosophy
1802	Royal Philosophical Society of Glasgow

Politics

1975	British International Studies Association
1951	David Davies Memorial Institute of International Studies
1884	Electoral Reform Society
1945	Federal Trust for Education and Research
1987	Institute of Welsh Affairs
1974	International Association for the Study of German Politics
1950	Political Studies Association
1868	Royal Commonwealth Society
1920	Royal Institute of International Affairs

Science general

1924	Association for Informational Management
1831	British Science Association
1956	British Society for the History of Science
1960	British Society for the Philosophy of Science
1799	Royal Institution of Great Britain
1660	Royal Society
1783	Royal Society of Edinburgh

Theology and Religious Studies

1908	Baptist Historical Society
1954	British Association for the Study of Religions
1904	Canterbury and York Society
1904	Catholic Record Society
1961	Ecclesiastical History Society
1981	European Association for Jewish Studies
1903	Friends Historical Society
1972	United Reformed Church History Society
1893	Wesley Historical Society

MONMOUTHSHIRE LIBRARIES

General Index

Note: In addition to the abbreviations listed at the beginning of the book, the following are used throughout the index; FE – Further Education; HE – Higher Education. Universities are listed under locations eg: Aberdeen, University of

INDEX OF ADVERTISERS

With over 1,000 titles in printed and digital format, **Kogan Page** offers affordable, sound business advice

www.koganpage.com

You are reading one of the thousands of books published by **Kogan Page**. As Europe's leading independent business book publishers **Kogan Page** has always sought to provide up-to-the-minute books that offer practical guidance at affordable prices.

The sharpest minds need the finest advice. **Kogan Page** creates success.

www.koganpage.com

You are reading one of the thousands of books published by **Kogan Page**. As Europe's leading independent business book publishers **Kogan Page** has always sought to provide up-to-the-minute books that offer practical guidance at affordable prices.